AIR TRANSPORT—A TOURISM PERSPECTIVE

Contemporary Issues in Air Transport

AIR TRANSPORT —A TOURISM PERSPECTIVE

Anne Graham
University of Westminster, London, United Kingdom

Frédéric Dobruszkes
Universite Libre de Bruxelles, Bruxelles, Belgium

Elsevier
Radarweg 29, PO Box 211, 1000 AE Amsterdam, Netherlands
The Boulevard, Langford Lane, Kidlington, Oxford OX5 1GB, United Kingdom
50 Hampshire Street, 5th Floor, Cambridge, MA 02139, United States

Library of Congress Cataloging-in-Publication Data
A catalog record for this book is available from the Library of Congress

British Library Cataloguing-in-Publication Data
A catalogue record for this book is available from the British Library

ISBN: 978-0-12-812857-2

For information on all Elsevier publications
visit our website at https://www.elsevier.com/books-and-journals

Publisher: Jonathan Simpson
Acquisition Editor: Brian Romer
Editorial Project Manager: Peter Adamson
Production Project Manager: Vijayaraj Purushothaman
Cover Designer: Matthew Limbert

Typeset by SPi Global, India

Contents

IV

REACHING THE DESTINATION AND ATTRACTIONS

List of Figures

List of Tables

Contributors

Daniel Albalate University of Barcelona, Barcelona, Spain
Thomas Budd Cranfield University, Bedford, United Kingdom
Jean-Michel Decroly Free University of Brussels (ULB), Brussels, Belgium
Frédéric Dobruszkes Free University of Brussels (ULB), Brussels, Belgium
David Timothy Duval University of Winnipeg, Winnipeg, MB, Canada
Xavier Fageda University of Barcelona, Barcelona, Spain
Frank Fichert Worms University of Applied Sciences, Worms, Germany
Andrew R. Goetz University of Denver, Denver, CO, United States
Anne Graham University of Westminster, London, United Kingdom
Nigel Halpern Kristiania University College, Oslo, Norway
Michael Hanke SkaiBlu, LLC, Consulting, Los Angeles, CA, United States
Isaac Levi Henderson Massey University School of Aviation, Palmerston North, New Zealand
Claire Humphreys University of Westminster, London, United Kingdom
Juan Carlos Martín University of Las Palmas De Gran Canaria, Las Palmas, Spain
David Metz University College London, London, United Kingdom
John F. O'Connell University of Surrey, Surrey, United Kingdom
David Ramos-Pérez University of Salamanca, Salamanca, Spain
Tim Ryley Griffith University, Nathan, Brisbane, QLD, Australia
Wai Hong Kan Tsui Massey University School of Aviation, Palmerston North, New Zealand
Augusto Voltes-Dorta University of Edinburgh, Edinburgh, United Kingdom
Walanchalee Wattanacharoensil Mahidol University International College, Nakhon Pathom, Thailand

Authors' Biography

Daniel Albalate holds an MSc in Economics (University College London, 2007) and a PhD in Economics (Universitat de Barcelona, 2008). He is currently an associate professor at the Department of Applied Economics at the University of Barcelona, where he serves as deputy director of the Observatory of Policy Analysis and Evaluation. His research interests focus on policy analysis and evaluation, particularly in the field of transportation.

Thomas Budd is a lecturer in Airport Planning and Management in the Centre for Air Transport Management at Cranfield University, UK. His main areas of expertise include airport strategic management, environmental planning and policy, airport surface access, and climate change adaptation and resilience. Thomas joined Cranfield in August 2014 having previously conducted his PhD research at Loughborough University, and held a research fellowship in the Centre for Transport Research at the University of Aberdeen.

Jean-Michel Decroly is a professor in Human Geography, Demography, and Tourism studies at the Free University of Brussels—ULB where he is also the director of the Applied Geography and Geomarketing Research Unit (IGEAT—DGES—Faculty of Sciences). His research interests are population and tourism dynamics in Europe, related to the logics of capitalism.

Frédéric Dobruszkes holds a PhD in Geography (2007) from the Free University of Brussels—ULB. He is currently an FNRS Research Associate and lecturer at the same institution. He is Head of the Brussels-based Interuniversity Centre for Mobility Studies (CIEM). His main research interests are transport geography, especially the dynamics of airline networks, low-cost airlines, social conflicts around aircraft noise, and air/rail competition.

David Timothy Duval is an associate professor in the Faculty of Business and Economics at the University of Winnipeg. He was previously an associate professor in the School of Business at the University of Otago in New Zealand. David's research interests focus on the economic and legal regulation of commercial air transport.

Xavier Fageda holds an MSc in Economics (University of Warwick, 2002) and a PhD in Economics (Universitat de Barcelona, 2004). He is currently an associate professor at the Department of Applied Economics at the University of Barcelona. His research interests focus on transportation, with particular interest in airline markets, regional and urban economics, and industrial organization.

Frank Fichert is a professor of Economics and Transport Economics at Worms University of Applied Sciences (Germany). He worked as a managing director of the Research Institute for Economic Policy at Mainz (1999–2004) and as professor for Economics and Air Transportation at Heilbronn University of Applied Sciences (2004–2009). He has published several papers on the transport sector and is the co-author of the leading German textbook on air transport management. His research focuses on competition and regulation in the air transport industry and the environmental issues of aviation.

Andrew R. Goetz is a professor in the Department of Geography and the Environment, as well as the Denver Transportation Institute and the Urban Studies program at the University of Denver. He is the co-editor of *The Geographies of Air Transport* (Ashgate, 2014), and co-author of *Denver International Airport: Lessons Learned* (McGraw Hill, 1997). He has written numerous journal articles and book chapters on air transport and airports, in addition to other transportation and urban studies topics.

Anne Graham is a professor of Air Transport and Tourism Management at the University of Westminster, London. One of her key areas of expertise and knowledge is air transport demand analysis and interrelations with tourism, and she has over 30 years' experience of lecturing, research, and consultancy on these topics. She has published widely with recent books including *The Routledge Companion to Air Transport Management*, *Airport Finance and Investment in the Global Economy*, *Aviation Economics*, *Managing Airports*, and *Airport Marketing*. Between 2013 and 2015 Anne was the editor-in-chief of the Journal of Air Transport Management.

Nigel Halpern is an associate professor in Air Transport and Tourism at Kristiania University College in Norway, and a visiting research fellow with the School of Aviation at the University of New South Wales in Australia. He has previously worked in tourism management, and with the licensing of airlines and tour operators. His main research interests are in marketing and strategy, interorganisational relations, and geographical dimensions of supply and demand. He has published widely on subjects in air transport and tourism. He is the co-author of *Airport Marketing* (Routledge 2013) and co-editor of *The Routledge Companion to Air Transport Management* (Routledge 2018).

Michael Hanke, formerly with United Airlines, and leading the carrier's worldwide e-commerce activities for United.com, is the founder and managing director of SkaiBlu, a US-based digital aviation consultancy. SkaiBlu's global client portfolio includes over 25 companies ranging from Airbus Industrie to Vietnam Airlines. Michael received his doctorate in Air Transportation from Cranfield University; his graduate studies were completed at the London School of Economics (MSc International Strategy and Diplomacy) and at Embry-Riddle Aeronautical University (MBA). He is a textbook author (*Airline E-commerce: Log On. Take Off*). Michael holds an FAA pilot license.

Isaac Levi Henderson is an assistant lecturer teaching in the areas of human factors, aeronautics, and air transport management. He is working towards a PhD at Massey University. His research covers topics relevant to the fields of aviation and tourism management.

Claire Humphreys is the head of Planning and Transport at the University of Westminster. She holds a PhD in Tourism Studies and has been teaching tourism for more than 20 years. She has written on a variety of different aspects of the tourism industry but has a particular interest in travel related to sports.

Juan Carlos Martín holds a PhD in Economics from the University of Las Palmas de Gran Canaria (Spain) and he is a Graduate in Mathematics from the University Autonoma of Madrid (Spain). He is currently a full professor at the Department of Applied Economic Analysis (ULPGC) and an active researcher at the University Institute Tourism and Economic Sustainable Development—TIDES. He has authored or co-authored more than 80 peer-reviewed papers and book chapters in the field of tourism and transport economics. He likes to teach international students.

David Metz is an honorary professor in the Centre for Transport Studies, University College London, where his research focuses on how demographic and technological factors influence travel demand. He spent part of his career as a senior civil servant in a number of UK government departments, both as policy advisor and scientist, including five years as Chief Scientist at the Department of Transport. His recent research has been summarised in a short book entitled *Transport Fast or Smart?* published in 2016.

John F. O'Connell is currently a reader of Air Transport at the University of Surrey where he leads the MSc in Air Transport Management. Prior to this, he was a senior lecturer in the Air Transport Department at Cranfield University for 10 years where he specifically lectured on Airline Strategy. He also lectured at Embry-Riddle Aeronautical University (extended campus in California) for a further five years and while at Embry-Riddle, he regularly lectured at the NASA Ames research facility at Moffett Field. He also has worked for the Boeing commercial aircraft company as an analyst for a number of years. He has completed a PhD on Airline Strategy at Cranfield University, together with an MSc in Air Transport Management from the same institution and an MBA (Aviation) from Embry-Riddle Aeronautical University. He also holds a pilot's licence and is a certified IATA instructor.

David Ramos-Pérez holds a PhD in Geography from the University of Salamanca, Spain (2006). He is an associate professor in Human Geography at the same university, where he lectures in the School of Tourism. The general focus of his research work is air transport geography, mainly the spatial impacts of market liberalisation, the provision of air services in remote regions, and the role of State aid to airlines in launching new routes.

Tim Ryley is a professor of Aviation at Griffith University in Brisbane, Australia. From over twenty years of transport research experience, Professor Ryley has been recognised internationally for his contributions in the fields of sustainable aviation, airport planning, airport surface access, airport operations, and air travel demand. He has been involved in many research and consultancy projects with airports in Australia and the United Kingdom.

Kan Wai Hong Tsui is a senior lecturer teaching aviation operations, and airline and airport strategies. His research covers different areas, and includes airline and airport demand forecasting, airport productivity and efficiency, and tourism activities and future trends and its relationship with air transport industry.

Augusto Voltes-Dorta holds a PhD in Economics from the University of Las Palmas de Gran Canaria (Spain), and an MSc in Airport Planning and Management from Cranfield University (UK). He is currently a Lecturer in Business Economics at the University of Edinburgh Business School. His main research interests include airport economics and air transport connectivity. In the area of tourism, he has investigated the potential for self-connectivity in European holiday markets, as well as the impact of ETA's dissolution on Spain's domestic tourism. He has published in many peer-reviewed journals such as Transportation Research Parts A, B, and E, as well as in Tourism Management.

Walanchalee Wattanacharoensil is currently an assistant professor in the Tourism and Hospitality Management Division, Mahidol University International College, Thailand. She had six years of professional experience in the aviation industry before joining academia. She conducted her doctoral studies on airport experience and its connection to the tourism experience at the School of Hotel and Tourism Management, the Hong Kong Polytechnic University. Her research interests include the service experience in travel and tourism contexts, the airport experience, the interconnected nature of the aviation and tourism industries, and tourist decision-making.

Series Editors' Preface

We are proud to introduce the exciting new book series entitled *Contemporary Issues in Air Transport* and the first volume in that series entitled *Air transport: A Tourism Perspective*. The aim of *Contemporary Issues in Air Transport* is to address the state of current thinking and future research direction across the full spectrum of air transport issues. The series will seek to commission the world's leading aviation scholars, practitioners, and policy makers to edit volumes that address the most challenging and controversial issues facing commercial air transport policy, planning, regulation, management, and operations worldwide. The series will investigate the theoretical and practical concerns relating to the contemporary issues of international air transport and will seek to create a world leading collection of titles that form a globally comprehensive insight into contemporary issues facing air transport regulators, owners, operators, and users worldwide.

We are therefore delighted to introduce the first volume in this series on Air Travel and Tourism which has been edited by Professor Anne Graham of the University of Westminster, United Kingdom, and Dr. Frédéric Dobruszkes of the Brussels Free University, Belgium. In just over 100 years commercial air transport has become the most important high-speed form of long distance travel, with 4.1 billion passengers flying on scheduled commercial flights worldwide in 2017 (ICAO, 2018). Aviation is intractably connected to global tourist activity with over half the 2.1 billion tourists who crossed an international border in 2017 being transported by air (ICAO, 2018). The scale of contemporary leisure air travel has profound implications for people, places, and the environment and intersects with debates surrounding cultural imperialism, environmental degradation, touristic development, destination marketing, and global public health.

This volume seeks to address the role played by air transport with respect to the present day tourist, whether that is on long-haul or short-haul flights. The volume takes an interesting approach, not least by focusing on the different stages of a tourist's journey—from the reason for undertaking a journey through to the final destination. Clearly, this encompasses a range of issues most notably the nature of the journey, such as visiting friends and relatives, the impact of technology, whether charter or low-cost carrier, airport subsidy, and the like.

The novelty of the volume is the focus on the integration of air transport and tourism since and whilst there is extensive literature relating to both the two areas have tended, on the whole, to be studied in silos. The volume is divided into themes based on four stages of a tourist's journey namely: the rationale for flying, choosing the transport mode by which to travel, the journey itself and all that entails such as accessing the airport and the airport experience, and finally, reaching the destination and the attraction that affords.

As series editors we have a vision for a world leading collection of volumes that focus on the contemporary issues facing air transport worldwide, offering academics, researchers, students, and practitioners with a real insight into the complex nature of an increasingly important area of worldwide activity.

Lucy Budd, Stephen Ison
Loughborough University, Loughborough,
United Kingdom

Reference

ICAO, 2018. Continued Passenger Traffic Growth and Robust Air Cargo Demand in 2017. ICAO, Montreal. https://www.icao.int/Newsroom/Pages/Continued-passenger-traffic-growth-and-robust-air-cargo-demand-in-2017.aspx. (Accessed July 26, 2018).

Acknowledgements

There are many people that we would like to thank who have been involved with producing this book:
The contributors who have given up their valuable time to write their chapters.
The Series Editors of Elsevier's *Contemporary Issues in Air Transport* (Stephen Ison and Lucy Budd) for inviting us to undertake such an exciting venture and having trust in us to deliver an interesting and insightful read.
Andrew Smith for suggesting the title of the book.
Finally, all family and friends who have tolerated the disruption in their lives and provided never-ending support for us whilst we have spent too many hours sitting in front of the computer screen. Special thanks must go to Ian, Lorna, Callum, Ewan, Luce, Joachim, and Helena.

CHAPTER

1

Introduction

*Anne GRAHAM**, *Frédéric DOBRUSZKES*[†]

*University of Westminster, London, United Kingdom [†]Free University of Brussels (ULB), Brussels, Belgium

CHAPTER OUTLINE

1.1 INTRODUCTION

This book provides a comprehensive, contemporary, and global analysis of the role of air transport for today's tourists. Long-haul tourists have very little choice but to travel by air (or go elsewhere), but air transport is an increasingly important mode for short-haul tourists as well, being encouraged by a more competitive airline industry and evolving airline business models. However, the relationship between air transport and tourism is complex and works both ways, with good air accessibility being a fundamental condition for the development of many tourist destinations, at the same time as the growth of tourism demand is essential for the well-being of many airlines and airports.

The book has a close fit within Elsevier's *Contemporary Issues in Air Transport* series as it is multidisciplinary, with an international authorship and content, and it makes both a theoretical and empirical contribution to knowledge. It is aimed to appeal to academic and practitioner audiences of both the air transport and tourism sectors, and particularly to those who are seeking a more rigorous insight into the current day complexities, synergies, and potential conflicts present within the relationship between the two sectors. Moreover, the issues covered are generally not limited to certain geographic regions and so the book has a truly global approach which is enforced by having a range of contributors from many places in the world.

The book adopts a novel and original approach to addressing these issues by systematically exploring the successive stages of the tourist's trip by investigating reasons for flying, then travelling decisions related to transport modes and airline/airport choice, then accessing airports and the airline/airport experience, and finally reaching the destination and attractions. This enables current and salient debates to be explored, for example, related to the underestimated influence of visiting friends and relatives (VFR) travel, the potential for self-connection, the influence of technology, the role of charters versus Low-Cost Carriers (LCCs), and public subsidies to support airport development, as well as many others. Cutting edge analysis is presented with future research directions, and policy and management implications, identified.

Therefore, the book has three key features to enable the acquisition of balanced and comprehensive knowledge of the role of air transport within tourism, and a thorough awareness of the links between theory and practice. These are as follows:

1. An analysis based on the successive stages of the tourist trip providing a full appreciation of all critical issues related to the air transport and tourism relationship.
2. A multidisciplinary (social sciences including geography and economics, planning, management, marketing) approach in order to fully appreciate the theoretical and policy concepts underpinning air transport and tourism development.
3. A multisector (airports, airlines, destination organisations, travel distributors) and global (developed countries, emerging markets) coverage to fully explore the practical implications of the linkages between air transport and tourism.

1.2 KEY SOURCES OF LITERATURE

The separate published literature related to the air transport and tourism sectors is extensive. However, most air transport publications do not explore in any detail the specific characteristics of tourists and the tourism industry, whilst tourism publications tend to treat air transport as one of a number of industry sectors that need consideration. Although a few texts do investigate the general relationship between transport and tourism, there is limited focus on air transport, and none of these offer a totally up-to-date and critical view of relevant contemporary issues. A review later briefly discusses the key sources of literature related to the air transport and tourism relationship and in doing so demonstrates that there is no current publication that deals exclusively and comprehensively with the integral and contemporary role that air transport plays for today's tourists. Hence this book is uniquely placed to fill this major gap.

One of the first insightful books related to the air transport and tourism relationship was jointly published by Routledge and the United Nations World Tourism Organisation (UNWTO) and was entitled *Aviation and Tourism Policies: Balancing the Benefits* (Wheatcroft, 1994). As the name suggests this only focused on policy issues, such as regulation, liberalisation, and protectionism, using an interesting case study approach with a novel analytical framework to evaluate the policies. A more recent unique comprehensive publication in this area is *Aviation and Tourism: Implications for Leisure Travel*, which in addition to considering industry and policies implications, pays attention to the broader external impacts and includes a number of case studies from different parts of the world (Graham et al., 2008). Overall, there is a greater range of tourism and general transport books (e.g. Lumsdon and Page, 2004; Duval, 2007; Page, 2009; Gross and Klemmer, 2014) but as stated before these only give limited coverage of air transport issues. In existence there is also the grey literature typically produced by government departments, industry organisations, or consultants that again touch on some aspects of the air transport and tourism relation. A notable example is the UNWTO's *Global Report on Aviation* (UNWTO, 2012). In addition, it is noticeable that recent books focused on air transport geography or economics (Bowen, 2010; Goetz and Budd, 2014; Doganis, 2010) do not comprehensively discuss the relationships with tourism, even though the issue appears in a scattered way throughout the pages.

There is greater coverage of the air transport and tourism relationship within academic journals. A few authors have chosen to look quite generally at some key and salient issues (Bieger and Wittmer, 2006; Duval, 2013) or to assess the general causality between direct air services and tourism demand (Koo et al., 2017). A more specific popular theme for analysis, considering case studies from all over the world, is the impact of air policy, especially regulation and liberalisation, on tourism flows (Papatheodorou, 2002; Forsyth, 2006; Warnock-Smith and Morrell, 2008; Warnock-Smith and O'Connell, 2011; Dobruszkes and Mondou, 2013; Zhang and Findlay, 2014; Dobruszkes et al., 2016). This links to other related research that has looked at the role played by airline strategy, competition, and alliance strategy in tourism development (Morley, 2003; Lian and Denstadli, 2010; Liasidou, 2012: O'Connell and Warnock-Smith, 2012). Another common research area is the influence of LCCs on tourism demand (Castillo-Manzano et al., 2011; Rey et al., 2011; Tsui, 2017; Young and Whang, 2011; Farmaki and Papatheodorou, 2015; Whyte and Prideaux, 2008). Airport and destination development has also been considered in relation to tourism growth (Almeida, 2011; Lohmann et al., 2009; Halpern, 2008; Costa et al. 2010). Whilst none of these articles cover the extensive range of issues considered in one place by this book, they are an invaluable complementary resource for developing more in-depth specific knowledge. (For a more extensive literature review on air transport and tourism please, refer to Spasojevic et al., 2018.)

1.3 ESTABLISHING COMMON DEFINITIONS

Most modes of transport serve other markets as well as the tourism market. For example, many railways handle a high proportion of commuter traffic, whilst the private car gets used predominately for local journeys for pleasure (e.g. recreation, visiting friends) and necessity (e.g. work, food shopping). However, air travel is somewhat unique as it deals almost exclusively with the tourism market, that is, if freight demand is excluded, and if established international definitions of tourism are accepted. This is partly because the nature of air travel means that passengers have to be travelling outside their *normal environment* which is a prerequisite for these formal international definitions of tourism. In 2017, 55% of all global tourist arrivals were by air (UNWTO, 2018).

The UNWTO has recommendations on how 'tourism' should be defined for the purpose of the collection of statistics. From the demand side it has the following definitions (UNWTO, 2010, pp. 99–100):

- A *traveller* is someone who moves between different geographic locations, for any purpose and any duration.
- A *visitor* is a traveller taking a trip to a main destination outside his/her usual environment, for less than a year, for any main purpose (business, leisure, or other personal purpose) other than to be employed by a resident entity in the country or place visited.
- A visitor is classified as a *tourist* (*or overnight visitor*), if his/her trip includes an overnight stay, or as a *same-day visitor* (*or excursionist*) otherwise.

More specifically within the European Union (EU), Regulation (EU) 692/2011 established a common framework for the systematic development, production, and dissemination of European statistics on tourism with definitions in line with these internationally recommended guidelines with the exception of a few Europe specific situations. These definitions are thus used for Eurostat publications (Eurostat, 2014). Moreover, the Organisation for Economic Co-operation and Development (OECD) also uses the same concepts in its reports (e.g. OECD, 2018).

In reality, within the 'tourism' sector, although such definitions have been well established for a number of years, they are not always universally applied and so this can produce inconsistencies and confusion when tourism data is analysed. Moreover, the air transport sector and the public at large tend to equate *tourism* with just personal travel, excluding business trips. In this book, the broader definition is generally accepted whenever possible (i.e. both personal and business demand = tourism demand) and the text aims to make it explicitly clear when just one type of tourism is being considered. However, given the very significant differences in the characteristics and needs of personal and business travellers, the overriding focus of this book is intentionally and undoubtedly personal tourism. Other texts, such as Beaverstock et al. (2010), deal with business tourism.

In addition, the difference in approach to data gathering within the two sectors, in spite of their close relationship, presents significant challenges when measuring and comparing demand. Air transport tends to use passengers or passenger-kilometres but often it is not possible to identify true origin and destination of travel or purpose. By contrast tourism demand is usually measured by looking at tourist numbers/arrivals, tourist-nights, or tourism expenditure but again this is not always split by purpose. So very often both the air transport and tourist data will not be at a sufficient level of disaggregation to consider personal air tourism specifically but in most cases it is this type of tourism that will dominate.

A further complication is in how the non-business or personal tourism is defined. UNWTO (2010) subdivides personal tourism into a number of different categories:

- Holidays, leisure, and recreation
- Visiting friends and relatives (VFR)
- Education and training
- Health and medical care
- Religion/pilgrimages
- Shopping
- Transit
- Other

Again, from a practical context, there tends to be inconsistencies in how such personal tourism is defined. Often two major categories will be used, namely, business and leisure, with leisure including all 'personal' categories listed before (Stock and Duhamel, 2005). Another popular alternative is when there are three main categories, namely, business, leisure, and VFR. Indeed, there are frequent debates as to whether VFR should come under the heading of *leisure* as, on the one hand, it usually involves an element of pleasure and may well be discretionary travel, whilst on the other hand, it may also be considered as some kind of obligatory travel, with this necessity element, arguably to some extent, making it more akin to business tourism. Globally using the UNWTO definitions in 2017, business and professional purposes accounted for 13% of trips; whereas leisure, recreation, and holidays accounted for 53%; VFR, health, religion, and other (27%); and not specified 7% (UNWTO, 2018). For each destination, however, these shares may vary considerably. Within this book since there is no consistent approach, a more flexible view has been adopted. In some cases, leisure tourism is assumed to be the same as personal tourism, whereas elsewhere a narrower definition has been used, particularly with VFR being considered separately. Again, whenever possible this is made explicit in the text.

All these divergences in understanding what is meant by 'tourism' of course complicates research and the dialogue between disciplines as well as between stakeholders. It is worth noting that the use of well-established, but broader (and thus vaguer), definitions, may be unintentional and only due to gaps in sources. But in other cases, it can be part of a strategy aimed at inflating the weight of tourism so politicians can capitalise on the alleged success of their policies (Dobruszkes et al., 2016).

Moving on to supply-side definitions, similarly there are some disparities in how the tourism industry is viewed. UNWTO (2010) states that it includes the following:

- Accommodation for visitors
- Food and beverage serving activities
- Railway passenger transport
- Road passenger transport
- Water passenger transport
- Air passenger transport
- Transport equipment rental
- Travel agencies and other reservation services activities
- Cultural activities
- Sports and recreational activities
- Retail trade of country-specific tourism
- Other country-specific tourism activities

Therefore, from a tourism viewpoint the tourist industry is said to include transport. By contrast the air transport sector, and to a certain extent the public at large, consider this somewhat differently with typically the tourism industry being associated with what goes on at the destination, and with transport being related to getting to and from the destination. This matches up with tourism expenditure data that usually only includes spending at the destination. Moreover, from a public sector viewpoint very often within government bodies and agencies there will be different departments or ministries associated with tourism and transport which subsequently leads to separate and independent strategies and initiatives being developed. As a consequence this can lead to poorly coordinated and sometimes even conflicting polices being established—this tends to be one of the fundamental problems facing these industries. The approach in this book is primarily to consider these two sectors as different industries, but at the same time acknowledging the close relationship between the two, which by necessity is a dominant theme that runs throughout all chapters.

1.4 STRUCTURE OF THE BOOK

As identified before, the book is divided into four themes representing the different stages of the tourist's journey. The chapters have been written by an international team of expert contributors, all with a proven experience of research and publication in their specialist areas. The exact mix of contributors has been carefully chosen to create a good blend of representation from different backgrounds. The chapters offer cutting edge critical debates based on original research and/or literature reviews. A balance has been sought between issues related to theoretical concepts and practical implications. Some overlap between chapters has been inevitable and desirable to ensure that together they provide a coherent and linked assessment of key issues, but this has been kept to a minimum.

1.4.1 Part I: The Rationale for Flying (Chapters 2–4)

The first chapter (Chapter 2) in this part written by Claire Humphreys considers the realms of contemporary tourism, by discussing the characteristics of the market, as developed nations experience market maturity and emerging economies provide new destinations and markets in earlier phases of development. It looks at economic disruptions, technological innovations, and other pull and push factors that determine demand, such as shifting patterns of demographic and geographic change. It concludes with an examination of the contemporary issues that have shaped the operation of the tourism industry, driven in part by changing attitudes to environmental and social sustainability.

The next chapter (Chapter 3) jointly authored by Frédéric Dobruszkes, David Ramos-Pérez, and Jean-Michel Decroly looks at reasons for flying. The authors review flying purposes based on available evidence, mostly from national surveys that cover international trips. They put into perspective certain beliefs, including the alleged dominance of business air travel, and highlight how reasons for flying vary across places, according to attributes and over time (both long-term structural changes and seasonal patterns).

The final topic in this part (Chapter 4), written by Anne Graham and David Metz, discusses concepts related to limits to growth from a demand viewpoint. Using a UK case study, the influence of time and income constraints in relation to both frequent and infrequent flyers is considered and evidence of demand maturity is investigated for a few specific UK markets. It is concluded that standard models of demand for air travel or tourism do not adequately reflect factors contributing to market maturity and the nature of frequent and infrequent flyers, and more understanding of such concepts is needed.

1.4.2 Part II: Before Travelling—Choosing Transport Modes, Airlines and Airports (Chapters 5–11)

This part begins with Chapter 5, authored by David Timothy Duval, and considers the impact of government policy and regulation. It does this by bringing together two broad themes with respect to the intersection of tourism and air transport. It first revisits the key characteristics of the relationship, including the influence of specific variables and elements, and finds that the arrangement of, and connectivity generated by, the international (and national) air transport system, can have a profound influence on the structure and scope of tourism. The second is consideration of the wider policy environment in which both coexist, suggesting that such a coexistence ultimately reveals government-sanctioned 'arranged mobility'.

The focus of the next chapter (Chapter 6), written by Daniel Albalate Del Sol and Xavier Fageda Sanjuan, then shifts to intermodal competition and tourism, by considering the important case of Spain. Empirical evidence shows the potentially detrimental effects that high-speed rail services may have on tourism demand, and in particular the negative net effect on domestic tourism because they lead to a substantial reduction of air transport in domestic flights that cannot be compensated for by rail services. Thus, the chapter concludes that diversifying the transport supply does not always imply better tourism outcomes, and intermodal competition must be considered when evaluating new transport projects.

The following chapter (Chapter 7) produced by Tim Ryley discusses the factors influencing the tourist choice of airport. It does this by considering the concepts associated with leisure travel, life stage, tourism trip type, and aviation choices within the airport context. Underpinning methodologies that can determine choice for air transport applications are assessed, as are a series of themes relating to air transport applications that have a focus on airport choice for tourists, such as the role of airport catchment areas, airport region strategic planning, and possible impacts of technology development.

In the next chapter (Chapter 8), authored by Augusto Voltes-Dorta and Juan Carlos Martín, attention is turned to the topical issue of self-connection. It is hypothesised that leisure travellers are expected to be one of the segments of demand most likely to benefit from self-connections, and so there is an investigation of the implications of self-connection from the perspective of the destination airports using data on European holiday markets in the Mediterranean region. The destination airports are ranked according to the potential benefits from self-connectivity by tapping into new origin markets to which they are not already connected in the traditional sense, showing how airports serving tourist destinations can identify new market opportunities.

Another important issue related to tourist choice is distribution trends which are considered by Michael Hanke in the next chapter (Chapter 9). This investigates how the transformation of the airline distribution ecosystem, fuelled by changes in the socioeconomic and demographic area, technology, disintermediation, global distribution systems and online travel agency developments, mobile distribution channels and emerging disruptors, is affecting the tourists that are travelling by air. Related concepts such as fare merchandising, ancillaries, and personalisation, as well as the growing importance of big data, new distribution capabilities, and artificial intelligence are explored.

The last two chapters in this part consider choices between different airline business models. The first one (Chapter 10) authored by John Frankie O'Connell provides an insightful and contemporary overview of the four different models, namely, LCCs, full-service network airlines, charter airlines, and regional airlines. It considers how the LCCs have caused the greatest seismic shift in airline history as they have reshaped the industry's competitive dynamics, whilst the legacy full-service airlines have incorporated specific traits of the LCCs but have retained their own value adding but product differentiating characteristics pivoted by their seamless hub and spoke connectivity. The charter airline's decline appears evident on the short-haul market, whilst the long-haul all-inclusive package holiday is resisting abatement due to its unique value proposition. For regional airlines, the chapter concludes that these will continue to primarily serve thin short-haul routes that are uneconomic for airlines with larger narrow-body aircraft.

Chapter 11, written by David Ramos-Pérez and Frédéric Dobruszkes, is the last chapter in this part. It focuses specifically on the role of charter airlines that have traditionally almost exclusively handled passengers travelling for holiday purposes. It analyses the diverse transformations of airlines involved with tourist flows in the context of aviation liberalisation, including so-called charter airlines or leisure airlines that now carry both package and seat-only passengers. The result is a continuum of different air carriers serving tourist routes after liberalisation. The authors then investigate the common belief that competition induced by low-cost carriers is shifting charter airlines towards long-haul markets, which is an idea that is challenged.

1.4.3 Part III: On the Go—Accessing Airports and the Airline and Airport Experience (Chapters 12–14)

The third part of this book moves on to considering issues related to passengers as they travel to airports, their experiences at airports, and the relationship between airlines and airports. The first chapter (Chapter 12), presented by Thomas Budd, looks at the role of different airport surface models where there is a need to balance often competing operational, strategic, and commercial requirements with the demands of different airport users. In particular, passengers pose a specific challenge due to the large number of trips generated, and the wide range of factors affecting their travel. Thus, the chapter examines the varying requirements and characteristics of air passengers in a surface access context at key stages of the door-to-door journey; ranging from pre-trip planning and mode choice to arrival and onward travel at their destination.

The next chapter (Chapter 13) authored by Walanchalee Wattanacharoensil explores the concept of the airport experience, as airports have started to move away from just applying a Level of Service (LoS) standard and service quality approach to enhance overall passenger satisfaction. The different dimensions of the airport experience are provided and the key drivers of the airport experience, both from a demand and supply side, are identified. Suggestions are made in terms of how airports can be effectively managed to fully take into account the passenger experience concept.

This part concludes with a chapter (Chapter 14), written by Frank Fichert, that describes the relationship between airports and airlines, with a specific focus on airports in typical leisure tourism regions and the changes induced by the rise of LCCs. Based on a discussion of objectives of the several entities along the value chain and an analysis of airline route choice, an airport's options for influencing airline decisions are presented. Common instruments like incentives within charging schemes and long-term contracts between airports and airlines are discussed, and some examples of partial vertical integration between airlines and airports are presented.

1.4.4 Part IV: Reaching the Destination and Attractions (Chapters 15–17)

Progressing through the passenger journey, the final part of the book considers issues related to reaching destinations and the role of tourist attractions. The first chapter (Chapter 15) authored by Nigel Halpern investigates the partnerships between destination management organisations (DMOs) and other tourism destination stakeholders with the air transport sector. Two main types of partnership, namely, marketing and funding partnerships are considered. Marketing partnerships are a joint commitment to strengthen awareness for the destination or the quality of air access, whilst funding partnerships provide financial aid or marketing support to encourage new routes that may not otherwise be launched. Numerous examples are provided and a detailed case study from Northern Norway is presented.

The next chapter (Chapter 16), written by Andy Goetz, considers the airport as an attraction in the context of an airport city or aerotropolis. It is explained that these two concepts have captured the imaginations of political leaders and economic development officials through the claims that airports are becoming the centres of urban regions, but such concepts are also subject to a range of economic, environmental, and social critiques. Three of the most well-known airport-oriented developments, located near airports serving Seoul, Dubai, and Amsterdam, are profiled in this chapter, which highlights their successes and shortcomings.

The final chapter (Chapter 17) in this part, presented by Isaac Levi Henderson and Wai Hong Kan Tsui, highlights the important but rarely researched relationship between tourism and niche aviation operations. The focus is on four key areas of tourism that are serviced by niche aviation operations, namely, adventure tourism, scenic tourism, heritage tourism, and space tourism. The nature of novelty and memorable tourist experiences is outlined and related to why niche aviation operations have become an important part of the tourism industry. Examples are provided to demonstrate how innovation in niche aviation operations could provide potential for further growth within the tourism and aviation industries.

Finally, this leads to the concluding chapter (Chapter 18). This reflects on the content of the book, viewing the air transport/tourism cross-relationships as a multifactor, multilevel process. It acknowledges that whilst some chapters have reinforced or confirmed some conventional understandings of these relationships, others have challenged these and brought new perspectives. The chapter concludes by identifying trends and uncertainties for the future.

So now all the preparations are done and we wish you a pleasant tourist journey.

References

Almeida, C., 2011. The new challenges of tourism airports—the case of Faro airport. Tour. Manag. Stud. 7, 109–120.

Beaverstock, J.V., Derudder, B., Faulconbridge, J., Witlox, F. (Eds.), 2010. International Business Travel in the Global Economy. Routledge, London.

Bieger, T., Wittmer, A., 2006. Air transport and tourism—perspectives and challenges for destinations, airlines and governments. J. Air Transp. Manag. 12, 40–46.

Bowen, J., 2010. The Economic Geography of Air Transportation: Space, Time, and the Freedom of the Sky. Routledge, Abington.

Castillo-Manzano, J.I., Lopez-Valpuesta, L., Gonzalez-Laxe, F., 2011. The effects of the LCC boom on the urban tourism fabric: the viewpoint of tourism managers. Tour. Manag. 32, 1085–1095.

Costa, T.F.G., Lohmann, G., Oliveira, A.V.M., 2010. A model to identify airport hubs and their importance to tourism in Brazil. Res. Transp. Econ. 26 (1), 3–11.

Dobruszkes, F., Mondou, V., 2013. Aviation liberalization as a means to promote international tourism: the EU-Morocco case. J. Air Transp. Manag. 29, 23–34.

Dobruszkes, F., Mondou, V., Ghedira, A., 2016. Assessing the impacts of aviation liberalisation on tourism: some methodological considerations derived from the Moroccan and Tunisian cases. J. Transp. Geogr. 50, 115–127.

Doganis, R., 2010. Flying Off Course: Airline Economics and Marketing, fourth ed. Routledge, Abingdon.

Duval, D.T., 2007. Tourism and Transport Modes, Networks and Flows. Channel View, Clevedon.

Duval, D.T., 2013. Critical issues in air transport and tourism. Tour. Geogr. 15 (3), 494–510.

Eurostat, 2014. Methodological Manual for Tourism Statistics. Eurostat, Brussels.

Farmaki, A., Papatheodorou, A., 2015. Stakeholder perceptions of the role of low-cost carriers in insular tourism destinations: the case of Cyprus. Tour. Hosp. Plann. Dev. 12 (4), 412–432.

Forsyth, P., 2006. Martin Kunz memorial lecture: tourism benefits and aviation policy. J. Air Transp. Manag. 12 (1), 3–13.

Goetz, A., Budd, L. (Eds.), 2014. Geographies of Air Transport. Ashgate, Farnham.

Graham, A., Papatheodorou, A., Forsyth, P. (Eds.), 2008. Aviation and Tourism: Implications for Leisure Travel. Ashgate, Aldershot.

Gross, S., Klemmer, L., 2014. Introduction to Tourism Transport. CABI, Wallingford.

Halpern, N., 2008. Lapland's airports: facilitating the development of international tourism in a peripheral region. Scand. J. Hosp. Tour. 8 (1), 25–47.

Koo, T.T.R., Lim, C., Dobruszkes, F., 2017. Causality in direct air services and tourism demand. Ann. Tour. Res. 67, 67–77.

Lian, J.I., Denstadli, J.M., 2010. Booming leisure air travel to Norway—the role of airline competition. Scand. J. Hosp. Tour. 10 (1), 1–15.

Liasidou, S., 2012. Decision-making for tourism destinations: airline strategy influences. Tour. Geogr. 15 (3), 511–528.

Lohmann, G., Albers, S., Koch, B., Pavlovich, K., 2009. From hub to tourist destination—an explorative study of Singapore and Dubai's aviation-based transformation. J. Air Transp. Manag. 15 (5), 205–211.

Lumsdon, L., Page, S. (Eds.), 2004. Tourism and Transport: Issues and Agenda for the New Millennium. Oxford, London.

Morley, C.L., 2003. Impacts of international airline alliances on tourism. Tour. Econ. 9 (1), 31–51.

O'Connell, J.F., Warnock-Smith, D., 2012. Liberalization and strategic change in air transport: an examination of current and future variations in tourist traffic to and from Egypt resulting from policy changes at Egypt Air. Tour. Econ. 18 (4), 845–870.

OECD, 2018. Tourism Trends and Policies 2018. OECD, Paris.

Page, S., 2009. Transport and Tourism: Global Perspectives, third ed. Prentice Hall, Harlow.

Papatheodorou, A., 2002. Civil aviation regimes and leisure tourism in Europe. J. Air Transp. Manag. 8 (6), 381–388.

Rey, B., Myro, R., Galera, A., 2011. Effect of low-cost airlines on tourism in Spain, a dynamic panel data model. J. Air Transp. Manag. 17, 163–167.

Spasojevic, B., Lohmann, G., Scott, N., 2018. Air transport and tourism—a systematic literature review (2001–2014). Curr. Issue Tour. 21 (9), 975–997.

Stock, M., Duhamel, P., 2005. A Practice-Based Approach to the Conceptualisation of Geographical Mobility. Belgeo 2005–1&2, 59–68. Available at https://belgeo.revues.org/12415. (Accessed February 11, 2018).

Tsui, K.W.H., 2017. Does a low-cost carrier lead the domestic tourism demand and growth of New Zealand? Tour. Manag. 60, 390–403.

UNWTO, 2010. International Recommendations for Tourism Statistics 2008. UNWTO, New York.

UNWTO, 2012. Global Report on Aviation. UNWTO, Madrid.

UNWTO, 2018. Infographics. Available at http://media.unwto.org/content/infographics. (Accessed May 27, 2018).

Warnock-Smith, D., Morrell, P., 2008. Air transport liberalisation and traffic growth in tourism dependent economies: a case-history of some US-Caribbean markets. J. Air Transp. Manag. 14 (2), 82–91.

Warnock-Smith, D., O'Connell, J.F., 2011. The impact of air policy on incoming tourist traffic: the contrasting cases of the Caribbean community and the Middle-East. J. Transp. Geogr. 19, 265–274.

Wheatcroft, S., 1994. Aviation and Tourism Policies: Balancing the Benefits. UNWTO/Routledge, Madrid/London.

Whyte, R., Prideaux, B., 2008. The growth in low-cost carrier services in Queensland: implications for regional tourism destinations. Tour. Recreat. Res. 33 (1), 59–66.

Young, J., Whang, T., 2011. The impact of low cost carriers on Korean island tourism. J. Transp. Geogr. 19, 1335–1340.

Zhang, Y., Findlay, C., 2014. Air transport policy and its impacts on passenger traffic and tourist flows. J. Air Transp. Manag. 34, 42–48.

PART I

THE RATIONALE FOR FLYING

CHAPTER

2

The Contemporary Tourist

Claire HUMPHREYS
University of Westminster, London, United Kingdom

CHAPTER OUTLINE

2.1 INTRODUCTION

Annually 9 billion domestic tourism trips and more than 1.1 billion international trips are taken (Euromonitor, 2016). Since the 1950s, when around 25 million cross-border trips were taken globally, the tourism industry has experienced virtually uninterrupted growth (UNWTO, 2016). Today more than half of the 1.1 billion international tourist arrivals are by air and the aviation industry is heavily influenced by the patterns of tourism demand.

This chapter examines the characteristics of the contemporary tourist and considers the trends and influences shaping travel patterns. This focuses predominantly on leisure tourism but the factors discussed often also relate to business tourists and those travelling to visit family and friends, whether staying overnight or travelling as day-trip excursionists. The chapter also explores some key issues affecting tourist behaviour and industry operations.

Globally domestic tourism far exceeds that of international tourism but nationally the significance of domestic tourism can vary substantially. For example, in the United States, Canada, Germany, the United Kingdom, and Japan, domestic tourism accounts for around 80% of total tourism consumption whereas Iceland, Poland, and Slovenia see about two-thirds of their tourism consumption coming from international tourists (OECD, 2016). However, appreciating the travel patterns of domestic tourists is challenging, with a lack of reliable statistics (Swarbrooke and Horner, 2007), due to challenges associated with surveying domestic tourists and a systemic lack of enthusiasm by local governments to invest funds in such data collection. Thus all too often the market characteristics, behaviour, and scale of travel taking place within national borders remain largely unknown.

As discussed in Chapter 1, whilst the main purpose of travel can be varied, international travel is often grouped into three categories, namely, leisure, business, and VFR (visiting friends and relatives) with the relative shares of each group remaining fairly consistent over time (Nawijn and Peeters, 2014). Each of these categories can experience different peaks and troughs through the year, creating seasonal patterns that the tourism and transport industries must consider when supplying products to meet demand.

The ever increasing numbers of tourists has led to more destinations investing public money in products and infrastructure designed to attract visitors (Saarinen, 2003). Tourism development is seen as a key driver of socio-economic progress, creating jobs and export revenues (UNWTO, 2016). This means that an expanding number of destinations are offering ever greater choice for the experienced traveller. Furthermore, with most travellers taking

Air Transport—A Tourism Perspective. https://doi.org/10.1016/B978-0-12-812857-2.00002-6

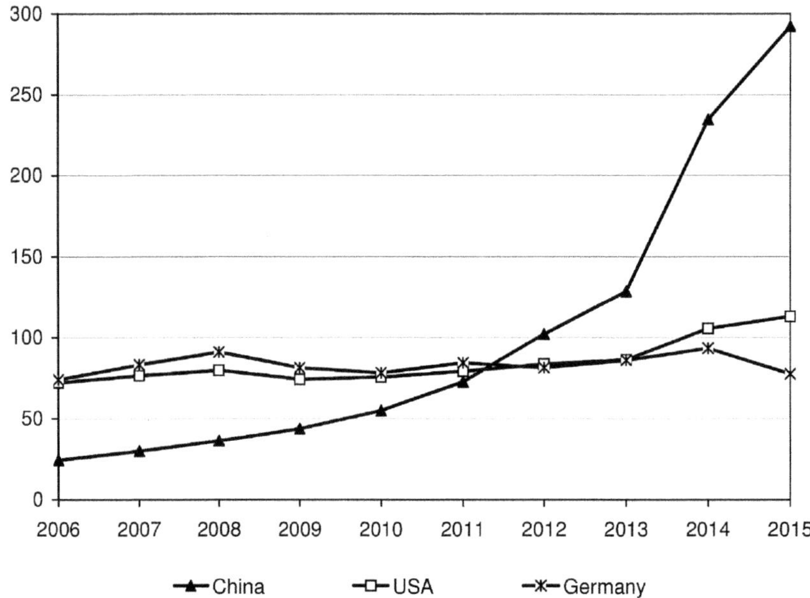

FIG. 2.1 Expenditure by residents of China, United States, and Germany on international tourism trips (US$ Billion). *(Source: UNWTO Tourism Highlights 2006–16.)*

international trips within their region, such growth also offers convenient destinations for markets from the newly emerging economies. Europe is still the most popular destination region, accounting for about half of all international tourist arrivals, with the Asia Pacific region in second place with almost one-quarter of global market share. As well as providing new destinations for existing markets, the emerging economies are fuelling the growth in tourism demand (Buckley et al., 2015). China, in particular, has experienced a rapid increase in outbound tourism (Fig. 2.1) and now tops the table for international tourism expenditure. China has also experienced substantial domestic tourism growth, with increasing incomes releasing suppressed demand and shaping travel preferences (Bihu et al., 2000; Cooper et al., 2005). The economic disparity between regions in China affects the types of travel product sought.

There is also greater influence from the millennial generation, searching for authentic cultural and social experiences that engage with local populations and use technology to inform choices (Moscardo and Benckendorff, 2010; Leask et al., 2014) (see Chapter 9). Whilst established and emerging destinations are aware of the demands by millennials, World Travel Monitor data suggests that demand patterns from this group are, in the main, not so very different from other older travellers (IPK International, 2016). Recognising the similarities and differences between markets is vital if businesses are to continue to meet the rapidly changing expectations of contemporary tourists.

2.2 CHARACTERISTICS OF CONTEMPORARY TOURISTS

The different stages of market maturity (Rovelstad and Blazer, 1983) mean that tourist characteristics vary enormously by region (see Chapter 4). The factors which will influence characteristics include availability of disposable income, the extent of prior travel experience, availability of leisure time and lifestage. The latter includes changes such as late-forming families in some regions, longer periods of living with parents, and more marriages without children.

For the mature markets of Europe and North America increased heterogeneity has been seen, as tourists have greater independence and individualism. There is also some level of spontaneity in travel—with short lead-time bookings now common when compared to the long-planned vacations of the past. One recent UK survey revealed that almost one-quarter of holidays were booked in the 3-week period before departure (Mintel, 2017). Similarly, an United States survey reported that less than one-third of airline bookings were made more than a month in advance of travel and for hotels three-quarters were booked in the week preceding arrival. Perhaps somewhat surprisingly 32% were booked on the same day as the stay (Sojern, 2013). This is perhaps a reflection of both the perishability of the product, a degree of homogeneity of product offering and easy cancellation terms offered by the hotel industry that encourages 'sophisticated last minute deal-seeking customers' to reserve accommodation with the likelihood of swapping to a new booking if a better deal is offered (Chih-Chien and Zvi, 2013, p. 17).

The emerging markets also offer new influences on the global travel industry. For example, air travel growth from the Asia-Pacific and Middle East regions far outstrips that of the United States (Martín, 2015). There is a suggestion that consumers from emerging markets demonstrate greater levels of involvement in the travel purchase process and limited travel experience means word-of-mouth recommendations often carry greater weight (Li, 2016). Once at a destination travel spending patterns are noticeably different, with higher retail spend on items such as electronics or cosmetics ahead of purchasing souvenirs. As with the developed markets there is a noticeable difference between generations of travellers and thus emerging economies also experience some market heterogeneity. Whilst it is useful to recognise the growing importance of the emerging economies on the travel industry there is a wide variety of travel trends which have an effect on all travellers regardless of origin.

2.3 TRENDS IN TRAVEL

A significant influence on the travel industry of recent years has been the increased incidence of terrorism at popular tourism destinations. In some cases tourists were a key target for many of the attacks (e.g. in Sousse (Tunisia) in 2015, Bali (Indonesia) in 2002, and Luxor (Egypt) in 1997) because it is likely to generate substantial media coverage, disrupt a source of revenue for the government and hit back at those nations often in opposition to the terrorist's ideals (Neumayer, 2004). In other cases attacks have occurred at destinations popular with tourists (e.g. Paris and Nice (France) in 2015 and 2016, London (England) in 2005, and New York and Washington (United States) in 2001). Such attacks may not deter international travel from taking place but instead divert visitors to alternative destinations (IPK International, 2016). There is also some evidence that domestic tourism can be curtained by terrorism but this effect is reduced as tourists learn to cope with frequent attacks (Adeloye and Brown, 2018). For many travellers the fear of terrorism is substantially greater than the likelihood of being a victim (Kozak et al., 2007) and over time tourists are learning to live with such uncertainties. Consequently, research by the World Travel and Tourism Council (WTTC) reveals that "on average, it takes approximately 13 months for a place to recover from a terrorist attack" (LaGrave, 2016).

The maturity of the tourism industry in developed economies has led to increased demand for customisable travel, as travellers seek greater independence. Experienced European travellers are increasingly preferring specialised holidays over mass-packaged holidays (CBI Market Intelligence, 2016). This is being driven by the ability to book low-cost flights and use online comparison websites to search out the most suitable accommodation. Consequently, travellers are purchasing the individual components of a trip independently or using the dynamic packaging services provided by travel retailers. Dynamic packaging is the process by which retailers put together flights, accommodation, and other travel components from numerous suppliers and sell the resulting package to consumers—one advantage for European travellers being that it gains protection under the Package Travel legislation (Holloway and Humphreys, 2016).

CASE STUDY 2.1 PACKAGE HOLIDAYS VS DIRECT BOOKING

Saga, a company established to provide products and services for the 'Over-50' market recognised the independent travel habits of their audience, producing travel advice on the pros and cons of booking packages over direct booking. They concluded:

- Package holidays tend to be cheaper because tour operators have negotiated deals for flights and accommodation. However, flights might be at unsociable times.
- One price for all aspects of the package, paid up-front, means greater transparency to the total holiday cost.
- European law (primarily the Package Travel Directive) provides greater protection against failure of travel companies.
- Tour operators providing packages often have local representatives to help if emergencies occur.
- Some customisation of packages is often possible but for the most part packages are usually of standard lengths (7/10/14 nights).
- Direct bookings allow greater freedom of choice.
- Direct bookings can better suit trips of irregular lengths or multi-city trips. They can also be better for shorter city breaks.
- Some suppliers will provide incentives (such as room upgrades, free wifi, or air miles) when customers book direct.
- Payment for hotels may not occur until departure which means costs can fluctuate between reservation and payment. Thus holiday costs are paid after the service is used rather than in advance.
- Direct bookings may not be covered by European legislation protection (or the ATOL scheme) thus travel insurance would be vital for protection against failure of suppliers.

Source: Saga (2016).

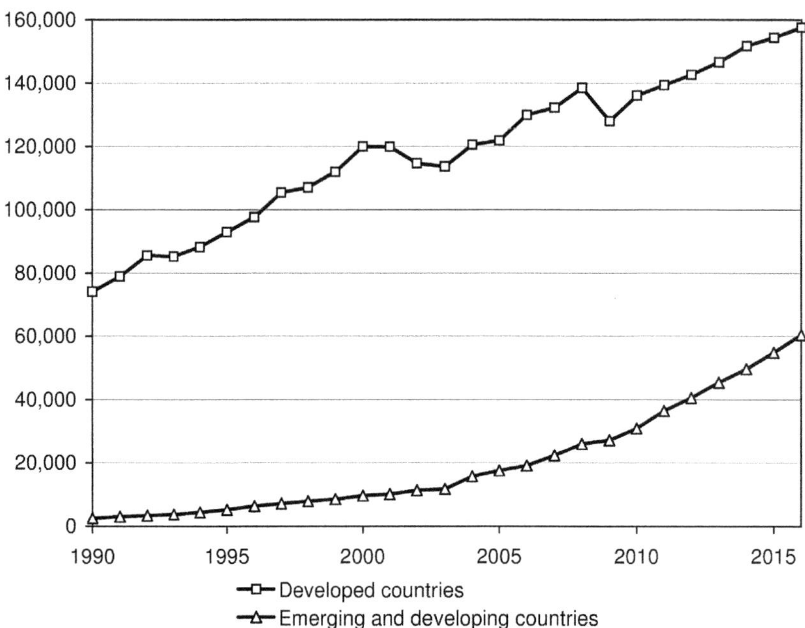

FIG. 2.2 Global consumer expenditure on package holidays (US$ million, current prices—fixed 2016 exchange rates). *(Source: Euromonitor (2017). Consumer Expenditure on Package Holidays: Statistics. London: Euromonitor.)*

Independent travel is being driven by the increased levels of prior travel experience and a desire for serendipitous opportunities for rewarding vacation experiences (Hyde and Lawson, 2003), often propelled by a search for authenticity and self-fulfilment. This has led to a rise in adventure travel reflecting 'the consumer shift away from material possessions towards an interest in actual experiences' (Euromonitor, 2016, p. 25) and the creation of destination event portfolios designed to appeal to local and tourist audiences.

The development of package holidays and charter airlines (introduced in the 1950s) (Chapter 11) inspired the rapid growth of international travel for the European markets over the following decades and it is important today in encouraging growth in developing nations. Euromonitor (2017) forecasts that spending on package holidays by the emerging and developing countries will expand to exceed US$637 billion by 2030, a tenfold increase of levels today (Fig. 2.2).

The effects of the 2008 global financial crisis influenced patterns of holiday-taking (Smeral, 2009), with reduced levels of discretionary spend leading to less long-haul travel from major European markets (Holloway and Humphreys, 2016), less tolerance of poor products or service experiences, and greater emphasis on value for money (OECD, 2016). A balance between speed, comfort, and cost continues to influence holiday choices and with around two-thirds of international trips made by Europeans lasting between 1 and 7 nights (IPK International, 2016) short-haul travel dominates. However, long-haul travel is now being stimulated by changes in the airline sector, with budget long-haul travel developing (CBI Market Intelligence, 2016) (see Chapters 9 and 10). Furthermore, air travel is increasing in value due to improved aviation technology (OECD, 2016).

The digital world is influencing consumer behaviour and tourism is an early adopter of digital innovation (see Chapter 9). Now information provision, price comparisons, real-time bookings, chatbots answering questions, and augmented reality all help to enhance the travel experience (Benckendorff et al., 2014). The development of digital platforms is driven by the benefits of network effects with complementary offerings that bring in a large number of users, increasing the value and significance of the platform. Companies such as Uber and Airbnb have created successful platforms to develop their business model and such systems are 'changing the relationships between consumers and producers, supporting cocreation and facilitating the more personalised experiences sought by consumers' (OECD, 2016, p. 31).

CASE STUDY 2.2 CHATBOTS AND THE TRAVEL INDUSTRY

The increased effectiveness of artificial intelligence has seen the creation of chatbots, computer programmes which mimic language styles to create quasi-conversations that replace traditional website searches. Hosted on a message system (Facebook messenger, text messages, etc.) an increasing number of chatbots are being developed by the tourism industry to help travellers book flights and hotels.

Intermediaries such as Skyscanner, Kayak, and Cheapflights have all developed chatbots for Facebook messenger, whereby customers respond to a series of text questions leading to a flight or hotel quote. KLM has also developed a Facebook messenger chatbot that provides flight status and boarding pass updates.

Although still in early stages of development, as artificial intelligence levels develop further and natural language processing improves so will the user experiences of such customer support tools.

Although some aspects of technology are seeing significant investment from the tourism industry, there are some limitations. It is forecast that more than one billion people globally will gain online access between 2016 and 2020, the majority using a mobile device. Yet, despite this predicted growth, travel companies generally have been slow to expand mobile-friendly websites, leading to often poor user experiences (Torres, 2017). Thus tourism businesses need to support travellers connecting to their websites and digital platforms via different wireless networks. Third and fourth generation (3G/4G) networks are widely available but can be slow, impacting user engagement with online resources (Picco-Schwendener and Cantoni, 2015). Mobile-optimised websites adapt the architectural layout to suit the screen size, rather than shrinking content to fit a smaller space. Consequently, the variety of content adjusts to suit the device, with enhanced usability increasing overall satisfaction (Groth and Haslwanter, 2015). Whilst these, and other, trends are affecting the tourism industry it is vital to consider their influence alongside a variety of factors affecting demand patterns.

2.4 FACTORS SHAPING DEMAND

Tourism demand is influenced by those factors which encourage the tourists to take a holiday or trip, and those which encourage visits to one destination ahead of others. These are commonly determined as push and pull factors, respectively (Dann, 1977; Gilbert, 1991). Pull factors reflect the appeal of the destination, influencing choice of one destination over others. This might be determined by the attractions offered, climate, culture, food, perceived value for money, safety and security, and other such influences. Push factors acknowledge a traveller's need for escape, relaxation, the opportunity to play, spend time with family, and interact with others (Crompton, 1979). It also suggests that education, self-development, and self-actualisation can stimulate travel. Historically some societies placed an inferred social status by the very nature of taking international holidays (Culler, 1981), particularly by air. However, with the advent of low-cost air travel making such trips available to a wider audience, social status is now more likely to increase through international trips to destinations perceived as exotic (Pappas, 2014).

Supporting the push factors previously discussed are travel facilitators, most significantly time and money (Holloway and Humphreys, 2016). Time free from work is deemed important to the quality of life—thus shorter working weeks and increased paid holiday has been seen with developed economies. Alongside availability of time is the availability of money. Demand for international travel closely tracks the economic conditions in major generating source markets and any increase in disposable income is likely to lead to an increase in tourism spending (OECD, 2016). Domestic travel, however, may experience counter patterns. For example, the United Kingdom saw an increase in domestic trip-taking and a parallel decline in overseas travel as the effects of the 2008 recession reduced income levels (Visit England, 2014). 'The growth of disposable income, the rise of the middle class in many emerging markets and changing attitudes of people towards travel' has enabled tourism to flourish (World Economic Forum, 2017, p. 24). Thus emerging economies will provide not only growing source markets but also new destinations which will pull tourists to their attractions and events.

Whilst the level of disposable income affects demand so too does the absolute cost of travel (Witt et al., 1991). One influence on cost is fluctuations in exchange rates and a country that is heavily reliant on one source market may consequently be susceptible when there are significant shifts in exchange rate between the two countries (WTTC, 2016). Tourists tend to have greater awareness of exchange rates with a country they plan to visit than awareness of the price of goods and services in their holiday destination (Quadri and Zheng, 2010). Whilst shifting exchange rates affect tourist demand, they also substantively affect tourism companies, many of which choose to hedge against extreme foreign exchange rates fluctuations to protect their cost margins (Patsouratis et al., 2005). For example, tour operators may need to pay airlines and hotels in dollars when their sales are in Euro, thus agreeing a forward contract to fix the exchange rate between the two currencies can minimise risk. The downside is missed benefits when the exchange rate moves in their favour. Without hedging volatile exchange rates can lead to travel businesses increasing prices charged to customers.

Alongside availability of time and money, the increase in international and domestic tourism can be attributed to changing demographics. Buckley et al. (2015, p. 63) acknowledge that, with more than 2 billion trips annually, China's domestic tourism is 'several times larger than all international tourism combined'. Global population growth expands markets but specifically rapid population growth in emerging economies and longer living populations in the developed economies combine to expand potential markets for tourism products (OECD, 2016, Tretheway and Mak, 2006). The global middle class is thus forecast to include an additional 3 billion people in the two decades ending 2031 (World Economic Forum, 2017). The rapid growth of the Chinese economy between 1980 and 2010 moved many millions of its residents out of poverty, with those earning high-than-average incomes choosing to participate in foreign travel (Mintel, 2016). Consequently, China is now the largest source market for Thailand, Japan, South Korea, and Russia. Similarly India has experienced substantive growth in outbound travel (from 13 million in 2010 to 18 million in 2014) (OECD, 2016).

A further influence is the growth of multigenerational travel—with parents, siblings, children, and grandchildren travelling together for shared experiences (Schänzel and Yeoman, 2015). This provides families who are geographically separated the opportunity to spend time together in environments that can more easily accommodate their varied needs. Two surveys completed in 2014 suggested that 18% of British and one-third of US respondents planned a multigenerational trip (defined as including at least three generations) (Kim, 2014; Goldstein, 2016). Furthermore, the growing number and affluence of grandparents means multigenerational trips allow them to share time and resources with their offspring.

The geographical separation of families through increased transnational migration has also led to increased travel, particularly VFR (Feng and Page, 2000). With a growing number of workers from low-income countries moving to work in wealthier regions, so an extended separation from partners and children becomes more common. Whilst decisions to work overseas may be a strategy designed to improve the socioeconomic circumstances of the family (Graham and Jordan, 2011) it may then require regular travel to bring these disconnected families together. In 2015 an estimated 2.7 million immigrants moved into the 28 European Union countries and a further 1.9 million moved from one EU country to another (Eurostat, 2017). Whilst this movement of people is not directly considered tourism the resulting VFR travel (either family visiting the foreign worker or the migrant returning home to see family) is substantial (Genç, 2013).

Whilst legally authorised travel has influenced tourism demand the growing refugee crisis is also affecting travel, leading to increasing border controls and visa restrictions. Nations impose visa restrictions based on their own assessment of security, political, cultural, and economic concerns in the countries of prospective visitors. Thus visa policies can have a 'restricting or encouraging effect on inbound mobility from foreign nations' (Karaman, 2016, p. 503). The European Union estimates that 6.6 million travellers annually are deterred from visiting the region due to cumbersome visa procedures (European Commission, 2014) whilst the travel ban announced by Donald Trump on taking office (and subsequent iterations not overturned in court) was forecast to deter international tourists from visiting the United States, consequently reducing tourism-related expenditure in 2017 by US$1.3billion (Horowitz, 2017). Significantly the World Economic Forum (2017) asserts that existing visa requirements are not directly enhancing national safety but are hindering tourism growth and job creation. However, visa-free travel is available for many travellers, with holders of passports issued by Singapore and Germany having the greatest freedom (Table 2.1).

Furthermore, the presence of high levels of refugee numbers can deter tourists from visiting and affect tourism operations (Pappas and Papatheodorou, 2017). As an example, in 2015–16 Greece saw vast numbers of refugees arrive at some of its islands and high-profile media reporting led to a reduction in number of tourist bookings. Consequently, holiday companies planned fewer charter flights to the affected islands and hotels saw occupancy levels plunge by as much as 70% (Hope, 2016). Media reports also suggested that the crisis deterred American tourists from taking Mediterranean cruises. Whilst such perceptions may be addressed over time to ameliorate influences on demand there are also some key contemporary issues that influence tourism operations today.

2.5 CONTEMPORARY ISSUES

Over the past few decades increased attention has been given to the responsibilities of tourism companies, particularly in regards to their impact on the environment and on host communities (World Economic Forum, 2017). Consequently, corporate social responsibility (CSR), ethical behaviour, and sustainability have all been given significant attention (Coles et al., 2013; Sandve et al., 2014; Manning, 1999). Although European consumers realise sustainable operations can be difficult to achieve, an increasing number of tourists are now expecting suppliers to at least attempt to implement sustainable practices (CBI Market Intelligence, 2016). Furthermore, the growing number

TABLE 2.1 Number of Visa-Free Countries Which Can Be Visited

Country of Issue of Passport	Number of Visa-Free Countries
Access to largest number of visa-free countries	
Germany, Singapore	159
South Korea, Sweden	158
Denmark, Finland, Italy, France, Japan, Norway, Spain, UK, USA	157
Austria, Belgium, Luxembourg, Netherlands, Portugal, Switzerland	156
Australia, Greece, New Zealand	155
Access to fewest number of visa-free countries	
Iran, Nepal, Sri Lanka, Sudan, Yemen	36
Somalia	35
Syria	30
Iraq	26
Pakistan	25
Afghanistan	22

(Source: Passport Index (2017). Global Passport Power Rank 2017. Available at https://www.passportindex.org/byRank.php. (Accessed July 6, 2017).)

of globetrotters means sustainable transport systems are important to controlling the overall level of emissions and impacts of tourism, and consequently more airlines are reporting their efforts at sustainability (PWC, 2011). There have also been common targets set to reduce aircraft carbon emissions and enhance fuel efficiency (World Economic Forum, 2017). Notwithstanding such enhancements air traffic increased by 80% between 1990 and 2014 and at that time was said to be responsible for about 2% of man-made carbon emission (Li and Cui, 2017). Consequently, the environmental efficiency gains per passenger kilometre have been overshadowed because total environmental impacts have substantially increased over the past 25 years (EEA et al., 2016).

CASE STUDY 2.3 BRITISH AIRWAYS

Like most firms, British Airways (BA) has reported on its responsible practices to highlight efforts to spread social and economic benefits. Its current corporate responsibility programme focuses on five themes:

1. To create sustainable and responsible communities
2. To promote well-being and inclusion
3. To conduct business responsibly
4. To reduce British Airways' environmental impact
5. To reduce waste and improve recycling

One aspect of this policy is to promote the health and well-being of employees (British Airways, 2017). Whilst this endeavour is a desirable goal in the summer of 2017 BA cabin crew announced several strikes because of a long-running dispute over pay. To try and break the strikes BA leased aircraft from Qatar Airlines, leading to claims that such actions were in contravention of its own CSR policy (Harley, 2017).

As tourism companies take greater interest in sustainability so there are a growing number of companies offering sustainability certification (OECD, 2016). These include:

- Earth Check
- Green Globe
- Rainforest Alliance
- Travelife Sustainability System
- Blue Flag

Certification schemes are developed by non-profit organisations, private tourism organisations, stakeholder groups and governments. For example, the UK Green Tourism scheme is operated by a not-for-profit association, and supported by the UK national tourist boards, to encourage attractions and accommodation providers to improve their sustainability credentials. With more than 100 recognised certification schemes for the tourism industry operating internationally there is plenty of opportunity for gaining accreditation and recognition (Jarvis et al., 2012). However, there is some criticism of many schemes which focus on improving the operating processes of businesses, or the way they measure, manage, and report efforts to operate more sustainably, rather than actually achieving the highest level of sustainability (Francis, 2017).

Moving on from sustainability to ethical responsibility, the tourism industry has frequently developed codes of conduct. The UNWTO Global Code of Ethics for Tourism provides a frame of reference to encourage responsible tourism. The key principles encourage mutual respect between societies; provide positive opportunities for individuals whilst avoiding exploitation of others; have respect for artistic, archaeological, and cultural heritage; provide equitable benefits for local communities; promote freedom to travel; and protect the rights of workers in the tourism industry. Implementation of these principles is encouraged through national legislation or dissemination via national tourism organisations. However, the voluntary nature of this code has moderated its wider application (UNWTO, 2015). As of June 2015, only 417 companies and associations had signed the Private Sector Commitment to the Code of Ethics. This included:

- AFTA—The Australian Federation of Travel Agents
- Air Malta
- All Nippon Airways
- Amadeus
- Club Méditerranée
- ECTAA—The European Travel Agents' and Tour Operators' Associations
- Iberia
- Japan Airlines
- NH Hotels
- RIU Hotels & Resorts
- Savoy Hotel and Resorts
- Sixt Rent a Car
- Thomas Cook AG
- TripAdvisor
- TUI AG

Whilst these companies are making a commitment towards improving their operations compared to other industries (such as retail, apparel, mining, or FMCG), tourism is 'less noticeable on indices like the Dow Jones Sustainability Index, FTSE4Good, CDP Climate Performance Leadership Index and Newsweek Green Rankings' (WTTC, 2017, p. 2). Thus, still greater effort is required to ensure responsibility is taken by national tourist associations, travel, transport and tourism operators.

Aligned to the issues of sustainability and ethics, in recent years slow travel has gained interest from some tourists. A desire to reduce carbon emissions and an increased focus on the tourist experience has encouraged people to travel more slowly overland, engaging with local communities en route to experience greater understanding and pleasure from travel (Dickinson and Lumsdon, 2010). Such travel affects choice of transport, the nature of accommodation sought in destinations (apartments and homestays ahead of hotels), and the variety of local activities engaged with (Buckley, 2011). Slow tourism is not just acknowledging the time taken to travel but a celebration of the time taken in the process of creating and savouring the tourism experience (Guiver and Mcgrath, 2016).

CASE STUDY 2.4 SLOW TOURISM IN THE EU

The European Union provided more than €3 million supporting a project developing Slow Tourism between Italy and Slovenia. This particular project attempted to encourage cross-border tourism in regard to bird watching, cycling, and river tourism. The investment was forecast to increase tourism in the region by 5%.

More than 250 tourism businesses joined the project which developed cycle routes, excursions by nature-friendly river boats, renovated boathouses, and added waterfront signposting and information points. Training activities for tour operators helped spread the concept of slow tourism as well as providing guidance on the development of slow tourism products in the region. The project also involved establishing marketing materials for tourists and promoting opportunities to international tour operators (via trade fairs).

Source: (Slow Tourism, 2014).

Debates about the concept of slow tourism often focus on the journey to the destination, considering distance travelled and mode of transport, and largely shunning long-distance air travel (Fullagar et al., 2012; Guiver and Mcgrath, 2016). However, slow tourism that encourages longer stays, with time spent in the locality and the use of public transport and local shops and restaurants, can perhaps trade off the flight used to reach the destination. More and more locations are advocating slow tourism as part of their offering, recognising that encouraging tourists to seek "more meaningful experiences rather than trying to tick off all the 'must-do' sights" (Caffyn, 2012, p. 77) can encourage engagement with the place, people, and local culture, thus offering greater community benefits.

Finally, a key contemporary issue to consider is that of the growth of the sharing economy and its impact on the tourism industry. A sharing economy (also known as a collaborative or peer-to-peer economy) is an economic model in which individuals are able to rent access to an asset owned by someone else (Heo, 2016). Citizens sharing resources has long existed but it is technology platforms, such as those offered by Airbnb and Uber, which has streamlined the process and allowed its effective growth. Thus some tourism services traditionally provided by businesses such as hotels and taxi companies are experiencing increased competition. Critics of the sharing economy argue that it creates reduced job security and unfair competition, with claims that health and safety, disability compliance, and taxes on revenue are avoided. Conversely supporters argue that it provides easy access to a wider variety of products, often of higher quality and lower price than those offered by traditional tourism businesses (Juul, 2017). It employs underutilised assets and can encourage the dispersal of tourism to less visited areas, expanding destination capacity in terms of accommodation, transport, hospitality, and travel experiences. Several sectors of the tourism industry are seeing competition from the sharing economy (Table 2.2).

Changing consumer behaviour has stimulated growing interest in the sharing economy. A Eurobarometer survey reported that half of respondents were aware of services provided by sharing platforms with almost one-fifth using these to purchase services. This level of use increases to around one-third when considering younger, more highly educated, urban living citizens (Eurobarometer, 2016). The sharing economy is also allowing more people to earn income from tourists, often by offering flexibility and unique local products, something which appeals to the millennial generation particularly (Zervas et al., 2017). This can mean increased economic opportunity for 'segments of the population that would otherwise not benefit directly' (OECD, 2016, p. 104). However, it is possible to look at the example of Airbnb to see that short-term accommodation rental can reduce the housing stock available to local residents, thus pushing up both property prices and rents, and shifting demand to less appealing locations (van der Zee, 2016). Local businesses such as shops, bars, and restaurants may lament the loss of the local population but can experience an increase in tourist numbers requiring their services. Consequently, the balance between these two may determine whether the overall effect is positive to their business, as whilst tourism can boost the local economy, it may come at a cost to other sectors.

In response to the growing number of properties promoted through Airbnb, the hotel industry has responded, albeit in a rather reactive manner (Amrish et al., 2017), with competitive pricing initiatives, innovative design and the launch of new brands that emphasise the local experience (Glusac, 2016). There is also effort to highlight factors that favour hotels, such as quality consistency and the necessity to abide by regulations ensuring hygiene and safety. Many governments have responded cautiously to the existence of Airbnb in an attempt to ensure protection in the public interest alongside maximising beneficial opportunities (Quattrone et al., 2016). Working with platform providers local governments have successfully imposed regulation on asset owners. For example, in Catalonia rental accommodation must be registered and meet minimum standards, with the local government fining platforms that advertise properties that do not conform. Some cities, such as Amsterdam and San Francisco, require platforms such as Airbnb to collect and remit occupancy taxes directly.

TABLE 2.2 Examples of Sharing Economy Platforms

Platform	Asset Shared
Airbnb	Short-term accommodation rental and travel experiences
Homeaway	Holiday home rental
Uber	Short-distance car rides
BlaBlaCar	Long-distance carpooling
EatWith	Scheduled communal meals in host homes
ToursbyLocals	Guided tours by knowledgeable residents

Whilst still in a relatively early stage the rapid growth of the sharing economy will require continued review of legislation by local and national governments. For many tourism business, competing with the sharing economy is just another of the many changes that reflects the dynamic nature of the tourism industry.

2.6 CONCLUSIONS

This chapter has highlighted that tourism is a rapidly expanding industry, already of a scale such that it dwarfs many other sectors. For example, in terms of direct GDP, tourism is double the size of the global automotive industry and in terms of employment it is twice as large as the global communications industry (WTTC, 2012). Tourism expansion is being driven both by the developed and newly emerging economies, with demand patterns varying due to a variety of push and pull factors, demographic changes, and migratory influences.

Alongside these changes to demand the industry is experiencing and responding to a variety of contemporary issues which are changing operational practices. Implementation of sustainable and ethical management practices is demanded whilst instability caused by terrorism, economic fluctuations, and increased competition continues to place additional pressures on travel and tourism businesses. Whilst technology may assist by offering possibilities for some efficiencies the level of investment required and speed of technological change may challenge all but the most forward thinking of companies.

In conclusion the movement of people for business, leisure, and VFR purposes is forecast to continue its meteoric rise (with international tourist arrivals predicted to reach 1.8 billion by 2030 (UNWTO, 2016)), thus requiring an increased supply of transport, accommodation, and other tourism services. Of prime importance is how changing market characteristics, desires, and expectations will shape the future supply.

References

Adeloye, D., Brown, L., 2018. Terrorism and domestic tourist risk perceptions. J. Tour. Cult. Chang. 16 (3), 217–233.

Amrish, M.M., Courtney, S., Xinran, L., 2017. The accommodation experiencescape: a comparative assessment of hotels and Airbnb. Int. J. Contemp. Hosp. Manag. 29, 2377–2404.

Benckendorff, P., Sheldon, P.J., Fesenmaier, D.R., 2014. The digital tourism landscape. In: Benckendorff, P., Sheldon, P.J., Fesenmaier, D.R. (Eds.), Tourism Information Technology. CABI, Wallingford.

Bihu, W., Hong, Z., Xiaohuan, X., 2000. Trends in China's domestic tourism development at the turn of the century. Int. J. Contemp. Hosp. Manag. 12, 296–299.

British Airways, 2017. Corporate Responsibility. Available at https://www.britishairways.com/en-gb/information/about-ba/csr/corporate-responsibility. (Accessed July 10, 2017).

Buckley, R., 2011. Tourism under climate change: will slow travel supersede short breaks? Ambio 40, 328–331.

Buckley, R., Gretzel, U., Scott, D., Weaver, D., Becken, S., 2015. Tourism megatrends. Tour. Recreat. Res. 40, 59–70.

Caffyn, A., 2012. Advocating and implementing slow tourism. Tour. Recreat. Res. 37, 77–80.

CBI Market Intelligence, 2016. CBI Trends: Tourism. CBI Market Intelligence, The Hague.

Chih-Chien, C., Zvi, S., 2013. On revenue management and last-minute booking dynamics. Int. J. Contemp. Hosp. Manag. 25, 7–22.

Coles, T., Fenclova, E., Dinan, C., 2013. Tourism and corporate social responsibility: a critical review and research agenda. Tour. Manag. Perspect. 6, 122–141.

Cooper, C., Fletcher, J., Fyall, A., Gilbert, D., Wanhill, S., 2005. Tourism Principles and Practice. Pearson Education, Harlow.

Crompton, J.L., 1979. Motivations for pleasure vacation. Ann. Tour. Res. 6, 408–424.

Culler, J., 1981. Semiotics of tourism. Amer. J. Semiot. 1 (1/2), 127–140.

Dann, G.M.S., 1977. Anomie, Ego-enhancement and Tourism. Ann. Tour. Res. 4, 184–194.

Dickinson, J., Lumsdon, L., 2010. Slow Travel and Tourism. Earthscan, London.

EEA, EASA and Eurocontrol, 2016. European Aviation Environmental Report 2016. Available at https://ec.europa.eu/transport/sites/transport/files/european-aviation-environmental-report-2016-72dpi.pdf. (Accessed January 29, 2018).

Eurobarometer, 2016. The Use of Collaborative Platforms. Available at http://ec.europa.eu/commfrontoffice/publicopinion/index.cfm/ResultDoc/download/DocumentKy/72885. (Accessed July 26, 2017).

Euromonitor, 2016. World Travel Market Global Trends Report. Euromonitor, London.

Euromonitor, 2017. Consumer Expenditure on Package Holidays: Statistics. Euromonitor, London.

European Commission, 2014. More Flexible Visa Rules to Boost Growth and Job Creation. European Commission, Brussels.

Eurostat, 2017. Eurostat: Migration and Migrant Population Statistics. Available at http://ec.europa.eu/eurostat/statistics-explained/index.php/Migration_and_migrant_population_statistics. (Accessed July 6, 2017).

Feng, K., Page, S.J., 2000. An exploratory study of the tourism, migration–immigration nexus: travel experiences of Chinese residents in New Zealand. Curr. Issue Tour. 3, 246–281.

Francis, J., 2017. Why I might create a Sustainable Tourism Certification Scheme. Available at https://www.responsibletravel.com/copy/sustainable-tourism-accreditation-schemes. (Accessed July 10, 2017).

Fullagar, S., Markwell, K., Wilson, E., 2012. Slow Tourism: Experiences and Mobilities. Channel View Publications, Bristol.

Genç, M., 2013. Migration and tourism flows to New Zealand. In: Matias, Á., Nijkamp, P., Sarmento, M. (Eds.), Quantitative Methods in Tourism Economics. Physica-Verlag HD, Heidelberg.
Gilbert, D.C. (Ed.), 1991. An Examination of the Consumer Behaviour Process Related to Tourism. Belhaven Press, London.
Glusac, E., 2016. Heotels vs. Airbnb: let the battle begin. In: New York Times. 20 July.
Goldstein, M., 2016. Multigenerational travel. In: Global Traveler. Global Traveller, Yardley, PA.
Graham, E., Jordan, L.P., 2011. Migrant parents and the psychological well-being of left-behind children in Southeast Asia. J. Marriage Fam. 73, 763–787.
Groth, A., Haslwanter, D., 2015. Perceived usability, attractiveness and intuitiveness of responsive mobile tourism websites. a user experience study. In: Tussyadiah, I., Inversini, A. (Eds.), Information and Communication Technologies in Tourism 2015: Proceedings of the International Conference in Lugano, Switzerland. Springer, London.
Guiver, J., Mcgrath, P., 2016. Slow tourism: exploring the discourses. Dos Algarves 27, 11–34.
Harley, N., 2017. Fresh British Airways strikes announced to coincide with the big summer getaway. In: The Telegraph. 6 July.
Heo, C.Y., 2016. Sharing economy and prospects in tourism research. Ann. Tour. Res. 58, 166–169.
Holloway, J.C., Humphreys, C.J., 2016. The Business of Tourism. Pearson, Harlow.
Hope, K., 2016. Migrant influx causes split in tourism fortunes for Greek islands. In: Financial Times. 1 July.
Horowitz, J., 2017. Trump is hurting American tourism. In: CNN Money. 7 June.
Hyde, K.F., Lawson, R., 2003. The nature of independent travel. J. Travel Res. 42, 13–23.
IPK International, 2016. ITB World Travel Trends Report. Berlin.
Jarvis, N., Weeden, C., Simcock, N., 2012. The benefits and challenges of sustainable tourism certification: a case study of the green tourism business scheme in the west of England. J. Hosp. Tour. Manag. 17, 83–93.
Juul, M., 2017. Tourism and the Sharing Economy. Available at http://www.europarl.europa.eu/RegData/etudes/BRIE/2017/595897/EPRS_BRI(2017)595897_EN.pdf. (Accessed July 26, 2017).
Karaman, A.S., 2016. The pernicious impact of visa restrictions on inbound tourism: the case of Turkey. Turk. Stud. 17, 502–524.
Kim, S., 2014. The rise of multi-generational holidays. In: The Telegraph. 10 September.
Kozak, M., Crotts, J.C., Law, R., 2007. The impact of the perception of risk on international travellers. Int. J. Tour. Res. 9, 233–242.
Lagrave, K., 2016. How terrorism affects tourism. In: Conde Naste. Available online at https://www.cntraveler.com/stories/2016-03-31/how-terrorism-affects-tourism. (Accessed June 11, 2018).
Leask, A., Fyall, A., Barron, P., 2014. Generation Y: an agenda for future visitor attraction research. Int. J. Tour. Res. 16, 462–471.
Li, X., 2016. Emerging-market research. J. Travel Res. 55, 419–426.
Li, Y., Cui, Q., 2017. Carbon neutral growth from 2020 strategy and airline environmental inefficiency: a network range adjusted environmental data envelopment analysis. Appl. Energy 199, 13–24.
Manning, T., 1999. Opinion piece: indicators of tourism sustainbility. Tour. Manag. 20, 179–181.
Martín, R., 2015. How Emerging Market Growth is Changing Tourism. https://www.weforum.org/agenda/2015/05/how-emerging-market-growth-is-changing-tourism/. (Accessed June 11, 2018).
Mintel, 2016. Travel and Tourism - China. Mintel, London, UK.
Mintel, 2017. Holiday Planning and Booking Process. Mintel, London, UK.
Moscardo, G., Benckendorff, P., 2010. Mythbusting: generation Y and travel. In: Benckendorff, P., Moscardo, G., Pendergast, D. (Eds.), Tourism and Generation Y. Wallingford CAB International, Wallingford.
Nawijn, J., Peeters, P., 2014. Rose Tinted Memories as a Cause of Unsustainable Leisure Travel. In: Gärling, T., Ettema, D., Friman, M. (Eds.), Handbook of Sustainable Travel. Springer, London.
Neumayer, E., 2004. The impact of political violence on tourism: dynamic cross-national estimation. J. Confl. Resolut. 48, 259–281.
OECD, 2016. OECD Tourism Trends and Policies 2016. OECD Publishing, Paris.
Pappas, N., 2014. The effect of distance, expenditure and culture on the expression of social status through tourism. Tour. Plan. Dev. 11 (4), 387–404.
Pappas, N., Papatheodorou, A., 2017. Tourism and the refugee crisis in Greece: perceptions and decision-making of accommodation providers. Tour. Manag. 63, 31–41.
Patsouratis, V., Frangouli, Z., Anastasopoulos, G., 2005. Competition in tourism among the Mediterranean countries. Appl. Econ. 37, 1865–1870.
Picco-Schwendener, A., Cantoni, L., 2015. Tourists and Muncipal Wi-Fi Networks (MWN): The Case of Lugano (Switzerland). In: Tussyadiah, I., Inversini, A. (Eds.), Information and Communication Technologies in Tourism 2015: Proceedings of the International Conference in Lugano, Switzerland. Springer, London.
Pwc, 2011. Building Trust in the Air: Is Airline Corporate Sustainability Reporting Taking Off? PriceWaterhouseCoopers, the Netherlands.
Quadri, D.L., Zheng, T., 2010. A revisit to the impact of exchange rates on tourism demand: the case of Italy. J. Hospital. Financ. Manag. 18, 47–60.
Quattrone, G., Proserpio, D., Quercia, D., Capra, L., Musolesi, M., 2016. Who Benefits from the "Sharing" Economy of Airbnb? In: Proceedings of the 25th International Conference on World Wide Web Montreal, Qubec. International World Wide Web Conferences Steering Committee, Canada.
Rovelstad, J.M., Blazer, S.R., 1983. Research and strategic marketing in tourism: a status report. J. Travel Res. 22, 2–7.
Saarinen, J., 2003. The regional economics of tourism in northern Finland: the socio-economic implications of recent tourism development and future possibilities for regional development. Scand. J. Hosp. Tour. 3, 91–113.
Saga, 2016. Package Holidays vs Direct Bookings: The Pros and Cons. Available at https://www.saga.co.uk/magazine/travel/travel-advice/package-holidays-vs-direct-bookings. (Accessed June 28, 2017).
Sandve, A., Marnburg, E., Øgaard, T., 2014. The ethical dimension of tourism certification programs. Int. J. Hosp. Manag. 36, 73–80.
Schänzel, H.A., Yeoman, I., 2015. Trends in family tourism. J. Tour. Futures 1, 141–147.
Slow Tourism (2014). Newsletter No 12. Available at http://www.slow-tourism.net/contentsite/docs/NW_12_ita-en.pdf. (Accessed July 26, 2017).
Smeral, E., 2009. The impact of the financial and economic crisis on European tourism. J. Travel Res. 48, 3–13.
Sojern, 2013. Travel Trends Report. Available at http://www.sojern.com/travel-insights/download/Q3_2013_Travel_Trends_Report_Sojern.pdf. (Accessed July 27, 2017).

Swarbrooke, J., Horner, S., 2007. Consumer Behaviour in Tourism. Butterworth Heinemann, Oxford.

Torres, R., 2017. Technology Trends and the Future of Travel, Global Economic Impact and Issues. WTTC, London.

Tretheway, M., Mak, D., 2006. Emerging tourism markets: ageing and developing economies. J. Air Transp. Manag. 12, 21–27.

UNWTO, 2015. Report of the World Committee on Tourism Ethics: Addendum 1 - Implementation of the Global Code of Ethics for Tourism. UNWTO, Madrid.

UNWTO, 2016. Tourism Highlights, 2016 ed World Tourism Organisation, Spain.

Van Der Zee, R., 2016. The 'Airbnb effect': Is It Real, and What Is It Doing to a City Like Amsterdam? The Guardian. 6 October 2016.

Visit England, 2014. Future of the Staycation–2014 and Beyond. London: Visit England. Available at https://www.visitbritain.org/sites/default/files/vb-corporate/Documents-Library/documents/England-documents/2013_summary.pdf. (Accessed January 29, 2018).

Witt, S.F., Brooke, M.Z., Buckley, P.J., 1991. The Management of International Tourism. Unwin Hyman, London.

World Economic Forum, 2017. The Travel and Tourism Competitiveness Report. World Economic Forum, Geneva.

Wttc, 2012. The Comparative Economic Impact of Travel and Tourism. World Travel and Tourism Council, London.

Wttc, 2016. Exchange Rate Trends and Travel and Tourism Performance. World Travel and Tourism Council, London.

Wttc, 2017. Understanding the Critical Issues for the Future of Travel and Tourism. World Travel and Tourism Council, London.

Zervas, G., Proserpio, D., Byers, J.W., 2017. The rise of the sharing economy: estimating the impact of airbnb on the hotel industry. J. Mark. Res. 54, 687–705.

CHAPTER

3

Reasons for Flying

Frédéric DOBRUSZKES, David RAMOS-PÉREZ†, Jean-Michel DECROLY**

*Free University of Brussels (ULB), Brussels, Belgium †University of Salamanca, Salamanca, Spain

CHAPTER OUTLINE

3.1 INTRODUCTION

Flying for leisure purposes has become commonplace in developed and emerging countries, as well as in oil monarchies, even though it mostly concerns specific social groups (i.e. people who can afford air tickets and need or want to travel). However, the different motivations for travelling by air—as in the hospitality industry—have received scant attention from scholars. It seems this issue interests mostly airports, public administrations, and airlines for marketing and development strategies. However, investigating the reasons for flying is actually key to understanding the cross-relationship between aviation and tourism.

Such research is challenging given the (un)availability of data. Most available sources are part of the grey, nonacademic literature that is dispersed and not always publicly available. Another critical issue is the starting point for investigation. One may consider 'travel' or 'tourism' statistics and isolate 'tourists' flying. However, as identified in Chapter 1, travel purpose and transportation modes rarely intersect in published reports. This is not an issue for those countries where people travel mostly by air (e.g. Australia, New Zealand, and the United States), but in other cases, the significant use of road and rail transport calls for modal-specific (or aviation-restricted) data.

More fundamentally, the very definition of 'tourism' and a 'tourist' is anything but stable, as also discussed in the introductory chapter. The use of the United Nations World Tourism Organisation (UNWTO) broader definition (a tourist is an overnight visitor, the exact travel purpose does not matter) of course produces larger numbers than with the definition that dominates the air transport sector and the public at large (tourists travel for personal purpose, so not for business). Moreover in many cases, basic facts can easily be found but with no given definition of 'visitors' or of 'tourists', so the reader has to find detailed reports (if any are available). For instance,

Air Transport—A Tourism Perspective. https://doi.org/10.1016/B978-0-12-812857-2.00003-8

the US National Travel and Tourism Office publishes a series of fact sheets related to arrivals and the spending of 'international visitors' that are not defined.[1]

This is the context in which this chapter proposes an overview of reasons for flying that alternates between empirical material and methodological issues. The next section introduces the split amongst air travel purposes as a discrete choice in various markets. The two following sections go further, accounting for the complexity due to multipurpose trips, on the one hand, and the variability in data across places and over time, on the other. The penultimate section summarises the various factors that shape flying propensity and purpose, and is followed by the conclusions and prospects for future research.

3.2 A SIMPLIFIED WORLD: FLYING PURPOSES AS A DISCRETE CHOICE

3.2.1 Classifying Air Passengers by Travel Purpose

Doganis (2010) proposes a classification of flying purpose that represents both academic and industry practice (Fig. 3.1). He first draws a line between business and leisure, and the demarcation comes basically from who pays for the tickets (employers vs households respectively) or from the first motivation of the trip (work-related trip vs escape from the everyday tedium of work). Then the leisure group can be split between visiting friends and relatives (VFR) and holiday tourism.

It can already be understood from these groups that the words are not neutral and are possibly ambiguous. For instance, VFR travel is a holiday for many people, and hopefully a leisure activity, but it can also be a social obligation (Janta et al., 2015). Many authors consider that VFR travel is underestimated (e.g. Jackson, 1990). Also, 'sports' are classified into 'other' by Doganis, but could also be 'business' (for professional players) and leisure (for supporters). The classification of a pilgrimage is also debatable. In US surveys, pilgrimages are treated as a single group. They could thus merge into 'other,' along with health treatments and migrations. This implicitly means that a pilgrimage would not be a leisure activity but a religious and social obligation. However, a pilgrimage can also be understood as an exciting activity, a crucial step in one's life and, beyond its sacred importance, a leisure activity. It is worth noting that alternative classifications may be based on temporal vs long-term (e.g. moving for education) mobilities, or on the constrained nature of the journey. Constrained trips relate to religious, social, and medical imperatives.

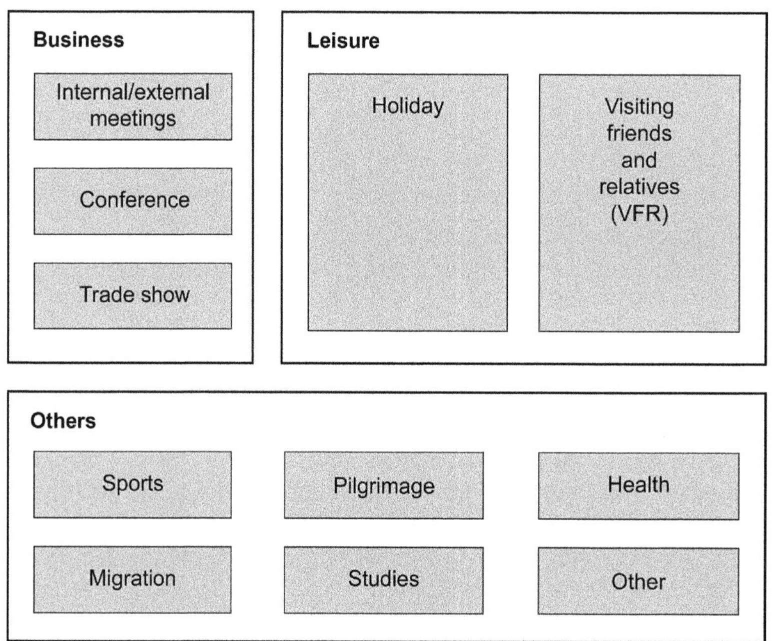

FIG. 3.1 Travel purposes by air. *(Based on Doganis, R., 2010. Flying Off Course: Airlines Economics and Marketing, fourth ed. Routledge, London and various surveys. The list is not exhaustive.)*

[1] See http://tinet.ita.doc.gov/outreachpages/inbound.general_information.inbound_overview.asp.

3.2.2 Collecting Data

The remainder of this chapter is based largely on empirical sources. Only information based on explicit methodologies have been considered. It is worth recalling that, in most cases, only restricted data are available for free (this involves, for instance, only aggregated figures, main travel purpose, older figures or one-quarter instead of annual figures). Indeed, several countries publish survey-based summaries but then sell detailed reports and customised analyses.[2] In the United States, for instance, the US Survey of International Air Travelers Program (which has surveyed air passengers every month since 1983)[3] publishes national, annual reports on both inbound and outbound flows that are priced at $1580 each, whilst Excel releases are priced at $4050 each. Customised printed tables start at $2365. In the United Kingdom, the Civil Aviation Authority (CAA) supplies annual departing passenger survey main results for free, and then sells more detailed figures from £345 + value added/sales tax. The gap between free and not-free statistics notably concerns the reasons for flying. Free data only makes the distinction between 'business' and 'leisure' (along with 'international' vs 'domestic'). In other cases, the travel purposes collected by public authorities are too broad. In Morocco, for instance, the form to be filled in by all arriving/departing passengers considers only four main travel purposes: tourism, business/conferences, education, and work. As a result, and in contrast with most other available data, no distinction is made between holidays and visiting friends.

In addition, the range of visitors covered varies. Many statistical sources assume passengers stay at least one night at their destination. Such assumptions exclude same-day trips, especially same-day business flights. It is also common that survey-based data exclude younger travellers. If a respondent is not asked with whom he or she is travelling, this would underestimate the volume of families travelling for leisure purposes. All this suggests that the information produced depends on the manner in which surveys are designed, and how respondents perceive their own activities. In other words, the data that follow should only be considered as orders of magnitude.

3.2.3 The Overall Situation

Table 3.1 presents the reasons for flying at country level. First, within the sample, it is clear that business is not the dominant reason for flying. Subject to markets (and possibly to the methods of acquiring information), business accounts for at best one-quarter of overnight air passenger travel. Domestic flights in Australia are the exception, with business travel being the main reason for flying. However, in general the small share of business travel is due to some extent to the frequent exclusion of same-day journeys, which typically account for a higher share of business travel, as evidenced by Australia's domestic figures (see the end of Table 3.1). Nevertheless, despite a growing structural need for long-distance communication in business (more multiunit companies, more interfirm relationships around collective projects, market spatial expansion, and increased communication with customers) (Aguilera, 2008), the purpose of business remains a secondary reason for flying.

As a result, flying for leisure is clearly the dominant motivation. It accounts for roughly 80% of the airline markets reported here, and even more for those places that are highly holiday dependent (such as the Seychelles). Within the leisure segment, 'holiday' accounts for about twice the share of VFR purpose. Interestingly, VFR represents roughly one-quarter of all air passengers. This could even be an underestimation since visiting friends and relatives could be perceived as going on holiday and because of multipurpose trips (see the next section).

There is little doubt that the expansion of air transport is a cause and consequence of economic, migratory, and tourist globalisation. However, these results contrast with the common emphasis put on aviation related to business travel, including between world/global cities and in the context of international activities (see Lassen, 2006; Beaverstock et al., 2009; Derudder and Witlox, 2014). To some extent, this body of literature has led to the implicit (and sometimes explicit) idea that passengers fly mostly for business purposes. Of course, airline revenues are probably often more dominated by business travel although unfortunately such financial data are usually held in 'commercial confidence' by the airline operators.

Finally, the share of other reasons for flying is limited and stable around 5%, which suggests the aforementioned groups indeed cover the main flying purposes.

In addition, Table 3.1 reveals interesting diverging results between country types and gives their location. The share of business is higher from Argentina and Mexico, because of there being less holiday purpose (from Mexico) and only a small VFR flow from Argentina. The latter could be explained by the distance from the United States.

[2] New Zealand is a useful counter example, with lots of data (including monthly data) available for free in both PDF and XLS file formats. See http://www.stats.govt.nz/browse_for_stats/industry_sectors/Tourism.aspx.

[3] See http://tinet.ita.doc.gov/research/programs/ifs/index.asp.

TABLE 3.1 Main Reason for Flying in Different Contexts

Market	Source	Business	Holiday	VFR	Others
Outbound flows					
US residents flying abroad (excluding Canada and Mexico) from 30 gateway airports (2015)	Survey of International Air Travelers	13%	53%	27%	7%
UK residents boarding at 11 airports, excluding connecting passengers (2015)	Annual departing passenger survey	17%	83% (leisure)		
Spanish residents flying from/to Spain (2016)	FAMILITUR—survey of residents' tourist mobility (n = 13,200)	16%	53%	27%	5%
Belgium, last outbound international flight (2010)	National mobility survey (n = 15,822)	7%	71%	18%	4%
Mexican residents travelling abroad by air (2015)	Bank of Mexico & SECTUR—survey on Mexican international outbound tourism (n = ?)	24%	48%	24%	4%
Argentinean residents travelling abroad from Buenos Aires airports (2016)	INDEC—International Tourism Survey (n = 65,292)	20%	66%	13%	2%
Seychelles residents travelling abroad; all modes included but air transport is ultradominant (2016). Includes both permanent and temporary departures	National Bureau of Statistics based on immigration disembarkation cards (n = 75,946)	13%	67% (holidays)		20% (of which 7% is 'end of contract')
Inbound flows					
Overseas residents visiting the United States (excluding Canada and Mexico) (2016)	Survey of International Air Travelers	18%	59%	18%	5%
Overseas residents flying back from the United Kingdom, boarding at 11 airports, excluding connecting passengers (2015)	Annual departing passenger survey	25%	75% (leisure)		
Foreign residents flying from/to Spain (2016)	FRONTUR—survey of nonresident arrivals and departures at Spanish airports (n = 313,671)	7%	87% (leisure and holidays)		7%
Overseas residents to Australia (2016)	International Visitors Survey (n = 40,000)	11%	50%	25%	14%
Overseas residents to New Zealand (2016), of which 99% came by air	NZ International Visitor Surveys (n = about 9800)	11%	56%	31%	2%
Foreign residents travelling to Mexico by air (2015)	Bank of Mexico & SECTUR—Survey on International Visitors arriving in Mexico (n = ?)	9%	75%	13%	3%
Foreign residents travelling to Argentina through Buenos Aires airports (2016)	INDEC—International Tourism Survey (n = 65,292)	20%	47%	28%	5%
Foreign residents travelling to Chile by air (2015)	SERNATUR—Report on International Tourists arriving in Chile (n = 42,300)	30%	48%	18%	4%
Overseas residents to Sri Lanka (2016), of which 98.7% came by air	Sri Lanka Tourism Development Authority based on Electronic Travel Authorisation System (ETA)	3%	83%	12%	2%
Overseas residents flying to Seychelles (2016)	National Bureau of Statistics based on immigration disembarkation cards (n = 302,288)	3%	93%	2%	2%
Domestic flows					
Domestic overnight trips within Australia (2016)	National Visitor Survey	41.3%	29.4%	26.7%	3.4%
Domestic day trips within Australia (2016)	National Visitor Survey	71.9%	12.0%	7.0%	9.1%

Note: 'Business' also includes conferences, workshops, and trade shows. 'Holiday' includes weddings and honeymoons, if any. 'Others' includes pilgrimages and education. When given, 'crews' and 'transit' have been excluded.
Source: Compiled by the authors.

Remoteness could also explain that air flows to Argentina and Chile account for much less holiday travel (in relative terms) than Mexico, which is much closer from the United States. Conversely, holidays largely dominate air travel to countries such as Sri Lanka and the Seychelles, given their specialisation in holiday tourism and lack of other business activities.

Finally, it is worth noting that there is a dearth of data relating to the poorest countries. Apart from the few figures included in Table 3.1, it was found that estimates made by consultants based on interviews and 'field works' lacked methodological details. For instance, SH&E (2010) supplies estimates of the typical reason for flying in Africa; holidays account for 5%, 2%, and 15% of domestic, regional, and intercontinental passengers, respectively. By contrast, business and VFR travel represents a much higher share than in the markets included in Table 3.1. Actually, there is no reason why conclusions derived from developed countries would work in undeveloped countries, particularly because the profile of passengers in poor countries differs significantly to that of passengers in wealthier countries. For instance, a survey performed at Goma Airport in the Democratic Republic of Congo amongst passengers boarding Congo Airways, found that 73% of them were males, 75% university graduates, 30% freelancers, and 25% employees of NGOs (Riziki et al., 2017). These figures diverge dramatically from results obtained in developed countries (see Table 3.5) and could affect flying purposes. The same authors also note that air fares in the Democratic Republic of Congo range between 30 and 60 eurocents per km, against about 20 eurocents in Europe and even 10 eurocents with low-cost airlines. SH&E (2010) also noted that air fares are much higher in Africa and in Latin America than within the United States. This confirms that air transport is more socially selective in poor countries. As a result, it cannot be claimed that the sample gathered into Table 3.1 would be valid everywhere.

3.3 ACKNOWLEDGING COMPLEXITY: FLYING FOR MULTIPLE PURPOSES

Previous statistics imply that surveyed travellers select a main purpose for travel. In the real world, though, the situation is more complex. For instance, people can travel primarily to their home country for a wedding, but then visit friends and relatives before possibly spending time in a tourist resort. In such a scenario it is impossible to predict the main travel purpose they would choose, which may involve an underestimation of VFR travel. Another example is travellers flying mainly for the purpose of business, but then taking advantage of the trip to undertake leisure activities. Scholars taking free time before or after a conference are a typical case of so-called extenders, and in some circumstances, the conference may only be an excuse to plan a holiday (Lassen, 2006; Tretyakevich and Maggi, 2011). Again, it is difficult to know which survey box would then be ticked. Clear instructions (e.g. the main purpose subject to the number of days spent for each subactivity or who paid for the air tickets, and thus made the trip possible) may help, provided these instructions are considered by travellers.

Some surveys account for this issue and make multiple choices possible. In the United States, for instance, the Survey of International Air Travelers asks respondents to tick both the main purpose of their trip (Q13A), then all other purposes (Q13B) with the clear statement, 'as many as apply'. Published results include single purpose (Q13A) and all travel purposes (Q13A+Q13B). Table 3.2 compares them and suggests an increase of nearly 30%

TABLE 3.2 A Comparison of Single and Multiple Reasons for Flying to/From the United States

	Inbound (2016)		Outbound (2015)	
Flying Purposes	**Main Purpose (%)**	**All Purposes (%)**	**Main Purpose (%)**	**All Purposes (%)**
Business	11.3	14.4	10	12
Convention/conference/trade show	6.7	9.0	3	4
Vacation/holiday	58.5	68.2	53	64
VFR	18.0	30.2	27	38
Education	4.4	6.4	4	7
Religion/pilgrimages			2	3
Health treatments			1	1
Total	98.9	128.2	100	129

Note: Figures exclude flows from/to Canada.
Source: Survey of International Air Travelers.

of reasons reported. This demonstrates the extent to which multipurpose air trips are a reality. All the reasons for flying are more frequent, provided respondents are allowed to report more than the main travel purpose. However, one of the most spectacular increases relates to VFR inbound traffic, even though very little, if any, is known about the hierarchy of motives.

Evidence of multipurpose trips also comes from a survey conducted by Ryan and Birks (2005) amongst 1297 passengers using Trans-Tasman low-cost air services from New Zealand's regional airports. About 75% of respondents reported a single purpose, but the other 25% reported at least two purposes. The most common combinations were holiday+VFR (6.4% of the total), business+conference (5.7%), holiday+conference (2.9%), visiting relatives+family occasion (2.8%), and business+visiting relatives (2.2%).

3.4 ACKNOWLEDGING COMPLEXITY: FLYING PURPOSES VARY ACROSS PLACES AND OVER TIME

Since travel purpose is shaped by various factors (see the next section) that are spatially heterogeneous, there is a priori no reason for observing a similar split everywhere. It has already been suggested that the split could be different in poor countries, but even considering developed countries only (as is mostly the case in Table 3.1), the reasons for flying can differ significantly amongst places.

Variability can first be observed amongst places of departure. In the United Kingdom, for instance, the business/leisure split varies significantly amongst airports, and thus amongst cities, with the leisure share ranging between 52% at London City Airport and 95% at East Midlands Airport (the average is 83%) (Table 3.3, 'UK residents'). These changes are likely to relate to the resident attributes and regional economic structures (including tourist amenities), but also to the airport specialisations within multiple-airport cities (such as London) or on a regional scale (e.g. East Midlands Airport focuses on low-cost carriers [LCCs]). It is thus not really surprising that the share of business travel is lower in less developed regions (e.g. postindustrial areas) or at LCC-focused airports (such as Luton and Stansted), even though several surveys have demonstrated that business travellers also consider flying with LCCs to some extent (e.g. Ryan and Birks, 2005; Kuljanin and Kalić, 2015), notably in the case of niche routes. Variability within the London metropolitan area is also noticeable. With London City being located literally within London's new business district (Canary Wharf) and close to the traditional one, it is not surprising that it accounts for the lowest share of leisure travellers. By contrast, Luton, Stansted, and Gatwick attract more leisure passengers because of cheaper flights, air links to tourist destinations, and poorer transport links to London's business districts. Also, Luton and Stansted are nearby working or lower middle-class districts and serve as airports for large areas between London and the

TABLE 3.3 Main Reasons for Flying From Various British Airports (2015)

	UK Residents		Overseas Residents	
Departure Airport	**Business (%)**	**Leisure (%)**	**Business (%)**	**Leisure (%)**
Birmingham	14	86	27	73
Bristol	15	85	22	78
Cardiff	9	91	26	74
East Midlands	5	95	11	89
Liverpool	10	90	10	90
London City	48	52	55	45
London Gatwick	12	88	19	81
London Heathrow	27	73	28	72
London Luton	13	87	16	84
London Stansted	13	87	16	84
Manchester	14	86	26	74
Total	17	83	25	75

Note: Connecting passengers are excluded.
Source: Computed from CAA Passenger Survey Report 2015's Table 2.2.

Midlands, including internationalised cities such as Cambridge. Heathrow shows an in-between profile, because it serves as a mega, nonspecialised airport. As London's main international gateway, it attracts a huge diversity of passengers because of its wide range of connections and efficient urban/regional rail services. Its location near to wealthy suburbs and the M4 motorway corridor (sometimes referred as the local Silicon Valley) is arguably also convenient for those passengers more sensitive to time and comfort than to price. Finally, Table 3.3 also shows that inbound and outbound traffic may show different patterns. At Birmingham Airport, for instance, the share of leisure travellers is higher amongst UK residents than amongst passengers travelling back to home.

The variability of reasons for flying can also be observed at the destination level, as evidenced by the last columns of Table 3.3 (overseas residents) and by US data—notwithstanding that only the first quarter is considered (Table 3.4).[4] Various attributes related to passengers and to places at the origin and destination, as well as characteristics of supply, arguably shape these patterns. Such attributes explain, for instance, that VFR travel is the highest to South America and Asia, and higher to the United Kingdom than France or Italy, given immigration patterns; that the Middle East is the arrival area with the largest share of religion/pilgrimage purpose, given that it accommodates Mecca where the Hajj (the pilgrimage that is one of the Islam's five pillars) takes place annually; that the Caribbean mostly attracts air passengers for holiday purposes. The share of business purpose is highest for China (where international US firms are significantly established) and the United Kingdom (a country that has kept close links with the United States).

Again, distance plays a significant role in shaping the reason for travel. The share of holiday travel tends to be higher for closer, beach-oriented destinations (see the Caribbean and Central America vs South America). Intercontinental holiday travel is nevertheless high to major heritage spots such as France and Italy, whose attractiveness is arguably large enough to counterbalance the distance.

In addition, the VFR share within Table 3.4 confirms that the US migratory basin is definitely global, since VFR is significant to all regions. Finally, the spatial patterns of education purpose seem more difficult to interpret,

TABLE 3.4 Main Reasons for Flying From the United States According to Destination (January–March 2012)

Destination	N	Business (%)	Convention, Conference, Trade Show (%)	Vacation, Holiday (%)	VFR (%)	Education (%)	Religion, Pilgrimage (%)	Health Treatment (%)	Other (%)
Europe	2843	22.5	6.0	32.6	25.2	11.2	1.5	0.3	0.8
France	411	16.6	4.2	47.0	14.6	15.6	1.9	0.2	0.0
Italy	357	10.5	5.3	45.6	11.0	23.6	3.5	0.0	0.4
United Kingdom	759	25.3	6.3	28.0	27.3	11.6	0.0	0.4	1.2
Caribbean	722	8.0	1.1	67.7	17.3	1.2	3.6	0.5	0.6
South Amer.	468	16.7	2.1	29.6	44.3	4.8	0.5	1.4	0.5
Central Amer.	375	16.0	0.6	49.7	19.2	4.7	5.6	1.1	3.2
Africa	446	10.7	1.7	32.0	32.8	10.1	6.5	1.0	5.1
Middle East	643	14.1	5.8	26.7	33.3	9.0	9.6	0.6	0.9
Asia	2614	21.0	4.7	21.5	45.2	5.4	0.8	0.7	0.6
China	336	31.6	3.0	16.9	39.3	6.3	0.1	1.5	1.3
Oceania	128	9.0	3.2	35.8	34.4	16.1	0.3	0.0	1.1
Total	10,102	19.2	4.5	32.5	31.1	8.8	2.2	0.6	1.0

Note: Business includes visiting customers, visiting suppliers, sales/marketing, and internal company meeting.
Source: Survey of International Air Travelers, US Travelers to overseas.

[4] Yearly data are on sale and too expensive for this research. It is worth noting that UK statistics may be biased by the fact that only the previous/following airport is considered, but not true origins and destinations in case of passengers are connecting somewhere. In addition, tourists taking part to multicountry trips also raise methodological issues (in some countries, only the destination country of the longest stay is recorded; in other countries, only the first country visited is considered).

even though academic institutes in Australia, New Zealand and South Africa are known to attract US students, even for short stays (a few weeks or months).

Since the purpose of flying is subject to both the origin and destinations of travel, it will vary at the actual origin–destination level, e.g. by airport-pairs or country-pairs. However, evidence related to this is scarce and when it exists, it is usually part of on-sale reports or customised data.[5]

Finally, flying purpose also varies over short- and long-term time horizons. Flying patterns naturally change within a given year, along with the weather at both origins and destinations (acting as push and pull factors), paid leave, school holidays (at least for families with children attending school or higher education), specific events on fixed (such as large music festivals and main sporting events), or variable (such as the Islamic Hajj) dates. This is evidenced by monthly travel purpose to New Zealand (Figs 3.2 and 3.3), for instance. In absolute figures, dramatic fluctuations affect leisure travel (both holiday and VFR), which is much higher over the Southern Hemisphere's winter. In contrast, business travel is more stable. Fluctuations are flattened when expressed in relative percentage terms, but still represent 15 points for VFR and 12 points for both holiday and business purposes.

However, the most important change in terms of mobility and social patterns actually refers to long-term trends. Indeed, long-term changes—including those amongst local/regional populations, lifestyles, economic structures, and air supply—are likely to have affected travel patterns in the sense that there is now a higher share of nonbusiness travel. Considering air passengers from Norway, for instance, Lian and Denstadli (2004) report that the share of leisure purpose increased from 34% in 1982 to 41% in 1998 for domestic trips and from 31% in 1986 to 40% in 1988 for international trips. A hypothesis is advanced that this change is due to four structural factors. First, there is an increase in the rate of participation in tourism in various countries, including China (UNTWO, 2017; Arlt, 2016). Second, travellers tend to fragment their holiday time into shorter, but more frequent, stays. Third, leisure passengers tend to consider air travel more often than before. This includes VFR travel when cheaper options have become available, such as between Europe and Morocco (Dobruszkes and Mondou, 2013). Finally, business travel tends to now

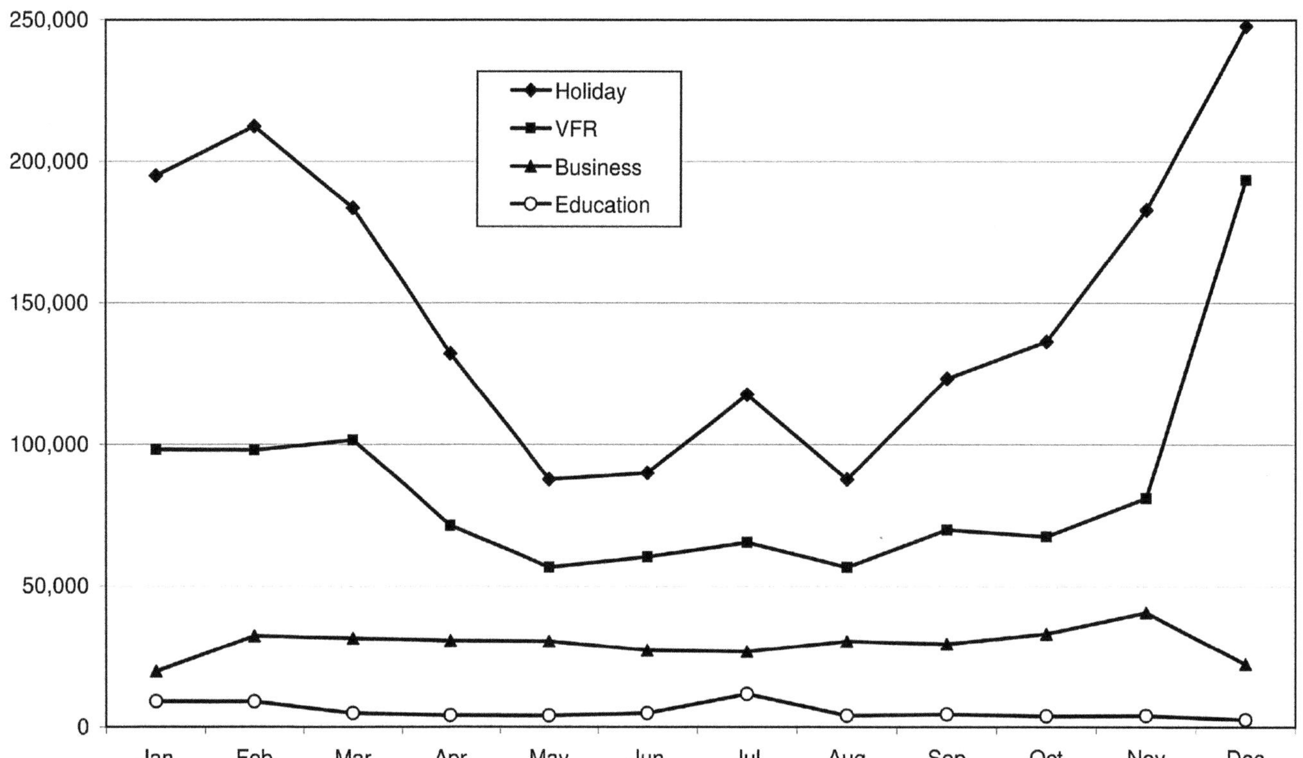

FIG. 3.2 Changes in travel purpose to New Zealand over 1 year by visitor numbers. *Note*: 99% travellers came by air, 1% by sea. *(Source: NZ International Visitor Survey.)*

[5] At best, there are some free statistics at the country-pair level but from/to only one given country. See, for instance, the detailed spreadsheets of the UK Travelpac series that combines transport mode, travel purpose, age, sex, and length of stay and independent vs. package traveller (https://www.ons.gov.uk/peoplepopulationandcommunity/leisureandtourism/datasets/travelpac).

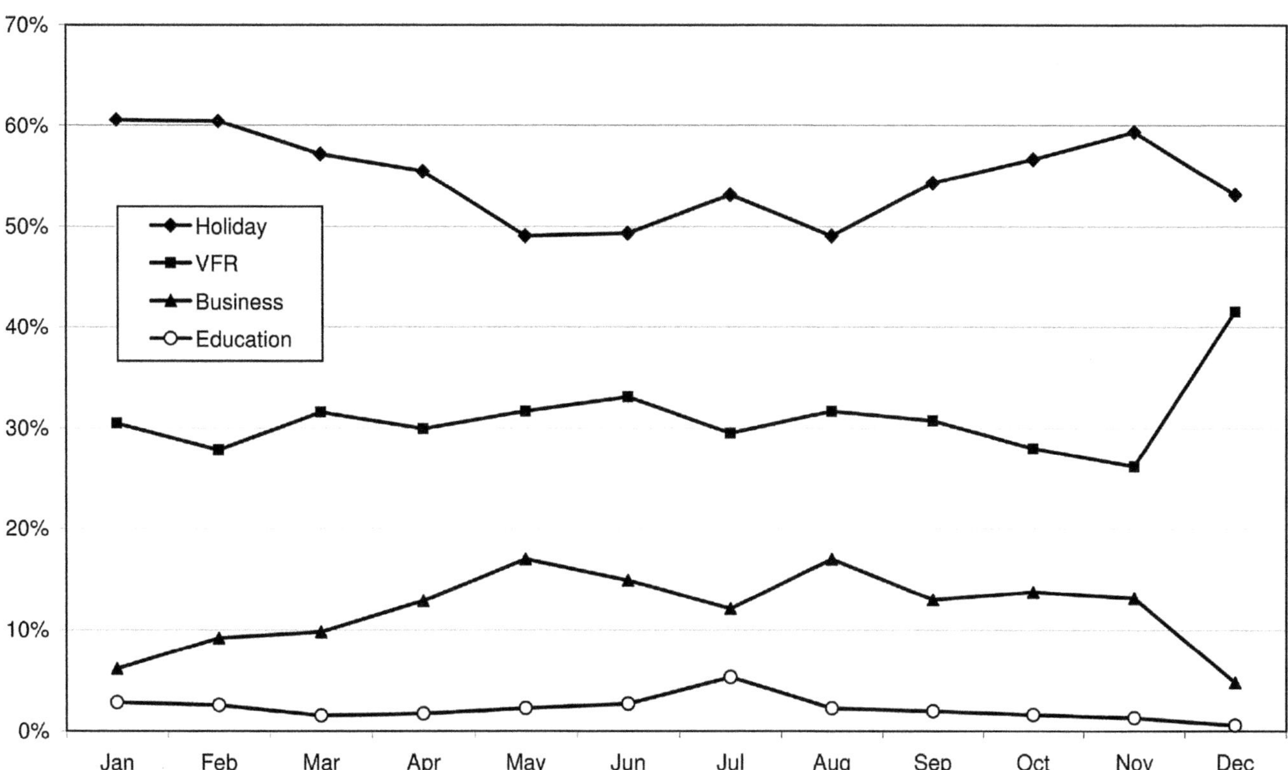

FIG. 3.3 Changes in travel purpose to New Zealand over 1 year by percentage share of visitor numbers. *Note*: 99% travellers came by air, 1% by sea. *(Source: NZ International Visitor Survey.)*

increase at a less rapid rate than leisure travel, or even stagnates in various markets. This may be due to the advent of ICT solutions and a general attempt to lower costs in order to maximise profits. Indeed, surveys of intra- and inter-firm communications firms suggest that developments in ICT-mediated relations have led to the use of face-to-face contact for only the 'most complex' interactions (Charlot and Duranton, 2006), which has induced a reduction in the number of business trips (Jones, 2013).

3.5 FACTORS AFFECTING FLYING PROPENSITY

3.5.1 Inhabitant Socio–Demo–Economic Attributes

Like travel purposes in general, flying purposes are shaped by various inhabitant or resident characteristics that affect how much, how often, and how far they may want, may need, and can travel (see also Chapters 2 and 4). Table 3.5 compares the propensity to fly—obtained by dividing the number of air travel trips by the total number of respondents[6]—from and within Switzerland across individuals' traditional attributes, and distinguishing between private and business purposes (the latter is probably underestimated because same-day travel is excluded). It converges mostly with various other available surveys performed in developed countries. First, figures confirm the aforementioned conclusions about the moderate share of business travel. In addition, age mostly restricts flying under 18 and over 64. Those aged 25–44 fly the most, but only because business travel is added to personal travel. As far as only flying for private purposes is considered, members of the 18–24 group are actually the most frequent air passengers. This tends to confirm the hypotheses that suggest that the mobility patterns of young adults have changed, notably since the advent of low-cost airlines and studies abroad, that have shaped long-distance social networks which are kept up by electronic social tools (Craps, 2017). Accordingly, flying has become commonplace amongst young adults.

However, if the 80+ group is excluded, the most relevant factor that shapes the propensity to fly is household income, with a 5.7 ratio between the lowest and highest groups. Very clearly, the wealthier inhabitants are, the more

[6] Therefore the ratio can be >1.

TABLE 3.5 Number of Air Trips by Swiss Residents Per Capita by Travel Purpose (2015)

Attributes	Private	Business	Others	All
Total	0.68	0.11	0.03	0.83
Gender				
Male	0.62	0.16	0.03	0.81
Female	0.74	0.07	0.03	0.84
Age				
6–17	0.56	(0.00)	0.02	0.58
18–24	0.96	0.03	0.10	1.10
25–44	0.89	0.18	0.03	1.10
45–64	0.69	0.18	0.02	0.89
65–79	0.43	0.02	0.01	0.46
80+	0.12	0.00	(0.01)	0.13
Household monthly income (CHF)				
<4001	0.27	0.03	0.02	0.32
4001–8000	0.63	0.05	0.02	0.70
8001–12,000	0.77	0.16	0.03	0.96
>12,000	1.26	0.41	0.05	1.72
Occupation				
Freelance	0.66	0.32	0.01	1.00
Familial colleague	0.58	(0.03)	0.00	0.61
Executive	0.92	0.36	0.03	1.31
Other employees	0.84	0.11	0.03	0.99
Trainee	0.60	0.00	0.04	0.64
Unemployed	0.68	(0.08)	0.06	0.81
Nonworking	0.46	0.01	0.03	0.50
Place of living				
Urban	0.77	0.11	0.03	0.91
Suburbs	0.60	0.10	0.03	0.74
Rural	0.47	0.11	0.03	0.61

Notes: $N = 17{,}060$ surveyed people who spend at least one night away from home. Occupational groups are given for 15+ respondents ($n = 15{,}185$). Between brackets: statistically not really reliable. Both domestic and international flows are included.
Source: OFS/Office fédéral de la statistique, 2017. Comportement de la population en matière de transports, Résultats du microrecensement mobilité et transports 2015. OFS, Neuchâtel.

they travel for both personal and business purposes. Partially overlapping the income factor, occupational groups also significantly shape flying propensity and purpose. Executives fly the most, and again for both personal and business reasons. This is not surprising considering their skills and/or management responsibilities that require them to attend meetings with partners or subsidiaries. In addition, their higher incomes mean flying for leisure is really an option. They are followed by self-employees, who form a heterogeneous group with lower/higher skills and lower/higher incomes. Also, some executives may actually work freelance for their employer for tax reasons. The gap between higher and lower occupational groups is not as big as by income though (the gap may, however, be larger according to distances flown). More surprisingly, the unemployed flying patterns are similar to the average, at least for private purposes. This may support the unproved hypothesis that suggested that low-cost airlines would democratise flying. It may also be due to the fact that some unemployed residents are foreigners flying to visit friends or relatives (VFR purpose) and make sacrifices to maintain social links with their home country.

Finally, the Swiss survey suggests that women fly a bit less for business reasons (which is coherent with gender inequalities on the labour market) but also a bit more for personal reasons (which should be investigated further), so the all-purpose propensity is eventually equal.

In summary, both flying propensity and flying motives are affected by basic social, demographic, and occupational attributes. In addition, these attributes also affect the destination choice for tourism, which is a socially driven process (Shaw and Williams, 2002). All other things being equal, they also affect the choice of transportation mode (see Chapter 6) since higher social–occupational travellers are usually more sensitive to travel time than travel cost, even though the digital revolution is changing the value of time, since it is now easier to take advantage of in-vehicle travel time to work (Wardman et al., 2016).

3.5.2 The Significance of Migration

Surprisingly, the aforementioned findings did not consider the presence of migrants as a key factor. The close relationship between migrations and VFR travel has been highlighted for a long time (Jackson, 1990; Williams and Hall, 2000), even though few econometric studies have actually considered it (Seetaram, 2012).[7] Yet several evidence-based studies have suggested a significant effect of migrants on air traffic to and from their home country (e.g. CAA, 2009; Forsyth et al., 2012; Seetaram, 2012; Boonekamp et al., 2018). This is due to the determination of such migrants to maintain social links with friends and relatives, and fulfil various obligations, such as attending funerals, weddings, birthdays, and degree ceremonies. In addition, some authors have found that migratory patterns related to former colonial links can still be observed to some extent in today's airline networks, and involve a high share of VFR travel (e.g. Ranély Vergé-Dépré and Roth, 2017).

VFR travel can be to or from the home country, and the relative importance is likely to be affected by social factors concerning visa issues (see later). For instance, a rich Australian family that sends its son or daughter abroad for education may have the budget to visit him/her at his/her destination, whilst the student could also visit his/her home country. In contrast, a poor African migrant who lives in Europe may hardly be able to afford his/her ticket to visit the family in his/her home country. Similarly, it would be too expensive for this migrant to pay for air tickets for the family, who would also need to get a visa.

Both airport and airline marketers are well aware of the economic importance of VFR travel. For instance, Porto Airport uses emigration patterns of people living in its catchment area to convince airlines to launch new routes (ANA, 2012a,b). In addition, it is known that low-cost airlines literally follow immigrants when shaping their network (Burrell, 2011; Dobruszkes, 2009b). In Belgium, for instance, it is significant that Ryanair connects Brussels South Charleroi Airport to Nador and Oujda in Morocco; many Moroccan immigrants to Belgium come from these areas that are otherwise not tourist destinations.

Beyond the migration–VFR relationship, it appears that migration can also boost non-VFR tourism travel, as evidenced by Dwyer et al. (2014) in the context of Australia.[8] Their econometric analyses concluded that in 2006, migration numbers had more impact on both inbound and outbound travel to/from Australia than income, relative price, and transportation costs, and even more impact than in 1991. Interestingly, specific models for VFR and non-VFR travel show that migration has a similar impact on both purposes and that, in contrast, income, relative price between origin and destination, and transportation cost have less impact on VFR travel than non-VFR travel, which confirms that VFR travel is needed more than non-VFR tourism. Thinking beyond this model, how can the positive impact of migration on non-VFR tourism travel be explained? On the one hand, on the inbound size, permanent migrants can promote, explicitly or implicitly, their new homeland when they travel to, or communicate with, their country of origin. In the same way, diasporic communities may shape ethnic neighbourhoods that contribute to tourism attractiveness of a destination (e.g. the 'Greek Precinct' and 'Chinatown' in Melbourne) and offer food and accommodation facilities managed by migrants from one community, which enhance the disposition to visit their compatriots. On the other hand, ethnic restaurants and other activities related to migrant communities can be a source of outbound tourism by generating a desire to discover the 'on the ground' heritage and cultural life of the countries from which the migrants come.

Finally, migrations may also induce roots tourism, even centuries later. This includes, for instance, descendants of African slaves visiting sub-Saharan Africa, descendants of white colonists visiting Ireland or the United Kingdom, Jews travelling to Israel, or Asian Americans visiting China (Handley, 2006; Maruyama and Stonza, 2010).

[7] Symptomatically, two models of air demand presented at the 2017 Air Transport Research Society world conference neglected migration as a potential factor.

[8] In the case of Australia, 'international travel' means 'flying' to 99% of the people.

3.5.3 Regional Economic Structures and Administrative Patterns (at Both Ends)

Apart from inhabitants' attributes, regional economic structures are also likely to shape flying patterns, both directly and indirectly. Directly, there is no doubt that the spatial patterns of multilocated firms, and of international trade, shape business travel whilst the presence or absence of tourism amenities and facilities (beaches, snowy mountains, hotels, heritage sites, etc.) inevitably affect the destination choices of tourists. Some business activities induce more need for long-distance travel, whilst others are too local to do so. Indirectly, regional economic patterns also influence national and international migrations and the concentration of specific social–occupational groups that may under- or overuse aircraft as a mode of transport.

A country's administrative architecture also affects the reasons for flying. In large countries or in the case of remote dependencies, the vertical organisation of the administration requires civil servants to travel between cities of different hierarchical status to attend various meetings. In addition, the availability or unavailability of medical facilities can push people to fly, all other things being equal. In the Canaries, Spain, for instance, no less than 7% of departing passengers from La Palma Airport flew for medical reasons (AENA, 2004).

3.5.4 Tourism Amenities

Whilst air mobility for leisure reasons has become rather commonplace in developed countries, after World War II it was reserved mainly for visiting places that had some specific resources. The attractiveness of tourist resources is a socially constructed process, and for a long time, sunny weather, sandy beaches, and ski resorts have been on top of the list of attractions. In fact, after the 1960s, extensive tourism development took place mainly at sunny destinations located on the so-called pleasure periphery (Turner and Ash, 1976). Since such destinations were located far from main outbound tourist markets, their development relied mainly on air links. Thus these tourist destinations usually benefitted from a level of air connectivity higher than expected according to their socioeconomic characteristics. Small islands are the best example of this, but other examples are peripheral regions such as Algarve (Portugal) or Cancun (Mexico), where only tourism activity can explain their diversity of air links. The air mobility of local residents on these islands and in these regions has been poorly studied. However, until the liberalisation of air transport markets, such supply was not available to local inhabitants but restricted to foreign tourists through charter flights included in package holidays. So the impact on residents' air mobility has been limited until recently. Within the EU, the end of restrictions imposed on charter services after liberalisation and fare reductions have probably pushed local demand for air transport in tourism destinations. However, the passenger structure of airports such as Faro is clearly dominated by inbound flows, which in 2012 fluctuated from 92.2% in the summer season to 68.7% in winter, according to a survey conducted by the airport (ANA, 2012a,b, 2013). Access to former surveys in order to perform diachronic studies is needed in order to evaluate possible changes and the diversity of reasons for flying.

The increasing attractiveness of major cities as tourism destinations, not only because of their cultural heritage, but also because of their urban life and diversity of amenities, has probably impacted on air mobility for leisure reasons to airports serving such cities recently touched by tourism development. Extensive research is needed because the available results are not conclusive. Porto, in the north of Portugal, is a good example of a city that has been transformed into a tourist hotspot recently. However, passenger surveys conducted by Porto Airport in 2004 and 2010 show only a slight increase in the number of passengers flying for tourism purposes (30.2%–32.3%). This is similar to the limited growth observed in those flying for business reasons (44.5%–46.0%), whilst VFR remained steady (20.3%–19.4%).

From the perspective of people living in outbound markets, charter services to tourist destinations played a key role in increasing the air mobility of the middle class in north-western Europe between the 1960s and 1980s (Garay and Cànoves, 2011; Doganis, 2010) (see Chapter 11). It is not only about reduced fares, but also about the decentralisation of charter flights' supply to regional airports (Pearce, 1987). These small airports in the United Kingdom, Belgium, the Netherlands, Germany, Denmark, and Sweden had a seasonal programme of charter flights to sunny destinations, easing accessibility to air mobility for those living in their catchment areas. During the charter sector's golden age, holidays were almost the only reason for flying from those airports, and more research is needed to establish whether some changes have taken place since liberalisation.

3.5.5 Supply-Side Characteristics

The characteristics of air services also affect purpose patterns, even though there may have been circular causalities between supply and demand. First, it is fair to assume direct air services between two places would influence the tourists' destination choice and thus affect the flying purpose mix aboard. However, there is little evidence to support this assumption. Based on econometric analyses and controlling for other factors, Duval and Schiff (2011) assessed the impact of new direct flights on the volume of international visitors to New Zealand for both 'holiday' and 'other' purposes from five different countries—Canada, Chile, Indonesia, South Korea, and Taiwan (one model was performed for each country of origin). It appears that direct air service availability is a significant factor only from some countries and for 'other' purposes only. This may imply that holiday purpose means more sensitivity to price (indirect routes are often cheaper) than to price and comfort. It could also be that in any case, New Zealand is so far away from most countries that indirect routes do not make a huge difference regarding the extent to which the destination is attractive. Koo et al. (2017) studied Australia, comparing inbound/outbound flows of tourists from/to 14 countries and dealing with the issue of endogenous relationships between supply and demand. They concluded that changes in direct services only affect outbound traffic, possibly due to the expansion of low-cost air services (the model did not control for air fares).

Several authors have examined the possible boost for tourism provided by low-cost airlines (as identified in Chapter 1). However surprisingly, very few authors have based their work on time series econometrics, whilst inappropriate statistics are regularly used; actually, the common practice is to show only before/after figures and/or to conduct surveys, and then to attribute all changes in air demand to the advent of cheaper flights (see Dobruszkes et al., 2016). The rare econometric studies that have been undertaken have shown that LCCs can boost flying for leisure purposes (see Lian and Denstadli, 2010, for flows to Norway; Rey et al., 2011, for flows from Western Europe to Spain; and Tsui, 2017, for domestic tourist flows within New Zealand). All other things being equal, LCCs would thus increase the share of leisure purpose from/to the markets they serve. Evidence also comes indirectly from surveys that compare passenger profiles between LCC and traditional airlines. For instance, Kuljanin and Kalić (2015) surveyed passengers at Belgrade Airport. Whilst gender, age, and trip duration are rather similar, there are significant differences in terms of education (lower level in LCCs), place of residence (LCCs are used more frequently by emigrants, for example, Serbians living abroad), occupation (less employees and more students, pensioners and unemployed in LCCs), and travel purpose (much more 'private' purpose and much less 'business' and 'tourism' purposes in LCCs—see Table 3.6). Here, LCCs are clearly associated with migration and VFR travel, even though how much both traditional and low-cost airlines serve the same or different markets is unknown (in other words, purpose splits may be affected by air fares, but also by inhabitant and place attributes at both ends). Similarly, Dobruszkes and Mondou (2013) found that the development of LCC services between Europe and Morocco boosted in the same proportion flows made by both foreign tourists (associated with holiday tourism) and by Moroccans living abroad (associated with VFR travel). Actually, LCC/VFRs' copresence has become commonplace on many 'ethnic' routes where LCCs literally accompany the migrants and may even fuel migrations (Burrell, 2011).

3.5.6 Institutional Issues

Finally, various institutional factors also affect the reasons for flying. One issue is how freely citizens can travel abroad. Some lucky travellers may simply use an ID, such as between most European countries. In most cases however, a passport is required and its cost may discourage the members of poorer households. As discussed in Chapter 2, in many cases, though, a visa is also needed, whether for the purpose of leisure (tourist visa) or work (business visa). In practice, there is no real distinction between a tourist and business visa, as long as they are both for short stays only: the basic requirements (valid passport), maximum length of stay, and fees are similar. In some destinations, business travellers must provide a letter of invitation from a local company. This means not only extra costs, but also dependence on the destination country's goodwill. Considering that a leisure trip is chosen by the travellers themselves, whilst a business trip is generally a constrained trip financially supported by a firm or public funds, it can be assumed that visa restrictions have a more negative effect on leisure trips than on business travel. Hence, restrictive visa policies

TABLE 3.6 Flying Purpose vs. Airline Type at Belgrade Airport (Spring, 2013)

Market	Traditional Airlines (%)	Low-Cost Airlines (%)
Business	43.4	14.2
Tourism	18.5	14.9
Private	33.2	67.5
Others	4.9	3.4

From Kuljanin, J., Kalić, M., 2015. Exploring characteristics of passengers using traditional and low-cost airlines: a case study of Belgrade Airport. J. Air Transp. Manag. 46, 12–18.

FIG. 3.4 Freedom to travel abroad within a visa (2017). *(Source: Map: F. Dobruszkes; Henley and Partners Visa Restrictions Index.)*

led by 'rich' countries to reduce illegal migrations (i.e. tourists who do not fly back to their home country) would increase the share of business travellers to these destinations. Conversely, less restrictions would favour leisure travel. Considering Turkey and 81 countries of origin over the 1995–2010 period, Balli et al. (2013) found a positive effect of a visa-waiving policy on international tourist flows, whilst controlling for various other factors. Fig. 3.4 shows the extent to which citizens are free to travel abroad without a visa. The overall picture suggests that, on average, inhabitants of rich countries are freer to travel abroad and would thus spend less money on visas.[9]

Institutional matters also refer to regulatory regimes imposed on (or offered) to the airlines. Aviation liberalisation tends to favour competition, route development, and lower fares, even though these alleged benefits may be spatially uneven and new monopolies may appear (Goetz and Vowles, 2009; Dobruszkes, 2009a). As a result, many authors and international organisations have claimed that aviation liberalisation is good for tourism development (Dobruszkes and Mondou, 2013). However, evidence is scarce because of the limited efforts applied to econometric methods, the confusion, as already discussed, between tourism definitions, little attention paid to changes in length of stays, and an overall belief that liberalisation is good in nature (see Dobruszkes et al., 2016). Having said that, findings are mixed (Duval and Schiff, 2011; Zhang and Findlay, 2014), which is likely because relationships between aviation liberalisation and tourism are very place dependent. For instance, open skies agreements between the United States and various African countries have only slightly affected the air market (and in some cases there are even no flights), in contrast with flights from the United States to Taiwan, El Salvador, Panama, and Iceland (Dobruszkes and Mwanza Wa Mwanza, 2007).

In addition, governments may also induce airline development through various policies. For instance, public authorities could lower airport charges to boost tourism or to counter a decrease in tourist arrivals, as was the case after the 1994 terrorist attacks in Turkey (Lobbenberg, 1995). Elsewhere, local and regional Spanish governments had widely subsidised airlines during the past decade to secure a minimum flight supply from a wide array of regional

[9] Latin America however, enjoys a better position than expected given its national income or level of development.

airports located across the country (Ramos-Pérez, 2016). The growth of incoming tourists was used to vindicate subsidies, but they also had an impact on the local population's propensity to fly, including the more frequent use of aircraft when travelling for holidays, as a survey conducted in 2006 at Zaragoza Airport showed (AENA, 2006). Governments can also directly develop a national airline for a wide range of motives, including positioning their country as a tourist destination. Gulf airlines are actual typical examples of such a strategy (Lohmann et al., 2009; Derudder et al., 2013). Insular countries such as the Seychelles and Mauritius followed the same strategy earlier, but at a less ambitious scale though (Lamy-Giner, 2014).

Finally, the provision of airline public service obligations (PSO) in peripheral regions can also increase the propensity to fly of people living in those areas. In the EU, PSO can include the imposition of a minimum supply of daily or weekly flights, a maximum fare and, in some cases, specific price discounts for local residents in order to relieve mobility restrictions derived from geographical isolation or remoteness (Williams, 2010). In the Canary Islands (Spain), a recent increase from 50% to 75% in the discount applied to air fares for local residents, has boosted interisland passengers. In a single year, from July 2017 to June 2018, interislands air routes added more than one million passengers. As a consequence of reduced air fares, VFR and leisure trips, but also domestic holidays within the archipelago, seem to have dramatically increased.

3.6 CONCLUSIONS

In this evidence-based chapter, the reasons for flying have been unveiled. The information is dispersed, not always comparable, mostly available in the local language and not always published. The cost of data is also restrictive. Despite these limitations, some key conclusions can be drawn.

First, arguably contrary to a collective unconscious belief, flying for business reasons is not dominant at the global and national levels, even though it can be more important from/to specific airports and along specific routes. Actually, leisure traffic is globally dominant, and the numbers of those flying for holiday purposes is larger than those flying to visit friends and relatives (VFR), even though VFR passengers are more numerous than business passengers and are probably underestimated.

Second, flying purpose is clearly place dependent. It involves attributes at both ends related to inhabitants, economic patterns and tourist amenities, plus institutional aspects. The factors that shape flying patterns play out on all geographical scales from districts to countries. Since they are spatially heterogeneous and do not play out in the same manner in all countries (see Duval and Schiff, 2011), the reasons for flying are not the same everywhere. Despite the impact at both ends of places on flying purposes, there was no data on travel purpose by country-, region-, or city-pairs. Reasons for flying also change over time, both short term (subject to seasons and special dates and days of the week) and long-term (following main social, economical, and political changes). In summary, this chapter confirms that there exists both a geography and a temporality associated with flying purpose. This means that surveys need to be carefully designed to avoid strong biases.

This chapter also reveals several avenues for future research. First, most data found relates to developed countries. Since reasons for flying are place dependent and air transport even more socially selective is poor countries, it is unlikely that findings from developed countries would apply elsewhere. In addition, available figures mostly concern international travel. Domestic markets are less known, notably because no entry or exit cards must be filled in by visitors. However, in 2016, domestic air travel accounted for 60% of the world's air passengers and 37% of the distances flown by passengers.[10] Based on seats offered by airport-pairs in June 2017, the top 30 included only four international routes, whilst the seven largest routes were domestic.[11] There is thus an urgent need to investigate domestic passengers too.

Finally, nearly all available splits of flying purpose are based on trips made. This neglects both distances flown and revenues generated for the industry. Yet the UK experience suggests that, based on distances flown within the United Kingdom, business purpose accounted for 55% in 2002–06 (Dargay and Clark, 2012). Although these figures only concern domestic travel (where surface alternatives exist), this is much more than any share of business travel in Table 3.1. Furthermore, the share of business class seats is higher in long-haul aircraft (Bowen, 2009). It is thus clear that distance- or revenue-based evidence would dramatically increase the importance of business travel.

[10] Computed from the ICAO 2016 Annual Report. Non-scheduled flights are not included but have become marginal.

[11] Computed by the authors from the OAG dataset.

References

AENA/Aeropuertos Españoles y Navegación Aérea, 2004. Aeropuerto de La Palma - Informe de Resultados de Encuestas. Año 2004. Semana tipo de marzo (SPCIR2004V0V). AENA, Madrid.

AENA/Aeropuertos Españoles y Navegación Aérea, 2006. Aeropuerto de Zaragoza - Informe de Resultados de Encuestas (ZAZIR2006V0). AENA, Madrid.

Aguilera, A., 2008. Business travel and mobile workers. Transp. Res. A 42, 1109–1116.

ANA/Aeroportos de Portugal, 2012a. Perfil do Passageiro Verao IATA 2012 - Aeroporto de Faro. ANA, Lisbon.

ANA/Aeroportos de Portugal, 2012b. Porto Airport. Porto Airport Marketing Department, Porto.

ANA/Aeroportos de Portugal, 2013. Passenger Profile IATA Winter 2012/13—Faro Airport. ANA, Lisbon.

Arlt, W.G., 2016. China's Outbound Tourism: History, Current Development and Outlook. In: Li, X. (Ed.), Chinese Outbound Tourism 2.0. CRC Press, AAP, Boca Raton, Oakville, pp. 3–20.

Balli, F., Balli, H.O., Cebeci, K., 2013. Impacts of exported Turkish soap operas and visa-free entry on inbound tourism to Turkey. Tour. Manag. 37, 186–192.

Beaverstock, J., Derudder, B., Faulconbridge, J., Witlox, F. (Eds.), 2009. International Business Travel and the Global Economy. Ashgate, London.

Boonekamp, T., Zuidberg, J., Burghouwt, G., 2018. Determinants of air travel demand: the role of low-cost carriers, ethnic links and aviation-dependent employment. Transp. Res. A Policy Pract. 112, 18–28.

Bowen, J., 2009. A people set apart: the spatial development of airline business class services. In: Beaverstock, J., Derudder, B., Faulconbridge, J., Witlox, F. (Eds.), International Business Travel and the Global Economy. Ashgate, London, pp. 11–30.

Burrell, K., 2011. Going steerage on Ryanair: cultures of migrant air travel between Poland and the UK. J. Transp. Geogr. 19 (5), 1023–1030.

CAA, 2009. International Relations: The Growth in Air Travel to Visit Friends or Relatives. Available from, http://publicapps.caa.co.uk/modalapplication.aspx?appid=11&mode=detail&id=3743. (Accessed February 11, 2018).

Charlot, S., Duranton, G., 2006. Cities and workplace communication. Some quantitative French evidence. Urban Stud. 43, 1365–1394.

Craps, A., 2017. Mobility practices of low-cost airlines' passengers. In: Cools, M., Limbourg, S. (Eds.), Proceedings of the BIVEC-GIBET Transport Research Days 2017. Towards an Autonomous and Interconnected Transport Future, Liège, 18–19 May, pp. 69–83.

Dargay, J., Clark, S., 2012. The determinants of long distance travel in Great Britain. Transp. Res. A 46, 576–587.

Derudder, B., Witlox, F., 2014. Global cities and air transport. In: Goetz, A., Budd, L. (Eds.), Geographies of Air Transport. Ashgate, Farnham, pp. 103–123.

Derudder, B., Bassens, D., Witlox, F., 2013. Political-geographic interpretations of massive air transport developments in Gulf cities. Polit. Geogr. 36, A4–A7.

Dobruszkes, F., 2009a. Does liberalisation of air transport imply increasing competition? Lessons from the European case. Transp. Policy 16 (1), 29–39.

Dobruszkes, F., 2009b. New Europe, new low-cost air services. J. Transp. Geogr. 17 (6), 423–432.

Dobruszkes, F., Mondou, V., 2013. Aviation liberalization as a means to promote international tourism: the EU–Morocco case. J. Air Transp. Manag. 29, 23–34.

Dobruszkes, F., Mwanza Wa Mwanza, H., 2007. Marginalisation et dépendance aérienne de l'Afrique sub-saharienne. Belgeo 2007 (2), 203–226.

Dobruszkes, F., Mondou, V., Ghedira, A., 2016. Assessing the impacts of aviation liberalisation on tourism: some methodological considerations derived from the Moroccan and Tunisian cases. J. Transp. Geogr. 50, 115–127.

Doganis, R., 2010. Flying Off Course: Airlines Economics and Marketing, fourth ed. Routledge, London.

Duval, D., Schiff, A., 2011. Effect of air services availability on international visitors to New Zealand. J. Air Transp. Manag. 17 (3), 175–180.

Dwyer, L., Seetaram, N., Forsyth, P., Brian, K., 2014. Is the migration-tourism relationship only about VFR? Ann. Tour. Res. 46 (3), 130–143.

Forsyth, P., Dwyer, L., Seetaram, N., King, B., 2012. Measuring the economic impact of migration-induced tourism. Tour. Anal. 17 (5), 559–571.

Garay, L., Cànoves, G., 2011. Life cycles, stages and tourism history: the Catalonia (Spain) experience. Ann. Tour. Res. 38 (2), 651–671.

Goetz, A., Vowles, T., 2009. The good, the bad, and the ugly: 30 years of US airline deregulation. J. Transp. Geogr. 17 (4), 251–263.

Handley, F., 2006. Back to Africa. Issues of hosting "roots" tourism in West Africa. In: Haviser, J.B., MacDonald, K.C. (Eds.), African Re-Genesis. Confronting Social Issues in the Diaspora. Routledge, London, pp. 20–31.

Jackson, R., 1990. VFR tourism: is it underestimated? J. Tour. Stud. 1 (2), 10–17.

Janta, H., Cohen, S., Williams, A., 2015. Rethinking visiting friends and relatives mobilities. Popul. Space Place 21 (7), 585–598.

Jones, A., 2013. Conceptualising business mobilities: towards an analytical framework. Rev. Transp. Business Manag. 9, 58–66.

Koo, T., Lim, C., Dobruszkes, F., 2017. Circular causality in aviation and tourism demand. Ann. Tour. Res. 67, 67–77.

Kuljanin, J., Kalić, M., 2015. Exploring characteristics of passengers using traditional and low-cost airlines: a case study of Belgrade airport. J. Air Transp. Manag. 46, 12–18.

Lamy-Giner, M.A., 2014. La desserte aérienne de deux petits Etats insulaires: les Seychelles et Maurice: Enjeux et restructurations. Cybergeo: Eur. J. Geogr. Available at http://cybergeo.revues.org/26490. (Accessed February 11, 2018).

Lassen, C., 2006. Aeromobility and work. Environ. Plan A 38, 301–312.

Lian, J.I., Denstadli, J.M., 2004. Norwegian business air travel–segments and trends. J. Air Trans. Manag. 10 (1), 109–118.

Lian, J.I., Denstadli, J.M., 2010. Booming leisure air travel to Norway—the role of airline competition. Scand. J. Hosp. Tour. 10 (1), 1–15.

Lobbenberg, A., 1995. The impact of turnround costs on inclusive tour prices. Tour. Manag. 16 (7), 501–505.

Lohmann, G., Albers, S., Koch, B., Pavlovich, K., 2009. From hub to tourist destination—an explorative study of Singapore and Dubai's aviation-based transformation. J. Air Transp. Manag. 15 (5), 205–211.

Maruyama, N., Stonza, A., 2010. Roots tourism of Chinese Americans. Ethnology 49 (1), 23–44.

Pearce, D.G., 1987. Mediterranean charters—a comparative geographic perspective. Tour. Manag. 8 (4), 291–305.

Ramos-Pérez, D., 2016. State aid to airlines in Spain: an assessment of regional and local government support from 1996 to 2014. Transp. Policy 49, 137–147.

Ranély Vergé-Dépré, C., Roth, P., 2017. L'avion, facteur d'unification du Bassin caraïbe? Mappemonde 120. Available at http://mappemonde.mgm.fr/120as3. (Accessed February 11, 2018).
Rey, B., Myro, R., Galera, A., 2011. Effect of low-cost airlines on tourism in Spain. A dynamic panel data model. J. Air Transp. Manag. 17 (3), 163–167.
Riziki, M.J., Dobruszkes, F., Mwanza Wa Mwanza, H., 2017. Pays en voie de développement et qualité de service d'une nouvelle compagnie d'aviation: le cas de Congo Airways (Airline service quality in developing countries: the case of Congo Airways). Les Cahiers Scientifiques du Transport 72.
Ryan, C., Birks, S., 2005. Passengers and low cost flights: evidence from the trans-Tasman routes. J. Travel Tour. Market. 19 (1), 15–27.
Seetaram, N., 2012. Immigration and international inbound tourism: empirical evidence from Australia. Tour. Manag. 33 (6), 1535–1543.
SH&E, 2010. Competitive Africa: Tourism Industry Research Phase II. Air Transport Sector Study. Report for the World Bank.
Shaw, G., Williams, A.M., 2002. Critical Issues in Tourism: A Geographical Perspective, second ed. Blackwell, London.
Tretyakevich, N., Maggi, R., 2011. Not just for business: some evidence on leisure motivations of conference attendees. Curr. Issue Tour. 15 (4), 391–395.
Tsui, W.K., 2017. Does a low-cost carrier lead the domestic tourism demand and growth of New Zealand? Tour. Manag. 60, 390–403.
Turner, L., Ash, J., 1976. The Golden Hordes: International Tourism and the Pleasure Periphery. Constable and Company, London.
UNTWO, 2017. Tourism Highlights: 2017 Edition. Available at http://mkt.unwto.org/publication/unwto-tourism-highlights. (Accessed February 11, 2018).
Wardman, M., Chintakayala, P., de Jong, G., 2016. Values of travel time in Europe: review and meta-analysis. Transp. Res. A 94, 93–111.
Williams, G., 2010. European experience of public service obligations. In: Williams, G., Bråthen, S. (Eds.), Air Transport Provision in Remoter Regions. Ashgate, London, pp. 99–113.
Williams, A., Hall, M., 2000. Tourism and migration: new relationships between production and consumption. Tour. Geogr. 2 (1), 5–27.
Zhang, Y., Findlay, C., 2014. Air transport policy and its impacts on passenger traffic and tourist flows. J. Air Transp. Manag. 34, 42–48.

CHAPTER

4

Limits to Growth

Anne GRAHAM[*], *David METZ*[†]

[*]University of Westminster, London, United Kingdom [†]University College London, London, United Kingdom

CHAPTER OUTLINE

4.1 INTRODUCTION

In considering the rationale for flying, it is very important to have a good appreciation of what the future may bring. Most global air travel and tourism forecasts predict a long-term rise in demand. For instance, Airbus (2017) is envisaging an average annual growth rate in passenger-kilometres of 4.4% until 2036. The United Nations World Tourism Organisation (UNWTO) is also predicting an annual rise of visitor numbers of 3.3% until 2030 (UNWTO, 2017). After many years of relatively steady growth, such forecasts generally assume that past traffic patterns and the relationship with key factors, such as economic growth, can be extrapolated into the future. However, they also assume that travel attitudes and behaviour do not change except when driven by these factors. If they do in fact change, this could have major implications for industry decisions, for example, concerning airport capacity or destination development, as well as policy areas related to the consumer, climate change, and tourism planning and management.

Within this context, very little attention has been given to any limits to future demand and so this chapter aims to investigate this issue. The next section introduces the key concepts related to limits to air travel growth, focusing on a demand viewpoint to fit in with this book's first theme that considers the rationale for flying. Also, some interesting relevant research findings from surface travel are briefly highlighted. In addition, an investigation of the wider tourism literature is presented to provide some insights into relevant travel decision-making behaviour since, as demand for air transport is derived, it is primarily the drivers of tourism demand that ultimately determine the airline traffic. This is followed by using the UK as a case study for considering these concepts related to limits to demand, which leads to some general conclusions being drawn.

4.2 THE KEY CONCEPTS

4.2.1 Air Travel Demand

Limits to air travel growth could potentially occur because of a number of reasons, from both a supply or demand perspective. Supply factors include insufficient airport capacity, such as the lack of runway slots or limited terminal

https://doi.org/10.1016/B978-0-12-812857-2.00004-X

capacity, or inadequate airspace capacity. They could also be related to environmental rather physical capacity limitations, for example, due to noise restrictions or air quality legislation. Other influential supply factors could include the absence of appropriate airlines or air routes, or inhibiting factors such as visa controls (as discussed in Chapters 1 and 3). Most of the attention of the previous research on growth limits has been on these supply-related factors.

Less frequent consideration has been given to limits to air travel growth from a demand viewpoint, which is the focus here. This can be linked to concepts such as market maturity and saturation. Here the general assumption is that the growth for products and services can be characterised by key lifecycle phases, starting with low growth with the initial introduction and limited consumer awareness and supply, then rapid growth as the product achieves greater market awareness and supply expands to fill the new market, and eventually slower growth once the product has become established and the market matures and finally approaches saturation, after which sales subsequently decline (Fig. 4.1; Kotler and Armstrong, 2017). In other words, market maturity can broadly be identified by declining growth rates of demand, whereas saturation can be considered to exist if there is no further growth.

A time series analysis of traffic data can detect whether any such relevant patterns of growth, such as an S-shaped curve or falling growth rates, are emerging. However, this may be misleading unless key drivers of demand, such as income or price, are taken into account. For example, demand may not increase when there are poor economic conditions, but then may return when the economic climate is better. As a consequence, some time ago Bowles (1994) discussed how one of the most commonly accepted measures of a mature market is one that grows by no more than the rate of economic growth of the country. At the same time, Rolls Royce (1994) defined a mature market as one where traffic growth is equal to the sum of income and yield growth, with any additional growth being defined as 'product' growth. Its Maturity Factor (MF), defined as income and yield growth divided by traffic growth, was used to quantify the extent of 'maturity' in a market. The MF would be 100% when the market is mature, but less than 100% in the presence of product growth. Meanwhile, Vedantham and Oppenheimer (1998) suggested a slightly different four-stage air transport model compared to the traditional links with product life, with the stages comprising latent demand (high growth rates), continual expansion (high growth rates), modal shifts (where aviation is the most efficient means of transport for consumers), and eventual maturity (when low growth rates appear).

Graham (2000) related the concept of the air product life cycle to the impact of income growth by suggesting a theoretical five-stage model of maturity and saturation using income elasticities. Income elasticity measures the demand response of the market to changes in the incomes of potential customers and so will tend to decrease as markets become more mature. Stage 3 of the model reflected movements towards maturity with declining elasticity values greater than one, followed by full maturity occurring at Stage 4 when the elasticity is 1. In other words, a totally mature market was defined as one which grows by no more than the income growth. Stage 5 was equated to market saturation, when the elasticity value is zero where any increase in income has no effect on demand. Eurocontrol (2013) used a similar approach but had slightly different definitions. They assumed that if an increase in income produced a smaller increase in demand, then the market was becoming mature, whereas if an increase in income caused no increase in demand, then the market was totally mature.

Hence this use of income elasticities can be applied to explore air travel growth limits due to constraints on income or alternative spending preferences. However, whilst many studies observe that income elasticity values can differ significantly between travel distance, type of traveller, and route, they rarely discuss concepts of maturity (Gallet and Doucouliagos, 2014; Gillen et al., 2008). Specifically, as regards frequent flyers there may also be constraints on time, or the need or desire to use time for other purposes. The time under consideration will be that spent away from the home or office, and the time available for holidays or visiting friends and relatives (VFR). The time constraint is likely

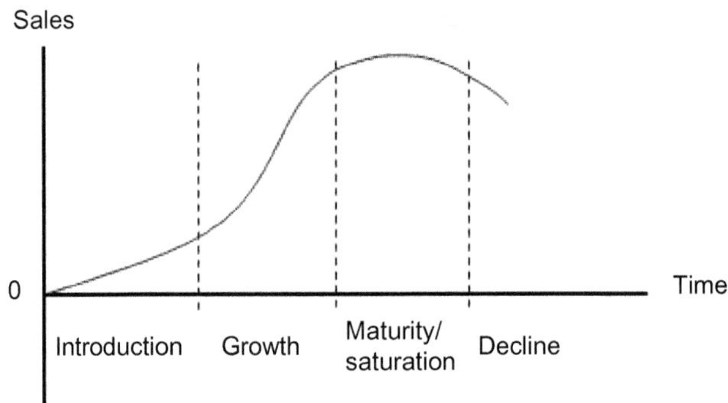

FIG. 4.1 The product life cycle. *(Adapted from Kotler, P., Armstrong, G., 2017. Principles of Marketing, Global Edition, 17th ed. Pearson, New York.)*

to vary for different segments, for example, being less of an issue for more elderly travellers in retirement. For short trips, such as weekend breaks, the time spent travelling may also be a constraining factor—to and from the airport, queuing and waiting at the airport, as well as time in the air. This is an issue rarely considered within the air travel research literature.

A further way to consider limits to air travel is by assessing travel propensity, or propensity to fly, being commonly defined as the air trips per capita. This value will not increase indefinitely but is likely to taper off as the market reaches maturity and approaches saturation. Propensity to fly will vary with the market, depending on a variety of factors such as living standards, demographics, and travel cost. Luxembourg, Norway, and Switzerland had the highest values in the world in 2013 (International Air Transport Association (IATA), 2014). By region North America had the highest trips per capita with a value of 1.63 followed by Europe with 1.21. Airbus (2017) confirmed that the average value for Europe was 1.2, with individual values elsewhere varying from 1.8 in the United States, compared to 0.4 in China and 0.1 in India. It is predicting that emerging markets travel will grow by an annual rate of 5.8% until 2036, compared with just 3.2% with advanced nations, resulting eventually in a narrowing of the gap between the travel propensity values of the population of these two different markets.

Meanwhile Morphet and Bottini (2014) assumed that market saturation would occur with 2–2.5 trips per capita for nonisolated markets, which were defined as countries where alternative transport modes are available. For isolated markets, for example, remote islands, where other modes of transport are not available or competitive, or where the market is artificially boosted by connectivity provided by a major hub, more than twice this value was assumed to represent saturation. Elsewhere Murphy and Wells (2010) suggested that the US domestic market for air travel was nearing saturation, which was expected at 2.4 trips per capita compared with the 2010 average of 2.2.

Two key determinants will influence the values of propensity to fly. These are the average number of trips and the proportion of the population that flies. As maturity is reached, the rate of increase of both these factors will slow. IATA (2014) observed that the average frequency of trips for high-income countries is 1.48 compared with 0.29 and 0.04 for middle- and low-income countries, respectively. However, it is usually assumed that there will always be a certain share of any population who will never travel by air for a number of reasons such as family or work circumstances, poor health/mobility, fear of flying, or just a lack of interest. Therefore there is likely to be a maximum proportion of the population who will travel. In the 1990s, James (1993) observed how the percentage of consumers who had flown in the United States had risen from one half to two-thirds in the 1970s but had been constant in the 70%–75% range since 1984—arguing that a 75% limit might be the most to be expected. Graham (1995) suggested that the maximum potential market, even in the wealthiest countries, was unlikely to exceed around 80% of the population, or in other words there would remain 20% of the population that never travelled.

However, in absolute terms, the number of people flying could vary because of population changes since demographic trends are key factors influencing travel patterns (Metz, 2016a). For example, certain developed economies are expecting to experience declines in population numbers in the future. For instance, Germany's population has been forecast to reduce from 82 million to 75 million by 2050 and Japan's population is predicted to shrink by a third by 2065 (The Economist, 2017; Demetriou, 2017). This may thus depress travel growth further, even if the travel propensity figures have reached a constant.

Empirical evidence to support these claims of a maximum travel participation level is hard to find, with little attention being given to people who are presently not flying or flying infrequently, the factors that influence these habits, and whether such people will fly more regularly in time to come. Any data that are available usually concern those who have not flown for only a certain period of time, typically one year. A key question is what proportion of these flew previous to this, and importantly what proportion is likely to fly in the future. It seems likely that some people will have never flown; some will have flown rarely or occasionally; others will regularly take annual holidays by air but may have missed a year for a particular reason such as illness; and for some the interval between annual holiday trips on occasions will be greater than 12 months. Some current infrequent flyers may have flown regularly in an earlier phase of life.

Rare research in this area for residents in the Netherlands, Belgium, and the German regions bordering the Netherlands examined when the last air trip had been taken or whether any residents had never flown (KiM Netherlands Institute for Transport Policy Analysis, 2015). The share of those who had not flown during the last year represented 43%, 45%, and 57%, respectively, in the three countries. Moreover, the percentage of those who had never flown ranged between 8%–16% and 35%–50% of the infrequent flyers said that they might not, or definitely would not, fly in the future. Fear of flying was the most cited reason for not flying, whilst the second most common cause was the cost of flying. Other reasons included poor health and concerns about the environment.

In summary, this short review of relevant literature demonstrates that limits to air travel is a concept relevant to both frequent and infrequent flyers. Table 4.1 lists some possible factors that could drive such limits. For frequent

TABLE 4.1 Factors Driving Possible Limits to Growth

Factors	Frequent Flyers	Infrequent/Nonflyers	Time Period
Cost of travel/budget constraints	May deter further travel	May deter ability to travel	Could be temporary
Time constraints	May deter further travel	May deter ability to travel	↓
Lack of knowledge of travel and booking options		May deter ability/motivation to travel	
Family/work/health circumstances	May deter further travel	May deter ability to travel	
Population changes	Decreases in the population may reduce absolute numbers of frequent travellers		
Motivation to travel by air	Frequent travel may reduce the motivation for further travel	Lack of motivation will result in no travel	
Fear of flying and security or safety concerns		May deter motivation to travel	
Environmental concerns	May deter further travel	May deter motivation to travel	Could be permanent

Source: Devised by authors.

flyers, typically from developed countries, limits associated with demand maturity and saturation may be expected to occur primarily because of constraints on income or time, and the need or preference to use these for other activities. These factors are likely to affect segments of the population in different ways. For example, for those who are retired the budget constraint may well play a role (as well as possibly health), whereas availability of time is unlikely to be an issue. The reverse situation may occur with busy senior management who are well paid. With infrequent flyers, a key issue is the time period under consideration and whether they are likely to fly in the future. Constraints related to income and time, as well as domestic circumstances and knowledge of travel may be overcome, whereas motivational attitudes and views towards the environment and safety/security of air travel may be more permanent. Focus is now briefly given to the experience of surface travel and then to broader tourism concepts, with the aim of providing more insights into this topic.

4.2.2 Experience of Surface Travel

It has been argued, for example by Metz (2013), that daily surface travel per capita in Great Britain and other developed economies has stabilised. In Great Britain for over 40 years there has been little change in average annual trip rate (about a thousand trips a year) or in average travel time (an hour a day). Also, the average annual distance travelled in Great Britain (by all modes except international aviation) increased from about 4500 miles per person per year in the early 1970s but has settled at about 7000 miles per person per year since the mid-1990s. Three-quarters of this distance is by car, hence car use per capita has ceased to grow, a phenomenon that is found for the developed economies generally and is known as Peak Car. This implies that the historic link between income and travel demand no longer holds and these findings in respect of daily travel are consistent with the propositions that (a) time constrains travel, there being many other activities to be fitted in to the 24 h of the day; and (b) demand for daily travel has saturated (Metz, 2010, 2016b). These findings confirm that maturity and saturation is a relevant issue for all modes of transport and that the experience of surface travel arguably may provide some indication of what may follow with air transport in the future.

4.2.3 Tourism Decision-Making

Attention is now turned to gaining a greater understanding of air travel demand by considering the tourist's decision-making process. A simple way of looking at this is to focus on the tourist's ability and willingness to travel, which leads on to the concepts of determinants and motivators (Swarbrooke and Horner, 1999). Determinants are factors that make it possible for people to travel, which can be related to economic and social conditions such as income and leisure time, and conditions set by the providers of travel services such as price and quality. Motivators are factors that make the consumer willing to travel and these will be related to personality traits, preferences, and attitudes. Many of these in turn are likely to be influenced by the socioeconomic and demographic characteristics of consumers.

These drivers of tourism demand and behaviour have been extensively studied but, as with air travel demand specifically, much of the attention has been on why people travel and the positive enabling factors, rather than investigating infrequent travellers or negative constraining factors. However, one of the most commonly used theoretical frameworks used within this limited travel constraints literature is the Leisure Constraints Model (LCM), which was developed in the late 1980s for all leisure activities (Godbey et al., 2010). It has subsequently been applied to a number of tourism cases (Nyaupane and Andereck, 2008).

The model has three categories of constraints, namely, intrapersonal constraints which are individual psychological and physical states, and attributes that affect preferences; interpersonal constraints that occur because of the unavailability of other people; and structural constraints (e.g. lack of time, money, opportunity, information, and access/proximity). It has been argued that the model is hierarchical in nature, with the constraints ordered sequentially so that each level of a constraint must either not exist, or be overcome, before going on to the next level. It is asserted that intrapersonal comes first, followed by interpersonal and then structural. Linking this with the concepts of motivators and determinants, it can therefore be argued that intrapersonal constraints or motivators influence leisure preferences whilst structural constraints or determinants influence leisure participation after the preference decisions have been made. Whilst not all the research agrees with the hierarchical sequence, there is some consensus with the intrapersonal–interpersonal–structural constraint typology which has been used, for example, to look at different market segments by geography, such as Portugal (Silva and Correia, 2008) and China (Lai et al., 2013); or by type of tourism or activity such as skiing (Gilbert and Hudson, 2000) or nature (Penningtom-Gray and Kerstetter, 2002). Lack of money and time are consistently identified as two of the key structural constraints.

Identifying constraints can be complex. For example, He et al. (2014) revealed that Japanese tourists with different sociodemographic characteristics faced diverse US-bound travel constraints. Meanwhile with a study of Spanish consumers, Alegre et al. (2010) argued that it is useful to not only examine the drivers of travel participation itself (e.g. income or budget), but also the factors that help to determine the degree of importance with which households perceive their budget constraints, such as the level of education, age, and barriers associated with poor health status. In Australia, Kattiyapornpong and Miller (2013) found that sociodemographic variables, which can perform as proxies for factors such as time limitations or preferences, can act in different ways to constrain or free different types of travel behaviour. They observed that there were significant levels of travel by even the most constrained groups, as well as significant amounts of nontravel by the least constrained sectors of society.

Linking to the discussion before concerning the time period or dimension of constraints to air travel, a basic assumption of the LCM is that obstacles prevent people from travelling, but if the obstacles can be removed, then they will travel. However, this has been challenged by some, suggesting that there are some people who just do not want to travel. For example, the research of Haukeland (1990) identified three types of Norwegian nontravellers based on social and economic constraints, but there was then was an additional fourth type of nontraveller that had no constraints but just preferred to stay at home. Haukeland's (1990) model was subsequently replicated using Canadian-based data by Smith et al. (2009).

Dolnicar et al. (2013) also questioned whether all people naturally had a desire to travel by looking at the relationship between holidays and the quality of life. They found that some may see a holiday as essential to the maintenance of a certain quality of life, Whilst others will not. In a study of Australian residents, they found that 30% said holidays did not enhance their quality of life. A few other researchers have argued that this is a difficult area to study, since there may be some element of social desirability bias that actually prevents nontravellers in revealing their lack of interest in travel. For example, Litvin et al. (2013) discussed whether this was the case with a US sample, as the reasons given for nonparticipation appeared to contradict the demographic characteristics of respondents.

McKercher (2009) also claimed that respondents in a survey of Hong Kong residents may have felt compelled to provide socially acceptable excuses for their nonparticipation, by indicating a lack of interest in travel, but then identifying a range of reasons for nonparticipation. He argued that this absence of the 'travel bug' in certain people could explain why, in spite of the efforts of the travel industry to remove obstacles to participation, a significant number of nontravellers remained. Later McKercher and Chen (2015), through evaluating the importance of travel within a set of 13 other leisure activities, found that some people did not consider travel to be a high enough priority for some to lead them to participate. They argued that this challenged the traditional constraints theory and helped explain why travel propensity rarely exceeded three-quarters of the population of developed economies. They concluded that it was priority rather than obstacles that were important, with travel being forsaken so that other higher priority needs could be meet.

More generally, evidence from Europe shows that, on average, just under 40% of EU residents did not participate in tourism in 2015 (Eurostat, 2017). The main reasons for not participating in tourism were given as financial which was identified by just over half the sample. Health was the second most important cause (stated by 20%) but 'no motivation', which is relevant to the discussion here, came a close third (18%). Other reasons were family, work, or study commitments. However, the data suffers from the same problems as identified with air travel, namely, that they only concern those who have not travelled for the last year, and nothing is known of previous travel patterns.

In essence, the general tourism literature very much mirrors the research on limits to air travel but provides additional consideration of the behaviour of travellers. Income/budget and time factors frequently appear as key constraints to travel in models such as the LCM. Moreover, there is a belief that there is a maximum level of participation in tourism, but with a real need to more fully understand the exact number, and motivation, of nontravellers. Finally, a recurrent theme within the literature is that the aggregation of data tends to hide significant factors, and, in particular, leads to a loss in awareness of behavioural sensitivity. Hence there is a need to disaggregate both the frequent and infrequent travel market as much as possible, as both tend to be very heterogeneous.

4.3 THE UK AIR TRAVEL MARKET

These three key interrelated recurrent themes, namely, income and time constraints, limits to travel participation, and behaviour by different markets, are now investigated by using the UK as a case study.

4.3.1 Relationship With Income and Time

With respect to the UK market, in spite of a popular belief that people are travelling more, and that there has been an increase in mobilities associated with VFR travel because of more people living, working, and studying abroad, evidence from the National Travel Survey (NTS) for England shows a relatively stable situation in terms of the number of international return air trips taken (Fig. 4.2). Therefore it is interesting to investigate further whether there is any evidence of limits to air travel demand in this market.

Growth and Income Trends

The official forecasts of the UK's Department for Transport (DfT) assume a certain degree of market maturity by using declining income elasticities related to judgement-based assumptions for different markets. Related to this, in 2010 the University of Westminster was commissioned by the DfT to investigate the available evidence on market maturity (University of Westminster, 2010). The findings discussed the date from which market maturity might take effect and the scale of the impact, suggesting that different segments of the UK market were exhibiting very different dynamics. The latest forecasts (DfT, 2017b) incorporate a range of assumptions based on declining income elasticities for different markets. Overall the income elasticity is predicted to decrease for 1.2 in 2016 to 0.9 in 2050 with the value for UK resident leisure travel falling from 1.4 to 1.0, and foreign leisure from 1.0 to 0.8. Sensitivity tests looking at

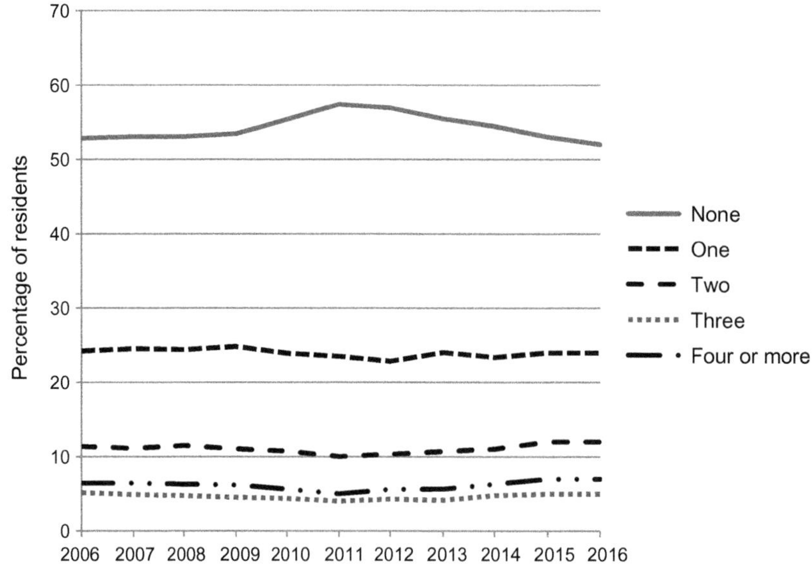

FIG. 4.2 International return air trips taken by English residents 2006–16. *(Source: NTS 2006–16.)*

making lower and higher maturity assumptions reduce the overall forecasts in 2050 from 410 million to 354 million and up to 445 million, respectively.

Earlier research by Graham (2000) using income elasticities concluded that the UK air international leisure travel market was only at the early stages of maturity, although the overall leisure travel market seemed to be much nearer to full maturity. Later, Graham (2006) discussed the potential impact of the rise of the low-cost carriers (LCCs), observing that there was a lack of evidence that these were appealing to the less wealthy previously nonflying parts of the population, but instead seemed to be encouraging more frequent flying. The UK Civil Aviation Authority (CAA) (2005) also investigated maturity and although there was some evidence that certain income elasticities had declined over time, it concluded that full maturity was still some way off. However, around this time, the CAA passenger surveys (CAA, 2008) showed that less than 1% of passengers were adults flying for the first time.

Time Constraints

As discussed before, an additional or alternative potential contributory factor to market maturity of travel may be time constraints. For air travel, it is not the hours in the day but the days in the year that may limit travel—not days of flying time but days away from responsibilities at home or work. To investigate the impact of possible time and other constraints, the University of Westminster undertook a pilot study in 2016 with the aim of gaining an understanding of the factors that limit air travel by individuals, distinguishing between business and nonbusiness or leisure travel. An online survey was created and administered to a convenience sample of 40 people who had taken at least four trips in the previous 12 months for any purpose. Semistructured telephone interviews were also administered to seven willing respondents (University of Westminster, 2016).

Although the sample size for the pilot survey was too small to support robust findings, the analysis pointed to the following conclusions:

- Time constraints are more important for leisure travel than are budget constraints, particularly permitted annual holidays from work.
- Business travellers tend to see such travel as obligatory, such that time constraints are seen as much less important.
- Other factors that limit leisure travel include older age and poorer health, and home and family commitments.

Here is a summary of some of the key comments of the respondents:

- Time constraints:

'I didn't have enough annual leave to take more', 'I ran out of holiday (work) and that is the reason why I did not take more non-business trips', 'Pressures of work are the only factors preventing me from taking more leave', 'Work commitments as well as not wanting to be to be away from home too often', 'Limited annual leave', 'Not enough time of university and/or work', 'Limited vacation days as self-employed', 'I work abroad and couldn't spend more time away from home'.

- Other constraining factors:

'Family commitments as well as work schedule'; 'Child care duties making it impossible to stay away longer than 10 days at a time. I would have preferred to make fewer trips, with longer stays', 'Important to find a good balance', 'It was very disruptive to my system as the jet lags kept me awake and hence tired for a very long time between trips. And just when I have adjusted I had to travel again and went into a vicious cycle of being tired', 'Family, pet and health commitments at home', 'I am responsible for the care of someone at home. Also I can only afford to take so much time away from work'.

4.3.2 Limits to Travel Participation

Fig. 4.2 showed that the NTS found that 52% of English residents took no flights abroad in 2016, whilst the Opinions and Life Style Survey (OPN) recorded the same figure of 52% in 2014 for all domestic and international flights (DfT, 2014, 2017a). There has been very little change with the NTS data in recent years and likewise the OPN figures have stayed within a narrow range. The CAA published the results of a survey in 2014 which looked at frequent and infrequent flyers in some detail (CAA, 2015). Frequent flyers were those who had flown in the 12 months preceding the survey, infrequent flyers were those who have not flown in the preceding 12 months. Overall the survey showed similar findings to the NTS and OPN data with 51% of UK residents being infrequent flyers. Younger people and older people were less likely to fly than those in mid-life and for the age groups 16–19 and 55+ (particularly 75+)

TABLE 4.2 UK Frequent and Infrequent Flyers by Age and Socioeconomic Group 2014

Age (%)	Frequent	Infrequent	Total	Socioeconomic Group (%)	Frequent	Infrequent	Total
16–19	47	53	100	Unemployed or between jobs	18	82	100
20–24	54	46	100	Homemaker	28	72	100
25–34	55	45	100	Unskilled manual	36	64	100
35–44	53	47	100	Skilled manual	46	54	100
45–54	53	47	100	Junior managerial	51	49	100
55–64	47	53	100	Middle managerial	62	38	100
65–74	48	52	100	Professional or senior managerial	61	39	100
75 Plus	27	73	100	Full time student	52	48	100

From CAA, 2015. Consumer Research for the UK Aviation Sector—Final Report. CAA, London.

there were more infrequent flyers than frequent flyers (Table 4.2). Moreover, in terms of socioeconomic groupings, the largest groups of infrequent flyers were junior managerial or skilled manual workers, with more frequent flyers than infrequent flyers with middle and senior managerial staff (Table 4.2). Around a third of the infrequent flyers had flown between 1 and 3 years ago and only 16% had actually never flown (Fig. 4.3).

Budget constraints were the most important reason for not flying, identified by nearly half of the infrequent flyers. Flying had not been an option when they made their travel plans for a further quarter of the sample. Personal circumstances, such as health issues or family changes, were more important reasons for nonflying than specific aviation factors, such as concerns about air travel (e.g. safety, security), accessibility and the impact of the environment (Fig. 4.4).

For future flying, the majority of infrequent flyers (55%) did not envisage any change in their flying habits, although 19% thought they would be flying more. However, very few of those (around 6%) who had not flown for 10 years, or had never flown, indicated that they would definitely fly more in the future. This supports the view that there may always be a certain percentage of the population that will not fly. Further analysis of this survey can be found in Graham and Metz (2017).

4.3.3 Air Travel Demand by Market Segment

As discussed before, much of the general research on limits to travel suggests that a disaggregated analysis might provide more insight because of the heterogeneous nature of air travel demand. As a very first step, and by way of illustration for the UK air market, this has been undertaken by visually assessing air flows by country from CAA passenger data, and by selecting a few markets that are perhaps showing signs of market maturity. Then visitor number

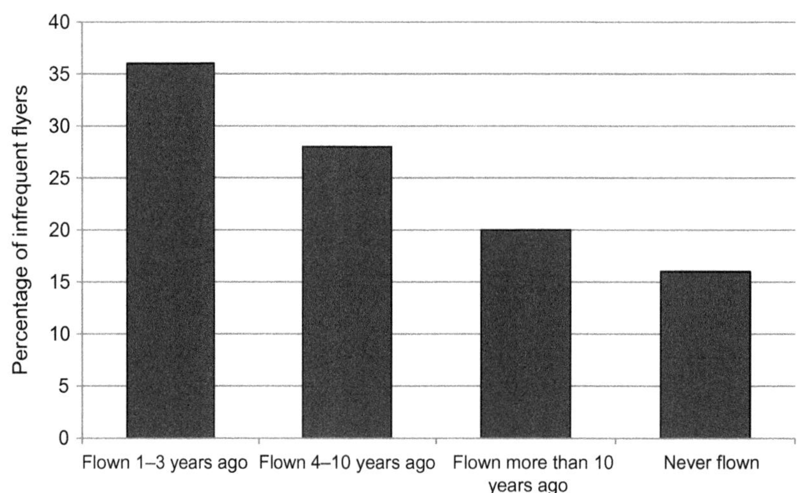

FIG. 4.3 Flying habits of UK infrequent flyers 2014. *(From CAA, 2015. Consumer Research for the UK Aviation Sector—Final Report. CAA, London.)*

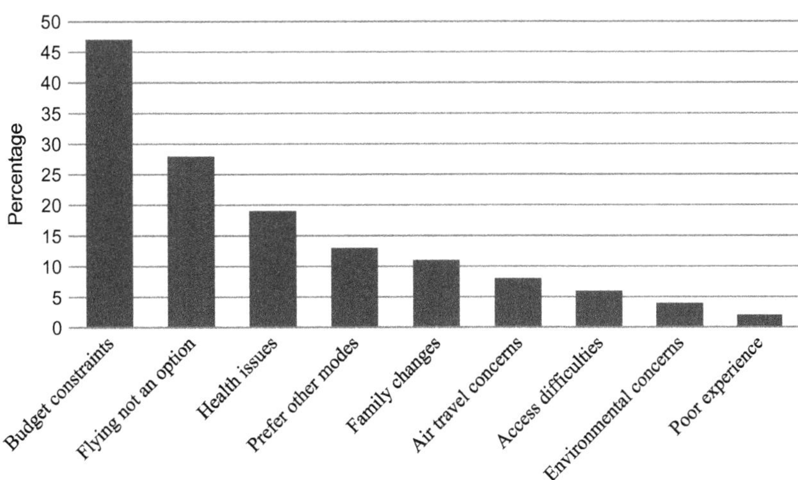

FIG. 4.4 Main reasons given by UK infrequent flyers for not flying 2014. *Note*: Respondents could provide multiple reasons. *(From CAA, 2015. Consumer Research for the UK Aviation Sector—Final Report. CAA, London.)*

data from the International Passenger Survey (IPS) for these selected routes, both incoming and outgoing, has been investigated to provide greater detail. It is important to note that the CAA data reports the point of uplift and discharge of each passenger, so the point at which a passenger disembarks from a particular service may not represent their ultimate destination. Moreover, the IPS operates on the basis that when a resident of the UK has visited more than one country, the entire visit is allocated to the country stayed in for the longest time.

Fig. 4.5 shows annual passenger numbers travelling between the United Kingdom and United States. After strong growth in the last century, there has been no further major increase subsequently. The downturns are primarily associated with 9/11 and with the impact of the recent financial crisis. Fig. 4.6 shows visitor numbers from the United Kingdom to the United States and from the United States to the United Kingdom, broken down by country of origin (UK residents and overseas residents) and by journey purpose (business and leisure). The total number of visitors is consistent with the passenger data shown in Fig. 4.5, recognising that every visit involves two trips. Interestingly again it shows that there has been no apparent overall growth with any of these submarkets, perhaps tentatively indicating market maturity.

Fig. 4.7 shows passenger numbers travelling between the United Kingdom and Japan. After strong growth in the last century, numbers fell back markedly before becoming somewhat more stable in recent years when the economic climate in Japan has become much more challenging and the population has been declining. Fig. 4.8 shows the breakdown of visitor numbers between the United Kingdom and Japan. The total is broadly consistent with the passenger numbers shown in Fig. 4.7. The main contributory factor to the fall in numbers is the marked decline in nonbusiness or leisure visits from Japan. Fig. 4.9 shows in more detail the trends for business visitors: broad stability for UK

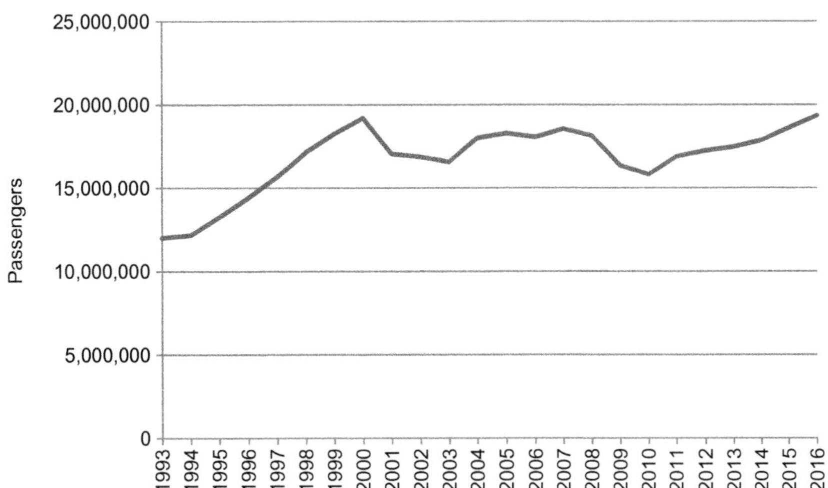

FIG. 4.5 Passenger numbers between the United Kingdom and the United States 1993–2016. *(Source: CAA passenger data 1993–2016.)*

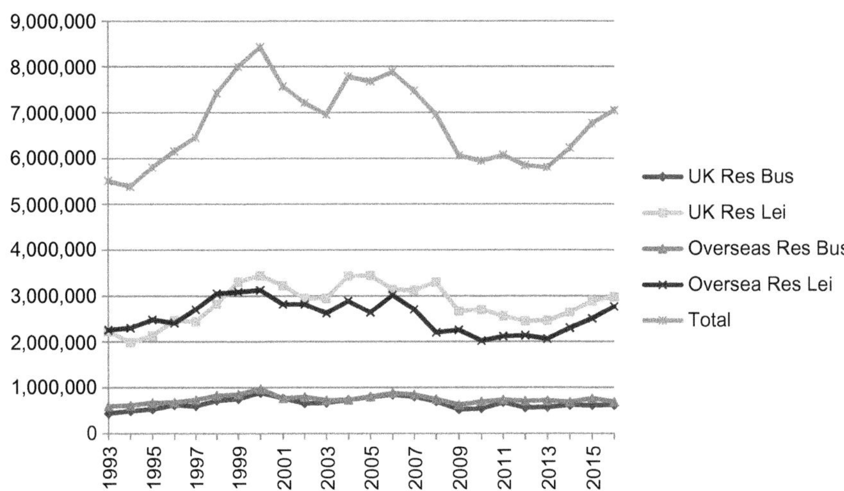

FIG. 4.6 UK residents visiting the US and overseas residents visiting the United Kingdom from the United States 1993–2016. *(Source: IPS visitor data 1993–2016.)*

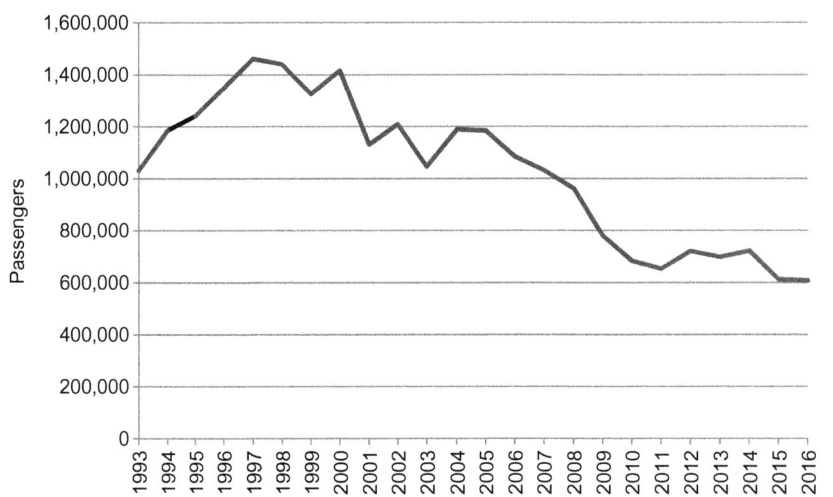

FIG. 4.7 Passenger numbers between the United Kingdom and Japan 1993–2016. *(Source: CAA passenger data 1993–2016.)*

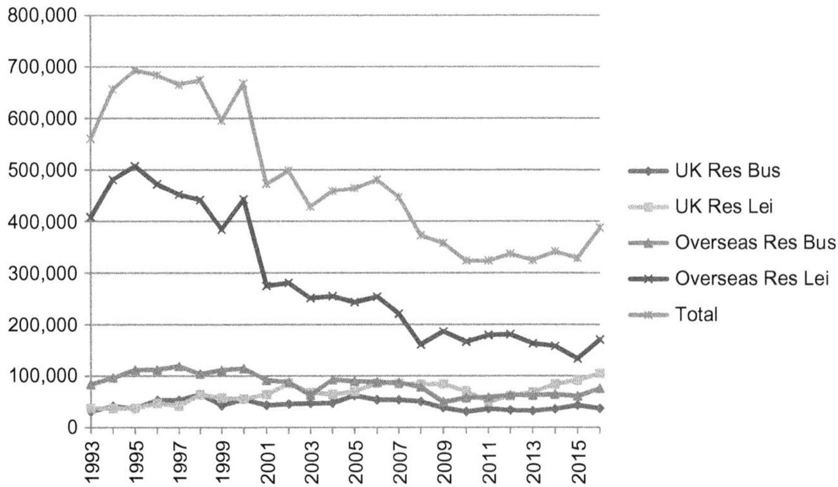

FIG. 4.8 UK residents visiting Japan and overseas residents visiting the United Kingdom from Japan 1993–2016. *(Source: IPS visitor data 1993–2016.)*

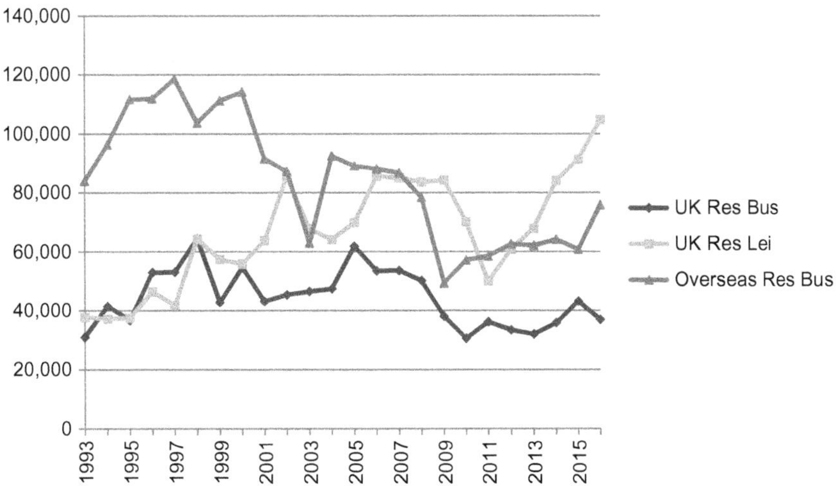

FIG. 4.9 UK residents visiting Japan and overseas residents visiting the United Kingdom from Japan 1993–2016 (excluding Japanese leisure travel and total numbers). *(Source: IPS visitor data 1993–2016.)*

residents travelling to Japan, significant decline in Japanese residents travelling to the United Kingdom. Fig. 4.9 also shows growth in numbers of UK residents visiting Japan other than for business. The situation here is more complex than for the United States. For instance, an increase in the proportion of passengers travelling between the United Kingdom and Japan via Middle East hubs could result in an apparent reduction in passenger numbers to and from Japan, but not in visitor numbers. Likewise, an apparent decline in passenger numbers from Narita may reflect a smaller number of inbound UK visitors beyond Japan travelling via Tokyo Narita airport. True origin–destination data, such as marketing information data transfer (MIDT) from the global distribution systems, would be useful data to use here for further analysis.

Similar trends showing cessation of growth can be seen for travel between the United Kingdom and Canada and the Caribbean. An analysis of disaggregated visitor numbers on these routes, which are generally less affected by indirect routings, might again provide greater insight. Overall, the market segments considered before are not typical, in that most others for the UK show continuing growth, but they are important and long established. It is possible that these are demonstrating evidence of market maturity, which over time may emerge in other market segments. As a first step the data tentatively shows some interesting trends, but more investigation is clearly needed, especially with regards to the extent to which UK residents in these cases are still travelling more, but merely going to different destinations, for example, due to shifting preferences, changes in exchange rates, or other economic factors. In addition, more true origin–destination data would help separate demand developments from changes in trips involving transfer connections (Fig. 4.10).

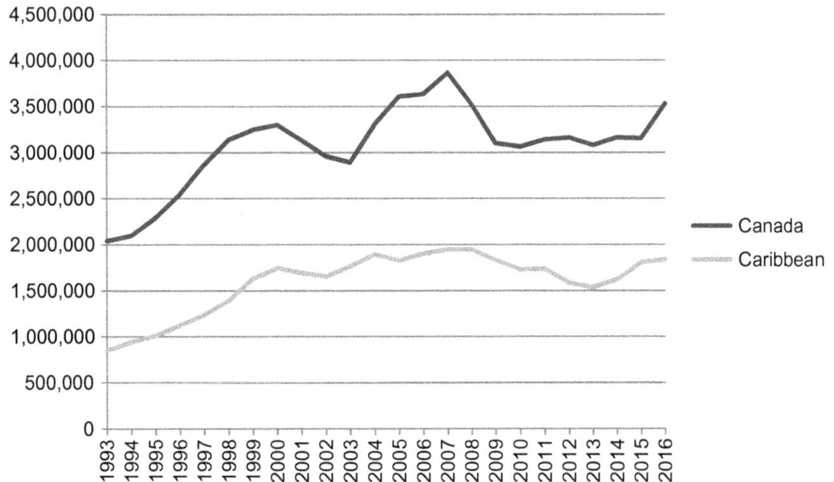

FIG. 4.10 Passenger numbers between the United Kingdom and Canada and the Caribbean 1993–2016. *(Source: CAA passenger data 1993–2016.)*

4.4 CONCLUSIONS

This chapter has aimed to highlight some of the key issues related to limits to travel from a demand perspective, as these are clearly very relevant when considering the rationale for flying. In doing so this has raised a number of unanswered questions. In general, more research is needed concerning how and when income and time constraints may have an impact on travel, and how motivational factors affect the patterns of both frequent and infrequent travel. Further understanding is needed to assess whether when constraints exist, they can be overcome, for example as suggested by the Leisure Constraints Model, or whether, as suggested by a number of other authors, there will always be a significant share of the population who will not travel.

The chapter has demonstrated that why people do not travel, generally or by air, is an understudied phenomenon, which is somewhat perplexing given the significant number of people that appear to not travel. An additional weakness with the limited research in this area is that it tends to treat frequent and infrequent travellers as homogeneous groups, whereas in reality there is a considerable amount of heterogeneity within both groups. Evidence of limits to travel in certain market segments may provide insight into what will happen for other markets in the future.

Specifically, for the UK outbound air travel market, there is some limited evidence of income constraints, with declining values of income elasticities, and perhaps time constraints as suggested from the pilot survey. Furthermore, it is apparent that the proportion of infrequent flyers has remained fairly constant over the last few years and is predicted not to change substantially—at least in the short term. There is also evidence of cessation of growth of demand for air travel for a few selected destinations accessed from the United Kingdom. These examples of growth cessation are consistent with the general concept of market maturity, which is a phenomenon that may be expected to emerge over time in other markets segments.

It seems unlikely that standard econometric models of demand for air travel or tourism adequately reflect factors contributing to market maturity and the nature of frequent and infrequent flyers. In general, such models assume continuity of behaviour between past and future, such that historic relationships between key parameters are conserved, with future demand then driven by exogenous variables such as population growth, income growth, oil prices, and other cost factors. However, the marked shifts in trends discussed before suggest that underlying travel behaviour is changing in ways that the models do not reflect. Accordingly, there is a need to understand better the factors that may contribute to market maturity, income, and time constraints, as well as patterns of frequent and infrequent travel, in order that models used to project future demand can be more fit for purpose.

References

Airbus, 2017. Global Market Forecasts 2017–2036. Airbus, Toulouse.

Alegre, J., Mateo, S., Pou, L., 2010. An analysis of households' appraisal of their budget constraints for potential participation in tourism. Tour. Manag. 31 (1), 45–56.

Bowles, R., 1994. Air travel: a growth or mature industry. In: Canadian Aviation Forecast Conference, Transport Canada. pp. 69–73.

CAA, 2005. Demand for Outbound Leisure Air Travel and Its Key Drivers. CAA, London.

CAA, 2008. Recent Trends in Growth of UK Air Passenger Demand. CAA, London.

CAA, 2015. Consumer Research for the UK Aviation Sector—Final Report. CAA, London.

Demetriou, D., 2017. Japan's Population to Strink by a Third by 2065. Available at http://www.telegraph.co.uk/news/2017/04/11/japans-population-shrink-third-2065/. (Accessed February 13, 2018).

DfT, 2014. Public Experiences of and Attitudes towards Air Travel 2014. DfT, London.

DfT, 2017a. National Travel Survey 2014. DfT, London.

DfT, 2017b. UK Aviation Forecasts. DfT, London.

Dolnicar, S., Lazarevski, K., Yanamandram, V., 2013. Quality of life and tourism: a conceptual framework and novel segmentation base. J. Bus. Res. 66 (6), 724–729.

Eurocontrol, 2013. Challenges of Growth 2013: Task 3—Scope, Scenarios and Challenges. Eurocontrol, Brussels.

Eurostat, 2017. Tourism Statistics—Participation in Tourism. Eurostat, Brussels.

Gallet, C.A., Doucouliagos, H., 2014. The income elasticity of air travel: a meta-analysis. Ann. Tour. Res. 49, 141–155.

Gilbert, D., Hudson, S., 2000. Tourism demand constraints: a skiing participation. Ann. Tour. Res. 27 (4), 906–925.

Gillen, D.W., Morrison, W.G., Stewart, C., 2008. Air Travel Demand Elasticities: Concepts, Issues and Measurement. Department of Finance, Canada.

Godbey, G., Crawford, D.W., Shen, X.S., 2010. Assessing hierarchical leisure constraints theory after two decades. J. Leis. Res. 42 (1), 111.

Graham, B., 1995. Geography and Air Transport. Wiley, Chichester.

Graham, A., 2000. Demand for air travel and limits to growth. J. Air Transp. Manag. 6 (2), 109–118.

Graham, A., 2006. Have the major forces driving leisure airline traffic changed? J. Air Transp. Manag. 12 (1), 14–20.

Graham, A., Metz, D., 2017. Limits to air travel growth: the case of infrequent flyers. J. Air Transp. Manag. 62, 109–120.

Haukeland, V.J., 1990. Non-travelers: the flip side of motivation. Ann. Tour. Res. 17 (2), 172–184.

He, L., Li, X., Harrill, R., Cardon, P.W., 2014. Examining Japanese tourists' US-bound travel constraints. Curr. Issue Tour. 17 (8), 705–722.

IATA, 2014. The Shape of Air Travel Markets over the Next 20 Years. Available at http://www.iata.org/whatwedo/Documents/economics/20yearsForecast-GAD2014-Athens-Nov2014-BP.pdf. (Accessed September 5, 2015).
James, G., 1993. US Commercial Aviation: A Growth or Mature Industry. In: 18th FAA Aviation Forecast Conference Proceedings, FAA-APO 93-2. pp. 182–202.
Kattiyapornpong, U., Miller, K.E., 2013. Socio-demographic constraints to travel behaviour. Int. J. Cult. Tour. Hosp. Res. 3 (1), 81–94.
KiM Netherlands Institute for Transport Policy Analysis, 2015. Determinants of Propensity to Fly and Airport Choice. Ministry of Infrastructure and the Environment, The Hague.
Kotler, P., Armstrong, G., 2017. Principles of Marketing, Global Edition, 17th ed. Pearson, New York.
Lai, C., Li, X.R., Harrill, R., 2013. Chinese outbound tourists' perceived constraints to visiting the United States. Tour. Manag. 37, 136–146.
Litvin, S.W., Smith, W.W., Pitts, R.E., 2013. Sedentary behavior of the nontravel segment: a research note. J. Travel Res. 52 (1), 131–136.
McKercher, B., 2009. Non-travel by Hong Kong residents. Int. J. Tour. Res. 11 (6), 507–519.
McKercher, B., Chen, F., 2015. Travel as a life priority? Asia Pac. J. Tour. Res. 20 (7), 715–729.
Metz, D., 2010. Saturation of demand for daily travel. Transp. Rev. 30 (5), 659–674.
Metz, D., 2013. Peak car and beyond: the fourth era of travel. Transp. Rev. 33 (3), 255–270.
Metz, D., 2016a. Changing demographics. In: Bleimer, M., Mulley, C., Moutou, C. (Eds.), Handbook on Transport and Urban Planning in the Developed World. Edward Elgar Publishing, Cheltenham, pp. 69–81.
Metz, D., 2016b. Travel Fast or Smart? A Manifesto for an Intelligent Transport Policy. London Publishing Partnership, London.
Morphet, H., Bottini, C., 2014. Propensity to Fly in Emerging Economies. Available at: https://www.pwc.com/en_GX/gx/capital-projects-infrastructure/pdf/pwc-propensity-to-fly-in-emerging-economies.pdf. (Accessed May 20, 2015).
Murphy, D., Wells, M., 2010. Is the US Domestic Air Travel Market Approaching Saturation? Theory and Evidence. . unpublished paper presented at Transportation Research Board (January).
Nyaupane, G.P., Andereck, K.L., 2008. Understanding travel constraints: application and extension of a leisure constraints model. J. Travel Res. 46, 433–439.
Penningtom-Gray, L.A., Kerstetter, D.L., 2002. Testing a constraints model within the context of nature-based tourism. J. Travel Res. 40 (4), 416–423.
Rolls Royce, 1994. Market Outlook. Rolls Royce, Derby, pp. 1993–2012.
Silva, O., Correia, A., 2008. Facilitators and constraints in leisure travel participation: the case of the southeast of Portugal. Int. J. Cult. Tour. Hosp. Res. 2 (1), 25–43.
Smith, W.W., Litvin, S.W., Nadav, S., Carmichael, B.A., 2009. Non-travellers: the flip side of motivation—revisited. Tour. Recreat. Res. 34 (1), 91–93.
Swarbrooke, J., Horner, S., 1999. Consumer Behaviour in Tourism. Butterworth-Heinemann, Oxford.
The Economist, 2017. Fading Echoes. Available at https://www.economist.com/news/finance-and-economics/21720578-rest-country-and-large-swathes-europe-will-face-similar-problems. (Accessed February 13, 2018).
University of Westminster, 2010. DfT Air Transport—Market Maturity—Summary Report. University of Westminster, London.
University of Westminster, 2016. Frequent Flyers and Time Constraints Research—Summary. . unpublished paper.
UNWTO, 2017. Tourism Highlights, 2017 Edition. UNWTO, Madrid.
Vedantham, A., Oppenheimer, O., 1998. Long-term scenarios for aviation: demand and emissions of CO2 and NOx. Energy Policy 26 (8), 625–641.

PART II

BEFORE TRAVELLING: CHOOSING TRANSPORT MODES, AIRLINES, AND AIRPORTS

CHAPTER

5

The Impact of Government Policy and Regulation

David Timothy DUVAL

University of Winnipeg, Winnipeg, MB, Canada

CHAPTER OUTLINE

5.1 INTRODUCTION

Future chapters in this book will perform a deep dive into the various machinations that characterise tourism (and aviation) as very complex international economic sectors and practices. This complexity is manifested in a range of services (epitomised through variations in scale, scope, and mode), but with the added complexity of numerous levels of competitiveness between actors focusing on product/service differentiation and markets served. Sector complexity in both is also very much defined by the sheer number of stakeholders, which is high in both but also noteworthy in that there is considerable cross-over and duplication. The conclusion from this is that both air transport and tourism draw considerable attention because of their importance and joint reliance upon each other.

This chapter attempts to situate a selection of current understandings and patterns of where tourism and aviation intersect. It contains two broad sections. The first considers the associative elements of the tourism–air transport relationship by discussing key drivers, the structure of the relationship itself and how this is manifested, business models of air transport companies and how this transfers into unique destination characteristics, the nature of commercial arrangements between destinations and air transport providers, and how government regulation is shifting the passenger experience. The second section argues that the tourism–air transport relationship is a function of international trade policy and political economy. It considers the arrangement of the international air service system, inside which tourism becomes a parallel by-product sitting alongside other economic activities. Given the existence of often heavy government oversight of how passenger air transport is permitted to operate, the chapter argues that tourism can ultimately be considered 'arranged mobility' that is governed, assessed, and permitted.

Air Transport—A Tourism Perspective. https://doi.org/10.1016/B978-0-12-812857-2.00005-1

5.2 THE TOURISM–AIR TRANSPORT RELATIONSHIP

To start, it is useful to attach some benchmark understandings of the nature by which tourism and air transport coexist and mutually support each other. A convenient yet salient starting point is the broad conceptual frameworks where there is seen critical bidirectional overlap and influence. Following this, the chapter then moves to isolate some examples of where it is possible to point confidently to air transport provision as a key driver of tourism development.

The key drivers (also discussed in Chapters 2–4) that underpin commercial air transport and tourism are arguably straightforward. These have been more or less interrogated in both the tourism and the transport geography literatures and can be said to include travel time, cost and network/amenity design, accessibility, and connectivity (see, for instance, Banister, 2011; Gillen and Morrison, 2005; Lederer and Nambimadom, 1998; Hall and Page, 2009; Redondi et al., 2011). Taken together, these lead to the conclusion that facilitating passenger throughput and destination accessibility determines success in driving visitor arrivals (Gilbert and Wong, 2003; Wang and Pitfield, 1999). As vectors of connectivity, these variables are fundamental to building successful tourism export sectors. In Indonesia, for instance, joint efforts by the national tourism ministry as well as airports and air navigation providers are seeking to increase the number of inbound air capacity (Jakarta Post, 2016). The tight relationship begs constant monitoring of external variables and correlation of policies that support aviation and its associated infrastructure. Nigeria's current economic climate, for example, remains uncertain following a drop in GDP growth in 2016 (Focus Economics, 2017), and the closing of the airport at Abuja and currency scarcity has worsened an already problematic situation with respect to accessibility (Vanguard Nigeria 2017).

Naturally, destinations which are geographically remote or, worse, difficult to access, rely heavily on air transport services and infrastructure to facilitate (Nutley, 2003). In economic geography, the initial work of Ullman in the 1950s introduced the concept of gravity which helped explain attractiveness of places relative to distance (Shaw and Hesse, 2010) and Tinbergen (1962, from Rauch 2016) explored this from the perspective of trade and exports. A general model of this approach appears commonly (in this case, adapted from Keum, 2010 and Head, 2007) as roughly: $F_{ij} = g\frac{m_i m_j}{d_{ij}}$, where F_{ij} represents the gravitational relationship (or 'market potential', as proposed by Boulhol et al., 2008, p. 8) between places i and j, m_i and m_j relate to some measure of economic performance and/or size of i and j, d_{ij} represents distance as a force affecting the relationship between i and j, and g is a constant (Keum, 2010). Previous research has sought to understand more clearly what is assumed to be a linear relationship between demand for air services and the relative attractiveness between two places as explained through such gravity models (e.g. Wojahn, 2001; see also Zhang and Findlay, 2014; Hazledine, 2009).

In the real world however, interactions between places and the spatiality of airline flows are much more complex than suggested by gravity models. First of all, interactions between places are shaped by various social, migratory, economic, and demographic factors that are not available worldwide at the appropriate scale. In addition, commercial operations determine network viability. The 'new economic geography' picked up on the need to contextualise behavioral (read: actual, rather than potential) reasons for place interactions (Boulhol et al., 2008, p. 8), for as Kanemoto (2013, p. 61) explains, in gravity-based approaches 'it was not clear whether or not the impacts are due to decreases in the costs of transporting differentiated products'. Indeed, there is support that lower air fares, in the short term, stimulate tourism growth (Forsyth, 2010; Forsyth et al., 2006), thus suggesting that distance may not always be an *exclusive* variable in assessing the attractiveness of a place (with a nod here to McKercher and Lew's [2003] well-cited tourism-based treatment of the distance decay curve and, more recently, Hazledine's [2017] comparative work that included a larger set of variables to determine attractiveness). Distance is an absolute that is shaped both commercially and politically; there are strong links between increased access and liberalisation, the latter of which is an implicit policy stance adopted by state governments in support of economic conditions that support competition. To this end, Piermartini and Rousova's (2008, p. 16) important work on the measurement of the effects of liberalisation found that (1) passengers decreased with distance, but that (2) distance is still a factor, such that

> there is robust evidence that liberalisation in the aviation market increases passenger flows. The effect is stronger for agreements signed by high income and middle income countries than for agreements by middle and low income countries. Furthermore, the effect is stronger for agreements among relatively close countries. This is an important result as passengers between relatively close countries are more likely to use direct flight connections.

In all, as Forsyth (2010) argues there is potential for agglomeration tendencies in the synergies between tourism product development and maturation and increased frequencies of air service provision to those destinations.

5.2.1 Systems Analysis and Value Chains

The call for more rigorous systems analysis in transportation is 20 years old (Stough and Rietveld, 1997), and it was Bieger and Wittmer (2006, Figures 4 and 5) who provided one of the more elegant conceptual frameworks that assisted in the linking of commercial aviation business models with those of destinations. At its core, the Bieger/Wittmer treatment still caries considerable merit, but the distinctions between some of the business models are, in 2017, perhaps somewhat less discrete (although, of course, this is not to suggest Bieger and Wittmer even deigned them to be discrete in their own right).

The structure of airline networks—and the business models to which they are applied (discussed later)—are necessarily dynamic in that they are informed by operational restrictions, demand for services (bidirectional), and opportunity cost. Airlines thus naturally form a critical component of the tourism value chain (with arguably vertical and horizontal applications and implications) because they are the vector by which tourism demand is realised. In this sense, the extent to which they have access to what Knieps (2014, p. 30) calls the 'complementary monopolistic airport infrastructures' in a nondiscriminatory manner is vital for the viability of a country or region's tourism sector. As evidence of this, in an interview with a high ranking government official responsible for linking infrastructure and tourism development in Nepal, the recognition of the importance of adequate air transport infrastructure in support of tourism is acknowledged in the aftermath of the devastating earthquakes in 2015:

> The tourism infrastructure in Nepal is a major setback to tourism growth. The condition of the only international airport—Tribhuvan International Airport (TIA)—is bleak in terms of both service and facilities for visiting tourists. Services and facilities inside TIA should be of international standard. Similarly, the tourism sector of any country heavily depends on the strength of the national flag carrier of that country. Nepal Airlines Corporation (NAC) is currently weak and flies to very few destinations. We don't have direct flights to Kathmandu from a majority of countries across the world. This directly affects the flow of tourists to Nepal. (The Himalayan Times, 2016)

5.2.2 Changing Business Models

Although it is discussed more fully in Chapter 10, several trends in business models for commercial air services that affect destination development can be identified. Airlines are constantly exploring options to diversify revenue opportunities and subsequently increase net returns and returns on capital (Tretheway and Markvhida, 2014). This is one of the reasons some established network airlines have introduced their own low-cost subsidiaries, such as Air Canada's Rouge, Jetstar (Qantas), and Level (IAG/British Airways). These low-cost derivatives (or so-called low-cost carriers, or LCCs) represent a new model: the so-called carrier within carrier (Graham and Vowles, 2006; Whyte and Lohmann, 2015) or airline within airline (Pearson and Merkert, 2014), taken up by established network carriers (Gillen and Gados, 2008) in the face of competitive pressures from 'stand-alone' LCCs. As Pearson and Merkert (2014, p. 25) note, however, this strategy can be difficult to execute:

> Many AWAs [airlines within airlines] materialised after the establishment of the LCCs with which they sought to compete. This can be seen worldwide. Late market entrance immediately means that they are at a disadvantage given that they cannot benefit from first-mover advantage and the promotion that is derived from being the 'consumer champion' from being the first to offer lower fares, for example as experienced by Southwest, Ryanair, Wizz Air (in Eastern Europe), and Air Asia. Late entrance, coupled with similar value propositions to the incumbent LCCs, may mean it is more difficult to appeal to passengers and thereby making it more challenging to gain sufficient traffic and revenue. This may mean that building market dominance is more challenging if not impossible, although market dominance must be coupled with profitability (sooner or later) than mere size for the sake of it.

Of course, the presence of LCCs on specific routings also benefits places of origin as well as destinations. Davison and Ryley (2010, p. 465) found that, in the case of the East Midlands in the United Kingdom, there was significant demand for low-cost services to various holiday destinations:

> There is a greater desire for cultural tourism-based destinations, illustrated by the popularity of Rome and Prague and evidence of a desire to trade between European city destinations. To maintain consumer interest, airlines need to continue to innovate, providing tourism destinations which meet these requirements.

Low-cost carriers have been important for increasing visitation and/or positioning destinations at the top-of-mind awareness for potential visitors. Castillo-Manzano et al. (2011), for instance, found that LCCs are not only substitutes for legacy carriers, but are in some instances actually preferred. As an illustration of mainstream public acceptance (and sometimes preference) for such models, more than half of all visitors to Spain in 2013 arrived via a low-cost carrier (Sinc, 2014). Despite the suggestion (Wilken et al., 2016) that long-haul stage lengths do not need the prized operational efficiency of faster turnarounds that characterise low-cost operations on shorter segments, long-haul models with a lower cost strategy are becoming more viable commercially, with roughly one dozen or so examples (e.g. China's Lucky Air, IAG's Level, Scoot from Singapore Airlines, and Jetstar by Qantas) (CAPA, 2017) (see Chapter 10). Yet a critical assessment of such initiatives might reveal more of an attempt by such operators to limit costs by muting consumer expectations of onboard amenities, thus espousing the perception of 'lower cost' that hovers near the conceptually problematic definition of the 'typical' low-cost carrier.

Regardless of the revenue model chosen (i.e. low cost vs dedicated network carriers), the operational benefits of deploying hub and spoke models has been shown to be often operationally efficient (see, for instance, Aguirregabiria and Ho, 2010). This introduces increasing opportunities for multiple hinterland spokes off main hubs to achieve some degree of adequate connectivity, thus providing opportunities for tourism growth if air services are able to operate at least somewhat profitably (Minato and Morimoto, 2011). The importance of airlift for hinterland destinations is made evident in the case of American Samoa. Currently only served twice a week by Hawaiian Airlines, the fact that the territory falls under the aeropolitical jurisdiction of the United States (i.e. it is not capable of negotiating its own air service arrangements) means that only US airlines are permitted to offer services from it to the US mainland. The result is that tapping into the lucrative US tourism market is difficult. The monopoly conditions as a result of a single carrier operating such services are a consequence of the size of the market and the cost of operating the flights (eTurboNews, 2015).

Just as there has been consolidation of network services and route structures through the use of hubs (e.g. Dennis, 2001), there has been a similar degree of consolidation taking place amongst carriers in the United States and Europe (Dennis, 2005; see also Fones, 2015). The operational merger announced in 2016 between Alaska Airlines and Virgin America is an example, and it has been suggested in media reports that continued consolidation and commercial mergers will result in fewer choices for travellers (LA Times, 2016). It was reported (Time, 2016) in February 2016 that 80% of the US domestic market is in the hands of the four large carriers (American, Delta, Southwest, and United). Several questions become paramount. For instance, what extent might this consolidation have on negotiations and market power that exist between airports and airlines? Smaller airports and upstart carriers might, at one time, have been able to arrange mutually beneficial commercial relationships, but when the size of one party increases there is a chance of power imbalance. Larger carriers (or those born as a result of consolidation) may find more value in competing directly with established legacy carriers at larger airports, thus diminishing the role that some smaller airports may play in network connectivity and, thus tourism.

5.2.3 Commercial Symbiotic Relationships

Given the cyclical and often unsteady nature of air service supply and demand (Dempsey, 2008b; Goetz and Vowles, 2009), it is not surprising that destinations have entered into direct commercial arrangements with air service providers. A public/private partnership can help secure access to an export-oriented supply chain that is necessary for the economic sustainability of tourism. Several examples of common commercial synergies in the airline–tourism relationship can be identified (see also Chapter 15):

1. Whilst destination marketing organisations are largely responsible for the marketing of their destinations from a tourism perspective, airlines are often very much part of the overall marketing horsepower of a particular place. For instance, Air Canada announced in May 2017 a campaign on social media entitled 'See: Canada'. Destination Canada, the country's DMO, announced in May 2017 a partnership with WestJet airlines (the second largest in the country) on joint marketing efforts (Newswire 2017).
2. A similar arrangement was announced in April 2017 between Singapore's Changi airport, Singapore Airlines, and the Singapore Tourism Board. The partnership was formed with the purpose of marketing Singapore as a stopover destination or even a 'twinning' destination (Xinhuanet, 2017). The partnership seeks to court travellers from China, Japan, and Australia and looks to spend up to $S34 million (Today Online, 2017). This arrangement may be important as Kuala Lumpur has steadily positioned itself as both a destination and mid-Asia hub for carriers moving passengers from that region (and the Antipodes) and Europe (Bowen, 2000).
3. It was reported (Caribbean News Now, 2017) in February 2017 that representatives from the Antigua and Barbuda Tourism Authority and the airport at St. John's (Antigua) travelled to the Routes Americas Conference held in the United States. These conferences are designed to bring together and facilitate meetings between tourism officials, airport authorities/companies, and airlines, with the intent of destinations to entice airlines to offer services to their respective countries or cities. In the case of Antigua and Barbuda, the example is interesting in that representatives from both the tourism sector and the airport were present, thus reinforcing the importance of collaboration to ensure commercial uplift.

5.3 THE CHANGING PASSENGER EXPERIENCE—IMPACTS ON TOURISM

It is not possible to escape a discussion of the tourism–air transport relationship without at least acknowledging how the passenger experience is changing at multiple stages of the journey. However, there are some distinctions that can be made in how the passenger experience is characterised. In absolute terms it refers, on the one hand, to the provision of onboard (or in-terminal, in the case of airports; see Correia et al., 2008) service culture and related experiences. As important as this is, however, there is another higher dimension to the passenger experience that reflects how government regulation and oversight of air transport is, or very well could be, changing the passenger environment and the ability of air transport providers and airports to frame positive passenger/guest experiences. Several examples illustrate this:

1. United States President Donald Trump issued a ban from early to mid-2017 on laptops from certain countries, which caused Emirates to reduce the number of flights to the United States as a result of a slump in demand (The National, 2017a). These kinds of regulatory edicts can have a direct impact on passenger routing, not to mention the lessening of available competitive options for passengers to choose from. In this particular case, the temporary ban also forced airlines and airports to adjust their own in-service provision. For instance, Emirates subsequently introduced laptop and tablet handling services on flights to the United States, where the airline would pack customer devices into the hold of the aircraft for passenger retrieval at their US destination. On some flights, Emirates also loaned tablets to passengers (The National, 2017b).
2. The United Airlines incident in 2017 in which a passenger was forcibly removed from a flight before takeoff highlighted countless issues with the application of rules and regulations and the relationship between airlines and ground security staff. It was an example of how claims through marketing of fair and proper treatment can be sidelined by negative incidents of such treatment.
3. The Canadian Government introduced in 2017 a Passenger Bill of Rights (Bill C-49). The intent of the Bill is to formalise the ability of the Canadian Transportation Agency, which will be charged with crafting regulations on passenger treatment, including compensation for delays and lost baggage. In so doing, Canada joins the European Union and the United States in having such formalised rules in place, although airlines have already provided such compensation measures as part of the competitive environment in which they operate.

What of the role of airports in the passenger experience? Globally, airports face the same shifting demand parameters as those faced by airlines, if only because both share the same customer. As will be outlined in Chapter 13, it is clear that airports are faced with the reality that they, too, must adapt. Notwithstanding their relationship with commercial tenants, airports fundamentally serve (or facilitate) two primary customer segments: airlines and passengers. Tension exists between these segments because passengers are often unable to distinguish the cause of any service failure during a journey. The result is that airports and airlines must constantly find ways to enhance the service experience in order to make it as seamless as possible. The challenge is that, despite the mutually beneficial arrangement between the two, airlines pay airports fees for use of the latter's facilities. When airports invest in terminal redevelopment or brownfield construction of new facilities, airline customers can understandably become concerned about how these new assets are ultimately funded (including the time horizon over which they are financed, and how) and whether they have a say in these new commercial initiatives. Further still are nonaeronautical revenues in the form of rent paid by airport retail operations or car park charges, all of which contribute to an airport's revenue and the passenger experience but over which many airline customers may not have much, if any, input.

5.4 GOVERNMENT POLICY FOR THE PROVISION OF AIR TRANSPORT

Whereas the previous section sought to crystalise the air transport/tourism relationship, this section argues that there can be no doubt that this relationship sits within a basin of (often very necessary) rules and regulations. Whilst it is true that business models and hub efficiencies obviously play an important role in airline route development (see, for instance, Weber and Williams, 2001), the role of government(s) cannot be discounted. Governments play a direct role in route development; they create the appropriate economic conditions to either limit or enhance competition through domestic policies enshrined in law or, internationally, through treaties. It is government regulation and oversight that ultimately determines how the air transport/tourism articulation point is freely able to move without friction.

5.4.1 The Case for 'Correcting' Market Imperfections

Notwithstanding the ability for firms to compete based on differentiation (Schnell, 2004), and indeed whether such differentiation is possible in all instances in the commercial aviation industry (e.g. Borenstein and Netz, 1999), the high initial capital cost of providing commercial air services often means the supply of those services rests with a small number of firms (even in the absence of regulatory hurdles). This situation almost always describes the commercial passenger aviation industry in many countries, the consequence of which can be imperfect competition (Meunier and Quinet, 2012; see also Dempsey, 1989). However, as Antoniou (2001, p. 78) argues, it problematically falls to government oversight to 'correct' such imperfections, but this in itself is also not without issue: 'Given the dubious track record of governments in the effort of restoring competition, the fundamental policy dilemma raised here is whether the potentially negative effects of the resulting monopolies are sufficiently large to warrant enhanced government intervention'. Further, Givoni and Rietveld (2009) provide a reminder that some imperfections are the consequence of strategic decisions made by carriers, particularly when market conditions, such as congestion at airports, act as a disincentive to increase capacity. Governments utilise various methods to correct market imperfections. Two are reviewed here: (1) direct and indirect subsidies (or risk shares) and (2) the legal provisions installed within legislation and their antecedent policies which govern market access.

5.4.2 Subsidies and Risk Shares

Financial subsidies and/or fiscal underwrites between destinations (usually spearheaded by governments) and airlines are not unusual. Whilst Warnock-Smith and O'Connell (2011, p. 272) found that "state ownership and influence in national carriers may in fact have a positive effect on levels of incoming tourism, especially if it is accompanied by increasingly liberal air service agreements and a withdrawal of blanket type state subsidies", Castillo-Manzano et al. (2011, p. 1093) argue that there is general support for airline subsidies in the case of attracting new entrants (particularly LCCs): 'On the basis of the position it has taken up in favour of LCCs, and despite the odd criticism, it should come as no surprise that the tourist sector shows almost generalised support for public administrations intervening to attract LCCs, even through the provision of direct subsidies'. Contracts to carry letter mail by air were, arguably, the catalyst for the development of commercial aviation in the United States in the first half of the 20th century (Goodrick, 1949) and, at present, public service obligations (PSO) contracts ensure secondary and tertiary European airports are serviced by commercial airlift (Wittman et al., 2016).

Subsidies, which can be alternatively referred to as operational underwrites or policy-based 'risk shares' (Duval and Winchester, 2011), exist for two reasons. First, there can be instances where air service provision to remote or rural destinations is untenable commercially because the size of the markets served are 'thin' and thus not economically sustainable (Nolan et al., 2005). Second, destinations and their associated governments may wish to ensure continuity of services by providing underwrites in exchange for some assurance of reliable and regular access (Wittman et al., 2016). A few examples of each can be identified:

1. As reported by Duval and Winchester (2011), the Cook Islands' underwrite of Air New Zealand services between Rarotonga and the United States offers an example of government underwrites/subsidies of foreign carriers. In this case, it was a lump sum subsidy and was installed because of the value the nonstop services brought to the Cook Islands. As noted by Duval and Winchester (2011, p. 89), 'removal of the LAX-RAR-LAX service would essentially remove Cook Islands' actual and perceived accessibility and connectivity'. In late 2016, criticism of the underwrite programme came in the form of an editorial in the Cook Island News (MeNair, 2016) suggesting that the net economic benefit of the underwrite was minimal and that it favoured only a portion of the island's economy.
2. There exist several examples of essential air service programmes in EU and United States. Such 'mechanisms' (to use Williams and Pagliari's 2004 characterisation) can be complex in their execution, but the basis of their structure allows for commercial airlines to bid for the right to offer services on specific routes. These services, which again often serve geographically remote destinations, are then underwritten by local or national governments. The aforementioned European PSO scheme is perhaps the best known. PSOs are enacted by Member States to specific services/routes or airports where commercial airlift would otherwise be rendered uneconomic, thus allowing States to offer operational subsidies to operators following a bidding process (Williams and Pagliari, 2004).
3. Accusations have been levied by various organisations that large airlines from the Middle East are effectively subsidised by their home governments. In the EU, the Europeans for Fair Competition group argue that these carriers are, importantly, *unfairly* subsidised, thus introducing market distortion and limiting competition.

A similar narrative has unfolded in the United States, where in 2015 the Partnership for Open & Fair Skies sought a 'level playing field' with respect to access by Middle East carriers. These are complicated issues (see Abeyratne, 2017, for a detailed account), as they strike at the heart of how a competitive aviation market should function, the role of trade agreements, and when the actions of one party are deemed to be in breach of these. Tretheway and Andriulaitis (2015, pp. 98–99) make the compelling case for multiple 'factors' which can be said to alter the playing field in international aviation and argue that these should not be corrected for in government policy. These include geography, the size of an airline, factors of production, the use of 6th freedom traffic (discussed later), and the availability of airport slots (Tretheway and Andriulaitis, 2015). de Wit (2014, p. 28) is in agreement:

> This is not a unique situation in international civil aviation because comparative advantages between states negotiating traffic rights are unavoidable, simply for geographical reasons. In the case of Dubai, the favourable location of its hub has allowed Emirates to develop a long-haul hourglass hub, which presents a much greater competitive threat to the European carriers than the same business model earlier developed by Singapore Airlines. Comparative advantages are the main factor for the explanation of this unlevel playing field and this throws a different light on the Commission's view that there is no reason to assume that European airlines are not able to operate viable hubs.

5.4.3 Market Oversight and Organisation—Aviation Competition and Trade Policies

Passenger movements through any international air transport system are ultimately governed by a series of international treaties that specify the nature and extent to which such services are permitted between two contracting States (Havel and Sanchez, 2011). Such agreements are founded in international law. They represent the structure within which air transport, and ultimately international tourism, operate and are judged to be robust and economically sustainable. This structure has been discussed at length elsewhere (see, for instance, Melville, 1998 and Dempsey, 2008a), as it forms the backbone of international air transport and, consequently, international tourism. It does, however, bear repeating here, albeit briefly, if only to illustrate how tourism can be said to be, more or less, 'arranged mobility.'

Perhaps the most pertinent and not-always-clearly-understood variable that influences tourism is the nature by which air transport networks are operationalised on behalf of commercial services. The underlying structure of tourism flows is ostensibly based within the notion of international trade. In this sense, air access becomes a tradeable good not unlike other services or goods which fall under the purview of arranged trade agreements involving two or more countries. These agreements (or arrangements, as they are sometimes called) contain provisions for route structures, capacity, frequency, and commercial designation (Dempsey, 2008a). Routings are defined through nine so-called freedoms of the air (see ICAO, 2018). As well, the extent to which to contracting states have agreed to certain route allowances, as per these freedoms of the air, is a consequential determination on the extent to which States have agreed to liberalise their formal air service exchange.

A more liberal approach to commercial passenger transport will feature agreement on more than a few basic (e.g. 3rd, 4th) Freedoms. A few examples illustrate this:

1. The seventh freedom is relatively rare (Piermartini and Rousova, 2011), but there are some reasons for this. Given it requires two sets of agreements, in this case between (1) Country A and Country C and (2) Country A and Country B, both Country B and Country C must be satisfied that services between them are undertaken by a commercial airline that is not a national or 'flag' carrier of either. It may be the case that neither Country B nor Country C has commercial airlines that are in a position to offer such airlift, in which case permissions associated with this freedom could be one of the few mechanisms for commercial access. Real-world examples are thus limited. For instance, whilst the air service agreement between New Zealand and Australia is perhaps one of the most open bilateral agreements in the world, it does not permit seventh freedom passenger services (although it does allow for seventh freedom cargo services) (Duval, 2011).
2. The eighth and ninth freedoms denote cabotage arrangements. As outlined by Havel and Sanchez (2011, note 72):

> Under the doctrine of cabotage, intra-state air routes are reserved exclusively for nationally owned and controlled air carriers. Air France, for example, cannot provide air service between New York and Chicago, except as an extension of an existing international service to New York from Europe. Air France also cannot, in providing that service, pick up any new U.S. domestic passengers in New York. A phenomenon of the history of trade, cabotage was invented with the deliberate mercantilist purpose of protecting domestic commerce from foreign competition.

The EU Third Package of liberalisation provides for cabotage services within the EU itself (Graham, 1997). Notwithstanding this often-used example, the operation of domestic routes by a foreign entity is more often provided for through domestic deregulation (and thus the establishment of a licenced domestic carrier) as opposed to such permissions being granted through air services agreements. As this author (2011:6) has pointed out elsewhere: 'States may be reluctant to grant such rights because the domestic flow of goods and passengers would be undertaken by foreign airlines. In addition, additional competition may drive prices down, but may ultimately result in incumbent airlines, with potentially small pools of capital, exiting the market if their costs cannot be covered'.

Whilst liberalisation can support increased flows of passengers and thus tourism (e.g. Dobruszkes and Mondou, 2013), there are instances where this has not occurred. Cuba potentially provides just such an example and points to the consequence for tourism of the relaxing of existing air transport restrictions which at one time were established as a result of decades-long politically motivated trade embargoes. As of August 2016, US carriers were offered limited access to the Cuban market, as specified by the US Government. As reported by Abiertas (2017), this led to a rush in seats when it was not entirely clear the demand was present. As reported by Peter Cerda (IATA) at the IATA AGM in 2017, the flows of traffic into Cuba are one way, leading to overcapacity (CAPA, 2018).

The Cuba example emphasises a potential dilemma when advocating for deregulation and liberalisation of mobility: the absence of a convincing control group and the complexity of air travel with respect to the number of predictor variables and conditions make it difficult to disentangle the policy effects. Policy makers, intent on ensuring the right economic and market conditions are in place to support passenger (and tourism) growth, must rely on available evidence that points to net social benefit. A conscious and commercial approach to airline route development has emerged as a consequence of liberalisation (Weber and Williams, 2001); however, in recent years there has been some concern about a relapse towards protectionism in aviation (de Wit 2014). Reuters (2016) reported the Lufthansa CEO as suggesting that protectionism was increasing as a reaction towards limited abilities for carriers to engage in mergers and acquisitions as a result of restrictions placed on foreign ownership of national carriers.

If it can be concluded that the 'patchwork' (Hafkoort, 1999) of bilateral and multilateral trade agreements in air services serves as the backbone by which tourism mobilities are manifested globally, and the fact that government policy towards these instruments of accessibility ultimately determines how efficient tourism mobilities can be, then some insight into government policy would shed some light on how air transport affects tourism. Two brief examples of New Zealand and Canada highlight contemporary approaches.

Nonresident entry into Canada for 2016 stood at over 30 million people, with the majority of these being Americans entering by automobile (Statistics Canada, 2017). Of non-US visitors, however, the vast majority (5.3 million) arrived by air. Facilitating these arrivals has been the willingness of the Canadian government to enter into liberal air service agreements. The overarching policy supporting this is called Blue Skies and emphasises air service arrangements featuring minimum restrictions with willing partner countries (Transport Canada, n.d.). The policy states quite clearly the relationship such open policies have with respect to tourism: 'Canada will continue to negotiate new ATAs and expand existing agreements to promote the interests of Canadian consumers, stakeholders, as well as our trade and tourism sectors'. Similarly, New Zealand worked to revise its international air policy in 2012 and argued for similar congruencies with its tourism sector:

> The objective of New Zealand's international air transport policy is to help grow the economy and deliver greater prosperity, security and opportunities for New Zealanders. This will be achieved by seeking opportunities for New Zealand-based and foreign airlines to provide their customers with improved connectivity to the rest of the world, and to facilitate increased trade in goods and services (including tourism). (New Zealand Ministry of Transport, 2015)

More recently, reminders of the economic and geographic position of regional centres in New Zealand with respect to the role aviation plays in tourism development (as well as wider economic development) have been levied by the New Zealand Airports Association. The solution, according to a white paper released in July 2017 (New Zealand Airports Association, 2017), includes such measures as active investment in airport infrastructure and direct underwrites of commercial services to remote destinations, both of which would be applied to eligible destinations meeting certain agreed-upon criteria. This proposal sits more or less onside with the EU PSO model and further underlines the importance of regional growth, or at least not growth in major urban centres at the expense of commercially problematic secondary routings.

5.4.4 Airports, Airlines, and Tourism—Synergies in Driving Growth?

Airports tend to operate as commercial ventures, yet they may not necessarily be structured as share capital corporations. Nevertheless, there is an expectation that airports would have a reasonable amount of interest in route development initiatives, if only because this assures them of passenger throughput and, thus utilisation of retail services in terminals run by companies which, in turn, pay rent to airport management companies in exchange for the right to operate in a terminal (Halpern and Graham, 2016). Halpern and Graham (2015) found in their survey of over 100 airports around the world that route development was a critical aspect of their operational planning. With both airports and airlines serving as 'interested parties' in the overall growth potential for tourism (and, it has to be said, in other more macroeconomic indices), it stands to reason that airports are critical pieces of infrastructure through which passengers pass. Their health as critical installations in the tourism–transport interface is paramount and thus worthy of attention from the perspective of government policy.

Neglect of airport sufficiency in the air transport system can have substantial consequences. Forward planning and strategies become paramount to ensure accessibility and connectivity (Frank, 2011, see also Ashley et al., 1995 and Graham, 1999). For instance, Bloomberg reported in June 2017 that record passenger growth in Thailand has put enormous fiscal and logistical pressure on the Suvarnabhumi and Don Mueang airports. Another example of the need for tourism and economic development planning to be in lock step with existing capacity constraints is the case of the Badgerys Creek airport development plan near Sydney, Australia. Billed as the much-needed second Sydney airport (which is already ranked as the busiest in the country), its development trajectory reveals a fascinating insight into the difficulties with long-term capacity planning for air transport infrastructure. The Badgerys Creek site was deemed the most suitable location for a second Sydney airport, and Sydney Airport (the company) was given right of first refusal by a previous Australian Government to develop the site (Australian Aviation, 2017). The airport company turned down the opportunity to develop the site because the economics could not justify the expense given the uncertainty of when suitable returns on investment would be forthcoming (ABC News, 2017). In the end, it will likely fall to the Australian central government to develop the site, thus illustrating that even when infrastructure such as airports are privatised it may fall to governments to absorb the heavy initial investment (ABC News, 2017).

5.5 CONCLUSION

This chapter has sought to use a modern lens to view the complex relationship between tourism and air transport. It has shown that, despite the mutual reliance and support, the nature of this relationship is far from simple, and it is in a near constant state of flux owing to changing market conditions, political interests, and changes in economic environments. This complexity is reflected in the variety of business models in the air transport sector (notwithstanding similar complexity in airport ownership models, which was not addressed here) as well as the complex policy environment in which governments enact some degree of regulatory control over many aspects of the sector (e.g. ownership, safety, security). If this chapter were to be written in 10 years' time, it is likely that the same actors, intent of ensuring tourism is retained as a positive export earner for most countries, would still be in place. However, unforeseen and disruptive events and economic conditions may well alter specific policy trajectories, hence it is vital that the mutual synergies be acknowledged and fostered.

References

ABC News, 2017. Badgerys Creek Airport: Why the Building of Sydney's Second Airport Has Fallen to the Government. Available at http://www.abc.net.au/news/2017-05-02/why-the-government-has-to-build-sydneys-badgerys-creek-airport/8489696. (Accessed May 30, 2017).

Abeyratne, R., 2017. The law of subsidies in air transport services. J. Int. Law Trade Policy 18 (1), 31–49.

Abiertas, P., 2017. US Citizens Can Finally Visit Cuba but Many Aren't *Quartz*. Available at https://qz.com/remote-login.php?login=755393d-6ce6996a0cdf0c0b3ff0daeee&id=39587363&u=969bcc929bba955ec9c7a5051735bd03&h. (Accessed April 10, 2017).

Aguirregabiria, V., Ho, C.-Y., 2010. A dynamic game of airline network competition: hub-and-spoke networks and entry deterrence. Int. J. Ind. Organ. 28, 377–382.

Antoniou, A., 2001. The air transport policy of small states: meeting the challenges of globalization. J. Air Transport. World Wide 6 (2), 65–92.

Ashley, D.J., Hanson, P., Velduis, J., 1995. A policy-sensitive traffic forecasting model for Schiphol airport. J. Air Transp. Manag. 2 (2), 89–97.

Australian Aviation, 2017. Federal Government Confirms It Will Build Badgerys Creek After Sydney Airport Passes on Right of First Refusal. Available at http://australianaviation.com.au/2017/05/sydney-airport-knocks-back-badgerys-creek-offer/. (Accessed August 21, 2017).

Banister, D., 2011. The trilogy of distance, speed and time. J. Transp. Geogr. 19, 950–959.

Bieger, T., Wittmer, A., 2006. Air transport and tourism—perspectives and challenges for destinations, airlines and governments. J. Air Transp. Manag. 12, 40–46.

Bloomberg, 2017. Thailand's Tourism Boom Puts a Strain on Its Airports. Available at https://www.bloomberg.com/news/articles/2017-06-27/lure-of-azure-waters-and-bangkok-nightlife-strains-thai-airports. (Accessed June 27, 2017).

Borenstein, S., Netz, J., 1999. Why do all the flights leave at 8 am?: competition and departure-time differentiation in airline markets. Int. J. Ind. Organ. 17, 611–640.

Boulhol, H., de Serres, A., Molnar, M., 2008. The contribution of economic geography to GDP per capita. OECD J. Econ. Stud. Available online at http://www.oecd-ilibrary.org/economics/the-contribution-of-economic-geography-to-gdp-per-capita_eco_studies-v2008-art9-en. (Accessed February 21, 2016).

Bowen, J., 2000. Airline hubs in Southeast Asia: national economic development and nodal accessibility. J. Transp. Geogr. 8, 25–41.

CAPA (Centre for Aviation), 2017. Long Haul Low Cost Becomes Mainstream as Full Service Airlines Gradually Embrace New Business Models. Available at https://centreforaviation.com/insights/analysis/long-haul-low-cost-becomes-mainstream-as-full-service-airlines-gradually-embrace-new-business-models-348105. (Accessed June 12, 2017).

CAPA (Centre for Aviation), 2018. Tweet from 4 June 2017. Available at https://mobile.twitter.com/CAPA_Aviation/status/871565175647739905. (Accessed June 2, 2018).

Caribbean News Now, 2017. Antigua-Barbuda Explores New Airline Partnerships. Available at http://www.caribbeannewsnow.com/headline-Antigua-Barbuda-explores-new-airline-partnerships-33656.html. (Accessed April 19, 2017).

Castillo-Manzano, J.I., Lopez-Valpuesta, L., Gonzalez-Laxe, F., 2011. The effects of the LCC boom on the urban tourism fabric: the viewpoint of tourism managers. Tour. Manag. 32, 1085–1095.

Correia, A.R., Wirasinghe, S.C., de Barros, A.G., 2008. Overall level of service measures for airport passenger terminals. Transp. Res. A 42, 330–346.

Davison, L., Ryley, T., 2010. Tourism destination preferences of low-cost airline users in the East Midlands. J. Transp. Geogr. 18, 458–465.

de Wit, J., 2014. Unlevel playing field? Ah yes, you mean protectionism. J. Air Transp. Manag. 41, 22–29.

Dempsey, P.S., 1989. Market failure and regulatory failure as catalysts for political change: the choice between imperfect regulation and imperfect competition. Washington Lee Law Rev. 46 (1), 1–40.

Dempsey, P.S., 2008a. The evolution of air transport agreements. Ann. Air Space Law 33, 127–193.

Dempsey, P.S., 2008b. The financial performance of the airline industry post-deregulation. Houston Law Rev. 45, 421–485.

Dennis, N., 2001. Developments of hubbing at European airports. Air Space Eur. 3 (1/2), 51–55.

Dennis, N., 2005. Industry consolidation and future airline network structures in Europe. J. Air Transp. Manag. 11, 175–183.

Dobruszkes, F., Mondou, V., 2013. Aviation liberalization as a means to promote international tourism: the EU-Morocco case. J. Air Transp. Manag. 29, 23–34.

Duval, D.T., 2011. The Principles of Market Access: A Primer on Air Rights. Centre for Air Transport Research, University of Otago.

Duval, D.T., Winchester, N., 2011. Cost sharing in air-service provision. J. Air Law Commerce 76, 77–96.

eTurboNews, 2015. American Samoa Tourism Suffering From Airline Monopoly. Available at http://www.eturbonews.com/54707/american-samoa-tourism-suffering-airline-monopoly. (Accessed May 2, 2016).

Focus Economics, 2017. Nigeria Economic Outlook. Available at http://www.focus-economics.com/countries/nigeria. (Accessed August 8, 2017).

Fones, R.W., 2015. Airline consolidations and competition law—what next? FIU Law J. 10, 446–465.

Forsyth, P., 2010. Tourism and aviation policy: exploring the links. In: Papatheodorou, A., Graham, A., Forsyth, P. (Eds.), Aviation and Tourism: Implications for Leisure Travel. Ashgate, Aldershot.

Forsyth, P., King, J., Rodolfo, C.L., 2006. Open skies in ASEAN. J. Air Transp. Manag. 12, 143–152.

Frank, L., 2011. Business models for airports in a competitive environment. One sky, different stories. Res. Transport. Business Manag. 1, 25–35.

Gilbert, D., Wong, R.K.C., 2003. Passenger expectations and airline services: a Hong Kong based study. Tour. Manag. 24, 519–532.

Gillen, D., Gados, A., 2008. Airlines within airlines: assessing the vulnerabilities of mixing business models. Res. Transp. Econ. 24, 25–35.

Gillen, D., Morrison, W.G., 2005. Regulation, competition and network evolution in aviation. J. Air Transp. Manag. 11, 161–174.

Givoni, M., Rietveld, P., 2009. Airline's choice of aircraft size—explanations and implications. Transp. Res. A 43, 500–510.

Goetz, A.R., Vowles, T.M., 2009. The good, the bad, and the ugly: 30 years of US airline deregulation. J. Transp. Geogr. 17, 251–263.

Goodrick, M.G., 1949. Air mail subsidy of commercial aviation. J. Air Law Commerce 16 (3), 253–279.

Graham, B., 1997. Regional airline services in the liberalized European Union single aviation market. J. Air Transp. Manag. 3 (4), 227–238.

Graham, B., 1999. Airport-specific traffic forecasts: a critical perspective. J. Transp. Geogr. 7, 285–289.

Graham, B., Vowles, T.M., 2006. Carriers within carriers: a strategic response to low cost airline competition. Transp. Rev. 26 (1), 105–126.

Hafkoort, J.R., 1999. The deregulation of European air transport: a dream come true? Tijdschr. Econ. Soc. Geogr. 90 (2), 226–233.

Hall, C.M., Page, S.J., 2009. Progress in tourism management: from the geography of tourism to geographies of tourism—a review. Tour. Manag. 30, 3–16.

Halpern, N., Graham, A., 2015. Airport route development: a survey of current practice. Tour. Manag. 46, 213–221.

Halpern, N., Graham, A., 2016. Factors affecting airport route development activity and performance. J. Air Transp. Manag. 56, 69–78.

Havel, B., Sanchez, G., 2011. The emerging *Lex Aviatica*. Georgetown J. Int. Law 42, 639–672.

Hazledine, T., 2009. Border effects for domestic and international Canadian passenger air travel. J. Air Transp. Manag. 15, 7–13.

Hazledine, T., 2017. An augmented gravity model for forecasting passenger air traffic on city-pair routes. J. Transp. Econ. Policy 51 (3), 208–224.

Head, K., 2007. Elements of Multinational Strategy. Springer, Berlin.

ICAO, 2018. Freedoms of the Air. Available at https://www.icao.int/Pages/freedomsAir.aspx. (Accessed June 2, 2018).

Jakarta Post, 2016. 30 Million Airline Seats Needed to Reach Target: Tourism Minister. Available at http://www.thejakartapost.com/travel/2016/11/07/30-million-airline-seats-needed-to-reach-target-tourism-minister.html. (Accessed November 7, 2016).

Kanemoto, Y., 2013. Evaluating benefits of transportation in models of new economic geography. Econ. Transp. 2, 53–62.

Keum, K., 2010. Tourism flows and trade theory: a panel data analysis with the gravity model. Ann. Reg. Sci. 44, 541–557.

Knieps, G., 2014. Market versus state in building the aviation value chain. J. Air Transp. Manag. 41, 30–37.

LA Times, 2016. Travel Groups Call on Congress to Review State of Airline Competition. Available at http://www.latimes.com/business/la-fi-review-state-of-airline-competition-20160205-story.html. (Accessed February 15, 2016).

Lederer, P.J., Nambimadom, R.S., 1998. Airline network design. Oper. Res. 46 (6), 785–804.

McKercher, B., Lew, A., 2003. Distance decay and the impact of effective tourism exclusion zones on international travel flows. J. Travel Res. 42, 159–165.

Melville, J., 1998. Identifying the regulatory effect of bilateral agreements on international aviation. J. Air Transp. Manag. 4, 39–46.

MeNair, M.-A., 2016. The case for ending airline subsidy. Cook Island News. Available at http://www.cookislandsnews.com/opinion/letters-to-the-editor/item/61348-the-case-for-ending-airline-subsidy/61348-the-case-for-ending-airline-subsidy. (Accessed June 13, 2017).

Meunier, D., Quinet, E., 2012. Applications of transport economics and imperfect competition. Res. Transp. Econ. 36, 19–29.
Minato, N., Morimoto, R., 2011. Sustainable airline strategy using portfolio theory: a case study of remote islands in Japan. J. Air Transp. Manag. 17, 195–198.
New Zealand Airports Association, 2017. Linking the Long White Cloud. Available at https://www.nzairports.co.nz/assets/Files/public/Linking-the-Long-White-Cloud-NZ-Airports-Position-paper-July-2017-FINAL-small-file.1.1.pdf. (Accessed August 21, 2017).
New Zealand Ministry of Transport, 2015. International Air Transport Policy Statement. Available at http://www.transport.govt.nz/air/iatrpolicystatement/. (Accessed August 21, 2017).
Newswire, 2017. Destination Canada and WestJet Announce Three Year Global Partnership to Inspire More Travellers to Explore Canada. Available at http://www.newswire.ca/news-releases/destination-canada-and-westjet-announce-three-year-global-partnership-to-inspire-more-travellers-to-explore-canada-621672233.html. (Accessed May 25, 2017).
Nolan, J., Ritchie, P., Rowcroft, J., 2005. Small market air service and regional policy. J. Transport. Econ. Policy 39 (3), 363–387.
Nutley, S., 2003. Indicators of transport and accessibility problems in rural Australia. J. Transp. Geogr. 11, 55–71.
Pearson, J., Merkert, R., 2014. Airlines-within-airlines: a business model moving east. J. Air Transp. Manag. 38, 21–26.
Piermartini, R., Rousova, L., 2008. Liberalization of air transport services and passenger traffic. In: World Trade Organization (Economic Research and Statistics Division), Staff Working Paper ERSD-2008-06.
Piermartini, R., Rousova, L., 2011. The sky is not flat: how discriminatory is the access to international air services? Am. Econ. J. Econ. Pol. 5 (3), 287–319.
Rauch, F., 2016. The geometry of the distance coefficient in gravity equations in international trade. Rev. Int. Econ. 24 (5), 1167–1177.
Redondi, R., Malighetti, P., Paleari, S., 2011. Hub competition and travel times in the world-wide airport network. J. Transp. Geogr. 19, 1260–1271.
Reuters, 2016. Lufthansa CEO says rising protectionism hampering M&A. Available at http://www.reuters.com/article/us-lufthansa-m-a-idUSKCN0YQ0FK. (Accessed August 21, 2017).
Schnell, M.C.A., 2004. What determines the effectiveness of barriers to entry in liberalised airline markets? J. Air Transp. Manag. 10, 413–426.
Shaw, J., Hesse, M., 2010. Transport, geography and the 'new' mobilities. Trans. Inst. Brit. Geographers NS 35, 305–312.
Sinc, 2014. Los vuelos 'low cost' han atraído más turistas a España, pero gastan menos. Available at http://www.agenciasinc.es/Noticias/Los-vuelos-low-cost-han-atraido-mas-turistas-a-Espana-pero-gastan-menos. (Accessed April 7, 2017).
Statistics Canada (2017). Non-resident travellers entering Canada. Available at http://www.statcan.gc.ca/tables-tableaux/sum-som/l01/cst01/arts34-eng.htm, CANSIM 427-0001. (Accessed June 2, 2018).
Stough, R.R., Rietveld, P., 1997. Institutional issues in transport systems. J. Transp. Geogr. 5 (3), 207–214.
The Himalayan Times, 2016. Nepal Has Enough Opportunities to Tap Tourists Who Visit Other South Asian Nations. Available at https://thehimalayantimes.com/business/nepal-enough-opportunities-tap-tourists-visit-south-asian-nations/. (Accessed November 7, 2016).
The National, 2017a. Emirates Cuts Flights to US over Laptop Ban. Available at http://www.thenational.ae/business/emirates-cuts-flights-to-us-over-laptop-ban. (Accessed June 1, 2017).
The National, 2017b. Emirates to Loan Tablets to Premium Passengers on US Flights after Ban on Electronic Devices. Available at https://www.thenational.ae/business/emirates-to-loan-tablets-to-premium-passengers-on-us-flights-after-ban-on-electronic-devices-1.42726. (Accessed June 1, 2017).
Time, 2016. Travel Groups Want Congress to Investigate Airline Competition (or Lack Thereof). Available at http://time.com/money/4204413/airline-competition-congress/?iid=sr-link1. (Accessed July 26, 2017).
Tinbergen, J., 1962. An analysis of world trade flows. In: Tinbergen, J. (Ed.), Shaping the World Economy. Twentieth Century Fund, New York.
Today Online, 2017. S$34m War Chest to Market Singapore as a Stopover Hub. Available at http://m.todayonline.com/singapore/s34m-war-chest-market-singapore-stopover-hub. (Accessed May 8, 2017).
Transport Canada (n.d.). The Blue Sky Policy: Made in Canada, for Canada. Available at https://www.tc.gc.ca/eng/policy/air-bluesky-menu-2989.htm . (Accessed June 16, 2017).
Tretheway, M., Andriulaitis, R., 2015. What do we mean by a level playing field in international aviation? Transp. Policy 43, 96–103.
Tretheway, M., Markvhida, K., 2014. The aviation value chain: Economic returns and policy issues. J. Air Transp. Manag. 41, 3–16.
Vanguard Nigeria, 2017. Airlines Current Challenges Impact Tourism, says NANTA President. Available at http://www.vanguardngr.com/2017/03/airlines-current-challenges-impact-tourism-says-nanta-president/. (Accessed April 19, 2017).
Wang, P.T., Pitfield, D.E., 1999. The derivation and analysis of the passenger peak hour: an empirical application to Brazil. J. Air Transp. Manag. 5, 135–141.
Warnock-Smith, D., O'Connell, J.F., 2011. The impact of air policy on incoming tourist traffic: the contrasting cases of the Caribbean community and the middle-east. J. Transp. Geogr. 19, 265–274.
Weber, M., Williams, G., 2001. Drivers of long-haul air transport route development. J. Transp. Geogr. 9, 243–254.
Whyte, R., Lohmann, G., 2015. The carrier-within-a-carrier strategy: an analysis of Jetstar. J. Air Transp. Manag. 42, 141–148.
Wilken, D., Berster, M., Gelhausen, M.C., 2016. Analysis of demand structures on intercontinental routes to and from Europe with a view to identifying potential for new low-cost services. J. Air Transp. Manag. 56, 79–90.
Williams, G., Pagliari, R., 2004. A comparative analysis of the application and use of public service obligations in air transport within the EU. Transp. Policy 11, 55–66.
Wittman, M.D., Allroggen, F., Malina, R., 2016. Public service obligations for air transport in the United States and Europe: connectivity effects and value for money. Transp. Res. A 94, 112–128.
Wojahn, O.W., 2001. Airline network structure and the gravity model. Transp. Res. E 37, 267–279.
Xinhuanet, 2017. Singapore's Airport, Airline, Tourism Authority Jointly Invest to Promote Inbound Travel. Available at http://news.xinhuanet.com/english/2017-04/17/c_136215340.htm. (Accessed May 8, 2017).
Zhang, Y., Findlay, C., 2014. Air transport policy and its impacts on passenger traffic and tourist flows. J. Air Transp. Manag. 34, 42–48.

CHAPTER

6

Intermodal Competition and Tourism

Daniel ALBALATE, Xavier FAGEDA

University of Barcelona, Barcelona, Spain

CHAPTER OUTLINE

6.1 INTRODUCTION

The role of transportation as an engine of economic growth for regions and cities has been extensively analysed. In this regard, transportation is crucial for economic growth because it may have positive effects in terms of higher productivity of private enterprises, lower transport costs for firms, and greater accessibility to territories. Furthermore, better transport connections between cities and regions may promote their economic links such as those related to trade, foreign direct investments, or tourism. In this chapter, there is an examination of the link between transportation and tourism and, in particular, an analysis of the interrelation between different transportation modes and the impact of such interrelation on tourism outcomes.

A number of previous studies have shown a significant relationship between transport infrastructure and tourism (Abeyratne, 1993; Chew, 1987; Della Corte et al., 2013; Khadaroo and Seetanah, 2007, 2008; Martin and Witt, 1988). Indeed, investment in any mode of transportation acts as one of the main determinants of tourist destination choice as it improves accessibility to a particular location. In general, improvements in accessibility of a tourist destination are expected to promote the revitalisation of urban tourism due to a reduction of the generalised cost of transportation. Thus tourism gains are amongst the most common positive economic externalities that are often claimed to be associated with transportation investments. No doubt, this expected improvement of the tourist attractiveness of destinations, if true, becomes an opportunity to renew the tourist supply for the industry (see Delaplace et al., 2014 and Feliu, 2012) and a positive external boost for the local economy (see Hernández and Jiménez, 2014).

In this chapter, in contrast with previous studies, empirical evidence is provided about the potentially detrimental effects that high-speed rail services may have on tourism outcomes. Competition between high-speed rail and air transportation may be fierce in short- and medium-haul routes. In this arena, high-speed rail may be very competitive

Air Transport—A Tourism Perspective. https://doi.org/10.1016/B978-0-12-812857-2.00006-3

in relation to airlines in terms of travel time and frequency, but not necessarily in terms of price. High-speed railways may have a negative effect on tourism because they could lead to a substantial reduction of air transportation supply.

The focus of the data is Spain, which is a relevant case study in the context of Europe, as it is the country with (i) the largest domestic air market, (ii) the most extensive high-speed rail network and, (iii) a high number of relevant leisure tourist enclaves.

The rest of this chapter is structured as follows. In Section 6.2 a detailed literature review is undertaken regarding the effects of transportation supply on tourism, intermodal competition between high-speed rail and airlines, and the result of such intermodal competition on tourism. Section 6.3 provides data about tourist enclaves, airport, and high-speed rail networks in Spain. Section 6.4 develops an econometric analysis of the substitution effect between air transportation and high-speed rail, whilst Section 6.5 conducts an econometric analysis of the outcome change for tourist enclaves affected by new high-speed railways. The last section is devoted to concluding remarks.

6.2 LITERATURE REVIEW: TRANSPORTATION AND TOURISM

The literature has paid attention to the role played by different modes of transportation in tourism outcomes and destination choices. This literature, which is broad, has considered all modes of transportation. Nonetheless, the interest here is in the role played by the potential intermodal competition between air transportation and high-speed rail, which has emerged as a fruitful area of recent research. Some studies have focused on the individual and separate effects of airline and airport investments, whilst others examine the potential contribution of high-speed rail projects to the tourist industry. Some others have paid more attention to the competitive and substitution effects produced by the introduction of high-speed rail in several medium-distance airline routes. However, only a few studies have considered the impact on tourism of the joint effect produced by the intermodal competition of these two modes. This section briefly reviews some of these works before developing a new approach to measuring how intermodal competition may affect tourism outcomes.

6.2.1 The Effect of Air Transportation and High-Speed Rail (HSR) on Tourism

On the one hand, a large proportion of tourists arrive at their final destination by air, so it is not surprising to find that air services have a significant impact on the number of tourist arrivals (Albalate and Fageda, 2016; Bieger and Wittmer, 2006; Dobruszkes and Mondou, 2013). The effect of air transportation on tourism outcomes is particularly strong when low-cost airlines are offering flights on the route (Chung and Whang, 2011; Donzelli, 2010; Rey et al., 2011). Thus there are no doubts about the contribution of air transportation to tourism outcomes.

On the other hand, the previous literature has also studied the link between new HSR stations and tourism outcomes. The role of new high-speed rail projects in promoting the revitalisation of tourism by improving accessibility is seen as a positive expected impact in the approach of recent studies such as Delaplace and Perrin (2013), Masson and Petiot (2009), and Bazin et al. (2010). For this reason, anticipated tourism gains from HSR are present in many recent studies (see Chen and Haynes, 2012; Edwards, 2012; Murakami and Cervero, 2012, amongst others). Nonetheless, the ex-post evaluation of the relationship between HSR and its effects is much more modest and controversial in terms of results. Examples of these recent ex-post research outcomes are Bazin et al. (2006), Bazin et al. (2013), and Delaplace et al. (2016) for France; Clavé et al. (2015), Albalate and Fageda (2016), Albalate et al. (2017), Guirao and Campa (2016), Padilla et al. (2016), and Saladié et al. (2016) for Spain; Pagliara et al. (2017) for Italy; and Kurihara and Wu (2016) for Japan.

In summary, air transportation is widely considered to play a very important role in terms of tourism impacts, whilst high-speed rail produces high expectations but moderate results. It is believed that this might be explained by the intermodal competition produced between these two modes of transportation, given that the main effect of new high-speed rail lines is to divert passengers from other modes of transportation—mainly from air services—to rail. For this reason, intermodal competition appears to be one of the most important elements in an analysis of the role of transportation infrastructure in tourism decisions and outcomes.

6.2.2 HSR vs. Air Transportation: Intermodal Competition

The literature on intermodal competition has been experiencing an important boost in the last few years. Most recent papers focus on the interaction between air transportation and high-speed rail, probably because high-speed rail represents a contemporary revolution in transportation technology that has been promoted in various countries around the world, attracting interest from both scholars and policy makers (Albalate and Bel, 2012). As a result, there is a growing body of literature examining the modal competition between HSR and air transportation (see Givoni and Dobruszkes, 2013, for a review) that stresses the former's ability to attract a relatively large market share of medium-distance travellers. This market share gain is obtained mainly at the expense of the airline industry. As a result, HSR has become a major determinant of market power loss (Zhang et al., 2014) and a major barrier to entry for airlines (Kappes and Merkert, 2013).

Evidence of sizeable losses in airline market shares and reductions in airline operations due to the opening up of HSR lines is documented for all countries with high-speed lines. The substitution effect is well documented from the pioneering inaugurations of HSR lines and continuing network developments in Japan (Albalate and Bel, 2012; Clever and Hansen, 2008; Fu et al., 2014; Taniguchi, 1992), and in several European countries, including France (Bonnafous, 1987; Klein, 1997; Vickerman, 1997), Spain (Albalate and Fageda, 2016; Jiménez and Betancor, 2012; Martín and Nombela, 2008; Pagliara et al., 2012; Román et al., 2007), Italy (Cascetta et al., 2011), and Germany (Dobruszkes, 2011; Ellwanger and Wilckens, 1993). Dobruszkes et al. (2014) and Albalate et al. (2015) also show this substitution effect using various econometric techniques for a sample of European routes. Similar impacts on air transportation have been documented in Asia, including Korea (Lee et al., 2012; Suh et al., 2005), China (Fu et al., 2012; Wu, 2013), and Taiwan (Cheng, 2010; Sun and Lin, 2018).

In contrast to the earlier studies that have identified a substitution effect, a few articles also found some possible complementarities between modes, showing that under certain circumstances HSR could complement rather than replace air transportation (Albalate et al., 2015; Dobruszkes and Givoni, 2013; Givoni and Banister, 2006). However, results of this complementarity are still scarce in the empirical literature.

6.2.3 The Role of Intermodal Competition on Tourism

HSR and air transportation typically have a specifically passenger-led orientation, hence their importance for the tourism industry. As argued, recent studies indicate that the main impact of HSR on mobility is to transplant existing airline passenger volumes, rather than to induce a higher number of new trips. Thus the interaction between airlines and HSR is of essential importance in any analysis of the impact of diversified transportation on tourism. Indeed, the fierce competition between these two modes of transportation may affect the overall impact on tourism. If the substitution effect produced by high-speed rail damages the airline industry it will definitely affect net tourism outcomes (Rey et al., 2011), with particular severity in the case of international tourists who use airports as the main international gateways (air transportation being the chief mode for long-distance mobility).

High-speed rail may have a higher influence on destination choices for those tourists situated at medium distances relative to their potential destinations: the ones more affected by the intermodal competition. These tourists may reasonably choose between high-speed rail and air transportation, or between high-speed rail and the road. It is well known that distance is a good predictor of the relative attractiveness of each mode of transportation. Whilst the road is clearly superior for short distances (up to 150 km), high-speed rail is able to gain a market share from that distance up to 600 km, at which point air transportation starts to be as competitive as HSR. This is why the impact of intermodal competition and its role on tourism might have a more relevant role for national tourists than for international tourists, particularly in the case of national networks that are not planned to connect to neighbouring countries, as in Spain. Indeed, Pagliara et al. (2015) studied the impact of HSR in Madrid on tourist destination choice by means of a revealed preference survey. Results indicate that the presence of HSR does not seem to be a key factor influencing the destination choice of tourists because most of them are international tourists that can only arrive by air transportation. However, the use of HSR appears to be attractive to international tourists for visiting nearby locations.

A similar conclusion is reached by Chen and Haynes (2015) when investigating the impact of the Chinese high-speed rail systems on its international tourism demand. These authors find very small demand elasticity with respect to the existence of HSR stations. Their results indicate that 'a 1% increase in HSR station[s] is associated with a 0.057% increase in international tourism arrivals, ceteris paribus' (Chen and Haynes, 2015, p. 59). Thus international tourism does not seem to be influenced by HSR availability and this presents a major barrier to anticipating positive impacts from rail transport on the tourism industry when considering all types of tourists, particularly those from abroad.

Hence, tourism decisions may be determined by the interaction between HSR and air transportation, but only for the distances in which this competition is reasonable. Positive impacts from HSR are expected, by increasing the overall number transport users or promoting a given type of visitor (high income, longer stays, etc.). However, HSR usually exerts a substitution or even predatory effect on air transportation for distances between 300 and 700 km. If HSR harms air transportation, above all alternative modes, due to its ability to attract a relatively large market share in medium distances, the supply of air services may drop, indirectly affecting the arrival of tourists, particularly those that do not have any choice between high-speed rail and air transportation due to distance and/or availability.

Albalate and Fageda (2016) already found inconsistent and weak direct effects of HSR on tourism in Spanish provinces due to negative indirect effects on air services, which may be a source of concern with respect to total tourist arrivals if HSR is not able to divert all these tourists to the rail (which is unlikely, as explained before, in the case of international tourists). According to results reported in most of the econometric models, the number of tourists grew at a similar rate over recent years in destinations (Spanish provinces) not connected to the HSR network as in destinations connected to it, indicating that factors other than the availability of this service may have a higher influence on the attractiveness of provinces for tourists. Similar results are also found in a recent study by Albalate et al. (2017), which considers tourist points—intensively tourist areas—instead of provinces, and their distance from high-speed rail stations. No clear effects on tourism were found to be produced by new HSR projects and, in many cases, airport investments proved to be a better alternative to promote tourism activity. Structural changes in air transportation, the role of hotel prices, and the size of municipalities all seemed to play a significant role in explaining local tourism, much more than the presence of a new high-speed rail.

6.3 THE EVALUATION OF INTERMODAL COMPETITION FOR DOMESTIC TOURISTS IN SPAIN

This chapter focuses on the impact of medium-distance intermodal competition on domestic tourism in Spain. Choosing Spain as a case study is particularly relevant given that it is one of the world's popular tourist destinations and has Europe's largest high-speed rail network (the second largest in the world, after China). According to UNWTO (2015), nearly 65 million visitors arrived in Spain in 2014, contributing more than €64 billion to the country's GDP (6.5% of total GDP). Given that Spain is a large country, it enjoys many tourist enclaves across the territory.

Although 80% of tourists arrive by air, road and domestic rail transport also play a significant role in facilitating their movements from airports to final or transit destinations (FRONTUR, 2015) and short excursions to surrounding areas. In fact, the road network density in Spain (in terms of motorway km per km^2 of land area) is well above the EU average of 28, and the country has spent nearly €50 billion over the last 25 years to develop the longest HSR network connecting more than 80 large and medium-sized cities, most of them provincial capitals. As explained in Albalate et al. (2015), Spain is one of the countries with the largest supply of transportation infrastructure in Europe.

In terms of airports, Fig. 6.1 shows the location of the airports managed by AENA-Enaire—excluding the few regional airports with low traffic volume. Also, in Fig. 6.2 (Moyano et al., 2016), the current network of high-speed railways and their locations is shown. Note that most of the HSR lines have as one of their endpoints the capital city of Madrid, providing a radial centralised network connecting the centre of the peninsula to the coast, where many tourist points are placed.[1] No connections between coastal resorts have been built, and no expectations for these types of nonradial corridors, that are more able to connect tourist points, are planned. Moreover, the network has not been designed to connect Spain to international destinations but has focused on connecting Madrid to the provincial capitals. Only one international connection is available, but it remains quite unattractive with respect to air and road transportation. This is the north-eastern connection to France through the Le Perthus Tunnel, today under financial distress due to the limited demand volume.

Regarding intermodal competition, note that Madrid-Adolfo Suárez and Barcelona-El Prat are the two main hubs of the Spanish airport system. Although there is no HSR station at these airport sites, they are well connected to the HSR network with fast and cheap public transportation services. As indicated, Madrid is served by all current HSR lines, but other relevant cities with important airports are also affected by HSR competition, including Barcelona, Málaga, Alicante and, to a lesser extent, Valencia and Seville. Thus some of the HSR lines have had an impact on the densest routes in the Spanish domestic market like Madrid–Barcelona (one of the densest in the world before the arrival of the HSR services), Madrid–Málaga, or Madrid–Valencia. For all these reasons, HSR could have significantly damaged the market share of air transportation for domestic flights, with an unknown impact on tourism outcomes.

In this chapter there is an evaluation of how the introduction of intermodal competition for medium distances has affected the number of domestic tourists in tourist points served by airports. Domestic tourists are the most exposed to intermodal competition in Spain, given the design of the network and the distances between cities. Thus evidence is provided of how the entrance of HSR has affected the choice of tourist destination for the Spaniards.

[1] However, note that there some bypassing services like, for instance, those connecting Barcelona with Sevilla.

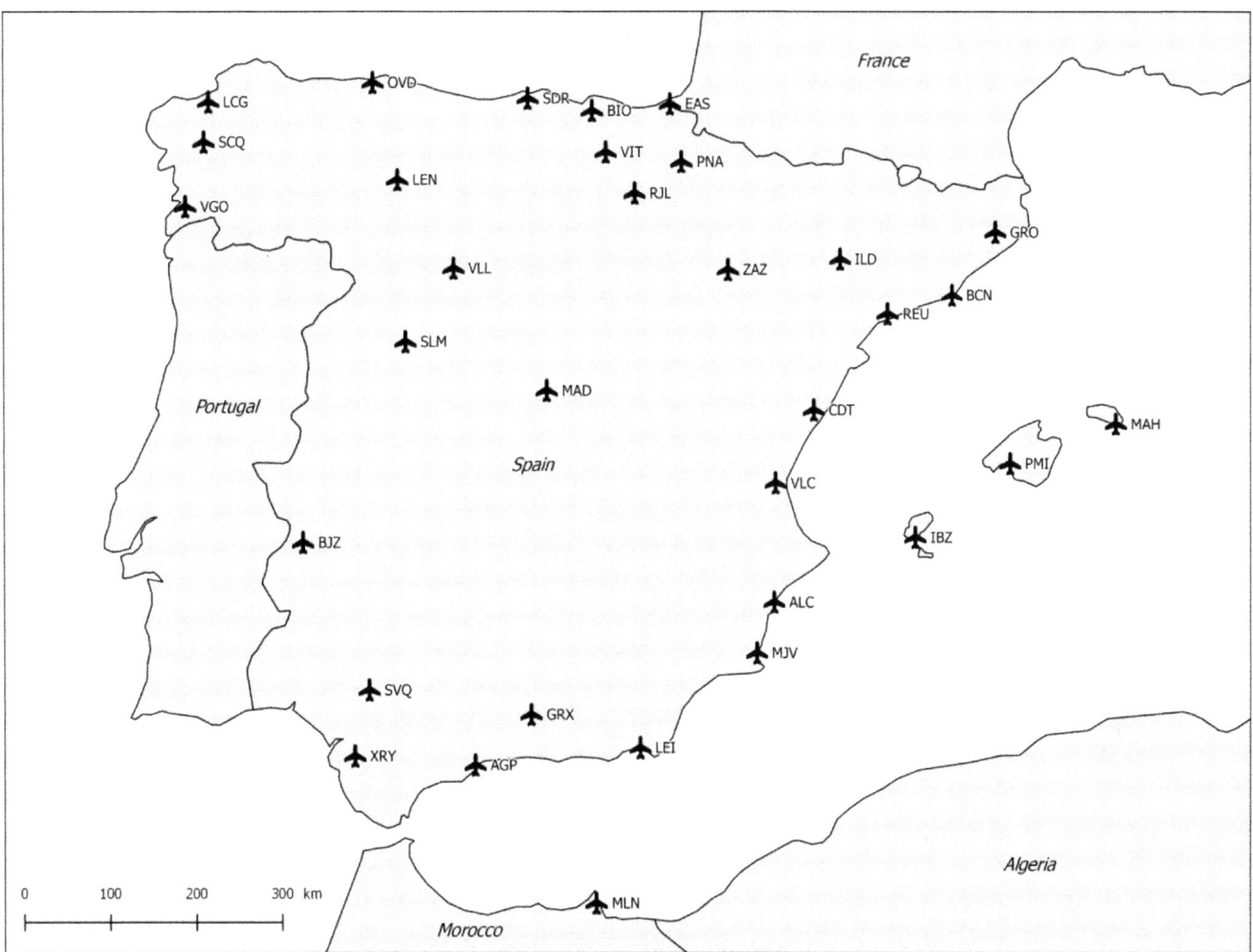

FIG. 6.1 Location of airports in Spain (airports with commercial traffic in 2017). *(Source: Natural Earth, OpenFlights.org, and OAG.)*

6.4 EMPIRICAL WORK

6.4.1 Measuring the Substitution Effect With the Entrance of HSR

In this section, there is an examination by means of a multivariate econometric analysis of the impact that HSR may have on the supply offered by airlines on Spanish domestic routes. The analysis is restricted to domestic flights because the HSR network in Spain is basically serving domestic routes, with only a recent connection to the south of France that is not continued with high-speed rail infrastructure between Perpignan and Montpellier.

For this analysis, advantage is taken of data provided by RDC aviation including the total number of seats, flight frequency, size of the aircraft at the airline-route level, and route distance (in kilometres). This dataset records information for the period 2005–16, on a monthly basis. Data for the presence of HSR have been obtained from the authors' own database, according to the dates of service inaugurations. Note that only Spanish routes within the mainland (excluding the Canary and Balearic Islands, and Ceuta and Melilla) are considered because it is solely in this geographical area that intermodal competition coming from trains is relevant. In fact, the islands and autonomous cities do not have any relevant railway network at all.

There is information for 147 routes, totaling 17,411 observations. It is also worth mentioning that the panel is unbalanced because some routes do not have air services in some months of the considered period. Thus observations are excluded for which the dependent variable has zero values. The equations to estimate effect for the airline *a* in route *k* in period *t* are as follows:

$$\log(Y)_{akt} = \alpha + \beta_1 \,\text{Distance}_k + \beta_2 \,\text{Squared\_Distance}_k + \beta_3 \,\text{HHI}_{kt} + \beta_4 \text{D}^{\text{HSR}}{}_{kt} + \beta_5 \,\text{Train\_time}_{kt} + \beta_6 \,\text{D}^{\text{HSR}} \,\text{X}\,\text{Train\_time}_{kt} + \eta^{'}_{ap} + \eta^{'}_{a} + \eta_{yt} + \eta_{qt} + \varepsilon_{akt} \tag{6.1}$$

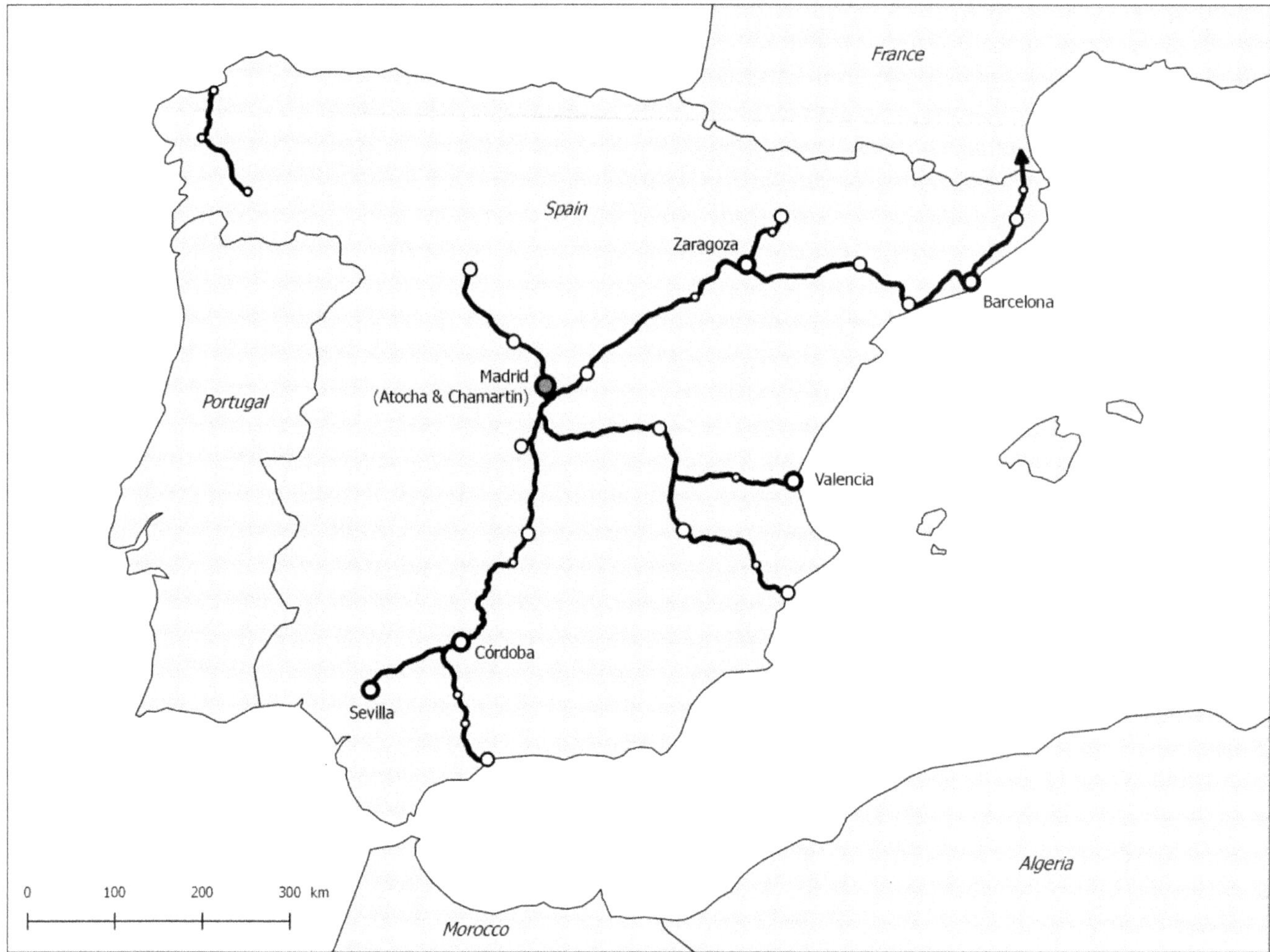

FIG. 6.2 High-speed rail network in Spain (2016). *(Source: Centro Nacional de Información Geográfica, Instituto Geográfico Nacional, and Moyano, A., Coronado, J., Garmendia, M., 2016. How to choose the most efficient transport mode for weekend tourism journeys: an HSR and private vehicle comparison. Open Transp. J. 10 (Suppl. 1, M8) 84–96.)*

Three different dependent variables are used: (i) the total number of seats, (ii) the total number of flights, (iii) the mean aircraft size. The dependent variable is expressed in logarithms so that the coefficient for the dummy of HSR can be interpreted as an elasticity.

Route distance (great-circle distance) is included as an explanatory variable. A negative relationship is expected between frequency and route length, whilst the coefficient of the distance variable should be positive with the mean aircraft size considered as a dependent variable. On longer routes airlines may prefer to reduce flight frequency and use larger aircraft whose efficiency increases with distance. In addition, since on long-haul routes intermodal competition with cars, trains, and ships is weak, airlines may be competitive with lower frequencies and larger aircraft (which is less costly for them). Having said this, a high proportion of routes in the sample are short-haul routes so that the competitiveness of air transportation in relation to cars and trains may increase with distance (see Bilotkach et al., 2010 for an econometric analysis on this issue). Thus it could also be the case that airlines increase frequency when route distance is higher. Taking all this into account, the expected sign of the distance variable is not clear a priori, particularly when the total number of seats is considered as a dependent variable. In order to test a possible nonlinear relationship between the supply of air services and distance, the squared distance is also included as an explanatory variable.

In addition, included as an explanatory variable, is the intensity of airline competition in the route through the Herfindahl–Hirschman index (HHI). This index measures the sum of the square shares of airlines operating in the route in terms of flight frequencies. Hence, a higher HHI implies weaker competition in the route. In the case of the frequency equation, a negative sign is expected, since fewer flights will be offered as competition on the route falls. Less clear is the expected sign of the HHI variable when the total number of seats and the mean aircraft size as dependent variables are considered.

Different types of fixed effects are added as controls. In this regard, airport (η'_{ap}), airline (η'_{a}), year (η_{yt}), and month (η_{qt}) are added as fixed effects. This allows control of unobserved heterogeneity that is time invariant or has a low variation over time, such as the demographic size and economic status of the cities, tourism intensity, and so on. It also allows controls of common time trends like the economic crisis that harmed all Spanish cities to a similar intensity and seasonal effects. Not included is route-fixed effect as this would be to imply a focus on variation of the data that in the case of one relevant variable, distance, is nil.

The main variable of the analysis is the dummy for HSR which takes the value, one, for routes affected by the presence of high-speed rail services. High-speed rail services are very competitive in short- and medium-haul routes so that they may capture part of the traffic that was channelled by airlines. Indeed, this dummy variable may capture the improvement that HSR represent (less time spend on the trip, more comfort, reliability, punctuality, frequency) in relation to convention train services. Thus a negative relationship is expected with the dependent variables.

Furthermore, there is an evaluation of how new rail infrastructure deployment is affecting the domestic airline market by including a variable measuring the in-vehicle time spent by train between the two end points in direct services, if they exist, or in the fastest services in the absence of direct services. This variable is called *Train_time*, and a positive relationship is expected with our dependent variables. Note that this variable has some correlation with the dummy for HRS but it is not high enough to expect a multicollinearity problem. The value of the correlation is 0.32. However, it is highly correlated with the distance variable (the value of correlation is 0.61). Thus part of the effect of this variable may be already captured by distance. The interaction between the dummy for HSR and the *Train_time* variable is also included. This variable allows measurement of the impact of the time spend on the trip for routes affected by the presence of HSR services.

The estimates may present heteroscedasticity and temporal and cross-sectional autocorrelation problems. The Breusch–Pagan/Cook–Weisberg test for heteroscedasticity and the Wooldridge test for autocorrelation in panel data are applied. Both tests show that there may be a problem of heteroscedasticity and autocorrelation, which must be addressed. Hence, the standard errors are robust to heteroscedasticity. Following Bertrand et al. (2004), an arbitrary variance–covariance structure is allowed by computing the standard errors in clusters by route, to correct for autocorrelation in the error term at both the cross-sectional and temporal levels.

Table 6.1 shows the descriptive statistics of the variables used in the empirical analysis. Data in this table show that the mean frequency is high (more than two flights per day) and the representative aircraft is large (more than 100 seats). Having said this, the heterogeneity in the sample is substantial, including high-density routes like those linking Madrid with Barcelona, Bilbao, Málaga, and Valencia and very thin routes like Málaga–Valladolid, Bilbao–Jérez, or Almeria–Zaragoza. Furthermore, it is also remarkable that the mean distance is relatively short (less than 600 km) so that high-speed rail services may be competitive in relation to the supply offered by airlines. Here, the longest route is Barcelona–Vigo (but still with less than 1000 km) and the shortest is Bilbao–Pamplona with about 100 km, a distance more favourable for the road. Finally, the mean level of competition in the route is relatively weak as the mean HHI is about 0.70. The HHI is 1 (the scenario of monopoly) in 41% of the routes. Finally, 10% of observations in the sample are affected by the presence of HSR.

Fig. 6.3 provides preliminary evidence about the impact of the HSR on the seats offered for a representative set of routes of the sample. The figure provides the numbers for the total seats offered by airlines on the route within

TABLE 6.1 Descriptive Statistics

Variable	Mean	Standard Errors	Minimum Value	Maximum Value
Seats	9876	15,751	34	213,544
Flight frequency	75	98	1	1314
Aircraft size	125	57	32	164
Distance	569	190	119	893
HHI	0.71	0.25	0.25	1
HSR	0.10	0.30	0	1
Train_time	424.38	218.70	73	960

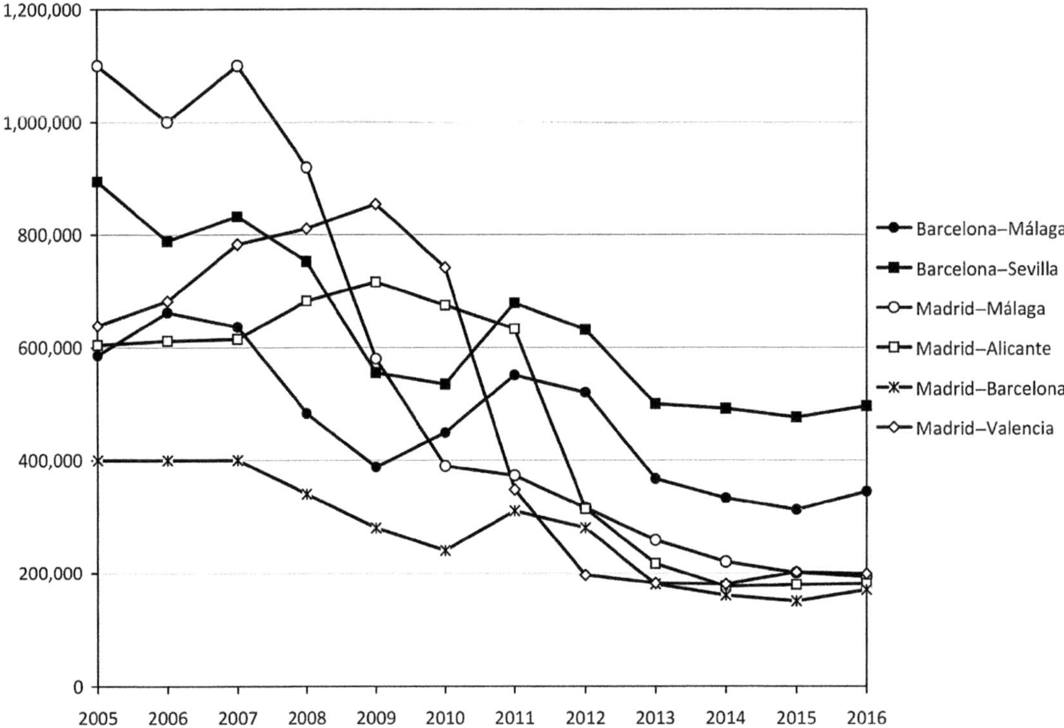

FIG. 6.3 Evolution of the total number of seats offered by airlines. *Note*: The numbers reported in the figure make reference to the total number of seats. The only exception is Madrid–Barcelona in which the numbers are divided by 10 to facilitate the visualisation of the figure. The startup date of the HSR lines is October 2009 (Barcelona–Málaga, Barcelona–Seville), January 2008 (Madrid–Málaga), October 2013 (Madrid–Alicante), October 2008 (Madrid–Barcelona), and January 2011 (Madrid–Valencia). *(RDC aviation.)*

the considered period (2005–15), on an annual basis. In all cases, the reduction in the number of seats offered by airlines is substantial after the entry of the HSR in the corresponding city pairing. In the initial year of HSR services, the supply of seats provided by airlines was reduced by 20% in Barcelona–Seville, 26% in Barcelona–Málaga, 37% in Madrid–Málaga, 31% in Madrid–Alicante, 18% in Madrid–Barcelona, and 53% in Madrid–Valencia. Part of the reduction in air capacity may be explained by the economic crisis that was especially severe in the period in which the HSR lines were opened (2008–13). However, air traffic has not recovered in recent years although the economic situation has improved a lot. Note that all the considered routes were dense routes (at least in terms of our sample) before the start of operation of HSR services, while the distance range for routes from Madrid is 300–500 km and about 900 km in routes from Barcelona.

Table 6.2 presents the results of the three different specifications of the equation that is estimated. Column II shows the results when the dependent variable is the total number of seats; column III when the dependent variable is flight frequency; and column IV when the dependent variable is the mean aircraft size. The overall explanatory power of the model is very high in the three estimations as the R^2 ranges from 0.71 to 0.81.

As expected, the distance variable is positive and statistically significant when the aircraft size is the dependent variable. However, the positive effect of distance on aircraft size is decreasing. It is positive but not statistically significant when the dependent variable is flight frequency. On longer routes, it seems that the demand increase due to the higher competitiveness of air services counterbalances the cost reduction that airlines may achieve from offering capacity with fewer flights and larger aircraft. Given that airlines increase frequencies and use larger aircraft on longer routes, it is not surprising that the distance variable is positive when the dependent variable is total seats. As in the case of aircraft size, such effect is decreasing.

Results for the HHI variable are more difficult to interpret. Contrary to expectations, this variable is positive and statistically significant when the dependent variable is flight frequency. Thus it seems that frequency competition is weak in the Spanish domestic market. This result is reinforced with consideration of the estimation where the dependent variable is the mean aircraft size. Indeed, airlines use smaller aircraft on more concentrated routes.

In any case, the main interest of the analysis is in the HSR variable. There is clear evidence of a substitution effect between domestic air services and high-speed services. The coefficient of the HSR variable is negative in the three equations, although it is not statistically significant when aircraft size is the dependent variable. The magnitude of

TABLE 6.2 Econometric Results

Independent Variables	Dependent Variable: Seats	Dependent Variable: Flight Frequency	Dependent Variable: Aircraft Size
Distance	0.003 (0.001)**	0.002 (0.001)	0.001 (0.0003)***
Squared_distance	−2.28e−06 (1.17e−06)**	−1.36e−06 (1.08e−06)	−9.28e−07 (3.03e−07)***
HHI	0.13 (0.13)	0.31 (0.12)**	−0.18 (0.06)***
D^{HSR}	−0.99 (0.19)***	−0.80 (0.19)***	−0.19 (0.13)
Train_time	−0.0003 (0.0002)	−0.0004 (0.0002)	0.00005 (0.0001)
D^{HSR} X Train_time	0.003 (0.0006)***	0.002 (0.0006)***	0.0002 (0.0003)
Intercept	2.00 (0.47)	−2.47 (0.43)***	4.47 (0.14)***
R^2	0.76	0.71	0.81
Number of observations	17,411	17,411	17,411

Notes: Standard errors are given in brackets (robust to heteroscedasticity and clustered by route). Airport, airline, year, and quarter fixed effects are added. Statistical significance at 1% (***), 5% (**), 10% (*).

the impact is remarkable. Airlines reduce seats by 99%, flights by 80%, and use aircraft that are 19% smaller, when they compete with high-speed rail services. Thus the latter seem to steal an important part of the demand that was previously channelled by airlines.

The variable for the time spent on the train is not statistically significant, perhaps because its effect is already captured by the distance variable. However, the interaction variable is positive and statistically significant which means that the effect of the time spent on the trip is positive for routes affected by the HSR services.

6.4.2 Evaluating Intermodal Competition on Tourism Outcomes

Overall, high-speed rail substantially damages the supply of air services. However, its net impact in terms of tourism outcomes remains uncertain. If high-speed rail is able to attract all the passengers lost by airlines and generate new trips then the overall effect should be positive. If it is only able to attract those passengers without adding new travellers then there should not be any significant effect on tourism from its introduction. If, on the contrary, it is not able to gain the passengers lost by airlines and does not add sufficient new travellers to compensate for that loss, the net impact of high-speed rail would be negative.

Table 6.3 displays a mean *t*-test comparing the sample with and without high-speed rail. Results indicate that numbers of tourists and overnights spent in tourist enclaves, in months and years in which a high-speed rail service is available, are statistically different and higher than numbers of tourists and overnights in enclaves, months, and years not served by high-speed rail lines. This expected outcome may be due to the fact that HSR might be placed precisely in places with larger amounts of tourists and visitors, for instance, in larger cities or populated areas. In addition, this analysis not only includes tourist enclaves where intermodal competition was introduced, but also tourist enclaves only served by airports between 2005 and 2015 and those served by high-speed rail for the whole period. This result, therefore, simply indicates that where a high-speed rail line is present the numbers of tourists and overnights are larger on average. Although this is informative, it does not speak about a change produced in tourism outcomes due to the introduction of intermodal competition.

TABLE 6.3 Two Sample *t*-test With Equal Variances—Tourism Outcomes for Tourist Enclaves Served by Airports With and Without High-Speed Rail Station in Spain (2005–15)

Group	Observations	Visitors	Overnights
With HSR	1070	126,736.4	259,608.1
Without HSR	2565	47,096.44	114,965.5
Difference	–	79,639.94***	144,642.6***
t-Statistic (difference)	–	33.02	25.95

Note: Statistical significance at 1% (***), 5% (**), 10% (*).

Thus in order to assess the evaluation of the net impact on tourism outcomes, an econometric time series analysis was conducted for each airport that received a new high-speed rail line competitor at some point between 2005 and 2015.[2] In this analysis attempts are made to evaluate the change in numbers of domestic tourists and overnights in the tourist enclaves served by the airport of reference, the closest to them. Thus only the 13 airports of reference that experienced intermodal competition from HSR are considered, and attributed to each airport was the information on the monthly number of domestic tourists and overnights of the closest tourist enclaves that form the tourist area served by the airport. Thus the total monthly number of domestic tourists and overnights are the two dependent variables. The equation considered for this analysis and replicated for each of the 13 airports experiencing HSR competition is the following[3]:

$$\log(\text{TOUR})_{mt} = \alpha + \beta_1 \text{HSR}_{mt} + \eta'_m + \text{Unemp}_t + \text{Year}_t + \varepsilon_{mt} \tag{6.2}$$

where TOUR_{mt} represents our two dependent variables for the month m and year t, and η'_m is a monthly fixed effect to account for seasonality. There are two other controls included. On the one hand, the Spanish unemployment rate to control for the economic cycle to account for the economic downturn produced by the global financial crisis. On the other hand, a time trend variable to capture anything related to time that could affect tourism outcomes. Log-transformation of the continuous variables—number of tourists and number of overnights—are used to obtain semielasticities. Indeed, the log-transformation of the dependent variable allows a quantification of the impact of the HSR variable (interpreting the coefficient) in terms of percentages of change. The Durbin Watson test rejects the presence of autocorrelation in all cases. Thus how the introduction of HSR affected tourism outcomes for the tourist areas served by the closest airport is measured.

Results are displayed in Table 6.4. Whilst results on the total numbers of tourists are mixed depending on the airport, results on the numbers of overnights and average duration of stays are more disappointing. High-speed rail has been able to moderately increase the amount of overall tourism in tourist enclaves served by the airports of A Coruña (31%), Albacete (11.6%), Alicante (10%), Barcelona (23.4%), and Valladolid (16.9%). In contrast, the high-speed rail net effect appears to be negative in the cases of León (−15.7%), Santiago (−24.6%), and Valencia (−8.8%). Finally, no significant effects on the overall number of tourists are identified in Girona, Málaga, Reus/Tarragona, Salamanca, and Vigo.

TABLE 6.4 Time Series Per Airport—Selected Results

Airport	Visitors	R^2	Overnights	R^2	Average Stay Per Tourist	R^2	Number of Observations
A Coruña	0.3119 (0.0461)**	0.81	0.2829 (0.0446)***	0.85	−0.0551 (0.0341)*	0.59	144
Albacete	0.1160 (0.0673)*	0.21	0.0499 (0.0797)	0.20	−0.1027 (0.0426)**	0.27	74
Alicante	0.1002 (0.0305) ***	0.91	−0.0250 (0.0291)	0.93	−0.5174 (0.0819)***	0.68	144
Barcelona	0.2339 (0.0354)**	0.54	0.1384 (0.0184)***	0.52	−0.1779 (0.0451)***	0.28	144
Girona	0.1061 (0.1061)	0.65	0.1081 (0.1667)	0.75	−0.0799 (0.4762)	0.67	64
León	−0.1569 (0.0645)**	0.86	−0.1587 (0.0626)***	0.85	−0.0005 (0.0475)	0.36	142
Málaga	0.0560 (0.0382)	0.92	0.0362 (0.0391)	0.94	−0.0621 (0.0742)	0.73	144
Reus/ Tarragona	−0.1668 (0.1294)	0.94	−0.1295 (0.1542)	0.95	0.1313 (0.1298)	0.91	75
Salamanca	−0.0096 (0.0661)	0.90	−0.0042 (0.0737)	0.87	0.0104 (0.0524)	0.45	100
Santiago	−0.2462 (0.0431)***	0.88	−0.3335 (0.0428)***	0.83	−0.1919 (0.0485)***	0.71	144
Valencia	−0.0882 (0.0386)**	0.79	−0.2092 (0.0547)***	0.81	−0.2643 (0.0690)***	0.70	144
Valladolid	0.16973 (0.0299)***	0.80	0.1347 (0.0320)***	0.77	−0.0566 (0.0232)**	0.27	143
Vigo	0.0940 (0.0748)	0.91	0.1190 (0.0769)	0.94	0.0416 (0.0600)	0.92	144

Notes: Standard errors are given in brackets (robust to heteroscedasticity). Monthly fixed effects to account for seasonality, the national unemployment rate, and a time trend have been assed. Statistical significance at 1% (***), 5% (**), 10% (***).

[2] Note that our tourism dependent variables include all types of purposes of travel for domestic travellers.

[3] Recall here that the provision of HSR services involves less air services so that the first model (Y_{akt}) is a logical step before the second one (TOUR_{mt}).

A more accurate measure of the impact on the tourism industry is by observing the change in the number of overnights, which avoids the effect of one-day visits that could imply low spending from tourists. Only in three cities are there positive and statistically significant effects after the introduction of high-speed rail: A Coruña (28.3%), Barcelona (13.8%), and Valladolid (13.5%). All the other tourist areas experience negative or nonsignificant impacts from the arrival of high-speed rail. Thus even if this intermodal competition may increase visitors, it can hardly be said to provide an increase of overnights. In fact, there is evidence of negative net impacts in León (−15.9%), Santiago de Compostela (−33.3%), and Valencia (−20.1%).

The previous result might be explained by the well-known fact that high-speed rail allows same-day returns, which might reduce the number of overnights. If that is true, it should be that the average stay of tourists decreases after the arrival of this mode of transportation. Thus the variable *average stay* is created by dividing the number of overnights by the number of tourists for each observation and a model is estimated in which the previous dependent variable is substituted by this new variable, to capture the mean length of stay in each area. The results displayed in Table 6.4 indicate that the introduction of intermodal competition in the form of high-speed rail generally reduces the average stay per tourist in most of the tourist enclaves. In seven airports there are statistically and negative impacts, whilst in no case is the impact is positive and statistically significant. The other six are not statistically significant at standard levels.

Since the literature has argued that high-speed rail may produce an increase of visitors but a reduction of the length of the stay due to its ability to efficiently facilitate a same-day return, the average stay was computed for the tourists for each area, month, and year and the analysis was reproduced in order to check whether the length of the stay changed with the introduction of this new transportation supply.

All these results seem to indicate that high-speed rail is not always able to attract all the passengers lost by airlines after the introduction of intermodal competition. Only in a few cases has the Spanish high-speed rail service been able to provide positive net effects after its introduction. In the majority of cases studied the net effect is nil or even negative. In addition, the introduction of intermodal competition delivers even more disappointing results in terms of net impacts on the number of overnights. As shown, this seems to be explained by the fact that high-speed rail is associated with a decrease in the average number of overnights per tourist.

6.5 CONCLUSIONS

High-speed rail and its impact on air transportation is gaining interest from both scholars and policy makers. Although the introduction of competition is generally positive for the user, here some concerns have been provided regarding the contribution of intermodal competition to the tourism industry. Although most papers tend to emphasise the possible contribution of high-speed rail to tourism, as if it was not damaging other modes of transportation, the ex-post evaluation is less optimistic and frequently disappointing.

In this chapter, there has been a study of the impact of the introduction of intermodal competition in the form of high-speed rail to tourist enclaves already served by airports. The analysis focuses on national tourists, considering the effects of high-speed rail on the supply of domestic flights. The results are consistent with most of the results in the literature, finding a substantial substitution effect that affects the number of seats, frequency of flights, and size of the aircraft. This effect should be considered when evaluating the role of high-speed rail—and that of intermodal competition—on tourism outcomes, given that the main effect it produces is a market share loss for the main mode of transportation used by tourists: air transportation. In fact, it is shown that the only way in which the introduction of intermodal competition may contribute to the tourist areas is by HSR attracting the demand lost by airlines and adding new travellers to the origin–destination pairs. The results indicate that it would not achieve this in many cases. In fact, it appears that high-speed rail has negative impacts in many of the areas studied and that it seems to reduce the average stay of tourists in those destinations.

The results imply that high-speed rail services, contrary to expectations, can have a detrimental effect on tourist outcomes, mainly due to the impact on air transportation. Instead of the expected benefits of intermodal competition, the results indicate that the damage inflicted on airlines may finally end up damaging the tourism industry, at least in terms of the choices made by national tourists that are the focus of this analysis. Indeed, the strong link between air transportation and tourism is well established in the literature.

According to the conclusions, public authorities and interest groups promoting high-speed rail projects—particularly those related to the tourism industry—should be more cautious about the expectations of tourism outcomes produced by high-speed rail where it may produce intermodal competition.

References

Abeyratne, R., 1993. Air transport tax and its consequences on tourism. Ann. Tour. Res. 20, 450–460.

Albalate, D., Bel, G., 2012. The Economics and Politics of High-Speed Rail. Lessons from Experiences Abroad. Rowman and Littlefield Publishers (Lexington Books), Lanham, MA.

Albalate, D., Fageda, X., 2016. High speed rail and tourism: empirical evidence from Spain. Transport. Res. A 85, 174–185.

Albalate, D., Bel, G., Fageda, X., 2015. Competition and cooperation between high speed rail and air transportation services in Europe. J. Transp. Geogr. 42, 166–174.

Albalate, D., Campos, J., Jimenez, J.L., 2017. Does the high-speed rail increase local visitors? Ann. Tour. Res. 65, 71–82.

Bazin, S., Beckerich, C., Delaplace, M., 2006. Analyse prospective des impacts de la Ligne Grande Vitesse Est-Européenne dans l'agglomération rémoise et en région Champagne-Ardenne. Rapport final pour le Conseil Régional Champagne-Ardenne, février, 495.

Bazin, S., Beckerich, C., Delaplace, M., 2010. Grande vitesse, activation des ressources spécifiques et développement du tourisme urbain: le cas de l'agglomération rémoise. Belgeo 1-2, 65–78.

Bazin, S., Beckerich, C., Delaplace, M., 2013. Desserte TGV et villes petites et moyennes, Une illustration par le cas du tourisme à Arras, Auray, Charleville- Mézières et Saverne. Les Cahiers Scientifiques du Transport 63, 33–62.

Bertrand, M., Duflo, E., Mullainathan, S., 2004. How much should we trust differences-in-differences estimates? Q. J. Econ. 119, 249–275.

Bieger, T., Wittmer, A., 2006. Air transport and tourism—perspectives and challenges for destinations, airlines and governments. J. Air Transp. Manag. 12, 40–46.

Bilotkach, V., Fageda, X., Flores-Fillol, R., 2010. Scheduled service versus personal transportation: the role of distance. Reg. Sci. Urban Econ. 40 (1), 60–72.

Bonnafous, A., 1987. The regional impact of the TGV. Transportation 14 (2), 127–137.

Cascetta, E., Papola, A., Pagliara, F., Marzano, V., 2011. Analysis of mobility impacts of the high-speed Rome-Naples rail link using within day dynamic mode service choice models. J. Transp. Geogr. 19 (4), 635–643.

Chen, Z., Haynes, K., 2012. Tourism industry and high speed rail, is there a linkage: evidence from China's high speed rail development. In: ASRDLF 2012 Conference Special Session on High Speed Rail, Tourism and Territories, 9–11 July, Belfort, France.

Chen, Z., Haynes, K.E., 2015. Impact of high-speed rail on international tourism demand in China. Appl. Econ. Lett. 22 (1), 57–50.

Cheng, Y.-H., 2010. High-speed rail in Taiwan: new experience and issues for future development. Transp. Policy 17 (2), 51–63.

Chew, J., 1987. Transport and tourism in the year 2000. Tour. Manag. 8 (2), 83–85.

Chung, J.Y., Whang, T., 2011. The impact of low cost carriers on Korean Island tourism. J. Transp. Geogr. 19, 1335–1340.

Clavé, S., Gutiérrez, A., Saladi, O., 2015. High-speed rail services in a consolidated Catalan Mediterranean mass coastal destination: a causal approach. In: Workshop on High Speed Rail and the City: Tourism and Dynamics Around Stations, January 21–23, 2015, Paris.

Clever, R., Hansen, M., 2008. Interaction of air and high-speed rail in Japan. Transp. Res. Rec. 2043, 1–12.

Delaplace, M., Perrin, J., 2013. Multiplication des dessertes TGV et Tourismes urbains et d'affaires, regards croisés sur la Province et l'Île-de-France. Recherche Transport et Sécurité 29, 177–191.

Delaplace, M., Pagliara, F., Perrin, J., Mermet, S., 2014. Can high speed rail foster the choice of destination for tourism purpose? In: EWGT2013—16th Meeting of the EURO Working Group on Transportation, Procedia—Social and Behavioral Sciences, 111, pp. 166–175.

Delaplace, M., Pagliara, F., La Pietra, A., 2016. Does high-speed rail affect destination choice for tourism purpose? Belgeo 3.

Della Corte, V., Sciarelli, M., Cascella, C., Del Gaudio, G., 2013. Customer satisfaction in tourist destination: the case of tourism offer in the City of Naples. J. Invest. Manag. 4, 39–50.

Dobruszkes, F., 2011. High-speed rail and air transport competition in western Europe: a supply-oriented perspective. Transp. Policy 18, 870–879.

Dobruszkes, F., Givoni, M., 2013. Competition, integration, substitution: myths and realities concerning the relationship between high-speed rail and air transport in Europe. In: Budd, L., Griggs, S., Howarth, D. (Eds.), Sustainable Aviation Futures. Emerald, Bradford, UK.

Dobruszkes, F., Mondou, V., 2013. Aviation liberalization as a means to promote international tourism: the EU–Morocco case. J. Air Transp. Manag. 29, 23–34.

Dobruszkes, F., Dehon, C., Givoni, M., 2014. Does European high-speed rail affect the current level of air services? An EU-wide analysis. Transp. Res. A 69, 461–475.

Donzelli, M., 2010. The effect of low-cost air transportation on the local economy evidence from Southern Italy. J. Air Transp. Manag. 16, 121–126.

Edwards, N., 2012. High Speed Rail Benefits That Add Up. Report for the Australian Greens.

Ellwanger, G., Wilckens, M., 1993. Hochgeschwindigkeitsverkehr gewinnt an Fahrt (high-speed traffic booms). Internationales Verkehrswesen 45 (5), 284–290.

Feliu, J., 2012. High-speed rail in European medium-sized cities: stakeholders and urban development. J. Urban Plann. Dev. 138, 293–302.

FRONTUR, 2015. Movimientos turísticos en frontera (Tourism at borders). Instituto de Estudios Turísticos. Available at http://www.iet.tourspain.es. (Accessed May 28, 2018).

Fu, X., Zhang, A., Lei, Z., 2012. Will China's airline industry survive the entry of high-speed rail? Res. Transp. Econ. 35 (1), 13–25.

Fu, X., Oum, T.H., Yan, J., 2014. An analysis of travel demand in Japan's inter-city market: empirical estimation and policy simulation. J. Transp. Econ. Policy 48 (1), 97–113.

Givoni, M., Banister, D., 2006. Airline and railway integration. Transp. Policy 13, 386–397.

Givoni, M., Dobruszkes, F., 2013. A review of ex-post evidence for mode substitution and induced demand following the introduction of high-speed rail. Transp. Rev. 33 (6), 720–742.

Guirao, B., Campa, J.L., 2016. Should implications for tourism influence the planning stage of a new HSR network? The experience of Spain. Open Transp. J. 2016 (10), 22–34.

Hernández, A., Jiménez, J.L., 2014. Does high-speed rail generate spillovers on local budgets. Transp. Policy 35, 211–219.

Jiménez, J.L., Betancor, O., 2012. When trains go faster than planes: the strategic reaction of airlines in Spain. Transp. Policy 23, 34–41.

Kappes, J.W., Merkert, R., 2013. Barriers to entry into European aviation markets revisited: a review and analysis of managerial perceptions. Transp. Res. E 571, 58–69.

Khadaroo, J., Seetanah, B., 2007. Transport infrastructure and tourism development. Ann. Tour. Res. 34, 1021–1032.

Khadaroo, J., Seetanah, B., 2008. The role of transport infrastructure in international tourism development: a gravity model approach. Tour. Manag. 29, 831–840.
Klein, O., 1997. Le TGV-Atlantique et les évolutions de la mobilité: entre crise et concurrence. Les Cahiers Scientifiques des Transports 32, 57–83.
Kurihara, T., Wu, L., 2016. The impact of high speed rail on tourism development: a case study of Japan. Open Transp. J, 35–44.
Lee, J.K., Yoo, K.E., Jung, S.Y., 2012. A study on the effect of high-speed railway launch to the air passengers' mode choice behaviour. In: Paper presented at the 16th ATRS World Conference, Tainan, Taiwan.
Martín, J.C., Nombela, G., 2008. Microeconomic impacts of investments in high speed trains in Spain. Ann. Reg. Sci. 41, 715–733.
Martin, C.A., Witt, S.F., 1988. Substitute prices in models of tourism demand. Ann. Tour. Res. 15, 255–268.
Masson, S., Petiot, R., 2009. Can the high speed rail reinforce tourism attractiveness? The case of the high speed rail between Perpignan (France) and Barcelona (Spain). Technovation 29 (9), 611–617.
Moyano, A., Coronado, J., Garmendia, M., 2016. How to choose the most efficient transport mode for weekend tourism journeys: an HSR and private vehicle comparison. Open Transp. J. 10 (Suppl. 1, M8), 84–96.
Murakami, J., Cervero, R., 2012. High-Speed Rail and Economic Development: Business Agglomerations and Policy Implications. UC Berkeley University of California Transportation Center UCTC.
Padilla, A.O., Rodríguez, D.B., Aracil, P.F., Morote, G.F., Galiano, J.C.S., 2016. High speed rail passenger profile in sun and beach tourism destinations: the case of Alicante (Spain). Open Transp. J. 10, 97–107.
Pagliara, F., Vassallo, J.M., Roman, C., 2012. High-speed rail versus air transportation, case study of Madrid-Barcelona, Spain. Transp. Res. Rec. 2289, 10–17.
Pagliara, F., La Pietra, A., Gomez, J., Vassallo, J.M., 2015. High speed rail and the tourism market: evidence from the Madrid case study. Transp. Policy 37, 187–194.
Pagliara, F., Mauriello, F., Garofalo, A., 2017. Exploring the interdependences between high speed rail systems and tourism: some evidence from Italy. Transp. Res. A, 300–308.
Rey, B., Myro, R., Galera, A., 2011. Effect of low-cost airlines on tourism in Spain, a dynamic panel data model. J. Air Transp. Manag. 17, 163–167.
Román, C., Espino, R., Martín, J.C., 2007. Competition of high-speed train with air transport: the case of Madrid–Barcelona. J. Air Transp. Manag. 13, 277–284.
Saladié, O., Clavé, S.A., Gutiérrez, A., 2016. Measuring the influence of the camp de Tarragona high-speed rail station on first-time and repeat tourists visiting a coastal destination. Belgeo (3).
Suh, S., Keun-yul, Y., Jeon-Hyun, K., 2005. Effects of Korean Train Express (KTX) Operation on the National Transport System. In: Proceedings of the Eastern Asia Society for Transportation Studies. Vol. 5, pp. 175–189.
Sun, Y.Y., Lin, Z.-W., 2018. Move fast, travel slow: the influence of high-speed rail on tourism in Taiwan. J. Sustain. Tour. 26 (3), 433–450.
Taniguchi, M., 1992. High speed rail in Japan: a review and evaluation of the Shinkansen Train. In: University of California Working Paper UCTC, No. 103.
UNWTO, 2015. World Tourism Organization. Online Statistics. Available at http://www.unwto.org. (Accessed May 28, 2018).
Vickerman, R., 1997. High-speed rail in Europe: experience and issues for future development. Ann. Reg. Sci. 31, 21–38.
Wu, J., 2013. The financial and economic assessment of China's high speed rail investments: a preliminary analysis. In: Discussion Paper 28, International Transport Forum, Paris.
Zhang, Q., Yang, H., Wang, Q., Zhang, A., 2014. Market power and its determinants in the Chinese airline industry. Transp. Res. A Policy Pract. 64, 1–13.

CHAPTER

7

Airport Choice

Tim RYLEY

Griffith University, Nathan, Brisbane, QLD, Australia

CHAPTER OUTLINE

7.1 INTRODUCTION

Individual travel motivations, particularly for leisure trips, relate to aspects such as location of friends and relatives, social commitments, flexibility of travel, and preferences for a particular surface access mode and airline. Aggregate leisure travel demand can change for a range of reasons including air fare fluctuations, specific events such as terrorism attacks, and wider trends of holiday destination preferences. Tourism opportunities for individuals have increased following the global rise in low-cost carriers. Typically, tourists can travel more cheaply and to more destinations. As secondary airports around metropolitan areas have developed, so travellers have a wider range of airports to choose from.

Individual travellers can be grouped according to distinct market segments that behave differently in response to price changes, typically split into business (further split into 'routine' and 'urgent') and leisure (further split into 'holidays' and 'visiting friends and relations') passengers. Therefore this chapter refers to the 'holidays' or leisure component of the traveller market segment. Whilst the focus is primarily on leisure travel, it is acknowledged that there is sometimes a blurring between the leisure and business traveller dichotomy. An example is when an individual goes on a trip which covers both categories, say a week at a business event followed by a week-long holiday in the same location (see Chapter 3).

This chapter discusses the factors influencing the tourist choice of airport. Following this introduction on the background tourist choice concepts, the airport context is summarised.

Underpinning methodologies that can determine choice for air transport applications are reviewed, before discussion on a series of themes relating to air transport applications that have a focus on airport choice for tourists: the role of airport catchment areas, airport region strategic planning, and possible impacts of technology development.

The focus within the chapter is on individuals as tourists and the underlying choices they make relating to air travel. Leisure travellers typically respond differently accordingly to a range of factors, and one is life stage that as

Air Transport—A Tourism Perspective. https://doi.org/10.1016/B978-0-12-812857-2.00007-5

individuals they go through. Four specific life stages that affect air travellers were identified in Davison and Ryley (2013): prefamily, family with children, empty nesters when children have left home, and retirement. Having children appears to be the life stage with the greatest effect on travel behaviour, as travellers have to be more organised, well planned, and less flexible with the choice of holiday destinations. This contrasts with the prefamily leisure travellers that comprise market segments such as young people wanting to party, student backpackers, and dual income couples. Life stage-based market segments will typically exhibit certain tourism behaviours. For instance, tourists in retirement are still more likely than other segments to use travel agents, package holiday offerings, travel from a local airport, and return to previous holiday destinations.

There are differences between the types of tourist trip people take, from weekend breaks, through to traditional 2 week summer holidays, and to longer term travelling such as student gap years. The type of tourist trip affects the destinations. A survey of East Midlands' residents of the United Kingdom (Davison and Ryley, 2010) focused on eight of the most popular low-cost carrier destinations. The destination types covered mainly weekend breaks (Berlin and Prague), a mix of weekend and week-long holidays (Edinburgh, Dublin, and Rome), and mainly week-long holidays (Malaga, Alicante, and Faro). A further interesting insight from this work is evidence of tourists trading between city destinations so that, for example, once they have visited one such as Rome they will then try another such has Prague.

The opportunities afforded by low-cost air travel have enabled many of the population in the United Kingdom to be able to make international leisure trips. A Civil Aviation Authority report (Civil Aviation Authority, 2006) examined the impact of low-cost carriers in the United Kingdom, including the types of people who benefit. There was growth in low-cost carrier-based leisure travel between 1995 and 2005 across all socioeconomic groups, but it was greater for the higher socioeconomic groups. The amount of travel by the lowest socioeconomic groups increased from 1.8 million United Kingdom leisure passengers in 1995 to 3.0 million in 2005, but the share decreased slightly from 8.7% to 7.7%.

The range of aviation choices that tourists face need to be conceptualised, from the time they consider a holiday up to and including when they actually travel. Such choices include: Which origin airport to fly from? Which destination airport to land at? How to get to these airports via surface transport? Which airline to travel with?

For some aviation choices there may be only one option, for example, if there is only one airline flying between the origin and destination airports (sometimes perceived within an airport-pair choice framework). There is still a choice in this, whether to take this flight or the default option of not travelling. A further choice option available in some situations is whether the individual could take an alternative transport mode to flying, most typically high-speed rail (see Chapter 6).

The two key characteristics affecting most air travel choices are cost and time (see some of the aviation choice reference examples such as Hess and Polak, 2005, and Proussaloglou and Koppelman, 1999). In addition, tourists value distances to and from the airports in relation to the holiday origin and destination. Passengers are interested in door-to-door travel time not just the duration of the flight.

The complexity increases if public transport is used for either surface access trip, as tourists also have to get to and from the public transport mode. Surface access modes of public transport options include taxi, bus, and rail. The travel behaviour issues for airport access are different from other surface transport contexts. For instance, when accessing airports individuals will often not use public transport as they have to take bags with them. A further complication is that surface access trips involve other individuals that can affect the tourist air travel choice process. Principal amongst them are meet-and-greet individuals, people travelling to and from airports to see off or welcome back an air traveller, typically a family member or friend.

7.2 THE ROLE OF AIRPORTS IN THE AVIATION SYSTEM

The main focus in this chapter is on individual tourist responses as a function of demand, but there are also links to the supply side, i.e. what is on offer to the traveller. The level of supply in an airport context covers a range of interrelated factors such as the underlying cost and availability of fuel, the types of aircraft available at the airport, the application and use of technology, airport management approaches, and airport capacity development and constraints (Kazda and Caves, 2007).

Airport development starts initially with an ad hoc single airport for a city. Over time further secondary airports are built, often for technical and political reasons. There are some currently city airport systems with two airports, a traditional large airport together with a smaller secondary one. Typical European airport systems examples include Frankfurt versus Hahn, Barcelona versus Gerona, and Brussels versus Charleroi.

Whilst there is development of individual airports, typically through their own Master plans, ideally wider strategic planning is required for city regions of two or more airports to ensure a more efficient use of resources and a better provision of air services. It can be hindered by airports in one system having different owners, for example, Brussels Airport (Brussels Airport Company) and Charleroi ('Brussels South', Government of Wallonia), where there is no overarching strategic policy body.

There are now many distinct multiairport regions around the world, and airports within the system tend to complement and compete with each other. de Neufville and Odoni (2013) identify 31 metropolitan regions in the world that generate more than 15 million originating passengers. The largest five regions, in order, are London, Tokyo, New York, Paris, and Los Angeles. For the largest region, London, the development of secondary airports has evolved to enable certain airports to have particular low-cost carriers and to serve certain markets: Gatwick (African and South American destinations), Stansted (Ryanair with a focus on low-cost carriers), Luton (EasyJet with a focus on holiday charters), and London City (access to financial district).

Airports vary in terms of public and private ownership, and opportunities for growth in terms of surrounding space available and the planning process. Their focus varies across different countries and regions of the world, as documented in Caves and Gosling (1999). One example is airports in Germany, where there is a lengthy planning process often constrained by an influential environmental lobby. Another example is the Greek airport system, which has a tourism and social trip focus, and many airports have strong local authority control.

Many tourism-based airports are focused primarily on inbound or outbound leisure travellers, as demonstrated by consumers near Northern European 'outbound' airports taking summer sun holidays via Southern European 'inbound' airports. Some airports do attempt to attract both inbound and outbound leisure travellers. One example, Cardiff International Airport, is likely to always predominate with outbound Welsh travellers going on holiday, but has been trying to build up Cardiff as a city-based tourist attraction (Davison et al., 2010).

de Neufville and Odoni (2013) outline how some major airports develop specific terminals with a sole focus on low-cost carriers and thereby primarily leisure travellers, such as Paris Charles de Gaulle Airport (terminal 3). These 'budget terminals' are often in stark contrast to high specification and expensive terminals that house legacy carriers, although it does not necessarily mean that airport charges will differ between terminals. As shown previously, some multiairport systems such as London (Luton) and Frankfurt (Hahn) have this scaled up with airports specifically dedicated to low-cost carrier services.

The economic viability of airports remains important, even following a period of growth in most regions worldwide. Airport income tends to be split into aeronautical and nonaeronautical revenue streams. Airports attempt to make as much income as possible from travellers via nonaeronautical revenue, typically through retailing and parking ventures. The desire of an airport to build shopping malls and generate parking revenue is an interesting tension when there are environmental as well as economic priorities.

7.3 METHODOLOGIES TO DETERMINE CHOICE FOR AIR TRANSPORT APPLICATIONS

This section reviews a couple of underpinning methodologies that can be used to determine choice for air transport, discrete choice modelling, and market segmentation. The first methodology is the development of discrete choice models, a widely accepted technique originating from economic consumer theory that has been used in transport research since the 1970s (see Ben-Akiva and Lerman, 1985; Louviere et al., 2000). The choices are deemed to be discrete because individuals make choices from a set of mutually exclusive and collectively exhaustive alternatives. In an aviation example, the destination airport choice for a holiday would be made from a discrete set of airport alternatives.

Quantitative data input to these choice models can either come from available revealed preference data or from specifically designed stated preference survey experiments, which enable the mental processes of consumers to be considered. Modelling based on stated preferences also has the advantage of enabling the analysis of hypothetical scenarios under experimental conditions. Stated preference-based discrete choice models can be utilised to predict consumer behaviour and forecast what travellers do under changed circumstances. For example, what will happen to demand if all air fares increase by 10%, or if journey time to and from the airport falls by 20%? However, forecasts generated from stated preference data can be subject to bias, typically if respondents state something in the experiment but act differently in practice.

Initial air travel choice modelling examples tended to focus on flight choice (Proussaloglou and Koppelman, 1999; Mason, 2000), airline choice (Hensher et al., 2001), and airport choice (Brooke et al., 1994; Hess and Polak, 2005).

Over time the models have taken on more complicated structures to take account of increasing complex behavioural aspects. For example, Hess et al. (2013) incorporate the three choices of airport, airline, and surface access transport mode into one nested model structure.

The second methodology concerns market segmentation, assuming that a market as a whole does not consist of homogeneous individuals. Typically, a market is segmented using the exploratory, statistical technique of cluster analysis and according to demographic variables such as age, gender, and income. These are the type of variables examined together with transport data and air travel characteristics, which can identify aviation-related passengers who share similar attitudes and characteristics, and future policy can be targeted accordingly. Cluster analysis has been applied to a range of aviation market segmentation examples, including Davison and Ryley (2013) and Budd et al. (2014). Some of the air travel discrete choice model examples also consider market segments, typically splitting the output according to the leisure and business traveller dichotomy, such as Brooke et al. (1994), or by using survey data solely targeting a particular market segment, such as business travellers in Mason (2000).

There are complexities associated with individual decision-making and behaviour that make applications, such as air transportation and tourists, difficult to analyse and model. For instance, discrete choice models have an assumption of rational decision-making which is not always the case. In addition, cluster analysis can seem to be simplistic and not take account of complexities such as within-segment variations, atypical consumers, and the way that people can change segment over time. A further assumption of both methodologies is that individuals act independently, whereas in reality they typically make decisions linking with other people, say family and friends close to them. The emergence of social media in recent years has reinforced this influence and associated techniques such as social network analysis offers opportunities to examine the relationships between individual decision-makers. It has recently been applied to transport examples (e.g. Ryley and Zanni, 2013), and so could be expanded into air transport and tourism research.

The quality of data collected is important for the outcomes of the methodological techniques to be applied, whether it is qualitative or quantitative in nature. Collecting new and original aviation data can mean that some difficulties arise if it is undertaken at an airport. Security procedures mean that it can be hard to access an airport, and the survey locations within terminals need to be considered to ensure a sample without bias. For instance, surveys need to be undertaken across a full section of terminals and departure gates to ensure a representative range of destinations are covered. They should also cover wider periods of time, as behaviour often changes across days of the week as well as months and seasons over a year.

Having the data collection effort away from airports, say direct targeting of households, can be easier and ensure a wider cross-section of the population, although some of the sample may be infrequent flyers or individuals who have never flown (for a discussion of these groups, see Chapter 4). Recent technological developments, such as information recorded on mobile devices and the associated big data capability will enable a greater quantity and a higher quality of data, and enable more advanced methodologies and improves outcomes for air transport and tourism applications. Despite the opportunities offered by big data, sample representativeness will still need to be ensured and appropriate analytical techniques applied in order to make the most of the expanded data.

7.4 AIR TRANSPORT APPLICATIONS WITH A FOCUS ON AIRPORT CHOICE FOR TOURISTS

This section provides more focus on themes bringing together air transportation applications with a focus on airport choice for tourists. Initially, the methodologies applied (choice modelling and clustering market segments) are considered, before a range of relevant themes are discussed. These cover the role of airport catchment areas, airport region strategic planning, and possible impacts of technology development.

7.4.1 Choice Modelling Case Studies

Many studies focus on tourists within the more general leisure trip market segment, as opposed to business travellers. One example is the stated preference choice modelling study by Proussaloglou and Koppelman (1999), based on telephone survey data of respondents in Chicago and Dallas. They developed a choice framework consisting of air carrier, flight schedule, and fare class and determined that leisure trip-makers have a lower willingness to pay for airline offerings, such as a frequent-flyer programme, than business travellers. A stated preference choice modelling study of business travellers by Mason (2000) provided insights into leisure trip-makers. It was demonstrated that business travellers from small-to-medium companies are attracted to low-cost carriers, showing that it is not just leisure trip-makers using this airline type.

A number of more specific airport choice studies have been undertaken, again covering business and leisure travellers. A particularly interesting case study is for the multiairport region of San Francisco (Hess and Polak, 2005). They studied the following three San Francisco airports (using 1995 data): San Francisco International (15 million passengers, 56%), Oakland International (7.7 million passengers, 29%), and San Jose Municipal (4.2 million passengers, 16%). There three significant attributes affecting choice are fare, frequency, and access journey time. Those not significant are access journey cost, flight time, number of operators on route, aircraft size, and airport on-time performance. Results were further split by resident and visitor passenger, in addition to the leisure and business traveller dichotomy. One outcome identified was a higher relative desire for greater daily flight frequencies by visitor leisure travellers than resident leisure trip-makers.

7.4.2 Clustering Market Segments of Tourists

Passengers naturally have a strong preference for the nearest airport, but passengers do trade between airports, especially if they have had a good previous experience. Parking costs and departure time can be more influential than flight cost, as shown by survey results split by market segment within Davison and Ryley (2010) from residents of the East Midlands region of the United Kingdom. The 'employed frequent flyers' and 'less mobile low earners' showed a particular preference for an early flight, whereas the more price sensitive 'retired annual holiday makers' preferred lower parking costs.

As also documented in Davison and Ryley (2010), these market segments have tourism preferences. 'Retired annual holiday makers' and 'retiring frequent flyer' segments did not mind returning to locations they have visited before and had been discouraged from flying due to recent changes in airport security. 'Frequent flyer' segments were demonstrated to be least satisfied by destinations from nearest regional airport and more likely to holiday abroad rather than in the United Kingdom. Perhaps a future trend could be the promotion of holidaying domestically rather than abroad (the so-called staycation—see Davison and Ryley, 2016 for further discussion), to infrequent flyers on environmental or financial grounds, if the cost of air travel increases.

7.4.3 Airport Catchment Areas

Passengers are willing to travel long distances to access airports, as documented by Ryley and Davison (2008). Most residents of the East Midlands region of the United Kingdom have used the local airports (East Midlands Airport, 88% and Birmingham International Airport, 79%), but it is of interest that many have also travelled further to access the London airports (Heathrow, 67%; Gatwick, 63%; Luton, 58%; and Stansted, 44%). This is typically a journey of between 1 and 2h travel time, with all London airports over 80 miles away. Many airports such as those in London now have large overlapping catchment areas. The spatial dimension of this has been demonstrated visually by 120-min mapping (using isochrones) of selected UK airports (Wiltshire, 2018). Thelle and Sonne (2018) have demonstrated that almost two-thirds of Europeans live within a two-hour drive of at least two airports, further demonstration of overlapping catchment areas accordingly and a high degree of choice in a dynamic airport system. Catchment areas can be measured by a range of indicators, for example, distance, travel time, and travel cost, and there is scope for further spatial analysis of this concept.

The catchment areas of airports are important from both an economic and environmental perspective. Future faster connections for passengers, say through a new public transport line or road building scheme, can lead to an increased airport catchment area. Depending on the type of surface access transport opportunities, the split can be more environmentally friendly and promoted accordingly. In determining future UK airport expansion between Heathrow and Gatwick airports (in the end Heathrow was recommended by the Government-appointed Commission), both airports presented plans with improved environmental surface access modal share, through further or newly developed public transport routes via High-Speed Rail and other train/bus service developments, to increase the catchment area (Ryley and Zanni, 2015b).

7.4.4 Airport Region Strategic Planning

Aviation strategic planning is often undertaken by regional policy makers in order to ensure efficient airport development. Recommendations for policy makers in the Australian state of Queensland (Donnet et al., 2018), which has tourism as one of the main industries, are based on US State examples. The States of Florida (CFASPP—Continuing Florida Aviation Systems Planning Process) and California (CASP—California Aviation System Plan) plans have clearly defined aviation strategies that assist integrated surface transport systems and funding allocations.

The study by Donnet et al. (2018) also identifies a clear airport hierarchy within Queensland, split between the North and South East regions of the State, the latter being the main focal point. The underlying concern behind the investigation is that the primary airport in Queensland, Brisbane, faces strong competition from the two major international airports of Sydney and Melbourne, which have strong State-based support. The tourism decision-making of passengers, including their airport entry point to Australia whether Sydney, Melbourne, or Brisbane, can therefore strongly influence national and regional aviation policy-making.

Any national airport hierarchy includes global and regional airports, and in different circumstances these airports complement and compete with each other. As a United Kingdom example, the regional airports of Cardiff International Airport and Bristol Airport compete with each other to some extent where their catchment areas overlap, but also have the shared goal of attracting local consumers whilst competing against the global London airports of Heathrow and Gatwick (Davison et al., 2010).

As shown by a survey-based study of passengers at the UK airport of Robin Hood Airport Doncaster Sheffield (Ryley and Zanni, 2015b), smaller regional airports are particularly focused on leisure travel, typically to summer sun destinations. These leisure travel-based airports are also more reliant on car-based travel, which tends to be the quickest and cheapest mode of transport. There tends to be a real or perceived lack of public transport alternatives. Whilst reducing private car journeys may yield environmental benefits, such strategies are largely at odds with commercial pressures to maximise the revenue potential of airport parking.

7.4.5 Technology Developments

Technological developments influence the airport choice of tourists. The potential of three technological innovations to reduce carbon emissions for airport surface access journeys was evaluated by Ryley et al. (2013). First, telepresence was considered, whereby relatives or friends could say goodbye to a traveller from home rather than travel to an airport to drop-off or pickup a passenger. Telepresence provides an alternative solution to face-to-face interactions, with remote communication between people with access to telepresence suites of dynamic video, motion-sensitive cameras, and surround sound. One suite could be located at home, the other at an airport, and they offer a more realistic three-dimensional experience than standard television viewing. Indeed, telepresence images are already being used at some airports for wayfinding. Telepresence may be a feasible technology for the year 2020 as market presence increases and installation and usage costs decrease.

Second, techniques to encourage public transport use, more environmentally friendly than motor vehicles, were investigated using the RFID (radio-frequency identification) tagging of luggage so that the bags could travel separately from passengers. This could assist tourists from being reliant on car-based travel, although security concerns still need to be overcome. Third, software could be developed to encourage ride-sharing, which could reduce the number of vehicles travelling to and from airport and knock-on effects such as congestion and pollution. This type of software is already available, but personal concerns of sharing travel with others need to be overcome for some population segments. These surface access examples illustrate the way that technology can change the tourist traveller experience at airports across a number of ways, with a range of economic, environmental, and social benefits.

7.5 CONCLUSIONS

The focus of this chapter has primarily been on individuals and the tourism choices they make, largely related to air travel. There is a complex combination of choices that tourists have to make incorporating surface access transport modes, airlines, and airports (origin and destination).

A multidisciplinary approach has been applied to the study of air travel-related tourist choices, principally from microeconomics (choice modelling), marketing (cluster analysis), and planning (airport region strategic planning). Many relevant studies focus on tourists within the traditional wider leisure trip-maker category, often contrasted against business travellers. The growth in secondary airports, in response to demand principally driven by leisure travel, has provided a greater choice for consumers in terms of origin and destination airports, as well as tourism destinations in a dynamic system. It has also encouraged tourists to travel further to access the origin airport in their home country.

The main focus within this chapter has been on airports within the air transportation and tourism system. Most airports focus on either tourist departures or arrivals, but some locations do focus on both, whether single-airport cities such as Cardiff or multiairport regions such as San Francisco. Airports have the challenge to compete and complement each other within a regional and national hierarchy, and this should be planned in order to make it an efficient system. Airports also need to be aware of technological developments, as illustrated in this chapter, in order to stay competitive and offer an attractive airport experience for leisure travellers.

This airport choice examination has highlighted some interesting and relevant further research opportunities. Air travel choices are becoming increasingly complex, and modelling should further respond accordingly to incorporate more origin and destinations options to the choice set of travellers. In addition, there should be more of a focus on spatial analysis. When considering the geography of where travellers live, the question of the individuals benefiting from the leisure travel advancements comes to the fore, that the opportunities should be available across all sections of society and not just the wealthy elite. Perhaps amongst the airport system response in an increasingly competitive environment there should be a renewed focus on state support for regional and less competitive airports.

References

Ben-Akiva, M., Lerman, S., 1985. Discrete Choice Analysis: Theory and Application to Travel Demand. MIT press, Cambridge.

Brooke, A.S., Caves, R.E., Pitfield, D.E., 1994. Methodology for predicting European short-haul air transport demand from regional airports. J. Air Transp. Manag. 1, 37–46.

Budd, T.M.J., Ryley, T.J., Ison, S.G., 2014. Airport ground access and private car use: a segmentation analysis. J. Transp. Geogr. 36, 106–115.

Caves, R.E., Gosling, G.D., 1999. Strategic Airport Planning. Pergamon, Oxford.

Civil Aviation Authority, 2006. No-frills Carriers: Revolution or Evolution? A Study by the Civil Aviation Authority. The Stationery Office, Norwich.

Davison, L.J., Ryley, T.J., 2010. Tourism destination preferences of low-cost airline users in the East Midlands. J. Transp. Geogr. 18 (3), 458–465.

Davison, L.J., Ryley, T.J., 2013. The relationship between air travel behaviour and the key life stages of having children and entering retirement. J. Transp. Geogr. 28, 78–86.

Davison, L.J., Ryley, T.J., 2016. An examination on the role of domestic destinations in satisfying holiday demands. J. Transp. Geogr. 51, 77–84.

Davison, L.J., Ryley, T.J., Snelgrove, M., 2010. Regional airports in a competitive market: a case study of Cardiff International Airport. J. Airport Manag. 4 (2), 178–194.

de Neufville, R., Odoni, A., 2013. Airport Systems. Planning, Design and Management, second ed. McGraw-Hill, New York.

Donnet, T., Ryley, T.J., Lohmann, G., Spasojevic, B., 2018. Developing a Queensland (Australia) aviation network strategy: lessons from three international case studies. J. Air Transp. Manag. 73, 1–14.

Hensher, D.A., Stopher, P.R., Louviere, J.J., 2001. An exploratory analysis of the effect of numbers of choice sets in designed choice experiments: an airline choice application. J. Air Transp. Manag. 7, 373–379.

Hess, S., Polak, J.W., 2005. Mixed logit modelling of airport choice in multi-airport regions. J. Air Transp. Manag. 11, 59–68.

Hess, S., Ryley, T.J., Davison, L.J., Adler, T., 2013. Improving the quality of demand forecasts through cross nested logit: a stated choice case study of airport, airline and access mode choice. Transportmetrica A Transp. Sci. 9 (4), 358–384.

Kazda, A., Caves, R.E., 2007. Airport Design and Operations. Emerald, Bingley.

Louviere, J.J., Hensher, D.A., Swait, J.D., 2000. Stated Choice Methods. Analysis and Application. Cambridge University Press, Cambridge.

Mason, K.J., 2000. The propensity of business travellers to use low cost airlines. J. Transp. Geogr. 8, 107–119.

Proussaloglou, K., Koppelman, F.S., 1999. The choice of air carrier, flight, and fare class. J. Air Transp. Manag. 5, 193–201.

Ryley, T.J., Davison, L.J., 2008. UK air travel preferences: evidence from an East Midlands household survey. J. Air Transp. Manag. 14 (1), 43–46.

Ryley, T.J., Zanni, A.M., 2013. An examination of the relationship between social interactions and travel uncertainty. J. Transp. Geogr. 31, 249–257.

Ryley, T.J., Zanni, A.M., 2015b. A passenger perspective of surface access issues at a regional airport in the UK: the case study of Robin Hood Airport Doncaster Sheffield. Int. J. Aviat. Manag. 2 (3/4), 241–255.

Ryley, T.J., Elmirghani, J., Budd, T., Miyoshi, C., Mason, K., Moxon, R., Ahmed, I., Qazi, B., Zanni, A., 2013. Sustainable development and airport surface access—the role of technological innovation and behavioural change. Sustainability 5 (4), 1617–1631.

Thelle, M.H., Sonne, M.L.C., 2018. Airport competition in Europe. J. Air Transp. Manag. 67, 241–248.

Wiltshire, J., 2018. Airport competition: reality or myth? J. Air Transp. Manag. 67, 232–240.

CHAPTER

8

The Option of Self-Connection

Augusto VOLTES-DORTA, Juan Carlos MARTÍN*[†]

[*]University of Edinburgh, Edinburgh, United Kingdom [†]University of Las Palmas De Gran Canaria, Las Palmas, Spain

CHAPTER OUTLINE

8.1 INTRODUCTION

Airline passengers are always looking for new ways to save in air fares, particularly those travelling for leisure purposes that are very sensitive to airline prices. With the widespread appearance of low-cost services and the concentration of arriving and departing flights in their home bases, many travellers started to create their own itineraries by combining multiple tickets from separate bookings and handling the baggage transfer themselves. This led to the emergence of self-connectivity as a popular way to travel, primarily for individual travellers who exhibit more flexible preferences regarding problematic areas like baggage issues and/or missed flight connections (OAG, 2016). The most common example of a self-connection is a passenger transferring between two low-cost carrier (LCC) flights, since the operation of flight connections has traditionally been considered uncharacteristic of the LCC business model due to cost reasons. However, self-connections can, in practice, apply to any other cases of interline connectivity beyond the scope of airline alliances or partnership agreements—throughout the paper this will be referred to as 'traditional connectivity'.

Factors like LCC dominance and price-elastic demand point to tourism destinations as the primary beneficiaries of self-connectivity. The scarce literature on the topic, however, places more attention on the opportunities for self-connectivity for the transfer airports than for the actual destinations. This chapter aims to provide a ranking of destination airports in (or around) the Mediterranean region according to the number of potential self-connecting links to origin markets in European countries. On top of the novel focus on destination airports, there is a contribution to the literature by complementing the analysis of airline connectivity with data on actual passenger demand market information data tapes (MIDT) to weight the importance of each origin market. This is a relevant improvement since not all self-connectivity is equally important for a destination airport (some origin markets are more attractive than others). Furthermore, the analysis is not restricted to low-cost connections, as it also included other types of self-connections that passengers can make: LCC with full-service carriers (FSC) and cross-alliance FSC. This leads to a more complete picture of the travel opportunities available to passengers, from which tourism-oriented

Air Transport—A Tourism Perspective. https://doi.org/10.1016/B978-0-12-812857-2.00008-7

airports can benefit as well. To that end, a connections-building (CB) algorithm has been developed that combines (MIDT) as well as OAG airline schedules for June 2016.

The rest of the paper is structured as follows: the next section provides a brief revision of the relevant literature on this topic. Thereafter, there is an introduction to the European case study, the supply and demand datasets, as well as the CB methodology. This is followed by the presentation of results, with particular focus on the ranking of airports according to arriving self-connecting frequencies, and a discussion of the main policy and managerial implications. Finally, the last section summarises the primary findings, addresses the limitations of the model, and proposes new paths for future research.

8.2 BACKGROUND

From an airline perspective, the emergence of self-connectivity fits with the current trend of many LCCs to go 'hybrid' and adopt many elements of the business model that is characteristic of full-service network carriers, such as price bundling, codesharing agreements, and connecting flights (Klophaus et al., 2012; Morandi et al., 2015; Fageda et al., 2015; Fichert and Klophaus, 2016). LCC/hybrid carriers like Vueling or Air Berlin did offer connect flights at one time (or indeed still do) in their main bases at Barcelona and Palma de Mallorca airports, respectively. Norwegian also introduced a connecting fee to facilitate transfers between their flights at selected locations and, more recently, the negotiations between Norwegian and Ryanair to develop low-cost long-haul connections at Gatwick airport have surfaced (CNN Money, 2017). The revealed interest by low-cost operators to tap into the market of self-connections capturing some of the rents currently enjoyed by the passenger triggers in part the objective of the research.

The business opportunity of self-connecting passengers has been recently picked up by a few European airports as well, such as London Gatwick and Milano Malpensa, which developed their own platforms to support passengers travelling with a combination of air tickets where the carriers do not provide flight transfers themselves (ViaMilano, 2016). In exchange for a fee (though this can also be offered for free), self-connecting passengers at Gatwick and Milano airports are offered two basic services: (1) baggage transfer between the feeding and the onward flights, and (2) an insurance policy that covers the risk of missing the onward flight in the event of a service disruption (Gattwick Airport, 2015). In order to book these services, passengers must search for flight connections employing dedicated online platforms that present self-connecting options to the passengers automatically. This removes the need for price-sensitive passengers to undertake an additional search effort to build their own travel itineraries and extends the market alternatives provided by online booking systems that mostly report traditional flight connections.[1]

From an airline perspective, it can be expected that they support these self-connection schemes if the additional interline connectivity brings economies of traffic density to their networks (Starkie, 2007). Airports providing these 'self-help-hubbing' services stand to benefit from increased nonaeronautical revenues linked to the extra connecting passengers (Malighetti et al., 2008). However, it is also worth noting the potential benefit to destination airports, which can benefit from more indirect arrivals via self-connections facilitated at other locations.

Several factors point to tourism destinations as the primary beneficiaries of self-connectivity. First, it has long been established that tourism demand is very sensitive to prices and particularly to the cost of travel (Ben-David et al., 2016). Second, holiday travel is a demand segment that, in Europe, has been heavily dominated by point-to-point LCC and charter services with limited traditional flight connectivity (Dobruszkes, 2013). Third, there is evidence that leisure passengers are willing to incur longer travel times in exchange for lower airfares (Fageda et al., 2015; OAG, 2016). Fourth, the advertising of self-connectivity at Gatwick and Milano airports is heavily targeted to Mediterranean tourism destinations, even those that are already well served by direct flights such as Barcelona or Rome (ViaMilano, 2016).

The scarce literature on the topic, however, places more attention on the opportunities for self-connectivity for the transfer airports (where the self-connection takes place) than for the other airports included in the itinerary. The most common methodological approach is to develop a CB algorithm that works with airline schedules to find competitive travel alternatives (Halpern and Graham, 2015). These algorithms search for all possible flight connections between predefined origin and destination airports. A simple approach to determine the validity of the identified connections is to set minimum and maximum connecting times (Seredynski et al., 2014). In this way, Malighetti et al. (2008) found that the majority of airline connectivity in Europe occurs outside the boundaries of airline alliances. Zeigler et al. (2017) also reached the same conclusion by showing that the potential interline connectivity between

[1] These search costs will, however, decrease as sites like Skyscanner now offer self-connections and unprotected flight transfers in their online search engines.

LCCs is higher than the traditional connectivity of scheduled FSCs in intra-European routes. They also argued that local policy makers should take into consideration these connectivity effects in the design of incentive contracts for LCCs at regional airports due to the ability to boost both originating and connecting traffic.

From the perspective of the hub airports, Malighetti et al. (2008) concluded that airports that are relatively 'central' to the European network were the ones with the highest potential for nontraditional connectivity (e.g. Munich, Paris-CDG, Stockholm, Helsinki). More recently, Suau-Sanchez et al. (2016) concluded that the dominance of LCC and reduced airline concentration boost airports' potential to host self-connections, whilst having a diverse destination mix is not a necessary condition. In addition, whilst long-haul self-connection opportunities are indeed available, most self-connectivity occurs in intraregional markets. Using a larger dataset of airline schedules, Maertens et al. (2016) found that the European LCC network has indeed increased its potential for self-connectivity in the last decade, and also identified Barcelona, Gatwick, and Stansted as the airports with the highest number of low-cost transfer opportunities. This paper went a step further providing information about the largest origin and destination markets by number of potential low-cost connections. Several airports serving tourism destinations appear in the top positions, like Barcelona, Malaga, Ibiza, or Catania. This indicates that the Mediterranean region is ripe for self-connectivity, as further confirmed by Suau-Sanchez et al. (2017), which also focused on ranking potential transfer airports in holiday markets.

Building on the concepts and methods developed by the studies before, this chapter provides a ranking of destination airports in (or around) the Mediterranean region according to the number of self-connecting links to European origin markets. From the perspective of airport operators and local tourism authorities, this type of analysis can be useful to obtain insights on the potential economic benefits brought by new flights, particularly if the destination is geographically isolated (e.g. island) and/or distant from major metropolitan centres (Suau-Sanchez and Burghouwt, 2012). The increased indirect connectivity brought by self-connections can improve the region's competitiveness as tourism destination (Hall, 2009).

8.3 DATA AND METHODOLOGY

8.3.1 Case Study and Datasets

The geographical dimension of the case study is delimited by the chosen origin and destination markets. The origin markets are represented by all commercial airports located in the European Economic Area. The destination markets are represented by all commercial airports serving coastal destinations in (or around) the Mediterranean region. The size of each origin market is measured by the total number of passenger bookings travelling from the relevant airport to the selected coastal destinations during the first week of June 2016. June is chosen as the sample month because its traffic level is the closest to the annual monthly average for the sample markets. Fig. 8.1 shows all airports included in our analysis according to the primary role as points of origin or destination. Data was available from these countries: Morocco, Algeria, Malta, Egypt, Jordan, Israel, Lebanon, Cyprus, Turkey, Greece, Croatia, Italy, France, Monaco, Spain, Gibraltar, and Portugal. All island destinations in these countries are included, even the Atlantic ones (Canaries, Madeira, and Azores). For mainland Spain, France, and Italy, only the airports serving Mediterranean destinations are designed as such (see the Appendix for more details).

The MIDT dataset includes 4.1 million passenger bookings in the above-defined markets obtained from the OAG Traffic Analyser. Each record contains information on the operating airlines, as well as the points of origin and destination, the connecting airports (up to two intermediate stops), and the number of passengers. The original sources of information for the MIDT dataset are Global Distributions Systems (GDSs) such as Galileo, Saber, or Amadeus, amongst others. MIDT is a common data source in the construction of airport route development reports (Halpern and Graham, 2015) and similar datasets have been employed in past studies to calculate air transport connectivity (e.g. Suau-Sanchez et al., 2016, 2017). However, the original sources of information beg the question as to whether LCCs would be adequately represented in the dataset since they are much less likely to use GDSs as distribution channel. In order to address this limitation, the raw data on passenger bookings has been adjusted by the provider (OAG Traffic Analyser) using a proprietary algorithm based on frequencies and supplied seats in each flight sector. The reliability of these adjustments was checked by calculating the overall market share of LCCs in intra-European markets that results from the adjusted MIDT data. Results were consistent with values reported by the European Commission (EC, 2014).

Table 8.1 provides a breakdown of bookings for the top 15 airlines, origin, and destination countries in our sample. United Kingdom, Italy, and Germany are the largest generators of air travel to Mediterranean destinations. Spain,

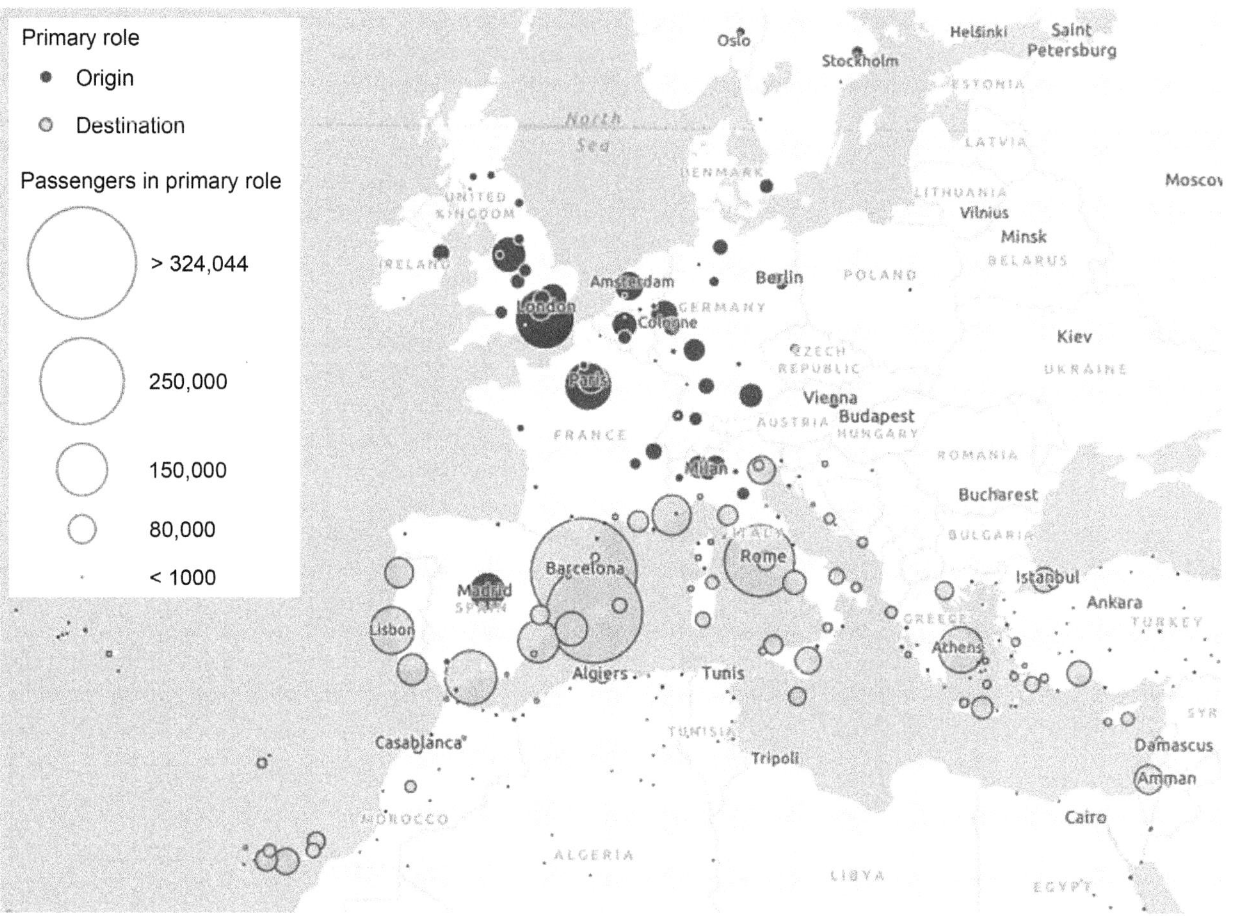

FIG. 8.1 Geographic distribution of origin and destination airports (first week June 2016). *(Source: MIDT)*

TABLE 8.1 Distribution of MIDT Bookings Per Airline, Origin, and Destination Country (First Week June 2016)

Origin Country	Bookings	%	Destination Country	Bookings	%	Airline	Bookings	%
UK	791,279	20.4%	Spain	1,416,026	34.4%	Ryanair	925,602	33.8%
Germany	606,817	15.7%	Italy	870,328	21.2%	easyJet	425,150	15.5%
Italy	605,143	15.6%	Greece	454,276	11.0%	Vueling	265,162	9.7%
Spain	492,264	12.7%	Portugal	362,413	8.8%	Alitalia	163,968	6.0%
France	449,280	11.6%	Turkey	271,287	6.6%	Air Berlin	115,772	4.2%
Greece	179,608	4.6%	France	238,950	5.8%	Aegean Airlines	112,250	4.1%
Switzerland	129,979	3.4%	Morocco	94,524	2.3%	Turkish Airlines	106,642	3.9%
Belgium	121,840	3.1%	Israel	83,781	2.0%	Jet2.com	89,633	3.3%
Netherlands	116,369	3.0%	Croatia	83,639	2.0%	TAP Portugal	88,843	3.2%
Portugal	100,591	2.6%	Algeria	56,604	1.4%	Thomas Cook	78,296	2.9%
Ireland	68,256	1.8%	Cyprus	54,695	1.3%	Lufthansa	77,445	2.8%
Sweden	59,092	1.5%	Malta	48,871	1.2%	Air France	76,762	2.8%
Denmark	52,002	1.3%	Tunisia	30,105	0.7%	British Airways	73,154	2.7%
Norway	49,223	1.3%	Egypt	28,888	0.7%	Monarch	71,031	2.6%
Austria	48,568	1.3%	Lebanon	17,283	0.4%	Iberia	68,381	2.5%
Total	3,870,311			4,111,670			2,738,091	

(Source: MIDT)

Italy, and Greece are the top traffic attractors on the European side, whilst Morocco is the top destination on the African side. As expected, intra-European markets are dominated by LCCs such as Ryanair and easyJet, which supports the hypothesis that a large number of self-connecting opportunities will be found amongst these airlines that do not typically operate transfer flights.

Further exploration of the demand dataset allows disaggregation of passenger bookings according to the type of itinerary. The vast majority of bookings (90.6%) are for nonstop travel, which is not surprising due to the relatively short travel distances around the Mediterranean. However, the amount of connecting passengers is not negligible (387 thousand per week) and represents an attractive segment of demand that destination airports could benefit from if self-connections become widespread in Europe.

The CB algorithm is built on a dataset of global flight schedules during the first week of June 2016, whose primary source is the OAG Schedules dataset. After simple data processing, the supply dataset comprises 655,987 unique records of scheduled passenger flight departures for 747 airlines that offered 89.7 million seats across a network of 2998 commercial airports. Each record indicates the operating airline, alliance membership (if applicable), flight number, origin and destination airport codes, aircraft type, number of seats, flight distance, departure and arrival times, and departure and arrival terminals (if applicable). Finally, there is also a dataset of minimum connecting times, including the airports' default values plus around 68,000 airline-specific exceptions. This was obtained from the OAG Connections Analyser.

8.3.2 Connection Builder

A CB algorithm was employed to find valid travel itineraries in the relevant markets. The parameters of the CB algorithm are summarised in Table 8.2. For each potential airport-pair combination between the sample airports (including those without MIDT passenger bookings), a search is made in the schedules dataset for all valid nonstop and one-stop flight combinations from the origin airport to the destination airport. No interline restrictions are imposed. For a traditional flight combination to be valid, it must meet the published minimum connecting times. For a self-connection itinerary, minimum connecting times are left-truncated at 2 hours. A flight combination is labelled as 'self-connecting' if either: (1) both arriving and departure airlines are LCCs (as indicated by ICAO, 2014), except the connecting services provided by Vueling at Barcelona, Air Baltic at Riga, and Eurowings at several of its German bases; or (2) the arriving and departure airlines are not part of the same alliance, except if the interline connection (e.g. as a result of codesharing out-of-alliance) is recorded in the minimum connecting times file as an exception.

First, in order to discard unrealistic flight combinations (Redondi et al., 2011; Seredynski et al., 2014; Grosche and Klophaus, 2015), maximum geographic detours and travel time increases are imposed. For airport pairs with MIDT bookings, a market-specific maximum geographic detour (ratio between indirect and nonstop flight distance) is calculated based on the real-world itineraries in the MIDT file. Second, a maximum travel time increase (ratio between total indirect travel time, including flight connections, and nonstop travel time) is calculated as the maximum travel time increase of all traditional flight combinations within a one-hour window with respect to the best weekly indirect travel time in each itinerary. The goal is to keep only the self-connecting flight combinations that are competitive in the sense that there is evidence that passengers are willing to accept these geographic detours and travel time increases in traditional flight connections. For airport pairs without MIDT bookings, the maximum geographic and travel time detours for indirect itineraries are determined by combining the individual maximum detours observed at the origin and destination airports, calculated separately from the existing MIDT records. The smallest values between the origin and destination airports will be used as the reference detours for the airport-pair itineraries without MIDT traffic. These itineraries are indeed relevant for the analysis because they signal an opportunity for the destination airport to tap into new origin markets from which they are not currently receiving any passengers despite having valid flight connections to it. The outcome of this stage is a dataset of 576,061 unique flight itineraries that the CB identified as valid travel options within the selected airport-pair markets.

TABLE 8.2 Parameters of the Connection Builder

1. No interline restrictions
2. Published minimum connecting times must be met (minimum 2 h for self-connections)
3. Maximum geographic detour per origin–destination market (calculated from MIDT itineraries)
4. Maximum travel time increase per origin–destination market
4a. Based on best weekly traditional connecting time (+ 1 h) in each individual itinerary

The next section aggregates these itineraries by destination airport and identifies the places with the highest development potential via self-connections, in terms of both available indirect frequencies and the ability to tap into additional pockets of passenger demand all over the European Economic Area. To that end, several simple indicators will be calculated: (1) Total arriving self-connecting frequencies (split between origin markets already served and new origin markets). (2) Number or 'hubs' that are linking the airport to new European origin markets via self-connectivity. (3) Hub leverage: ratio between new origin markets and number of hubs. This number provides an indication of how many new markets can be reached for each direct transport link to a European hub. To the extent a given hub is also the main base of a LCC, the results provide a measurement of how valuable it is, on average, for the destination airport to maintain its relationship with the LCCs that are creating these self-connecting travel opportunities, both within their own networks or in combination with onward carriers. (4) Coverage of origin markets: indicates the proportion of total potential European passenger demand that the destination airport is connected to. The size of each origin market is measured by the total number of passenger bookings departing from a given origin airport. This figure is split in two components: current markets (origin points already being served as per the MIDT data) and new markets (new origin points not served and only reachable by self-connection). A large increase in coverage means that the relevant carriers can self-connect passengers from large origin markets that are not currently served directly or by means of traditional connections. (5) Largest self-connecting airline (this refers to the airline that operates the second leg of the flight that arrives to the tourism destination), with an indication of the amount and percentage of self-connecting frequencies to new origin points. In most cases, this number becomes a second measurement of the potential value of low-cost self-connections to the destination airport.

8.4 RESULTS AND DISCUSSION

Table 8.3 presents the ranking for the top 10 destination airports according to the number of arriving self-connecting itineraries from European markets. Similar to the results of Maertens et al. (2016), the results reveal that airports in major tourism destinations like Barcelona, Tel Aviv, Rome, or Palma de Mallorca are amongst the ones that would receive the largest amount of self-connecting frequencies, ranging from 10 up to 16 thousand different one-stop itineraries per week. This is largely due to the strong complementarity between their home carriers' schedules (i.e. Vueling, Alitalia, and Air Berlin, respectively) with the schedules of other nonpartner airlines that create self-connecting opportunities elsewhere. The vast amount of self-connecting frequencies, however, is not particularly beneficial for the major airports due to the overlap with origin markets already served with nonstop flights or traditional connections (this is seen in the low proportion of 'new origins' over 'total' under 'self-connecting frequencies'). Indeed, large European airports are well connected to the rest of the continent. For the top three airports mentioned before, the increase in demand coverage ranges between 2.4% and 5.8%, whilst the largest benefit belongs to Ibiza Airport (Spain) with 7% (see 'new origins' column under 'coverage'). This means that self-connections arriving at Ibiza connect that airport to new origin markets that represent 7% of the total passenger demand to Mediterranean destinations. This small contribution is also seen in the hub leverage indicators, as most large tourism destinations can only self-connect to between one and two new origin markets per associated hub (see 'origins/hub' column under 'hub leverage'). Thus it is clear that the benefit of self-connections, if evaluated at the destination level, is not going to be concentrated in the large airports, despite the large number of itineraries coming in.

A second way to approach this analysis is to rank the sample destinations according to the potential to reach unserved markets. These results are presented in Table 8.4 and now include the top 20 airports sorted in descending order by the percentage increase in demand coverage from self-connecting frequencies (see 'new origins' column under 'coverage'). The figures reveal that the airports that stand to benefit the most are those in Northern African destinations, such as Morocco or Algeria, and well as Greek, Italian, and Spanish islands. Amongst the top destinations, Zakynthos (Greece), Constantine (Algeria), and Paphos (Cyprus), which are currently self-connected to unserved origin points, represent between 27% and 42% of the total European demand.[2] In these cases, most of the valid self-connecting frequencies are indeed to new origin markets so there is an interesting potential to develop these opportunities that are 'hidden' in the complexity of European airline schedules. Table 8.4 also presents how these airports have a much higher level of hub leverage, potentially reaching by self-connection between three and four new origin markets for each existing link to a European gateway (in the top cases above 10 new origin markets—see 'origins/hub' column under 'hub leverage'). Of all the different regions, Spanish islands, such as Menorca, Fuerteventura, or Lanzarote benefit slightly less due to their good connectivity to the continent.

[2] The case of Nador (Morocco) is a singular one since the airport is primarily a travel point for Moroccan migrants in the summer months, rather than serving a fully developed tourist destination.

TABLE 8.3 Top 10 Destination Airports With the Most Arriving Self-Connecting Frequencies (First Week of June 2016)

Airport	Country	Self-Connecting Frequencies			Hub Leverage			Coverage		Largest Self-Connecting Airline		
		Total	Current Origins	New Origins	New Origins	Hubs	Origins/hub	Current Origins	New Origins	Name	Freqs New Origins	% Increase
Barcelona (BCN)	Spain	17,829	15,738	2091	100	134	0.7	92.4%	4.0%	Vueling (VY)	819	9.6%
Tel Aviv (TLV)	Israel	14,718	13,811	907	85	69	1.2	90.9%	5.5%	El Al (LY)	445	6.1%
Rome (FCO)	Italy	14,508	13,013	1495	86	109	0.8	89.7%	5.8%	Alitalia (AZ)	521	9.3%
Palma (PMI)	Spain	10,972	9302	1670	134	112	1.2	95.4%	2.4%	Air Berlin (AB)	181	8.6%
Lisbon (LIS)	Portugal	9147	7557	1590	109	73	1.5	92.6%	4.5%	TAP (TP)	882	16.4%
Malaga (AGP)	Spain	8825	7034	1791	130	95	1.4	95.8%	2.0%	Vueling (VY)	197	12.1%
Ibiza (IBZ)	Spain	8797	3762	5035	148	69	2.1	91.3%	7.0%	Vueling (VY)	773	44.5%
Nice (NCE)	France	7979	7191	788	90	76	1.2	90.6%	3.8%	easyJet (U2)	191	7.5%
Athens (ATH)	Greece	7615	6748	867	114	84	1.4	90.2%	5.9%	Aegean (A3)	334	9.0%
Alicante (ALC)	Spain	7182	4767	2415	161	92	1.8	91.9%	6.5%	Norwegian (D8)	446	27.5%

TABLE 8.4 Top 20 Destination Airports With Largest Increase in Demand Coverage From Self-Connections (June 2016)

Airport	Country	Self-Connecting Frequencies			Hub Leverage			Coverage		Largest Self-Connecting Airline		
		Total	Current Origins	New Origins	New Origins	Hubs	Origins/hub	Current Origins	New Origins	Name	Freqs New Origins	% Increase
Nador (NDR)	Morocco	1141	131	1010	139	11	12.6	33.8%	57.1%	Air Arabia Maroc (3O)	708	89.6%
Girona (GRO)	Spain	1117	94	1023	132	31	4.3	32.0%	46.7%	Ryanair (FR)	593	91.1%
Constantine (CZL)	Algeria	1599	200	1399	108	10	10.8	45.4%	41.9%	Air Algerie (AH)	1206	87.3%
Paphos (PFO)	Cyprus	2799	733	2066	144	30	4.8	53.4%	32.0%	easyJet (U2)	567	74.7%
Zakynthos (ZTH)	Greece	1420	238	1182	134	36	3.7	56.7%	27.8%	Thomas Cook (MT)	327	94.8%
Hurghada (HRG)	Egypt	1595	440	1155	111	28	4.0	64.1%	26.7%	Condor (DE)	137	46.4%
Chania (CHQ)	Greece	2029	720	1309	174	45	3.9	66.8%	25.6%	Ryanair (FR)	355	65.4%
Brindisi (BDS)	Italy	1903	435	1468	106	24	4.4	71.3%	23.3%	Ryanair (FR)	642	85.7%
Kos (KGS)	Greece	2173	533	1640	160	51	3.1	72.5%	22.4%	Thomson (TOM)	399	92.6%
Tenerife Norte (TFN)	Spain	2680	1472	1208	63	14	4.5	69.5%	22.2%	Binter Canarias (NT)	486	47.7%
Lamezia Terme (SUF)	Italy	2063	791	1272	92	27	3.4	74.0%	19.3%	Alitalia (AZ)	321	47.1%
Algiers (ALG)	Algeria	5635	4152	1483	100	40	2.5	79.8%	16.9%	Air Algerie (AH)	875	23.0%
Beirut (BEY)	Lebanon	4067	3009	1058	106	30	3.5	77.1%	16.9%	Middle East Airl. (ME)	454	21.2%
Menorca (MAH)	Spain	3295	1690	1605	143	50	2.9	79.4%	16.5%	Air Europa (UX)	254	29.6%
Olbia (OLB)	Italy	3241	2231	1010	116	46	2.5	77.7%	16.2%	Meridiana fly (IG)	362	22.3%
Casablanca (CMN)	Morocco	6734	4914	1820	142	50	2.8	81.8%	15.9%	Royal Air Maroc (AT)	1425	27.0%
Lanzarote (ACE)	Spain	3742	1853	1889	157	52	3.0	82.0%	15.6%	Ryanair (FR)	377	53.0%
Fuerteventura (FUE)	Spain	2903	1356	1547	140	53	2.6	80.4%	15.1%	TUIfly (X3)	250	54.5%
Heraklion (HER)	Greece	7142	1709	5433	168	73	2.3	81.0%	15.1%	Aegean Airlines (A3)	918	68.1%
Kerkyra (CFU)	Greece	3070	1286	1784	175	66	2.7	77.8%	15.0%	easyJet (U2)	459	76.0%

Whilst the new origin markets reached via self-connections depend on the destination under analysis and its existing flight network, it is worth separating them in two broad categories: (i) smaller markets in Eastern European countries that become more accessible and (ii) new points in countries already accessible from the destination that nonetheless represent larger origin markets. More insight is provided in Figs 8.2–8.5 that show the detailed results for four case study destinations: Lanzarote (Canary Islands, Spain), Heraklion (Crete, Greece), Olbia (Sardinia, Italy), and Casablanca (Morocco).

Lanzarote airport (ACE) serves the homonymous Spanish island, located off the Atlantic coast of Morocco and with an economy largely based on tourism. With a level of traffic in excess of 5 million annual passengers, the airport is well connected directly to its main origin markets: United Kingdom, Mainland Spain, and Germany. However, self-connectivity can open the door to markets in the Baltic countries, Poland, and Iceland, whilst also helping to reach more origin points in larger markets like the United Kingdom, Italy, and Greece. Heraklion (HER) is the main airport in the Greek island of Crete and serves around 6 million annual passengers with strong seasonality. The picture drawn by the results is different than in the case before, the Eastern European markets present much less frequencies, whilst the bulk of new origin points clearly shifts to Western Europe: Spain, France, Italy, United Kingdom, and Portugal. Casablanca (CMN) is the largest of the four selected airports, with recorded levels of traffic above 8 million annual passengers and the lowest seasonal effects as it serves not only a well-developed tourism destination but also the largest city and economic capital of Morocco. Olbia (OLB), on the other hand, is a relatively smaller airport, serving around 2 million annual passengers, most of them holiday travellers. In both airports, the distribution of frequencies to new origin markets is clearly concentrated in the United Kingdom. Thus it appears that, from an origin markets perspective, budget holidaymakers from British secondary cities are the ones that could benefit the most from self-connections, particularly if departing from airports dominated by LCCs. This result makes sense due to the congestion at London Heathrow steadily pushing regional frequencies outside the UK's primary hub and the drastic reduction of domestic 'traditional' connectivity.

In view of these results, it is clear that self-connectivity uncovers new potential origin points that the airports and airlines may want to target. As presented in Table 8.4, frequencies to new origin markets by the primary carriers at each airport represent between 20% and 95% of their total self-connecting frequencies (*%increase* column).

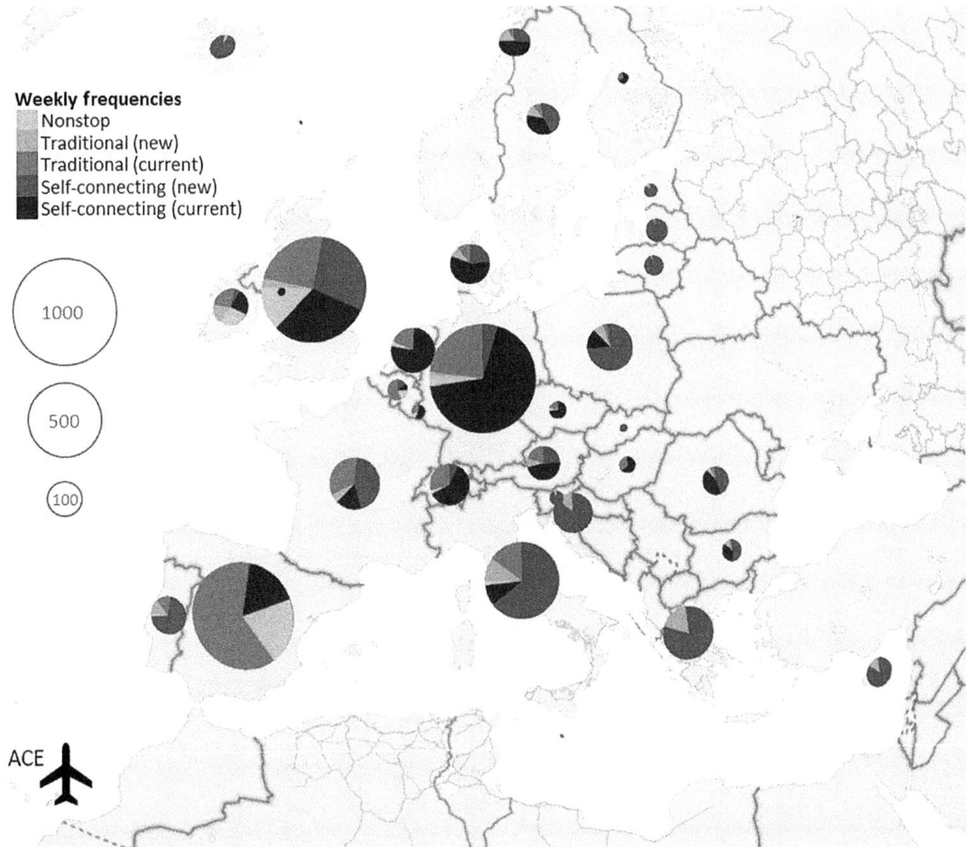

FIG. 8.2 Distribution of valid arriving frequencies to Lanzarote Airport (ACE) according to origin country.

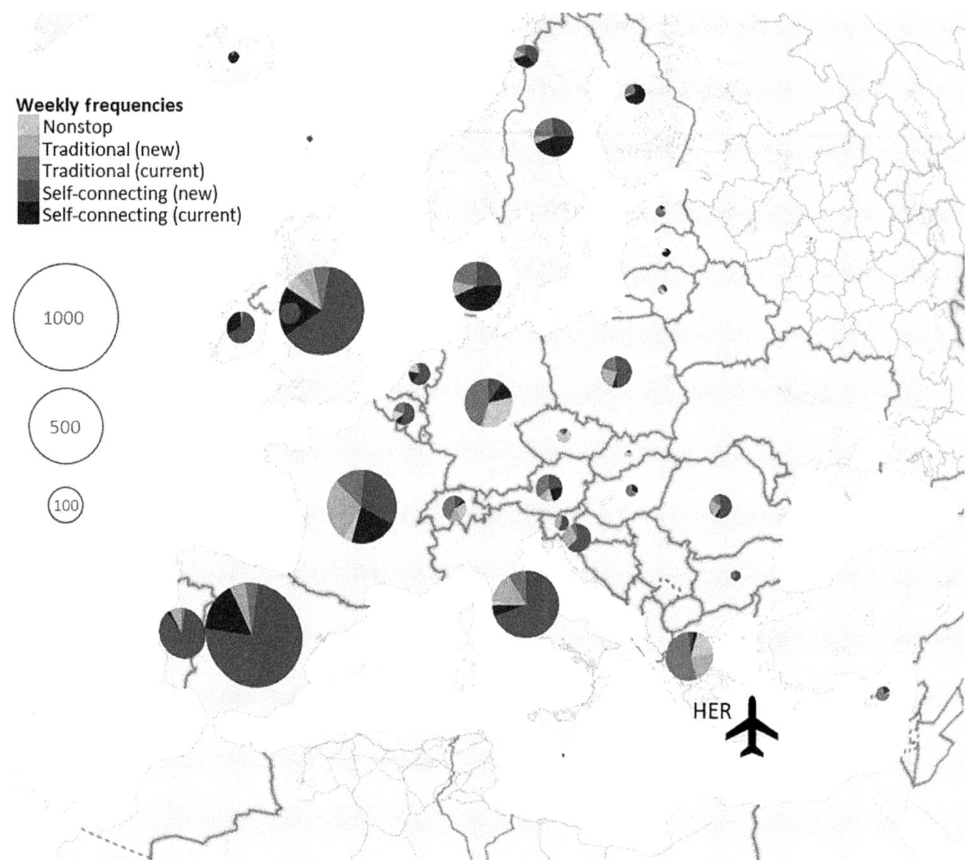

FIG. 8.3 Distribution of valid arriving frequencies to Heraklion Airport (HER) according to origin country.

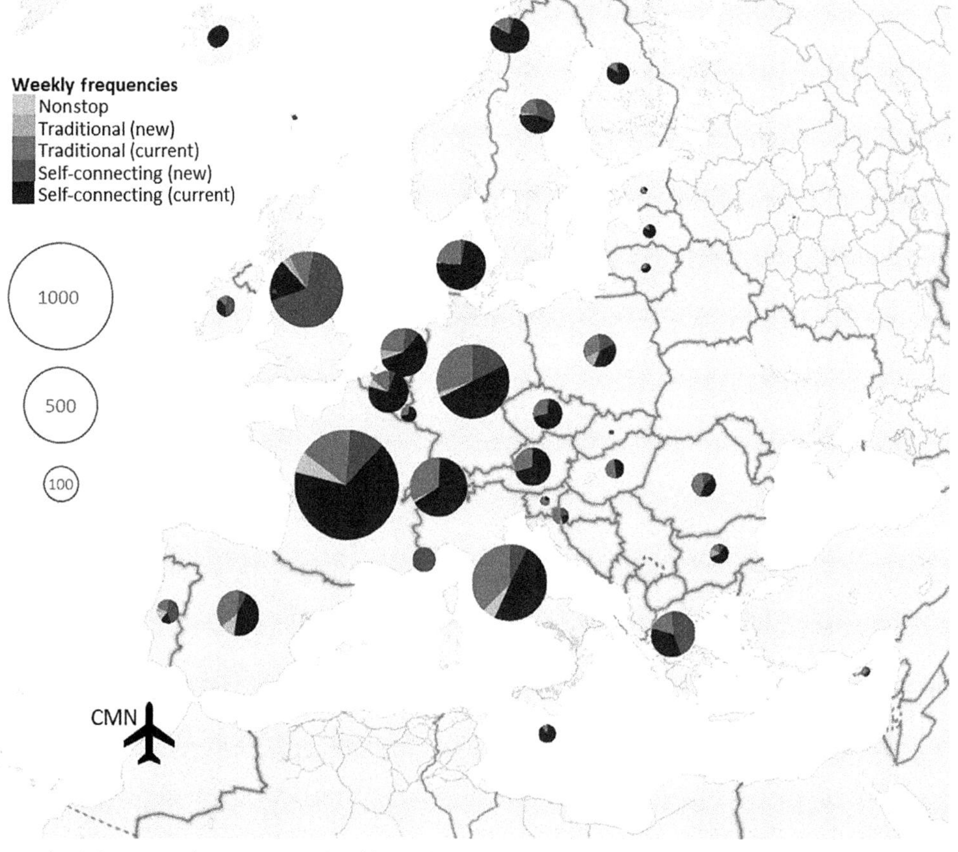

FIG. 8.4 Distribution of valid arriving frequencies to Casablanca Airport (CMN) according to origin country.

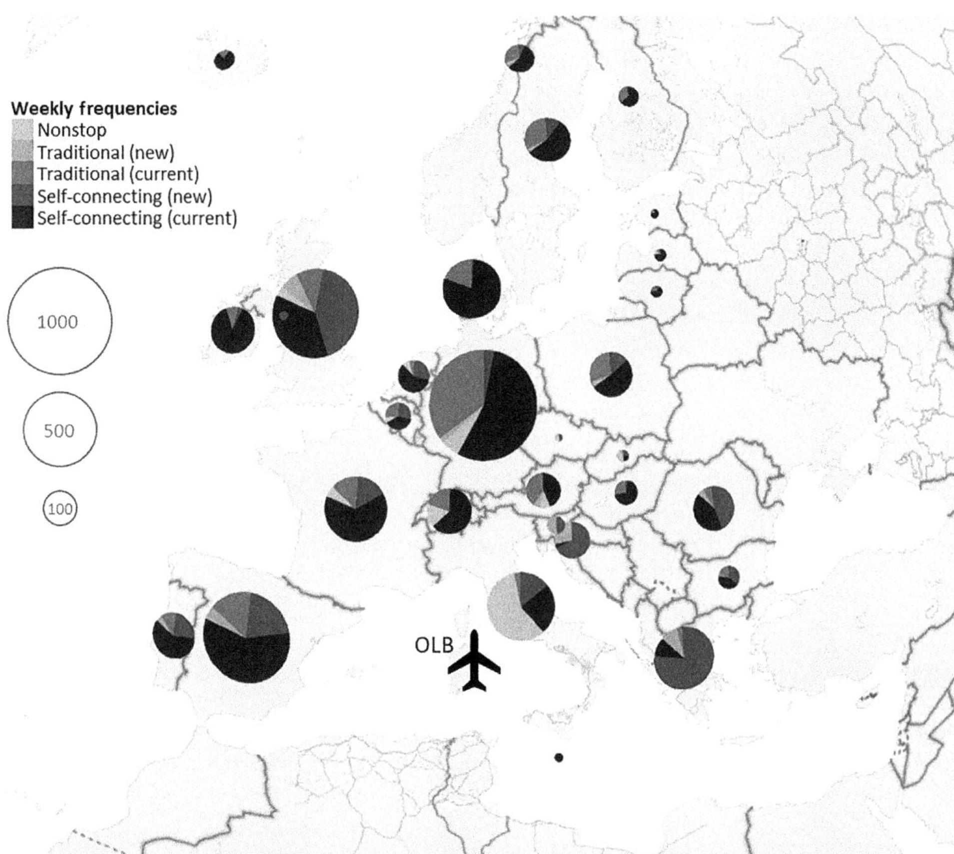

FIG. 8.5 Distribution of valid arriving frequencies to Olbia Airport (OLB) according to origin country.

In addition, note that self-connectivity is not the exclusive territory of LCCs (such as Ryanair and easyJet) and full-service airlines (e.g. Alitalia) can also be relevant in this area. Depending on the attractiveness of the markets, the airlines could use these arguments to negotiate more favourable economic conditions with airport operators or local tourism authorities. In that regard, it is also worth mentioning the case of Girona (GRO), which is second overall in the ranking. After being one of the major Ryanair bases for many years, the LCC significantly cut its frequencies at GRO in favour of the primary airport in Barcelona (Dobruszkes et al., 2017). This substantially reduced its connectivity to European origin markets. The demand coverage in June 2016 was only 32%, but self-connections can help the airport tap into an additional 46.7% pocket of demand. The fact that these frequencies are provided primarily by Ryanair helps to put into perspective the role that the LCC can still play at the airport despite the sharp reduction in the number of nonstop flights. In the current context of projected congestion at Barcelona airport, the objective of making GRO a stronger alternative to the primary destination in the region could benefit from self-connectivity, particularly if the itineraries are competitive in terms of pricing, and access times to Barcelona are improved with the opening of the new high-speed rail station at GRO airport that is projected.

8.5 CONCLUSION

This chapter aims to provide a ranking of airport destinations in (or around) the Mediterranean region according to the increase in indirect connectivity to origin markets created by the availability of self-connecting travel options for leisure passengers. The paper aims to fill a gap in the literature by shifting the focus on the analysis from the intermediate airports (where the self-connection takes places) to the destination airport. Furthermore, the analysis is not restricted to low-cost connections, but also includes other types of self-connections that passengers can make, such as low cost with full service. In order to judge the attractiveness of each new origin market, data on actual passenger demand (MIDT) for June 2016 is combined with OAG Schedules to identify the self-connecting frequencies.

Results show that airports in major destinations, like Barcelona, Rome, or Palma de Mallorca, are amongst the ones that would receive the most self-connecting frequencies, largely due to the complementarity between their home carriers' schedules with the schedules of other nonpartner airlines. This vast amount of self-connections, however, is not particularly beneficial due to the overlap with origin markets already served with traditional connections. When ranking the sample destinations according to the potential to reach unserved markets, the figures reveal that the airports that stand to benefit the most are those in Northern African destinations, such as Morocco, and well as Greek, Italian, and Spanish islands. These destinations could leverage up to four new origin markets for each existing link to a European gateway, thus enhancing their own competitiveness on account of the improved accessibility. Whilst the new markets reached via self-connections depend on the destination under analysis, it is worth separating them in two broad categories: (i) smaller markets in Eastern European countries that become more accessible and (ii) new points in countries already accessible that nonetheless represent larger origin markets, particularly within the United Kingdom.

Tourism authorities in destination cities may want to target the new 'hidden' markets with dedicated marketing campaigns. If the potential size of the new market is sufficiently large, for example, secondary UK cities, these campaigns could be carried out in the origin airports. However, for most new markets in Eastern Europe that are not particularly large, promotion of self-connecting routes could be delivered more efficiently by consolidating efforts at the relevant hubs with the collaboration of the operating airline(s). Depending on the actual figures, LCCs (and their self-connection partners) could use their 'hub leverage' to negotiate more favourable conditions with airport operators or local tourism authorities for facilitating the self-connections, perhaps with some degree of exclusivity.

The research, however, has a few limitations. First, the relevance of self-connections themselves for the development of leisure travel in Europe may be diluted in the future by LCCs actually incorporating these opportunities into their own menu of services rather than let the passengers or intermediate airports capture these rents via self-connecting platforms. For example, Ryanair is currently piloting connections between its own flights at several of its European bases and news has surfaced of negotiations with other major LCCs to facilitate interline connectivity as well. From a methodological perspective, it is also worth noting that our definition of self-connections does not rely on comprehensive information on existing interline agreements, such as those provided in IATA databases that were not available to the researchers. Whilst that information is generally transparent and can be easily found in the relevant airlines' websites, further research should employ a consistent source of data to improve the accuracy of our estimates. Another suggestion for further research is to expand the scope or analysis to long-haul markets, such as those between Europe and America or Asia-Pacific, where there are low-cost airlines already operating (like Norwegian at Gatwick or Iberia/Level in Barcelona) in strong competition with established network carriers. The prospect of saving in air fares by means of self-connections between low-cost airlines can also make this travel option popular in long-haul markets.

References

Ben-David, N., Teitler-Regev, S., Tillman, A., 2016. What is the optimal number of hotel rooms: spain as a case study. Tour. Manag. 57, 84–90.

CNN Money, 2017. Norwegian Eyes Low-Cost Airline Pact With Ryanair and Easyjet. (1 February).

Dobruszkes, F., 2013. The geography of European low-cost airline networks: a contemporary analysis. J. Transp. Geogr. 28, 75–88.

Dobruszkes, F., Givoni, M., Vowles, T., 2017. Hello major airports, goodbye regional airports? Recent changes in European and US low-cost airline airport choice. J. Air Transp. Manag. 59, 50–62.

EC, 2014. New State Aid Rules for a Competitive Aviation Industry. In: Competition Policy Brief February 2014. European Commission.

Fageda, X., Suau-Sanchez, P., Mason, K., 2015. The evolving low-cost business model: network implications of fare bundling and connecting flights in Europe. J. Air Transp. Manag. 42, 289–296.

Fichert, F., Klophaus, R., 2016. Self-connecting, codesharing and hubbing among European LCCs: from point-to-point to connections? Res. Transp. Business Manag. 21, 94–98.

Gattwick Airport, 2015. Available at http://www.gatwickairport.com/at-the-airport/flight-connections/gatwick-connects/. (Accessed March 8, 2016).

Grosche, T., Klophaus, R., 2015. Hubs at risk: exposure of Europe's largest hubs to competition on transfer city pairs. Transp. Policy 43, 55–60.

Hall, P., 2009. Looking backward, looking forward: the city region of the mid-21st century. Reg. Stud. 43, 803–817.

Halpern, N., Graham, A., 2015. Airport route development: a survey of current practice. Tour. Manag. 46, 213–221.

ICAO, 2014. List of Low-Cost Carriers. Available at http://www.icao.int/sustainability/Documents/LCC-List.pdf. (Accessed April 2, 2017).

Klophaus, R., Conrady, R., Fichert, F., 2012. Low cost carriers going hybrid: evidence from Europe. J. Air Transp. Manag. 23, 54–58.

Maertens, S., Pabst, H., Grimme, W., 2016. The scope for low-cost connecting services in Europe—is self-hubbing only the beginning? Res. Transp. Business Manag. 21, 84–93.

Malighetti, P., Paleari, S., Redondi, R., 2008. Connectivity of the European airport network: "Self-help hubbing" and business implications. J. Air Transp. Manag. 14, 53–65.

Morandi, V., Malighetti, P., Paleari, S., Redondi, R., 2015. Codesharing agreements by low-cost carriers: an explorative analysis. J. Air Transp. Manag. 42, 184–191.

OAG, 2016. Self-Connection: The Rise and Roadblocks of a Growing Travel Booking Strategy, OAG Reports. Available at https://www.oag.com/self-connection. (Accessed March 31, 2017).

Redondi, R., Malighetti, P., Paleari, S., 2011. Hub competition and travel times in the worldwide airport network. J. Transp. Geogr. 19, 1260–1271.
Seredynski, A., Rothlauf, F., Grosche, T., 2014. An airline connection builder using maximum connection lag with greedy parameter selection. J. Air Transp. Manag. 36, 120–128.
Starkie, D., 2007. The dilemma of slot concentration at network hubs. In: Czerny, A., Forsyth, P., Gillen, D., Niemeier, H.-M. (Eds.), How to Make Slot Markets Work. Ashgate, Aldershot.
Suau-Sanchez, P., Burghouwt, G., 2012. Connectivity levels and the competitive position of Spanish airports and Iberia's network rationalization strategy 2001-2007. J. Air Transp. Manag. 18, 47–53.
Suau-Sanchez, P., Voltes-Dorta, A., Rodríguez-Déniz, H., 2016. Measuring the potential for self-connectivity in global air transport markets: implications for airports and airlines. J. Transp. Geogr. 57, 70–82.
Suau-Sanchez, P., Voltes-Dorta, A., Rodríguez-Déniz, H., 2017. An assessment of the potential for self-connectivity at European airports in holiday markets. Tour. Manag. 62, 54–64.
ViaMilano, 2016. Available at http://www.flyviamilano.eu/en/viamilano-transit-service/. (Accessed March 8, 2016).
Zeigler, P., Pagliari, R., Suau-Sanchez, P., Malighetti, P., Redondi, R., 2017. Low-cost carrier entry at small European airports: low-cost carrier effects on network connectivity and self-transfer potential. J. Transp. Geogr. 60, 68–79.

APPENDIX: TOURIST AIRPORTS IN MAINLAND SPAIN, ITALY, AND FRANCE

Country	Code	Airport
France	MRS	Marseille Provence
France	NCE	Nice
France	MPL	Montpellier Mediterranee
France	PGF	Perpignan
France	TLN	Toulon/Hyeres
France	BZR	Beziers
Italy	BRI	Bari
Italy	FCO	Rome Fiumicino
Italy	NAP	Naples Capodichino
Italy	PSA	Pisa
Italy	SUF	Lamezia Terme
Italy	TRS	Trieste
Italy	VCE	Venice Marco Polo
Italy	CIA	Rome Ciampino
Italy	GOA	Genoa
Italy	PSR	Pescara
Italy	AOI	Ancona
Italy	BDS	Brindisi
Italy	REG	Reggio Di Calabria
Italy	RMI	Rimini
Italy	TSF	Venice Treviso/Sant'angelo
Italy	VIF	Vieste
Spain	AGP	Malaga
Spain	ALC	Alicante
Spain	BCN	Barcelona
Spain	IBZ	Ibiza

Continued

APPENDIX: TOURIST AIRPORTS IN MAINLAND SPAIN, ITALY, AND FRANCE—CONT'D

Country	Code	Airport
Spain	PMI	Palma de Mallorca
Spain	VLC	Valencia (ES)
Spain	GRO	Girona
Spain	LEI	Almeria
Spain	MJV	Murcia
Spain	MAH	Menorca
Spain	REU	Reus

CHAPTER

9

Distribution Trends

Michael HANKE

SkaiBlu, LLC, Consulting, Los Angeles, CA, United States

CHAPTER OUTLINE

9.1 INTRODUCTION

Airline distribution is concerned with making an airline's supply available to the travelling public. An airline's supply is the product of three ingredients: seat inventory, fares, and flight schedule. The management of the industry's supply is in the midst of a significant transformation phase. The next few years may well see major changes in how airlines sell to value-seeking travellers. Arguably, the future commercial success of an airline will largely depend on how effectively it manages distribution in coming years.

Dealing with the 'standard' topics in airline distribution—revenue generation, distribution costs, global distribution system (GDS) connectivity, relationship management of third-party retail/referral channels with online travel agencies (OTAs), and meta-search engines—will not suffice any longer. This approach would be too insular and prevents an airline from successfully managing disruptive forces stemming from changes amongst travellers, technology, and the airline business. Instead, distribution needs to adopt a wider view when developing and maintaining a marketplace for its airline. At the same time, distribution also needs to be in closer alignment with related airline disciplines such as marketing, sales, product development, revenue management/pricing, e-commerce, and web customer service.

Air Transport—A Tourism Perspective. https://doi.org/10.1016/B978-0-12-812857-2.00009-9

The discussion briefly covers the history of airline distribution and then sheds light on trends in areas that the airline distribution community should anticipate moving forward by considering, in turn, marketplace growth and changes, the technology landscape innovations, traveller expectations, and airline distribution participants and processes.

9.2 AIRLINE DISTRIBUTION: A BRIEF HISTORY

The history of airline distribution is less than 100 years old and goes back to the early days when commercial passenger transport started in the 1920s. Back then, distribution was concerned with offering the airline supply to a small, wealthy demographic comprising mostly celebrities, royalties, politicians, and wealthy businessmen. Channels used to sell tickets included the phone, city ticket offices (generally accommodated in hotels to be closer to the airline's target audience), airport ticket offices and, of course, travel agencies. The latter were particularly useful in growing airlines' distribution networks due to their large geographic coverage, their experience in selling transport services to the public (maritime shipping and trains had already been part of a travel agency's product portfolio since the 1840s when the modern travel agency was born with UK-based Thomas Cook), and their ability to offer additional travel products and services.

Until the early 1950s, this ecosystem remained largely unchanged. However, with the advent of high-speed, large capacity jet transport, airline travel entered the initial stages of becoming a mass market. As a result of airlines now dealing with a much larger and growing audience, distribution had to be adjusted and go 'electronic'. This enabled airlines to manage the increased volume and complexity of inventory and pricing data more efficiently and effectively. The first carrier to move in this direction was American Airlines. It de facto laid the seeds for today's digital distribution principles with the launch of the computer reservations system (CRS) Sabre in 1964. Table 9.1 presents several key milestones and events that occurred in airline distribution since then.

9.3 MARKETPLACE GROWTH AND CHANGES

The global travel market is huge and growing. Travel and tourism supports 292 million jobs, contributes to 10% of world GDP (World Travel and Tourism Council, 2017), and was expected to generate $1.3 trillion in bookings in 2017 (PhocusWright, 2017). The top five global source markets include the United States, China, Japan, Germany, and the United Kingdom. Combined, they account for almost 60% of the total global travel bookings (Fig. 9.1).

Across all regions, air travel is growing and projected to almost double from 3.8 billion passengers in 2016 to 7.2 billion in 2035 (IATA, 2016a, b). Rising consumer demand as a result of growing economies and discretionary incomes, population growth, and the new middle class in emerging markets are all key drivers of this development (see also Chapter 2). This means that the Asia Pacific region is forecast to be the source of almost half of the new passengers over the next 20 years. Notably, China is expected to replace the United States as the world's largest aviation market around 2024, with India displacing the UK for third place in 2025 (IATA, 2016a, b). In essence, airline distribution needs to be prepared for a much more geographically diverse customer base.

Digital channels play significantly into the travel growth story. They are estimated to generate close to 50% of total travel sales in 2017 with online sales steadily growing and reaching $817 billion in 2020. North America, Asia Pacific, and Western Europe are the dominant players for global digital travel sales with Asia Pacific solidifying its lead throughout 2020 and claiming a 40% share (Fig. 9.2). The airline sector is travel's most penetrated online segment. The United States and Europe are close to plateauing with a 2017 online penetration rate of 60% and 50%, respectively. Asia Pacific is increasing much faster with half of their airline bookings expected to be generated online by 2020 (PhocusWright, 2017). A combination of factors have been enabling and driving this growth in online travel distribution (Fig. 9.3).

9.4 TECHNOLOGY LANDSCAPE AND INNOVATIONS

9.4.1 Mobile Devices

The enthusiastic embrace of mobile devices by both consumers and companies is significant and in many ways reminiscent of the internet boom years from the mid-1990s to the early 2000s. Mobile, with smart phones and tablets, is a disruptive factor and its adoption amongst travellers is high (depending on the country, it is close to or exceeds

TABLE 9.1 Historical Developments in Airline Distribution

Timeframe	Key Developments
1960s	• 1964 launch of American Airlines' in-house CRS called Sabre. • Other major CRSs emerging are Abacus (acquired in 2015 by Sabre), Apollo/Galileo, Worldspan (these three would later be grouped under the 'Travelport' brand), Amadeus, and Travelsky
1970s	• Initiated by United Airlines with Apollo, CRSs are externalised. Carriers enable travel agencies access to their CRSs by installing special desktop terminals in the latter's offices • The industry's first 'business-to-business (B2B)' information exchange and marketplace were born. Through a CRS, a travel agency could realise similar efficiencies as airlines when searching and booking tickets for their clients
1980s	• Throughout the 1980s, the CRSs evolve into more complex GDS. The emergence of electronic data interchange (EDI) standards enables the real-time communication with GDSs that now featured different types of multiple travel suppliers such as airlines, hotels, and car rentals • Over 80% of a carrier's revenue comes from the traditional travel agency sector
1990s	• Airlines launch their first official websites and, pioneered by Alaska Airlines and the former British Midland in 1995, provided travellers direct access to their reservation systems for the first time. Shoppers could now manage on their own crucial steps of the travel life cycle including search and purchase • Airlines in the United States cut travel agency commission, these decline steadily from 10% since 1996 • A new player, the online travel agency, embodied by Expedia and Travelocity enters the marketplace in 1996
2000s	• *E*-ticketing grows and represents half of carriers' sales in the early 2000s • Kayak as the first meta-search engine launches in 2004. LCC/ULCCs, meta-search engines, and social media companies become integral parts of the distribution ecosystem • The first challengers to GDSs, so-called Global New Entities (GNEs) appear on the scene in 2005. They present themselves to airlines as low-cost alternatives to the then existing GDSs. Airlines leverage them in their ongoing cost reduction battles with GDSs from which they extract discounts on distribution fees • Around 2005, airlines begin to embrace a retailer approach in distribution. Fare families with prespecified product/service benefits were offered to travellers. Air Canada was the first major network carrier to tie certain benefits such as advance seat selection, fare refundability, and baggage allowance with particular fare products. Following were branded fares and unbundled à la carte fares that have become integral to what is now referred to as fare merchandising • With the 2007 iPhone release by Apple, mobile computing goes mainstream and airlines launch their first mobile sites, giving rise to a new distribution channel
2010s	• In 2011 Google enters the travel distribution space through its acquisition of ITA, a software company that drives the launch of Google.com/Flights, a new travel meta-search engine • In 2012 IATA via resolution 787 introduces the New Distribution Capability (NDC) programme. It advocates a replacement of the old EDIFACT-based transmission with an XML-based transmission standard that enables a modernisation of the way airlines distribute their offerings. Airlines are provided with the ability to decommoditise their supply through product differentiation and brand enhancements. At the same time, third-party outlets including travel agencies are offered new rich airline content they can access • During the 2010s, major carrier groups launch various direct distribution initiatives. These aim at bypassing GDSs and capturing bookings directly through an airline's booking platform, often in conjunction with a financial incentive for the booker • Consolidation in the marketplace leads to growing hybridisation of players with mergers and acquisitions amongst OTA, meta-search engines, and GDSs

80% for smart phones, tablets range between 50% and 65%) (Fig. 9.4). In most mature online travel markets such as the United States and United Kingdom, for example, travellers use mobile mostly for search and shopping but the large majority of bookings are still handled via desktops. Emerging markets on the other hand—China is an example—do not have such entrenched booking habits. In their case, travellers have leapfrogged desktops/laptops and use mobile as their key primary devices for bookings (Fig. 9.5).

Mobile adoption is expected to climb and be driven by the 'mobile-first' millennial travellers. Interestingly, some travellers have already abandoned desktops/laptops altogether in favour of exclusive smartphone and tablet computing. Amongst global leisure travellers, this share amounted to 23% in 2015. It is therefore not surprising that some carriers such as KLM already openly talk about a 'mobile-only' strategy. Their CEO Pieter Elbers is on record for stating that 'Whatever people do, it should fit in this small machine' whilst also noting that there is even a future where customers might not visit an airline's digital property (be it website or mobile) at all but instead interact via generic nonairline owned digital platforms such as Facebook or WeChat (CAPA, 2016). For those travellers still using multiple devices—for instance, in the United States, the share of households with 3+ or 5+ devices is 65% and 33%,

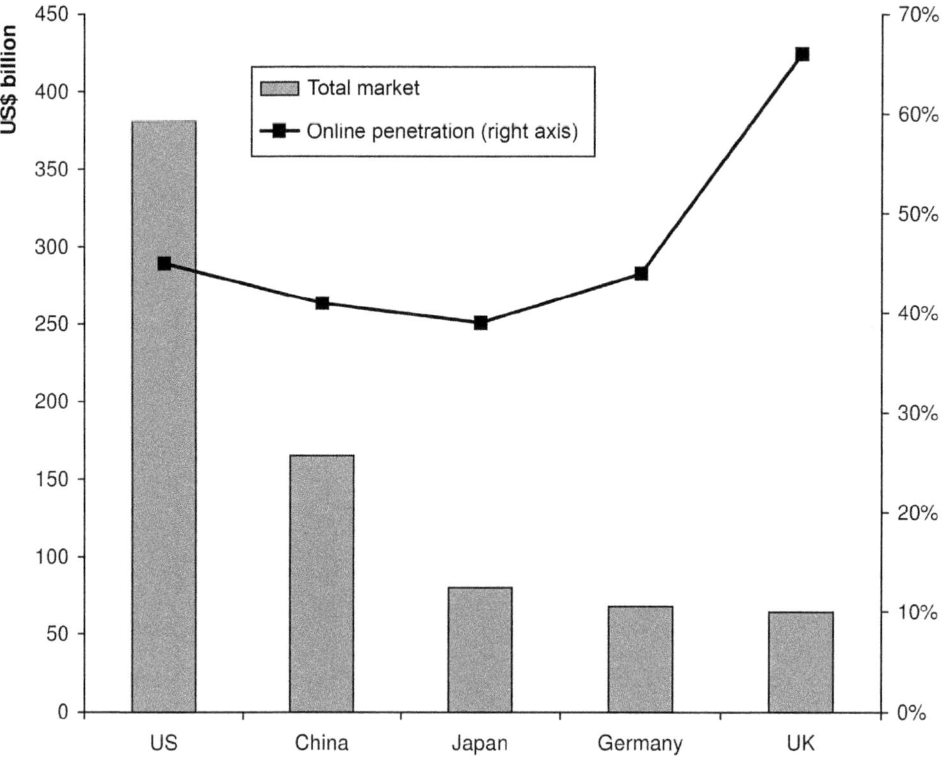

Note: These five markets account for almost 60% of global travel bookings

FIG. 9.1 Total bookings (US$ billion) and online penetration for leading travel markets (2017). *(Adapted from PhocusWright, 2017. Phocus Forward, the Year Ahead in Digital Travel, White Paper. Available at www.phocuswright.com. (Accessed August 27, 2017).)*

respectively (Expedia, 2015)—and toggle interchangeably between them, airlines need to improve the connectivity between them, thus allowing a seamless sharing of shopping activities.

It is probable that the airline distribution's current perspective of mobile as a separate channel will eventually disappear in the next few years. To be fully prepared for a postmobile world, however, many airlines have to step up and improve their mobile presence for a more user friendly environment. A survey amongst European travellers revealed many frustrations with mobile devices, the top frustration being a too small screen to see pictures and videos, followed by too slow download connection (Tnooz, 2014). Airlines need to discard their still too text heavy mobile designs and introduce visually based flight shopping and booking features. Pictures, diagrams, and maps would be key components in this context. Furthermore, voice empowered interaction via artificial intelligence applications are also likely to play a more prominent role in conjunction with intelligent personal assistants (IPAs) (more on this in the discussion about Artificial Intelligence later).

9.4.2 Big Data

Big data coexist with concepts such as 'targeting', 'one-to-one marketing', 'merchandising', and 'personalisation'. Since the advent of the commercial internet in the 1990s, the scale, speed, and frequency by which data are collected has significantly increased (and continues to do so). Today, supported by e-tag-driven technology, airlines capture traffic sources going to/from their digital properties (third-party websites, search engines, social networks, emails, advertising campaigns), they know about a traveller's geography via IP addresses, mobile and wearable devices, and they track the digital clickstream of travellers to learn of their site surfing and conversions. Additionally, airlines collect vast amounts of data from their passenger service systems including frequent flyers programmes, reservations systems, and departure control systems. Often they also purchase demographic and psychographic data from third parties and combine them with their primary data sources.

Data are highly critical for airlines. Essentially, they can be utilised for digital profiling and establishing a better insight into travellers' behaviours and preferences. Amongst other things, this allows the unique tailoring and personalisation of

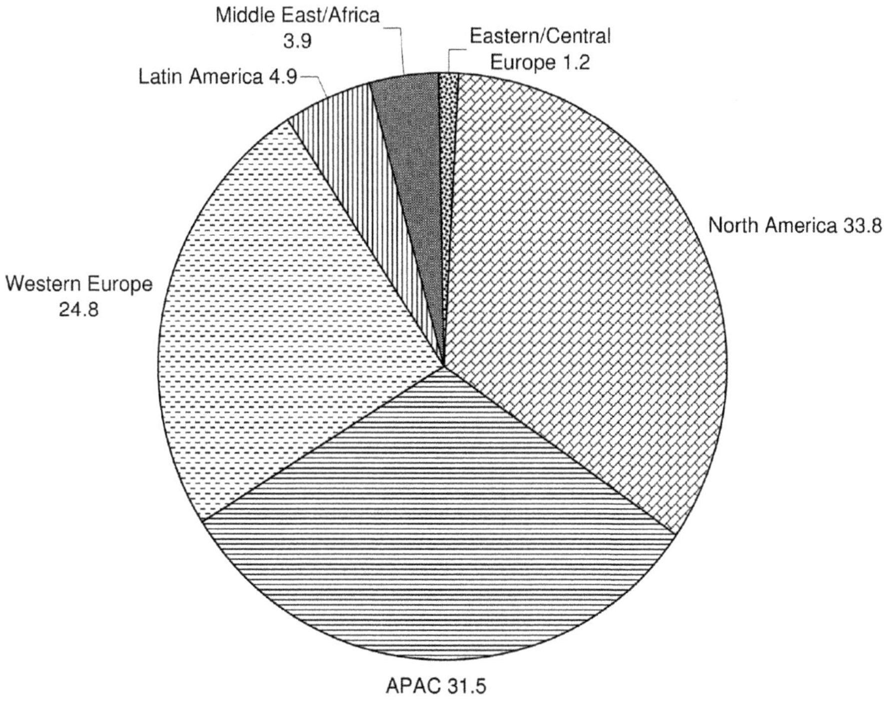

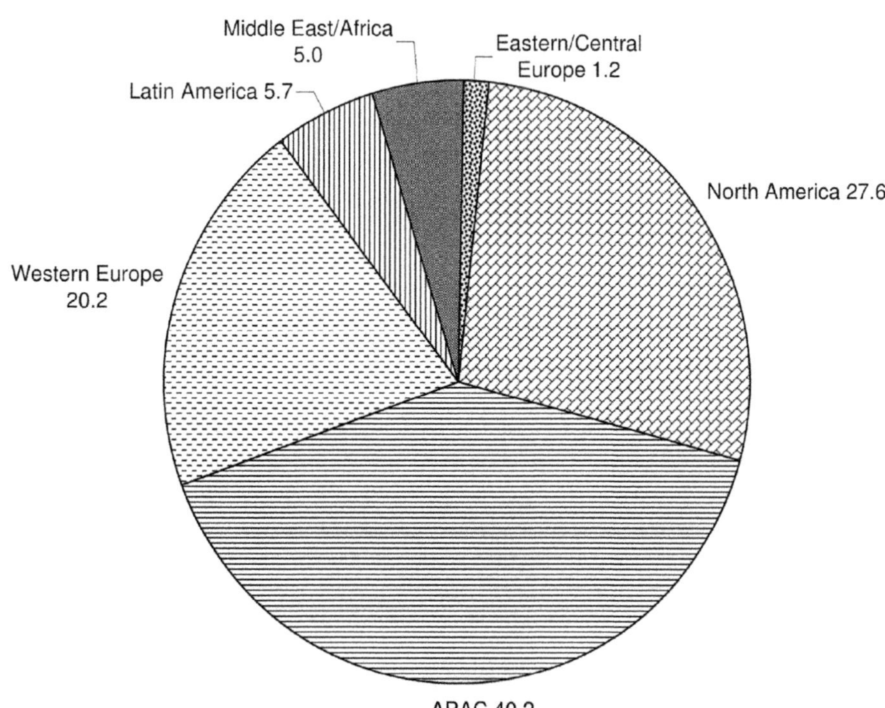

FIG. 9.2 Estimated global digital travel sales—2016 and 2020. *(Adapted from eMarketer, 2016. By 2020, Digital Travel Outlays Will Top $817 Billion Globally. Available at https://www.emarketer.com/Article/By-2020-Digital-Travel-Outlays-Will-Top-817-Billion-Globally/1014251. (Accessed September 14, 2017).)*

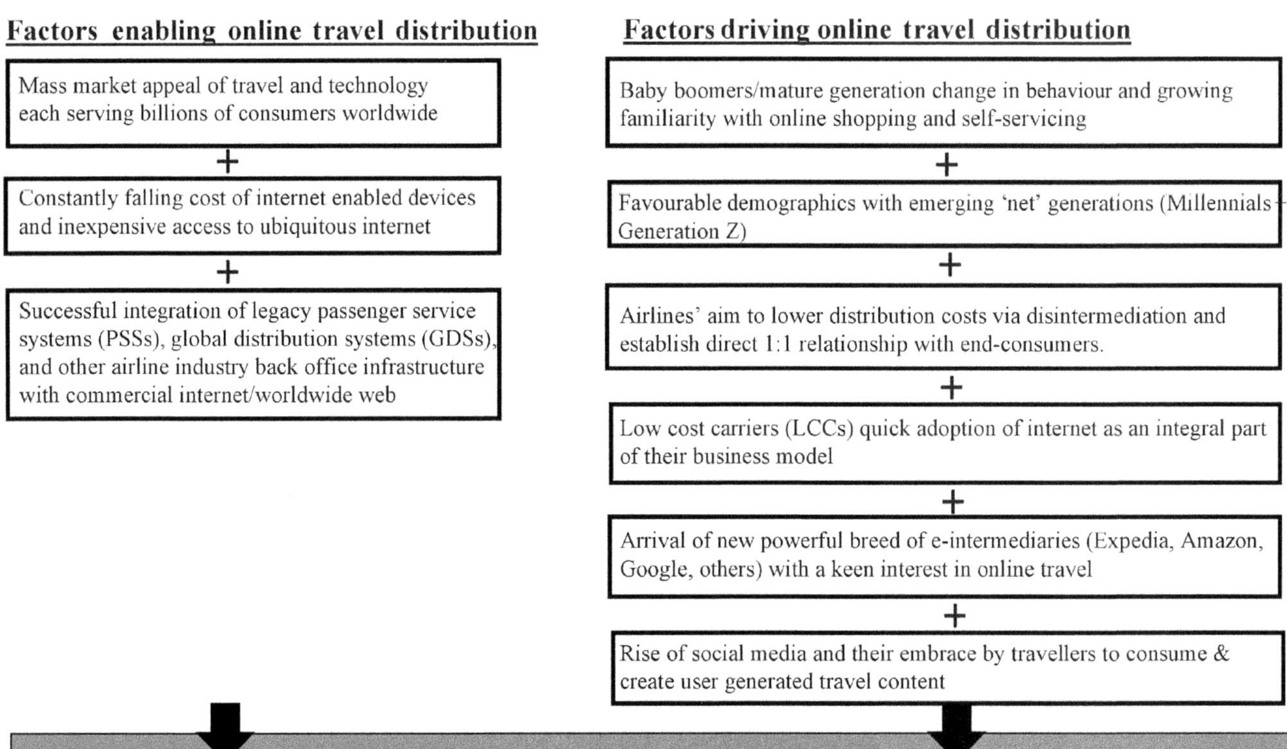

FIG. 9.3 Enablers and drivers of online travel distribution.

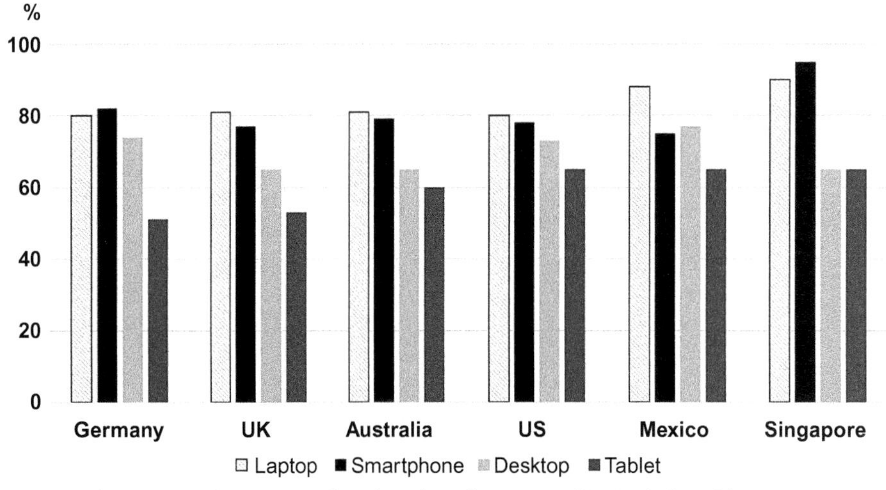

FIG. 9.4 Mobile device ownership amongst leisure travellers for selected countries (2015). *(Adapted from IATA, 2016a. What We Do—The Future of Airline Distribution 2016–2021. Available at https://www.iata.org/whatwedo/airline-distribution/ ndc/Documents/ndc-future-airline-distribution-report.pdf. (Accessed September 15, 2017).)*

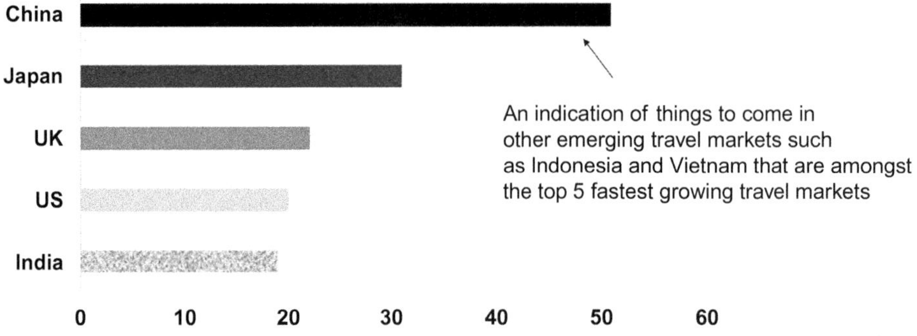

FIG. 9.5 Mobile travel gross bookings (2016)—Top five countries. *(Adapted from PhocusWright, 2017. Phocus Forward, the Year Ahead in Digital Travel, White Paper. Available at www.phocuswright.com. (Accessed August 27, 2017).)*

offerings to travellers. Areas such as pricing, products, and customer service have now become decommoditised. This development reflects a new level of intelligence applied to the airline business including airline distribution. Transforming relationships with travellers and making them more meaningful based on internet ubiquity, database connectivity and algorithm applications is a key element in an airline's future success. A growing number of carriers take cues from the online retailer Amazon, a leader in this area. Amazon is well known for excelling in the digital profiling of shoppers and offering them individualised purchase recommendations. An estimated one-third of Amazon's sales come from its recommendation and personalisation systems (Schoenberger and Cukier, 2013).

Clearly, airlines have ample data. In theory, this 'fuel' of the digital economy that has become a key driver to the many new technologies such as mobile, artificial intelligence, and the Internet of Things, should, arguably, enable the industry to deliver better service to travellers including personalisation. However, the reality is different. Take as an example the industry's customer satisfaction scores. In 2017, US airlines as an industry earned a score of 75 on the American Customer Service Index's 100-point scoring system. It is the best score the nation's airlines have ever received, but they are still in the bottom third of more than 40 sectors measured in the US economy (American Customer Service Index, 2017). Furthermore, in a survey for IATA, travellers in different countries responding to the question how effectively airlines apply personal information to deliver offers and service customers expect the highest score on a scale of 1 to 5 was 3.2 (Mexico) followed by 2.6 (UK), 2.4 (United States), and 2.1 (Brazil) (IATA, 2016a, b). Meanwhile, although personalisation has been an airline business top priority for some time now, the ability to make it happen is still weak at many carriers. In one industry survey, only one of the 23 surveyed airlines in that research claimed to provide truly personalised offers (Diggin Travel, 2017).

There are several reasons for this situation. These include multiple and disconnected airline databases, organisational siloes that prevent critical data sharing, lack of proper IT infrastructure, inadequate in-house analytics talent, and maybe also the still underlying approach of the industry to view its business through the lens of a logistics company as opposed to that of a customer service company. A case in point, albeit an extreme one, was the violent removal of passenger David Dao from an overbooked United Airlines flight last year. This was an interaction based on customer data that factored in his degree of FFP loyalty and ticket price paid, to accommodate a United flight crew who had to travel to another location.

Big data—and by extension personalisation—arguably offer airlines compelling advantages. They can sell more by selling differently and be of greater relevance to their target audience. In order to make this happen, airlines need to focus on remedying internal organisational and managerial shortcomings. The establishment of a company-wide approach for the consistent collection and single-view usage of customer data, possibly under a centralised leadership in the company ('Chief Data Officer'), will have to be an important step in this direction. At the same time, the industry needs to overcome growing concerns amongst the travelling public and legislators in many countries about data privacy and economic discrimination issues. This issue is already high on the legislative agenda in the European Union (EU). Effective May 2018, companies including airlines operating to/from/within the EU needed to take account of the tightening of data privacy laws. These may make it more difficult to collect certain data and do personalised offerings. Another concern for the airlines is the significant fines if a company is found noncompliant (up to 4% of global revenue) and the need to report data breaches within 72 h after occurrence.

9.4.3 Artificial Intelligence (AI)

Closely related to Big Data is artificial intelligence, the intelligence of machines or devices. AI has the potential to significantly affect airline travellers throughout the whole travel cycle. For example, speech recognition applications are one AI area and they are available today with the increasingly popular intelligent personal assistants (IPAs) incorporated in mobile devices. An IPA is essentially a software programme that completes certain tasks for its user, provides answers to a user's questions, and even gives recommendations. Google Assistant, Apple Siri, Microsoft Cortana, Baidu Duer, and Amazon Alexa are all examples and the possibilities where they could arguably add value to airline travellers are wide ranging (Fig. 9.6). To achieve all potential benefits, airline distribution will have to find ways to interact with voice applications.

Since 2008, when Alaska Airlines as the first carrier in the world launched an AI-based customer service representative on alaskaair.com called 'Jenn', the number of airlines working other AI-supported applications, notably bots and virtual assistants (VAs), has steadily increased. As these become ever more sophisticated in their natural interactions for both voice and text-based usage, it is probable that airlines will feature them as part of their future distribution platforms.

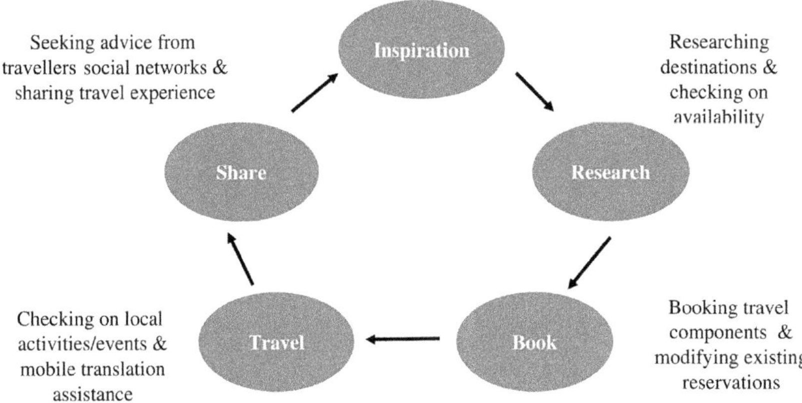

FIG. 9.6 Adding voice to mobile travel applications. *(Adapted from Rose, N., 2010. Why Voice Interaction Will Change Mobile Travel. Available at www.traveltechnology.com/2012/01. (Accessed August 2, 2017).)*

9.4.4 Wearables

The world of wearables is quite diverse. Although smart watches have caught many headlines, wearables also include earbuds/headphones, items embedded in clothing and contact lenses (Fig. 9.7). Features associated with wearable computing are still small in numbers since this platform has not entered the mainstream yet. Nevertheless, the outlook for wearables is arguably positive as, according to IDC, the number of units expected to be shipped globally may grow to approximately 240 million in 2021. The bulk of these are smart watches (Lamkin, 2017). For now, it seems that existing features found today on mobile platforms are extended to wearables such as a smartwatch. Due to their small interface, booking features—as currently used—are unlikely on wearables. Nevertheless, it is important to remember that wearables allow airlines to collect unique data about travellers such as their current location, conditions, and circumstances. Offers for on-the-go and in-destination promotions would be feasible according to a traveller's location, interest, and bio state.

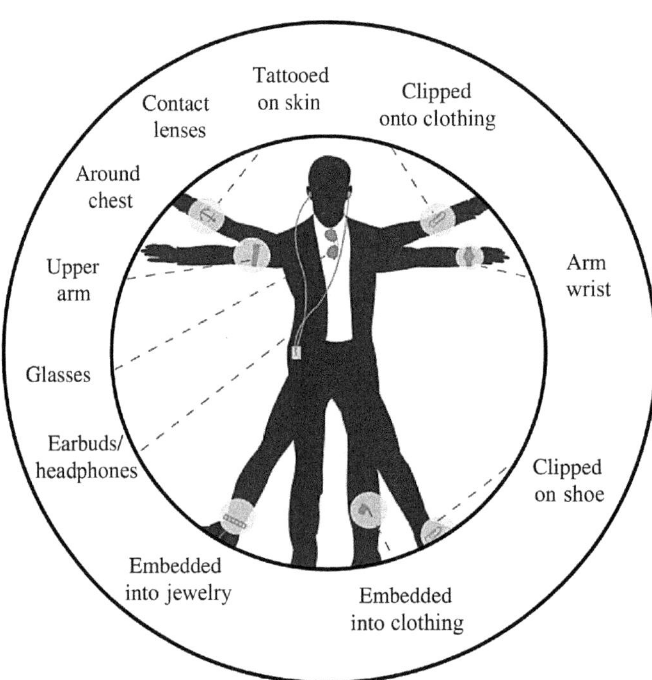

FIG. 9.7 Different types of computing wearables. *(Adapted from Dr4ward, 2013. What is the modern Vitruvian man for all wearable technology? Available atwww.dr4ward/dr4ward/2014/03. (Accessed September 1, 2017).)*

9.4.5 Virtual Reality

Virtual reality has taken on many different forms. In the online travel marketplace, virtual worlds, website avatars, holograms, and augmented reality are common areas of application. As far as virtual worlds are concerned, airlines may be attracted to them because of the opportunity to promote their brands and also sell their products/services (albeit in virtual form). However, the heydays of popular virtual worlds such as Second Life that managed to attract major corporate entities are gone. The presence of airlines including those of TAM and KLM that had opened operations there in 2007 and 2008, respectively, quickly faded once it became evident that it would not be the new future of marketing. Furthermore, the emerging popularity of social media showed that people were more interested in interacting with other people in the real world. There is some speculation that Second Life might be reincarnated because it is working on integrating the virtual reality headset by Oculus Rift, a company that was acquired by Facebook in 2014. If and when that occurs and virtual worlds again might attract mainstream consumer interest, some carriers possibly may revisit the idea of a virtual world presence. In the foreseeable future, however, virtual worlds are not an area for airline distribution in any significant way.

Holograms and augmented reality also apply virtual elements. Since 2011, several airports in Europe and the United States have introduced holograms of real-life customer service staff to speed up security queues (see also Chapter 13). The holograms are typically projected on life-size surfaces, modelled after real airport staff, and assist departing passengers in the security zones. The possibility that airlines may one day deploy holograms in an airport and offer last minute upgrades to travellers in the gate area is not far-fetched. Augmented reality has also become increasingly common with airlines in recent years. In essence, it is technology that superimposes computer generated images on a person's real view, thus creating a composite view of real and virtual scenes. In 2017 Air New Zealand launched a beta test for equipping its flight attendants with a HoloLens headset that could identify passengers through facial recognition, calling up details about their destination, allergies, their current emotional state (calm, anxious), and even the time since they got their last beverage.

Virtual reality provides for an artificial, software, generated environment that is presented to the user in such a way that their belief is suspended and they accept it as the real environment. On a computer, virtual reality is primarily experienced through two of the five senses: sight and sound. According to estimates by IDC, global shipments for virtual reality headsets are to increase from 7.4 million in 2016 to almost 49 million in 2021 (Businesswire, 2017). Airlines have already incorporated VR into their distribution efforts. For example, since November 2015, Virgin Atlantic has started offering a virtual reality application. Built in partnership with Microsoft for Windows smart phones and tablets, it sells the airline's Upper-Class experience to people who have not purchased a ticket yet. Corporate client offices, roadshows, and corporate lobby locations are some of the ground venues for experiencing the VIP check-in at London Heathrow, the carrier's airport lounge 'Club House' and the aircraft cabin of Upper-Class. The airline wanted to provide for an engaging experience to business travellers where they are during the day. These developments are an indication that VR could expand beyond games and 3D movies which are its key domains of application so far. It is likely that more airlines will begin to test virtual reality technology for inflight and on the ground applications, and distribution will partake in these initiatives.

9.4.6 Internet of Things (IoT)

The Internet of Things is about everyday objects being connected to the internet. This enables unprecedented tracking, data collection, analysis, and control. In the context of the online travel marketplace, this means that more things than ever could be connected to travellers, be it in an airport or elsewhere. One key device part of the IoT revolution can be a traveller's smartphone.

This everyday object connectivity requires significant infrastructure in smart devices, location technology, and intelligent software that can deal with massive amounts of data, and find a relevant solution for an individual web traveller in a specific context. For example, the use of beacons, which potentially can allow airlines to reap the benefits of being able to match location with other information, is predicted to rise. SITA estimates that the share of airlines leveraging IoT will be 44% in 2018 (SITA, 2015). Beacons are part of the proximity-sensing infrastructure that also includes cellular, near-frequency communication (NFC) and wi-fi at airports that airlines have been busy deploying in recent years. Many more related projects are in the works and pave the way for the IoT. Some 76% of airlines appear to understand the concept of IoT and 86% assume that its benefits will become clear within the next 3 years (SITA, 2015).

The goal of IoT is to improve the travel experience of web travellers and minimise/eliminate 'pain points' as much as possible. Airlines are working on 'beaconising' their apps, and once implemented, travellers will potentially start to enjoy some of the stated benefits. One example involves the transformation of booking and shopping to 'smart' retail. IoT can be used to offer individualised promotions by airport retailers as the traveller walks by certain stores. It could point to the nearest restaurant based on a traveller's dining preferences (with access to reviews by other travellers) and advise how much time could be spent in duty-free shopping before heading to the gate and not delaying a flight departure (see also Chapter 13).

9.5 TRAVELLER EXPECTATIONS

To serve expectations successfully requires an understanding of who the travellers are, what their requirements are, and also how they digitally 'tick'. The leisure travel market is commonly made up of certain subgroups ranging from adventurers to high-end travellers, each with their set of unique customer needs. These subgroups can be subjected to further segmentation factors such in the geographic, sociodemographic, and digital area. Within this context, a few issues relevant for airline distribution can be highlighted.

9.5.1 Novice Travellers

Many travellers, especially from emerging markets and developing economies countries, have never booked a flight before. These inexperienced travellers have no preconceived notions of how to go about shopping and purchasing an airline ticket and other ancillary services. Some of them might not even have a bank account or use traditional forms of payments such as debit or credit cards. Preferences such as dealing with a fully integrated travel agency services versus a do-it-yourself booking engagement, and what digital devices are used for shopping/booking are important to know. Many first-time travellers might not have any idea about traditional travel agencies or desk/laptops. For instance, in Asia, it is likely that they leapfrog straight to mobile and use a combination of apps, text, and voice platforms although some travellers might actually be prepared to engage a travel agent and pay them for their services.

In order to serve these new travellers optimally, airlines' distribution need to focus on deploying shopping and booking processes that are simpler than what is generally available today. In mature travel markets like the United States and United Kingdom, when booking a 4-day leisure trip, it is claimed that the average leisure consumer spends today around 42 h online—the equivalent of a full work week—by dreaming about, researching, planning, making a reservations, and then sharing their experiences whilst travelling or when they get back home (Boston Consulting Group, 2013). This cannot be expected to be the standard for novice travellers. Clearly, there must be less time consuming and more intuitive ways when shopping for an airline ticket.

Take, for example, the innovative approach by former Brazilian airline TAM (now part of the LATAM group) to reach the rapidly growing middle class in their country. In 2011, it started selling tickets through low-end retail chain Casas Bahia and at bus stations, allowed customers to pay in multiple instalments, and even provided 'how to fly' advice to first-time flyers (Acioli, 2011). In Africa, airlines such as Kenya Airways have partnered with mobile payment services M-PESA and Airtel Money to allow people without a bank account via SMS to purchase airline tickets (MPesa, 2016). When discussing forms of payment—they are a key component in airline distribution— it needs to be mentioned that most carriers appear to lack a clear strategy in this area and view them from a cost minimisation perspective as opposed to revenue growth opportunity. For example, when asked in a recent survey whether they accepted 12 forms of payment, on average carriers work with 4.4 led by credit and debit cards. Only a few airlines feature gift card programmes and none allow multiple forms of payment for a single transaction (Cataldo, 2017).

9.5.2 Millennial Travellers

In the next 5–10 years, millennials—those born between 1980 and 1994—will enter their peak earning, spending, and travelling years. In the United States, for example, they account for more than 83 million people, making them the single largest population cohort before baby boomers with 75 million (US Census Bureau, 2015). Amongst travellers in key travel markets, the share of millennials is significant (Fig. 9.8).

Millennials, like no other previous generation, personify the digital traveller (Boston Consulting Group, 2013; Tourism Intelligence, 2014). It is claimed that around 80% of them consider travel reviews important, some 57% update social media every day whilst travelling, and 32% use smart phones for travel bookings. Additionally, they are also known to engage in more travel research and comparisons over the internet and are less concerned than nonmillennials about sharing personal information online such as brand preferences, where they live, and personal hobbies, to name just a few. Millennials are associated with a phenomenon called the Do-it-yourself (DIY) traveller,

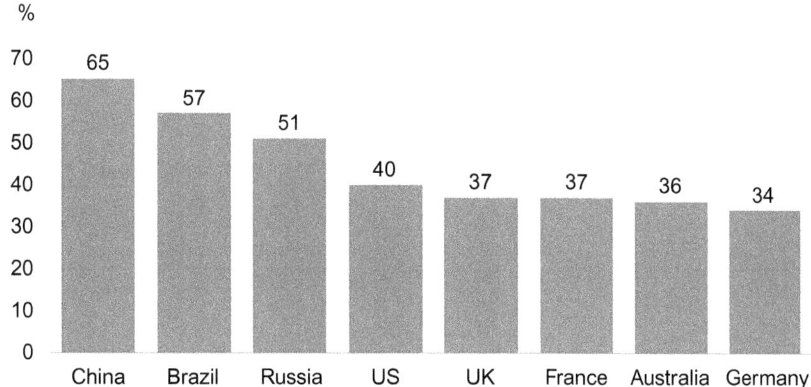

FIG. 9.8 Millennials—Share of leisure travellers. *(Adapted from Phocuswright, 2016. Mobile, Millennials, and Emerging Markets: The Next Wave in Global Travel, White Paper/Webinar. Available at www.phocuswright.com. (Accessed August 20, 2017).)*

sometimes also referred to as the 'silent traveller'. Due to the omni-presence of mobile devices and social media, DIY travellers can research and book online, check-in via mobile, self-check their luggage, and fly without interacting with anyone. Distribution needs to recognise the digital edginess and self-reliance of millennials, and airlines with a well-developed digital presence should find a ready audience with millennials. However, millennials appear to gravitate more towards intermediaries such as OTAs and not airlines when it comes to booking airline tickets: 37% prefer booking through OTAs compared to 24% direct through the airlines whilst older travellers' share through OTAs and airlines is 28% and 42%, respectively (PhocusWright, 2015). Moving forward, airline distribution needs to do a better job capturing millennials via relevant tactics including more attractive prices and a wider selection of offerings (Fig. 9.9).

9.5.3 Older Travellers

As societies around the world age due to higher life expectancy and lower fertility rates, airlines will serve an increasing number of older travellers. In 2015, 8.5% of the world population was 65 years of age or older. This proportion is projected to grow to 12% in 2030 (US Census Bureau, 2015). Whilst Europe already occupied 22 spots out of the 25 oldest countries in the world in 2015, the Asia Pacific region is quickly catching up. In 2030 Japan, Hong Kong, South Korea, and Taiwan will be amongst the oldest countries in the world whilst China's 65 years of age population will have almost doubled from 137 million (10% of its total population) in 2015 to 239 million (17%) in 2030 (US Census Bureau, 2015). At the same time, the population aged 80 and older will have quadrupled in some countries such as Brazil, China, India, South Korea, and Vietnam (US Census Bureau, 2015).

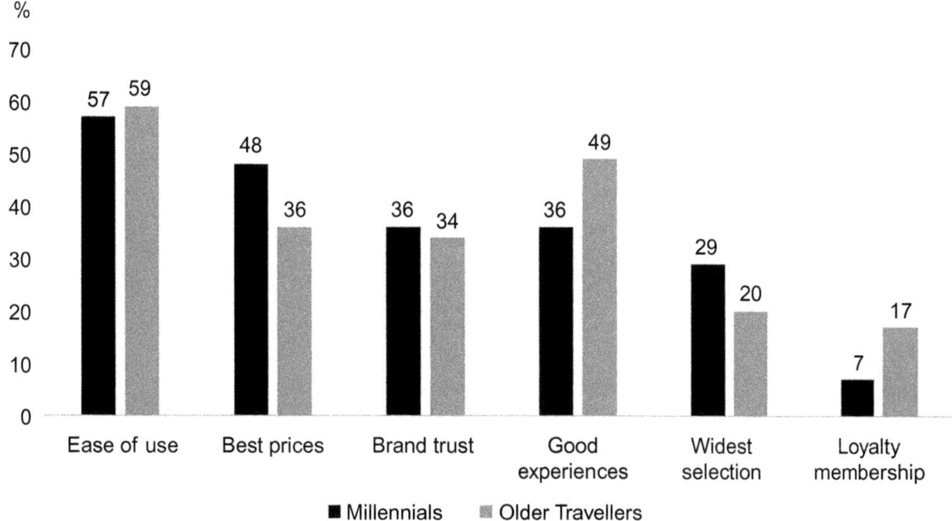

FIG. 9.9 Millennials vs. older travellers—Reasons for online shopping. *(Adapted from PhocusWright, 2015. The Year Ahead in Digital Travel, White Paper. Available at www.phocuswright.com. (Accessed August 28, 2017).)*

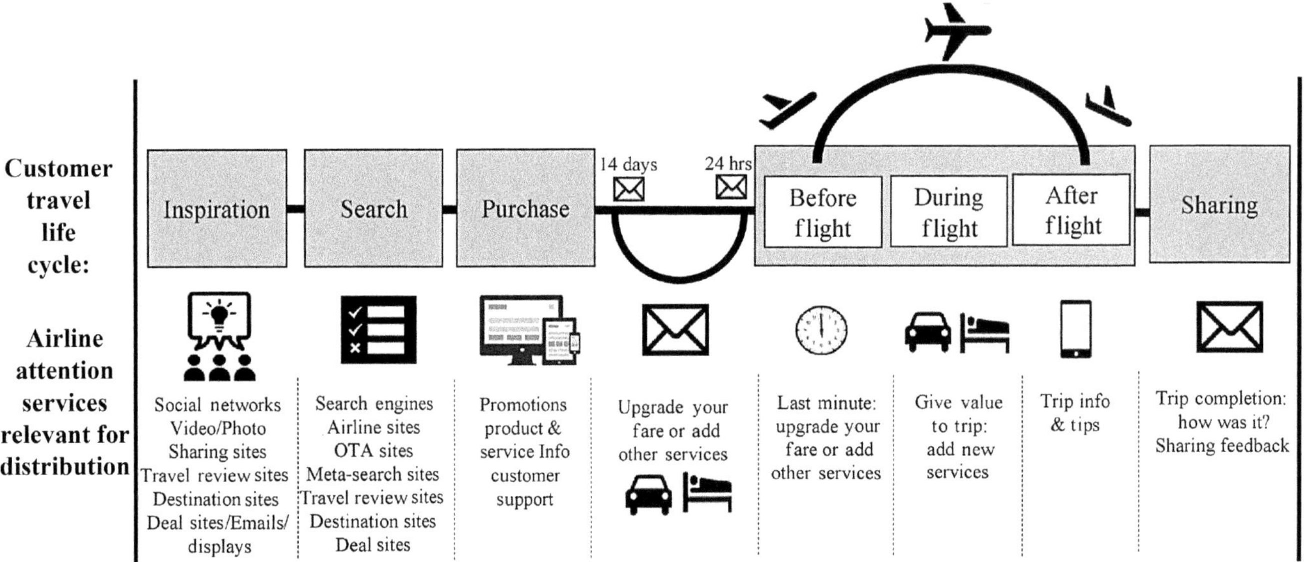

FIG. 9.10 The travel life cycle and airline offerings.

On the upside for airlines, 'greying' societies mean more leisure passengers since a larger portion of seniors are likely to embark on travel. Older travellers tend to book their trips more in advance than their younger peers although last minute decisions appear to be also common if fare specials are available, and if there is an opportunity to do a multigenerational trip with children and/or grandchildren. At the same time, older travellers have some unique requirements that need to be taken into consideration. For example, their limited physical mobility may result in preferring nonstop flights over connecting flights, or if connecting flights are part of the itinerary, more time should be allowed to cover the distance between gates. In such circumstance, the possibility of reserving wheelchair services as part of the booking process would be relevant. Later flight departures could be offered to senior travellers so they do not have to leave their home before sunrise. In this case, presenting premium seats for increased comfort or priority boarding to minimise waiting in queues could be well received. The above are just a few examples where distribution could further personalise offerings to older travellers.

9.5.4 Selling Through the Entire Travel Life Cycle

Traditionally, a carrier's distribution efforts focused narrowly on a customer's ticket shopping and booking stages. However, with today's shift to arguably a retail mind-set in the industry, airlines that want to create additional revenue opportunities for themselves need to embrace a wider perspective, and accommodate a customer's journey long before the shopping process begins and after the trip is completed. The travel life cycle is a construct that captures the various stages of a customer's journey whilst simultaneously identifying opportunities for an airline to sell (Fig. 9.10). One area where airline distribution could also tap into is the so-called in-destination market—it includes everything that travellers do once they have arrived, ranging from spa treatments and city tours to scuba diving. Globally, this market is valued at $112 billion annually. Furthermore, with inflight connectivity poised for substantial growth amongst many carriers, the inflight stage is another opportunity for airline distribution. It is estimated to generate $130 billion in ancillaries by 2035 (Inmarsat, 2017). To be successful in their efforts to monetise the participation in the various travel life cycle stages whilst also enhancing their brands, the airline offerings above everything else have to be relevant—this means timely and personalised.

9.6 AIRLINE DISTRIBUTION PARTICIPANTS AND PROCESSES

Today's airline distribution ecosystem is made up of a complex network of participants, each with their unique economic model focus, offerings spectrum and set of customer needs (see Fig. 9.11). The pressure points on this system are manifold and come from different directions. A few keys issues related to this are discussed as follows.

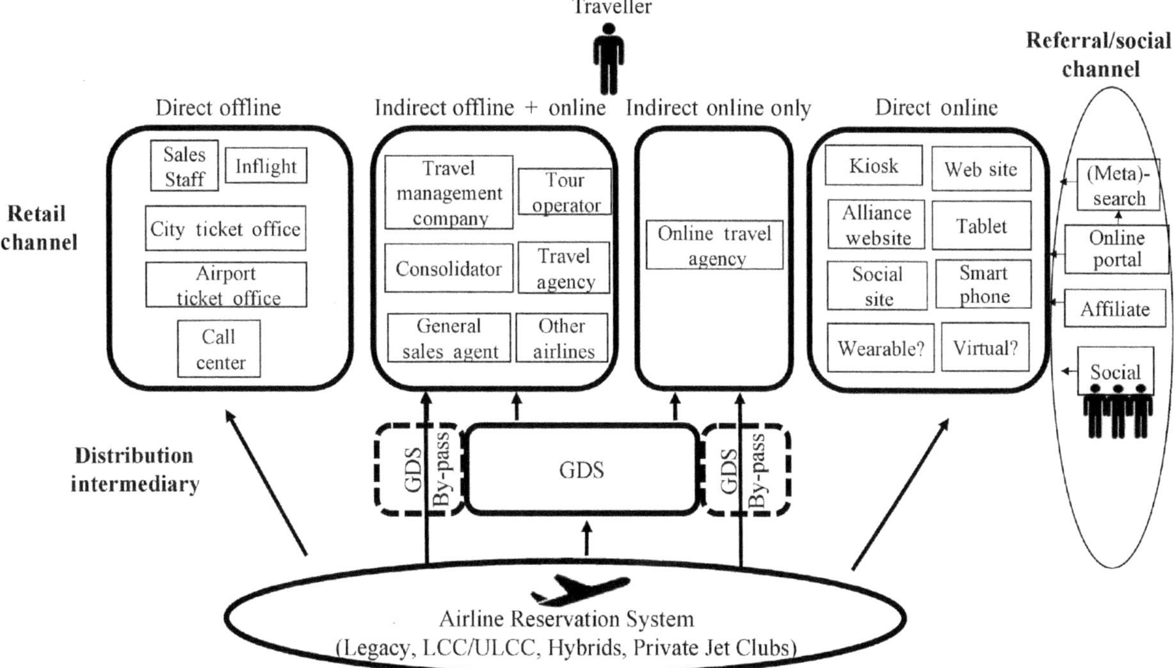

FIG. 9.11 The airline distribution ecosystem and key drivers affecting participants.

9.6.1 Differentiation Through Retailing: The Growing Role of Ancillaries

For many airlines, distribution is not any longer only about selling standard fare products. Today, they position themselves more as retailers in the marketplace that engage in what is referred to 'fare merchandising'. This retailer approach involves à la carte fare add-ons, branded fares, and fare families with prespecified products and services.

Revenue generation beyond the actual ticket sale has existed for many years in the airline industry. It commonly included the fees levied for excess baggage, ticket changes, prepaid tickets, and unaccompanied minors. With the emergence of LCCs in the late 1980s, however, a whole new and wider perspective was brought to this extra or ancillary revenue (see Chapter 10). In their strategy to compete against established legacy carriers, LCCs offered drastically lower fares by removing components of the airline fare product that were traditionally included in the base fare. In the past, airline customers have never considered these elements as part of a bundle since airlines have always marketed products, not bundles of components. This clearly changed when LCCs started unbundling fares and introduced à la carte fares.

An à la carte fare product essentially features separate and itemised elements of the airline fare product for which an airline customer now pays extra. In recent years, carriers have enhanced the à la carte menu with a variety of travel-related items. They include airport lounge vouchers, inflight wi-fi passes, priority boarding, and mileage boosters, to name a few examples. Besides offering à la carte products and services, several airlines have also started to repackage items and now market fare families and branded fares. Importantly, whilst LCCs are still the main adopters of fare merchandising, legacy carriers have come to embrace it as well. In October 2015, Lufthansa became the first European legacy airline to unbundle services by introducing a three-tier fare system. This allows the company to not only compete more directly on the actual fare but also charge more for nonticket items including checked bags and seat reservations. Introducing such services incur minimal costs and can therefore be an additional profitable revenue stream for airlines. The importance of ancillaries cannot be underestimated, being a major contributor to the airline industry's revenue generation. For 2016, ancillaries grew by 7.8% over 2015 and amounted to $67.4 billion or 9.1% of total revenue (Fig. 9.12).

By selling merchandise fares, an airline acknowledges that a seat is not any longer just a seat but actually a unique product. The days are gone when a seat was viewed as a commodity with the fundamental differentiator being whether the seat was in economy, business, or first class. Each airline will have to develop its own approach as to how to unbundle/repackage its fare products and price the different components. Fare merchandising can potentially offer an airline several benefits. Importantly, it may allow an airline to achieve two main objectives that are discussed.

- Revenue maximisation

The revenue streams from fare merchandising can be significant for a carrier. For example, in 2016, Southwest Airlines realised $2.9 billion in revenue from various ancillary sources including fare merchandising. Delta Airlines, in the second half of 2016, generated more than $300 million alone from Comfort Plus, its rebranded extra legroom economy class seats (CarTrawler, 2016). Further insight to how an ultra-low cost carrier (ULCC) maximises revenues from fare merchandising is provided by Spirit Airlines. With almost 40% of their total annual revenue coming from ancillaries, they are amongst the world's leading carriers in this field. They have found the price elasticity of the primary purchase (the ticket) to increase significantly for fare levels of $99 and higher. If the base is less than $99, concern for the price levels of secondary add-ons is much less significant. With this approach, the carrier not only increases its load factor but also generates substantial ancillary revenue (Hanke, 2016). When discussing revenue maximisation from fare merchandising, there is also the opportunity for an airline to offset other cost increases quickly. An example is fuel price upswings that make à la carte fares also attractive to airlines. During the 2008 fuel crisis, many US carriers swiftly introduced charges for checking a second bag.

- Product differentiation and brand enhancement

With the ability to offer more choices in actual merchandising, an airline may not only differentiate itself in the marketplace from the competition, but may also provide a unique value proposition for web travellers. Fare merchandising allows the 'decommoditisation' of the airline seat, making it possible to strengthen their brand. There are certainly benefits from the incremental revenue streams that come from fare merchandising but equally important should be the realisation that fare merchandising is also about earning trust with web travellers, matching fares of competitors (most often LCCs), and providing for additional value.

Overall, introducing and managing fare merchandising has had a profound impact on the airline distribution community. Table 9.2 provides for an overview of what the implications are for specific players.

9.6.2 IATA's New Distribution Capability (NDC) Programme

The recent IATA New Distribution Capability (NDC) initiative involves the adoption of an important XML-based messaging standard that should help establish a base for a distribution of ancillaries on a consistent basis and large scale. As a result of pressure from member airlines, IATA had been looking for quite some time to address carriers' limitations in terms of distributing new internet-enabled differentiated product/service offerings and providing access to full and rich air content. The existing GDSs had been focused on delivering standard, commoditised content to travel agencies and therefore could not (or would not) accommodate the retailing solutions airlines wanted to offer. Against this background, IATA launched the NDC programme with IATA Resolution 787 in the autumn of 2012.

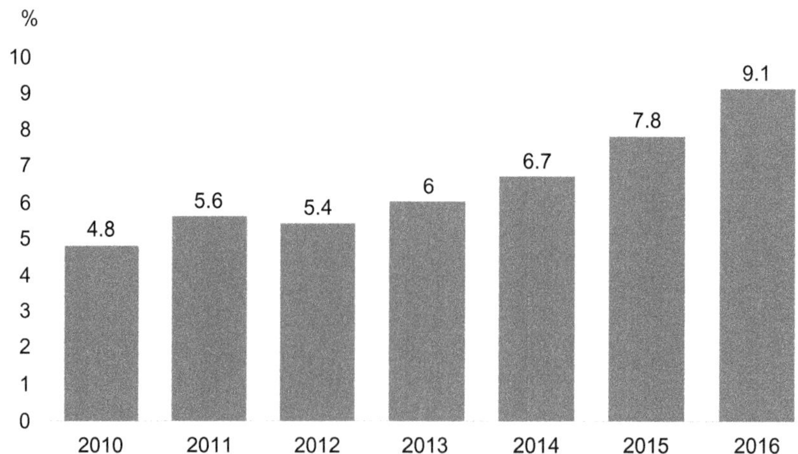

FIG. 9.12 The growing importance of ancillary revenue. *(Adapted from CarTrawler, 2016. Ancillary Global Estimate. Available at https://www.cartrawler.com/ct/media/2016/11/CarTrawler-ancillary-series-global-estimate-report-29-november-2016-en.pdf. (Accessed September 3, 2017).)*

TABLE 9.2 Implications of Fare Merchandising

Party	Impact
Travellers	The number of fare choices has certainly gone up and travellers need to decide for various aspects of each booking what they want (or not). Travellers would be challenged in their comparison shopping as an 'apple-to-apple' comparison has become more difficult and time consuming. This could open the door to new forms of content aggregation by third parties
Travel agencies (off and online)	Traditional travel agencies and OTAs would be required to upgrade or replace their current technical systems in order to integrate the merchandise fare products and move away from offering standard, nonmerchandise fare products to the travelling public. Part of this upgrade would involve the decision whether or not to 'direct connect' to an airline's internal reservations system and/or modified GDS that could also handle merchandise fares. Like travellers, travel agencies are likely to spend more time on the booking process due to the increased number of choices
Global distribution systems	GDSs would need to continue investing in platform technology upgrades/training to be able to handle airline-specific merchandise fare products for further distribution amongst travel agencies. The question is: Are GDSs acting fast enough and is their upgrade sufficient in terms of scale and scope?
Travel meta-search engines	Low fare search results may not be accurate, thus a modification of search algorithms reflecting a traveller's search for merchandise fare products would seem critical. With new devices like Amazon Echo and the growing popularity of intelligent personal assistants such as Siri, meta-search needs to break new ground if they want to stay relevant. One possible scenario of dealing with fare merchandising is through the adoption of direct booking solutions where airlines present their branded ancillaries on the meta-search engine's platform. UK meta-search provider Skyscanner claims a 20% conversion boost with airlines that have adopted this approach with the company (Arslanian, 2017)
Travel management companies	They might have to modify their corporate client databases and profiles as well as upgrade their booking platforms and technical systems to handle merchandise fare products. The booking process, as in the case for regular travel agencies, is likely to take longer and increases cost
Airlines	Overhauling their internal reservations platforms to offer ancillary suppliers merchandise fare products is crucial, reorient their company culture, and adjust intra/interdepartmental processes to adopt a retailing approach. Importantly, if carriers want to grow their ancillary revenue significantly, they have to find ways (including commission-base incentives) to selling them through travel agencies

The NDC programme advocates an XML-based transmission standard that enables a modernisation of the way airlines distribute their offerings. Specifically, airlines are provided with the ability to decommoditise their supply. At the same time, third-party channels including travel agencies, travel content aggregators such as meta-search engines, and corporate buyers are offered new rich airline content they can access (Fig. 9.13). In essence, IATA's 787 Resolution for NDC has four mandates at its core to overcome the industry's current distribution gap:

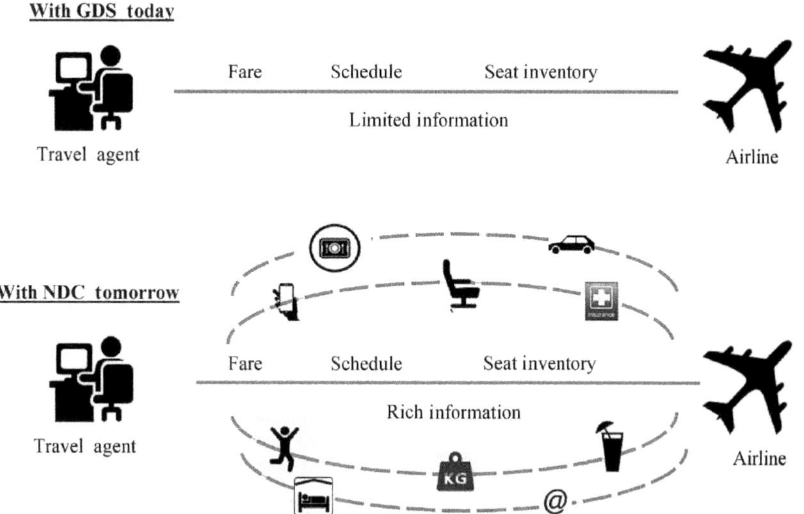

FIG. 9.13 The Impact of NDC—Decommoditising airline distribution.

- Allow individual airlines to determine their own prices and the nature of those products/services offered depending on who the requestor is and what they are requesting.
- Facilitate the implementation of a shopping basket capability for a shopper to add or remove items from their basket as they choose. The different choices may trigger a repricing of the products offered by a carrier.
- Support the distribution of new products and the changes and amendments of existing orders.
- Facilitate a transparent display of products being offered and enable comparison amongst different products.

The NDC programme and associated XML standard is voluntary and no IATA member *has* to adopt it. Anyone wishing to continue using the existing transmission standard EDIFACT can do so. As of Spring 2017, 31 airlines had signed up for participating in an NDC pilot including Aer Lingus, American, Hainan Airlines, Qatar Airways, and Swiss International. IATA expects to have 90 NDC carriers in place by 2020 (May, 2016). In the meantime, issues such as who will ultimately pay for the adoption and ongoing operation of this technology standard by many of the worldwide 60,000 travel agencies still need to be settled. This means that NDC is not a guaranteed success. If NDC fails to catch on, it is likely that airlines will simply move forward individually with building platforms that enable the offering of ancillaries and personalised products and fares.

9.6.3 Direct Distribution

Airline sales and distribution is expensive and covers a complex web of cost items (Fig. 9.14). Many airlines have managed to slash their distribution costs by half in a 10–15 year time frame but these costs are still a major issue. It is in this context that the Lufthansa Group applied a so-called distribution cost surcharge of €16 (almost $18) per ticket as of September 1, 2015. Thus any leisure and corporate agency handling bookings via a GDS has to either absorb this extra charge or pass it on to the traveller. Not surprisingly, GDSs and many travel agencies are particularly concerned about loss of income as a result of this move. However, this needs to be seen in the light of the airline's attempt to gain a higher share of the profits. According to the carrier, 70% of its tickets are handled through indirect distribution. Also, a direct booking with Lufthansa costs €2 versus €18 for bookings through third-party channels that involve a GDS. Against this background, the incentive to shift ticket sales to direct distribution and save on costs is understandably strong. Lufthansa also became the first carrier in the world to strike a direct connect relationship with Google Flights whereby travellers using the search engine platform could book their tickets directly via a 'Book on Google' button.

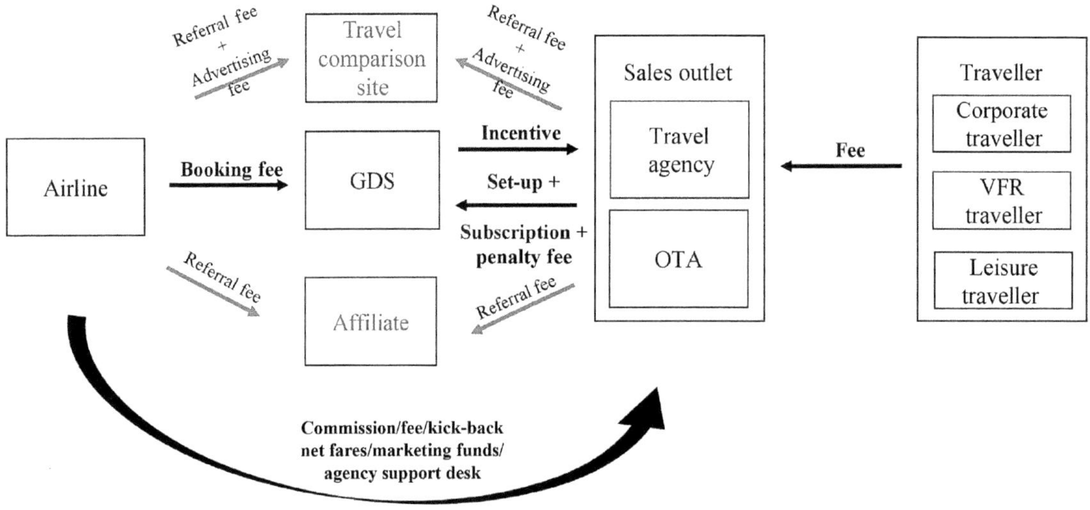

FIG. 9.14 The cost of sales and distribution.

Other carriers are likely to follow similar approaches. For example, British Airways (BA) and Iberia have implemented a GDS surcharge of £8 on agency bookings not made via the carriers' website or direct channels. BA and Iberia said the surcharge would not apply if the GDS used content created using NDC technology that gives airlines greater control of how fares and products are displayed. GDSs have said that they are working to find a deal to integrate such content. Meanwhile, American Airlines announced in summer 2017 that it would pay travel management companies (TMCs) a \$2-per-segment incentive if they book through a NDC-supported connection to the carrier. More recently, the Air France–KLM group has also started assessing GDS surcharges effective April 1, 2018. Implicit in this focus on direct distribution is not only the airline industry's dissatisfaction with GDSs but with OTAs as well. A common concern is that they seem to be seen as too price focused and sellers of airline offerings as commodities, as opposed to branded fares or carrier specific ancillary products.

As a result of these direct distribution initiatives, SkaiBlu Consulting estimates that the share of airlines' website and mobile devices is likely to increase over the next few years whilst that of third parties including those of OTAs will decline (Fig. 9.15). However, as some legacy carriers' direct web sales shares go up, there will most likely be a plateauing of around 50%–55%. In other words, it is unlikely that many legacy carriers will ever reach more than 45%—55% of direct web sales. The reasons include corporate travel, group travel, and tours/packages that for the most part are still distributed via offline channels. Moreover as much as the move away from GDSs and travel agencies may be praised as a cost saving measure, it is important to remember that customer acquisition cost is likely to go up. This is the result of an airline's increased advertising engagement with search channels and other media formats, especially outside a home market where a carrier's brand is generally less known. This is a major trade-off to be considered.

Meanwhile the direct sales shares of LCCs are expected to fall further over the next few years by several percentage points. Key reasons for this development are that LCCs are pursuing more and more the corporate travel market. Southwest announced in 2016 that they want to attract more business travellers and increase their contribution to overall sales from 35% to 40% by 2018. easyJet's business sales accounts today for 25% of the company's revenue and they have just established a new organisation exclusively focused on business travel. Even Ryanair has been aiming increasingly at business travellers. Corporate travel is still largely handled via traditional intermediaries including GDSs, corporate travel agencies, and travel management companies (TMCs), hence the slight decline of some LCCs' direct web sales shares.

With all of this development, OTAs, especially Expedia and Priceline who control a combined global OTA booking share of over 50%, are very unlikely not to change. They are expected to become larger and to continue to make further acquisitions. Past examples from 2015 include Expedia purchasing Travelocity and Orbitz, whilst Priceline invested \$500 million in Chinese OTA Ctrip. In 2016 Ctrip acquired a controlling stake in Chinese competitor eLong and also bought the Indian OTA MakeMyTrip. Interestingly, OTAs expand now vertically and focus on meta-search engines—Google's looming presence is certainly a driver. Priceline's Kayak has just bought the Momondo Group (they operate the Momondo and Cheapflight meta-search engines) whilst Ctrip bought UK-based Skyscanner. Former distinctions of

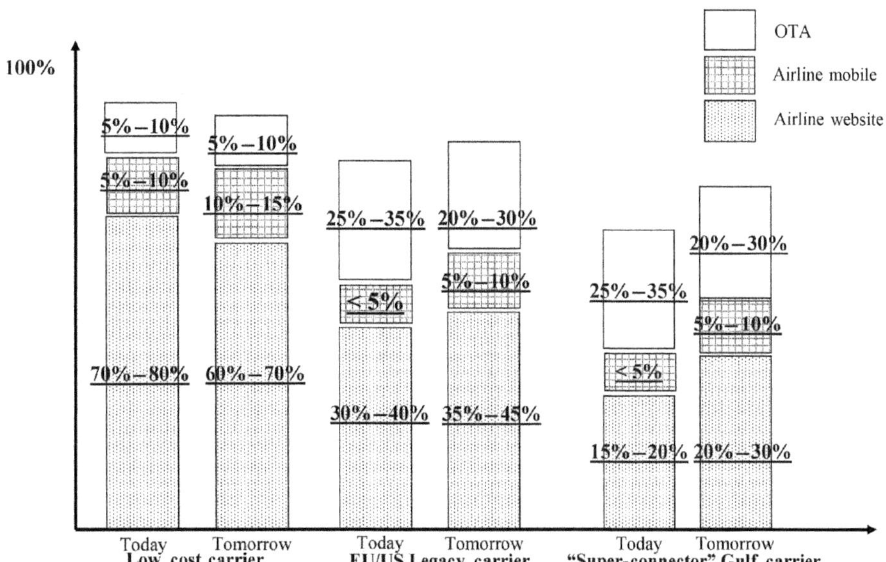

FIG. 9.15 Airlines' share of direct e-sales: Today vs. tomorrow.

who does what in the distribution funnel (search vs. shopping vs buying) are likely to be more 'muddied' because of the increased hybridisation of today's OTAs. Companies that might become a target for an acquisition in the near future include the LastMinute Group (they operate several OTAs and meta-search engines) from the UK, Spanish eDreamsOdigeo with Opodo and Liligo, as well as meta-search engine players Wego from Singapore and Ixigo from India.

At the same time, growing in size is certainly no protection against disruption that may make intermediaries such as OTAs less significant players at one point. One potential game changer for the future may come from a technology called blockchain. It is mostly known as the platform for Bitcoin, the cryptocurrency but it can have other areas of application as well. Essentially, Blockchain is a database that contains a continuously growing list of data records and transactions. Importantly, there is no need for a central entity to validate transactions when the participants can agree and validate them. In a travel context, this could mean that GDSs and OTAs might not play the intermediary role in the future they occupy today. TUI, the world's largest travel company has even publicly stated that blockchain has the potential to break the near-monopolistic hold of Priceline, Expedia, and Airbnb through the introduction of decentralised databases where transactions with suppliers like airlines are executed on the basis of 'smart contracts' (Skift, 2017).

In the foreseeable future, it is likely that several e-sales and distribution arrangements will exist side by side. Airlines may well continue working in traditional ways with intermediaries including agencies (off- and online) and GDSs. At the same time, there will be more setups in place for direct distribution. They include an NDC-based direct connect with third-party retailers and facilitated by airline technology providers such as Farelogix and others that offer applications to bridge the different platforms involved. Direct distribution is also likely to mean that airlines will look for ways to make their own direct online presence more competitive with increased ancillaries and personalisation features (Fig. 9.16). In this regard, the role of merchandising engines will be significant.

All three e-sales and distribution arrangements are likely to be governed by a cost control imperative whereby airlines will look to accomplish the following:

- renegotiate more favourable terms with existing partners including GDSs and agencies;
- shift volume to lower cost channels (direct connect and direct online sales);
- reduce costs through increased efficiencies like cloud computing.

It should be emphasised that e-sales and distribution is not only about cost efficiency, but also involves important value addition. This is because more airlines and intermediaries will be able to offer ancillary sales and use enhanced big data insight to do more targeted offerings.

9.6.4 New Disruptors

Besides existing participants in today's airline distribution system, a new breed of players has joined, dabbled, or expressed interest in the online travel space in recent years, namely, a group collectively referred to as CAFGAA (Concur, Apple, Facebook, Google, Amazon, and Alibaba). The degree of their engagement varies but what they all

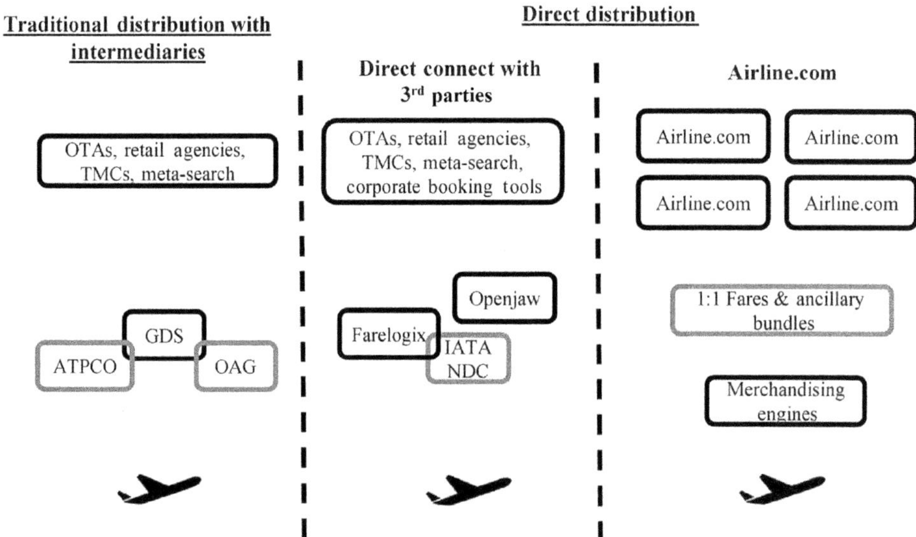

FIG. 9.16 The future of airline distribution—the coexistence of multiple solutions.

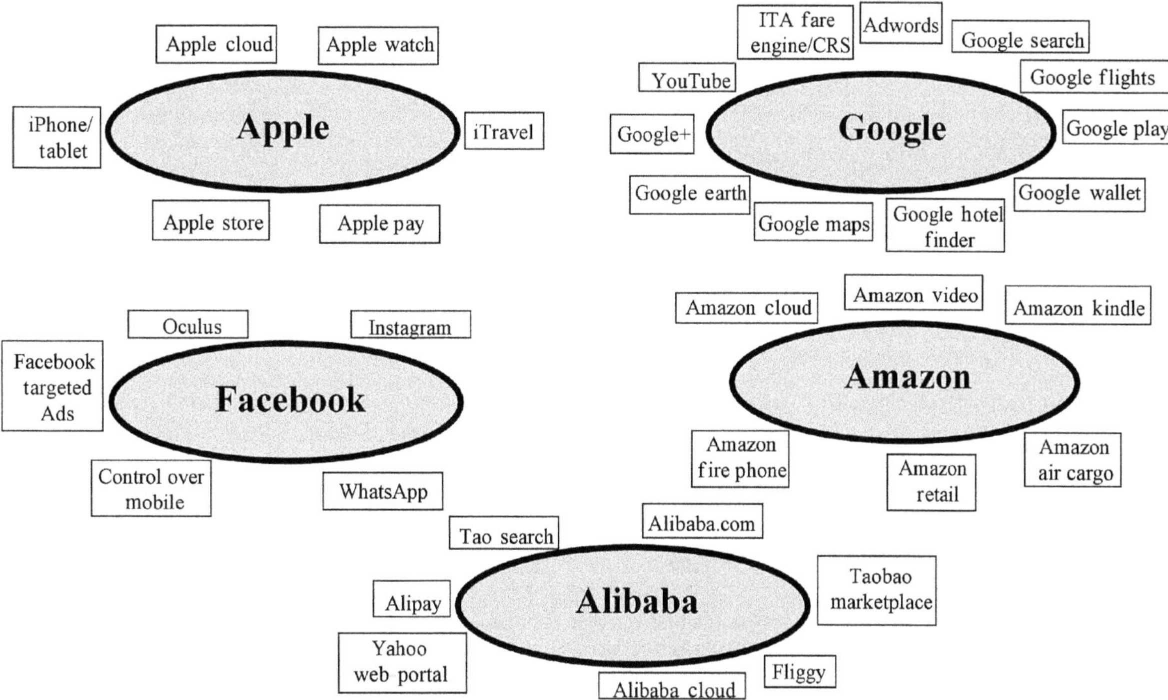

FIG. 9.17 The new disruptors in airline distribution.

have in common is powerful brand recognition in the marketplace, a large customer base, a thorough understanding of technology coupled with marketing expertise and knowledge, and significant financial resources. They are all known to be highly effective disruptors and certainly have the potential to rewrite the rules of the game for e-sales and distribution. A particular issue is the power of these companies' proprietary ecosystems that make it relatively easy to integrate and expand travel products and services (Fig. 9.17). There are also other potential players such as Airbnb which launched in November 2016 their first product beyond accommodation called 'Trips'. This new travel service platform covers homes, places, and experiences. The company has signalled its intention to become a full-service travel company by adding other travel products like flights, restaurant bookings, and car hire. Meanwhile, in October 2016, Uber announced 'Elevate', the development of a flying taxi network that is planned to launch in 2026 (see also Chapter 2 for a discussion of these sharing economy platforms).

9.7 CONCLUSION

This chapter has examined how fuelled by multiple external macro factors such as technology, politics, sociodemographic changes, and the global economy, the airline industry as a whole and distribution in particular, is likely to be disrupted to a degree and with a pace not seen for many years. In order to manage the challenges ahead and use the ongoing transformation to a company's competitive advantage, airline distribution needs to stay closely tuned to major developments in the external environment. At the same time, it needs to transcend existing siloes and insular approaches. More than ever, close cooperation with other key disciplines including marketing, revenue management, and e-commerce is pivotal.

References

Acioli, R., 2011. Middle Class Takes Flight With TAM. Available at http://sparksheet.com/brazil%E2%80%99s-middle-class-takes-flight-qa-with-tam%E2%80%99s-manoela-amaro/. (Accessed September 22, 2017).

American Customer Service Index, 2017. ACSI: Low-Cost Carriers Lead Legacy Airlines for Passenger Satisfaction. Available at http://www.theacsi.org/news-and-resources/press-releases/press-2017/press-release-travel-2017. (Accessed April 2, 2018).

Arslanian, D.P., 2017. Flight Metasearch—Hard Landing Into a New Business Model. Available at https://www.tnooz.com/article/flight-metasearch-new-business-model/. (Accessed September 30, 2017).

Boston Consulting Group, 2013. The Digital Road to Earning Travellers Trust. Available at https://www.bcgperspectives.com/content/interviews/transportation_travel_tourism_digital_economy_bolden_dylan_digital_road_to_earning_travelers_trust/. (Accessed September 30, 2017).
Businesswire, 2017. Worldwide Shipments of Augmented Reality and Virtual Reality Headsets. Available at http://www.businesswire.com/news/home/20170619005183/en/Worldwide-Shipments-Augmented-Reality-Virtual-Reality-Headsets. (Accessed September 11, 2017).
CAPA, 2016. Global Aviation Summit Responding to Digital Disruptions. Available at https://centreforaviation.com/insights/analysis/klm-ceo-pieter-elbers-at-the-capa-acte-global-aviation-summit-responding-to-digital-disruption-309846. (Accessed September 29, 2017).
CarTrawler, 2016. Ancillary Global Estimate. Available at https://www.cartrawler.com/ct/media/2016/11/CarTrawler-ancillary-series-global-estimate-report-29-november-2016-en.pdf (Accessed September 3, 2017).
Cataldo, G., 2017. Payments: Airlines' Under-appreciated, Under-leveraged Asset. Available at https://www.tnooz.com/article/payments-airlines-under-appreciated-under-leveraged-asset/. (Accessed October 1, 2017).
Diggin Travel, 2017. Airline Ancillary Revenue Leaders. In: Global Airline Ancillary Survey.
Expedia, 2015. Meetings & Conventions. Available at http://www.meetings-conventions.com/uploadedFiles/MobileWhitepaper_ExpediaMediaSolutions.pdf. (Accessed September 13, 2017).
Hanke, M., 2016. Airline E-Commerce: Log on.Take off. Routledge, New York.
IATA, 2016a. What We Do—The Future of Airline Distribution 2016–2021. Available at https://www.iata.org/whatwedo/airline-distribution/ndc/Documents/ndc-future-airline-distribution-report.pdf. (Accessed September 15, 2017).
IATA, 2016b. IATA Press Room. Available at http://www.iata.org/pressroom/pr/Pages/2016-10-18-02.aspx. (Accessed September 4, 2017).
Inmarsat, 2017. News. Available at https://www.inmarsat.com/news/34067/. (Accessed October 1, 2017).
Lamkin, P., 2017. Wearable Tech Market To Double By 2021. Available at https://www.forbes.com/sites/paullamkin/2017/06/22/wearable-tech-market-to-double-by-2021/#5820aac1d8f3. (Accessed September 23, 2017).
May, K., 2016. Half of Airlines Will Move to NDC and Agencies Love It. Available at https://www.tnooz.com/article/half-of-airlines-will-move-to-ndc-and-agencies-love-it/. (Accessed September 20, 2017).
MPesa (2016). Book And Buy Kenya Airways Ticket Via Mpese Online Ticket Booking. Available at http://www.mpesacharges.com/book-and-buy-kenya-airways-ticket-via-mpesa-online-ticket-booking/. (Accessed September 28, 2017).
PhocusWright, 2015. The Year Ahead in Digital Travel, White Paper. Available at www.phocuswright.com. (Accessed August 28, 2017).
PhocusWright, 2017. Phocus Forward, the Year Ahead in Digital Travel, White Paper. Available at www.phocuswright.com. (Accessed August 27, 2017).
Schoenberger, M.V., Cukier, K., 2013. Big Data. John Murray, London.
SITA, 2015. Airline IT Trends Survey 2015. https://secure.sita.aero/globalassets/docs/surveys-reports/airline-it-trends-survey-2015.pdf. (Accessed September 23, 2017).
Skift (2017). Blockchain Will Disrupt Expedia and AirBnB. Available at https://skift.com/2017/07/11/blockchain-will-disrupt-expedia-and-airbnb-tui-ceo-says/. (Accessed September 20, 2017).
Tnooz, 2014. Available at https://www.tnooz.com/article/phocuswright-european-traveler-technology-trends/. (Accessed September 4, 2017).
Tourism Intelligence (2014). Generation Y: The New Face of Business Travel. Available at http://tourismintelligence.ca/2014/06/30/generation-y-the-new-face-of-business-travel/. (Accessed September 3, 2017).
US Census Bureau, 2015. Newsroom and Press Releases. Available at https://www.census.gov/newsroom/press-releases/2015/cb15-113.html. (Accessed September 7, 2017).
World Travel and Tourism Council, 2017. Economic Impact Analysis. Available at https://www.wttc.org/research/economic-research/economic-impact-analysis/. (Accessed September 12, 2017).

CHAPTER

10

The Role of the Different Airline Business Models

John F. O'CONNELL

University of Surrey, Surrey, United Kingdom

CHAPTER OUTLINE

10.1 INTRODUCTION

Commercial aviation has reached a milestone as it celebrates its 100-year anniversary. Few industries have had such an impact on society as it connects people, cultures, and business across continents. The value chain within the air transport industry is wide ranging as over 1400 scheduled airlines, 26,000 aircraft in service, 3900 airports, and 173 air navigation services providers are engaged to interconnect all corners of the globe that facilitate the movement of people and cargo (ICAO, 2017). The airline industry propels prosperity through a spectrum ranging from economic expansion to cultivating tourism, in an increasingly environmental aware society. It has become a key pillar of the tourism sector as it provides a vital link between the tourist-generating destinations and the home country, which has been continuously sparked by its increasing affordability. Simply put, 'tourism cannot happen without transport options to bring tourists to a destination'. The academic literature is replete with the strong correlation between air services (both route availability and airfares) and its impact on the number of tourist arrivals (Albalate and Fageda, 2016; Yin et al., 2015; Dobruszkes and Mondou, 2013; Bieger and Wittmer, 2006; Button and Taylor, 2000). Information about how passenger demand interacts with available capacity can help destinations target advertising and promotional efforts. Koo et al. (2013) reported that air transport capacity is considered as one of the key factors in tourism forecasting, along with other key determinants of tourism demand such as income.

Worldwide, air travel has grown at a bustling pace over the last 100 years—it took 50 years for the industry to reach 1 billion passengers (1930s to 1987) and only took 20 years to get to 2 billion (1988–2005), whilst the industry achieved the 3 billion passenger milestone in <10 years (2006–13). IATA (2018a) stated that over the last 10 years, it averaged growth rates of 5.5%, whilst in 2017 it soared to 7.6%, although unevenly spread across the globe. A plethora of reasons underpin this relentless augmentation that includes low air fares; higher disposable incomes; enlarging middle

Air Transport—A Tourism Perspective. https://doi.org/10.1016/B978-0-12-812857-2.00010-5

class in large emerging markets such as China[1] and India[2]; liberalisation which has removed the shackles of pricing constraints and market entry in various areas; airline cooperative arrangements; whilst flight frequencies, together with incessant competition have all aggregated to incentivise the traveller to partake in even more journeys.

The scale of the global air transport industry is notable as 3.8 billion passengers travelled by air in 2016 on 35 million scheduled flights that operated on 54,000 routes and which transported 53 million tonnes of freight (ICAO, 2017). Likewise, tourism has encountered virtually uninterrupted growth over time, despite occasional shocks, demonstrating the sector's strength and resilience. International tourist arrivals have increased from 25 million globally in 1950 to 1235 million[3] by 2016, whilst its international tourist receipts surged from US$2 billion in the 1950s to US$1220 billion by 2016 which has a multiplier catalytic effect into the global economy (UNWTO, 2017). The segmentation of these trips from a global perspective reveals that over half of all international tourist arrivals in 2016 (53% or 657 million visitors) was for holidays, recreation, and other forms of leisure, whilst another 27% travelled for other reasons that include visiting friends and relatives (VFR), religious/pilgrimages, and for health treatment, whilst another 13% reported travelling for business and professional purposes whilst the remaining 7% of arrivals was not specified (UNWTO, 2017; see also Chapter 3). At a regional level the segmentation follows a similar pattern as Zhang (2015) found that 45% of the visitors to Australia came for holidays, whilst 25% intended to visit friends and relatives.

The landscape of travelling for tourism purposes has evolved considerably over the decades as the top 15 country destinations absorbed 98% of all international tourist arrivals in the 1950s, whilst in the 1970s the proportion was 75% and by the new millennium, it had fallen to <60% (Airbus, 2017). According to the World Tourism Organisation, international tourist arrivals are now growing faster than overall GDP growth. Tourism is ever evolving and changing as Dubai, for example, is a relatively new tourism market, welcoming 15.8 million tourists in 2018, with 2 million emanating from India alone (Gulf News, 2018), whilst Emirates Airline is the catalyst for tourism development in the Gulf capital (O'Connell and Bueno 2016; O'Connell, 2011a,2011b). Meanwhile in developing economies such as the Philippines, 6.6 million international tourists visited the island in 2017, 11% higher than the previous year—the national flag carrier Philippine Airlines commenced a partnership with the domiciled tourism board to encourage foreign leisure travellers to visit the Philippines (Business World, 2018; Philippine Airlines, 2017).

Air transport has often become the preferred mode of transport for international travel. In the 1980s and 1990s the majority of trips were taken by surface modes such as road, water, or rail, however that began to change thereafter to air. Fig. 10.1 shows that 48% of tourists travelled by air in the mid-2000s, but registered 54% by 2016 and forecasts indicate that it will climb to 62% by 2036 when there will be >2.4 billon international arrivals worldwide (UNWTO, 2017; Leahy, 2017). The growth on the air transport side was largely triggered by a shift in the regulatory policy from bilateral agreements to multilateral arrangements to an open skies[4] platform which was necessary in-part to accommodate the surge[5] in global tourism. For example, the Open Skies agreement by ASEAN (Association of South East Asian Nations) was recently fully ratified following its implementation that began in 2009. The agreement supports increased competition and connectivity within the region, providing passengers the benefits of lower fares and greater itinerary and service-level choices. Subsequently, it allowed low-cost carriers to gain compelling traction, whilst full-service network carriers have significantly increased their frequencies as a consequence of the freer regulatory environment. Zhang and Findlay (2014) have strongly argued that such liberalisation builds up a strong tourism industry. Undoubtedly there is a growing interdependency between aviation and tourism which are becoming more and more interwoven. The outlook for strong air travel demand is consistent with broad consumer demand trends and travel and tourism outlooks.

By the end of 2016, 3.81 billion passengers were transported by different types of airline business models as presented in Table 10.1 and each has a different set of structural dimensions, operating characteristics, and passenger specifications. The remaining discussion will describe the underlying characteristics and changing dynamics of low-cost carriers, full-service network airlines, charter airlines, and regional airlines.

[1] Almost 1.6 billion passengers are expected to travel within China in 2036, almost four times the number of passengers that travelled by air in 2016. Meanwhile the outbound China market is predicted to double to over 200 million travellers annually by 2020 (Airbus, 2017).

[2] The number of domestic Indian passengers is expected to grow almost six times in the next 20 years, reaching the level as domestic United States is today (Airbus, 2017).

[3] The geographical breakdown of these arriving international tourists in 2016 is as follows: Europe, 616 million; Asia and the Pacific, 308 million; the Americas, 199 million; Africa, 58 million; and the Middle East, 54 million (UNWTO, 2017).

[4] Open Skies means the liberalisation of the rules and regulations of bilateral agreements, with the aim of creating a free-market environment. The open skies agreements include several 'freedoms of the air'.

[5] The recent open skies agreement between China and Australia, for example, has changed the tourism dynamics between these two countries as China has now become Australia's fastest growing and highest spending international visitor market. Around 1.3 million Chinese tourists visited Australia in 2017 spending around US$7.7 billion during their stay (China Daily, 2017).

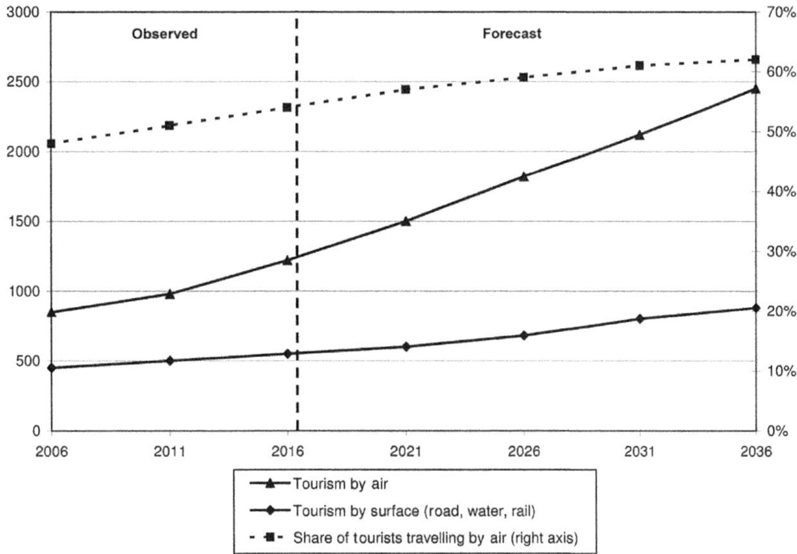

FIG. 10.1 International tourist arrivals by transport mode 2006–2036. *(Source: UNWTO. Untwo tourism highlights, 2017 Edition, 2017. Available at https://www.e-unwto.org/doi/pdf/10.18111/9789284419029. (Accessed February 29, 2018); Leahy, J. Growing horizons global market forecasts, 2017–2036. 2017. Available at http://www.airbus.com/content/dam/corporate-topics/publications/backgrounders/2017-06-09_GMF2017_John_Leahy.pdf. (Accessed March 29, 2018).)*

TABLE 10.1 The Number of Passengers Transported by the Different Airline Business Models 2003 versus 2016

	2003	2016	% change (2003–16)
Full-service airlines	1300 million	2660 million	105
Low-cost carriers	178 million	972 million	440
Regional airlines	147 million	109 million	−26
Charter airlines	83 million	69 million	−17
Total	1.7 billion	3.81 billion	124

Source: O'Connell analysis from ICAO, IATA, AEA, ATA, AAPA, AACO, Low Cost Carrier databases.

10.2 LOW-COST CARRIERS

There are now three categories of low-cost carriers (LCCs) in the world today which are the conventional LCC, ultra LCC, and long-haul LCC, and each of these will be discussed in detail later. The ultra and long-haul LCCs are newly formed derivatives or extensions of the conventional model. There is an extensive literature portfolio that provides evidence about the strong effect that low-cost airlines have on tourist outcomes. There seems little doubt that the rapid development of LCCs worldwide has had a significant impact on the tourism sector in terms of the transportation of air travellers and the promotion of tourist destinations that include both mature and emerging markets which are underpinned by low air fares (Tsui, 2017; Eugenio-Martin and Inchausti-Sintes, 2016; Dobruszkes and Mondou, 2013; Chung and Whang, 2011; Doganis, 2010; Donzelli, 2010; O'Connell and Williams, 2005). From a regional perspective there is strong evidence of the interrelationship as results from Young and Whang (2011) affirm that LCCs stimulated new demand to the South Korean tourist island of Jeju. Graham and Dennis (2010) remarked that the flow of tourists to Malta has increased because of LCCs. Meanwhile, Rey et al. (2011) confirmed that after the entrance of LCCs, the average number of tourists travelling from EU-15 countries to Spain had substantially increased.

10.2.1 The Conventional Low-Cost Carrier

Low-cost carriers have now been entrenched in the global landscape for more than four decades, supported by the adaptation of widespread deregulation policies in their domiciled markets. They have produced, arguably, the greatest paradigm shift in airline history. They have reshaped the competitive dynamics of the short-haul market and have been largely responsible for increased growth in air transport activity over the last 30 years. They operate on a

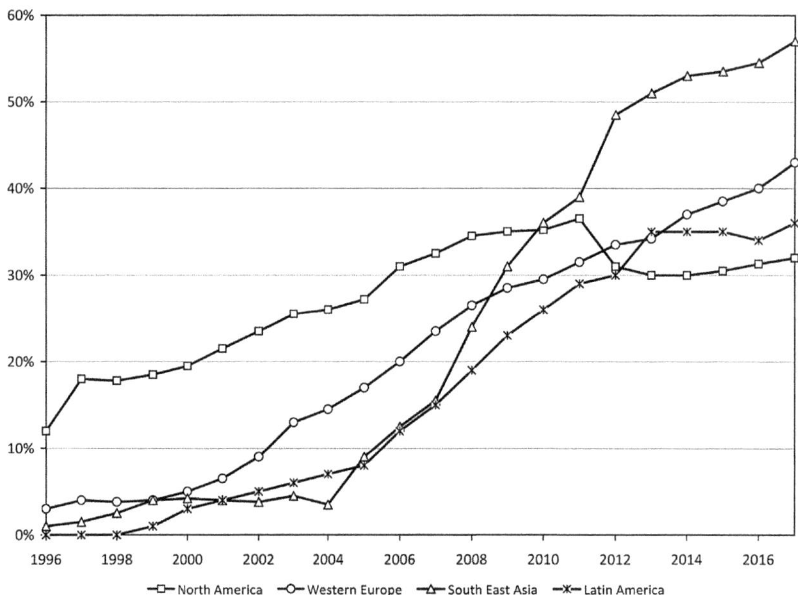

FIG. 10.2 Market share (in terms of seats) of low-cost carrier's worldwide from 1996 to 2017. *(Source: Author analysis from OAG data in 2018.)*

very different operating platform than that of full-service airlines as they enshrine the concept of 'low cost' into their organisational culture and offer low fares in exchange for eliminating many of the traditional passenger services. The academic literature widely covers the low-cost carrier business model which encapsulates the following characteristics: simplified fleet (one aircraft type), direct bookings via the website, debundled flight products to capitalise on ancillary revenue generation, high aircraft utilisation, maintaining strong pressure on labour productivity (lower salaries whilst retaining high output), absence of unions, secondary airports, point-to-point routes, high seat density, multiple bases, short sector lengths, operate multiple daily flight sectors, fast turnarounds, outsourcing, and so on (Button et al., 2018; O'Connell and Connolly, 2016; Fageda et al. 2015; Pearson et al. 2015; O'Connell and Warnock-Smith 2013; de Wit and Zuidberg, 2012; Doganis, 2010; O'Connell and Williams, 2005; Morrell, 2005; Doganis, 2005). Southwest Airlines formulated this innovative and robust business model back in 1971, which has subsequently been replicated all over the world. The business model reengineered the operating cost[6] structure into a lean, efficient, and highly productive business model paralleled with operational simplicity and high productivity (both aircraft and staff). It has gained considerable scale by extracting the gains generated from lower unit costs and then churning these advantages into lower fare offerings.

Table 10.1 presents that low-cost carriers have transported around 972 million passengers worldwide in 2016, up by a rapid 440% when compared to 2003 levels. The LCCs are continuing to add capacity at, arguably, alarming rates as Ryanair, for example, added 5000 more flights in the 12-month period from April 2016 to April 2017 according to OAG analysis. Fig. 10.2 gives a diagrammatical representation by seat capacity of the speed at which these low-cost carriers are expanding with 57% of South East Asia infiltrated by such business models by 2017, whilst they have captured 43% of the Western Europe market, together with 32% of North America whilst commanding 36% of the Latin American market.

These budget carriers are growing passenger traffic in two ways: first by stimulating new demand and second by diverting passengers away from full-service airlines, regional carriers, and charter airlines in the form of substitute traffic. The LCC business model is beginning to evolve as Ryanair which had strictly adhered to its strategy of removing complexity from its core competency for decades is now allowing customers to book Air Europa flights from its website, which enables them to book flights from 15 European cities via Madrid to 16 countries in North, Central, and South America, including Argentina, Brazil, Cuba, Mexico, and the United States. A more integrated phase is currently underway whereby Ryanair customers will be able to connect onto Air Europa long-haul flights through Madrid. Meanwhile Ryanair's point-to-point strategy is also beginning to evolve as passengers can *book connecting Ryanair flights* without having to go landside whilst their checked baggage will also be transferred onto the

[6] In 2017 the unit cost in terms of CASK (measured in €cents) is as follows: Wizz Air €3.18, Ryanair €3.24, easyJet €5.5, IAG €6.6, Air France–KLM €7.6, Lufthansa's €8.2 cents. Meanwhile Southwest's unit costs were around 20% lower than those of American Airlines and 17.5% lower than United Airlines. All stage lengths were adjusted for these unit cost calculations (author calculations).

connecting flight. This has been offered at Rome Fiumicino, Bergamo and Porto and could be spread out to its other 80+ hubs across Europe challenging the network of full-service carriers—this strategy is similar to what Southwest offers throughout their network in the United States. However, the Irish LCC is also trialling connections to other airlines that have intercontinental networks. Planned interline agreements with Norwegian and Aer Lingus that are due to begin in the summer of 2018 (Ryanair, 2018; Flightglobal 2018; Ryanair, 2017).

In addition, Ryanair may be setting the seeds of another step change in evolving its business model which may allure other LCCs to follow suit as it is growing its presence at primary airports. It has added bases in Athens, Brussels, Lisbon Rome Fiumicino, Amsterdam Schiphol and recent entered into the Lufthansa stronghold that belongs to the domain of Frankfurt Main airport (Bettini et al. 2018; Dobruszkes et al. 2017; Dziedzic and Warnock-Smith, 2016). As the strategies evolve the line between the full service and LCC become ever more blurred. The low-cost carriers strive not to compete directly against each other as OAG analysis reveals that Ryanair only directly overlaps with easyJet on 74 routes on its network. Ryanair only competes directly with Vueling on 62 and with Wizz Air on 30 routes. The LCCs are increasingly attacking the networks of the full-service airlines and this is significantly contributing to their mounting pressures that are ever relenting.

Low-cost carriers have also been synonymous with strong financial performance as many of the budget carriers have operating margins[7] that are considerably higher than network airlines. The high financial returns being reaped by the low-cost carriers has attracted investors, which has allowed them to become well capitalised and invest in enlarging their fleets. This is evident when assessing their ordering portfolio, as Ryanair is set to grow from 430 aircraft by mid-2018 to 569 737s over the coming years, whilst easyJet is set to expand from 185 A320s to 319, and Wizz Air intends to grow its fleet from 93 A320/321 aircraft to 368units by the same period. In addition, all three LCCs are ordering the next-generation aircraft which are accompanied with higher seating capacities, further exacerbating the overcapacity dilemma. Combined, these LCCs will add 518 more aircraft to the EU short-haul market, mounting further pressure onto full-service network airlines as their short-haul traffic which acts as a feeder mechanism to their long-haul operation is being severely threatened. In Asia, it is even more pronounced with Lion Air having 402 short-haul aircraft on order, AirAsia with 388, VietJet Air with 178, and India's IndiGo has a vast 442 narrowbody aircraft to be delivered over the coming years. Some primary airports in the region have also reacted to the shifting passenger dynamics by building dedicated low-cost carrier terminals to accommodate the new entrant wave of LCCs that seeks cost efficiencies at every level. Zhang et al. (2008) argued that the terminal at Kuala Lumpur International airport (now replaced) proved to be beneficial for AirAsia as it contributed to the company's cost reduction and output expansion. CAPA (2012) gives a defined numerical value on the cost savings gained by LCCs in using such a terminal by stating that Japan's Osaka Airport produced usage fees that were 40% lower when compared to the mainline terminal.

10.2.2 The Ultra Low-Cost Carrier

The conventional low-cost carrier model has been further segmented by the engineering of an 'ultra low-cost carrier' (ULCC) which has become increasingly popularised in the United States by Spirit Airlines, Allegiant Air, and Frontier Airlines. In a 2014 report, the US Government Accountability Office stated that these carriers are delineated because of their lower base fares and their high fees for ancillary services (GAO, 2014). Bachwich and Wittman (2017) proposed that three pillars were necessary in order to define the categorisation of an ULCC. First, they achieve significantly lower costs than LCCs or other network carriers. Second, they aggressively collect ancillary revenue for unbundled services. Finally as a result of lower base fares, they realise lower unit revenues than other carriers, even when ancillary revenues are taken into account. Author analysis reveals that there was a 32% cost per available seat mile differential between Southwest and Spirit in 2017, indicating the magnitude of the ULCC lean business model—the greatest cost saving emanated from labour. Ancillary revenues are game-changing strategies for the industry (Reales and O'Connell, 2017; Warnock-Smith et al. 2017; O'Connell and Warnock-Smith 2013—see also Chapter 9). The ULCC have utilised ancillaries to the maximum by charging for the most basic unbundle product including carry-on bags. Spirit generated 46.4% of its revenues from Ancillaries ($50 per passenger) in 2016 whilst Frontier and Allegiant derived 42.4% and 40%, respectively (Ideaworks, 2017). Research by Bachwich and Wittman (2017) through an econometrics model concluded that when there is an ULCC presence in a market, it triggered base fares to decline by 21%, as compared to an 8% average reduction for LCC presence. Hemmerdinger (2017) states that

[7] The following airline models show the spread of operating margins for 2017: Allegiant Air, 15.1%; AirAsia, 19.8%; Ryanair, 23.1%; Southwest, 16.6%; Wizz Air, 15.7%; WestJet, 9.8%; IAG, 11.9%; Lufthansa Group, 8.4%; Singapore Airlines, 3.5%; United Airlines, 9.3 (Source: 2017 annual accounts).

WestJet's proposed ULCC called Swoop will enter the Canadian market with fares that are 40% lower than current. These models are now proliferating throughout the world with Volaris and VivaAerobus in Mexico together with Jetlines and EnerJet in Canada.

10.2.3 The Long-Haul Low-Cost Carrier

As the short-haul markets get crowded, low-cost carriers are seeking out new growth opportunities elsewhere and a natural progression for the business model would be to expand into long-haul markets whose embryonic developments are currently unfolding at Norwegian[8] and AirAsia X. Boeing (2017) assessed that >90% of the current LCC capacity resides in the short-haul segment. However that is set to change rapidly as CAPA (2018a,b) identified that there are now >160 widebody aircraft operating scheduled long-haul low-cost services under 21 operator's[9] certificates from 17 countries in 2018.

As market structures become more complex and consumer behaviours continue to evolve low-cost long-haul (LCLH) business models are fast emerging throughout the world and are addressing a different passenger segmentation by extending affordable travel into long-haul destinations. There has been a renewed interest in LCLH as the liberalisation of intercontinental regulatory frameworks is expanding whilst at the same time new generation fuel-efficient aircraft have come to market. These new generation aircraft were designed to link new city pairs that bypass hubs traditional fortress hub airports that were dominated by full-service network airlines. The cost savings between the new and old generation aircraft are apparent as Boeing (2015) argues that the 787 offers 20% greater fuel efficiency than its 767 predecessor. The scholarly literature validates that LCLH operators may achieve a 20%–25% reduction in costs over traditional full-service network airlines, whilst in short-haul markets its much more divergent, registering 40%–60% (Wensveen, 2011).

The long-haul markets served by these LCCs are much more challenging than operating in short-haul markets, as entities such as capital costs for these expensive widebodies[10] are much higher when compared to their narrowbody counterparts. Moreover the network needs support in the form of feed traffic because just operating on a point-to-point basis significantly risks reducing the load factor. The high aircraft utilisation rates that materialise from fast turnaround times on the short-haul markets does not transpire in the long-haul sectors as the longer stage lengths pertaining to the LCLH means that the turnaround times occupy a much smaller proportion of aircraft's day. It is unable to operate multiple flight sectors per day due to its long stage length, which is an important trait that it enjoys in the short haul. Important cost items such as fuel and marketing represent a much higher share of costs for long haul, whilst staff and ground costs are a considerably smaller share of total costs on long haul. Typically, there are relatively few premium seats[11] on LCLH compared to traditional full-service airlines, thus reducing the revenue potential, especially on routes with significant demand for premium service like London to New York. However, OAG analysis reveals that the majority of the LCLHs in Southeast Asian markets are mostly operating on medium-haul routes that are <3800 nautical miles—in fact just 6 out of the 69 routes are deployed on longer routes. By positioning these widebodies on medium-haul routes, it puts them in direct competition with narrowbodies that have lower unit costs which ultimately impacts on overall profits.

The fare becomes the key pivotable cornerstone that sets the new entrant lean business model apart and it is the principal differentiator that attracts the passenger—Dewberry and Hou (2012) show that Asian long-haul low-cost carrier fares are on average 32% lower than those of their full-service carrier counterparts. De Poret et al. (2015) established that the financial viability of the long-haul low-cost carrier rested on high seat density, cargo revenues, and dependence on ancillary revenues. Earlier Asian-based LHLCs such as Oasis Hong Kong and Viva Macau failed in 2008

[8] Norwegian Air Shuttle is now the fastest-growing airline on routes between Europe and the United States. Its US network from Europe is set to grow from 44 routes in the summer 2017 to 55 routes in summer 2018. As of the end of December 2017, Norwegian has added over 850,000 seats on routes connecting Europe and the United States, almost five times as many as its closest rival, British Airways (Anker Report, 2018). This excessive seat supply by Norwegian is also influenced by the fact that it has a much denser seat capacity on its aircraft when compared to BA as its cabin is void of business and first class compartments—see footnote 11.

[9] The following LCLH airlines all operate with widebody aircraft as at May 2018 and include: Jetstar, AirAsia X, Scoot, Norwegian Air Shuttle, Air Canada Rouge, Cebu Pacific, Norwegian Air International, Jin Air, Azul, Thai AirAsia X, Indonesia AirAsia X, NokScoot, Lion Air, WestJet, Beijing Capital, Eurowings, Wow Air, Level, Norwegian Air UK, Thai Lion Air, French Bee (Source: CAPA, 2018a,b).

[10] The following are the manufacturer list price set in 2017: B787-8 ($224.6 million), B787-9 ($264.6 million), A330-300 ($256.4 million), A350-800XWB ($272.4 million). (Source: Air Transport World, 2017).

[11] The following are the seat configurations for the 787-9 in 2018 for British Airways and Norwegian. British Airways: First class, 8; Business class, 42; Premium economy, 39; Economy, 127. Norwegian Air Shuttle: Premium economy, 35; Economy, 309 (SeatGuru, 2018).

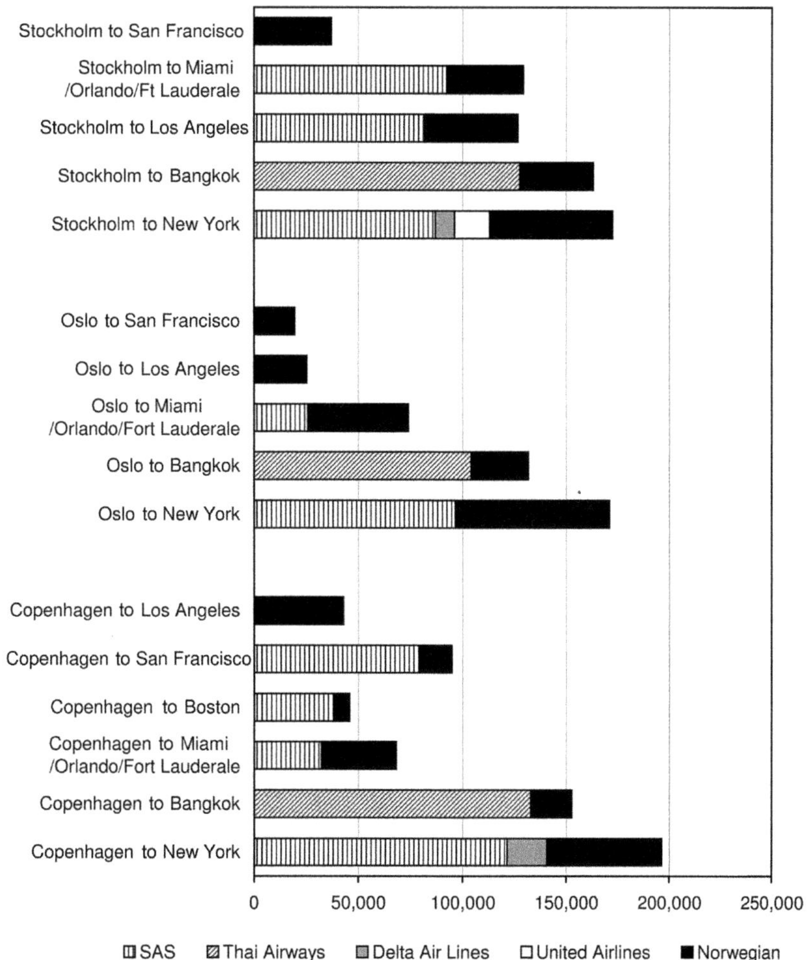

FIG. 10.3 Market penetration of Norwegian from Scandinavia in terms of seats (Summer 2017 vs. Summer 2018). *(Source: Author analysis from OAG.)*

and 2010, respectively, due to a lack of feed traffic and relentless competition with full-service airlines (Whyte and Lohmann, 2015; Daft and Albers, 2012; Wensveen and Leick, 2009). Low-cost long-haul carriers such as Norwegian, AirAsia X,[12] and Cebu Pacific which incubated as short-haul operators are now evolving to the next developmental stage by providing short-haul feeder traffic to support their long-haul routes. Airline Business (2017a) describes how Norwegian is offering connectivity beyond its London Gatwick hub as its bank structure is engineered so that arriving passengers from Singapore can connect to Norwegian's European destinations whilst similarly it can gather feed from its European and North American network for the service to Singapore. AirAsia X leverages its overall network, as 56% of its long-haul passengers are connecting in Kuala Lumpur with around 67% of those connecting passengers coupling from AirAsia to AirAsia X whilst the remaining 33% are transiting from AirAsia X to AirAsia X (AirAsia X, 2016). AirAsia has big aspirations as it has 70 widebodies (60 A330-900s and 10 A350-900s as of mid-2018) to be delivered together with 388 narrowbodies and a visionary master plan might foresee it becoming a global LCC super-connector as it exponentially enlarges the footprint of its international network, challenging the dominance of established legacy airlines such as the Arabian Gulf carriers, that are specifically modelled on capturing sixth freedom traffic. This style of operation is being copied by other LHLC worldwide as Philippine-based Cebu Pacific has 15% of its traffic connecting from long-haul destinations to its domestic market (CAPA 2018a,b).

Figs 10.3 and 10.4 highlight the expeditious penetration of Norwegian and AirAsia X, respectively, from their home base over a 12-month period from the summer of 2017 to the summer of 2018 on key intercontinental markets.

[12] Besides its domiciled base at Kuala Lumpur, it has joint ventures (JVs) with Indonesia AirAsia X and Thai AirAsia X. It has further aspirations to utilise the AirAsia X outposts in India to conjoin with Europe and for its affiliate in Japan to penetrate into the US West Coast (Flightglobal, 2017).

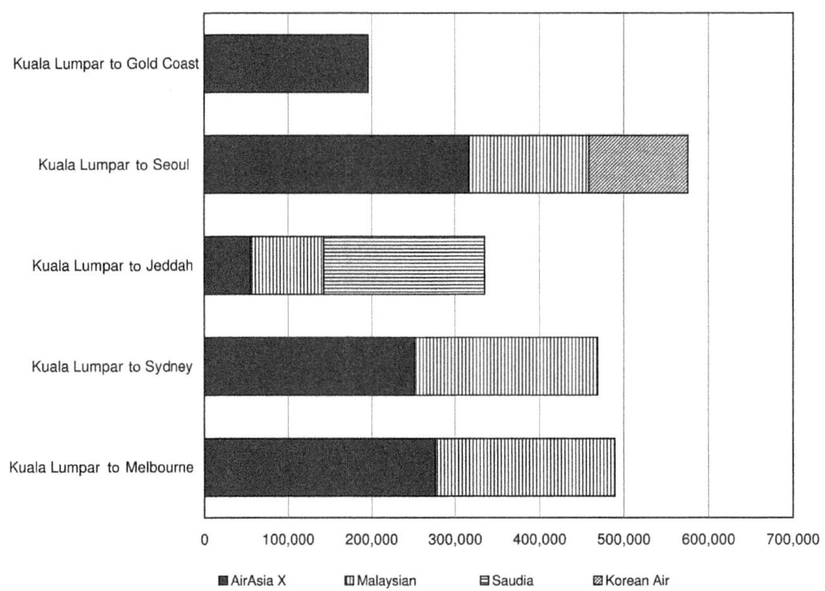

FIG. 10.4 Market penetration of AirAsia X from Kuala Lumpur in terms of seats (Summer 2017 vs. Summer 2018). *(Source: Author analysis from OAG.)*

Norwegian and AirAsia X have grown the traditional and well-established routes like the Scandinavian capital cites (Stockholm, Oslo, Copenhagen) to New York and Kuala Lumpur to Melbourne, whilst simultaneously triggering new demand by operating to new destinations that were not deemed feasible or overlooked by the legacy airlines such as AirAsia X's route from Kuala Lumpur to Australia's Gold Coast whilst Norwegian operates solely on routes that include: Stockholm to San Francisco, Oslo to San Francisco and Los Angles, Copenhagen to Los Angeles.

Twenty years earlier, full-service airlines largely dismissed the threat of LCCs on their short-haul markets but are now quickly reacting to the long-haul threat by creating their own low-cost long-haul subdivision as witnessed by Singapore Airlines,[13] Qantas, Air Canada, Korean Air, Lufthansa, Hainan Airlines, and IAG.

10.3 FULL-SERVICE NETWORK AIRLINES

Full-service airlines have been largely responsible for bringing tourists to distant destinations and are a critical component to the tourism value chain. In the summer of 2018, British Airways, for example, served 29 destinations in North America, 21 in Latin America, 18 in Africa, 11 in the Middle East, and 15 in Asia—the extensive network that is operated nonstop creates a multiple array of tourist destination permutations which produces an enticing opportunity for vacation travellers. Thailand, for example, has exponentially grown its tourist traffic over the past two decades as it welcomed 7.8 million visitors in 2007, burgeoning to over 35 million by 2017 of which European and American tourists represented 27% and 6%, respectively—the vast majority of these arrived by full-service airlines (Thailand Ministry of Tourism and Sports, 2018).

Full-service airlines have a long legacy as they were mostly set up by governments as far back as the 1930s, or even earlier, and many continue today to be the flag carriers of their respected countries. They have been the world's dominant airline business model for decades but they are being continuously challenged as new disruptive airlines continue to enter the global marketplace equipped with leaner cost structures, high productivity mandates, and best practice efficiencies that trigger structural shifts within the industry that distinctly affects the full-service airlines. As the global airline industry continues with its restructuring, its financial performance has improved notably since the financial crisis in 2008.

Over the decades, full-service network airlines have been synonymous with underperforming financial returns due to a plethora of underpinning criteria that included government interference, bureaucratic management,

[13]Singapore Airlines, for example, setup Scoot in 2012. By mid-2018 it operated 24 short-haul aircraft and 16 787s in a two-class configuration and has a further 39 A320 neo's and 4 787s on order. It currently operates to 65 destinations in 19 countries but it predominantly serves mid-range destinations from Singapore but is operating to Athens and Honolulu with ambitions to replicate this long-haul flying activity to other European cities (Flightglobal, 2018).

overstaffing, inefficiencies, low productivity, no clear strategy, strong unions, high wages, poor service quality, and high fares which contributed to amassing successive losses year after year. They were identified with the term 'legacy' which is often associated with outdated practices (Doganis, 2010; Doganis, 2005; O'Connell, 2011a, O'Connell, 2011b; O'Connell, 2007). They have emerged from decades of regulation and remain riddled with high cost structures. Passengers have become more demanding down through the decades and can now select from a large pool of competitors. It was difficult for network airlines to maintain their high levels of service standards due to their need for widespread cost cutting because of the low returns that the industry historically generated. The dual effect of high costs and the complexity of the business model are making it very difficult for full-service airlines to effectively defend their territory especially in short-haul markets.[14] This vulnerability continues to be vigorously exploited by the LCCs and this effect has been replicated in many parts of the world that have deregulated their markets.

However, the majority of full-service airlines are now gaining financial traction and generating stronger margins. Overall, the industry is now creating economic value as IATA forecasts 2018 to be the 4th consecutive year of above-cost-of-capital returns for investors, which demonstrates that the industry is changing into a leaner, flexible, and more competitive entity (IATA, 2017). It has also been helped by the strengthening global economic outlook, favourable fuel prices, liberalisation including antitrust immunity, equity investments, consolidation and drop in jobs, new employment contracts following airlines' restructuration plans to avoid bankruptcy, joint ventures, ancillary revenues, network restructuring, and so forth. Embraer (2017) shows the changing landscape by identifying that the cost gap between traditional full-service and budget airlines has fallen by an average of 40% in 10 years both in the United States and Europe, partly because the full-service airlines have abandoned old differentiators like free baggage and in-flight catering on short-haul flights. The growing intersection led airlines to a broader scope and variety of their products and services to fight for the same passengers.

The bulk of the world's traffic continues to be carried by full-service airlines (2.66 billion passengers) and their principal differentiator and core competency is their hub and spoke apparatus which facilities the seamless movement of passengers through a central hub. The traffic emanates from both their own network and from the networks of other carriers via code share agreements or through alliance/equity partnerships. A hub is a highly efficient means of coordinating incoming 'spoke' traffic with departing flights at a carriers' home base. The strategy involves combining point-to-point traffic with transferring passengers originating from the points at the end of each spoke of the hub. Whereas the point-to-point traffic terminates at the hub, the transferring passengers pass through and depart to other domestic or international destinations on the hub's spoke network. The science involves the synchronisation of incoming flights to provide maximum feed for departing aircraft waiting to take-up their multiorigin share of incoming passengers. This form of scheduling creates a bank of many incoming flights arriving almost simultaneously, followed by a wave of departures. This method serves as an effective traffic multiplier (Akca, 2018; O'Connell and Bueno, 2016; Logothetis and Miyoshi, 2016; Alderighi et al., 2005; Dennis, 1994).

Author analysis of MIDT data reveals that approximately 40% of all long-haul passengers carried by Lufthansa are directly originating at its hubs in Frankfurt and Munich, whilst about 60% are transfer passengers. Under a hub and spoke network, the carrier operates flights from smaller markets to a hub airport, timing arrivals close together so that passengers can then connect to flights from the hub to other markets. A major advantage of the hub-and-spoke system for the carrier is that it gives the carrier the ability to generate more traffic over light-density and high-density routes. However, this strategy demands a variety of aircraft sizes to accommodate different markets, which triggers fleet complexity. Lufthansa, for example, operates 277 aircraft that include A319, A320, A321, A330, A340, A380, A350, B747, Fokker, whilst it has orders/options for additional 777s and CS100s—this complexity adds layers of cost for training, spare parts, maintenance, crew optimisation.

Airline services have been generally characterised by customer segmentation. Therefore the full-service airlines have multiple passenger cabins ranging from first class, business, premium economy,[15] and economy. However, the

[14]Discussions at airline conferences in Europe indicate that most of the short-haul operations by full-service airlines in Europe are loss making. Air France–KLM, for example, posted short-haul losses of €300 m in 2015, with the majority of these losses stemming from Air France.

[15]Premium economy is a separate class of seating and service that differs from the standard economy class product. It offers about 5–7 in. of extra legroom as well as additional amenities, which can include wider seats, more recline, leg rests, more channels on the in-flight entertainment system with larger screens, laptop power ports, and premium food service. Premium economy is generally 35% more expensive than the standard economy fare. The 3 US Majors and around 36 different European carriers (including several sister brands) together with 19 Asia-Pacific airlines now offer either a dedicated premium economy section or an enhanced economy product on their widebody aircraft by mid-2018. Virgin Atlantic, one of the premium economy pioneers now has the largest premium economy section of any operator with the 66 seats on board its 747-400s. Meanwhile India's Vistara is the world's first carrier to offer a premium economy cabin on its narrowbody aircraft that it uses in the Indian domestic market.

lines between first class and the ever-improving business class are becoming ever more blurred with first[16] class disappearing altogether except for specific branded carriers with extensive long-haul networks like BA, Emirates, Lufthansa, and Singapore Airlines. These carriers pursue high yield passengers and as a result the business model incorporates the following traits: large networks; interconnectivity that is further augmented through alliance partnerships and code share feeders; a wide array of distribution channels (e.g. travel agents, online travel agents, call centres, websites); a wide spectrum of amenities for business passengers (e.g. airport lounges, fast track security, limousine service); personalisation; flexible[17] tickets; a vast portfolio of in-flight products (e.g. flat beds, quality food and beverage, advanced in-flight entertainment systems with multiple channels, internet, and mobile phone connectivity); convenient airports; frequent flyer programmes; and so forth. Therefore providing service quality has become pinnacle in remaining competitive. Revenue from premium traffic (first and business class) remains an important income generator and can account for 30%–40% of total passenger revenue, whilst the vast majority of this comes from business class (CAPA, 2017b). The Telegraph (2017) reported that premium traffic between the Europe to Middle East market produces 7.7% of passengers but represent almost 37% of the revenue.

Full-service network airlines also transport cargo[18] and remain an important component of the business model. Around three-quarters of air cargo is transported by airlines that combine passenger and cargo divisions, with cargo typically generating up to 9% of the revenues of the industry (IATA, 2018b). However, this varies significantly from carrier to carrier as European carriers such as British Airways and the Lufthansa Group generated 4.7% and 7.7%, respectively, of their total revenues from cargo in 2017, whilst US-based carriers like American and United each generated around 2%. However, many Asian carriers generate a large proportion of their revenues from cargo. China Airlines, Cathay Pacific, Korean Air, EVA Air, for example, generated 27%, 24%, 23%, 21%, respectively, of their revenues from cargo in 2016 according to the author's analysis. Air cargo has been a difficult industry to extract high returns as it is exposed to an array of impeding factors that include cyclical downturns, overcapacity, falling yields, low load factors—measuring 49.1% in November 2017 (IATA, 2018c), directionality issues, supply chain bottlenecks, power of freight forwarders, security, customs checks, excessive paperwork, and so forth. There is also a structural change taking place as more cargo is now being transported in the belly hold of widebody aircraft as new fuel-efficient aircraft come to market. Currently around 45% of freight is carried via belly hold capacity but this is expected to increase significantly over the coming years (Airline Business, 2017b). As a consequence passenger airlines with dedicated cargo operations are increasingly divesting from their full freighter fleet due to the strong fluctuations in the air cargo market and the ample belly capacity of new long-haul passenger aircraft.

Full-service network airlines are bound to remain an important entity over the coming decades. They are an essential component in reaching distant tourist markets due to their extensive international networks that are further supplemented by code share agreements through alliance and equity partners where the remotest tourist site can be integrated into the network. They are increasingly being forged in order to adapt to a continuously changing competitive landscape that is becoming increasingly ferocious. They need to rely on producing added value and consumer-driven product differentiation beyond the basics of the LCC product.

10.4 CHARTER AIRLINES

Charter airlines are normally owned by tour operators such as the TUI Group. These tour operators are large-scale businesses that combine two or more travel services (e.g. transport, accommodation, catering, entertainment, and sightseeing) and sell them either through travel agencies or directly to final consumers as a single product called a 'package holiday'. This seamless integrated business conglomerate allows for significant savings through economies of scale as each stakeholder works to optimise synergies and reduce risk across the multifaceted enterprise resulting in a lean but value-adding package holiday. There are about 45 charter airlines operating commercial aircraft seating over 80 passengers in Europe (Flightglobal, 2017). Barrett (2008) explains that charter carriers are also known as nonscheduled airlines and were considered as the first low-cost model. They operated under a different regulatory

[16] Amongst the big three US carriers, Delta has phased out international first class altogether, United is eliminating it in 2018, and American offers it on only a small number of flights. Elsewhere in the world, airlines including Cathay Pacific, Lufthansa, Air India, Qantas, Singapore Airlines, Emirates are all reducing the number of first-class seats. Qatar Airways has first class only on its A380 fleet.

[17] Ticket flexibility is provided for the business class passenger who wishes to change the travel date or time and reserves the right to cancel the trip and receive a full refund.

[18] Approximately 62.5 million tonnes will be transported by air in 2018. This represents <1% of world trade by volume, but over 35% by value (IATA, 2018b).

environment by circumnavigating the bilateral constraints as well as the price mechanisms imposed by IATA, which allowed them to expand rapidly (Williams, 2002, 2008, 2011).

Charter airlines usually offer flights as part of a holiday package that integrates the flight, hotel accommodation, meals, airport transfers, as well as providing entertainment and escorted tours to places of historical and social significance. Doganis (2010) states that the high volume of vacationers allows tour operators to amass substantial bulk discounts on hotel accommodation, thus creating considerable economies of scale. Europe generates half of the world's international tourist traffic which has more than doubled in just 5 years to 616 million and as a consequence, most of the charter activity emanates from this continent. Williams (2002, 2008, 2011) stated that the development of inclusive tour charter flights has been a significant factor in the development of holiday tourism to/from Europe. The United Kingdom is one of Europe's largest leisure tourism markets from both an inbound and outbound perspective; consequently, this market is a good indicator of transformation. Indeed, the landscape is rapidly changing as data from the UK CAA (2017) revealed that the overall UK Charter market has declined from 34.5 million passengers in 2001 to 11.2 million by 2016, which clearly portrays that this business model is in decline. It fell by a huge 27% alone in 2016, which was the biggest rate of decline over the 15-year period. CAPA (2017a) confers that the decline of the charter market throughout Europe is very significant as charter flights accounted for only 3.4% of total flights in Europe in 2016, which was considerably less than half of the 7.7% share taken by charter flights in 2005.

The short haul and long haul are the two specific markets that are affecting charter airlines in different ways, and the dynamics being encountered are very divergent. First in the short-haul market, charters have been directly competing with the LCCs (see Chapter 11). Monarch Airlines is an example of the demise of charters on the short-haul markets. It was a well-established 50-year-old UK charter airline with its fleet composed entirely of short fleet aircraft that became insolvent in late 2017 as its business model focused exclusively on the short-haul UK-Mediterranean/North African routes which was in direct competition with the LCCs. To compete in its new environment, Monarch adapted[19] by evolving their business model to that of a scheduled low-cost carrier. Monarch's CEO stated that its restructuring from charter to scheduled flying was primarily because 'short-haul charter flying is on its way out' (Airline Business, 2017c; Taylor, 2015).

O'Connell and Bouquet (2015) provide a detailed explanation for this decline by finding that dynamic packaging has played a key role in the demise of charter airlines on these short-haul leisure markets (see also Chapter 2). Dynamic packaging is the term used when passengers are able to self-assemble their own package of travel products including flights, accommodation, car rental, travel insurance, tourism themes which are seamlessly coalesced through one transaction via the airlines' own website. This mechanism allows vacationers to bypass the package holidays offered by charter airlines. As a consequence, this has forced the charter airlines to diversify and seek out alternative tourist sites in distant continents. Previous to this consumers had to visit many independent websites or book a package holiday that had all the vacation components under a single price. Graham (2008) has argued that consumers are seeking more flexibility in tourism products because they are becoming more experienced in travelling and they are becoming more sophisticated and demanding, whilst Ayazlar (2014) ascertains that today's passengers want to customise and self-manage their own personal holidays. This process has created a seismic shift in the charter airline business model, particularly on short-haul markets.

In the long-haul market, charters have been much more successful and have enjoyed longevity of high demand over the years. The Office for National Statistics (2016) found that around 6 million long-haul holiday visits were made by UK residents in 2016, representing 13.4% of the total UK holiday visits, and this number of vacationers has remained constant over the last number of years. Passengers are more willing to book an all-inclusive package for long-haul destinations as the complexity associated with languages, laws, geopolitics, cultures differ significantly from the home country. Therefore these holidaying tourists are far more likely to book through a tour operator, especially for retired vacationers. They have the added reassurance of an enjoyable stay as the tour company plants a holiday representative at the resort to smoothen any irregularities or unforeseen difficulties, which provides a key differentiator from that of a self-assembled holiday package from an airline website. As a consequence the long-haul all-inclusive package holiday provided by charter airlines has retained its attraction and appeal to society—data from the mature UK market indicate that they have consistently captured around 40% of the international holiday market over the last two decades (Office for National Statistics, 2016). The question is whether this long-haul charter market can be replaced by long-haul low-cost carriers who operate to distant holiday destinations. Research from

[19] In 2000 < 10% of Monarch's passengers flew on their scheduled services, but by 2016, it had reverted to almost 100% (OAG analysis by the author). Before its demise it operated 14 routes to Portugal from the UK where it was in competition with 3 carriers, whilst its Spanish routes to Malaga from both Birmingham and Manchester had 7 airlines operating which significantly challenged its positioning in the marketplace (Airline Business, 2017c).

Rodrıguez and O'Connell (2017) concluded that this will not be the case in the near future and found that age segmentation will play a big role in determining this criteria as their research deduced that older generation (>56 years of age) were significantly more willing to book their holiday through a tour operator that provides an all-inclusive package, rather than separately aggregating all these individual travel products from the website of a low-cost long-haul carrier.

However, charter airlines are very exposed to terrorist[20] incidents and after an attack the immediate impulse of vacationers who had booked a vacation to the afflicted zone is to assess their itinerary. O'Connor et al. (2008) measured such an assessment through a survey and found that 70% of the respondents would not continue with the planned trip. However, holiday packages are sold many months ahead of the departure date and consequently these vacation packages are very difficult to reallocate, because charters operate on a platform of horizontal integration whereby airline reservations, hotel rooms, and catering are bundled into a single basket and often into a specific tailor-made package. Airlines strictly follow Government warnings and frequently cancel/reschedule flights or administer additional security measurements—in late 2015 easyJet following a UK Government guideline prohibited passengers from checking-in luggage on flights returning from the Egyptian resort of Sharm El-Sheik following an attack on a Russian airliner until security measures at the airport were elevated (Calder, 2015).

However, two pivotal cornerstones that differentiate charter airlines, especially in the United Kingdom, are their ATOL affiliation and their destination expertise. First, the Air Travel Organiser License (ATOL) is a safeguard against insolvency or bankruptcy of a tour operator. All tour operators and travel companies selling holiday packages including flights in the United Kingdom are required by law to hold this licence. It will ensure that consumers already abroad can complete their holidays and be repatriated to their homeland at no extra cost and those who have paid for their holidays but have not yet departed will receive a full refund. Second, charters are destination 'Knowledge Brokers' as they provide a vertically integrated platform that encapsulates a wide spectrum that includes flight, hotel, meals, entertainment, tour representative, and so forth giving the business model a hierarchical significance over other airline business models. However, many of the full-service airlines such as British Airways, Virgin Atlantic, Emirates, Etihad Airways[21] have holiday divisions that now compete vigorously with charter airlines.

10.5 REGIONAL AIRLINES

The fleet type generally differentiates the regional airlines from the other types of airline business models as they operate aircraft that generally have <130 seats composed of a mix of turboprop and regional jets. From a worldwide perspective, these regional carriers interlink these remote regions with tourists and provide a much appreciated catalytic effect in proving economic prosperity, employment, and have become key drivers of the socioeconomic development of these rural areas. The passenger's decision for choosing the most suitable holiday option depends on a variety of factors such as the consumer profile, the distance to the final destination, the transport options, and the price of services (Dwyer et al. 2004; Forsyth et al. 2006). Halpern (2010) states that these remote regions are blessed with natural resources like beaches, mountains, wilderness, and wildlife which can be exploited for the development of inbound tourism with air travel being the fastest and most efficient means of gaining access to the destination.

The number of in-service, regional aircraft with 50–130 seats has grown by nearly 40% since 2005 (Ascend, 2016). The underpinning criteria for such growth include economic prosperity following the 2009 recession, an increase in passenger traffic originating from clusters of secondary cities, and an increased focus on fuel efficiency. The European Regional Airline Association (2015) reports that 50% of passengers worldwide fly sectors below 500 nautical miles (NM) and 30% fly sectors below 300NM, which are ideal sector lengths for regional aircraft. In 2017 the member airlines that comprise the association grew their total number of operated routes to 1673, which was a 15% increase over the previous year, which in turn increased their overall capacity by 4.4%. The equipment operated by these

[20]Turkey, for example, had long been an attractive destination for European holidaymakers, but the combination of an attack on Istanbul Ataturk airport, followed thereafter by the attempted coup in the summer of 2016, led to a 37% decrease in foreign visitor numbers over the previous year (Republic of Turkey ministry of culture and tourism, 2016). Meanwhile, Russia initiated a total suspension of flights to Egypt following the shooting down of a MetroJet aircraft from Sharm El-Sheikh whilst many other carriers remain reluctant to serve the resort. Tourism across the North African corridor is blanketed with political unrest and potential terror threats which have forced the charters to source new appealing markets elsewhere, substantially escalating its marketing budget.

[21]Etihad Holidays, introduced a revolutionary platform labelled 'sunshine guarantee' for holidaying in Abu Dhabi from 1st May until 30 September—2016 if it rains, consumers will be refunded (Etihad Holidays, 2016).

European[22] regional operators averaged flight sectors of just 1.25 h with aircraft that have an average seating capacity of 79 seats, which is ideal for serving thin markets in peripheral city airports—in fact 26% of their seats targeted tertiary airports in 2017 (European Regional Airline Association, 2018). In China, over 50% of the routes carry only 100 passengers which is a huge opportunity for regional operators (Toh, 2017).

Regional airlines serve a dual role by feeding passenger traffic into the hubs of full-service airlines and by operating on low-density routes from peripheral communities which are unprofitable for the full-service carriers. The partnerships between regional airlines and full-service carriers differ considerably throughout the world. In the United States, regional airlines provide feeder services to American Airlines,[23] for example, with a large number of these US regional affiliates also serving a number of other US Majors[24] at the same time. These US regional airlines transported almost 155 million passengers in 2016 with an aggregated fleet size of 1995 aircraft (1661 regional jets and 294 turboprops) that provide around 42% of all scheduled departures in the US domestic market. They served nearly every US airport[25] (622 airports) of which two-thirds (415 airports) relied exclusively on the regional airline service for their community's only scheduled service (Regional Airline Association, 2017).

Gillen et al. (2015) declares that the US Majors have a dual approach when securing a contract with regional airlines. First, they pay the regional airline a fixed fee for each departure, fixed fee for each passenger, with additional incentives based on completion of flights, on-time performance, and baggage handling performance. Second, there is an option for a revenue-sharing arrangement, where the two carriers negotiate a proration formula, whereby the regional airline receives a percentage of the ticket revenue for those passengers travelling. These contracts generally last for 2 years and passengers travelling on the regional airline earn the network airline's frequent flyer points. However, the pilots at the mainline carriers such as American Airlines have a strict contract clause with the regional operators, to whom they outsource flying. These contracts regulate the type of aircraft that are operated and which routes they serve. There are two important limits that must be adhered prior to the contract being sanctioned which mandate that the maximum seat limit is set at 76 seats, whilst its Maximum Take-Off Weight (MTOW) must not exceed 86,000 lbs. The scope clause particularly favours the Bombardier's CRJ900 and Embraer's E-175 as these two aircraft types fit under the scope clause. However, aircraft such as the Mitsubishi MRJ90 and E-175 E2 exceed the 86,000 lb. scope limit which is problematic for these manufacturers in gaining traction into the fleets of the 26 US regional carriers.

The structure is different in Europe and Asia as regional airlines are designed primarily to feed traffic only to their parent company (Lufthansa CityLine pledges allegiance solely to Lufthansa, whilst Australia's Sunstate Airlines serves only Qantas). There are also independent regional airlines such as FlyBe that pursue niche markets and also provide leased aircraft in the livery of SAS and Brussels Airlines. FlyBe offers unique connectivity to many of its network points, as it is developing a series of interline and code share partnerships with long-haul carriers such as Virgin Atlantic and Cathay Pacific. Its agility means that it can react quickly to opportunities as it commenced domestic service from Heathrow to Edinburgh and Aberdeen, filling the void of Virgin Atlantic's outsourced subsidiary Little Red which exited and it is now expanding this domestic network to other long-haul partners. Europe's regional airlines operate 1.1 million flights a year and carry just 62 million passengers using a fleet of 765 aircraft contributing €52 billion to European GDP (McNamara, 2016). OAG data indicates that Europe's regional airlines supply around 12% of the intra-European seats, whilst the 10 largest[26] regional airlines account for 70% of all regional seats. During a typical week in June 2012, regional airlines operated 18,780 feeder flights to the European hubs of full-service network airlines, which is sizeable considering that Ryanair operated around 1300 during this period. Two-thirds of KLMs Cityhopper passengers, for example, transfer to/from its parent KLM mainline airline, whilst the remaining is point to point without transfer.

[22]Europe's biggest Regional Airline operators in 2017 and their share of the Region airline market: Hop, 5.1%; FlyBe, 4.5%; Lufthansa CityLine, 2.8%; KLM Cityhopper, 2.8%; Wideroe, 2.3%; SAS (regional division), 2.1%; Austrian (regional division), 2.1%; Air Nostrum, 2.1%; Lot Polish Airlines (regional division), 1.9%; Others, 74.4% (Source: OAG analysis by author).

[23]American Airlines regional brand is American Eagle, which in turn has 9 different operating partners in American Eagle livery that include Air Wisconsin, Envoy Air, ExpressJet Airlines, Mesa Airlines, Piedmont, PSA, Republic Airlines, SkyWest Airlines, and Trans States Airlines.

[24]For example, SkyWest Airlines provides services (with number of daily flights in parenthesis) for Alaska Airlines (135), Delta Air Lines (913), American Airlines (310), and United Airlines (817). Skywest Airlines carried 35.9 million passengers in 2017, with a fleet of 431 aircraft (SkyWest Airlines, 2018).

[25]US regional airports accounted for 19% of seats in 2017 (Anna.aero, 2018).

[26]These 10 regional airlines (with % of total regional seats) include Lufthansa Regional, 15%; Flybe, 11%; HOP!, 10%; Wideroe, 5%; KLM cityhopper, 8%; Iberia Regional (Air Nostrum), 5%; Swiss Global, 5%; Alitalia Cityliner, 4%; Finnair (Norra), 4%; Binter Canarias 3%. (Source: OAG analysis by author).

Regional airlines have a lower operating cost on a per trip basis as there is not enough demand to fill a larger aircraft like a 737 or 320. The operating cost for a 740-km trip on a regional jet with 86 seats is around $4330 compared to a narrowbody aircraft with 170 seats, whose operating costs amount to $6575 in 2015 (European Regional Airline Association, 2015). A notable exclusivity for regional airlines in Europe is that they are often the only service provider on thin routes as research from OAG analysis uncovers that regional airlines were the sole operator on over 40% of the total routes with many availing of economic compensation under the Public Service Obligation (PSO) schemes, which are available for 232 routes in Europe.

Finally, the landscape surrounding the larger sized regional airlines appears solid as they have the 'right fit' aircraft (with <120 seats) that operate on short sectors often with high daily frequencies on thin routes that do not justify the use of large narrowbody equipment—these attributes particularly favour the high yield business passenger.

10.6 CONCLUSION

This chapter has discussed the four main airline business models, namely, low-cost carriers, full-service network airlines, charter airlines, and regional airlines—each has a different set of structural dimensions, operating characteristics, and specifications.

The LCCs have caused the greatest seismic shift in airline history as they have reshaped the industry's competitive dynamics and have forced airlines to evolve and adapt in order to function in the new operating environment. Traditional low-cost carriers have themselves become fragmented by constructing derivatives which are comprised of ultra low-cost carriers and low-cost long-haul carriers that are targeting specific passenger segments with low fares. These embryonic business models are quickly gaining traction in the global market place and are placing increasing competitive pressure on the other airline business models. In particular, the LCLHs are now moving into the coveted territory of the long-haul market of the full-service airlines which was their last remaining domain and this has triggered ripple effects as flag carriers themselves are moving fast to setup their own LCLH subsidiaries. The LCLHs have engineered their bank structure at their hub airports such that their own short-haul traffic feeds into their long-haul network. This is replicating the full-service hub and spoke mechanism but invariably at a lower unit cost which transpires into lower fares tempting passengers to switch to the cheaper option, furthering the challenge for full-service airlines.

The legacy carriers themselves have in turn mirrored parts of LCCs by unbundling the fare and selling individual components, such as seat selection, bags, and so forth, causing the two airline business models to become blurred, particularly on short-haul markets. To compound the obscurity, LCCs are now beginning to feed full-service carriers that are members of the global alliances whose primary objective is to distribute passengers to each other's network. Undoubtedly there is a convergence between the two business models that is favouring LCCs, which will increase their market penetration. However, the flag carriers retain certain value adding and consumer-driven product differentiation far beyond the basics of the LCC product such as seamless hub and spoke connectivity supported by alliance affiliation, multiple cabins including business class, vast array of flight products and distribution channels, superior customer service, cargo logistics capability, and so forth.

The charter airlines are, arguably, becoming an unworkable entity in the short market as they compete against the LCCs. Passengers are self-assembling their own customised package of travel products via websites, thereby creating a seismic shift in the fate of charters particularly to destinations that are in the network range of the LCCs. However, the long-haul charter operations continue to thrive, particularly for the older generation as they are more willing to book all-inclusive package holidays in distant continents as the complexity associated with languages, customs/laws, differ significantly from the home country. However, a key question is what disruptive effect will LHLCs have in the near future.

Finally the regional airlines are bespoke and unique due to the category of aircraft that they operate which usually have <130 seats. They serve a dual role by feeding passenger traffic into hub airports and by operating on thin low density routes from peripheral communities that are uneconomic for full-service airlines or LCCs, which solidifies their positioning in the marketplace thereby giving the business model longevity and sustainability. The regional carriers are either independent or subsidiaries that belong to full-service airlines. In the United States, some of the independent entities provide feeder services to each of the three big US Majors, whilst in Europe and in Asia, regional carriers usually pledge allegiance solely to their parent affiliate.

References

Air Transport World (2017). Airbus and boeing average list prices 2017. Available at http://atwonline.com/data-financials/airbus-and-boeing-average-list-prices-2017. (Accessed April 17, 2018).

AirAsia X (2016). Annual Report, 2015. Available at http://www.airasiax.com/. (Accessed April 19, 2018).

Airbus (2017). Horizons global market forecasts, 2017–2036. Available at http://www.airbus.com/content/dam/corporate-topics/publications/backgrounders/Airbus_Global_Market_Forecast_2017-2036_Growing_Horizons_full_book.pdf. (Accessed March 27, 2018).

Airline Business, 2017a. Asia-Europe back on Airlines radar. Airline Business 33 (5), 26–27. June.

Airline Business, 2017b. Turning up the volumes. Airline Business 33 (8), 36–38. October.

Airline Business, 2017c. Monarch a casualty amid leisure market saturation. Airline Business, 8–9. November.

Akca, Z., 2018. Comparative analysis with a new hub connectivity measure considering revenue and passenger demand. J. Air Transp. Manag. 67, 34–45.

Albalate, D., Fageda, X., 2016. High speed rail and tourism: empirical evidence from Spain. Transp. Res. A 85, 174–185.

Alderighi, M., Cento, A., Nijkamp, P., Rietveld, P., 2005. Network competition—the coexistence of hub-and-spoke and point-to-point systems. J. Air Transp. Manag. 11 (5), 328–334.

Anker Report (2018). Norwegian dominates Europe-US growth in S18; total capacity up 6%, 8th January. Available at https://img1.wsimg.com/blobby/go/f91e7ea1-3ed0-4ecd-a54c-55cff9d5319a/downloads/1c8qab5v5_571278.pdf. (Accessed March 2, 2018).

Anna.aero (2018). US regional airports accounted for 19% of seats in 2017; ULCCs report greatest growth; Pittsburgh and Cleveland are on the up, 31st January. Available at http://www.anna.aero/2018/01/31/us-regional-airports-accounted-for-24-of-all-seats-in-2017/. (Accessed March 30, 2018).

Ascend (2016). Aircraft and Airline Data. Available at http://www.ascendworldwide.com/what-we-do/ascend-data/aircraft-airline-data/ascend-online-fleets.html. (Accessed March 27, 2018).

Ayazlar, R.A., 2014. Dynamic packaging applications in travel agencies. Procedia Soc. Behav. Sci. 131, 326–331.

Bachwich, A.R., Wittman, M.D., 2017. The emergence and effects of the ultra-low cost carrier (ULCC) business model in the U.S. airline industry. J. Air Transp. Manag. 62, 155–164.

Barrett, S., 2008. The Emergence of the Low Cost Carrier Sector. In: Graham, A., Papatheodorou, A., Forsyth, P. (Eds.), Aviation and Tourism: Implications for Leisure Travel. Ashgate, Aldershot, pp. 103–118.

Bettini, H.F.A.J., Silveira, J.M.F.J., Oliveira, A.V.M., 2018. Estimating strategic responses to the march of a low cost carrier to primary airports. Transp. Res. E 109, 190–204.

Bieger, T., Wittmer, A., 2006. Air transport and tourism perspectives and challenges for destinations, airlines and governments. J. Air Transp. Manag. 12, 40–46.

Boeing (2015). Boeing: about the 787 family. Available at http://www.boeing.com/boeing/commercial/787family/background.page. (Accessed March 26, 2018).

Boeing (2017). Current market outlook 2017–2036. Available at http://www.boeing.com/resources/boeingdotcom/commercial/market/current-market-outlook-2017/assets/downloads/cmo-2018-3-20.pdf. (Accessed March 26, 2018).

Business World (2018). Philippines' tourist arrivals hit 6.6 million in 2017, up by 11%, 9th February. Available at http://bworldonline.com/tourist-arrivals-philippines-hit-6-6-million-2017/. (Accessed April 20, 2018).

Button, K., Taylor, S., 2000. International air transportation and economic development. J. Air Transp. Manag. 6 (4), 209–222.

Button, K., Kramberger, T., Grobin, K., Rosi, B., 2018. A note on the effects of the number of low-cost airlines on small tourist airports' efficiencies. J. Air Transp. Manag. 72, 92–97.

Calder, S. (2015). Sharm el Sheikh Flight Suspensions: easyJet tells passengers they can fly home tomorrow—without their luggage, 5th November. Available at. http://www.independent.co.uk/news/uk/home-news/sharm-el-sheikh-flight-suspensions-easyjet-tells passengers-they-can-fly-home-tomorrow-without-their-a6723026.html. (Accessed April 1, 2018).

CAPA (2012). Osaka Kansai Airport LCCT to open on 28-Oct-2012. Available at http://centreforaviation.com/news/osaka-kansai-airport-lcct-to-open-on-28-oct-2012-167345. (Accessed March 27, 2018).

CAPA (2017a). Charting the decline of charter Part 1: UK non-scheduled air services reach lowest ever share, 11 July. Available at https://centreforaviation.com/insights/analysis/charting-the-decline-of-charter-part-1-uk-non-scheduled-air-services-reach-lowest-ever-share-353324. (Accessed April 4, 2018).

CAPA (2017b). First class airline travel. Is it dead? Airlines should expand their brands with premium perks. 18th December. Available at https://centreforaviation.com/insights/analysis/first-class-airline-travel-is-it-dead-airlines-should-expand-their-brands-with-premium-perks-390280.(Accessed March 16, 2018).

CAPA (2018a). Long-haul low cost airlines: World Airways to be us' first, 16th March. Available at https://centreforaviation.com/insights/analysis/longhaul-low-cost-airlines-world-airways-to-be-us-first-405559.(Accessed March 17, 2018).

CAPA (2018b). Is the long haul low cost model sustainable in the long term? 14th March. Available at https://centreforaviation.com/insights/video/is-the-long-haul-low-cost-model-sustainable-in-the-long-term-647. (Accessed March 17, 2018).

China Daily (2017). Chinese visitors' spending in Australia hits all-time high: survey, 12th December. Available at http://www.chinadaily.com.cn/a/201712/12/WS5a2f8f61a 3108bc8c 6726f32.html.(Accessed February 28, 2018).

Chung, J.Y., Whang, T., 2011. The impact of low cost carriers on Korean Island tourism. J. Transp. Geogr. 19, 1335–1340.

Daft, J., Albers, S., 2012. A profitability analysis of low-cost long-haul flight operations. J. Air Trans. Manag. 19, 49–54.

De Poret, M., O'Connell, J., Warnock-Smith, D., 2015. The economic viability of long-haul low cost operations: evidence from the transatlantic market. J. Air Transp. Manag. 42, 272–281.

de Wit, J., Zuidberg, J., 2012. The growth limits of the low cost carrier model. J. Air Transp. Manag. 21, 17–23.

Dennis, N., 1994. Airline hub operations in Europe. J. Transp. Geogr. 2 (4), 219–233.

Dewberry, P. and Hou, Y. (2012). Long-haul, low-cost airlines-flight tested. Bank of America, Merrill Lynch, 10 July.

Dobruszkes, F., Mondou, V., 2013. Aviation liberalization as a means to promote international tourism: the EU—Morocco case. J. Air Transp. Manag. 29, 23–34.

Dobruszkes, F., Givoni, M., Vowles, T., 2017. Hello major airports, goodbye regional airports? Recent changes in European and US low-cost airline airport choice. J. Air Transp. Manag. 59, 50–62.
Doganis, R., 2005. The Airline Business, second ed. Abingdon, Routledge.
Doganis, R., 2010. Flying Off Course: Airline Economics and Marketing, fourth ed. Routledge, New York.
Donzelli, M., 2010. The effect of low-cost air transportation on the local economy evidence from Southern Italy. J. Air Transp. Manag. 16, 121–126.
Dwyer, L., Forsyth, P., Madden, J., Spur, R., 2004. Evaluating tourism economic effectiveness and old approaches. J. Tour. Manag. 73, 307–317.
Dziedzic, M., Warnock-Smith, D., 2016. The role of secondary airports for today's low-cost carrier business models: the European case. Res. Transp. Bus. Manag. 21, 19–32.
Embraer (2017). Embraer market outlook 2017. Available at http://www.embraer (http://outlook2017.com/wp-content/uploads/2017/07/Embraer-Market-Outlook_2017.pdf, 14 April 2018) market outlook2017.com/wp-content/uploads/2017/07/Embraer-Market-Outlook_2017.pdf.(Accessed April 14, 2018).
Etihad Holidays (2016). Abu Dhabi, sunshine guaranteed. Available at http://www.etihadholidays.co.uk/deals/deal.aspx?deal=156&vendor=EYH&gsvacationtype=AH01&promocode=SUNSHINE2016 (Accessed March 23, 2018).
Eugenio-Martin, J.L., Inchausti-Sintes, F., 2016. Low-cost travel and tourism expenditures. Ann. Tour. Res. 57, 140–159.
European Regional Airline Association (2015). The case for investing in the regional airline industry. Available at: http://www.eraa.org/sites/default/files/the_case_for_investing_in_the_regional_ airline_industry_september_2015.pdf. (Accessed February 22, 2018).
European Regional Airline Association (2018). Yearbook, the Annual Directory of ERA. Available at https://www.eraa.org/publications/yearbook. (Accessed February 24, 2018).
Fageda, X., Suau-Sanchez, P., Mason, K.J., 2015. The evolving low-cost business model: network implications of fare bundling and connecting flights in Europe. J. Air Transp. Manag. 42, 289–296.
Flightglobal (2017). Subscription Database. Available at: www.flightglobal.com/. (Accessed March 18, 2018).
Flightglobal (2018). Subscription Database. Available at: www.flightglobal.com/. (Accessed March 27, 2018).
Forsyth, P., King, J., Rodolfo, C.L., 2006. Open skies in ASEAN. J. Air Transp. Manag. 12, 143–152.
GAO (2014). Airline Competition, GAO-14-515, June. Available at https://www.gao.gov/assets/670/664060.pdf. (Accessed March 26, 2018).
Gillen, D., Hasheminia, H., Changmin, J., 2015. Strategic considerations behind the network-regional airline tie ups—a theoretical and empirical study. Transp. Res. B Methodol. 72, 93–111.
Graham, A., 2008. Trends in leisure travel demand. In: Graham, A., Papatheodorou, A., Forsyth, P. (Eds.), Aviation and Tourism: Implications for Leisure Travel. Ashgate, Aldershot.
Graham, A., Dennis, N., 2010. The impact of low-cost airline operations to Malta. J. Air Transp. Manag. 16, 127–136.
Gulf News (2018). 15.8 million people visited Dubai in 2017, April 11. Available at http://gulfnews.com/business/sectors/tourism/15-8-million-people-visited-dubai-in-2017-1.2169807. (Accessed March 29, 2018).
Halpern, N., 2010. The marketing of small regional airports. In: Williams, G., Brathen, S. (Eds.), Air Transport Provision in Remoter Regions. Ashgate, Aldershot, pp. 77–98.
Hemmerdinger, J., 2017. Ultra-competitive? Airl. Bus. 33 (5), 29–33.
IATA (2017). Airlines forecast to create value for investors for 4th year, 8th December. Available at https://www.iata.org/publications/economics/Reports/chart-of-the-week/chart-of-the-week-08-Dec-2017.pdf. (Accessed March 14, 2018).
IATA (2018a). 2017 marked by strong passenger demand, record load factor. 1st February. Available at http://www.iata.org/pressroom/pr/Pages/2018-02-01-01.aspx. (Accessed March 2, 2018).
IATA (2018b). Air cargo strategy. Available at http://www.iata.org/whatwedo/cargo/Documents/cargo-strategy.pdf.(Accessed March 8, 2018).
IATA (2018c). November peak season air freight demand up 8.8%, 10th January. Available at http://www.iata.org/pressroom/pr/Pages/2018-01-10-01.aspx. (Accessed March 9, 2018).
ICAO (2017). Aviation benefits 2017. Available at https://www.icao.int/sustainability/Documents/AVIATION-BENEFITS-2017-web.pdf. (Accessed February 27, 2018).
Ideaworks (2017). The 2017 Car Trawler Yearbook of Ancillary Revenues. Available at http://www.ideaworkscompany.com/wp-content/uploads/2017/09/2017-Ancillary-Revenue-Yearbook.pdf. (Accessed March 5, 2018).
Koo, T.R., Tan, D.T., Duval, D.T., 2013. Direct air transport and demand interaction: a vector error-correction model approach. J. Air Transp. Manag. 28, 14–19.
Leahy, J. (2017). Growing horizons global market forecasts, 2017–2036. Available at http://www.airbus.com/content/dam/corporate-topics/publications/backgrounders/2017-06-09_GMF2017_John_Leahy.pdf. (Accessed March 29, 2018).
Logothetis, M., Miyoshi, C., 2016. Network performance and competitive impact of the single hub—a case study on Turkish Airlines and Emirates. J. Air Transp. Manag. 14, 1–9.
McNamara, S. (2016). Europe's biggest airline? Air Transport World. 19th October. Available at http://atwonline.com/blog/europe-s-biggest-airline. (Accessed March 3, 2018).
Morrell, P., 2005. Airlines within airlines: an analysis of US network airline responses to low cost carriers. J. Air Transp. Manag. 11 (5), 303–312.
O'Connell, J.F., 2011b. Airlines: an inherently turbulent industry. In: O'Connell, J.F., Williams, G. (Eds.), Air Transport in the 21st Century. Ashgate, Farnham, pp. 59–96.
O'Connell, J.F., Bouquet, A., 2015. Dynamic packaging spells the end of European charter airlines. J. Vacat. Mark. 21 (2), 175–189.
O'Connell, J.F., Bueno, O.E., 2016. A study into the hub performance Emirates, Etihad Airways and Qatar Airways and their competitive position against the major European hubbing airlines. J. Air Transp. Manag. 50, 1–12.
O'Connell, J.F., Connolly, D., 2016. The strategic evolution of Aer Lingus from a full-service airline to a low-cost carrier and finally positioning itself into a value hybrid airline. Tour. Econ. 23 (6), 1296–1320.
O'Connell, J.F., Warnock-Smith, D., 2013. An investigation into traveler preferences and acceptance levels of airline ancillary revenues. J. Air Transp. Manag. 33, 12–21.
O'Connell, J.F., Williams, G., 2005. Passengers' perceptions of low cost airlines and full service carriers: a case study involving Ryanair, Aer Lingus, Air Asia and Malaysia Airlines. J. Air Transp. Manag. 11 (4), 259–272.

O'Connor, N., Stafford, M.R., Gallagher, G., 2008. The impact of global terrorism on Ireland's tourism industry: an industry perspective. Tour. Hosp. Res. 8 (4), 351–363.
O'Connell, J.F. (2007). The strategic response of full service airlines to the low cost carrier: threat and the perception of passengers to each type of carrier, (Ph.D. Thesis). Cranfield University, Cranfield, UK.
O'Connell, J.F., 2011a. The rise of the Arabian Gulf carriers: an insight into the business model of Emirates Airline. J. Air Transp. Manag. 17 (6), 339–346.
Office for National Statistics, 2016. Travel Trends 2016. UK Statistics Authority, London. Available at https://www.ons.gov.uk/peoplepopulationandcommunity/leisureandtourism/articles/traveltrends/previousReleases. (Accessed April 11, 2018).
Pearson, J., O'Connell, J.F., Pitfield, D., 2015. The strategic capability of Asian network airlines to compete with low-cost carriers. J. Air Transp. Manag. 47, 1–10.
Philippine Airlines (2017). PAL encourages the world to experience the heart of the Filipino, 22nd September. Available at https://www.philippineairlines.com/AboutUs/newsandevents/ethof. (Accessed March 30, 2018).
Reales, C.N., O'Connell, 2017. An examination of the revenue generating capability of co-branded cards associated with frequent flyer programmes. J. Air Transp. Manag. 65, 63–75.
Regional Airline Association (2017). RAA Regional Airline Association, 2017 Annual Report. Available at https://c.ymcdn.com/sites/www.raa.org/resource/resmgr/2017pubs/RAA_AnnualReport_v13.pdf. (Accessed March 3, 2018).
Republic of Turkey ministry of culture and tourism (2016). Tourism statistics. Available at https://www.kultur.gov.tr/EN,153017/tourism-statistics.html. (Accessed March 9, 2018).
Rey, B., Myro, R., Galera, A., 2011. Effect of low-cost airlines on tourism in Spain. A dynamic panel data model. J. Air Transp. Manag. 17, 163–167.
Rodrıguez, A., O'Connell, J.F., 2017. Can low-cost long-haul carriers replace charter airlines in the long-haul market? A European perspective. Tour. Econ. 24 (1), 64–78.
Ryanair (2017). Ryanair website to sell Air Europa long haul flights, 23 May. Available at https://corporate.ryanair.com/news/ryanair-website-to-sell-air-europa-long-haul-flights/. (Accessed February 26, 2018).
Ryanair (2018). Connecting flights service from Milan and Rome extended with 27 more routes, 16 February. Available at https://corporate.ryanair.com/news/connecting-flights-service-from-milan-and-rome-extended-with-27-more-routes/. (Accessed April 1, 2018).
SeatGuru (2018). Seat maps. Available at https://www.seatguru.com/. (Accessed March 23, 2018).
SkyWest Airlines (2018). Facts. Available at http://www.skywest.com/about-skywest-airlines/facts/. (Accessed April 16, 2018)..
Taylor, I. (2015). Big interview: monarch restructure reflects future of flying. Travel Weekly, 1 October. Available at http://www.travelweekly.co.uk/articles/56780/big-interview-monarch-restructure-reflects-futureof-flying. (Accessed March 29, 2018).
Thailand Ministry of Tourism and Sports (2018). Tourism statistics of Thailand. Available at: http://www.mots.go.th/mots_en57/main.php?filename=index. (Accessed April 2, 2018).
The Telegraph (2017). Is this the beginning of the end for the first class plane cabin? The Telegraph. 1st November. Available at https://www.telegraph.co.uk/travel/news/beginning-of-the-end-for-first-class/. (Accessed April 9, 2018).
Toh, M., 2017. Secondary chance. Airl. Bus. 33 (8), 32–33.
Tsui, K.W.H., 2017. Does a low-cost carrier lead the domestic tourism demand and growth of New Zealand? Tour. Manag. 60, 390–403.
UK CAA (2017). Airline Data Annual Reports 2017. Available at https://www.caa.co.uk/Data-and-analysis/UK-aviation-market/Airlines/Datasets/UK-Airline-data/2017/Airline-data-annual-reports-2017/. (Accessed March 19, 2018).
UNWTO (2017). Untwo tourism highlights, 2017 Edition, Available at https://www.e-unwto.org/doi/pdf/10.18111/9789284419029. (Accessed February 29, 2018).
Warnock-Smith, D., O'Connell, J.F., Maleki, M., 2017. An analysis of ongoing trends in airline ancillary revenues. J. Air Transp. Manag. 64, 42–54.
Wensveen, J.G., 2011. Air Transportation: A Management Perspective. Ashgate, Burlington, VT.
Wensveen, J.G., Leick, R., 2009. The long-haul low-cost carrier: a unique business model. J. Air Transp. Manag. 15 (3), 127–133.
Whyte, R., Lohmann, G., 2015. Low-cost long-haul carriers: a hypothetical analysis of a 'Kangaroo' route case study. Transp. Policy 3 (2), 159–165.
Williams, G., 2002. Airline Competition: Deregulation's Mixed Legacy. Ashgate, Farnham.
Williams, G., 2008. The future of charter operations. In: Graham, A., Papatheodorou, A., Forsyth, P. (Eds.), Aviation and Tourism: Implications for Leisure Travel. Ashgate, Aldershot, pp. 85–102.
Williams, G., 2011. Comparing the economic and operating characteristics of charter and low-cost scheduled airlines. In: O'Connell, J.F., Williams, G. (Eds.), Air Transport in the 21st Century. Ashgate, Aldershot, pp. 185–195.
Yin, M., Bertolini, L., Duan, J., 2015. The effects of the high-speed railway on urban development: international experience and potential implications for China. Prog. Plan. 98, 1–52.
Young, J., Whang, T., 2011. The impact of low cost carriers on Korean island tourism. J. Transp. Geogr. 19, 1335–1340.
Zhang, A., Hanaoka, S., Inamura, H., Ishikura, T., 2008. Low-cost carriers in Asia: deregulation, regional liberalization, and secondary airports. Res. Transp. Econ. 24, 36–50.
Zhang, Y., 2015. International arrivals to Australia: determinants and the role of air transport policy. J. Air Transp. Manag. 44, 21–24.
Zhang, Y., Findlay, C., 2014. Air transport policy and its impacts on passenger traffic and tourist flows. J. Air Transp. Manag. 34, 42–48.

CHAPTER

11

The End of European Charter Airlines: Myths and Realities

David RAMOS-PÉREZ, Frédéric DOBRUSZKES*†

*University of Salamanca, Salamanca, Spain †Free University of Brussels (ULB), Brussels, Belgium

CHAPTER OUTLINE

11.1 INTRODUCTION

In December 2013, preliminary annual results of TUI Travel, Europe's largest tour operator, which owns some of the main European charter airlines, reported a 20% increase in profits. Its chief executive, Peter Lang, attributed that rise to the renaissance of package holidays (Clancy, 2013). In fact, according to the UK International Passenger Survey, package holiday trips by air by UK residents increased by 25.6% between 2010 and 2015. Even more interesting is the fact that package holidays to European destinations increased by 36.5%, reaching 11.5 million trips in 2015, increasing their UK market share from 72.8% to 79.1% of all package holidays abroad.[1]

These figures not only show a growing tour operator industry, but also support the survival of so-called charter airlines, even though their status can (and will) be debated. Obviously, package holiday passengers are not carried only by charter airlines. However, these passengers remain the core travelling component of airlines whose brand names, to most observers, evoke the thought of charter flights. Ironically, the end of charter airlines has been predicted since the end of the 1990s, when easyJet's founder, Stelios Haji-Ioannou, pointed out (in December 1998) that charter airlines would no longer exist in the UK within 10 years (Aviation Strategy, 1999). He was then only echoing the arguments of a growing number of academics and consultants, who argued that air transport market liberalisation within the European Union and changes in tourism demand behaviour would lead to the end of package holidays and charter airlines. It was supposed that the emerging low-cost airlines would cater extraordinarily well for the increasing

[1] Authors' calculations from International Passenger Survey data at http://www.ons.gov.uk/ons/rel/ott/travelpac/index.html

demand for less standardised, post-Fordist holidays (Ioannides and Debbage, 1997). Both these factors would threaten the future of charter airlines for short- and medium-haul destinations, but leave some opportunities for long-haul services to long-haul destinations (Williams, 2001, 2008) in the new tourism peripheries (Gormsen, 1997).

Undoubtedly, so-called charter airlines have lost market share within the European Single Aviation Market (DLR, 2008), which could signal a 'structural decline' of inclusive tours (Aviation Strategy, 2015). But despite the dispersal of low-cost carriers to main tourist destinations (Dobruszkes, 2013) and increasing demand for individual holidays through dynamic packaging (O'Connell and Bouquet, 2015), European 'charter airlines' currently seem far less likely to disappear than they did a decade ago, as the figures in the opening paragraph suggest. However, it is clear that charter business models have been adapted to limit their decline. Strategies have included the consolidation process in the European leisure industry, which has led to a concentration in two major groups (namely, TUI and Thomas Cook) with all the major charter airlines.

These apparently contrasting narratives raise two questions that are at the core of this chapter. First, what does 'charter airline' now mean after air transport liberalisation? This is not a common question, considering that charter airlines' *raison d'être* was to get round protectionism affecting the so-called regular airlines. Investigating this is complicated by the pervasive and confusing use of inherited concepts by scholars, the industry, and within some official statistics. However, clarifying concepts and current business models is an important step in achieving a better understanding of tourism patterns, long-distance travel, and the aviation business for tourism purposes.

Second, how have charter airlines reorganised their network within the framework of liberalisation, increased competition from LCCs, and declining package holidays? Although a trend to leave short-haul routes and focus on long-haul routes has been widely claimed as their only survival strategy, the literature lacks an analysis of the evolution of charter airline networks at the city-pair level. Assessing what has (or has not) changed after the development of LCC services to short- and middle-haul tourist destinations could confirm (or not) the aforementioned trend.

The rest of this chapter is organised as follows. In the next section, the existing literature on charter airlines' evolution after liberalisation is reviewed, and the charter concept itself is briefly examined. In Section 11.3 the methodology and data used are introduced, and there is a discussion concerning issues about data availability for charter airlines. In Section 11.4 the results of the two study cases are presented. Finally, the results are discussed in Section 11.5 where conclusions are drawn.

11.2 CHARTER AIRLINES: AN INFINITELY VARIABLE BUSINESS

The foundation of charter airlines lies in the 1944 Chicago Convention, which has strongly shaped the regulatory regime of commercial aviation. The convention introduced a distinction between 'scheduled flights' and 'nonscheduled air services'. The provision of 'scheduled flights' was clearly related to the goodwill of the States involved, since:

> No scheduled international air service may be operated over or into the territory of a contracting State, except with the special permission or other authorisation of that State, and in accordance with the terms of such permission or authorisation (Article 6).

In contrast, 'nonscheduled flights' could possibly be operated in a more flexible environment considering that:

> Such aircraft, if engaged in the carriage of passengers, cargo, or mail for remuneration or hire on other than scheduled international air services, shall also, subject to the provisions of Article 7, have the privilege of taking on or discharging passengers, cargo, or mail, subject to the right of any State where such embarkation or discharge takes place to impose such regulations, conditions or limitations as it may consider desirable (Article 5).

Doganis (1973) reports that attitudes towards the authorisation of nonscheduled flights varied significantly amongst countries. In Europe, a larger step towards their liberalisation was taken with the 1956 'Multilateral Agreement on Commercial Rights of Non-Scheduled Air Services in Europe' signed in Paris by the European Civil Aviation Conference (ECAC) Member States. At the time, the ECAC had 19 members, and thus involved a much larger space than the then imminent European Economic Community. The agreement lifted the 'regulations, conditions or limitations' stipulated in Article 5 of the Chicago Convention for aircraft registered in an ECAC member state and operating 'international flights for remuneration or hire, on other than scheduled international air services' between ECAC members[2] provided they were engaged in various activities that notably included 'the transport

[2] Contracting States can stipulate whether outlying islands in the Atlantic Ocean and islands with semiindependent status are included or not.

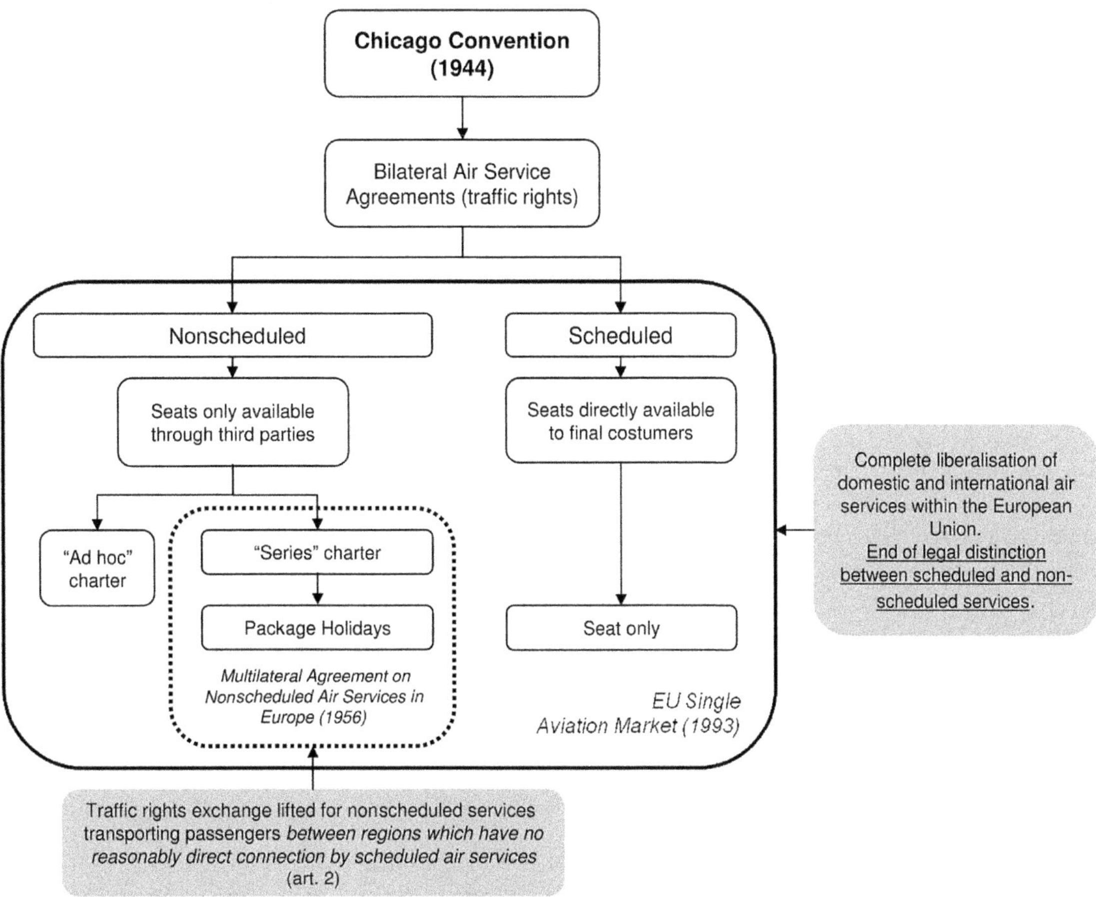

FIG. 11.1 An interpretive framework for scheduled, nonscheduled, and charter services within Europe. *(Source: Devised by authors.)*

of passengers between regions which have no reasonably direct connection by scheduled air services'. This clause made it possible to avoid the need for exchanging air traffic rights through bilateral agreements (Fig. 11.1), which encouraged charter airlines to launch new air routes. However, Doganis (1973) states that even under this agreement, several countries were not so open to nonscheduled operations. In addition, IATA attempted to regulate the nonscheduled business of its member airlines, especially charter air fares. This encouraged IATA airlines to set up new charter airlines that were not members of IATA.

Interestingly, the distinction made by the two aforementioned agreements refers to the 'scheduled' versus 'nonscheduled' nature of flights. Many scholars, observers, and public authorities also use the adjectives 'regular' and 'nonregular', respectively. In most cases, at least in Europe prior to the 1993 market liberalisation, the airlines concerned were 'national flag airlines' and 'charter airlines'. The principle of a charter airline is well known: a person or organisation that charters a flight for own use. A distinction is usually made between 'ad hoc' and 'series' charter flights. Ad hoc flights offer 'à la carte' services; for instance, for a corporation that offers its employees a trip or for a sports team going to a match. Series flights are repetitive and have typically been developed as a key component of tour operators' (TOs) inclusive packages, combining flights, accommodation, local transportation, food, and various activities (Fig. 11.1).

Taking advantage of a less protectionist environment, of lower cost operations, and of social transformations in Western societies, passenger charters grew dramatically during the 1960s and 1970s in two main markets—between Northern and Southern Europe and over the Atlantic. According to Doganis (1973, 2010), charter airlines accounted for one third of trans-Atlantic passengers at the 1977 peak and up to 50% of all international intra-European passengers by 1975/1976. In the early 2000s, they were still flying to various European resorts when only a few of these were serviced by other airlines (Dobruszkes et al., 2006).

In Europe, ad hoc flights have always been marginal. Charter flights have been dominated by 'series charters' serving stable flows of leisure passengers. As Doganis (2010) points out, 'they normally had a set timetable and were operated as regular series of flights'. In many cases, indeed, charter flight schedules are known, even though they may be indicative and subject to changes. The integration of air transport and of large hotels dedicated to mass tourism fundamentally involves the regular feed of a destination with tourists. In this sense, charter flights need to be operated regularly. Consequently it is clear from this discussion that 'scheduled/nonscheduled' and 'regular/nonregular' expressions are confusing.

In fact, for years the main difference between flag (scheduled) and charter airlines was that the charter capacity was not directly available to final customers (Fig. 11.1). Charter airlines only traded their seats to tour operators, which then proceeded with a joint sale of seats, accommodation, food, and transfers in tourist-originating countries. These so-called package holidays became intimately associated with European charter airlines, and for years their services were known as Inclusive Tourist Charters (ITC). Similarly, ad hoc flights were by nature accessible only to people invited by the person or organisation that chartered the flight. However, this distinction in the way charter flight seats were sold also became confusing during the late 1970s. A more liberal approach then lifted some restrictions on seat-only sales by charter airlines, and some of them also got traffic rights to offer scheduled flights. For example, by the end of the 1980s, UK charter airlines were selling up to a 20% of their supply as seat-only, and Britannia Airways was already servicing some main tourist routes as conventional 'scheduled' services (Learmount, 1987).

In addition, it is worth noting that charter flights were operated by charter airlines but also, to some extent, by flag airlines. An example of this was when millions of Muslims went to Mecca for the annual pilgrimage. Finally, flag airlines also sold to the TOs some seats within their conventional 'scheduled' flights. These flights could thus be considered as mixed flights, even though they were legally defined as 'scheduled flights'. So in the end, on the eve of major changes in regulatory regimes, the provision of tourist air mobility[3] was more diverse than is usually considered (Fig. 11.2).

This framework was changed subsequently by the movement towards more aviation liberalisation. Of course, the process has been uneven in terms of both geography (i.e. places concerned) and the degree of liberalisation. However, easier access to the market and more freedom to set air fares has made it possible for airlines, whatever business model they adopted after liberalisation, to operate more routes without the constraint of establishing a charter airline. Conversely, charter airlines were not necessarily forced to operate charter flights anymore. To some extent, they could 'regularise' themselves.

The most extreme experience of international aviation liberalisation came from the EU, which by 1993 had removed virtually all types of restrictions for community carriers operating intra-EU air services.[4] The EU law simply

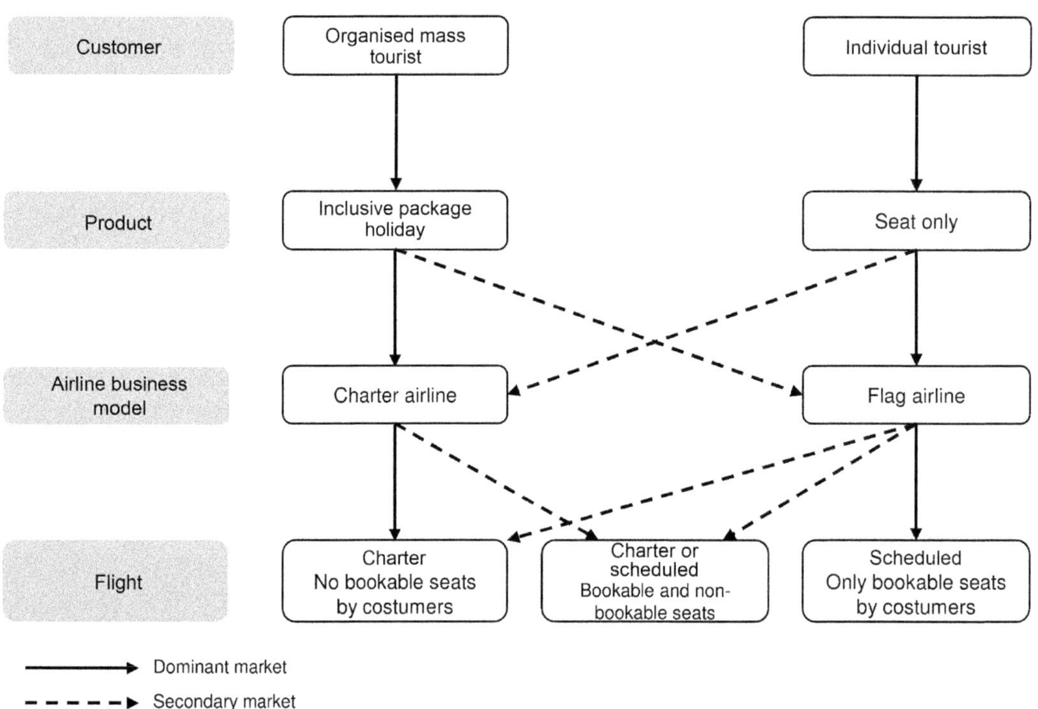

FIG. 11.2 The provision of tourist air mobility during charter's golden age. *(Source: Devised by authors.)*

[3] A simplified version of Cohen's (1974) typology of tourists has been used to define customers in the diagram, considering only 'Organised Mass Tourists' and 'Individual Tourists'.

[4] Domestic flights were fully liberalised by 1997 at the latest.

does not distinguish between scheduled and nonscheduled airlines and flights anymore. In the first stage, however, charter airlines did not disappear. According to Lobbenberg (1995), a continuum of air carriers could be observed, ranging from traditional Inclusive Tourist Charter airlines (selling all their supply to tour operators) to flag airlines, which were completely independent from tour operators. Between both, some carriers opted for mixed models, combining seat-only and package holiday customers in the same aircraft. Examples included Britannia, Hapag-Lloyd, and Condor.

In the second stage, low-cost carriers (LCCs) emerged as a key outcome of aviation liberalisation. Offering seat-only flights at even lower fares than charters, they dramatically expanded to a point at which they accounted for one-third of intra-European air services around 2008, whilst Ryanair and easyJet became the two leading airlines based on the volume of intra-European seats supplied[5] (Dobruszkes, 2013). In terms of networks, the LCCs adopted various strategies and penetrated various types of markets, including routes traditionally operated by charter airlines to Mediterranean resorts and the Canaries from Northern Europe. LCCs were thus widely mentioned as a major threat to charter airlines (Williams, 2001). Changes in tourist behaviour within a post-Fordist context of tourist development, with individual and more frequent holidays of shorter stays (Ioannides and Debbage, 1997; Graham, 2008), can explain the appeal of tourist routes for low-cost carriers. Arguably, the low-cost business model is a much better match for the more flexible needs of tourists than the pure charter one. Moreover, new mobility patterns and temporal migrations related to the increasing number of second homes bought by North Europeans in mature tourist destinations (King et al., 1998; O'Reilly, 2000; Benson and O'Reilly, 2009) have fed demand for air travel through the seat-only product instead of package holidays.

According to several observers, charter airlines could not resist competition from the LCCs in the short- and medium-haul markets. As a result, the intra-European charter business was expected to be redeployed in the long-haul air market that the LCCs did not serve (Williams, 2001, 2008). However, more than 20 years after EU liberalisation, tour operators continue to sell package holidays, and some airlines still charter a high proportion of their capacity for them. But some major changes have occurred during this time. Whilst airlines that focus only on package holidays still exist, almost all the former charter airlines now carry both package and seat-only passengers. Furthermore, low-cost airlines, such as easyJet, which previously sold seats to final customers only, now also sell some capacity to tour operators (Clark and Dunn, 2015), a trend also observed in Japan, for instance (Wu, 2016). After a wave of mergers and consolidation on a European scale, the original charter airlines are now commanded by two major travel groups (TUI and Thomas Cook), which are vertically integrated with many of the main charter airlines. Furthermore, tour operators are no longer restricted to the use of their in-house airlines. They also contract blocks of seats with a diversity of airlines, from the former charter airlines to low-cost carriers. As an example, Doganis (2010) reported that in 2007, Condor (one of the largest charter airlines in Europe at the time) sold about 40% of its capacity to the TO it belonged to (namely, Thomas Cook). The remaining capacity was sold as seat-only seats (36%) and to other TOs (24%).

After all these changes and transformations, Lobbenberg's (1995) seminal idea of a continuum of different air carriers serving tourist routes after liberalisation remains relevant. More recently, Lohmann and Koo (2013) also concluded that a continuum of different business models was more accurate than a strict categorisation of airlines. In fact, the nature of the so-called charter airlines has certainly become less clear than before the liberalisation of European aviation (Papatheodorou and Lei, 2006), as is summarised in Fig. 11.3.[6] Symptomatically, most former European charter airlines do not advertise themselves anymore as charter airlines, as evidenced by the contents of their websites. Leisure airlines or holiday carriers are now concepts widely preferred by scholars, public authorities, and consultants. Similarly, the International Air Carrier Association (IACA), once founded as a trade association of European and North American charter airlines (Haanapel, 1978), and which still defends the interests of such airlines, clearly bans 'charter' from its vocabulary. This does not prevent several of its member airlines being part of the Thomas Cook or TUI travel group and welcoming a significant share of package passengers. These airlines, though, are now significantly advertised as seat-only airlines as well. However, their common feature could be the way their network is shaped. According to Doganis (2010), advance contracts with the TOs are still the main driver of their network geography.

Nevertheless, little remains known about the changes in the network geography of the former charter airlines. How much could they resist the changes within the EU? And how much were they forced to migrate to long-haul destinations? This will be analysed in the remaining parts of this paper.

[5] Including the EU27, Norway, Iceland, and Switzerland, the latter three having joined the liberalised EU aviation market.

[6] Whilst agreeing with the idea of a continuum of business models, there is a need for clarity reasons and to stress what still individualises former charter airlines, to differentiate them in Figure 11.3 from the other four business models widely acknowledged in the literature on air transport liberalisation in the European Union: full-service network carriers, low-cost carriers, regional carriers, and hybrid carriers (DLR, 2008).

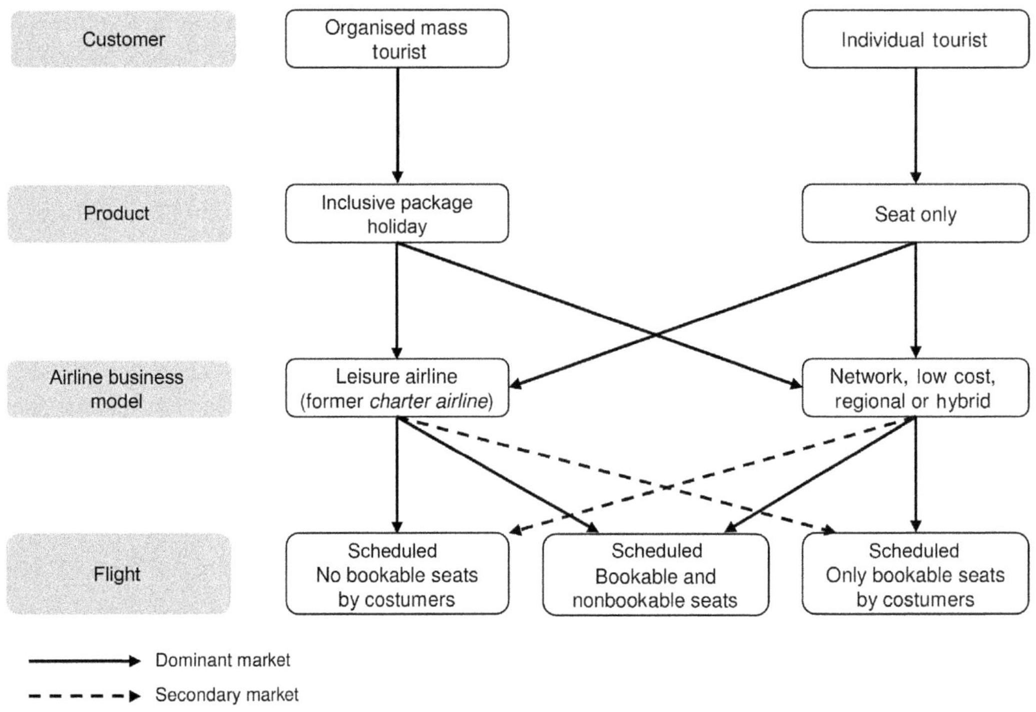

FIG. 11.3 Today's role of the European former charter airlines. *(Source: Devised by authors.)*

11.3 FROM A VAGUE CONCEPT TO POOR STATISTICS

11.3.1 How to Track Charter Airlines

A major issue when working with charter airlines is choosing the appropriate data to capture real changes and avoid misinterpretation. As for demand, in the early 1970s, Doganis (1973) rightly pointed out that 'distinctions between scheduled and non-scheduled traffic as defined by the ICAO in 1952 have become so blurred as to be meaningless'. According to a 1952 ICAO Council definition, 'a scheduled international air service is a series of flights that possesses all the following characteristics:

(a) It passes through the airspace over the territory of more than one State;
(b) It is performed by aircraft for the transport of passengers, mail or cargo for remuneration, in such a manner that each flight is open to use by members of the public;
(c) It is operated, so as to serve traffic between the same two or more points, either (i) according to a published timetable, or (ii) with flights so regular or frequent that they constitute a recognisably systematic series'.

On the other hand, nonscheduled services were simply defined as 'a commercial air transport service performed as other than a scheduled air service'.

Although the method of sale of available capacity is included within the scheduled service definition ('open to use by members of the public'), in practical terms, regulatory criteria were used to distinguish between scheduled and nonscheduled flights, because they were subject to different regulations. In Europe, whilst scheduled and nonscheduled services were strictly disconnected and tourists' air mobility was a restricted charter business, this traffic distinction offered reliable information to distinguish between charter airlines and other operators. In fact, statistical reports published by the ECAC during the 1970s enabled the development of the original charter airlines to be traced from 1965 onwards.

However problems arose by the late 1970s, when restrictions on seat-only sales by charter airlines were lifted, charter services became so frequent that they constituted systematic series, and flag airlines began to operate leisure-oriented services, as explained previously. Difficulties in monitoring charter airlines increased further in 1993, when intra-EU air market liberalisation came into force. At this time, all restrictions on community carriers operating intra-EU services were removed and the distinction between scheduled and nonscheduled traffic became completely useless in analysing charter airline trends.

Furthermore, EU Member States were obliged to transmit air transport data in a standardised way to the Statistical Office of the European Communities (EUROSTAT) in 2003 only (OJEU, 2003). From 1993 to 2003 no common criteria existed, and airlines, airports, and Member States were free to decide how they classified traffic figures (ICAO, 2013). For example, in relevant countries for former charter airlines, such as Germany, the distinction between scheduled and nonscheduled was eliminated for intra-EU flights, and from 2000 all flights were considered scheduled. Arguably, the German shift in reporting traffic data from nonscheduled to scheduled services due to an administrative decision has had an impact on the apparent traffic growth shown for other 'scheduled' air carrier passengers and the decline in charter airlines over the first decade of the 21st century.

However, definitions of scheduled and nonscheduled services for EU statistics established in 2003 have not solved the difficulties found in tracking the charter airlines because they simply copy the ICAO definition from 1952. Only the fifth edition of the ICAO Reference Manual in Statistics, published in 2013, considers this problem for the very first time. Forty years after Doganis' call, an official recognition of the limits of incumbent scheduled and nonscheduled concepts has been made. A new definition of both concepts has been proposed, and is now clearly based, as Doganis has already suggested, on the method of sale of available capacity (ICAO, 2013):

- Scheduled revenue flights. Flights scheduled and performed for the purpose of remuneration according to a published timetable, or which are so regular or frequent as to constitute a recognisably systematic series, and are open to direct booking by members of the public; and extra section flights occasioned by overflow traffic from scheduled flights.
- Nonscheduled revenue flights (excluding on-demand flights). Charter flights and special flights offered for remuneration other than those reported under scheduled flights. They include any items related to blocked-off charters and exclude air taxi, commercial business aviation, or other on-demand revenue flights.

Interestingly, nonscheduled airlines are no longer defined by exclusion, and now constitute a more complex category, which is more in line with reality. A new kind of nonscheduled flight is included (namely, blocked-off charter) to define 'flights where the whole capacity is blocked off for charter sale on flights published as scheduled flights but carried out as charter flights on the same or similar routing and operating time'. This category applies to the traditional European series charter of the 1970s and 1980s, but nowadays charter and other airlines supply a mix of seats open to direct booking with blocks of seats sold to tour operators. Pure charters are a rarity, at least in Europe (in contrast, these traditional charters still exist, for instance, in Asia, even though they are challenged by recent aviation policies—see Wu et al., 2018).

Whilst the conceptual evolution of both definitions is appreciated, they continue to be useless for tracking the evolution of charter airlines, particularly after air transport market liberalisation within the European Union and changes in tourism demand behaviour. This implies that when working with demand statistics, nonscheduled figures are no longer synonymous with former charter airlines services. Furthermore, nonscheduled statistics are not representative of package holiday volumes. Ignoring these issues could lead to serious misinterpretations of reality.

As a result, the only way to move forward is to use disaggregated data on flights and passengers by airline at the route level. However, datasets for nonscheduled services at the route level have always been difficult to access. In a seminal study about nonscheduled flows at route level, carried out by the French Institut du Transport Aérien (ITA), routes with traffic of at least 20,000 nonscheduled passengers in 1979 were registered. Official statistics reported by each country were used, but inadequacy or lack of data was found for Greece, Italy, Portugal, Yugoslavia, Belgium, Sweden, Denmark, and Norway. Precise statistics were provided only by the Federal Republic of Germany, the Netherlands, France, the United Kingdom, and Spain (Cambau and Lefèvre, 1981). Pearce (1987a,b) found similar difficulties when analysing Mediterranean charter geography.

Today, after European market liberalisation, difficulties have increased for commercial reasons. In Sweden, for instance, national confidentiality legislation prevents the disclosure of statistics on routes with less than three operating carriers (Swedish Transport Agency, personal communication). Besides, due to the changes in tourists' air mobility reported previously, there is also a need for data at the route level to be broken down by operating airline. Such level of disaggregation is rarely available, and should it be available the prices charged by administrations holding such data usually obstructs meaningful research.

11.3.2 Data and Methods Used

The above discussion suggests that demand-side data on charter airline networks is scarce. The situation is at least better on the supply side, and this is relevant when investigating changes in airline network strategies. Many scholars and industry consultants have been using global databases edited by the Official Airline Guide (OAG) company, but a major problem arises due to its focus on scheduled flights. Although some flights from former charter airlines have been considered at least from 1995, this is far from capturing all the operations of these airlines. For some countries and/or airlines OAG data offers a reliable picture at least from the year 2000, as has happened with Germany. But it is not the case for the United Kingdom, where large differences arise, depending on the airlines and years considered: for example, British charter airlines are not included in the OAG databases before January 2004.

Some calculations have been made to check the reliability of the OAG data for selected years. For Germany, due to rules on confidentiality procedures relating to disaggregated data at the airline level, a comparison has been undertaken of a sample of OAG data containing all flights between Germany and Spain with actual figures from the Spanish airports, using official statistics provided by AENA, the state-owned company that manages commercial airports. The results show a high level of reliability with the OAG data, with only minor differences observed that can be related to last-minute increased or reduced capacity (Table 11.1).

As for the United Kingdom, the official statistics at the airline level from the UK Civil Aviation Authority (CAA) have been compared with OAG data. The results are less promising than in the previous case (Table 11.2). Whilst first Britannia and then Thomson data are completely reliable, other charter airlines are totally missing in 2004. Moreover, as different waves of consolidation have affected charter airlines during recent years, mergers need to be considered in order to perform homogeneous comparisons. However, the lack of reliability of OAG data for UK charter airlines does not make it possible to join data from different carriers to evaluate the impact of mergers. Indeed, this is not a minor issue, because Thomson Airways has its origins in two major British airlines, Britannia Airways and First Choice Airways, which merged in 2007.

TABLE 11.1 Coverage of the OAG Database for Main German Charter Airlines: Comparison With AENA Records

	August 2004				August 2017			
Airline	**AENA**	**OAG**	**Gap**	**% OAG**	**AENA**	**OAG**	**Gap**	**% OAG**
Air Berlin	1856	1884	*28*	*101.5*	1900	2073	*173*	*109.1*
Hapag-Lloyd	1114	1100	*−14*	*98.7*	–	–	–	–
Condor	1058	1000	*−58*	*94.5*	783	780	*−3*	*99.6*
LTU	534	487	*−47*	*91.2*	–	–	–	–
Hapag-Lloyd Express	383	382	*−1*	*99.7*	–	–	–	–
Germania	9	1	*−8*	*11.1*	449	421	*−28*	*93.8*
TUI Fly	–	–	–	–	848	850	*2*	*100.2*
Germanwings	151	151	*0*	*100.0*	253	245	*−8*	*96.8*
Eurowings	–	–	–	–	1286	1243	*−8*	*96.8*

Source: Authors' calculations from OAG Max and AENA statistics.

TABLE 11.2 Coverage of the OAG Database for Main UK Charter Airlines: Comparison With CAA Airline Statistics

	August 2004				August 2017			
Airline	**CAA**	**OAG**	**Gap**	**% OAG**	**CAA**	**OAG**	**Gap**	**% OAG**
Britannia	5014	5228	*214*	*104.3*	–	–	–	–
First Choice	4183	0	*−4183*	*0.0*	–	–	–	–
Thomson Airways	–	–	–	–	7449	7338	*−111*	*98.5*
Thomas Cook	3172	0	*−3172*	*0.0*	4803	4700	*−103*	*97.9*
Monarch Airlines[a]	2993	0	*−2993*	*0.0*	0	4400	*4400*	–
MyTravel Airways	4253	0	*−4253*	*0.0*	–	–	–	–
Astraeus	1019	0	*−1019*	*0.0*	–	–	–	–
Excel Airways	2082	0	*−2082*	*0.0*	–	–	–	–

[a] *Traffic results for Monarch Airlines are not included in CAA Statistics for August 2017. Financial problems which led to the bankruptcy of the airline in October 2017 may explain missing data.*

Source: Authors' calculations from OAG Max and UK CAA statistics.

In order to improve the reliability of the OAG database, the real data of operated flights by each British airline at the route level has been explored, derived from UK Flight Punctuality Data supplied by the CAA and available online.[7] The problem here is that only 10 airports are covered by these statistics up to 2013, so charter flights from some regional airports are also missing, as presented in Table 11.3. Besides, UK Flight Punctuality Data only include information about flights operated, but not seats supplied.

In spite of these flaws, the OAG database has been expanded with information about British airlines derived from UK Flight Punctuality Data. By integrating this data with the OAG database a much higher level of reliability was obtained, because coverage for the merged operations of Britannia and First Choice increased from 54.5% to 87.6% of total flights.

Greater reliability is impossible to achieve for the seat supply and only detailed estimates were calculated for First Choice long-haul services. By comparing UK Punctuality Statistics with data on aircraft utilisation by individual airlines also provided by the CAA it was possible to allocate the number of seats to each frequency operated, due to the homogeneity of the long-haul fleet used by First Choice (Boeing 767-300ER, 258 seats).

Considering the observed data shortcomings, and the possibilities to increase data reliability, it was decided to conduct this research as a case study of Thomson and Condor. Both represent two major tourist outbound markets in Europe, the United Kingdom, and Germany.[8] Furthermore, they represent different adaptation strategies of former charter airlines to European market liberalisation. Both have been integrated into one of the two major European tour operators, but whilst the current Thomson airline was formed from the 2008 merger of Britannia and First Choice, Condor remained as Lufthansa's leisure subsidiary between 1959 and 2000, and then was gradually acquired by Thomas Cook between 2000 and 2003. In addition, the distribution of LCCs in the UK's air market differs notably from that in Germany's market, with 39.6% and 18.3%, respectively, of all seats offered in 2016.[9] Therefore Condor and Thomson experience dissimilar competition pressure from low-cost carriers.

The evolution of recent traffic also shows different patterns: both Condor and Thomson reached a peak in passenger numbers in 2005–06, followed by a clear decline until 2009, but whilst Condor has experienced significant growth from 2009 onwards, except for a slightly decrease in 2016, Thomson has only reduced the rate of decay (Fig. 11.4). In fact, the British charter airline is much smaller than the previous merged ones, showing that consolidation has meant a cut in capacity.

Thus, in the remaining part of the chapter, comparisons are made of Thomson and Condor's network evolution, by performing a disaggregate analysis at the route level, including an assessment of route range[10] variations

TABLE 11.3 Coverage of the UK Flight Punctuality Data for Main UK Charter Airlines: Comparison With CAA Airline Statistics

	August 2004				August 2017			
Airline	**CAA**	**UK Punct.**	**Gap**	**% Punct.**	**CAA**	**UK Punct.**	**Gap**	**% Punct.**
Britannia	5014	3308	*−1706*	*66.0*	–	–	–	–
First Choice	4183	3047	*−1136*	*72.8*	–	–	–	–
Thomson Airways	–	–	–	–	7449	7213	*−236*	*96.8*
Thomas Cook	3172	2974	*−198*	*93.8*	4803	4706	*−97*	*98.0*
Monarch Airlines	2993	2789	*−204*	*93.2*	0	4412	*4412*	–
MyTravel Airways	4253	3311	*−942*	*77.9*	–	–	–	–
Astraeus	1019	867	*−152*	*85.1*	–	–	–	–
Excel Airways	2082	1948	*−134*	*93.6*	–	–	–	–

Source: Authors' calculations from UK CAA statistics and UK flight punctuality data.

[7] http://www.caa.co.uk/Data-and-analysis/UK-aviation-market/Flight-reliability/Datasets/UK-flight-punctuality-data/

[8] Leisure airline rankings published annually by Airline Business confirm that both airlines are the main operators in the British and German markets, as they used to be, at least from the end of the 1970s (Cambau and Lefèvre, 1981).

[9] Computed by the authors from OAG, based on all regular air services from and within the two countries.

[10] For the purposes of this paper, long haul is defined mainly according to CAA (2007) criteria. Thus, all those routes connecting UK and German origins with destinations outside Europe, outside North Africa, and outside the Middle East have been considered as long-haul routes. 'Europe' also includes Russia West of the Urals and Turkey; 'North Africa' only includes Morocco, Algeria, Tunisia, Libya, and Egypt; and 'Middle East' only includes Israel, Lebanon, Jordan, and the Syrian Arab Republic. A definition based on journey time or distance could be used, but this would mean long-haul routes could differ amongst airports, which makes no sense for the objectives of this study. For instance, if long-haul routes with a stage length of more than 4000 km were chosen, as Wilken et al. (2016) explained, flights to Sharm el Sheikh (Egypt) from Glasgow would be considered as long haul (4368 km), whereas from London to Gatwick they would be short and medium haul (3869 km).

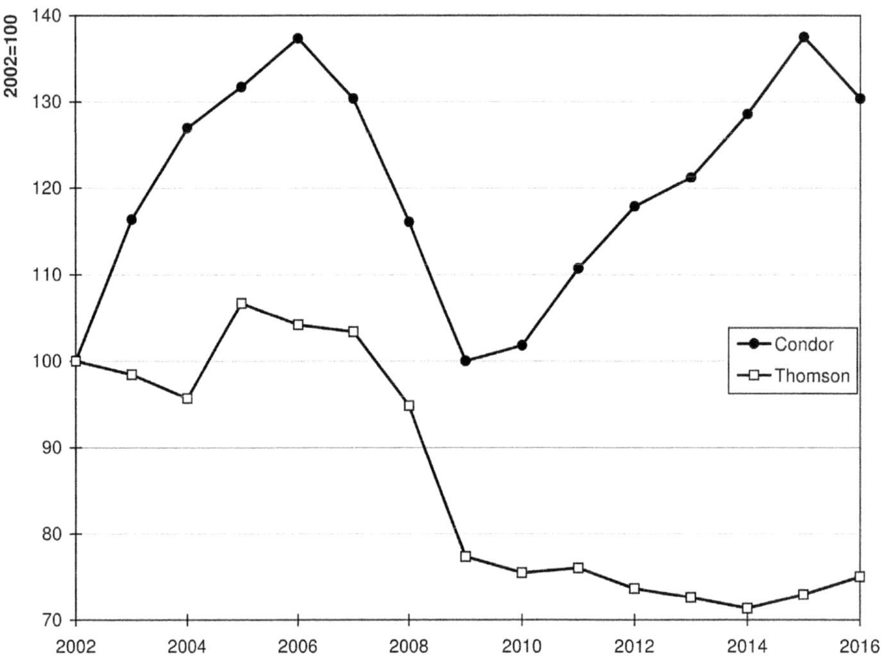

FIG. 11.4 Thomson vs Condor—Passenger Evolution (2002 = 100). *(Source: Airline Business rankings and UK CAA statistics.)*

(short/medium-haul versus long-haul) and changes in the number and nature of airlines competing with Thomson and Condor at the city-pair level. Selected years for the analysis are determined by data availability, but using 2004 as the base year for examining changes is quite applicable, because charter traffic and package holidays peaked in the United Kingdom between 2001 and 2004. A time span of 10 years can be considered reasonable for evaluating structural changes at the route network level; thus 2014 is the other reference year. Moreover, as seasonal differences between summer and winter are quite relevant when studying leisure charter airlines, data for both January and August was computed each year.

11.4 THE DESTINY OF FORMER CHARTER AIRLINES: COMPARING THOMSON AND CONDOR

11.4.1 The Alleged Shift to Long-Haul Flights

Table 11.4 introduces the main changes in the provision of air services by Thomson and Condor, making the distinction between short/medium-haul services and long-haul ones. Considering absolute figures, Thomson has clearly reduced its short/medium-haul business in terms of seats supplied, but in the context of a stable number of winter destination and of more numerous summer destinations. With the long-haul business, Thomson has clearly developed its presence in terms of both destinations offered and seats supplied.

At the same time, Condor has sharply decreased its number of short/medium-haul routes but slightly increased its number of seats in this market, which suggests more frequencies and/or larger aircraft use. In the meantime, the airline has increasingly developed its long-haul business, in both the number of destinations and seats.

In the end, the absolute amount of long-haul operations is without any doubt higher in 2017 than in 2004. However, it is also very clear when using any metric, that the short- and medium-haul market still dominates services supplied by the two airlines considered. This picture is better highlighted by Fig. 11.5,[11] even though just the number of flights is plotted. It suggests that both Thomson and Condor's shift to long-haul services is a slight move rather than a sharp change in operations. This result clearly contradicts recurrent claims expressed by other scholars.

Nevertheless, Condor has always been much more focused than Thomson with these services. Figures for August 2017 are a good example of that, because long-haul seats accounted for 11.6% of Thomson's total supply whilst in

[11] In order to make an accurate comparison, Thomson's figures for year 2004 include First Choice flights and seats, because both airlines were merged in 2008. Data presents evidence that consolidation led to significant cuts in capacity. Because of the length constraint, only August is shown.

TABLE 11.4 Condor and Thomson Main Indicators (Departing Flights)

Thomson[a]						
Winter season	*Jan 2004*	*%*	*Jan 2017*	*%*	*Gap*	*Growth %*
City-pairs[b]	162		177		15	*+9.3*
Short/medium-haul	130	*80.2*	132	*74.6*	2	*+1.5*
Long-haul	32	*19.8*	45	*25.4*	13	*+40.6*
Seats[c]	355,445		303,379		–52,066	*–15*
Short/medium-haul	322,266	*90.7*	217,768	*71.8*	–104,498	*–32*
Long-haul	33,179	*9.3*	85,611	*28.2*	52,432	*+158.0*
Average stage flown (km)	2645		3278		628	*+23.9*
Summer season	*Aug 2004*	*%*	*Aug 2017*	*%*	*Gap*	*Growth %*
City-pairs[b]	279		365		86	*+30.8*
Short/medium-haul	258	*92.5*	326	*89.3*	68	*+26.4*
Long-haul	21	*7.5*	39	*10.7*	18	*+85.7*
Seats[c]	982,934		781,930		–201,004	*–20*
Short/medium-haul	946,151	*96.3*	691,261	*88.4*	–254,890	*–27*
Long-haul	36,783	*3.7*	90,669	*11.6*	53,886	*+146.5*
Average stage flown (km)	2261		2627		366	*+16.2*
Condor						
Winter season	*Jan 2004*	*%*	*Jan 2017*	*%*	*Gap*	*Growth %*
City-pairs[b]	139	*100.0*	107	*100.0*	–32	*–23*
Short/medium-haul	98	*70.5*	54	*50.5*	–44	*–45*
Long-haul	41	*29.5*	53	*49.5*	12	*+29.3*
Seats[c]	142,550	*100.0*	209,985	*100.0*	67,435	*+47.3*
Short/medium-haul	95,398	*66.9*	107,785	*51.3*	12,388	*+13.0*
Long-haul	47,153	*33.1*	102,200	*48.7*	55,048	*+116.7*
Average stage flown (km)	4284		5349		1065	*24.9*
Summer season	*Aug 2004*	*%*	*Aug 2017*	*%*	*Gap*	*Growth %*
City-pairs[b]	224	*100.0*	207	*100.0*	–17	*–7.59*
Short/medium-haul	193	*86.2*	160	*77.3*	–33	*–17.10*
Long-haul	31	*13.8*	47	*22.7*	16	*+51.6*
Seats[c]	413,904	*100.0*	496,700	*100.0*	82,796	*+20.0*
Short/medium-haul	368,746	*89.1*	392,911	*79.1*	24,165	*+6.6*
Long-haul	45,158	*10.9*	103,789	*20.9*	58,631	*+129.8*
Average stage flown (km)	2487		3130		644	*+25.9*

[a] *In 2004 data from Britannia and First Choice have been joined to allow reliable comparison.*
[b] *Number of routes includes stopping routes.*
[c] *Number of seats avoids double counting due to stopping flights, considering only first origin and final destination.*
Source: OAG Max (January and August 2004); OAG Analyser (January and August 2017).

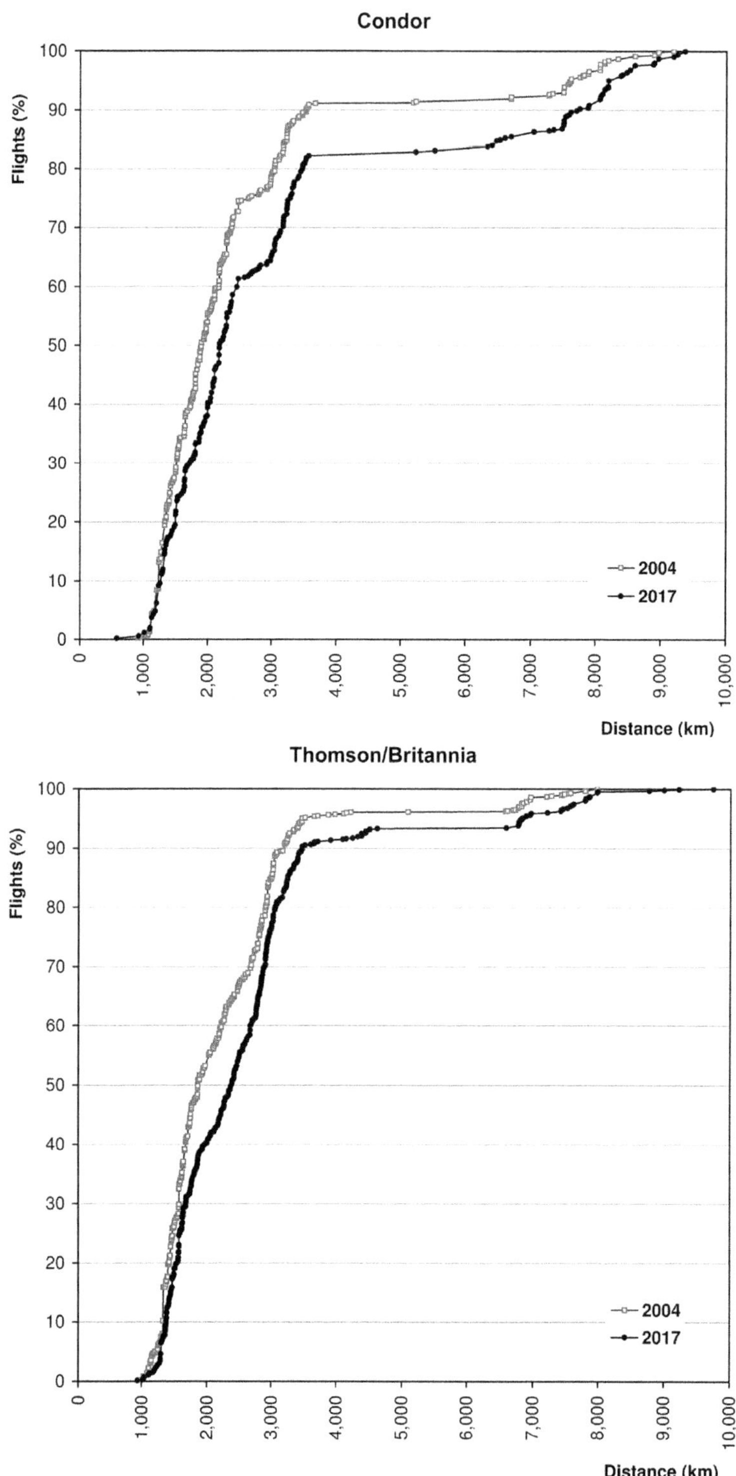

FIG. 11.5 Cumulative distribution of Condor and Thomson services according to distances flown—August 2004 vs 2017. *(Source: Authors' calculations from OAG Max and UK CAA statistics.)*

Condor's case they accounted for 20.9%. In fact, Condor's relative growth in capacity on such services is larger than Thomson reported, and absolute figures show that the German airline recorded a larger increase. Moreover, Condor's average trip length not only grew at a higher pace than Thomson's during the summer season (26% vs 16.2%), but also in the winter season (Table 11.4).

Regarding the geography of long-haul services, Condor has created a more diversified network than Thomson (Fig. 11.6), including much more than the classic routes to Caribbean resorts in the Dominican Republic, Mexico, Cuba,

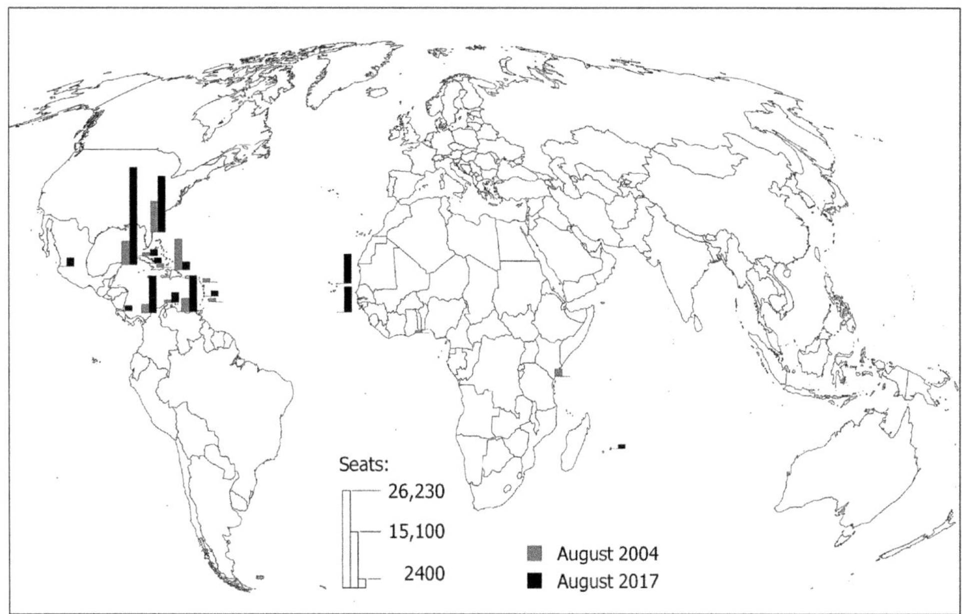

FIG. 11.6 Thomson's flight supply on Long-Haul routes—August 2004 vs August 2017. *(Source: Authors' calculations from OAG Max and UK CAA statistics.)*

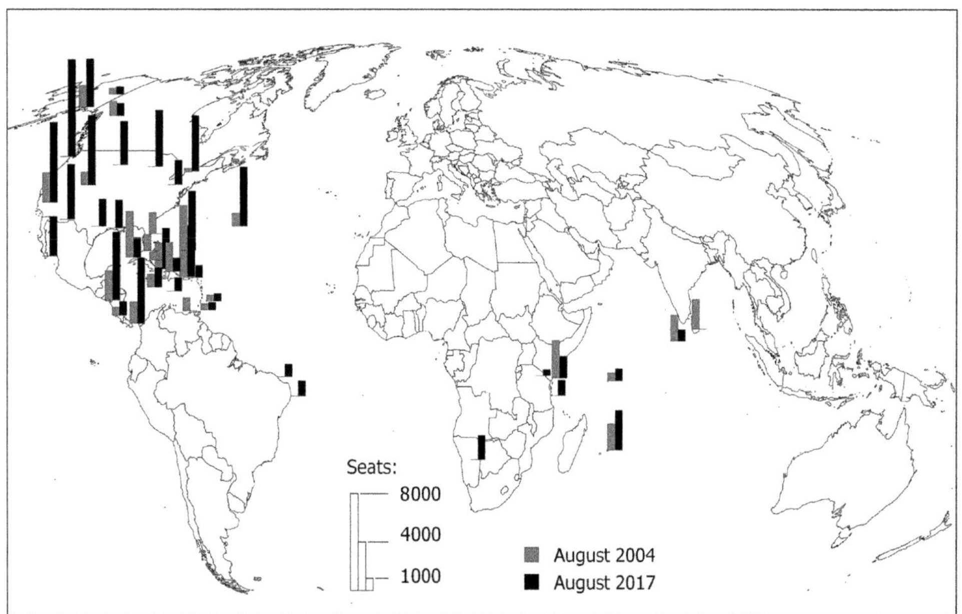

FIG. 11.7 Condor's flight supply on long-haul routes—August 2004 vs August 2017. *(Source: Authors' calculations from OAG Max and UK CAA statistics.)*

and Jamaica. Routes connecting its Frankfurt and Munich bases to tourist destinations in North America, Central America, Brazil, and East Africa (Fig. 11.7) were developed and strengthened between 2004 and 2017 (Fig. 11.8).

11.4.2 Low-Cost Carrier Competition: Cannibalisation of Former Charter Airlines or New Balance?

The next step of the analysis is to investigate the potential role of LCCs in the trend unveiled in the previous section. Figs 11.9 and 11.10 show route changes at the city-pair level during the 13-year period considered.

When analysing routes in 2017 there is a differentiation between dropped routes and discontinued routes. *Dropped* routes are those Condor or Thomson abandoned but which are still offered by other airlines. *Discontinued* routes are those abandoned by Condor or Thomson and not currently supplied by any other airline. The first conclusion

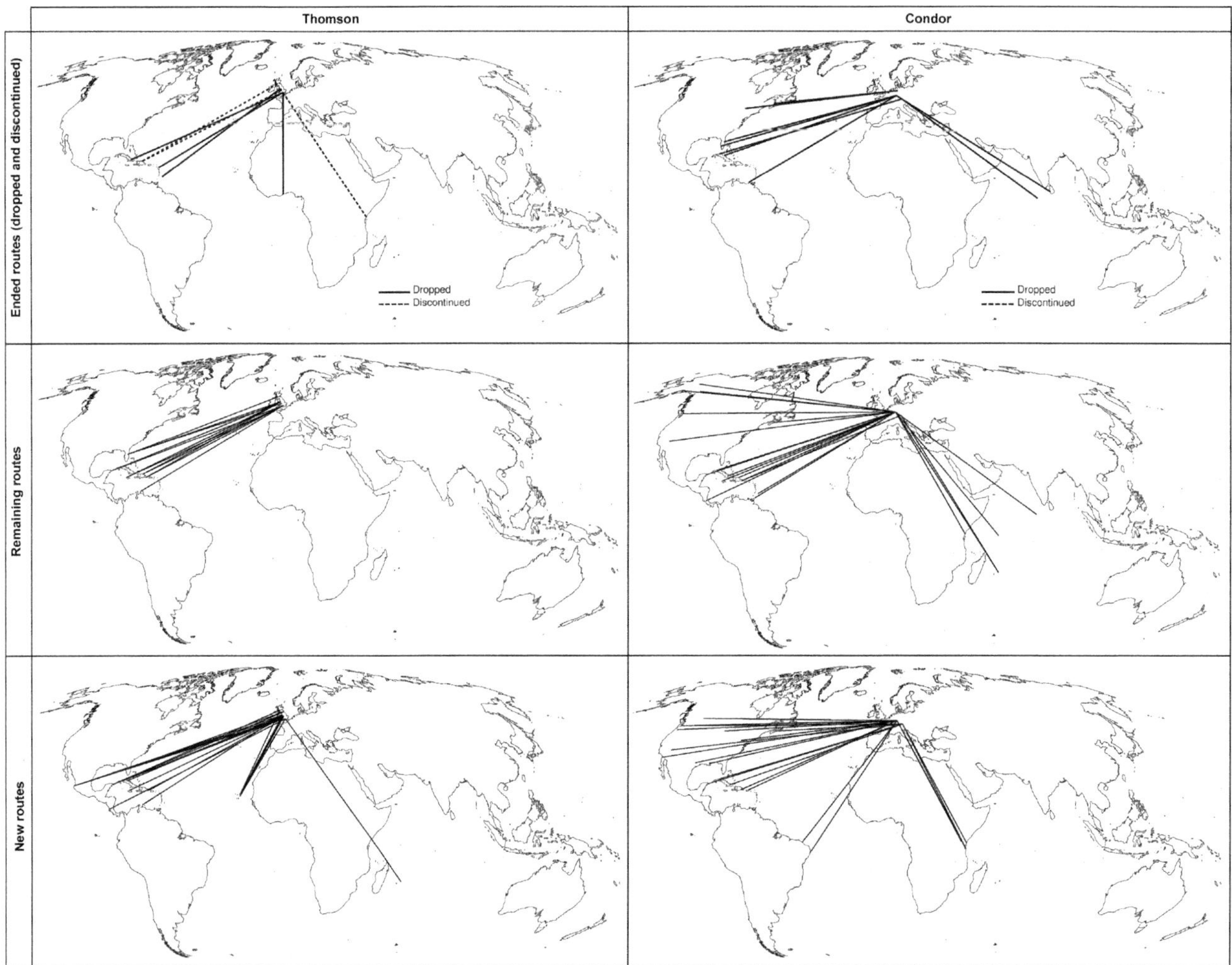

FIG. 11.8 Condor and Thomson's route network changes on long-haul routes—August 2004 vs August 2017. *(Source: Authors' calculations from OAG Max and UK CAA statistics.)*

derived from the analysis is the high number of discontinued routes: 23% of Condor's routes and 56% of Thomson's belong to that group. The end of Condor's services to the Bulgarian Black Sea resorts or the closure of Thomson's bases in Coventry or Durham can be cited as examples of routes completely discontinued (Fig. 11.10). Therefore besides LCC competition, important factors contributing to the elimination of air links appear to be the tour operators' and airlines' strategic planning and the economic performance of the routes.

Focusing on dropped routes, it can be observed that the LCC presence can be associated with 80% of Thomson's abandoned routes still operated by other carriers. The LCC market share is above 25% on all but one of these routes, and even exceeds 75% with eight of them (Table 11.5). Routes from new LCC airport bases showed more propensity to be dropped, as in the Liverpool case, affecting mainly destinations in Spain and Portugal (Fig. 11.10). Finally, on at least four routes that Thomson abandoned, other leisure airlines remain as the only operators, showing the limits of LCCs to be present on all short- and medium-haul leisure-oriented routes. However, the main LCCs are still expanding, so their absence may simply mean a temporary absence on the former charter airlines' short/medium routes.

As for Condor's dropped routes, the LCC presence is a minor explicative factor, because LCCs can only be associated with 14.5% of these routes. Air Berlin, an ex-charter airline that evolved into a hybrid network airline, emerged as Condor's main competitor: it was offering services on 26 out of 76 routes that Condor dropped (34.2%), and on 11 of them it was supplying more than 40% of total capacity. In fact, similar calculations for the year 2014, before financial difficulties began affecting Air Berlin,[12] show a higher presence of Air Berlin on routes formerly operated by Condor.

[12] Air Berlin ceased all operations late October 2017.

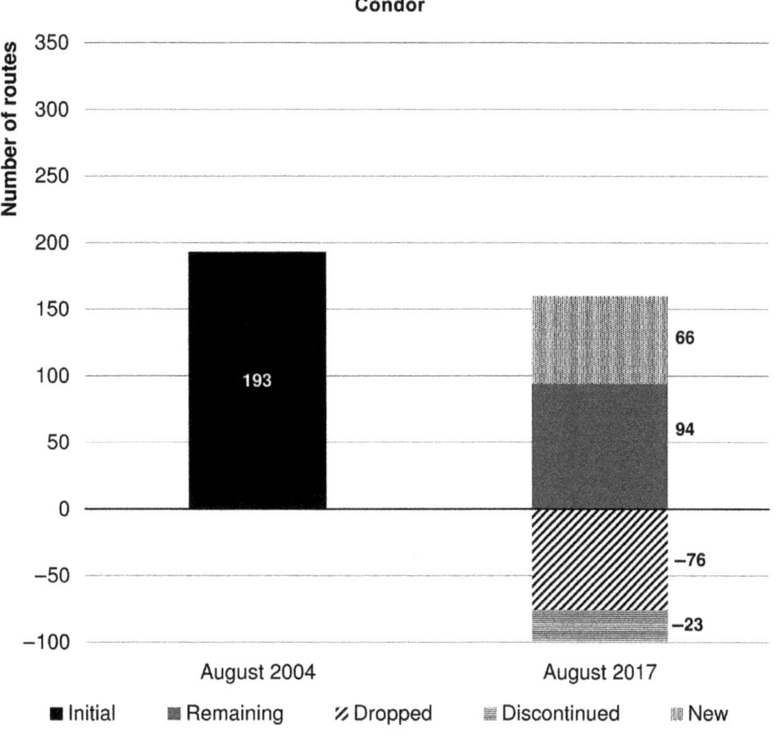

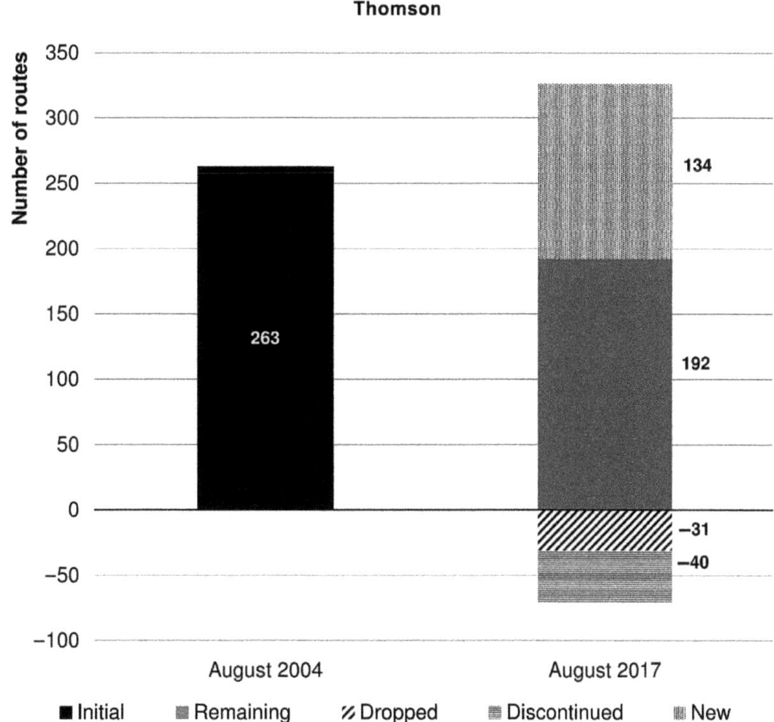

FIG. 11.9 Condor and Thomson's route network changes (short- and medium-haul range). Note: Dropped routes are those Condor or Thomson abandoned but which are still offered by other airlines. Discontinued routes are those abandoned by Condor or Thomson and not currently supplied by any other airline. *(Source: Authors calculations from OAG Max and UK CAA statistics.)*

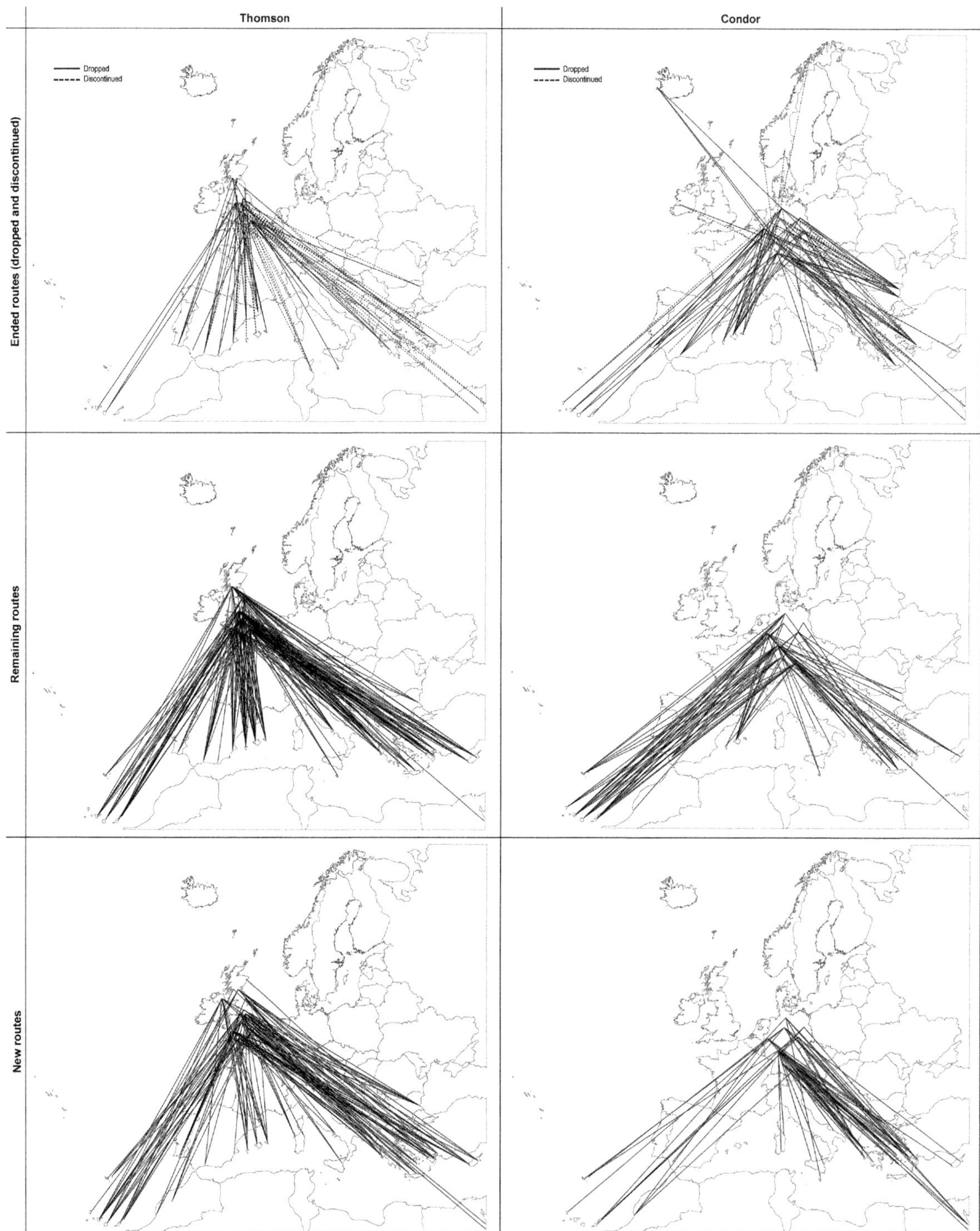

FIG. 11.10 Condor and Thomson's route network changes on short- and medium-haul routes—August 2004 vs August 2017. *(Source: Authors' calculations from OAG Max and UK CAA statistics.)*

New routes that opened between August 2004 and August 2017 constitute 41% of both Condor and Thomson's routes operated in 2017, but they represent a lesser proportion of capacity (21.4% and 22.3%, respectively). Whilst the number of new routes opened is 66 and 134, only 19 and 10 destinations (mainly Greek, Italian, and Croatian ones) were added, respectively, in 2017. Four new departing airports have been included in Thomson's network, but none in Condor's network. On the other hand, the German airline has abandoned

TABLE 11.5 LCC Market Share in Thomson and Condor Dropped Routes—August 2004–17

	Routes	
LCC Share (%)	**Condor**	**Thomson**
0.0	65	6
0.1–24.9	2	1
25–49.9	7	9
50–74.9	1	7
75–100	1	8
Total	76	31

Source: Authors' calculations from OAG & CAA data (August 2004 and August 2017).

eight departing airports, focusing on nine departing airports, showing a large route network rationalisation. These figures evidence a new combination of departing and arriving airports already served as a main trend for newly opened routes.

Route openings favour city-pairs without competition from LCCs, especially in Condor's case. As can be seen in Fig. 11.11, 94.3% of new routes and seats supplied by Condor and more than 62.1% of those supplied by Thomson belong to this category. Furthermore, when opening a new route, any airline prefers a monopolistic position if possible, and former charter airlines are not an exception (Fig. 11.11). Such strategy helps develop an understanding as to why former charter airlines are facing much less competition from low-cost airlines in newly opened routes than in inherited ones. Only 5.7% and 34.6% of seats supplied by Condor and Thomson on new routes are challenged by LCCs, whilst the average figures for the whole network are 22.7% and 66.1%, respectively.

From a geographical perspective, destinations in Greece and Spain have clearly benefitted from new routes added on short- and medium-haul range (Fig. 11.10). Whilst new routes to Greece basically involved the same destinations in the islands for both airlines, some differences arise in the case of Spain. Condor only opened new routes to the Canary Islands and Thomson diversified by including the Balearic Islands and Spanish mainland. Condor's choice can be understood as a way to avoid low-cost competition, because on longer routes, such as those involving the Canary Islands and the Greek islands, the LCC market share used to be less than on the shorter ones involving destinations such as Faro or Alicante. As for Thomson, the opening of new bases in Doncaster and Bournemouth, which are less affected by LCC operations, could explain such new destinations.

On a second level are Egypt and Turkey. This is a relevant issue because both countries had not liberalised air links with the European Common Aviation Area (ECAA) at the time, and bilateral agreements remain to rule the opening of new routes. For former charter airlines it is easier to grow in these markets than in liberalised ones, such as Morocco, where European low-cost airlines have recorded impressive growth since 2007 (Dobruszkes and Mondou, 2013).

Most of the routes operated by Condor and Thomson in August 2017, almost 59%, are inherited routes that already existed in August 2004. Between 77.7% (Thomson) and 78.6% (Condor) of seats supplied are concentrated on these routes, showing the sound stability of both networks.

As pointed out before, competition from LCCs is more intense on these remaining routes than on the new ones, and the bulk of capacity supplied on these routes is affected by LCC competition. However, major differences between airlines can also be identified, with Thomson facing more intense competition from such carriers (Fig. 11.11). Once again, Air Berlins' role is important here: if it had been considered as a LCC, the differences found between Condor and Thomson would have disappeared, with 73.4% of routes and 61.3% of seats supplied by Condor on remaining routes avoiding LCC competition.

Another important difference is the intensity of competition each airline faces: 80.3% of Condor seats facing low-cost competition are supplied on routes where the LCC market share is below 25%, whilst 27.1% of Thomson seats are in the same situation (Table 11.6).

Monopoly routes are infrequent amongst inherited city-pairs and are usually low-frequency connections (mainly one weekly flight) representing a low share of capacity, and involving secondary airports at the origin or at destination. Finally, from a geographical point of view, the inherited routes of both airlines show a high concentration in only three countries (Fig. 11.10), Spain and Greece again, now joined by Funchal and Faro in Portugal.

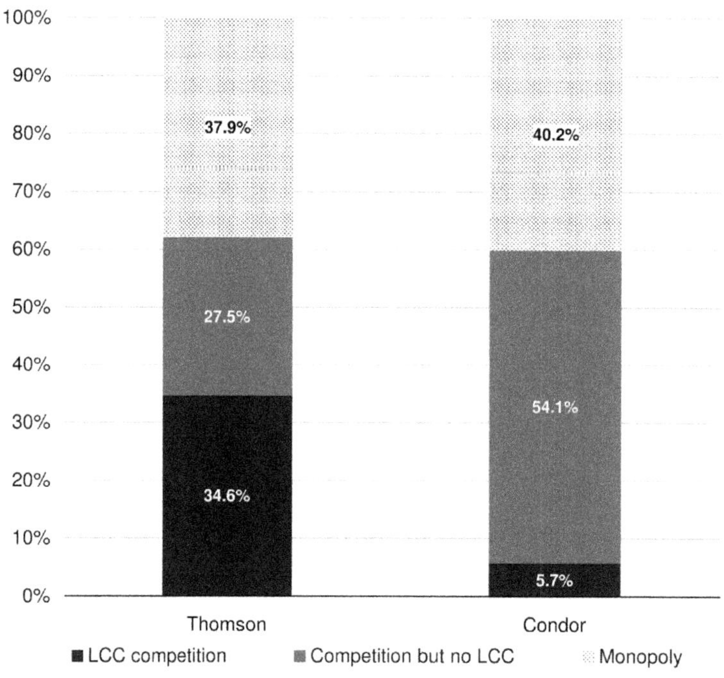

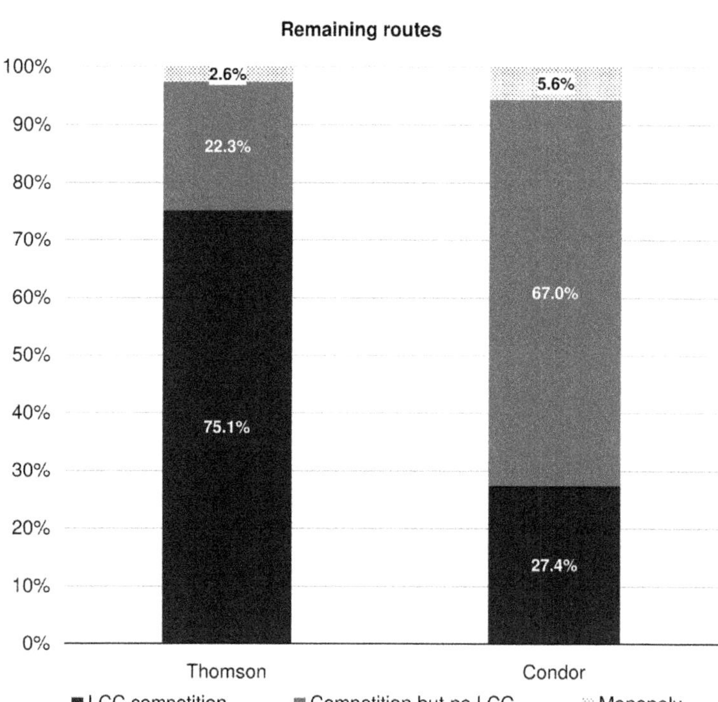

FIG. 11.11 Seats affected by competition in new and remaining routes (%). *(Source: Authors' calculations from OAG Max and UK CAA statistics.)*

TABLE 11.6 LCC Market Share in Thomson and Condor Remaining Routes—August 2004–17

	Condor		Thomson	
LCC Share (%)	**Routes**	**Seats**	**Routes**	**Seats**
0.0	79	226,830	72	133,987
0.1–24.9	11	68,667	32	109,334
25–49.9	4	16,740	53	207,947
50–74.9	0	0	30	79,129
75–100	0	0	5	7031
Total	94	312,237	120	403,441

Source: Authors' calculations from OAG and CAA data (August 2004 and August 2014).

11.5 DISCUSSION AND CONCLUSIONS

Following air transport market liberalisation in the EU, some misunderstanding emerged concerning the concept of charter airlines. As has been shown, an in-depth approach about what 'charter' really means nowadays was necessary to shed light on the confusion created by the use of such concepts imported from preliberalisation times. At least within the EU, charter airlines are not the same carriers that emerged in the 1950s to circumvent protected air markets and supply affordable leisure trips to tourists through package holidays commercialised by tour operators. These former charter airlines show inherited features from the past, and contracts with tour operators are still a significant driver of their network geography. But a growing percentage of their capacity is now directly available to final consumers, restraining the effectiveness of the 'nonscheduled' category included in official statistics to study its evolution. Moreover, the survival of package holidays and the growing hybridisation of air transport business models have led traditional scheduled airlines and low-cost players to sell blocks of seats directly to tour operators, a practice once considered limited mostly to charter airlines. Thus tracking package holiday trends at the route level has evolved into an impossible task that only a new method of collecting statistics could resolve, as Doganis already proposed in 1973.

Currently, the use of supply-side data (seats and flights) is arguably the best way to track charter airlines and changes in its route network. Using such data, case study research based on two main European charter airlines was conducted in order to revisit claims made about the impact of liberalisation on the network geography of the charter airlines. The analysis has been carried out at route level, which is the main uniqueness of this research related to charter airlines.

The results of the analysis suggest that the alleged move of former charter airlines to long-haul flights is limited, even though it could still be in an early phase. During the 13-year period studied, long-haul supply grew at a higher pace than short- and medium-haul supply in both airlines. Excluding Condor's winter season schedule, long-haul supply does not reach a market share of 30% in any season or airline. Clearly, long-haul operations are now more relevant for both airlines than they were 13 years ago, as the increase in the average stage flown demonstrates. However, short- and medium-haul services have remained dominant, both in absolute and relative terms. But some differences also emerge between both airlines: whilst Condor combines an increasing specialisation in the long-haul market with gains in short- and medium-haul capacity, Thomson has cut seats and capacity in that range. The merger of Britannia and First Choice in 2008 to form Thomson could have resulted in network redundancies and overcapacity in short- and medium-haul services, which were also suffering from the low-cost carrier's expansion into the leisure market.

The results also show that in Europe, competitive pressure from LCCs differs notably from one carrier to another. Obviously, as Condor's strategy was considerably more focused on long-haul markets since the beginning of the century, and the LCC market share in Germany is lower than in the United Kingdom, it has felt less pressure from such airlines. But calculations on short- and medium-haul routes that were stopped between 2004 and 2014, reveal that between one-third and a half of them have been discontinued and are not operated for other airlines anymore. The LCC presence on the rest of the stopped routes—those that are called dropped routes—is far from being exclusive. By now, if it is clear that LCCs have forced the former charter airlines to rethink their network to some extent, but they have not really driven them away towards the long-haul market.

However, European low-cost airlines are still expanding. As a result, Thomson and Condor's move to other short/medium routes that are not currently served by LCCs can simply be a short-term respite. On the other hand, new leisure/charter airlines from Central and Eastern Europe are entering the market, supplying a growing capacity within the intra-EU market, not only from their home countries (Taylor, 2016; Taylor and Ciechański, 2015a,b) but also from Northern and Western European countries (Bugnot, 2012).

Research founded on analyses of 'scheduled' and 'nonscheduled' passenger categories within former charter airlines have tended to under-represent the actual role of short-haul operations for former charter airlines. As these operations have mainly transited to the 'scheduled' category, authors have assumed that 'nonscheduled' and long-haul services were the only market niche for former charter airlines. Moreover, such analyses have focused on the British case, and have ignored the diversity of outbound tourist markets within Europe, including the less mature ones in Central Europe. Thus a larger geographical diversity of former charter/leisure airlines needs to be considered in future research. New data sources need to be explored to increase the coverage of charter airline operations. Only further trends in networks operated by both former charter airlines and LCCs will allow more accurate conclusions to be made on substitution processes and on the respective roles of these two groups of airlines.

Acknowledgements

Some of the results reported here come from a three-month research fellowship of David Ramos-Pérez at the Free University of Brussels (ULB) to develop the project 'Tourism and air transport in the Euro-Mediterranean area: a geography of competition between charter and low-cost airlines (1990-2013)', financed by the Spanish Ministry of Education, Culture and Sports (José Castillejo Program, reference CAS14/00107).

References

Aviation Strategy, 1999. Consolidation pace increases for Europe's charter airlines. Aviat. Strateg. 18, 7–9. Available at https://www.aviationstrategy.aero/newsletter/Apr-1999/3/Consolidation_pace_increases_for_Europe's_charter_airlines. (Accessed June 19, 2018).

Aviation Strategy, 2015. The beginning of the end for Europe's charter airlines. Aviat. Strateg. 204. Available at https://www.aviationstrategy.aero/newsletter/Mar-2015/3/The_beginning_of_the_end_for_Europe%E2%80%99s_charter_airlines. (Accessed June 19, 2018).

Benson, M., O'Reilly, K., 2009. Migration and the search for a better way of life: a critical exploration of lifestyle migration. Sociol. Rev. 57 (4), 608–625.

Bugnot, F., 2012. Ces compagnies charter de l'Est qui profitent du ciel français. L'Echo Touristique. May 25th, Retrieved on November 13th, 2015. http://www.lechotouristique.com/article/ces-compagnies-charter-de-l-est-qui-profitent-du-ciel-francais,51337.

CAA, 2007. Connecting the Continents—Long Haul Passenger Operations From the UK (CAP 771). Civil Aviation Authority, London. Available at http://publicapps.caa.co.uk/docs/33/CAP771.pdf. (Accessed June 19, 2018).

Cambau, D., Lefèvre, G., 1981. Panorama of World Non-Scheduled Passenger Transport. Part Two: Major Origin-Destination Flows (ITA Study, 1981/4). Institut du Transport Aérien, Paris.

Clancy, R., 2013. TUI Travel profits boosted by return of package holiday. The Telegraph. Retrieved on December 10th, 2014. http://www.telegraph.co.uk/finance/newsbysector/retailandconsumer/leisure/10507500/TUI-Travel-profits-boosted-by-return-of-package-holiday.html.

Clark, O., Dunn, G., 2015. Fresh packaging. Airl. Bus. 31 (8), 39–41.

Cohen, E., 1974. Who is a tourist? A conceptual clarification. Sociol. Rev. 22 (4), 527–555.

DLR (German Aerospace Center), 2008. Airline Business Models—Topical Report. European Commission, Brussels.

Dobruszkes, F., 2013. The geography of European low-cost airline networks: a contemporary analysis. J. Transp. Geogr. 28, 75–88.

Dobruszkes, F., Mondou, V., 2013. Aviation liberalization as a means to promote international tourism: the EU–Morocco case. J. Air Transp. Manag. 29, 23–34.

Dobruszkes, F., Schepens, V., Decroly, J.-M., 2006. Éléments pour une géographie de l'offre charter européenne face à la concurrence des compagnies low-cost. In: Bernier, X., Gauchon, C. (Eds.), Transport et tourisme. Collection Edytem, Chambéry, pp. 65–76.

Doganis, R., 1973. Air transport—a case study in international regulation. J. Transp. Econ. Pol. 11 (2), 109–133.

Doganis, R., 2010. Flying Off Course. Airline Economics and Marketing, fourth ed. Routledge, London.

Gormsen, E., 1997. The impact of tourism on coastal areas. GeoJournal 42 (1), 39–54.

Graham, A., 2008. Trends and characteristics of leisure travel demand. In: Papathedorou, G.A., Forsyth, P. (Eds.), Aviation and Tourism. Implications for Leisure Travel. Ashgate, Aldershot, pp. 21–33.

Haanapel, P., 1978. Ratemaking in International Air Transport. A Legal Analysis of International Air Fares and Rates. Kluwer, Deventer.

ICAO, 2013. Reference Manual on the ICAO Statistics Programme, fifth ed. International Civil Aviation Organization, Montreal.

Ioannides, D., Debbage, K., 1997. Post-Fordism and flexibility: the travel industry polyglot. Tour. Manag. 18 (4), 229–241.

King, R., Warnes, A.M., Williams, A.M., 1998. International retirement migration in Europe. Int. J. Popul. Geogr. 4 (2), 91–111.

Learmount, D., 1987. Classy charter. Flight Int. 131 (4052), 33–35.

Lobbenberg, A., 1995. Strategic responses of charter airlines to single market integration. J. Air Transp. Manag. 2 (2), 67–80.

Lohmann, G., Koo, T.T.R., 2013. The airline business models spectrum. J. Air Transp. Manag. 31, 7–9.

O'Connell, J.F., Bouquet, A., 2015. Dynamic packaging spells the end of European charter airlines. J. Vacat. Mark. 21 (2), 175–189.

O'Reilly, K., 2000. The British on the Costa del Sol. Routledge, London.

OJEU, 2003. Regulation (EE) no 437/2003 of the European Parliament and of the Council of 27 February 2003 on statistical returns in respect of the carriage of passengers, freight and mail by air. Off. J. Eur. Union L66, 1–8.

Papatheodorou, A., Lei, Z., 2006. Leisure travel in Europe and airline business models: a study of regional airports in Great Britain. J. Air Transp. Manag. 12 (1), 47–52.

Pearce, D.G., 1987a. Mediterranean charters—a comparative geographic perspective. Tour. Manag. 8 (4), 291–305.

Pearce, D.G., 1987b. Spatial patterns of package tourism in Europe. Ann. Tour. Res. 14 (2), 183–201.

Taylor, Z., 2016. Air charter leisure traffic and organised tourism in Poland: are charters passé? Morav. Geogr. Rep. 24 (4), 15–25.

Taylor, Z., Ciechański, A., 2015a. Transport lotniczy w obsłudze polskich touroperatorów—część I (Air transport in the servicing of polish tour operators—part I). Prz. Geogr. (Polish Geog. Rev.) 87 (2), 255–278.

Taylor, Z., Ciechański, A., 2015b. Transport lotniczy w obsłudze polskich touroperatorów—część II (Air transport in the servicing of polish tour operators—part II). Prz. Geogr. (Polish Geog. Rev.) 87 (4), 569–588.

Wilken, D., Berster, P., Gelhausen, M.C., 2016. Analysis of demand structures on intercontinental routes to and from Europe with a view to identifying potential for new low-cost services. J. Air Transp. Manag. 56, 79–90.

Williams, G., 2001. Will Europe's charter carriers be replaced by "no-frills" scheduled airlines? J. Air Transp. Manag. 7 (5), 277–286.

Williams, G., 2008. The future of charter operations. In: Graham, A.P., Forsyth, P. (Eds.), Aviation and Tourism. Implications for Leisure Travel. Ashgate, Aldershot, pp. 85–102.

Wu, C., 2016. How aviation deregulation promotes international tourism in Northeast Asia: a case of the charter market in Japan. J. Air Transp. Manag. 57, 260–271.

Wu, C., Jiang, Q., Yang, H., 2018. Changes in cross-strait aviation policies and their impact on tourism flows since 2009. Transp. Policy 63, 61–72.

PART III

ON THE GO: ACCESSING AIRPORTS AND THE AIRLINE AND AIRPORT EXPERIENCE

CHAPTER

12

The Role of Airport Surface Access in the Passenger Journey

Thomas BUDD

Cranfield University, Bedford, United Kingdom

CHAPTER OUTLINE

12.1 INTRODUCTION—THE SURFACE ACCESS CHALLENGE

The hardest thing in aerial travel, nowadays, is not to fly, but to get quickly to and from the airport.
(Everyday Science and Mechanics magazine, 1931, p. 647)

From the very earliest days of commercial air transport, planners have concerned themselves with facilitating seamless transitions for passengers changing between surface and air transport. This is more of an issue today than it has ever been, given that the world's largest airports now generate millions of miles of surface access (also called 'ground access') travel from the many thousands of airport passengers accessing and egressing these sites every day.

Due to their considerable size and specific operating requirements, airports have generally been sited towards the edge of, or even some considerable distance from, the major cities they serve. London's Gatwick Airport (around 35 miles from central London) and Oslo's Gardermoen (30 miles from central Oslo) in Europe are such examples, with similar scenarios found at many other airports worldwide. For airport surface access this poses an inherent challenge, in so much that road, rail, and other surface modes are typically designed to converge in the centre of urban areas (i.e. often some distance from where airports are located). Airports are often significant trip generators within a region, and as demand for air travel has grown, airports have needed to facilitate growing numbers of journeys to and from sites that were located primarily for their suitability for aircraft, rather than surface transport. For airports located in more remote sites (e.g. former military bases) or in very rural areas, this issue can be even more profound.

From an infrastructural perspective, an airports' surface access system constitutes several key components. Depending on the airport and the prevailing national regulatory conditions, these may be owned and operated by the airport operator or a third party. The immediate road network surrounding the airport forms the first major component, including on-airport roads, highways/motorways, and any additional roads connecting these. For airports

Air Transport—A Tourism Perspective. https://doi.org/10.1016/B978-0-12-812857-2.00012-9

with rail access, the same principle applies. Further infrastructural components of the surface access system include public transport terminals, including bus, coach, or rail stations. Provision for passengers being dropped-off/picked-up will typically be offered on the forecourt close to the passenger terminal. Car parking facilities (including taxi and car rental) will also typically be offered by all but the very smallest of airports. In some cases, on-airport access systems will also be provided for passengers by Automated People Movers (APM). These are driverless or automated systems designed to facilitate the mass movement of airport users between terminals, provide access to satellite or other remote areas of the airport (e.g. boarding gates), and/or to provide connections to railways stations or other mass transit nodes. Accompanying wayfinding provision in the form of directional signs and information boards will also be included as part of an airports surface access arrangements.

From the perspective of the airport operator, surface access planning and provision can be viewed as being driven by three key interrelated factors. The first of these relates to the operational imperative associated with ensuring the safe flow of passengers and other airport users in a timely and efficient manner. Unreliable journey times and problems of congestion will inevitably have negative knock-on implications for the smooth operation of the airport as a whole. The second key driver of surface access relates to strategic and competition factors, in so much that passengers are an airport's primary customer, and will reside within, or need to travel to, the wider catchment area. Airports that are able to utilise their catchment area by facilitating convenient, reliable, and cost-effective surface access for their passengers will have a competitive advantage over airports where this is not the case, all other things being equal. This may be especially important for airports located in a single multiairport region and/or those catering to similar markets (e.g. low cost or long haul).

For large airports or those located in regions where there are few alternative airports to fly from, the geographical extent of an airport's catchment area may be extremely large. In some cases, passengers may travel several hours to access their airport of choice by either private car, long-distance coach, or national or international rail services, including high-speed ones (e.g. to Amsterdam, Frankfurt, and Paris CDG airports). Where an airport serves a particular destination not offered by other airports in the region and/or offers more attractive air fares, passengers may also be willing to accept a lengthy journey to and from the airport. This 'exurban' market, as Coogan et al. (2008) define it, can be challenging to plan for from a public transport perspective, as passenger trip origins are generally fewer in number and more dispersed than regions (typically urban areas) closer to the airport.

The third key driver of surface access provision, and the main focus of this chapter, relates to surface access' role as a key component of the passenger experience. For the international leisure tourist or business traveller, their journey to or from the airport will represent one of the first experiences, or final memories, of an airport, region, or country. The highly time sensitive nature of these journeys, combined with the financial penalties associated with missing a flight, mean that the journey to the airport can often be the most stressful part of a passengers' journey. Anxieties associated with missing a flight or reaching their destination are likely to be more acute for infrequent travellers or those unfamiliar with the airport or regional transport system. For short-haul air travel, in some cases the journey to and from the airport can also cost as much, and take as long, as the flight itself. Relaxed, satisfied passengers will in turn yield operational and strategic planning benefits for the airport, as mentioned, and may lead to other benefits including increased dwell time (and commercial spend) in terminal retail outlets.

This chapter will examine the role of surface access in the passenger journey. Specifically, it addresses how the varying requirements and characteristics of passengers determine their behaviour and travel decisions at different stages of the journey. With reference to selected real-world examples, the chapter will also highlight various challenges facing airport managers with regards to surface access provision. Following a similar approach to the book as a whole, the chapter is organised according to the different stages of the passenger surface access journey; starting at the point of origin at the pretrip planning stage and concluding with the arrival and onward travel at the point of destination. The chapter concludes by examining likely future trends in a surface access context and the difficulty of planning and uncertainty.

12.2 THE VARYING REQUIREMENTS AND CHARACTERISTICS OF PASSENGERS

12.2.1 Pretrip Planning and Mode Choice

Passengers represent the majority of surface access journeys at an airport, with the remaining trips undertaken by the other major airport user groups; airport employees, people dropping-off/collecting other passengers (so called meeter-greeters), and cargo, supply, delivery, and other commercial vehicles. Passengers changing or transferring between flights at an airport are not considered in a surface access context as they do not require surface travel to and from the airport in question. This is why at large hub airports the proportion of surface access passengers will typically be lower than airports that predominantly serve point-to-point originating and destination (O–D) markets. For example, in 2016 over 75 million passengers passed through London Heathrow, of which just over 27 million (or 36.1%) were connecting to other flights. In comparison, at Manchester Airport, a regional airport in England's northwest, only 2.9% of the airport's 21.6 million passengers used the airport to connect to other flights (Civil Aviation Authority, 2017).

Surface access passengers are conventionally classified as being either originating (outbound) or terminating (inbound) passengers. This distinction matters primarily as a reflection of whether or not the passenger is likely to have access to a private vehicle when starting their trip. Clearly, a passenger arriving at an airport is less likely to have access to their own vehicle than someone starting their journey from their home or place of work. As a result, an airport with a predominant focus on originating/outbound traffic will likely need to accommodate a larger proportion of private vehicles than an airport with a strong focus on inbound passengers (e.g. airports located in popular tourist destinations with comparatively small resident populations).

Regarding the factors that govern decisions about how to travel to the airport, as already mentioned, the time and financial costs associated with being late or missing a flight mean that passengers are highly time sensitive and hence require a mode of transport that is affordable, efficient, and reliable. Overall, it is posited that passenger mode choice is a function of perceptions regarding the relative cost, comfort, and convenience of competing modes (Ashford et al., 2013). These findings are variously supported by research showing that travel time, cost, and comfort/convenience are pivotal considerations when deciding how to travel (e.g. see Psaraki and Abacoumkin, 2002; Pels et al., 2003; Tam et al., 2005; Chang-Jou et al., 2011). Importantly, whilst the overall door-to-journey time *is* an important consideration for passengers, the reliability of that journey may be valued as highly, if not more so, by some passengers and/or in certain circumstances. In other words, a passenger may be happy to sacrifice a slightly longer journey for one that they consider to be more reliable and less susceptible to delays.

In addition to factors of time and cost, there may be important mediating factors relating contextually to the nature of the passenger's trip that influence decisions about travelling to the airport. Arguably the most important of these contextual factors relates to whether the passenger is travelling for leisure or business purposes. People travelling for leisure purposes, especially those staying away for a few days or more, are more likely to be carrying larger luggage items with them than a business traveller, who will typically only be staying away from home for a relatively short period of time. Generally speaking, passengers encumbered with heavy or bulky luggage will favour using a private car (where available) or a taxi than public transport. Even relatively small suitcases designed to fit into the overhead 'bins' on an aircraft can be problematic to take on some public transport services, which may be crowded and/or provide little space for luggage storage. This issue is recognised as a key challenge in encouraging more passengers to use public transport (Coogan et al., 2008, p. 107).

> A major impediment to the choice of a public mode for ground access is a lack of baggage accommodation.

Leisure passengers are also more likely to be travelling as part of a group (e.g. with family and friends) than the business traveller. Hence, it may be more cost efficient for the passenger to share the cost of using a car or a taxi, than pay for separate tickets on public transport. Business and leisure passengers may also vary in terms of their relative sensitivity to time and cost factors. Research here shows that business passengers generally place a higher value on journey time than they do on the cost of their trip (e.g. see Pels et al., 2003; Hess and Polak, 2006). This will typically cause business passengers to favour the mode that offers the most efficient journey time. For example, in London the premium nonstop express rail service, 'The Heathrow Express', is targeted primarily with the business user in mind, with an accompanying premium price point to reflect this. The preference for shorter journey times over cost considerations is easy to understand, given that business travellers may need to travel on a regular basis and, crucially, will usually have their travel costs paid for by their employer or third party (Coogan et al., 2008).

A relatively new phenomenon in a surface access context is that of the airline-operated private luxury limousine services. These are currently offered by a small selection of full-service network carriers (e.g. Emirates, Qatar, and Etihad Airways) at selected airports to passengers travelling in either business or first-class cabins (or equivalent). Passengers travelling to/from a specified distance from the airport can prebook a chauffeur-driven car from their point of origin/destination at no additional cost over and above the price of the airfare. For these passengers, there is clearly little incentive to choose to travel by any other mode, hence the traditional mode choice considerations are virtually redundant. Alongside the traditional transfer coach, which is most commonly associated with so-called package holidays, the airline-operated limousine represents one of only a small number of examples where the surface access portion of a passengers' trip is provided by the airline or tour operator, and where the price is incorporated with the price of the air fare.

12.2.2 The Journey to the Airport

Passengers generally favour using private cars because of the perceived comfort, availability, flexibility, reliability, improved personal safety and security, low-marginal costs, ease of transporting heavy luggage, and the short door-to-door journey times they provide (Kazda and Caves, 2008; Humphreys and Ison, 2005). Taxi use is generally higher for passengers than for other airport users for similar reasons (de Neufville and Odoni, 2003). When discussing the share of journeys made by different modes at airports, private cars and taxis are commonly grouped together and termed 'private vehicle trips', reflecting the characteristics of the vehicle itself and the 'private', as opposed to shared, nature of the journey.

At airports worldwide, private vehicle trips represent the vast majority of passenger surface access journeys. In 2005 Humphreys and Ison showed that at large airports in Europe (defined as those handling >10 million passengers per year), around 65% of all journeys were made by private vehicles. In 2016, 60.7% of passenger journeys at Heathrow were undertaken by private vehicle (CAA, 2017). This figure is typically much higher for smaller regional or secondary airports where lower passenger numbers make it harder to sustain economically viable public transport services (see Fig. 12.1). Whilst there are examples of large airports where public transport mode shares are higher, for example, Tokyo Narita in Asia or Oslo Gardermoen in Europe, and public mode shares at some airports have improved over the past decade, the growth in overall demand over the same time period largely outweighs these changes.

This reliance on private vehicle journeys poses considerable challenges for decision-makers, most notably in terms of minimising the potential for traffic congestion around airports and the associated negative implications for reduced local air quality and increased greenhouse emissions. Peaks in surface access traffic will typically follow prevailing airline schedules, with peaks in activity in the morning (06:00–08:00) for passengers on the first 'wave' of departing flights, and a similar peak in the evening at the end of the working day. Where these coincide with peaks in normal commuter traffic, the potential for traffic congestion and unreliable journey times is greatly enhanced.

The coinciding of airport and nonairport-related peaks in traffic can also be a problem with regards to public transport, where airport passengers carrying luggage may have to share buses and railway carriages with nonairport users. Often, these services will not be adequately configured to store higher volumes of luggage, adding difficulty and stress to the journeys of both the airport and nonairport user. To try and alleviate these problems, there have been some attempts to develop facilities whereby passengers can check in their luggage at off-site locations, including major railway stations, before proceeding to the airport. Perhaps the most notable example of such a scheme is Hong Kong's 'in-town check-in' facility, which serves Hong Kong International airport via their MRT subway system at no additional charge to the passenger. However, similar facilities elsewhere have generally been less successful. In 1999 a downtown check-in facility at London's Paddington railway station was opened for passengers travelling to Heathrow by train. However, the facility did not receive sufficient patronage to make it economically viable and

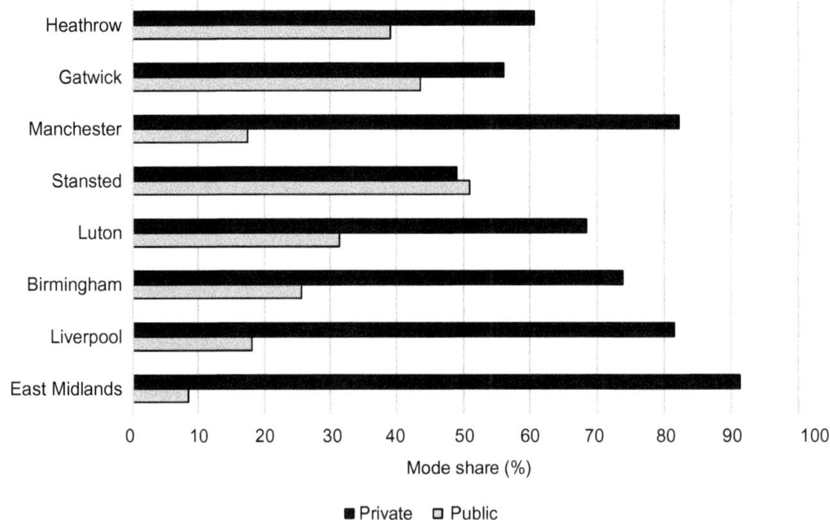

FIG. 12.1 Passenger mode shares at selected UK airports. *(From Civil Aviation Authority, 2017. CAA Passenger Survey Report, Available at: https://www.caa.co.uk/uploadedFiles/CAA/Content/Standard_Content/Data_and_analysis/Datasets/Passenger_survey/CAA%20Passenger%20Survey%20 Report%202016.pdf. (Accessed December 1, 2017).)*

it was subsequently closed in 2004 (Coogan et al., 2008). Increased security concerns following the 2001 terrorist attacks in New York, and the subsequent fall in demand for air travel, combined with increasing availability of online ticketing and check-in procedures over this period have limited the potential for more widespread adoption of these facilities at other airports.

An alternative system for handling luggage is offered in Switzerland, where the national railway company SBB allows passengers travelling from either Zurich or Geneva airport to check-in their luggage at their local railway station. Inbound passengers can then also collect their luggage at their railway station on their return. Third-party commercial operators (e.g. Airportr) may also offer passengers the chance to have their luggage transported to and from the airport for a fee at some airports.

Unsurprisingly, services that operate directly to/from an airport will be preferred by passengers over those where it is necessary to change modes (e.g. bus to train, train to train, etc.). This is known as the 'interchange penalty', whereby the likelihood of a passenger choosing to use public transport diminishes significantly if they are required to change modes along the way. Clearly, the more changes that are required, the less attractive the service becomes to the passenger.

By comparison, dedicated airport express services offer direct or even nonstop services to/from an airport and a city or major urban area. These can be operated by rail, bus, or in some rare cases driverless/autonomous vehicles (e.g. the Incheon 'Maglev' train in South Korea). Examples of express rail services include the Heathrow Express (London), Arlanda Express (Stockholm), and Narita Express (Tokyo). These will be configured specifically with the needs of the airport passenger in mind (i.e. space for storing luggage, low-step access, and single deck) and are less likely to be shared with large numbers of nonairport users, given the few stopping points and their comparatively high price. However, these may be ill suited for passengers wishing to travel to locations other than the city centre. Research from the United States estimates that <30% of passenger trips to/from airports begin or end in the downtown region (LeighFisher et al., 2010).

Whilst express rail services are more commonly associated with major airports and those serving longer haul routes, smaller regional or secondary airports are more likely to operate some form of express bus service. These are typically far less cost intensive to construct, operate, and maintain, but retain similar characteristics in terms of offering passenger-oriented services to predominantly downtown destinations. Ticket prices on express services tend to be priced higher than comparative regional services, which typically offer more connections to the wider catchment area but are generally slower (in terms of door-to-door journey time) and may be tailored less towards the needs of the airport passenger.

Of the UK's large airports, Stansted has the highest proportion of journeys made by public transport, including by rail, bus, and coach (50.9%; CAA, 2017). Whilst it may be tempting to suggest that high public transport use is a direct function of the perceived preferences of the 'typical' low-cost passenger (i.e. price sensitive and willing to trade some comfort and convenience for reduced costs), the research is inconclusive in this regard. Whilst it is true that low-cost carriers have helped make air travel accessible to a broader populace, generally speaking, passengers flying with low-cost carriers are by no means more or less likely to be from any other socioeconomic background than people travelling with any other carrier. For example, easyJet's first route from the United Kingdom to Nice was targeted to serve people who owned a second home in France (a market they continue to serve very well), and a significant share of low-cost winter traffic in the United Kingdom is to skiing and winter sports destinations.

In certain circumstances, it has been suggested that low-cost passengers may even pose additional surface access challenges by being prepared to travel further to access their departure airport to take advantage of the lower fares offered (e.g. see Transportation Research Board of the National Academies et al., 2011). Instead, it seems likelier that the trip characteristics typically associated with short-haul air travel, combined with the provision of readily available, reliable, affordable public transport services, *can* in some cases be favourable to increased public transport use. In the case of Stansted, public transport mode shares are boosted by having a strong focus on inbound passengers (who are less likely to have access to a car), with a significant share of passengers needing to travel to/from London (i.e. a large market conducive to higher volume public transport).

12.2.3 At the Airport

One of the first requirements a passenger will have of the on-site surface access system is a clear and easily navigable signing and wayfinding system. This will typically consist of permanent static directional signs (e.g. located on approach roads) and variable message signs (VMS) displaying pertinent contextual information (e.g. the location of areas with available car parking spaces). Whilst the majority of passengers will ultimately need to reach security screening in the terminal, there are a myriad of other passenger flows that an airport's wayfinding infrastructure needs to accommodate. These may include transitions between terminals, car parking and public transport facilities, as well as between airport hotels, business centres, or cargo and maintenance areas. The growing number of passengers, combined with the wide range of airport sizes and configurations can make this even more challenging. There are various principles airports can adhere to when designing their wayfinding system (see Case Study 12.1, adapted from Gresham, Smith and Partners et al., 2011).

CASE STUDY 12.1 BEST-PRACTICE IN AIRPORT WAYFINDING

The general core principles of good airport wayfinding can be summarised as follows. While these principles represent good practice in wayfinding design generally, it is important that special considerations are given to the needs of the airport user. For example, there is generally a greater reliance on the use of symbols and/or multilingual signs in airport settings than elsewhere, given that passengers may not be able to understand the local language.

Conspicuous—the color and light on the sign should contrast with the background so that they are easily visible.

Concise and comprehensible—passengers are unlikely to spend more than a few seconds looking at a sign. It is important to avoid possible ambiguity when using symbols.

Legible and location—signs must be readable from the distance at which the user is first likely to be looking for them, and located at relevant decision points along the passenger.

(From Gresham, Smith and Partners, Texas Transportation Institute, Human Factors North Inc., Big Sky Inc., Society for Environmental Graphic Design, Mineta San Jose International Airport, 2011. Wayfinding and Signing Guidelines for Airport Terminals and Landside (ACRP, 52), Transportation Research Board of the National Academies, Washington, DC.)

For passengers parking their car at the airport, facilities will generally be differentiated according to how long the vehicle will be left parked. Long-term parking facilities, where a vehicle will typically be left for 24h or more, are generally located further from the terminal building and connected via a shuttle bus. In Europe and North America, it is also common for third-party providers to operate off-site car parks. These are often priced competitively compared with comparable facilities offered by the airport, but they may be located much further from the airport. Generally speaking, the requirement for longer term parking is more commonly associated with use by leisure passengers, who may be staying away from home for some time.

In contrast, short-term parking facilities (<1h to a few days) will be located much closer to the terminal building to allow quicker access (normally on foot). These facilities will be priced to deter passengers from leaving their vehicles for longer periods of time. Their added convenience, combined with the shorter nature of these trips, means that short-term parking facilities are often favoured by business passengers. Various 'value-added' services, including car washing or valeting, are also commonly offered by airports to generate additional revenue and may be available in either short- or long-term facilities.

Whilst perhaps not a primary concern for passengers, the predominance of private car journeys at airports has profound implications in terms of increased greenhouse gas emissions and reduced local air quality. The need to reduce private car journeys on environmental grounds has long been recognised in national Government policy, especially in Europe, and meeting mode share targets is now commonly a prerequisite for receiving planning approval for expansion projects. Herein lies a potential conflict of interests on the part of the airport operator. On the one hand, increasing policy and regulatory pressure encourages airports to reduce private vehicle use, whilst on the other hand, the commercial realities of running an airport mean that passenger car parking represents a vital revenue stream, accounting for as much as 25% of total revenues in some cases (Jacobs Consultancy et al., 2009). Successfully balancing these competing pressures consequently represents "...perhaps one of the most difficult problem areas to face airport management (Ashford et al., 2013, p. 411)". Relatively few examples exist of airports who have been able to dramatically reduce emissions from their surface transport activities (see Case Study 12.2).

CASE STUDY 12.2 STOCKHOLM ARLANDA'S EMISSION CAP

Sweden's largest airport, Stockholm Arlanda, is unique in that it is the only airport in the world operating under an enforced cap on the level of emissions it can produce. In 1991 the Swedish government approved the construction of an additional third runway at the airport on the condition that greenhouse gas emissions did not exceed 1990 levels for a period of at least 10 years after the runway was completed in 2001. This was to include emissions from aircraft landing/taking off and from all surface access traffic, in addition to emissions from heating/lighting and airport vehicles. Whilst Swedavia, the airport operator, have been successful in meeting these obligations whilst simultaneously growing passenger numbers (from

15 million passengers in 1990 to nearly 25 million in 2016), this is largely a result of improvements in aircraft technology and the ability to accommodate more passengers on fewer, but larger, aircraft. Over the same period, the airport operator acknowledges that the proportional and total role of surface access emissions has grown. This is despite numerous innovative policies developed by the airport, including the 'Ecotaxi' initiative, where priority to pick up passengers is based on the environmental efficiency rating of the individual taxi (Swedavia Airports, 2017).

Environmental and congestion problems may be increased at an airport if the passenger chooses to be dropped-off and/or picked-up by a friend or relative in a private car. This is to say that the passenger is left/collected at the terminal curbside or the vehicle is parked for a short duration whilst the passenger is accompanied to/from the terminal. Whilst this may be convenient for the passenger, these 'kiss-and-fly' trips, as they are also referred to as, generate additional vehicle traffic and can exacerbate problems of congestion. They also provide little (if any) financial contribution for the airport operator. In a study of the five largest airports in the United Kingdom, Budd (2016) found that millions of additional 'meeter–greeters' travel to and from airports for the sole purpose of dropping-off and collecting passengers (see Table 12.1). This represents something of a hidden element of surface access travel, given that data on the extent of these trips is rarely recorded or published.

Consequently, airports are increasingly seeking means by which they can reduce the volume of drop-off/pick-up journeys. One mechanism commonly employed, especially at regional or secondary airports, is to charge passengers a fee to be dropped-off/picked-up outside the terminal. For example, at London Luton Airport, a fee of £3.50 (around US $4) is charged for cars to access the terminal for a period of 10 min, with an additional charge of £1 (US $1.40) for every minute thereafter. However, there is little to suggest that the implementation of these charges actually discourages the use of drop-off/pick-up in reality, and they have proven largely unpopular with airport users. Budd et al. (2014) found that passengers who currently favour being dropped-off/picked-up (collectively termed the 'Dogmatic Drop-offs') showed strong attachments to using their cars, have low perceptions of the environmental problems of car use, and consequently show little potential to change their travel behaviour (Case Study 12.3).

CASE STUDY 12.3 PERCEPTIONS OF SURFACE ACCESS AS PART OF THE WHOLE TRIP

For passengers, the surface access component of their journey represents only part of a much longer (and generally more expensive) journey. As a result, it can be difficult to frame travel behaviour decisions about surface access in the same way that other journeys might be. Consider the long-haul passenger, who is likely to have already spent large amounts of money on their flight and accommodation. Here, the surface access component of their journey may account for only a relatively small portion of the total time and financial outlay for the trip. In comparison, the journey to work is often the only journey a person will make in a day and is typically a trip people make regularly. In this scenario, it is easy to see how a person's relative valuation of time and cost factors may vary.

The effects of this juxtaposition may also apply in an environmental context, given that passengers travelling to airports are doing so with the explicit intention of going on to undertake an activity that is itself widely regarded as being environmentally damaging (i.e. flying). Convincing passengers of the need to travel by alternative modes of transport for environmental reasons may be challenging, seeing that the surface element of their journey may represent only a fraction of the total emissions for their entire journey. By comparison, the environmental role of surface access travel may be perceived as merely a 'drop in the ocean'.

TABLE 12.1 'Meeter–Greeters' as a Percentage of Total Passengers at Five UK Airports, 2014

	Total Passengers	Meeter–Greeters	% of Total
Heathrow	73,164,000	4,453,156	6.1
Gatwick	37,886,000	951,642	2.5
Manchester	21,660,000	795,872	3.7
Stansted	19,899,000	688,176	3.5
Luton	10,400,000	194,541	1.9
Total	163,009,000	7,083,387	4.3

From Budd, T., 2016. An exploratory examination of additional ground access trips generated by airport 'meeter-greeters'. J. Air Transp. Manag. 53, 242–251.

For passengers arriving by public transport, there are a number of important design requirements that an airport needs to consider over and above the provision of key infrastructure (rail and bus terminals, waiting areas, and ticketing facilities). The positioning of these facilities relative to the passenger terminal is clearly an important planning consideration. As passengers will typically be travelling with luggage, it is necessary to minimise walking distances and the number of changes in level required to access the terminal, and to provide shelter from the weather. Where possible, passengers should also be physically separated from vehicle or other traffic flows. This obviously has important safety implications but also yields operational benefits in terms of ensuring smoother traffic flows on airport roads. Public transport options are likely to be less attractive in comparison to private vehicle modes if the former are located further from the terminal than the latter. Consequently, there is a strong case for prioritising terminal access to public transport users over those using a private vehicle. This philosophy is evident at airports including Amsterdam's Schiphol, where railway passengers can almost instantaneously access the very heart of the terminal complex via a single escalator from platforms located beneath the terminal.

At some larger airports passengers may also require the use of Automated People Mover (APM) systems. These may resemble light-rail or urban trams in appearance and are fully automated, driverless systems used for moving large volumes of passengers between key areas of an airport. Landside APM may be used to connect separate terminals or provide connections to key landside facilities, including car parks or public transport terminals. Airside APM typically provide connections to remote or satellite aircraft gates/stands whilst maintaining suitable connection times for passengers connecting between flights. APM have been crucial in enabling airports to expand their facilities and, subsequently, facilitate large-scale airline hubbing operations. APM typically operate on fixed guideways or tracks and are electrically powered, meaning that there may be local air quality benefits over systems where passengers are transported by a shuttle bus. There are many examples of APM currently in operation at airports worldwide, with the majority of these implemented airside (e.g. in Atlanta, Las Vegas, and Orlando in the United States). By comparison, landside APM are generally less common, but are in evidence at airports including London Gatwick (United Kingdom), Paris CDG (France), New York JFK and Newark (United States), Dusseldorf (Germany), and Chicago O'Hare (United States). Singapore's Changi airport is relatively unusual in that it has both airside and landside APM systems in operation (Lea and Elliott, Kimley-Horn, and Associates Inc. and Randolph Richardson Associates, 2010).

Reduced walking distances and connection times within the airport may be especially valued by passengers with reduced mobility or those with other requirements affecting their ability to navigate the airport. These passengers can include a very broad spectrum of conditions and abilities, including wheelchair users or those who require additional help walking, passengers who may be visually or hearing impaired, or those with autism or forms of dementia. Whilst not purely a concern for older passengers, the stress affecting someone undertaking a journey may be felt more acutely by an older person due to the normal physical and psychological deterioration associated with the ageing process. Research by Mein et al., (2014) highlights four prevalent issues for older passengers:

Wayfinding—unfamiliarity with a complex environment, comprehension of directional signs/information screens, and understanding key terminology.

Fatigue—having to stand in queues, long walking distances, and handling heavy luggage.

Technology and equipment—understanding and using self-service devices and using escalators and moving walkways.

Amenities—ready access to washroom facilities and use of congested environments.

For the reasons outlined, private cars and taxis are strongly favoured by older passengers over public transport modes. Generally, the ageing population and the increased number of older people using air travel poses broad design, operational, and technical challenges for providers. Namely, there are questions as to how airlines and airports can best accommodate the specific physical and psychological needs of this demographic in a cost-efficient and operationally workable manner. This may include provision of additional seating in waiting areas and at key transition points in the airport, staffed information desks, and assistance at self-service devices, as well as audible alerts at escalators and moving walkways. Some airports also operate systems whereby passengers are able to self-identify as requiring additional assistance, and are given a visible yet discrete identifier (normally a coloured lanyard or badge) that alerts airport staff that the passenger may require additional help. In terms of surface access, this could mean assistance with purchasing of tickets, identifying the correct shuttle bus, or finding a suitable taxi on arrival.

12.2.4 Arrival and Onward Travel

As mentioned, the arriving passenger represents a key market for public transport at airports given that these passengers are less likely to have access to a private car for their onward journey. It is important that steps are taken to accommodate this important market segment by ensuring that that there are regular, reliable public transport services available when passengers require them. However, this is considerably easier said than done, especially when passengers may be travelling very early in the morning or late at night (i.e. when public transport services are generally less frequent). In most cases an airport operator will have little direct control over the timetabling and schedule arrangements of the bus and rail companies that serve the airport, but it is important that airports work closely with transport providers where possible to ensure suitable service provision.

In some cases, airlines may encourage the use of onward travel by public transport by selling tickets for these services to passengers onboard the aircraft. Tickets may be offered at a discounted or preferential rate over the 'walk-up' fare, with the airline typically receiving commission on any tickets sold. Low-cost carriers have been especially quick to adopt this model. In Europe, easyJet operate their 'easyBus' service, a self-styled low-cost airport transfer bus service at London's Gatwick, Stansted, and Luton Airport; Manchester Airport; as well as Geneva, Milan Malpensa, and Pisa Airport.

It is common for hotels surrounding an airport to be served by a purposely operated hotel 'shuttle' style bus or mini-van service. These may operate on a scheduled or on-demand basis and may be offered free of charge or for a fee. These services are required even where the distance between the hotel and the airport terminal is relatively small, given that it can be difficult to access these sites on foot.

For airports located in traditional holiday destinations, a considerable share of passengers may be travelling on prearranged tour coaches. These will typically be included as part of a holiday package booked through a tour operator or travel agent and will transfer passengers directly to and from their accommodation. The highly seasonal and uneven nature of the demand at these airports (which may be relatively quiet throughout the rest of the year) can make efficient management of capacity challenging. This may be compounded by the fact that the typical operating characteristics of coaches vary significantly from other road vehicles and require considerably more vertical and horizontal space for parking and manoeuvring. For example, coaches will typically require passengers to access the side of the vehicle in order to load and unload their luggage. This can pose both operational and safety challenges, especially if passengers need to access the traffic side of the vehicle to do this.

Conversely, for passengers who are not part of a tour party, taxis and minicabs are also widely used. From a definitional perspective, taxis are considered distinctive from minicabs in that the latter describe private hire cars that are booked in advance (these drivers are commonly seen in the arrivals hall of airports waiting for passengers who booked the journey). Typically, minicabs will be left in short stay car parking facilities. In contrast, taxis operate on a 'first-come-first-served' basis and will typically have designated waiting areas (or 'ranks') close to the front of the terminal building. Airport operators will generally have commercial agreements with taxi and minicab operators granting the company licences to either drop-off and/or collect passengers from the airport. The ease and convenience offered by taxis may be favoured by arriving passengers, who are less likely to be familiar with using public transport in the region. In some countries, there may be problems of unlicenced drivers seeking to solicit business, usually by offering cheaper fares than the licenced alternatives. Aside from the commercial issues this can cause, there are obvious safety implications for passengers using vehicles and drivers that are unlicenced, unregulated, and uninsured for the purpose at hand. The recent growth in the popularity of transport technology providers, including Uber (see Chapter 2), is a new manifestation of the planning and policy challenges airports face.

A relatively small, albeit still significant, share of passengers will rent private cars for their travel. Rental car facilities will typically be located in designated parking areas or as part of larger shared facilities, which are often located away from the terminal. Airports will generally receive commercial revenues from rental car firms in a similar fashion to other airport tenant companies.

12.3 FUTURE TRENDS AND PLANNING FOR UNCERTAINTY

The quotation at the very start of this chapter, taken from a popular US consumer magazine from the first half of the 20th century, provides a reminder that the journey to and from the airport, and the challenges associated with it, have formed a fundamental component of air travel since the very earliest days. As this chapter has shown, the challenges faced by contemporary decision-makers in terms of meeting the varied needs and requirements of passengers, reconciling often conflicting commercial and environmental goals, and in particular increasing the share of journeys by public transport, are considerable and in all likelihood will remain a key challenge for the foreseeable future.

For airport operators, providing passengers with the opportunity, or context, in which they can choose a form of travel that is convenient, reliable, and affordable is a fundamental planning goal. Yet this relies to a significant extent on the continued provision of key infrastructure and services, which can be considered as both a prerequisite for, and a great enhancer of, strategic development. This is of course inherently difficult. Whilst there is a generally held consensus that demand for air travel will continue to rise, even with the most sophisticated forecasting techniques, experience shows that it is difficult to reliably predict the nature and scale of future trends in air traffic, which ultimately determine the type and configuration of the surface access system required by an airport.

Inevitably, the problems of forecasting become more acute the further into the future one seeks to predict. Unfortunately, these longer timescales are those most commonly associated with infrastructure planning. For airports located in mature air transport markets, prevailing planning, political, and economic climates can compound this problem, often making the delivery of large-scale, lengthy infrastructural projects prohibitively difficult. Airports must increasingly make the best of what they have in this regard. As a result, there is growing recognition of the value of flexible design and operating practices in surface access and airport planning in general (see de Neufville, 2016). The general principles of flexible design revolve around the ability to easily accommodate changes (especially increases) in capacity or capability requirements. For example, this can be achieved by incorporating additional space in design concepts that allow for increases in capacity, or designing multifunctioning facilities so that spaces can be reconfigured for different uses if necessary. Crucially, adaptive planning procedures are also put in place that recognise that original plans may need to adapt and evolve in response to changes in the market over time.

Sources of this uncertainty range from very broad macroeconomic forces (e.g. demographic changes and the needs of an ageing population), to changes in market conditions (e.g. the entry or exit of a carrier), or even social and cultural changes. Future legislative and regulatory environments also provide a key source of uncertainty. This may include increased environmental, security, or accessibility regulation, but need not even relate directly to the air transport industry. Unpredictable, infrequent 'shock-events' like wars, terrorist attacks, geopolitical instability, or natural disasters also have the potential to significantly alter the planning landscape for airports.

In a surface access context, technological change and rapidly evolving consumer practices is perhaps one of the key sources of uncertainty. This is particularly evident in the area of vehicle technology, where recent years have seen a gradual shift towards the uptake of hybrid or fully electric powered vehicles. This has resulted in the growing trend for provision of electric charging points in airport car parking facilities, for example, with the potential for inductive (i.e. wireless) charging technology to be implemented in the future. In terms of wayfinding, the proliferation of smartphones and other connected personal devices already also offers the potential for more personalised navigation, perhaps bringing into question the role of traditional wayfinding systems. Technological advances in computer booking and reservation systems have also enabled airports to introduce more sophisticated inventory and yield management systems for their car parks, coupled with similar advances in ANPR (Automatic Number Plate Recognition) technology, which is now widely employed at airports. In the future, more complex vehicle-tracking and location technologies may also be adopted. Looking further ahead, accommodating autonomous vehicle technologies (either part or fully driverless) may pose additional challenges, not least in terms of ensuring passenger safety during any transitional period where cars driven by humans and fully driverless vehicles share the same space.

In the meantime, the journey to and from the airport remains an essential component of the passenger journey. There is a need for airports to examine and comprehend the underlying determinants of a passenger's travel behaviour, and the factors governing these decisions, in order to make more efficient and better targeted planning decisions in a way that makes best use of the existing surface access system and catchment area. For passengers, surface access travel will most likely remain a necessary, if not entirely welcome, part of their overall journey.

References

Ashford, N.J., Stanton, H.P.M., Moore, C.A., Coutu, P., Beasley, J.R., 2013. Airport Operations, third ed. McGraw-Hill, London; New York.

Budd, T., 2016. An exploratory examination of additional ground access trips generated by airport 'meeter-greeters'. J. Air Transp. Manag. 53, 242–251.

Budd, T., Ryley, T., Ison, S., 2014. Airport ground access and private car use: a segmentation analysis. J. Transp. Geogr. 36 (1), 106–115.

Chang-Jou, R., Hensher, D.A., Hsu, T.-L., 2011. Airport ground access mode choice behaviour after the introduction of a new mode: a case study of Taoyuan International Airport in Taiwan. Transp. Res. E 47 (3), 371–381.

Civil Aviation Authority, 2017. CAA Passenger Survey Report. Available at https://www.caa.co.uk/uploadedFiles/CAA/Content/Standard_Content/Data_and_analysis/Datasets/Passenger_survey/CAA%20Passenger%20Survey%20Report%202016.pdf. (Accessed December 1, 2017).

Coogan, M.A., MarketSense Consulting LCC, Jacobs Consultancy, 2008. Ground Access to Major Airports by Public Transportation, ACRP (Airport Cooperative Research Programme) Report 4. Transportation Research Board of the National Academies, Washington, DC.

de Neufville, R., 2016. Airport systems planning and design. In: Budd, L., Ison, S. (Eds.), Air Transport Management. Ashgate, Aldershot, pp. 61–78.

de Neufville, R., Odoni, A., 2003. Airport Systems: Planning, Design and Management. McGraw-Hill, New York.

Everyday Science and Mechanics, 1931. Airport Docks for New York. vol. 11. Gernsback Publications, New York, p. 647.

Gresham, Smith and Partners, Texas Transportation Institute, Human Factors North Inc, Big Sky Inc., Society for Environmental Graphic Design, Mineta San Jose International Airport, 2011. Wayfinding and Signing Guidelines for Airport Terminals and Landside (ACRP, 52). Transportation Research Board of the National Academies, Washington, DC.

Hess, S., Polak, J.W., 2006. Airport, airline and access mode choice in the San Francisco Bay area. Pap. Reg. Sci. 85 (4), 543–567.

Humphreys, I., Ison, S., 2005. Changing airport employee travel behaviour: the role of airport surface access strategies. Transp. Policy 12 (1), 1–9.

Jacobs Consultancy, Walker Parking Consultants, Mannix Group, DMR Consulting, 2009. Guidebook for Evaluating Airport Parking Strategies and Supporting Technologies, ACRP (Airport Cooperative Research Programme) Report 24. Transportation Research Board of the National Academies, Washington, DC.

Kazda, A., Caves, R.E., 2008. Airport Design and Operation, second ed. Emerald, Bingley.

Lea and Elliott, Kimley-Horn and Associates Inc., Randolph Richardson Associates, 2010. Guidebook for Planning and Implementing Automated People Mover Systems at Airports., *Airport Cooperative Research Programme (ACRP) Report 37*. Transportation Research Board of the National Academies, Washington, DC.

LeighFisher, Dowling Associates Inc., JD Franz Rsearch Inc., WILTEC, 2010. Airport Curbside and Terminal Area Roadway Operations, Airport Cooperative Research Programme (ACRP) Report 40. Transportation Research Board of the National Academies, Washington, DC.

Mein, P., Kirchhoff, A., Fangen, P., 2014. ACRP Synthesis of Airport Practice 51: Impacts of Ageing Travellers on Airports. Transportation Research Board of the National Academies, Washington, DC.

Pels, E., Nijkamp, P., Rietveld, P., 2003. Access to and competition between airports: a case study for the San Francisco Bay area. Transp. Res. A 37 (1), 71–83.

Psaraki, V., Abacoumkin, C., 2002. Access mode choice for relocated airports: the new Athens International Airport. J. Air Trans. Manag. 8 (1), 89–98.

Swedavia Airports, 2017. Stockholm Arlanda: Environment. Available at https://www.swedavia.com/arlanda/environment/#gref. (Accessed November 8, 2017).

Tam, M.L., Tam, M.L., Lam, W.H.K., 2005. Analysis of airport access mode choice: a case study in Hong Kong. J. East. Asia Soc. Transport. Stud. 6 (1), 708–723.

Transportation Research Board of the National Academies, Lian, J.I., Rønnevik, J., 2011. Airport competition—regional airports losing ground to main airports. J. Transp. Geogr. 19 (1), 85–92.

CHAPTER

13

The Airport Experience

Walanchalee WATTANACHAROENSIL

Mahidol University International College, Nakhon Pathom, Thailand

CHAPTER OUTLINE

13.1 INTRODUCTION

Significant economic growth and airline supply factors, such as the emergence of low-cost carriers (LCCs), have increased the demand for air travel and resulted in airport management having to cater for these increasing passenger numbers and the changing nature of demand. Given the increasingly competitive environment and a shift of revenue focus towards the nonaeronautical side, passengers now play a much more crucial role in the airport business. Industry research asserts that 'a happy passenger spends more' (DKMA, 2014) and so it is inevitable that airport management is aiming to enhance the customer experience. Modern airports not only provide infrastructure for airlines, but also serve as places of experiential interest for air travellers (Brilha, 2008; Graham, 2014; Zenglein and Müller, 2007). As such, the airport has become a multipurpose site where passengers can be exposed to a wide range of activities, which significantly contribute to the airport's nonaeronautical revenue (for instance, through its catering, retailing, and even its car parking facilities).

Since the early 2000s, the airport experience (AE) has emerged as a new concept for airport management to help them improve passenger satisfaction. During this period, a positive airport experience has increasingly been considered, particularly by international hub airports, as a key factor to enhance revenues from both airlines and passengers—especially transferring ones. A positive airport experience has also, arguably, become a factor that draws local residents and airlines to an airport when multiple alternative choices of airports exist. Moreover, the concept of the airport experience can be considered in relation to the tourism destination, by focusing on the increasing role of airports within the tourism industry. Within this context, it can be argued that enhancing the airport experience can create a positive effect on the image of a destination.

In the following section, the development of various concepts applied in the airport terminal from a service quality approach to the holistic approach of airport experience is examined, together with different definitions and dimensions associated with the airport experience.

13.2 DEFINITIONS AND DIMENSIONS OF THE AIRPORT EXPERIENCE

13.2.1 From Airport Service Quality to Airport Experience

To enhance service quality at the airport, the Level of Service (LoS) standard introduced by the International Air Transport Association (IATA) and the Airport Council International (ACI) used to be virtually the sole objective key measurement to monitor an airport's operational service performance. In the case of LoS, service is perceived as being the occupancy of the 'space' and 'time' of airport facilities. Under LoS, the mechanism to obtain a better monitoring of service performance is to increase the satisfactory results of two dimensions, namely, 'Holding facilities' (which measure the occupancy of space in square-metres per passenger) and 'Processing facilities' (which measure the waiting time in minutes per passenger) (IATA and ACI, 2017). However, the application of LoS has been criticised over its approach to service improvement, as it is initiated mainly from both a technical and a management perspective, without any integration of the opinions of passengers. As a result, airports decided to utilise an airport service benchmarking mechanism, called Airport Service Quality (ASQ), to enhance their service quality, service efficiency, and customer satisfaction. ASQ is a global benchmarking programme used by a wide range of airports in order to measure passenger satisfaction when they travel through an airport. It uses a quantitative survey to measure airport performances, using different criteria associated with the airport's operations.

Airports also use Skytrax world airport rankings as a means to assess their performance from the passenger viewpoint. By gathering opinions from a large number of air travellers using different service criteria, both ASQ and Skytrax allow airports to gain a better insight into the criteria of airport services that air travellers perceive as being significant to them. An understanding of how air travellers perceive the airport services enhances the airport opportunity to better meet their passenger demands; and as a result, it should lead to higher passenger satisfaction levels (Graham, 2014). Case Study 13.1 provides brief explanations for LoS, ASQ, and Skytrax.

CASE STUDY 13.1 AIRPORT SERVICE QUALITY MEASURES

Level of service (LoS)

The LoS standard is a guidance framework, based on the joining of forces of IATA and ACI, for the planning of airport terminal facilities, as well as for the monitoring the operational service performance of existing facilities. The LoS framework basically specifies the minimum service requirements at 12 terminal subsystems, namely, departure hall, check-in for economy, check-in for business, self-check in kiosk, passport control for departure and arrival, security, airside passenger concourse, baggage claim, customs control, public arrival hall, and transfer security. It uses a two-dimensional matrix for measurement: the processing facilities (measuring space and waiting time) and the holding facilities (measuring space and occupancy). Its general objectives are to provide optimum passenger facilities and to avoid the under or overusage of the terminal infrastructure.

Airport service quality (ASQ)

ASQ, initiated by ACI, is a global benchmarking programme that measures passenger satisfaction based on performances within the airport. The quantitative survey uses 34 criteria attributes and asks passengers to rate specific service-related topics and overall satisfaction while in the airport. The latest data from 2016 indicates that there are over 300 airports from 85 countries participating in ASQ.

Skytrax

Skytrax was established in 1989 and is based in London, United Kingdom. The World Airport Awards began in 1999, when Skytrax launched its first global airport customer satisfaction survey. In the 2016–17 survey, Skytrax reached out to 13.82 million airline passengers of 105 different nationalities who completed the survey. The survey covered 555 airports worldwide, and evaluated traveller experiences using different airport service and product key performance indicators—from check-in, arrivals, transfers, shopping, security, and immigration—through to departure at the gate.

From International Air Transport Association (IATA), 2017. Level of Service Concept. Available at: http://www.iata.org/services/consulting/airport-pax-security/Pages/level-of-service.aspx. (Accessed June 1, 2018); Airport Council International-Airport Service Quality (ACI-ASQ), 2017. Airport Service Quality. Available at: http://www.aci.aero/Customer-Experience-ASQ. (Accessed May 29, 2018); Skytrax World Airport Awards, 2017. The 2017 World Airport Awards: Methodology. Available at: http://www.worldairportawards.com/Awards/awards_methodology.html. (Accessed May 31, 2018).

Despite its good intentions, this service quality approach has recently come under criticism for not being adequate enough to provide an in-depth understanding about passengers and how to really enhance passenger positive impressions at the airport. This is because service quality places too much emphasis on individual processes and services, but does not provide a holistic picture, and nor does it reflect what a passenger actually perceives and experiences during their airport journey. As stated by DKMA (2014), a sole focus on improving service quality to enhance passenger satisfaction can be problematic and can create a distorted view of passenger satisfaction with only a specific vision of an operation. The service quality approach treats different touch points as separate units. By addressing each unit as a criterion for performance measurement, airport management consequently manages them independently. However, this does not reveal how passengers perceive their overall satisfaction of the airport. More recent studies have shown that passengers want to have a smooth and seamless journey (DKMA, 2014; BCG, 2016; OECD, 2016; SITA, 2016). When passengers travel through an airport, they encounter and interact with a wide range of activities and services, and do not rationally perceive their airport journey as separate functions. This means that airports had to find a new way to look at the overall passenger journey, in which a more holistic and experiential approach is required. This is the reason why the term *passenger airport experience* has been introduced as a new holistic concept in order to enhance passenger levels of satisfaction.

13.2.2 Current Definitions of Airport Experience

As aforementioned, the airport experience concept has been widely debated in the past decade or so, as witnessed, for example, at meetings of Airport Council International-North America (see ACI-NA, 2017) and Future Travel Experience events (see FTE Global, 2018). As a result, several attempts have been made to produce a formal definition of the term. An activity-based approach can define one perspective of the airport experience. Harrison et al. (2012) gave an operational definition of airport experience as being the activities and interactions that passengers undergo in an airport. These key activities are classified as *necessary* (compulsory processes in the airport terminal that a passenger must complete in a set order, such as check-in, immigration, and security) and *discretionary* (other activities that can be optional and unordered, such as watching the aircraft, eating/drinking, and duty free shopping). Boudreau et al. (2016, p. 4), on the other hand, defined the airport experience as a net impression of all of the experiences a passenger has in an airport, as judged by 'a passenger's individual standards, expectations, and perceptions'. This definition, nevertheless, can still be problematic as it looks at the airport experience from the service quality point of view, where the outcome of experience is equivalent to the difference (gap) between what a passenger perceives and what they expect. When scrutinising the term from customer experience literature, airport experience differs from service quality because the term *experience* represents a holistic perspective that a passenger encounters in the airport sphere, whereas service quality is a measurement of variables using specific criteria (Fodness and Murray, 2007; Graham, 2014). Accordingly, airport experience is subjective in nature (Parandker and Lokku, 2012; Verhoef et al., 2009) and needs to be defined based on the holistic judgement of passengers. Therefore another alternative of viewing airport experience is to focus on the smooth connection of sequential processes, which is referred to as a *seamless journey* (OECD, 2016).

13.2.3 Dimensions of the Airport Experience

Different studies related to service management have attempted to understand the dimensions of experience, but there is still paucity within the airport context. Generally understanding dimensions allows for a wider range and more comprehensive perspective on a particular topic, which may bring about the potential for an innovative approach to enhance value. The same applies to the dimensions of airport experience. Recently, Wattanacharoensil et al. (2017) attempted to identify the experience dimensions, drawing from the service experience literature proposed by Helkkula (2011), to provide alternative insights within the airport context. They argued that the airport experience comprised a process dimension, a phenomenon dimension, and an outcome dimension. The definitions of each experience dimension are explained as follows:

(1) Experience as a process includes key phases or stages in the passenger airport process involving three key activities:

  a. Functional activities: this is what Harrison et al. (2012) introduced as necessary activities that passengers must go through in a set order, such as check-in, bag drop, immigration, security, and boarding for departure activities.

  b. Servicescape: this refers to the interior of the functional design of the airport, particularly the signage, and the walking distance of the areas for the necessary or functional activities, such as immigration, security, and the boarding gate.

  c. Personal service: this refers to interactions with customer service staff or airport personnel during the airport journey, particularly involving necessary or functional activities.

(2) Experience as a phenomenon refers to hedonic and aesthetic aspects in relation to discretionary activities, which cover the leisure activities as well as atmosphere, food, and retail areas, which enhance the passenger hedonic and aesthetic experience.

(3) Experience as an outcome refers to the four experiential aspects that can be associated with a passenger as a result of their experiences in the airport terminal. The four types of outcomes of experience comprise perception, memory, emotion, and fairness.

Wattanacharoensil et al. (2017) confirmed that experience as a process (functional, servicescape, and service provision) is highly associated with the emotional and the memory outcomes of passengers. An unsatisfactory airport experience in the necessary functions (e.g. unpleasant experiences during check-in, security, immigration and the boarding processes; confusing airport navigation; unfriendly departure staff; or unpleasant experiences during the baggage claim, and immigration on arrival) will significantly influence the negative feelings of passengers towards that particular airport and will remain in their memories, which can influence a passenger's desire to return to that airport or their choice of airport in the future.

Airports providing leisure and recreation (represented by the hedonic and aesthetic aspects in the consumption experience or experience as a phenomenon) are also strongly associated with the passenger's emotions, but the significance of the negative experience is not as strong as in the first category (experience as a process). The findings imply that a passenger will seriously perceive and appreciate the hedonic and aesthetic aspects that an airport provides, once the process dimension meets a satisfactory level.

Passengers also experience four key outcomes on their airport journey: perception, memory, emotion, and fairness. Details of the four outcomes are shown in Fig. 13.1. Amongst the four aspects of outcomes, fairness outcomes were found to be particularly important to passengers. Price, physical spaces and settings, treatment by service personnel, and the handling procedures affect the way passengers perceive fairness and justify their experience at the airport. Unfair feelings lead to negative experiences and can occur when:

(1) Passengers feel that they are handled very poorly by the service staff (interactional justice).

(2) The handling procedures are delivered but do not help passengers (procedural justice).

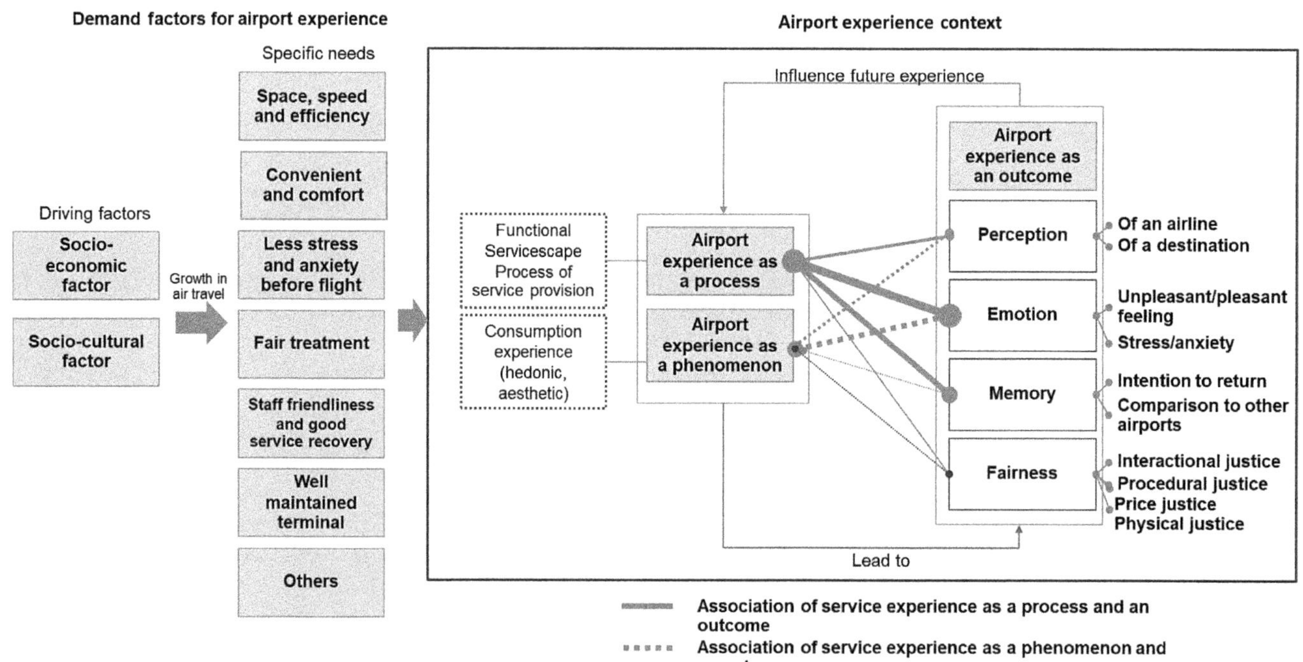

The thickness of the lines indicates in the Airport Experience.
Context box represent a strong association.

FIG. 13.1 Framework of the passenger airport experience. *(Modified from Wattanacharoensil, W., Schuckert, M., Graham, A., Dean, A., 2017. An analysis of the airport experience from an air traveler perspective. J. Hosp. Tour. Manag. 32, 124–135.)*

(3) Passengers feel that they are being overcharged when buying necessary items (food and water) in the airport terminal (price justice).
(4) Passengers perceive that the airport design and the use of space have worsened conditions, such as an overly cramped boarding gate (physical justice).

13.3 FACTORS AFFECTING THE AIRPORT EXPERIENCE

The airport experience phenomenon is driven by both demand and supply factors. On the demand side, given that a significant number of people now have the ability to travel, socioeconomic factors are key drivers of demand (see Chapter 2). Indeed, the International Civil Aviation Organisation (ICAO) reported that the rapid growth in tourism and air transport is due to higher incomes and a growing middle class in emerging economies, which have encouraged higher consumption expenditure (OECD, 2016). Growth is not restricted to only specific high-income markets such as Western Europe, the United States, or Oceania but has rapidly moved to Asia, emerging BRICS countries, especially with the accelerating progression of China, and other developing nations. So possibilities for air travel are diverse and people can travel to all key geographic regions, both for leisure and for trade purposes. Consequently, this leads to a significant demand for airports to support this growth. Moreover, a consequential factor arising from the emerging economic growth is that air travel is not limited only to specific cultural groups—mainly from the very high to high-income countries as in the past—but goes beyond this to the mid to lower income levels. The emergence of LCCs has altered perceptions of flying and has made air travel a truly global phenomenon.

The growing number of experienced travellers has also affected the level of expectations related to the passenger journey. Since the airport is the first place which air travellers encounter when arriving at a destination, the airport is claimed to be an ambassador which gives first and last impressions to visitors who visit the destination (Levine, 2016); and the passenger airport experience can be perceived as an important part of the overall travel experience as well as the tourism experience (Tussyadiah and Fesenmaier, 2009). Drivers from the demand side can be addressed further down to the level of individual travellers, which are affected by their demographic and cultural influences. For instance, Crotts and Erdmann (2000) found that international visitors from masculine cultures (with a high masculinity index according to Hofstede's framework) tended to demand more airport services compared to visitors from feminine cultures. Jiang and Zhang (2016) also found that passengers aged 50 and above require more essential service items and more comfort from the airport.

On the other hand, drivers from the *supply* side are a catalytic factor that pushes the implementation of the airport experience. This includes the roles of international bodies in air transport such as IATA and also the availability of information technology (IT) (see also Chapter 9). Indeed, in order to cope with the increasing number of passengers, various organisations have put forward ideas that enhance service efficiency in the airport operations, thus creating a better passenger experience. A major example is the Fast Travel Initiative which was introduced by IATA in 2007. Its purpose is to provide choice, convenience, and control through self-service options in six areas in the airport terminal, namely, check-in, bags ready-to-go, document check, flight rebooking, self-boarding, and bag recovery. Currently 41% of global passengers are being offered all the Fast Travel self-service options (IATA, 2017).

Additionally, it is not an understatement to state that IT is a crucial stimulus for the airport experience and shifts the current practice of airport operations to a new level, ultimately to the *smart* airport concept. IT and digital transformation, arguably, allow airports to enhance the passenger experience and alleviate frustration. For instance, if internet access is made available during the waiting time for check-in or passport-check, airport passengers could become more tolerant of long queues (Jiang and Zhang, 2016). The Fast Travel Initiative works well because of the robust support of IT, which helps to reduce the time burden of passengers. The introduction of mobile technology as a global movement has also dramatically changed the way travellers communicate, as well as consume products, services, and experiences. Boudreau et al. (2016) identified ways that technology can help airports enhance the airport passenger experiences as shown as follows:

- Improving airport efficiency: as seen from the implementation of self-service technology (SST) kiosks, or the improvements in the passenger-processing system.
- Easing navigation: the use of IT to help with signage or digital wayfinding.
- Reducing waiting time: utilising technology to monitor waiting time and to expedite processes.
- Providing necessary and real-time information: such as the flight time, flight schedules, baggage on the belt, and special discounts in the duty free.
- Soliciting customer feedback: using social media to engage with passengers in open communication, and to receive feedback.

- Streamlining the customer experience: using mobile applications to order food online or providing payment options at the parking facility to streamline the process.
- Enhancing customer service: facilitating airport staff to be able to handle customer requests immediately and effectively through pad devices or wearable technologies.

Smartphones have become an important component leading to a better airport experience for passengers. The introduction of airport smartphone applications can, arguably, enhance seamless travel as passengers can access on-time information when they navigate through the airport or be informed of special promotions at the duty-free shops. According to SITA (2016), 83% of passengers carry smartphones and as a consequence, airports and airline operators see the opportunities in connecting with passengers in this way. Smartphones have redefined the customer experiences (Wang et al., 2012) and empowered passengers to have more flexibility and control over airport operations in a way never before deemed possible. Moreover, through smartphones, passengers can proactively search flight information and access any necessary information, both in normal and disruptive situations (Future Travel Experience, 2014).

Table 13.1 and Case Study 13.2 provide details on the current use of technologies that can enhance the passenger airport experience. The concept of common use (CU), such as common use self-service (CUSS) and common use passenger processing systems (CUPPs), is employed at numerous airports to improve operational efficiency and to allow passengers to have considerable control and flexibility over certain basic functions, such as the check-in process. Moreover, radio-frequency identification (RFID), near-field communication (NFC), and i-Beacon technology are utilised in the airport environment. RFID can be used to streamline performance in baggage tracking and security gate processing in the airport. NFC uses magnetic field induction to enable communication amongst devices when touched together (TechTarget Network, 2017). Several airports are using NFC to facilitate passenger boarding at the gate or accessing the airline lounges. According to SITA (2017), NFC technology will help increase the sharing of mobile boarding passes from between 2% and 3% in 2011 to between 50% and 80% by 2018. i-Beacon technology is a technology that uses Bluetooth low energy and geo-fencing to trigger the display of location-relevant information on devices at the right time, and in the right situation (SITA, 2017). A number of airports have used i-Beacon to enhance the retail experience and airport navigation, as well as ensuring that passengers receive real-time flight information. Wearables are also expected to play a crucial role in the passenger experience through the use of smart wearables

TABLE 13.1 Types of Key Technologies That Can Enhance Airport Experience

Types of Technology	Description	Applications in the Airport	Purpose(s)/Benefit(s) on Airport Experience
CUTE—common-use terminal equipment	Common use (CU) is a proposed concept introduced by the International Air Transport Association (IATA), which determines the flexible and shared use of airport facilities through shared technology and infrastructure Common use terminal equipment (CUTE) is a common software and network airport solution that enables airlines and handling agents to access their own applications from workstations with printers being shared by all users. CUTE was introduced in 1984 for passenger check-in and boarding	Airline and airport management develop a system allowing passengers from different airlines to share the check-in kiosk. CUTE and CUPPS enhance efficiency of the check-in process	Improving efficiency
CUPPS—common-use passenger processing system	CUPPS was introduced by IATA in 2009 and was developed to simplify common implementation usage by promoting a model in which airlines would have a single application that could run on any CUPPS certified platform. The aim was for CUPPS to set a standard and to replace the Common Use Terminal Equipment (CUTE) standard; given that there were at least seven CUTE platform suppliers and managing as well as adapting platforms posed difficulties for airline managements		

TABLE 13.1 Types of Key Technologies That Can Enhance Airport Experience—cont'd

Types of Technology	Description	Applications in the Airport	Purpose(s)/Benefit(s) on Airport Experience
CUSS kiosk—common-use self-service	CUSS is a shared kiosk offering airport check-in to passengers without the need for ground staff. CUSS can be used by several participating airlines in a single terminal	CUSS allows passengers to conduct a self-check in for numerous airlines	Improving efficiency Reducing wait time
RFID	Use of radio waves to read and capture information stored on a tag attached to an object	Improves the timing and accuracy of baggage transfer from the check-in counter to the aircraft	Improving efficiency
i-Beacon with airport application	i-Beacon is technology that uses Bluetooth low energy and geo-fencing to trigger the display of location-relevant information on devices at the right time and in the right situation	Identifying passenger location and sending relevant information to the passenger Locating passengers in the airport if they are late arriving at the gate; or navigating them through the airport Sending notifications or promotional coupons as passengers enter close-by areas Communicating actual waiting times of queues Personalised updates Alert passengers of real-time information with regard to flight schedules, baggage claim, and boarding gates; as well as triggering mobile boarding passes	Providing necessary information at the right time Reducing the length of time taken Passenger customisation
Wearables	Electronic devices that can be worn by an individual, such as Google glasses or smart watches	Providing fast customer service: smart watches used with i-Beacon help identify the exact location of staff and communicate specific tasks to that staff member's location in the airport, which enhances customer service efficiency	Easing navigation Improving customer services
Near field communication (NFC)	A short-range wireless connectivity standard that uses magnetic field induction to enable communication between devices when they are touched together	Boarding at the gate, or gaining entry into the airline lounges	Enhancing queue efficiency Reducing wait time
Robots	A machine designed to execute one or more tasks automatically, with speed and precision	Robots can do many functions depending on how they are programmed. Robots help passengers check-in, giving directions and information about boarding times, serving food and drink, dancing to entertain, and help cleaning the area	Better passenger service Better communication of important information Keeping the terminal clean

From Beaconstac, 2016. 10 Airports Using Beacons to Take Passenger Experience to the Next Level. March, Available at: https://blog.beaconstac.com/2016/03/10-airports-using-beacons-to-take-passenger-experience-to-the-next-level/. (Accessed May 26, 2018); Future Travel Experience, 2016a. Nice Côte d'Azur Airport Leverages Retail Benefits of Beacon Technology. Available at: http://www.futuretravelexperience.com/2016/02/nice-cote-dazur-airport-leverages-retail-benefits-of-beacon-technology/. (Accessed June 2, 2018); Future Travel Experience, 2016b. New Mia App Provides Travellers With Personalised Travel Assistant. Available at: http://www.futuretravelexperience.com/2016/02/mia-app-provides-travellers-with-personal-travel-assistant/. (Accessed June 2, 2018); Future Travel Experience, 2017a. Gatwick's Beacon Installation Provides Partners With Blue Dot Navigation And Augmented Reality Wayfinding. Available at: http://www.futuretravelexperience.com/2017/05/gatwick-airports-beacon-installation-enables-blue-dot-navigation/. (Accessed June 2, 2018); Future Travel Experience, 2017b. Houston Airports Launches Turn-By-Turn Airport Wayfinding Technology. Available at: http://www.futuretravelexperience.com/2017/07/houston-airports-launches-turn-by-turn-airport-wayfinding-technology/. (Accessed June 3, 2018); International Air Transport Association (IATA), 2014. Common Use. Available at: https://www.iata.org/whatwedo/passenger/Documents/Common-Use-Fact-Sheet-October2014.pdf. (Accessed June 3, 2018); Royal Aeronautical Society, 2017. Rise of the Airport Robots. Available at: https://www.aerosociety.com/news/rise-of-the-airport-robots/. (Accessed June 3, 2018); SITA, 2017. SITA Shows the Way for iBeacon Technology at Airports. Available at: http://www.sita.aero/pressroom/news-releases/sita-shows-the-way-for-ibeacon-technology-at-airports. (Accessed June 1, 2018); TechTarget Network, 2016. Robots. Available at: http://whatis.techtarget.com/definition/robot-insect-robot-autonomous-robot. (Accessed June 1, 2018).

such as Google Glass and Smartwatch, which are expected to be introduced in 2018 (FlightView, 2015). Robots have now been introduced in the areas of customer service and also to reduce the burden of the cleaning tasks from cleaners in the airport terminal.

Despite the positive application of IT, technological challenges to enhancing passenger experience still exist. According to CAPA-SITA (2013), information availability and accuracy can be a problem. The issue of the accuracy of data given to passengers, such as real-time information on the flight status or about flight delays, the collaborating issues amongst the different stakeholders in the airport environment who provide the meaningful data, and system compatibility for seamless access to data from different units are still found to be problematic and challenging, and need to be overcome.

CASE STUDY 13.2 AIRPORT I-BEACON, WEARABLES, AND AUGMENTED REALITY EXAMPLES

Côte d'Azur Airport (NCE) launched a beacon-enabled application (app) at the opening of its newly refurbished Terminal 1 retail area. The airport has installed several beacons across the terminal to send contextual retail information and promotions to passengers, on the basis of their location in the terminal.

Miami International Airport (MIA) launched the beacon-enabled app to improve passenger experience by providing personalised updates, directions, tips on the basis of their location, and needs at the airport.

Hong Kong International Airport (HKG) was among the first airports in Asia to test the iBeacon technology. The airport has installed more than 50 beacons at Terminal 1 to trigger location-relevant messages to passengers. The airport also uses interactive navigation maps to guide passengers along common navigation paths, such as public transport points, check-in counters, immigration, boarding/arrival gates, and baggage claim areas.

Tokyo Haneda Airport (HND) Japan Airline staff are provided with smart watches to enhance their effectiveness in assisting passengers. The beacons and smart watches help identify the exact location of staff and to assign and communicate specific tasks to their location in the airport. This unique initiative led to Japan Airlines being the first airline to use beacons to improve operational efficiency.

Gatwick Airport (LGW) invested in upgrading and modernising infrastructure, and in simplifying the passenger experience and optimising operations. By communicating with mobile apps, the augmented reality (AR) wayfinding tool allows passengers to use the camera function on their device to view directions to their destination within the terminal.

From Beaconstac, 2016. 10 Airports Using Beacons to Take Passenger Experience to the Next Level. March, Available at: https://blog.beaconstac.com/2016/03/10-airports-using-beacons-to-take-passenger-experience-to-the-next-level/. (Accessed May 26, 2018); Future Travel Experience, 2016a. Nice Côte d'Azur Airport Leverages Retail Benefits of Beacon Technology. Available at: http://www.futuretravelexperience.com/2016/02/nice-cote-dazur-airport-leverages-retail-benefits-of-beacon-technology/. (Accessed June 2, 2018); Future Travel Experience, 2016b. New Mia App Provides Travellers With Personalised Travel Assistant. Available at: http://www.futuretravelexperience.com/2016/02/mia-app-provides-travellers-with-personal-travel-assistant/. (Accessed June 2, 2018); Your London Airport Gatwick, 2017. Press Releases. Available at: http://www.mediacentre.gatwickairport.com/press-releases/2017/17_05_25_beacons.aspx. (Accessed June 2, 2018).

Competition within the airport industry, and a stronger emphasis on revenue and profit generation, are amongst the key reasons for why the airport experience has become a key focus for airports. Passengers constitute a large captive market and contribute significantly to nonaeronautical revenue (Graham, 2014). As ACI (2016a) reported, the global nonaeronautical revenue share in the year 2015 was 39.8% and accounted for US$60.42 billion—the most important item was retail concessions, which accounted for 26%. A positive relationship between the increase in nonaeronautical revenue and passenger satisfaction has been revealed, in that when the global passenger satisfaction level increases by 1%, the average growth of nonaeronautical revenue increases by 1.5% (ACI, 2016b). Highly satisfied passengers will potentially spend extra time at the airport and might also spend more money. Moreover, a passenger's positive airport experience has a knock-on benefit to an airport. It enhances passenger satisfaction, the potential for future revisits to a destination, and the dissemination of positive word-of-mouth communication. Also travellers' views on their experience influence their choice of airline and the airport, as well as helping the airline determine which airport to choose as a transfer hub. One example is Changi airport in Singapore, where many passengers particularly select airlines to travel on that use the airport as a transfer hub, due to a positive airport experience (Star2.com, 2016).

13.4 MANAGING THE PASSENGER AIRPORT EXPERIENCE

Currently, an increasing number of passengers expect, or at least desire, international airports to provide an efficient, seamless, and hassle-free experience. Identifying the relative satisfaction of passengers and connecting this to service quality measurements in a particular area can help to boost passenger satisfaction to a certain level. In this respect, airport management needs to consider improving areas that are less satisfactory, but which are important to passengers (Boston Consulting Group (BCG), 2016; Graham, 2014). A survey conducted by BCG (2016) revealed that there are five areas in the airport terminal which passengers find relatively important, but typically suffer from low levels of satisfaction. These areas are (1) arrival immigration, (2) security, (3) the retail area, (4) baggage collection, and (5) the gate holding area. However, airports may well perform differently in these areas and so specific research should be conducted to reveal passenger needs and associated performance at an individual airport level (Graham, 2014).

As discussed in the previous section, attempting to understand passengers from a service quality approach is open to criticism. This only rectifies the service problem from each area of the service touch points, which may undermine the overall experience of passengers. Therefore airport management needs to look beyond the concept of each service function and consider the smooth connection of each activity throughout the whole passenger airport journey. Accordingly, the management challenge regarding the passenger experience is a complex route involving myriad interactional points of service personnel, key airport functions, and the interaction of technologies (Boyarsky, 2016). Therefore managing the overall passenger experiences requires careful planning, understanding dialogues, and cooperation from the related parties. A fundamental step for airport management is to establish dialogues about 'types of experience that airport management wants their passengers to have' (Passenger Terminal Today, 2015). This should be regarded as a strategic decision that needs to be communicated to other related parties (e.g. retailers, immigration, and ground handling agents) to deliver services and experiences that support the airport's position accordingly. This approach also assists airport management in identifying partners who are a good 'fit' with its stated customer experience objectives (Passenger Terminal Today, 2015). Case Study 13.3 shows how airport management at Changi Airport collaborates with different parties to enhance the passenger experience.

CASE STUDY 13.3 ENHANCING THE PASSENGER EXPERIENCE AT CHANGI AIRPORT

Singapore Changi Airport was labelled as the world's best airport for 2017 by Skytrax and second best airport in the Asia-Pacific Region in the 2016 ACI-ASQ awards. In fact it has been voted as the world's best airport every year since 2013 by Skytrax (see Skytrax, 2017). Changi states that it uses technology, nature, art, and architecture combined with an array of services, attractions, and distractions to enhance passenger airport experiences.

For services, Changi Airport Group (CAG) collaborates with over 200 agencies and companies which collectively have a workforce of 28,000. Changi has a number of missions to fulfil as an important gateway to Singapore including ensuring the integrity of immigration functions at the airport. CAG is committed to delivering the *One Changi Experience*. It emphasises seeking the support of the leadership of its partners, ensuring an engaged Changi workforce, and achieving constant dialogue with its customers. Clear communication of the airport's vision and mission, and a requirement that all related parties share the same airport identity, are two of the key mechanisms that CAG has identified can encourage such positive collaboration.

The Corporate Information & Technology and Corporate & Marketing Communications divisions of Changi airport have introduced a single login ID across the key digital platforms—One Changi ID. Through this single login ID, air travellers can conveniently connect and use Changi Airport's digital platforms. Some of the current key digital platforms include iShopChangi (an online shopping portal), iChangi mobile app, the Changi Rewards loyalty card programme, and the Changi Airport website. The digital transformation journey aims to bring about better customer experiences. Not only is this expected to bring advantages to air travellers in Changi airport, but CAG also receives a significant benefit as the single login ID enables a consolidated view of the customers in the database, which was not possible previously, when the individual systems maintained their own set of user databases.

It is the aim of Changi airport to give opportunities to the passengers to enjoy the airport facilities, and to provide an enhanced experience, according to each passenger's available time. For example, if the passenger has 2–3h to spare, they can shop in a variety of shops. If they have 4–5h, the passenger can experience a nature trail, watch a film, or have a massage. If they have more than 5h, the passenger can leave the airport and visit the city on an arranged sightseeing tour. Moreover, Changi airport has recently improved the intermodal passenger experience. It has done this by collaborating with different travel and industry partners to ease the transfer of passengers via coach and ferry services via fly-coach and fly-cruise concepts to nearby destinations, such as Indonesia and Malaysia.

From Changi Airport Singapore, 2017a. Airport Experience. Available at: http://www.changiairport.com/en/airport-experience.html. (Accessed March 11, 2018); Changi Airport Singapore, 2017b. A Seamless Digital Experience Through One Changi ID. Available at: http://www.changiairport.com/corporate/media-centre/resources/publication/changi-journeys/issue-7/a-seamless-digital-experience-through-one-changi-id.html. (Accessed February 1, 2018); Changi Airport Singapore, 2017c. Changi Sees Growth Potential for Trips Connecting Traveller Via Air, Land and Sea. Available at http://www.changiairport.com/corporate/media-centre/resources/publication/changi-journeys/issue-8/changi-sees-growth-potential-for-trips-connecting-traveller-via-air-land-and-sea.html. (Accessed May 26, 2018); Changi Airport Singapore, 2017d. One Changi Experience. Available at: http://www.changiairport.com/content/dam/cacorp/publications/Annual%20 Reports/2011/CAG-AR2011-Corp.pdf. (Accessed May 29, 2018).

TABLE 13.2 Maslow's Hierarchy of Needs as Applied to Airports

Level	Examples of Airport Components	Related Parties
Level 5: Self-actualisation	Special facilities such as garden, entertainment, relaxation room, and the creation of a sense of place	Airport management Architect or interior design company Service provider companies
Level 4: Esteem	Airport lounge for specific groups Relaxing and pleasant rest areas Well-designed servicescapes Valet parking	Airport management Service provider companies (Lounge, parking services)
Level 3: Social	Friendly and courteous services to enhance airport image Friendly security and immigration personnel Variety of concessions—duty free, food and drinks Caring for families and elderly passengers	Airport management Ground handling agents Immigration authorities Retail and concessions
Level 2: Safety	Accurate and timely information Improved airport access Wayfinding and navigation in the terminals Security and safety screening technologies	Airport management Airlines Air traffic control Security companies
Level 1: Physiological	Capacity of infrastructure—enough space Clean facilities—new and clean restrooms Adequate gate areas Basic concessions Good airline and ground services On-time performance	Airport management Cleaning companies Retail and concessions Airlines Ground handling agents

Modified from Boudreau B., Detmer G., Tam S., Box S., Burke R., Paternoster J., Carbone L., 2016. ACRP Report 157: Improving the Airport Customer Experience, Washington, DC, Transportation Research Board.

In order to manage the airport experience, Boudreau et al. (2016) proposed a hierarchical way for airport management to consider the airport's positioning and availability of resources. Adapted from Maslow's hierarchy of needs theory, physiological, safety, social, esteem, and self-actualisation levels related to airport management are identified. A positive airport experience at higher levels can be achieved when performance at a lower level is achieved. The lowest level (physiological) represents the basic elements that the airport must fulfil before moving on to the next step, which is in line with the research of BCG (2016); the highest self-actualisation level is when value-added factors come into play after the performance at the lower levels has been accepted. Table 13.2 provides details of each level and shows the related responsible parties that need to collaborate to ensure a positive experience.

Other factors that contribute to the passengers' positive or negative experiences during their airport journey are the purpose of travel, age, and psychological aspects (stress, anxiety, or fear of flying). Passengers may feel stressed when using so many different airport functions. Bogicevic et al. (2013) conducted a study using data mining techniques on 1095 traveller comments to identify the dissatisfying factors within the passenger experience. It was found that a passenger's positive airport experience is threatened by three key factors, namely, location for the security check procedures, poor signage, and long waiting lines. However, levels of satisfaction with potentially stressful processes can vary at different airports, depending on the airport servicescape, the internal design of the service flow (space and queue management), and the design of the terminal. Fig. 13.2 illustrates the different levels of dissatisfaction derived from research of the key areas of checking/bag-drop and security/border control. Inevitably, passengers find some parts in the airport journey more stressful than others, and unsurprisingly the check-in and security/immigration processes are commonly identified as being the two most stressful and least satisfactory parts of the passenger airport journey (see, e.g. Bogicevic et al., 2013; Graham, 2014; Travel Tech and Amadeus, 2011). Amongst many other things, managing the passenger's level of stress and anxiety can be a factor that airport operators have at least some partial control over, and the introduction of the Fast Travel Initiative and other technological enhancements can, potentially, help alleviate this stress and frustration.

A good airport experience can also create a positive connection with the tourism destination. Research by Wattanacharoensil et al. (2017) revealed that air travellers perceived airports and their airport experience in relation to a tourism destination in three different ways:

First, passengers look at the airport as an ambassador or as a representation of a destination. This is supported by the fact that airports are generally perceived as the first and last impressions of a destination to local hosts and

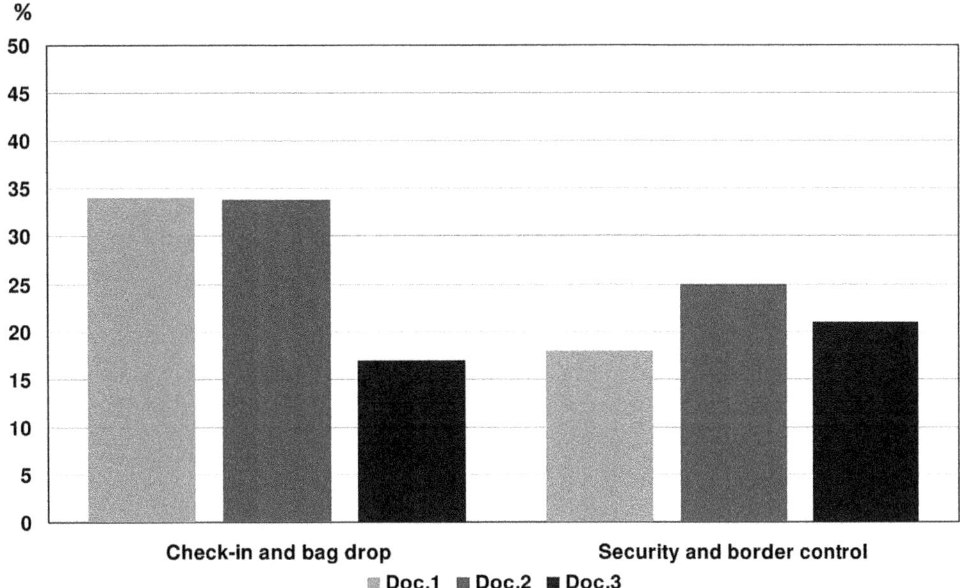

Doc.1: CAPA-SITA 2013: Six Indian airports (% indicating level of stress) $n = 500$;
Doc.2: Travel Tech and Amadeus 2011: General information (% indicating negative experience by passengers) n = unknown (from online survey of over 35,000 North American air travellers);
Doc.3: ORC 2009, p. 27: Four UK airports (% indicating passenger dissatisfaction) $n = 1619$;

FIG. 13.2 Level of dissatisfaction with the key areas of the airport journey: departure checking/bag-drop and security/border control. *(From CAPA-SITA, 2013. CAPA-SITA white paper on technology & innovation in Indian aviation. Transforming the Passenger Experience: Technology in Indian Aviation in 2015. Available at: https://www.sita.aero/resources/type/white-papers/capa-sita-report-on-transforming-the-passenger-experience. (Accessed May 26, 2018); ORC International, 2009. Research on the Air- Passenger Experience at Heathrow, Gatwick, Stansted and Manchester Airports. ORC International, London; Travel Tech and Amadeus, 2011. Navigating the Airport of Tomorrow. Amadeus IT Group SA. Available at: http://www.amadeus.com/AirportOfTomorrow. (Accessed June 2, 2018).)*

visitors as previously stated. Evidence of negative phrases, such as 'you are an embarrassment' and 'not a good face' of the country/city, was highlighted by passengers, indicating the representative role.

Second, passengers see airports as the interpretative location of the tourism/destination slogan and image. Passengers perceive airport service processes as a point of comparison to the destination slogan, or the image that the destination projects. In other words, passengers view the airport according to their mental perception of the characteristics of a destination. For instance, when passenger visited an airport when the associated destination had the image of 'Land of smiles', or 'Efficient society', these certain characteristics were compared to the airport's performance and evaluated by passengers accordingly. Comments such as 'my experience at airport [X] is thus a simple testimony of what this society is all about, efficient and organised' and "...unfriendly, robotic staff with no sense of humanity—welcome to the 'Land of smiles'", were elicited from passengers when they experienced the airport service performance and compared it to the characteristics of the destination.

Third, passengers also assess their actual experience of airports, and compare it to the positive tourism promotional message of a destination, thus indicating a more integral role of the airport to the tourism destination. Evidence showed that passengers who received the tourism promotional message prior to visiting a destination, and who then encountered poor experiences during the airport arrival, conveyed dissatisfaction and disappointment towards the management of the destination. A comment such as 'How can a government promote tourism but ignore fundamental services (too long queue in the airport immigration) to those tourists!' supported this criticism. Therefore, arguably, it can be inferred that passengers do not see airports as a separate entity from a destination like some shopping complex, but regard airports as an integral and internal part of the tourist experience.

Overall this discussion demonstrates the role that an airport plays with the tourist's perception of a destination and establishes that the airport experience is part of the whole tourism experience. It can be argued that if passengers perceive and assess tourism and airports as a collaborative unit, then a good airport experience can indeed enhance the positive perception of a traveller towards a destination.

13.5 CONCLUSION

This chapter provides an overview of the importance of the airport experience and identifies related issues that can potentially allow airports to better serve their passengers. The evolution from a service quality to airport experience approach has been explained, since the opportunity to enhance the overall passenger satisfaction cannot occur when service touch points are looked upon as separate units. Instead they must be viewed in a holistic form as part of a seamless journey. A crucial point that cannot be neglected in relation to the airport experience is the need for collaboration amongst the related parties that are involved in key airport activities. In order to achieve this, a clear definition of the airport experience has to be clearly identified and communicated to the other related parties. Moreover the essence of the airport experience has the potential to significantly affect the tourism destination and as a consequence (and as argued by OECD, 2016), the airport operator and tourism authorities should work more closely to mentally connect the image and characteristics of a destination within the airport interior and its associated operations.

Despite being a current and topical phenomenon, airport experience research is still quite limited and requires further attention by academia, especially in comparison to the number of research outputs related to airport service quality. The paucity in the literature creates the obvious need for more in-depth studies, both related to the demand and supply aspects of airport experience. Some of the research questions that should be addressed are, for instance: What are the different cultural perceptions of the airport experience in different geographic regions? How does the airport experience at the regional and international hub airport differ? How does airport experience for a LCC passenger differ from a full-service carrier? How can airports enhance stakeholder collaboration to create a seamless journey? What are the roles of IT in the airport experience enhancement? How can airports measure airport experience? The list of questions is indeed long and moreover, further research on how the airport experience can enhance the image of a tourism destination is another potentially interesting area to explore.

References

Airport Council International (ACI), 2016a. The voice of the world's airports. In: Airport Economics at a Glance. Available at http://www.aci.aero/Data-Centre/Airport-Statistics-Infographics. (Accessed May 26, 2018).

Airport Council International (ACI), 2016b. Delivering a Unique Customer Centric Experience. Available at http://aci-na.org/sites/default/files/BIT-session5-Gauthier.pdf. (Accessed May 29, 2018).

Airport Council International-North America (ACI-NA), 2017. ACI-NA/AAAE Airport Customer Experience Symposium. Available at http://www.aci-na.org/event/aci-naaaae-airport-customer-experience-symposium. (Accessed January 26, 2018).

Bogicevic, V., Yang, W., Bilgihan, A., Bujisic, M., 2013. Airport service quality drivers of passenger satisfaction. Tour. Rev. 68 (4), 3–18.

The Boston Consulting Group (BCG), 2016. The Connected Airport: The Time Is Now. The Boston Consulting Group, Inc. Available at http://img-stg.bcg.com/BCG-Connected-Airport-Jan-2016_tcm9-145248.pdf. (Accessed May 26, 2018).

Boudreau, B., Detmer, G., Tam, S., Box, S., Burke, R., Paternoster, J., Carbone, L., 2016. ACRP Report 157: Improving the Airport Customer Experience. Transportation Research Board, Washington, DC.

Boyarsky, B., 2016. Developing a Customer-Experience Vision. Available at http://www.mckinsey.com/business-functions/marketing-and-sales/our-insights/developing-a-customer-experience-vision#_=_. (Accessed June 1, 2018). March.

Brilha, N.M., 2008. Airport requirements for leisure travellers. In: Graham, A., Papatheodorou, A., Fortsyth, P. (Eds.), Aviation in Tourism: Implications for Leisure Travel. Ashgate, Aldershot, pp. 167–176.

CAPA-SITA, 2013. CAPA-SITA white paper on technology & innovation in Indian aviation. In: Transforming the Passenger Experience: Technology in Indian Aviation in 2015. Available at https://www.sita.aero/resources/type/white-papers/capa-sita-report-on-transforming-the-passenger-experience. (Accessed May 26, 2018).

Crotts, J.C., Erdmann, R., 2000. Does national culture influence consumers' evaluation of travel services? A test of Hofstede's model of cross-cultural differences. Manag. Serv. Qual. 10 (6), 410–419.

DKMA, 2014. Why Focusing on Improving the Passenger Experience. Available at http://www.dkma.com/en/images/downloads/customer-service/Why%20focus%20on%20the%20passenger%20experience.pdf. (Accessed June 1, 2018).

FlightView, 2015. Convenience & Choice: What Travelers Want Most (and are Willing to Pay for) Throughout Their Journey. Available at http://cdn2.hubspot.net/hubfs/278711/Convenience-and-Choice-in-Travel-July2015.pdf. (Accessed May 26, 2018).

Fodness, D., Murray, B., 2007. Passengers' expectations of airport service quality. J. Serv. Mark. 21 (7), 492–506.

Future Travel Experience, 2014. Is Mobile Technology Making It More Difficult for Airports and Airlines to Define Their Own Passenger Experience?. Available at http://www.futuretravelexperience.com/2014/02/mobile-technology-making-difficult-airports-airlines-define-passenger-experience/. (Accessed June 1, 2018).

Future Travel Experience Global (FTE Global), 2018. Redefine Your Passenger Experience and Business Performance Strategies in Vegas. Available at http://www.futuretravelexperience.com/fte-global/. (Accessed June 3, 2018).

Graham, A., 2014. Managing Airports: An International Perspective, fourth ed. Routledge, London.

Harrison, A., Popovic, V., Kraal, B.J., Kleinschmidt, T., 2012. Challenges in passenger terminal design: a conceptual model of passenger experience. In: Proceedings of the Design Research Society (DRS) 2012 Conference. Department of Industrial Design, Faculty of Architecture, Chulalongkorn University, Bangkok, pp. 344–356.

Helkkula, A., 2011. Characterising the concept of service experience. J. Serv. Manag. 22 (3), 367–389.

International Air Travel Association (IATA), 2017. Fast Travel: Fact Sheet June 2017. Available at http://www.iata.org/whatwedo/passenger/fast-travel/Documents/Fast-Travel-factsheet-June%202017%20final.docx.pdf. (Accessed January 29, 2018).

International Air Transport Association and Airport Council International (IATA & ACI), 2017. Improved Level of Service Concept. Available at https://www.iata.org/services/consulting/Documents/cons-apcs-los-handout.pdf. (Accessed June 2, 2018).

Jiang, H., Zhang, Y., 2016. An assessment of passenger experience at Melbourne Airport. J. Air Transp. Manag. 54, 88–92.

Levine, A., 2016. First impressions: when an airport gets it right. Forbes. Available at https://www.forbes.com/sites/andrewlevine2/2016/01/03/first-impressions-when-an-airport-gets-it-right/#6bf8d3fe7788. (Accessed June 2, 2018).

OECD, 2016. Seamless transport to enhance the visitor experience. In: OECD Tourism Trends and Policies 2016. OECD Publishing, Paris.

Parandker, S.R., Lokku, D., 2012. Customer experience management. In: Services in Emerging Markets (ICSEM), 2012 Third International Conference. IEEE, Mysore, pp. 44–49.

Passenger Terminal Today, 2015. Defining the Passenger Experience. Available at http://www.passengerterminaltoday.com/opinion.php?BlogID=1425. (Accessed January 29, 2018).

SITA, 2016. Air Transport Industry Insights: The Future is Connected. Available at https://www.sita.aero/globalassets/docs/surveys--reports/360-degree-report-the-future-is-connected-2016.pdf. (Accessed June 1, 2018).

SITA, 2017. SITA Shows the Way for iBeacon Technology at Airports. Available at http://www.sita.aero/pressroom/news-releases/sita-shows-the-way-for-ibeacon-technology-at-airports. (Accessed June 1, 2018).

Skytrax World Airport Awards, 2017. The 2017 World Airport Awards: Methodology. Available at http://www.worldairportawards.com/Awards/awards_methodology.html. (Accessed May 31, 2018).

Star2.com, 2016. Flyers Choose to Shop and Relax at the Airport. Available at http://www.star2.com/travel/malaysia/2016/07/09/flyers-choose-to-shop-and-relax-at-the-airport/. (Accessed June 1, 2018).

TechTarget Network, 2017. Near Field Communication (NFC). Available at http://searchmobilecomputing.techtarget.com/definition/Near-Field-Communication. (Accessed June 1, 2018).

Travel Tech and Amadeus, 2011. Navigating the Airport of Tomorrow. Amadeus IT Group SA. Available at http://www.amadeus.com/AirportOfTomorrow. (Accessed June 2, 2018).

Tussyadiah, I.P., Fesenmaier, D.R., 2009. Mediating tourist experiences: access to places via shared videos. Ann. Tour. Res. 36 (1), 24–40.

Verhoef, P.C., Lemon, K.N., Parasuraman, A., Roggeveen, A., Tsiros, M., Schlesinger, L.A., 2009. Customer experience creation: determinants, dynamics and management strategies. J. Retail. 85 (1), 31–41.

Wang, D., Park, S., Fesenmaier, D.R., 2012. The role of smartphones in mediating the touristic experience. J. Travel Res. 51 (4), 371–387.

Wattanacharoensil, W., Schuckert, M., Graham, A., Dean, A., 2017. An analysis of the airport experience from an air traveler perspective. J. Hosp. Tour. Manag. 32, 124–135.

Zenglein, M.J., Müller, J., 2007. Non-Aviation Revenue in the Airport Business–Evaluating Performance Measurement for a Changing Value Proposition. Berlin School of Economics, Berlin.

CHAPTER

14

The Airline–Airport Relationship: Allocating Risks and Opportunities in a Vertical Partnership

Frank FICHERT

Worms University of Applied Sciences, Worms, Germany

CHAPTER OUTLINE

14.1 INTRODUCTION

A key feature of all transport services is their dependence on a dedicated infrastructure. For tourism destinations, if located at a larger distance from the home regions of their (potential) visitors, the existence of a (sufficiently dimensioned) airport is an indispensable condition for welcoming travellers. Moreover, the airport infrastructure has to fulfil certain technical and regulatory requirements (e.g. runway length, security control) as well as tourists' expectations with respect to service quality. In addition to the airport, other air transport infrastructure facilities are needed (in particular air traffic control), but this will not be further discussed in this chapter. However, the existence of an airport is only a necessary, but not a sufficient condition for connectivity; airline services are required as well.

Traditionally, the provision of airport infrastructure is separated from the provision of airline services. In most parts of the world, both industries have gone through a process of considerable change over the last decades. The provision of air transport services has been liberalised on many domestic markets (first in the United States in 1978), in the European Union (EU) and between some neighbouring countries (e.g. Australia and New Zealand), as well as on an international level (open skies agreements). Amongst others, liberalisation has enabled new business models, in particular the rise of low-cost carriers (LCCs) (see Chapter 10). In parallel, and at least partly as a consequence of

Air Transport—A Tourism Perspective. https://doi.org/10.1016/B978-0-12-812857-2.00014-2

airline liberalisation, many airports have matured from 'pure' providers of infrastructure to market-oriented (commercialised) entities, with an increasing importance of 'commercial' revenues (in particular from shops and restaurants inside the airport and car parking).

This chapter deals with the relationship between airlines and airports in a liberalised and commercialised environment, paying special attention to the linkages with the tourism industry. First, the objectives of airlines and airports are discussed, in particular with respect to tourism policy. Second, basic information on different business models of airports is provided, again with a specific focus on tourism flows. The third part of the chapter deals with the route development strategies of airlines, followed by a comprehensive discussion of an airport's options to influence these decisions. This part will cover different marketing activities as well as a large variety of financial incentives within and outside an airport's charging scheme, referring also to the legal framework in the European Union. The next section deals with options for a (partial) vertical integration between airports and airlines. Before the conclusions, risks and opportunities from the perspective of the different stakeholders are discussed.

The chapter will elaborate on the relationship between airports and airlines in a general way, but mostly with the European situation as a reference point. Examples will be used to illustrate specific trends and the use of selected instruments, again usually referring to the European Union.

14.2 OWNERSHIP AND OBJECTIVES OF OWNERS

Although liberalisation and privatisation are two major trends in the air transport industry over the last decades, still many airports and even airlines are partially or even fully owned by states, regional bodies, and/or municipalities. Therefore a first step in analysing the relationship between airlines and airports is a discussion of ownership structures and the corresponding objectives of the respective entities.

In North America, the EU, and also some parts of Australasia, many airlines are in full private ownership. In particular, all low-cost carriers are privately owned (the only exceptions being low-cost subsidiaries of (partially) state-owned full-service network carriers). However, in Africa, the Middle East, large parts of Asia and Latin America, and even in the EU, 'traditional' airlines often are either fully publicly owned or have only been partially privatised.

For fully privatised airlines it can be assumed that they aim at maximising profits. On the other hand, if the government is involved as a shareholder, the airline usually will also have to consider overall policy goals. In the case of tourism destination countries this typically will include improving the accessibility of the airline's home country for visitors from abroad (for one example, see Government of Malta, 2017). Competition with other airlines as well as budget constraints might limit an airline's ability to serve the overall policy objectives if they are not in line with market requirements.

Regarding airports, the situation is even more complex. On a worldwide basis, most airports are publicly owned, with a share of privatised airports between 1% (North America) and 31% (Europe) (ACI, 2017). However, in particular many large- and medium-sized European airports have been fully or at least partially privatised, therefore serving the majority of passengers in Europe (for details, see ACI Europe, 2016). Moreover, there are several examples for Public–Private Partnerships, that is, a private firm investing in a state-owned airport and/or operating it. These long-term agreements can take different forms (e.g. management contracts, concessions, Build–Operate–Transfer models), but usually the contract period is limited, giving the government an opportunity to change the terms of the contract or even regain full public ownership and control. However, also for fully privatised airports the relationship with the government is crucial for airport managers, since business opportunities are heavily dependent on policy decisions, especially with respect to larger investment in runways or terminals and operating restrictions (e.g. night curfews).

In addition to (regional) employment, gross value added, and—in some cases—military functions, the major role of an airport from the perspective of policy makers is to enable connections to other regions, facilitating business as well as private travel. For leisure tourist destinations, in particular those located in regions where from a visitor's perspective air transport is the only suitable way of travelling, an airport's capacity and connectivity might be a limiting factor for tourism development. For example, the concession contract between the Greek government and a joint venture formed by the German airport operator Fraport and a Greek company obliges the private concessionaire to significantly expand the capacity of the 14 airports covered by the agreement (most of them located on islands) as well as to improve the quality of their passenger service facilities (Fraport, 2017). This clearly aims at enabling and attracting a larger number of tourist arrivals in the respective regions.

Several studies have analysed whether airports are operating under economies of scale (for an overview, see Lechmann and Niemeier, 2013). Although the empirical evidence is somehow mixed, at least for airports with less than three to five million passengers decreasing average costs can be assumed. Moreover, the revenues of airports with less than three million passengers often are not sufficient to make the airport profitable. For airports with less than one million passengers it is quite often not even possible to cover the operating costs. Therefore these airports usually depend on public funding, causing state aid issues which will be discussed in more detail in subsequent parts of the paper.

However, it is in the general interest of each (not capacity restrained) airport to increase passenger numbers since—given the high share of fixed costs—the additional aeronautical as well as nonaeronautical revenue contributes to increasing profits or reducing losses. A negative effect on the economic performance of an airport might only occur if either the growth in passenger numbers requires capacity enhancing investment (with additional costs exceeding additional revenue) and/or the airlines manage to capture the additional revenue by specific agreements with the airport. The second aspect will also be discussed in more detail later.

14.3 AIRPORT PASSENGER CHARACTERISTICS, BUSINESS MODELS, AND IMPLICATIONS FOR AIRPORT MANAGEMENT

There are several ways of defining and delineating business models of airports. With respect to the topic of this chapter, the shares of incoming and outgoing travellers matter. Especially in many 'sun and beach' destinations, the large majority of passengers are tourists from abroad. This may also lead to a high degree of seasonality in regions with pronounced peak and off-peak periods (e.g. the Mediterranean). Since most major cities in industrialised countries are also popular destinations for visitors (e.g. New York, London, Paris, Berlin) airports within the respective regions do not only serve a large number of business travellers but also many outgoing and incoming leisure tourists as well as other private travellers (esp. visiting friends and relatives—VFR). Finally, some cities or regions in industrialised countries may not attract a large number of (foreign) tourists, leading to a high share of outgoing travellers at the airport. Depending on these structural characteristics of demand, the different types of airports will also use specific strategies in their relations to the airlines.

The prevailing groups of passengers at an airport also determine the market shares of airlines following different business models. Before the emergence of low-cost carriers, most European tourists were flying to 'sun and beach' destinations on charter airlines (for the example of Faro airport in Portugal see Almeida, 2011) (see also Chapter 11). Even today, nonscheduled flights as part of a package holiday play an important role for many countries, for example, in Northern Africa (for the example of Tunisia, see Oxford Business Group 2016, p. 151). However, for Intra-European travel the emergence of low-cost airlines accompanied by new booking options for hotels and other accommodations via the internet has caused dramatic changes in the entire tourism industry (O'Connell and Bouquet, 2015). A growing number of travellers book their flights and their accommodation separately. Low air fares to a specific destination will in many cases boost demand for the destination ('generating' travel demand). Consequently, route decisions of LCCs and therewith also the relationship between airports and low-cost airlines have gained importance. Nowadays, many tourist destination airports are characterised by a high or even dominant share of low-cost traffic (for the example of Faro, see Almeida, 2011). Moreover, the boundary between charter airlines and low-cost carriers is blurring, since—if not restricted by bilateral Air Service Agreements—many charter airlines nowadays also sell tickets to individual passengers (leisure airlines).

In large cities and metropolitan areas the situation is different. The respective regions are usually served by traditional network carriers, charter flights, and low-cost carriers. Whereas in some regions one airport accommodates all types of airlines, elsewhere neighbouring airports concentrate on specific market segments, in particular 'regional' or 'low cost' airports with a focus on low-cost carriers. However, fundamental changes may even occur within a relatively short period of time, for example, Ryanair's rather recent move towards serving primary and even hub airports (Dobruszkes et al., 2017).

Finally, many regional or low-cost airports located in industrialised countries outside the large metropolitan regions to a large degree depend on outgoing leisure tourists and some VFR traffic. Examples include UK airports like Bournemouth, and German airports like Paderborn-Lippstadt and Kassel.

14.4 AIRLINE ROUTE POLICY

'Traditional' airlines (FSNCs) and low-cost carriers follow a totally different approach with respect to their network structure. FSNCs operate most or even all of their flights out of one (or sometimes two or even more) hub airport(s). This might also include connections to typical holiday destinations, but—since (at least on short-haul routes) these origin and destination (O&D) markets usually are rather competitive and passengers are price sensitive—a FSNC's focus is rather on serving transfer passengers on those markets than on selling tickets to O&D travellers.

Due to specific investment, the dependence on a large local market as well as infrastructure requirements for hub operations, FSNCs are usually 'tied' to their hub airport(s). On the other hand, low-cost carriers often are considered to be 'footloose' (Humphreys et al., 2006), that is, they are serving point-to-point markets from many different airports and might rather easily switch aircraft from one route to another. Within the European common aviation market, carriers like Ryanair, easyJet, and Wizz Air operate on many city-pair markets outside their home countries and show a high degree of flexibility in opening as well as abandoning routes or even bases. Since the market segment of low-cost traffic has grown significantly over the past years, the number of newly served connections outweighs the number of routes that have been ceded. In general, larger low-cost airlines base aircraft (and crews) at several airports, leading to some stability in their network structure, but also some of those bases have been switched in the past (Malighetti et al., 2016).

From the perspective of an airline, the opening of a new route is always a trial-and-error process. Although route decisions are based on market research and demand modelling, revenue might be below forecasts and/or costs might be higher than expected. In general, in the first months or even years after the opening of a new route, its profitability is often low since (potential) passengers first have to be aware of the new travel opportunity. Moreover, an airline will have to take some investment, in particular marketing efforts. Compared to the opening of new routes, the risk of expanding services on a given route (e.g. increasing the number of weekly flights) is usually lower, but still not negligible.

14.5 AIRPORT OPTIONS FOR INFLUENCING AIRLINE ROUTE AND BASE CHOICE

14.5.1 Overview of Potential Strategies

There are several options for an airport to influence airlines' decisions on the opening (and also expansion) of routes and/or the establishment of a base. First, as part of their overall marketing endeavours many airports employ route development managers, trying to identify potentially profitable connections and attracting new airlines, often referred to as the air service development (ASD) process (see Halpern and Graham, 2013, 2015). Although many general market data is available to airlines as well as to airports, route development managers employed by an airport can build a specific expertise on local travel requirements (e.g. information on business connections between local firms and their customers and suppliers, indicating a demand for business travel). Moreover, they might also assist an airline when getting in touch with large potential customers or other business partners. In addition to direct bilateral contacts, regular route conferences serve as a multilateral platform for bringing airlines and airports together.

Second, many airports offer direct or indirect financial benefits, especially for newly opened routes, route service expansions, or new entrants, that is, airlines not having served this airport before. In general, a multitude of options exist for granting advantages to an airline, in particular the (regulated) charging scheme, nonregulated service contracts (especially ground-handling provided by the airport and/or rental agreements on airport facilities). Moreover, airports may offer one-off (nonrecurring) as well as repeated payments, or the covering of costs which otherwise would have to be borne by the airline (e.g. staff accommodation and/or training, marketing activities). Furthermore, there are some possibilities for contracts which are not formally linked to an airline's route decision but might be considered as part of an overall 'package deal' by the contracting parties, for example, an airport (or a regional body) might buy advertising space at the airline's website or the onboard magazine after the airline has started to serve the airport or an additional route.

A particular form of assistance might comprise an airport's marketing activities for promoting a new route or a new airline serving the airport. The airport uses its regular means of communication (e.g. press releases or airport magazines) and/or might start a dedicated marketing campaign with specific advertisements of different kind. These campaigns could also be a joint project between the airport and the airline. Depending on the expected share of incoming and outgoing passengers, other stakeholders might be involved. In particular, tourism development organisations sometimes promote their destination at the other point of a newly established route (see Chapter 15). Again, a cooperation with the respective airline is possible (e.g. 'spend your vacation in destination X, now airline Y offers direct flights from airport Z'). Some airports have published (rather general) marketing support schemes (e.g. Abruzzo Airport, n.d.; AENA, n.d.; Shannon Airport 2017, Cork Airport, 2018, have even published detailed tables for calculating marketing support payments), whereas for other airports there is even less information publicly available on the preconditions for granting such kind of assistance and their magnitude.

14.5.2 Charging Schemes and Contractual Agreements Between Airports and Airlines

A growing number of airports include different types of incentives in their aeronautical charging scheme (Malina et al., 2012; Fichert and Klophaus, 2011). Common incentives are a reduction of (some) aeronautical charges for newly opened routes and/or growing passenger numbers on a route or of an airline. In line with the overall regulatory framework for airport charges (e.g. in the EU), regulators usually make sure that these incentives are not discriminatory. Depending on the legal framework for setting airport charges in a jurisdiction, specific arrangements with an airline might require an active role of the state or a regional body. For example, reductions in airports charges at Charleroi airport (Belgium) were granted to Ryanair under an agreement with the Walloon region (see European Commission, 2004).

Given the uncertainty about the profitability of new routes mentioned before, an airport's financial assistance after the opening of a new route might be seen as a risk-sharing mechanism between the airline and the airport. Depending on the specific arrangement, the airport might even assume the entire risk. Quite often, airlines and airports agree on medium- to long-term contracts, where airlines guarantee a certain number of flights per period, a certain seat capacity offered, and/or a certain number of aircraft based at the airport in exchange for an airport's commitment on keeping charges below a certain level, guaranteeing service levels and/or opening hours, investing in the airport infrastructure and/or providing financial assistance to the airline.

From an institutional economics perspective, these contracts can be seen as a mutual attempt to prevent strategic behaviour. Since both sides usually have to take some kind of specific investment (e.g. infrastructure expansion by the airport, planning and marketing activities by the airline and/or the airport), without a contractual agreement a holdup situation might occur after the opening of a route, with the airport and/or the airline trying to improve their economic results by increasing charges or reducing operations, respectively. The negotiating position of the airport depends on many structural determinants, in particular the degree of competition from neighbouring airports (or competing regions, especially in the case of 'sun and beach' destinations) and the overall (potential) market share of the respective airline at the airport.

Although it is publicly known that specific contracts between airports and (low cost) airlines are widespread (for the example of Poland, see Huderek-Glapska and Nowak, 2016), their provisions are typically considered a business secret. However, some of these agreements have become subject to investigations on state aid, and several decisions were published by competition authorities or courts. A path breaking case handled by the European Commission covered the contractual agreement between Ryanair and Charleroi airport in Belgium. The contract included, besides others, a commitment on the reduction of airport charges for 15 years, one-off payments by the airport, and a discount on ground handling fees in exchange for Ryanair's contractual obligation to offer a certain number of flights over the respective period (Gröteke and Kerber, 2004).

14.5.3 Competitive Distortions and Legal Framework in the European Union

Specific contracts between an airport and an airline basically might cause two types of competitive distortions. First, if not all airlines serving an airport are given the same advantages, the preferred treatment of one airline might disturb competition between airlines, in particular if the favoured airline already has a large market share at the respective airport. At least in the EU, directive 2009/12/EC on airport charges aims at prohibiting charging schemes which include discriminatory elements. Specific requirements with respect to incentives for new routes can be found in the 2014 guidelines on state aid to airports and airlines (European Commission, 2014). However, some charging schemes seem to be 'tailor made' for a dominant airline at a specific airport. For example, Frankfurt-Hahn airport (a low-cost airport in the extended Frankfurt region with a local market share of Ryanair exceeding 80%) levies no movement charges if 90% of an airline's flights have a turnaround time at the airport of less than 30 min (which should usually be the case for Ryanair) and for passenger charges a volume discount is granted, favouring Ryanair as the by far largest airline at the airport (Flughafen Frankfurt-Hahn, 2012). Moreover, in unregulated business segments, for example, provision of ground handling services or renting of airport facilities, there is less transparency and a discriminatory behaviour is more difficult to identify.

Second, in case of a subsidised airport it might be argued that benefits granted by this airport to its airline customers will distort competition with neighbouring airports as well as with other airlines operating out of neighbouring airports where charges are cost recovering and no additional support is granted. As a consequence, there might be a pressure at the neighbouring airport to also reduce charges below a cost recovering level (such 'race to the bottom' effects are also discussed for local tax rates or subsidies).

The EU has already taken several measures in order to prevent competitive distortions caused by specific agreements between (subsidised) airports and airlines as well as by airport subsidies in general. Already in 2005 'Community guidelines on financing of airports and start-up aid to airlines departing from regional airports' were published (European Commission, 2005). With respect to start-up aid for new routes, the Commission assesses an airport's strategy based on a private investor test. Therefore if agreements between airports and airlines improve the profitability of an airport (i.e. reduce losses or even increase profits) they are considered to be compatible with European law.

With respect to public funding, already the 2005 guidelines made a distinction between airport infrastructure, the operation of airport infrastructure, and ground handling services. The 2014 guidelines, which have replaced the 2005 guidelines, are more restrictive and state that, after a transition period, the operating costs of an airport should not be subsidised, except for those airports providing services of general economic interest or allowing for connectivity of regions with special requirements. Regarding infrastructure provision, the guidelines define a maximum share of subsidies, primarily based on the size of an airport, again allowing for a transition period. Airports with more than five million passengers per year are expected to finance their investment without additional public funding.

Since the 2014 guidelines limit the public funding of airports, the potentials for granting favourable conditions to airlines are declining. Moreover, some airports might even exit the market, in particular airports with significant overlaps in their catchment area, due to the guidelines' additional restrictions against the 'duplication of unprofitable airports' (European Commission, 2014, p. 19). With respect to start-up aid to airlines, the 2014 guidelines limit the magnitude of the discount (maximum 50%) as well as its duration (maximum three years).

14.6 VERTICAL INTEGRATION

The connection between an airport and an airline with the (supposedly) highest degree of stability is a (partial) vertical integration. Basically three options exist. First, the airport and the airline might have the same owner. The typical case is state ownership, for example, in Middle East countries like the United Arab Emirates, ensuring a strategic link also to the governmental tourism development organisation (Lohmann et al., 2009). It can be assumed that conflicts between the airport and the airline on the allocation of risks and opportunities are minimised in such a constellation. For example, whereas European hubs usually apply a reduced passenger charge for transfer passengers (which might be a consequence of the higher intensity of competition in the transfer market), in Dubai transfer passengers are exempted from passenger charges, providing a clear benefit for the state-owned airline (Partnership for Open & Fair Skies, 2015). In Europe there is only very limited evidence of full vertical integration. Manston airport (UK) was bought by a private investor in 1998 but did not become profitable in the following years. In 2003 the company owning the airport also acquired a low-cost airline (EUJet) which operated out of Manston. However, the entire company continued to make losses and went bankrupt in 2005 (Kent County Council, 2015).

Second, the airline might own shares of the airport (or vice versa). Whereas, to the best knowledge of the author, there is no example for an airport holding shares of an airline, there is one example for an airline having acquired minority shares of an airport (Lufthansa with Fraport, the operator of Frankfurt airport). Especially for hub airports, this vertical relation might strengthen the airline's position in influencing decisions which will affect one of their key resources (e.g. airport expansion projects).

Third, airlines might invest in terminal or other infrastructure at an airport. In the United States, airlines and airports usually agree on long-term 'use and lease' contracts for terminal infrastructure (for recent developments, see Messina and Smith, 2016). In Europe, joint ventures are sometimes used, for example, in the case of Munich airport's second terminal (with Lufthansa as the partner of the airport operator). A specific situation can be found in Bremen (Germany), where Ryanair won a public tender for operating a dedicated low-cost terminal, investing approximately 10 m Euro (Niemeier and Njoya, 2011). Joint ownership of a terminal usually requires that this part of the airport infrastructure is exclusively used by the respective airline (and—if applicable—its alliance partners). From the airline's perspective, it is possible to influence the design of the respective infrastructure based on its specific requirements. Moreover, being shareholder of a terminal also lets the airline participate in the nonaeronautical revenues generated at this facility. From a competition policy perspective, a (partial) vertical integration also causes some concerns, since the airport might have an incentive to provide privileges to its 'partner airline', negatively influencing the situation of (potential) competitors (Kuchinke and Sickmann, 2007).

14.7 DISCUSSION OF RISKS AND OPPORTUNITIES

Given the different objectives of the relevant stakeholders, there are several risks as well as opportunities associated with the design of the airline-airport relationship. First of all, the cooperation between airports and airlines (sometimes complemented by tourism development organisations and/or other regional bodies) aims at increasing passenger numbers (as a precondition for reaching other objectives). Although in many cases a traffic generation—especially due to new or extended low-cost services—could be observed, there are also examples for routes which have been ceased if they turned out to be economically nonviable. Such developments might be a consequence of changes outside the control of the cooperating entities (e.g. overall political situation), but also due to determinants which can be influenced by the airline or the airport, respectively (e.g. service quality).

If passenger numbers (or average yields) are below expectations, the type of relationship between the airport and the airline matters. If only unilateral incentives exist (e.g. discounts for new routes within the charging scheme), the airline (in particular a low-cost carrier) might ask for a higher financial contribution of the airport, reduce its capacity, or simply abandon the route. However, in case of a contract between the airport and the airline, the specific provisions matter, for example, whether the airline is only obliged to offer a certain number of frequencies or whether also passenger volumes have been agreed on. Moreover, the contract might comprise consequences in case of low passenger numbers, for example, additional payments by the airport. As stated before, the allocation of risks between the airport operator and the airline will to a large degree be influenced by the competitive situation of the airport.

Second, even if passenger numbers meet or even exceed previous expectations, some stakeholders may not benefit from this development. Many airports rely on increasing nonaeronautical revenues due to higher passenger numbers, outweighing discounts on aeronautical charges and additional payments to the respective airlines. Consequently, in case of low nonaeronautical revenues per passenger, an airport might even sustain higher losses as a consequence of increasing passenger numbers. Especially with respect to passengers travelling on low-cost airlines, two opposing hypotheses might be stated. On the one hand, it might be argued that LCCs, in general, attract a higher share of passengers with an income below average (or in general customers not able or not willing to spend much money during their vacation), resulting in low spending also at the airport. Moreover, the relatively low share of business travellers on low-cost carriers is also expected to have a negative effect on average nonaeronautical revenues. On the other hand, passengers of a low-cost airline usually pay relatively low fares, so they might be able to spend more at the airport, maybe also buying goods which they will consume during the flight (since LCCs do not offer free drinks or other amenities). In addition, some LCCs operate routes to regional airports not served by 'traditional' carriers. On these routes the LCC passengers might show a spending profile similar to passengers of network airlines, for example, due to a high share of VFR passengers. Empirically, Yokomi et al. (2017) show for UK airports that LCC traffic generates relatively less nonaeronautical revenue than non-LCC traffic.

Finally, even if airlines as well as airports benefit (economically) from increasing passenger numbers, the effect on tourism might be dissatisfying for the regional stakeholders. First, the share of outgoing passengers might be higher than expected. Especially in industrialised countries, some regional stakeholders were hoping for more visitors in the airport region, but passenger flows are largely dominated by outgoing travellers. Second, in spite of a large number of incoming tourists, the visitors might not stay in the airport region but continue to neighbouring regions in order to spend their vacation. Third, even if the number of tourist in the region increases, their average spending in the region may be relatively low, and/or their average stay might be relatively short (for the example of Morocco, see Dobruszkes and Mondou, 2013). With respect to passengers travelling on low-cost airlines, similar arguments might be brought forward as already stated before regarding an airport's nonaeronautical revenue. Empirically, the various effects are difficult to capture and to distinguish. With respect to passenger numbers, Rey et al. (2011) show a positive relation between low-cost flights and the number of tourists visiting Spain but without a further regional differentiation.

14.8 CONCLUSIONS

The relationship between airports and airlines is complex. At first sight, they both aim at increasing passenger numbers. However, as long as they are not vertically integrated—like for example in the Gulf countries through state ownership—there is always a potential dispute on the distribution of risks and opportunities.

The emergence of low-cost carriers, especially in Europe but also elsewhere, complemented with improved opportunities for self-booking of hotels and other types of accommodation has led to dramatic changes in the entire travel value chain. On the one hand, LCCs have proven to be able to 'generate' traffic, that is, to significantly increase the number of passengers and therefore in most cases also the number of tourists. On the other hand, these low-cost carriers are not confined to serve specific airports or even countries. Therefore airports, for example, in typical 'sun and beach' destinations do not only compete with neighbouring airports but also with airports in similar destinations in other regions. Consequently, the negotiating power of large low-cost airlines usually is considered to be quite strong. The large number of incentives within airport charging schemes as well as other types of support for airlines newly serving or growing at an airport might serve as an indicator for this type of competition. Especially for smaller airports (regional airports as well as low-cost airports) increasing passenger numbers may not lead to reduced losses, especially if additional nonaeronautical revenues remain small or are passed through to the airlines.

Since the losses of regional and low-cost airports are mostly covered by the government, contracts between (regional) airports and (low cost) airlines have been subject to criticism and also many investigations by competition authorities. Meanwhile, regulations have been amended (at least in the EU), aiming at a lower degree of airport subsidies. Assuming that these rules will not be softened, the negotiating power of low-cost airlines could be reduced to some degree. It remains to be seen, whether this will also affect tourism flows.

References

Abruzzo Airport (n.d.). Commercial Policy Development Routes. Available at http://www.abruzzoairport.com/docs/it/Commercial_Policy_Development_Routes.pdf. (Accessed June 3, 2018).

ACI Europe—Airports Council International Europe, 2016. The Ownership of Europe's Airports. ACI Europe, Brussels.

ACI—Airports Council International, 2017. Airport ownership, economic regulation and financial performance. In: Policy Brief 2017-01. ACI, Montreal.

AENA (n.d.). Marketing Support Initiatives. Available at http://www.aena.es/csee/ccurl/960/288/Marketing%20Support%20Initiatives.pdf. (Accessed June 3, 2018).

Almeida, C., 2011. The new challenges of tourism airports—the case of Faro airport. Tour. Manag. Stud. 7, 109–120.

Cork Airport, 2018. Route Support Cork Airport Route Support Scheme ("RSS") Long-Haul Operations. Available at http://www.corkairport.com/docs/default-source/About-Us-Docs-/cork-airport-long-haul-route-support-scheme-2018.pdf?sfvrsn=0. (Accessed June 3, 2018).

Dobruszkes, F., Mourou, V., 2013. Aviation liberalization as a means to promote international tourism: the EU-Morocco case. J. Air Transp. Manag. 29, 23–34.

Dobruszkes, F., Givoni, M., Vowles, T., 2017. Hello major airports, goodbye regional airports? Recent changes in European and US low cost airline airport choice. J. Air Transp. Manag. 59, 50–62.

European Commission, 2004. Commission decision of 12 February 2004 concerning advantages granted by the Walloon Region and Brussels South Charleroi Airport to the airline Ryanair in connection with its establishment at Charleroi. Off. J. Eur. Union L137, 1–62.

European Commission, 2005. Community guidelines on financing of airports and start-up aid to airlines departing from regional airports. Off. J. Eur. Union C312, 1–14.

European Commission, 2014. Guidelines on state aid to airports and airlines. Off. J. Eur. Union, C99/3–34.

Fichert, F., Klophaus, R., 2011. Incentive schemes on airport charges—theoretical analysis and empirical evidence from German airports. Res. Transp. Bus. Manag. 1, 71–79.

Flughafen Frankfurt-Hahn, 2012. Entgeltordnung. Available at http://www.hahn-airport.de/sycomax/files/512457_Flughafen%20Frankfurt-Hahn%20Entgeltordnung%202012.pdf. (Accessed June 3, 2018).

Fraport, 2017. Fraport Greece Begins 40-Year Concession at 14 Greek Regional Airports. Available at https://www.fraport.com/content/fraport/en/our-company/media/newsroom/archive/2017/fraport-greece-begins-40-year-concession-at-14-greek-regional-ai.html. (Accessed June 3, 2018).

Government of Malta, 2017. Air Malta. Available at https://tourism.gov.mt/en/aviation/Pages/Aviation-Entitities/Air-Malta.aspx. (Accessed June 3, 2018).

Gröteke, F., Kerber, W., 2004. The case of Ryanair—EU state aid policy on the wrong runway. ORDO 55, 313–331.

Halpern, N., Graham, A., 2013. Airport Marketing. Routledge, London/New York.

Halpern, N., Graham, A., 2015. Airport route development: a survey of current practice. Tour. Manag. 46, 213–221.

Huderek-Glapska, S.A., Nowak, H., 2016. Airport and low cost carrier business relationship management as a key factor for airport continuity: the evidence from Poland. Res. Transp. Bus. Manag. 21, 44–53.

Humphreys, I., Ison, S., Francis, G., 2006. A review of the airport-low cost airline relationship. Rev. Netw. Econ. 5 (4), 1–8.

Kent County Council, 2015. Manston Airport Under Private Ownership: The Story to Date and the Future Prospects. Available at https://www.kent.gov.uk/__data/assets/pdf_file/0003/29541/Manston-Airport-position-statement.pdf. (Accessed June 3, 2018).

Kuchinke, B., Sickmann, J., 2007. The joint venture terminal 2 at Munich Airport and the consequences: a competition economic analysis. In: Fichert, F., Haucap, J., Rommel, K. (Eds.), Competition Policy in Network Industries. LIT, Berlin, pp. 123–154.

Lechmann, M., Niemeier, H.-M., 2013. Economies of scale and scope of airports—a critical survey. J. Air Transp. Stud. 4 (2), 1–25.

Lohmann, G., Albers, S., Koch, B., Pavlovich, K., 2009. From hub to tourist destination—an explorative study of Singapore and Dubai's aviation-based transformation. J. Air Transp. Manag. 15 (5), 205–211.

Malighetti, P., Paleari, S., Redondi, R., 2016. Base abandonments by low cost carriers. J. Air Transp. Manag. 55, 234–244.

Malina, R., Albers, S., Kroll, N., 2012. Airport incentive Programmes: a European perspective. Transp. Rev. 32, 435–453.

Messina, J.F., Smith, E.T., 2016. Emerging trends in airport-airline use and lease agreements in the USA. J. Airport Manag. 10 (3), 273–282.

Niemeier, H.-M., Njoya, E.T., 2011. Do dedicated low cost passenger terminals create competitive advantages for airports? Res. Transp. Bus. Manag. 1, 55–61.

O'Connell, J.F., Bouquet, A., 2015. Dynamic packaging spells the end of European charter airlines. J. Vacat. Mark. 21 (2), 175–189.

Oxford Business Group, 2016. The Report Tunisia 2016. Oxford Business Group, Oxford.

Partnership for Open & Fair Skies, 2015. Restoring Open Skies: The Need to Address Subsidized Competition from State-Owned Airlines in Qatar and the UAE. Available at http://www.openandfairskies.com/wp-content/themes/custom/media/White.Paper.pdf. (Accessed June 3, 2018).

Rey, B., Myro, R.L., Galera, A., 2011. Effect of low cost airlines on tourism in Spain. A dynamic panel data model. J. Air Transp. Manag. 17 (3), 163–167.

Shannon Airport, 2017. Short-Haul Operations Route Support Scheme (RSS). Available at http://www.shannonairport.ie/gns/business/aviation-development/route-support-schemes.aspx. (Accessed June 3, 2018).

Yokomi, M., Wheat, P., Mizutani, J., 2017. The impact of low cost carriers on non-aeronautical revenues in airport: an empirical study of UK airports. J. Air Transp. Manag. 64, 77–85.

PART IV

REACHING THE DESTINATION AND ATTRACTIONS

CHAPTER

15

Partnerships Between Tourism Destination Stakeholders and the Air Transport Sector

Nigel HALPERN

Kristiania University College, Oslo, Norway

CHAPTER OUTLINE

15.1 INTRODUCTION

This chapter examines how destination management organisations (DMOs) and other tourism stakeholders are partnering with the air transport sector to promote and encourage aviation tourism development. The chapter consists of four main sections. The first section provides background on why DMOs and other tourism stakeholders are increasingly forming partnerships with the air transport sector. The second and third sections consider two main types of partnership that are used: marketing partnerships and funding partnerships. Example initiatives and issues are examined, and a case study relating to funding partnerships is provided. The fourth section provides a conclusion.

15.2 BACKGROUND

The leading organisational entity for many destinations is a DMO, often called a Tourism Authority, Tourism Board, or Convention and Visitors Bureau. A DMO may be created as a single public authority, a full private company, or through a public/private partnership, and they exist at a national, regional, or local level depending on the needs of the destination and the level of decentralisation of public administration (UNWTO, 2017). DMOs have traditionally been responsible for destination marketing. However, many of them are now also strategic leaders in destination development and responsible for developing strategic frameworks from which to guide and coordinate destination management activities (UNWTO, 2007). As an example, Destination NSW, DMO for the state of New South Wales in Australia, recognises that to realise the state's goal of doubling Chinese tourism expenditure, strategies are needed to support and stimulate growth in airline capacity to Sydney from primary hubs and other major cities in China (see Table 15.1).

Air Transport—A Tourism Perspective. https://doi.org/10.1016/B978-0-12-812857-2.00015-4

TABLE 15.1 Destination NSW China Tourism Strategies—Aviation

Strategy	Activities
Continue to pursue a multiairline development approach, with tiered level support for marketing based on current and committed capacity, frequency, and routes	• Dedicate resources to developing cooperative partnerships under MOU agreements with airline partners
Encourage additional capacity from primary markets of Beijing, Shanghai, and Guangzhou	• Collaborate with Sydney Airport Corporation and Tourism Australia in encouraging existing carriers to add additional services on Sydney routes
Encourage direct capacity from secondary cities	• Engage with new airline partners including third country and low-cost carriers
Invest in route development activities	• Increase investment in cooperative marketing with airline partners • Assist sustainability of services by working in partnership with Sydney Airport Corporation to target the Sydney-based management of Chinese carriers and Qantas to provide contacts and assistance that can help them build the two-way traffic • Seek opportunities to obtain additional financial investment for aviation opportunities through Tourism Australia's Aviation Development Fund • Work with industry partners to support charter services from developing markets

Modified from Destination NSW, 2012. China Tourism Strategy 2012–20, Destination NSW, Sydney.

As seen from the example in Table 15.1, part of a DMO's strategy is likely to be focused on accessibility, which along with location, attractive product and service offerings, quality experiences, and community support, is unique to destination success (Bornhorst et al., 2010). Not all destinations rely entirely on air access. However, for destinations targeting markets that do, airlines (or tour operators that own or purchase capacity from airlines when bundling tour packages together) are key suppliers, and supplier relations are a key factor for DMO success along with effective management, strategic planning, organisational focus and drive, proper funding, and quality personnel (Bornhorst et al., 2010).

Airlines have a fair amount of power over tourism stakeholders in a destination. They have relatively mobile assets (aircraft and crew) and a choice of destinations, especially in more liberal markets where they have greater freedom over decisions on where they fly to and from (see Chapter 5). They also tend to be large companies, increasingly deal directly with the consumer in origin markets, and may be the main suppliers of tourists to a destination. This compares to tourism stakeholders in a destination that are often small- and medium-sized enterprises, operating from a relatively fixed location, and dependent on airlines to bring in the tourists. In addition, many destinations are geographically separated from source markets and therefore rely on services from foreign airlines. To reduce asymmetrical power in relations between tourism stakeholders and airlines, DMOs can represent stakeholder interests collectively, and then develop partnerships with airlines.

The need to collaborate and form partnerships is much greater than ever before. DMOs exist to bring more tourists and tourism expenditure to the destination. However, they are competing with a growing number of destinations, each with their own DMO, and often on a diminishing public sector budget. Many DMOs are therefore under greater pressure to develop partnerships within and outside the destination to pool resources (financial and nonfinancial) and to effectively perform their role as a DMO. Some DMOs are even mandated to develop partnerships, and rely heavily, if not entirely on investment from the private sector. Furthermore, one organisation rarely controls all stages of the tourism value chain, so there are vested interests and potential benefits to be gained by tourism stakeholders in a destination from working together rather than pursuing personal agendas (e.g. see d'Angella and Go, 2009).

Of course, airports as providers of infrastructure for air services can play a key role in supporting tourism development in a destination (e.g. see Halpern, 2008; Lohmann et al., 2009) and are likely to be a key stakeholder for their DMO. Traditionally considered as public utilities for the safe and efficient movement of aircraft, passengers, and cargo, airports are increasingly operated as commercial businesses seeking to grow traffic and generate sufficient returns on investment. As a result, many airports are focused on route development (also known as air service development), which is the process associated with attracting new routes or growing, retaining or influencing change to existing services (Halpern and Graham, 2015). Whilst airports work towards establishing relationships of their own with airlines (see Chapter 14), they also stand to benefit from working with their DMO and other tourism stakeholders, and many airports view this as an important part of their own route development activities. For instance, in their survey of route development experts at 124 airports worldwide, Halpern and Graham (2016) found that the use of strategic marketing partnerships (e.g. collaborations with tourism and other stakeholders) is one of the most widely used route development activities by airports when marketing themselves to airlines; used by 96% of airports (44% 'to a great extent').

Then there are the airlines. Despite sustained long-term growth in demand for air transport, much of that growth has been a result of deregulation/liberalisation (see Chapter 5), and increased privatisation and competition, along with reduced government support means that profit margins and returns on investment have been lower than in other industries (Tretheway and Markhvida, 2014), even during recent years when profit margins have improved—due partly to lower fuel prices. Therefore although much of the power in route development is with an airline (Tan et al., 2017), they potentially have a lot to gain from working with DMOs and other tourism stakeholders, including airports, and receiving as much support as possible from them and other value chain partners, for instance, to establish and promote routes. This is more important than ever given that airlines have arguably become more risk averse since the global financial crisis but also because of ongoing uncertainty due to high costs of capital or fuel hedging losses (Duval and Winchester, 2011). Indeed, airlines increasingly view route development efforts as being most successful when they include all three key stakeholders: airlines, airports, and tourism destination stakeholders. This is commonly referred to in industry as the 'Golden Triangle in Air Service Development' (e.g. see Mayes, 2011).

Further insight on the importance of tourism and aviation partnerships was provided at the World Routes Tourism Summit in China in 2016 (see Hamill, 2016) where Alfredo Gonzalez, Vice President of Sales and Global Development at Visit Florida pointed out that expanding routes is always on the radar for airlines, but that it is difficult to achieve without tourists to fill the aircraft. He emphasised the importance of working together, stating that tourism and airlines is the future of working together—no one can do it alone. Arik De, Head of Commercial at AirAsia X Berhad stated that whilst financial packages are important for partnerships, the key thing is being able to work together. Similarly, Khalil Lamrabet, Director Aviation Business Development at Dubai Airports stated that partnerships should not be restricted to incentives. Airports can help by showcasing and being the shop window to the destination and should seek to provide added value to airlines and passengers. He also emphasised that support from both sides, airports and tourism authorities, minimises the risk factors for airlines, and means that airports and tourist destinations are better placed for business. In a recent study, Spasojevic et al. (2018) surveyed 100 route development experts and found that partnership is the most important of 17 different leadership attributes for achieving successful route development.

Mayes (2011) recognises important factors for aviation and tourism partnerships, stating that there need to be common goals, a clear shared strategy and targets, equality amongst the partners, longevity of the partnership, a joint approach by DMOs to airlines and tour operators, and from the DMO's perspective, there should be a true understanding of the market and the customer needs of target airlines and tour operators. However, partnerships do not always succeed, and reasons for the failure of tourism partnerships in general are commonly associated with a lack of time and investment in the partnership, changes in priorities, poor communications, unrealistic timetables, unrealistic expectations of partnership benefits, or a lack of detailed partnership planning (Morrison, 2013). The latter typically involves a number of key stages such as the formation of a destination partnership planning team, a review of partnership needs and desired benefits, the setting of partnership goals, identification of potential partners, preparation of a draft written partnership proposal, appointment of a partnership leader, commencement of discussions with most appropriate partners, modification of the proposal as necessary and the move towards consensus, preparing a contract or memorandum of understanding (MOU) (MOU agreements will be considered in more detail in the next section of this chapter), appointing a partnership leadership team, and evaluating the results of the partnership (Morrison, 2013). For partnerships that are well planned and successful, there are many potential benefits. However, there are also many barriers and potential challenges that may affect even well-planned partnerships (see Table 15.2).

TABLE 15.2 Potential Benefits and Barriers and Challenges in Tourism Partnerships

Benefits	Barriers and Challenges
Accessing customer databases	High turnover rate of principals
Accessing new markets	Huge diversity of the tourism sector
Better serving customer needs	Imperfect information communications
Enhancing image	Independence and self-interest
Expanding social responsibility	Lack of adequate funds
Increasing budgets	Long-term payoffs
Increasing market appeal	Measurement difficulties
Increasing pool of expertise	Subsector differences
Sharing facilities and sharing information	Uneven partner benefits

Based on Morrison, A.M., 2013. Marketing and Managing Tourism Destinations, Routledge, Abingdon.

The issues mentioned thus far on planning, key stages and potential benefits, barriers and challenges, relate to partnerships in general so many of the issues will be revisited when examining partnerships used specifically for aviation tourism development in the following sections of this chapter. Similarly to Duval (2013) in his review of critical issues in air transport and tourism, this chapter focuses on two main types of partnership: marketing partnerships based on joint activities that support and stimulate growth in demand for airlines, which subsequently grows tourist arrivals and expenditure in the destination; and funding partnerships that subsidise the establishment and marketing of new routes for a time-limited period in order to secure and grow new connections to the destination.

15.3 MARKETING PARTNERSHIPS

Many high-profile agreements have been signed by DMOs or government departments and national or overseas airline partners that are viewed as being key to bringing tourists to the destination (see Table 15.3). There are many reasons for engaging in such partnerships (e.g. see Riege et al., 2002). The focus of aviation and tourism agreements seems to be to increase the budget for marketing through the pooling of funds, enhancing tourists' image of and interest in the destination, accessing new markets, or better serving existing markets.

Based on a review of the agreements listed in Table 15.3, areas of cooperation and activities undertaken typically include joint marketing and promotions (i.e. for brand awareness via tactical and digital marketing, including the development and use of collateral material such as destination images or videos that can be used in airline advertising campaigns or shown on airline in-flight entertainment systems); joint participation in airline and airport networking events or travel trade exhibitions; joint roadshows (i.e. to meet with other prospective partners such as tour operators and distributors); sharing information and conducting joint market research and product development; joint familiarisation trips such as for overseas tour operators or media; stakeholder education such as training on how to promote and market the destination to tourists (i.e. for airline staff, or local or overseas stakeholders such as travel agents and tour operators); and launching special offers, competitions, incentive travels, and holiday packages. There is also often a focus on the airline agreeing to include the destination in their fleet expansion plans, add new routes, or improve existing levels of service. Whilst DMOs or government departments may conduct direct activities as part of the agreement, the focus is largely on indirect marketing via the airlines and their distribution channels, which is a common approach for national marketing partnerships in international travel and tourism (Riege and Perry, 2000).

DMOs may have agreements with multiple airline partners, along with other partners such as land or sea-based transport or distribution providers to reflect different strategic objectives, although it is worth noting that DMOs prefer to focus on a few specific partners and target markets because of limited financial resources and because it is difficult to position a destination to appeal to all markets (Reige and Perry, 2000). The agreements will often work

TABLE 15.3 Agreements Signed Between DMOs or Government Departments and Airlines in 2017

DMO/Authority	Airline(s)	Main Purpose
Ministry of Tourism Indonesia	Jetstar Group (Jetstar Airways and Jetstar Asia)	Promote growth in international tourism to Indonesia (TTG Asia, 2017)
Sabah Tourism Board	Royal Brunei Airlines	Promote activities for tourists from Melbourne to Borneo (The Borneo Post, 2017)
Seychelles Tourism Board	Kenya Airways	Promote tourism and intra-Africa traffic to the Seychelles (Kenya Airways, 2017)
Tanzania Tourist Board	Air Tanzania	Promote Tanzania domestically and internationally. Not just as a safari destination, but as the best destination in Africa (Air Tanzania, 2017)
Tourism Authority of Thailand	EVA Air	Promote Thailand as a short-haul destination for Taiwanese tourists and a long-haul destination for tourists from North America (EVA Air, 2017)
Tourism Authority of Thailand	Singapore Airlines	Promote travel to Thailand from Australia, New Zealand, Singapore, and South Africa (Singapore Airlines, 2017)

towards the development of joint activities that support wider campaigns and form part of an overall integrated approach to marketing and promoting the destination. Activities are often funded by a combination of cash and marketing in-kind from public and private sources, and with each partner contributing something to the agreement. This is the case with Visit Britain who in 2015/16, generated *GBP 12.7 million* in cash and marketing in-kind to help with a range of campaigns to showcase Britain internationally. Visit Britain's travel and tourism partners at that time included Air India, British Airways, Brittany Ferries, easyJet, eDreams (Opodo), Emirates, Etihad, Eurostar, Expedia, Hostelworld, Hotels.com, P&O Ferries, Qatar Airways, STA Travel, Trafalgar, and Virgin Atlantic (Visit Britain, 2017). Example campaigns with airline partners and a summary of activities is presented in Table 15.4.

DMOs may also develop agreements with local strategic partners such as airports. For instance, in 2017, the Tourism Authority of Thailand signed an agreement with Airports of Thailand (which owns and operates six international airports in Thailand that account for more than 90% of the total visitor arrivals to the country) to grow the number of airlines and passengers travelling to, from, and through Thailand and to promote Thailand as the aviation

TABLE 15.4 Visit Britain's 2015/16 Campaigns With Airline Partners

Airline Partner	Campaign	Activities
British Airways and American Airlines	British Famous campaign to drive visits from the United States to Britain	Four online videos across multiple platforms in the United States featuring British comedian Diane Morgan trying to 'make it' in America, whilst promoting Britain along the way. The videos drive online traffic to www.BritishFamous.com—a hub filled with destination content from Visit Britain and tactical fares and offers from American Airlines and British Airways, converting the inspiration to visit into bookings
British Airways	Campaign to support a new nonstop British Airways flight to London from New Orleans	Visit Britain and British Airways sculptures in New Orleans; strategic public relations and media activities including a social media engagement campaign using the hashtag #BALovesNOLA and a media and influencer event to promote the route; an installation of iconic British people, places, and things set against New Orleans landmarks; competition for a free trip and four-night stay for two in London
British Airways	#OMGB (Oh My GREAT Britain) Home of Amazing Moments campaign to drive visits to Britain from South Africa	Discounted air fares with British Airways of up to 20%; competition for a trip for two from South Africa to the United Kingdom with the opportunity to experience an amazing moment such as riding the world's fastest zip line in Wales, relaxing at a spa in Cardiff, living like royalty at a Scottish castle, or soaking up the atmosphere at a Manchester United football game
British Airways, Etihad, Flight Centre, Hainan Airlines, and Qatar Airways	#OMGB (Oh My GREAT Britain) Home of Amazing Moments campaign to drive visits to Britain from regional gateways in the United Arab Emirates, India, Australia, and New Zealand	Showcasing what Britain has to offer through activities with Etihad and Qatar Airways and through bespoke itineraries focusing on culture, countryside, and food and drink that are featured in Flight Centre stores throughout Australia; promoted travel between Beijing/Shanghai and London with British Airways through digital and social media targeting social pioneers and cultural adventurers
Virgin Atlantic (and Marketing Manchester)	It all starts in Manchester campaign to drive visits from the United States to Manchester and the North	Showcase Manchester and the North through four holiday films based around sport, culture, outdoor activities, and nightlife shot in a first person camera phone in a social media tone; the campaign ran across Instagram and Facebook, supported with digital banners on various travel websites in the United States driving consumers to engage further on the content hub; website content was grouped by the four key themes with a focus on practical information and links through to comprehensive itineraries showing users how to experience their #OMGB moments in Manchester and the North, including places to stay and how to get around Manchester and the surrounds

Based on examples available at Visit Britain, 2017. Global Partnership Campaigns. Available at: https://www.visitbritain.org/global-partnership-campaigns. (Accessed September 19, 2017).

hub of Asia (TAT News, 2017). The two partners publicised their marketing and promotional activities via media and distribution channels such as their respective websites, print publications, and social media. They also agreed to undertake joint marketing at airline and airport networking events and travel trade exhibitions that they attend. Both parties agreed to formulate a joint annual action plan to identify specific activities to be undertaken in various markets and to meet each month to ensure that the plan is being properly implemented. A key part of the agreement was to share information on market trends and traveller demographics through their respective databases and global networks. In association with this, the Tourism Authority of Thailand agreed to conduct extensive market research about visitor experiences in Thailand. In a similar agreement, Tourism New Zealand and Christchurch Airport committed NZD 6 million in 2016 to jointly promote New Zealand through Christchurch Airport (see Tourism New Zealand, 2016).

Agreements rarely involve the tripartite combination of a DMO, airline, and airport—the so-called golden triangle that was highlighted in the previous section of this chapter as being important for aviation tourism development, although admittedly, airports will often be members of their respective DMO anyway. A recent exception to this is the SGD 33.75 million agreement between Singapore Airlines, Changi Airport Group, and Singapore Tourism Board in 2017 (Singapore Tourism Board, 2017). The three partners agreed to extend an ongoing partnership that is aimed at promoting inbound travel to Singapore.

Agreements should be strategic and therefore over a longer term period, for instance of three or more years, and often in writing. This is important given that formal contracts and stable involvement in DMO activities are a prerequisite for sustainable relationships between DMOs and their primary stakeholders (d'Angella and Go, 2009; Sheehan and Ritchie, 2005). Agreements are therefore typically formalised by a MOU (sometimes called a letter of intent) that is signed by the various parties involved and typically commits them to a 2- to 3-year agreement, often with an option to extend or expand the agreement at the end of that period. Unlike a contract, a MOU is not legally binding. However, it is more formal than a so-called gentleman's agreement. It expresses an interest in working together and acts as a tool for implementing the partnership.

In terms of benefits, a MOU formalises the partnership, which was recognised in the previous section of this chapter as being a key stage in the destination partnership process. It is also recognised as a key ingredient of successful destination partnerships (Morrison, 2013). It ensures that all parties agree on their roles and the areas of cooperation. This will help to avoid potential future misunderstandings or conflict. It also provides a framework for how decisions will be made and will help to keep the partnership focused on its purpose and goals, and on track with activities to be actioned. As with the MOU between Singapore Airlines, Changi Airport Group and Singapore Tourism Board, it provides a framework that can be extended or expanded, for instance, over additional years or by allowing additional partners to join, therefore providing a more strategic and holistic long-term perspective. The agreement is typically released to the media via a press release and other activities to raise awareness for it. This can increase the profile of the agreement and its partners and add credibility to, and generate interest in, any planned initiatives. The agreement is likely to improve communications between the respective partners and allows for a joint response to any queries. It also communicates the purpose and goals of the agreement to stakeholders in the destination, allowing them to align their products and services accordingly so that they too can benefit from it.

A major challenge for such agreements is if stakeholders in the destination do not agree or buy-into the purpose and goals of the agreement. This can create disagreements and potential conflict, and would mean that activities to target and deliver certain markets to the destination are not met with the necessary products and services needed to cater for them on the ground. Similarly, agreements with one partner mean that other potentially useful partners, for instance other airlines, are sidelined, and may decide to offer their services elsewhere. On the other hand, it could be argued that they will also benefit from increased awareness for the destination without needing to contribute to, or be a part of the agreement. In some cases, it may be argued that such agreements act as state aid and have the potential to distort competition.

Other potential challenges are that the agreement assumes partners can work together effectively and efficiently, which is not always the case, for instance, due to the diversity of partners and their potential self-interest but also because of difficulties in communication (Morrison, 2013). In addition, a MOU is often a short and concise document with broad statements of intent rather than dealing with day-to-day practicalities. Achieving the intended outcomes may therefore prove difficult, especially if precise actions and timescales are not agreed upon. Measuring the outcomes of the agreement and any specific activities that are conducted can also be difficult as it is not always easy to quantify the impacts and to isolate them from other changes that are taking place in the destination.

15.4 FUNDING PARTNERSHIPS

Marketing partnerships are typically a joint commitment to work together to achieve something, normally in destinations that are seeking to strengthen awareness for their destination or the quality of air access. However, there are many destinations that find it difficult to attract air services in the first place and their tourism industry may suffer as a result. In such circumstances, subsidising air services may be necessary (Duval and Winchester, 2011). A subsidy is a form of economic intervention, which in an aviation context is defined by Gössling et al. (2017, p. 2) as 'any form of financial aid or in-kind support extended to the aviation sector or its supply chain'.

In terms of route development, many forms of subsidy are used, for instance, airport-based incentives such as fee waivers or discounts and marketing support offered to airlines by airports (see Chapter 14). Airport-based incentives are often focused on developing air services that generate revenue for the airport but not necessarily for inbound tourism. There are government-based programmes such as Public Service Obligations and Essential Air Services (see Bråthen and Halpern, 2012). These programmes aim to guarantee a minimum level of public air service to small or remote communities rather than supporting commercial inbound tourism. Government policies may also impact on aviation-related tourism flows (see Chapter 5). However, government policies, government-based programmes, and airport-based incentives are rarely formed through partnerships between tourism destination stakeholders and the air transport sector, and are therefore beyond the scope of this chapter.

A number of schemes then fit into what can be called community-based incentives which includes marketing support from public authorities to airlines to carry out campaigns for the promotion of tourism (see Ramos-Pérez, 2016), travel banks where private businesses and individuals pledge to purchase a certain number of tickets or a percentage of the travel budget of a private business (see Klophaus, 2016), and minimum revenue guarantees that are used to offer airlines a minimum revenue guarantee to protect against potential losses. Minimum revenue guarantees are typically administered by an airport and funded by a mix of local support, airport incentives, and government grant money, and sometimes by private tourism stakeholders such as hotels and resorts seeking to guarantee air services for their guests (see Ross, 2016). Route development funds (RDFs) also fit into the category of community-based incentives and are the focus of this section.

RDFs are based on a collaborative and coordinated partnership involving the public and private sector, and the so-called golden triangle of airlines, airports, and tourism destination stakeholders. Whilst marketing partnerships tend to focus on strengthening awareness for the destination or the quality of air access, RDFs tend to focus on encouraging the introduction of new routes. The routes should contribute to regional economic development by focusing on inbound tourism and/or the generation of new business links. Unlike government-based programmes that focus largely on unprofitable domestic public services, RDFs focus on direct international services, possibly with foreign carriers as opposed to depending on national carriers, and on routes that should become profitable over time. They may be established at a national, regional, or local level. The main idea is that stakeholders in the destination pool resources and provide financial aid or marketing support to airlines to share risk during the early stages of establishing a new route when investment costs are high for the airline and when the route is not so well known to target markets. They therefore encourage new routes that may not otherwise have been launched, which although based on a different approach, is a similar desired outcome to that of other forms of subsidy such as airport-based incentives, government-based programmes, and other community-based incentives.

RDFs are typically managed by a DMO or government authority and have a Board of Directors with representation from key destination stakeholders such as DMOs, government authorities, economic development agencies, employer's or business organisations, airports, and other public or private companies. Ensuring that the many stakeholders get along with each other, feel that they are a valued member of the partnership, and stay focused on a common purpose may be problematic for some destinations, especially if individual stakeholders have different views on how to develop tourism in the destination. Most RDFs are focused on offering financial aid to airlines when establishing a new route to the destination. However, there may also be an offer of marketing support that airlines can use to promote the destination (see Table 15.5). To access the funds, airlines typically need to meet strict criteria. Marketing support is normally offered as a one-off grant, whilst aid for new routes may be offered for specific routes that are named by the fund (e.g. as with the Canary Islands Flight Development Fund) or for any route that meets specific criteria to an airport or airports in the destination (e.g. as with the Icelandic Route Development Fund). Various models exist for calculating the amount of financial aid or marketing support for new routes, as is seen in some of the examples in Table 15.5.

TABLE 15.5 Example RDFs

Destination—Scheme	DMO(s) Involved	Brief Description
Copenhagen—Copenhagen Connected	Wonderful Copenhagen Visit Denmark	Launched 2010. Part of a national programme for Denmark called Global Connected (with separate schemes called Copenhagen Connected and West Denmark Connected). Total budget of DKK 127 from 2010 to 2018. Supports airlines marketing Denmark as a destination, new routes, and familiarisation trips. Also, funds marketing partnerships (Visit Copenhagen, 2017)
Canary Islands—Flight Development Fund	Canary Islands Tourism	Launched 2014. A budget of EUR 3.7 million for 24 new routes in 2017 to support the start-up of new scheduled direct air routes between the Canary Islands and specific international airports. The amount of funding varies per route and is often paid as a lump sum grant or over a period of years, for example, up to EUR 169,772 paid as one sum for a new route to La Palma from Paris (Canary Islands Tourism, 2017)
Iceland—Icelandic Route Development Fund	Promote Iceland Visit East Iceland Visit North Iceland	Launched 2016. Offers route and marketing support for scheduled international routes to Akureyri and Egilsstaðir. No details on total budget. However, EUR 3 is offered in support for each landed passenger (and up to a total of ISK 50 million annually or EUR 200,000 over a 3-year period). Marketing support of at least ISK 10 million for each route is also offered (Ministry of Industries and Innovation, 2016)
Northern Ireland—Air Route Development Fund	Tourism Ireland	Announced 2016. A budget of GBP 4 million over a 3-year period to support the development of new unserved routes with a high potential for inbound tourism and business in Northern Ireland (Invest NI, 2016)
Northern Norway—Charter Fund Scheme	Northern Norway Tourist Board	Launched 2014. Initial annual budget of NOK 10 million over 3 years to support tour operators organising charter flights to airports in Northern Norway. Reimburses tour operators up to 25% of total charter costs when cabin factor is below 80% (NNR, 2016)

Some RDFs are successful in attracting investment from the private sector, which provides valuable financial support for route development. However, RDFs typically rely on a primary source of public investment for the fund, for instance, from a national government department or a regional or local administration, and should therefore comply with any regulations or guidelines on state aid. In Europe, guidelines on the provision of state aid to airlines for launching a new route are stringent, for instance, the route must contribute to a well-defined objective of common interest, there should be a need for state intervention, the aid must be appropriate as a policy instrument, it should have an incentive effect, the amount of aid should be limited to the minimum necessary, and it should not have undue negative effects on competition and trade (see section 5.2 of EC, 2014; also see Chapter 14).

There is still a fair amount of uncertainty about the legal practice of the European guidelines, and notification and the subsequent approval of RDFs in Europe should therefore go through the EFTA Surveillance Authority (ESA). For DMOs, this can be a complex and time-consuming process that is likely to require costly legal advice and other assistance, for instance, from consultants. In fact, the same can be said about the entire process associated with developing, managing, and evaluating a RDF, which is illustrated by the case study in the next section of this chapter (see also AviaSolutions, 2006a,b).

There are also likely to be challenges associated with the partnership. For instance, airports may not be keen on third parties such as a DMO becoming involved in their relationship with airlines. Besides, the airport may have its own incentive scheme already (see Chapter 14) and may not want to compromise this, or their relationship with existing airline customers by having a separately administered RDF for their airport that may have different objectives and target different airline customers to their own incentive scheme. There may also be a reluctance to share commercially sensitive information (e.g. about the airports finances or details of the contracts that it has with airlines) although this should not be major issue for airports because the financial arrangements for a RDF normally fall outside of the commercial agreement that an airport has with its airlines. Any tensions over such issues are likely to diminish over time and as the partnership develops a certain level of trust (AviaSolutions, 2006a).

For airlines, any decision to operate to a destination needs to make commercial sense, especially in an era when they are more reluctant to take risks (Duval and Winchester, 2011) (see also Tan et al., 2017 for a tool that can help tourism destinations and air service development teams to evaluate the risks from the perspective of the airline and its network). Whilst the presence of start-up aid or marketing support may help to mitigate financial risk, it is not likely to be decisive in influencing their decision to serve the destination. There will still need to be clear evidence of sufficient demand for the route (e.g. see Halpern and Graham, 2016). This is supported by AviaSolutions (2006a) who, in their assessment of RDFs in Scotland and Northern Ireland, found that the key message from airlines is that although financial incentives in the early years of the route mean that it is more likely to be considered, basic route fundamentals also need to be in place in terms of demand (both inbound and outbound), and passenger yield.

This links to a wider debate on whether there is a tendency to overemphasise the dependence of tourism on aviation. In an analysis of the Danish RDF initiative Global Connected, and based on interviews with industry experts, Hvaas (2014) suggests that funding is rarely influential and that there are threats of unidirectional traffic, cannibalisation, and inappropriate metrics with such programmes. As a result, Hvaas suggests that a more sustainable approach would be for destination stakeholders to cooperate to develop inbound tourism products and services to match the needs of an airline's customer groups. Related to this is the debate on whether air traffic drives demand for tourism or whether tourism is the influencing factor for air traffic. Evidence suggests that influences are not one directional (e.g. see Bieger and Wittmer, 2006) and that although increased air traffic can influence tourism demand (e.g. see Koo et al., 2017), air traffic alone is not a sufficient tool for improving demand for tourism, for instance, whilst LCCs have been found to act as a driver for visitation [albeit with possible negative side effects such as a decrease in average length of stay (Dobruszkes and Mondou, 2013), or an increase in seasonal concentration of traffic (Halpern, 2011)], successful development of tourism is also dependent on other factors influencing demand (Farmaki and Papatheodorou, 2015). In this respect, Christchurch Airport has an interesting initiative that is focused on providing support to tourism companies on New Zealand's South Island that are making the most of opportunities from the rapidly growing Chinese market, which is a key target market for the South Island (see Christchurch Airport, 2017). Called the Christchurch New Horizons Fund, it has an annual budget of NZD 100,000 and is initiated by Christchurch Airport as part of the 'South' initiative (that involves all 13 South Island regional tourism organisations working collaboratively in tourist markets). Successful recipients, which for 2018 includes companies offering wildlife tours, glacier guiding, and scenic rail journeys, each receive assistance with product development, marketing materials and travel, valued at NZD 25,000, and a year's collaborative activity with the airport.

Returning to the issue of financial risk to airlines, AviaSolutions (2006a) found that airline's perceived financial risks associated with serving regional markets are particularly high and are exacerbated by the belief that some regional markets do not have a good track record of successful introduction of international services. This is important given that it is often regional markets that are the main drivers of RDFs. Interestingly, AviaSolutions (2006a) also found that whilst funds are seen by airlines as helping to reduce financial risk, a more important benefit is that the RDF increases the profile of route development in the media or political and business forums, and that this can help to improve awareness for the initiative, and encourage potential partners such as airports to contribute to it. The increased level of engagement between managers of the fund and potential airlines may also encourage airports to raise their own levels of engagement with airlines or encourage airports to assist with engagement activities relating to the fund, for instance, partnering with the DMO to raise awareness for the fund at airline and airport networking events or travel trade exhibitions.

The user rather than the tax payer is normally expected to pay for international travel so there will need to be accountability for the use of any public funds. The RDF should therefore try to reduce the public burden by also seeking new sources of private sector investment. There will also need to be measurable benefits for the region and its tourism stakeholders. Any economic benefits generated by the fund, for instance, additional tourist expenditure and jobs, will need to be balanced against social or environmental concerns that stakeholders may have.

RDFs have been recognised as being able to stimulate new routes with wider economic benefits to their region (e.g. see Hvaas, 2014; Scott Wilson, 2009). However, the effectiveness of RDFs is sometimes questioned because several routes end up being seasonal versus year-round or discontinued after the funding period has expired (Pagliari, 2005). This is important given that consistency of air services over time is a key concern to destinations reliant on air access, along with price and capacity (e.g. see Fuellhart and O'Connor, 2013). Whilst a lack of profitability (linked to weak demand) is typically cited as being the cause for air route suspension (e.g. see de Wit and Zuidberg, 2016), Lohmann and Vianna (2016) suggest that DMOs and airports can influence demand and that this, in addition to stakeholder involvement in general, can play a key role in maintaining route viability and avoiding air route suspension, although they also point out that whilst DMOs and airports can influence demand, airlines have the final decision. Airlines may of course be tempted to switch to other airports to chase funding opportunities elsewhere so contracting airlines to commit to the route for a minimum period after the funding period expires is an important part of any RDF. One of the greatest concerns relating to RDFs is that they may create market distortions as some routes may have started without the funding anyway. There is therefore a risk that the market becomes overreliant on subsidies.

In terms of measuring the effects of a RDF, isolating the impact of new routes from other changes taking place in the destination can be a challenge. In addition, growth at airports with the RDF may result in reductions in traffic at airports in surrounding areas meaning that although one destination may benefit, the wider region or country may not. There may also be the problem of tourists flying to a destination on a route that benefits from the fund but then move on to other destinations therefore having only marginal benefits for the destination providing the aid (e.g. see Francis et al., 2004).

Developing a successful funding initiative will depend on support from stakeholders. Castillo-Manzano et al. (2011) found that tourism businesses at destinations served by five regional airports in Spain were generally supportive of subsidising the introduction of low-cost carrier routes by local public administrations (55% of respondents said 'yes, with all the means at their disposal', 23% said 'yes, but not with subsidies', and 15% said 'no, the emergence of new flight connections and of new airlines should be a natural process with no interference from public administration'). However, support is likely to vary by destination as it depends to a large extent on local factors such as the existing level of air service provision and the settlement and industry structure in the region, for instance, the level of dependency on aviation tourism development.

Effects on the existing (or potential) level of air service provision is also an important consideration because increased competition, for instance, resulting from low-cost carrier entry, is found to be a contributing factor to the exit of tour operators (cannibalisation) and to the profitability of network carriers (Farmaki and Papatheordorou, 2015). Similarly, attracting tour operators may affect existing scheduled carriers that may be operating to the destination with very thin margins and any reduction of demand for their services may result in them cancelling routes or reducing their level of service, which could have a negative impact on the destination because of reduced connectivity for residents and businesses. Funding partnerships should therefore be careful not to upset existing airlines or deter potential airlines that are not able to access the aid. Bieger and Wittmer (2006) advocate the matching of airline business models to tourist destinations to maximise synergies between them. However, this is increasingly complicated by the merging of airline business models (see Jean and Lohmann, 2016; Lohmann and Koo, 2013), for instance, where tour operators are increasingly selling seats only or selling packages that include flights on low-cost carriers. Tourism businesses surveyed by Castillo-Manzano et al. (2011) were asked what type of airline is most useful for the economic growth and development of their city. Nineteen percent of respondents said low-cost carriers, 12% network carriers, and 68% both. Again, strategic decisions will need to be made depending on the local situation. However, for destinations that want to develop a diversified tourism offering, multiairline strategies will be important.

CASE STUDY 15.1 THE CHARTER FUND SCHEME FOR NORTHERN NORWAY

The Charter Fund Scheme for Northern Norway was conceived in January 2010 at the Avinor Conference in Alta, and developed over several years with the assistance of consultants and law firms, and various meetings and prestudies, before being launched at the end of October 2014. The objective is to provide financial support to tour operators arranging charter flights to airports in Northern Norway, thereby helping to boost tourism and the number of jobs supported by the tourism industry, and prevent a current trend for depopulation in the region (ESA, 2013).

Norway is a member of the common European aviation market and must therefore comply with European Union guidelines on state aid to airports and airlines according to EC (2014), which replaced EC (2005). In line with these guidelines, approval for the scheme was granted by ESA in 2013 for a duration of 3 years, and on condition that an evaluation report regarding the effects of the scheme on tourism, depopulation, and competition was submitted upon its expiry (see ESA, 2013). The evaluation was made in 2017 and subsequent amendments were approved by ESA, including a prolongation from 2017 to 2020 (see ESA, 2017).

The scheme is administered and marketed by the regional DMO—the Northern Norway Tourist Board (NNR), a company established in 2009 to market and develop tourism in Northern Norway. Fifty-one percent of NNR shares are held by the three county administrations for the region: Nordland, Troms, and Finnmark. Remaining shares are held by private stakeholders including Rica Hotels, Thon Hotels, and the shipping and explorer voyage operator Hurtigruten (NNR, 2017). According to ESA (2017), the scheme is included in the budgets set by the three county administrations and with an annual amount of NOK 10 million. Aid from the budget is allocated by a committee that includes NNR, the airport operator Avinor (a wholly owned state limited company under the Norwegian Ministry of Transport and Communications that is responsible for 45 state-owned airports, 27 of which are in Northern Norway), and the Tourism Northern Norway branch of the Norwegian Hospitality Association (NHO Tourism), which is the largest employer's and trade organisation in Norway.

Aid is provided in the form of grants that reduce risk to tour operators establishing air services to the region. The amount of aid is calculated according to two key factors: average cabin factor and total charter costs. Under the scheme, tour operators are required to set a break-even point at 80% of the cabin factor, which the scheme considers to be the industry standard. This can be debated given that many larger tour operators such as Thomson Airways (part of the TUI Group) and Thomas Cook Airlines (part of the Thomas Cook Group) typically achieve annual average load factors of over 90%. From 2005 to 2016, they achieved annual load factors of 88.4% to 94.1% and 87.9% to 94.1%, respectively (UK CAA, 2017). The scheme reimburses the tour operator up to a maximum of 25% of the total charter costs, that is, the financial obligations of the contract between the tour operator and the airline. The level of aid decreases to zero if a cabin factor of 80% or more is reached. The scheme is therefore designed to reduce risk when load factor is between 60% and 80% (see Table 15.6).

To date, the scheme has been marketed nationally and internationally through the channels of NNR, Avinor, and the government's national development agency Innovation Norway, for example, through personal meetings with multiple tour operators and airlines in countries including Belgium, France, the Netherlands, Spain, Italy, Russia, the UK, Switzerland, Germany, Austria, and Israel (NNR, 2017).

According to ESA (2013), key conditions of the initial scheme were that applicants are the tour operator but all applications must be supported by three parties (the tour operator, the airline, and the destination provider); minimum aircraft size of Boeing 737 category or larger; minimum length of stay of tourists of 2 nights; a 'land arrangement'—confirmation that the tour package includes expenditure of at least NOK 800 per tourist with a local commercial provider of tourist services; and a minimum of two flights in the package programme schedule—with priority going to longer package programmes. After evaluating the scheme, several changes were made (see ESA, 2017). The minimum aircraft requirement of Boeing 737 category or larger was repealed because of the challenging landing conditions at many airports in the region, and therefore greater suitability of smaller aircraft at many airports; the minimum length of stay of tourists was increased from 2 to 3 nights to more effectively induce tourist spending; and the minimum value of land arrangement was increased from NOK 800 per tourist to NOK 1500.

Evaluation of the scheme provided an analysis from October 2014 to December 2016 (see ESA, 2017). Twelve applications were received covering both summer and winter seasons, and five package programmes were concluded. A total of 34 flights were operated to four airports (Bodø, Evenes, Tromsø, and Alta). The evaluation recognises that the relatively low number of flights means it is difficult to evaluate the impact on local tourism companies. However, an assessment is made of the scheme's effect on increased economic activity estimating more than 20,000 additional guest nights in the region and a total value creation of NOK 24.1 million. NOK 2.5 million was paid out in aid, which means that the fund has provided a return of almost NOK 10 for each kroner invested by the county administrations. Interviews with travel agents that made bookings for international tour operators and tour operators themselves confirmed that the scheme, by reducing risk, induced additional rotations that would not have been carried out in its absence, therefore contributing to an increase in the number of tourists to Northern Norway. Of course, the calculations relating to the return on investment do not take into consideration any costs associated with creating, promoting, administering, and evaluating the scheme, which are likely to be substantial.

As mentioned in the previous section, a potential criticism of such schemes is that they only stimulate a short-term effect and services are reduced or withdrawn after the funding period expires. It is too early to answer this as the scheme is still operative. However, one of the reasons for prolonging the scheme has been to provide time for a more permanent stabilisation or increase in the basis for employment (see ESA, 2017). This is because the nature of charter operations and reaction of the local service industry is long term and certainly beyond the initial 3-year period of the scheme. The period needs to be long enough for charter operators to commit long term and for the region to become more established in the eyes of tourists, and with charter operators subsequently able to deliver a sufficient volume of tourist demand to the region so that the local industry is then willing and able to commit to investing in tourism (ESA, 2017).

It is interesting to note that whilst NHO Tourism was involved as a partner, the organisation's aviation branch, NHO Aviation publicly criticised the scheme in a letter to ESA (see NHO Aviation, 2012). NHO Aviation argue that the region is already served by a scheduled network of flights (and some commercially operated charter flights) that provide connectivity, even to particularly remote areas, and a significant proportion of foreigners travel on existing scheduled services to the region already. Indeed, airline schedules as of September 2017 show that at the four airports that served charters receiving aid from the fund between 2014 and 2016, mainline carrier SAS operates 109 weekly arrivals from Oslo using Boeing 737-600/700/800 aircraft whilst low-cost carrier Norwegian operates 92 weekly arrivals using Boeing 737-800s. There are also many regional and connecting flight options with SAS, Norwegian, and other operators such as Widerøe. It could of course be argued that the need to transfer via Oslo rather than having direct international routes acts as a deterrent to tourism (e.g. see Spencer, 2009). Hence the need to offer start-up aid to charters providing direct international routes.

NHO Aviation also argue that such a scheme is more likely to increase rather than prevent or reduce migration in Northern Norway because many existing connections to the region are vulnerable to small traffic or income reductions that may result from any diversion to new, subsidised charter flights, which could result in a reduced overall transport offer to the region and therefore negatively affect settlement and industry structure. It can also be argued that a limited new charter business will have relatively small effects on the local community anyway. Subsidising charter operations with public money may distort competition and make it difficult to start new scheduled routes. It also favours foreign versus Norwegian companies as charter traffic is typically incoming from operators based in other countries. The subsidies for routes to airports in Northern Norway also discriminate with airports in other parts of Norway, many of which are in areas with the same challenges in

TABLE 15.6 Example of Aid Per Rotation From the Scheme According to Cabin Factor and Sales Revenue

Cabin Factor (Percent)	Sales Revenue NOK (EUR)	Aid From the Scheme NOK (EUR)
50	187,500 (€19,181)	75,000 (€7676)
55	206,250 (€21,096)	75,000 (€7676)
60	225,000 (€23,021)	75,000 (€7676)
65	243,750 (€24,939)	56,250 (€5756)
70	262,500 (€26,858)	37,500 (€3837)
75	281,250 (€28,786)	18,750 (€1918)
80	300,000 (€30,705)	0 (€0)

Assumptions: Boeing 737-800 used from London to Northern Norway; estimated net cost to the airline in its agreement with the tour operator is NOK 300,000 per flight rotation; aircraft carries a maximum of 186 passengers (with an 80% break-even point set at 149 passengers). Figures in Norwegian Kroner (NOK) are converted to Euros (EUR) using a rate of 1 NOK = 0.1023 EUR according to XE Currency Converter Live Rates on 14 December 2017.

Data from ESA (EFTA Surveillance Authority), 2017. EFTA Surveillance Authority Decision No 143/17/COL of 13 July 2017 on a Prolongation and Modification of the Charter Fund Scheme for Northern Norway from 1.11.2017 to 31.12.2020 (Norway), EFTA Surveillance Authority, Brussels.

terms of population and industry development, although the fact that most airports in Norway are owned and operated by one company, Avinor, reduces this argument.

15.5 CONCLUSION

This chapter examines the ways in which DMOs and other tourism stakeholders collaborate with the air transport sector using marketing and funding partnerships for aviation tourism development. Marketing partnerships are a joint commitment to strengthen awareness for the destination or the quality of air access, whilst funding partnerships provide financial aid or marketing support to encourage new routes that may not otherwise be launched. The partnerships are based on the pooling of resources by the public and private sector to develop a collaborative and coordinated approach to aviation tourism development. They are likely to be most effective when based on strategic long-term efforts, and the so-called golden triangle of air service development that includes airlines, airports, and tourism destination stakeholders. Agreements should be formalised, for instance, by a MOU or contract. Partnership outcomes should be measurable, although it is often difficult to isolate the impacts of the partnership from other changes that are taking place in the destination.

Despite the obvious importance and widespread use of marketing partnerships for aviation and tourism, there is very little academic literature on the subject. Several papers have recognised the use of marketing partnerships in aviation and tourism (e.g. Duval, 2013; Tan et al., 2017; Spasojevic et al., 2018). However, unlike funding partnerships, there is a distinct lack of theoretical and empirical research on the subject. It is clearly an area of potential interest and provides opportunities for future research, especially regarding how agreements are developed and implemented, the benefits and challenges associated with them, and the potential outcomes that they have on aviation tourism development.

Both types of partnership seek to grow air traffic on the basis that it will contribute to tourism. However, successful development of tourism is also dependent on other factors influencing demand. Therefore a more sustainable approach might be for destination stakeholders to cooperate on developing tourism products and services in the destination to match the needs of target passengers of airlines. Only then does it make sense to develop marketing and funding partnerships with the air transport sector.

References

Air Tanzania, 2017. TTB and ATCL Sign MoU for Travel and Tourism Promotion. Available at http://www.airtanzania.co.tz/news/ttb-and-atcl-sign-mou-for-travel-and-tourism-promotion. (Accessed September 19, 2017).

AviaSolutions, 2006a. Bergen Route Development Forum Steering Group: Review of Existing UK Route Development Funds. AviaSolutions, Old Woking.

AviaSolutions, 2006b. Bergen Route Development Forum Steering Group: Route Development Plan and Management Arrangements. AviaSolutions, Old Woking.

Bieger, T., Wittmer, A., 2006. Air transport and tourism—perspectives and challenges for destinations, airlines and governments. J. Air Transp. Manag. 12 (1), 40–46.

Bornhorst, T., Brent Ritchie, J.R., Sheehan, L., 2010. Determinants of tourism success for DMOs & destinations: an empirical examination of stakeholders' perspectives. Tour. Manag. 31 (5), 572–589.

Bråthen, S., Halpern, N., 2012. Air transport service provision and management strategies to improve the economic benefits for remote regions. Res. Transp. Bus. Manag. 4, 3–12.

Canary Islands Tourism, 2017. Flight Development Fund. Available at http://turismodeislascanarias.com/en/flight-development-fund. (Accessed September 19, 2017).

Castillo-Manzano, J.I., López-Valpuesta, L., González-Laxe, F., 2011. The effects of the LCC boom on the urban tourism fabric: the viewpoint of tourism managers. Tour. Manag. 32, 1085–1095.

Christchurch Airport, 2017. New Opportunities And New Horizons For Tourism Operators. Available at http://christchurchairport.co.nz/media/873929/christchurch_airport_-_new_opportunities_and_new_horizons_for_tourism_operators.pdf. (Accessed September 19, 2017).

d'Angella, F., Go, F.M., 2009. Tale of two cities' collaborative tourism marketing: towards a theory of destination stakeholder assessment. Tour. Manag. 30, 429–440.

de Witt, J.G., Zuidberg, J., 2016. Route churn: an analysis of low-cost carrier route continuity in Europe. J. Transp. Geogr. 50, 57–67.

Dobruszkes, F., Mondou, V., 2013. Aviation liberalization as a means to promote international tourism: The EU-Morocco case. J. Air Transp. Manag. 29, 23–34.

Duval, D.T., 2013. Critical issues in air transport and tourism. Tour. Geogr. 15 (3), 494–510.

Duval, D.T., Winchester, X., 2011. Cost sharing in air-service provision. J. Air Law Comm. 76, 77–96.

EC (European Commission), 2005. Communication from the Commission: Community Guidelines on Financing of Airports and Start-up Aid to Airlines Departing from Regional Airports (2005/C 312/01). Off. J. C 312/48, 9.12.2005. EC, Brussels.

EC (European Commission), 2014. Communication from the Commission: Guidelines on State Aid to Airports and Airlines (2014/C 99/03). Off. J. C 99/03, 4.4.2014. EC, Brussels.

ESA (EFTA Surveillance Authority), 2013. EFTA Surveillance Authority Decision No 303/13/COL of 10 July 2013 Concerning a Charter Fund Scheme for Northern Norway (Norway). EFTA Surveillance Authority, Brussels.

ESA (EFTA Surveillance Authority), 2017. EFTA Surveillance Authority Decision No 143/17/COL of 13 July 2017 on a Prolongation and Modification of the Charter Fund Scheme for Northern Norway from 1.11.2017 to 31.12.2020 (Norway). EFTA Surveillance Authority, Brussels.

EVA Air, 2017. EVA Air and TAT Sign MOU Aimed at Boosting North American Tourism. Available at http://www.evaair.com/en-global/about-eva-air/news/news-releases/2017/2017-01-05-eva-air-and-tat-sign-mou-aimed-at-boosting-north-american.html. (Accessed September 19, 2017).

Farmaki, A., Papatheodorou, A., 2015. Stakeholder perceptions of the role of low-cost carriers in insular tourism destinations: the case of Cyprus. Tour. Hosp. Plan. Dev. 12 (4), 412–432.

Francis, G., Humphreys, I., Ison, S., 2004. Airports' perspectives on the growth of low-cost airlines and the remodeling of the airport-airline relationship. Tour. Manag. 25, 507–514.

Fuellhart, K., O'Connor, K., 2013. Air services at Australian cities: change and inertia 2005-2010. Geogr. Res. 51 (1), 37–48.

Gössling, S., Fichert, F., Forsyth, P., 2017. Subsidies in aviation. Sustainability 9 (8), 1–19. 1295.

Halpern, N., 2008. Lapland's airports: facilitating the development of international tourism in a peripheral region. Scand. J. Hosp. Tour. 8 (1), 25–47.

Halpern, N., 2011. Measuring seasonal demand for Spanish airports: implications for counter-seasonal strategies. Res. Transp. Bus. Manag. 1 (1), 47–54.

Halpern, N., Graham, A., 2015. Airport route development: a survey of current practice. Tour. Manag. 46, 213–221.

Halpern, N., Graham, A., 2016. Factors affecting airport route development activity and performance. J. Air Transp. Manag. 56, 69–78.

Hamill, L., 2016. Why Tourism and Aviation Partnerships are Vital for Business. Available at http://www.routesonline.com/news/29/breaking-news/269069/why-tourism-and-aviation-partnerships-are-vital-for-business/. (Accessed September 19, 2017).

Hvass, K.A., 2014. To fund or not to fund: a critical look at funding destination marketing campaigns. J. Dest. Market. Manag. 3, 173–179.

Invest NI, 2016. Announcement of £4 Million for Air Route Development. Available at https://www.investni.com/news/announcement-of--4million-for-air-route-development.html. (Accessed September 19, 2017).

Jean, D.A., Lohmann, G., 2016. Revisiting the airline business model spectrum: the influence of post global financial crisis and airline mergers in the US (2011-2013). Res. Transp. Bus. Manag. 21, 76–83.

Kenya Airways, 2017. Kenya Airways Signs a Marketing MOU with Seychelles Tourism Board. Available at https://www.kenya-airways.com/about-us/media-room/press-release/kq-signs-a-marketing-mou-with-seychelles-tourism-board/. (Accessed September 19, 2017).

Klophaus, R., 2016. Air travel banks: a public-private partnership approach to air services development at smaller airports. J. Airport Manag. 10 (2), 200–208.

Koo, T.T.R., Lim, C., Dobruszkes, F., 2017. Causality in direct air services and tourism demand. Ann. Tour. Res. 67, 67–77.

Lohmann, G., Koo, T.R., 2013. The airline business model spectrum. J. Air Transp. Manag. 31, 7–9.

Lohmann, G., Vianna, C., 2016. Air route suspension: the role of stakeholder engagement and aviation and non-aviation factors. J. Air Transp. Manag. 53, 199–210.

Lohmann, G., Albers, S., Koch, B., Pavlovich, K., 2009. From hub to tourist destination—an explorative study of Singapore and Dubai's aviation-based transformation. J. Air Transp. Manag. 15, 205–211.

Mayes, N., 2011. Public-private partnerships: Implications for air service development. In: State of the Industry Conference. Caribbean Tourism Organisation, St. Martin.

Ministry of Industries and Innovation, 2016. The Icelandic Route Development Fund. Available at https://eng.atvinnuvegaraduneyti.is/subjects/the-icelandic-route-development-fund/. (Accessed September 19, 2017).

Morrison, A.M., 2013. Marketing and Managing Tourism Destinations. Routledge, Abingdon.

NHO Aviation, 2012. NHO Luftfart kritiserer offentlig finansiert støtteordning for charterreiser til Nord-Norge i brev til Eftas overvåkingsorgan. Available at http://nholuftfart.no/uttalelser/nho-luftfart-kritiserer-offentlig-finansiert-stoetteordning-for-charterreiser-til-nord-norge-i-brev-til-eftas-overvaakingsorgan-article1427-185.html. (Accessed September 19, 2017).

NNR (Northern Norway Tourist Board), 2016. The Charter Fund Northern Norway. Available at http://www.nordnorge.com/corporate/en/newsfactsstatistics/?Bransje=510. (Accessed September 19, 2017).

NNR (Northern Norway Tourist Board), 2017. Annual Report. 2016 Northern Norway Tourist Board, Alta.

Pagliari, R., 2005. Developments in the supply of direct international air services from airports in Scotland. J. Air Transp. Manag. 11 (4), 249–257.

Ramos-Pérez, D., 2016. State aid to airlines in Spain: an assessment of regional and local government support from 1996 to 2014. Transp. Policy 49, 137–147.

Reige, A., Perry, C., 2000. National marketing strategies in international travel and tourism. Eur. J. Mark. 34 (11/12), 1290–1305.

Reige, A., Perry, C., Go, F.M., 2002. Partnerships in international travel and tourism marketing: a systems-oriented approach between Australia, New Zealand, Germany and the United Kingdom. J. Travel Tour. Market. 11 (1), 59–77.

Ross, T., 2016. Airline Revenue Guarantees Jump to $5.7 Million. Available at http://www.steamboattoday.com/news/airline-revenue-guarantees-jump-to-5-7-million/. (Accessed September 19, 2017).

Scott Wilson, 2009. Evaluation of the Scottish Air Route Development Fund. Scott Wilson, Glasgow.

Sheehan, L., Ritchie, B., 2005. Destination stakeholders: exploring identity and salience. Ann. Tour. Res. 32 (3), 711–734.

Singapore Airlines, 2017. TAT and Singapore Airlines Sign MOU to Boost Travel to Thailand. Available at https://www.singaporeair.com/en_UK/us/media-centre/press-release/article/?q=en_UK/2017/January-March/jr0317-170227. (Accessed September 19, 2017).

Singapore Tourism Board, 2017. $34m Three-Year Tripartite Partnership to Strengthen Singapore's Destination Appeal and Drive Visitor Traffic. Available at https://www.stb.gov.sg/news-and-publications/lists/newsroom/dispform.aspx?ID=702. (Accessed September 19, 2017).

Spasojevic, B., Lohmann, G., Scott, N., 2018. Air transport and tourism—a systematic literature review (2001-2014). Curr. Issue Tour. 21 (9), 975–997.

Spencer, D.M., 2009. Airport stops and flights on small airplanes as inhibitors or tourism-related air travel: a case study. Tour. Manag. 30, 838–846.

Tan, D.T., Koo, T.T.R., Duval, D.T., Forsyth, P.J., 2017. A method for reducing information asymmetry in destination–airline relationships. Curr. Issue Tour. 20 (8), 825–838.

TAT News, 2017. TAT and Airports Authority sign MoU to Promote Tourism, Share Research. Available at http://www.tatnews.org/tat-airports-authority-sign-mou-promote-tourism-share-research/. (Accessed September 19, 2017).

The Borneo Post, 2017. Brunei Airlines, Sabah Tourism Board to Develop Tourism. Available at http://www.theborneopost.com/2017/03/29/brunei-airlines-sabah-tourism-board-to-develop-tourism/. (Accessed September 19, 2017).

Tourism New Zealand, 2016. Tourism New Zealand and Christchurch Airport Sign $6m Commitment in New JV. Available at http://www.tourismnewzealand.com/news/tourism-new-zealand-and-christchurch-airport-sign-6m-commitment-in-new-jv/. (Accessed September 19, 2017).

Tretheway, M.W., Markhvida, K., 2014. The aviation value chain: economic returns and policy issues. J. Air Trans. Manag. 41, 3–16.

TTG Asia, 2017. Jetstar, Indonesia Ink MoU on Tourism Promotion. Available at http://www.ttgasia.com/2017/05/09/jetstar-indonesia-ink-mou-on-tourism-promotion/. (Accessed September 19, 2017).

UK CAA (Civil Aviation Authority), 2017. Airline Financial Tables 2005–2016. Available at https://www.caa.co.uk/Data-and-analysis/UK-aviation-market/Airlines/Datasets/UK-Airline-financial-tables/Airline-financial-tables-2014-2015/. (Accessed September 19, 2017).

UNWTO (United Nations World Tourism Organisation), 2007. A Practical Guide to Tourism Destination Management. UNWTO, Madrid.

UNWTO (United Nations World Tourism Organisation), 2017. Destination Management & Quality Programme: Conceptual Framework. Available at http://destination.unwto.org/content/conceptual-framework-0. (Accessed September 19, 2017).

Visit Britain, 2017. Global Partnership Campaigns. Available at https://www.visitbritain.org/global-partnership-campaigns. (Accessed September 19, 2017).

Visit Copenhagen, 2017. About Copenhagen Connected. Available at http://www.visitcopenhagen.com/global-connected/copenhagen/about-copenhagen-connected. (Accessed September 19, 2017).

CHAPTER

16

The Airport as an Attraction: The Airport City and Aerotropolis Concept

Andrew R. GOETZ

University of Denver, Denver, CO, United States

CHAPTER OUTLINE

16.1 INTRODUCTION

The airport has been transformed over time from a simple aviation facility to a major activity centre that serves multiple purposes. They have become centres for commercial activity and catalysts for urban development, as travellers and businesses have been drawn to airports and their surrounding areas because of the growth in importance of air transport and its accessibility advantages. As global tourism has expanded, airports have increasingly expanded their focus to cater to tourist needs and interests. Just as the airports themselves have changed over time, the land use patterns around them have also changed. Previously peripheral to urban development, airports have become much more integrated with cities and urban regions. More recently, the airport city and aerotropolis concept have been introduced claiming that airports are becoming the new centres of large urban regions, eclipsing traditional central business districts in economic importance.

This chapter will discuss how airports and their surrounding areas have become greater attractions by identifying the key factors and processes that have contributed to this evolution. After considering changes in the role and functions of airports and land use near airports, the limits to airport attractiveness and sustainability implications of airport development will be discussed. The chapter will then interrogate the airport city and aerotropolis model through critical examination of their concepts and discussion of three aerotropolis cases: New Songdo City near Seoul Incheon International Airport in South Korea, Dubai South near Al-Maktoum International Airport in the United Arab Emirates, and the Zuidas District near Amsterdam Airport Schiphol in the Netherlands.

Air Transport—A Tourism Perspective. https://doi.org/10.1016/B978-0-12-812857-2.00016-6

16.2 THE ROLE AND FUNCTION OF AIRPORTS: FROM DERIVED DEMAND TO DESTINATION

First and foremost, airports are air transport facilities that must ensure a safe, reliable, efficient, and pleasant travel experience for the public. Whilst airports have become many things over time, their central role and purpose remains air transport, and all of the necessary requirements that come with this primary function. Historically, they have been simply a place to access airline service, thus constituting a derived demand. Exceptions included people who would visit airport observatory decks to watch aircraft take off and land. Over time, however, airports added other functions that increased their attractiveness for purposes other than just accessing air transport.

As a consequence of the remarkable breakthroughs in aviation technology since the Wright Brothers first flew their heavier-than-air powered aircraft in 1903, air transport has grown dramatically and airports have needed to become larger and more specialised. The increase in size and speed of aircraft has necessitated wider and longer runways, taxiways, terminals, and concourses. Likewise, the growth and commercial success of air transport has led to the need for bigger and more numerous airports. Since the practical operation of aircraft requires airspace clearance for aircraft to take off and land, airports have a large impact zone that determines what can and cannot be located at or near an airport. As a result, airports are major land consumers and affect land use not only on the airport site itself but also for a large buffer zone surrounding the airport.

With the growth of air transport and the increased volume of passenger traffic, airports became sites of significant commercial activity. In years past, concessionaires at airports provided a limited amount of basic services and amenities, such as food and drinks, currency exchange, newspapers and magazines, and other sundry items catering to the traveller. Ground transport services in the form of taxis, buses, trains, vans, and rental cars were established to facilitate access to final destinations. As airports grew in size and passenger volume, the number and range of commercial establishments at airports expanded. Specialised 'duty-free' shopping, in which international travellers could purchase limited quantities of particular items, such as alcohol, tobacco, chocolate, perfume, and cosmetics, without paying value-added taxes or excise duties, became a popular and rewarding commercial activity at airports (Frethy, 2004). Recognising the lucrative profit potential of commercial enterprises, airports have expanded the range of concessions greatly to include clothing, electronics, bookstores, art galleries, specialised restaurants, and many other retail offerings, thus creating a shopping mall atmosphere in terminals and concourses. Whilst most airport concessions are aimed at the air traveller, airport workers as well as 'meeters and greeters' add to the customer market base. As a result, the airport has become a retail destination which now hosts a wide range of commercial establishments that would typically be found in central business districts or other specialised commercial centres.

A concomitant factor related to commercialisation has been the airport privatisation movement, which itself is part of the larger neoliberal policy turn that started with airline deregulation in the 1970s. The airline industry had historically been characterised by state-owned or state-regulated carriers in which entry, exit, routes, fares, and other operational aspects were controlled by national aviation authorities. The pattern of state ownership and control also extended to airports, sometimes by national airport authorities, but in many cases local or provincial governments or regional airport authorities. After the shift in macroeconomic policy towards neoliberalism led to deregulation of regulated airlines in the United States and privatisation of many state-owned airlines in Europe, Asia, and other parts of the world, many state-owned airports became privatised in one form or another. As of 2014, at least 450 airports worldwide had some form of private sector participation in their management or ownership (US GAO, 2014). In 2016 International Airports Council-Europe found that over 40% of European airports had at least some private shareholders, and that these airports handled three out of every four passengers (Jankovec, 2016; Poole, 2016). In the United States, airport ownership has remained with local governments or regional authorities, but there has been a substantial increase in public–private partnerships in which many airport functions have been privatised through contractual arrangements.

As part of efforts to maximise revenues, airports have encouraged more commercialisation, thus increasing nonaeronautical revenue. Historically, airports received most of their revenue from aeronautical sources, including landing fees and lease payments from airlines using passenger and cargo facilities. Today, airports receive an increasing percentage of their revenues from nonaeronautical sources, including concessions, automobile parking and rental car fees, and engineering services and utilities (de Neufville and Odoni, 2003; Graham and Ison, 2014).

This shift has been occurring at least in part due to increased competition amongst airports to attract more airline services, including low-cost airlines. Under deregulation, airlines have the freedom to choose which markets to serve, thus airports and their regions have become more entrepreneurial in their approach to recruiting airlines and ensuring more frequent and reliable air service for their communities. As part of efforts to entice and retain airlines, airports have tried to keep landing and other fees for airlines low so as to be competitive with other airports that are also seeking increased airline service. In some cases, airports have provided financial incentives or subsidies to airlines for initiating new air service. This downward pressure on aeronautical revenues has increased pressure for airports to maximise nonaeronautical revenues. Airports have discovered that increasing the number of passengers through encouraging more airline service will result in greater commercial revenues, thus incentivising their airline recruitment strategies.

The commercial growth and diversification of airports has led to a greatly expanded role and the creation of 'mini-cities' within the largest ones. In addition to a robust retail environment, airports contain many other services and functions, including airport administrative offices, airline services, security personnel and facilities, local police and fire departments, postal services, hotels and entertainment facilities, meeting spaces, leisure and fitness facilities, and other specialised uses such as museums and chapels. Outside of the terminal and concourses, but still on airport property, land has been utilised for other purposes, including aircraft maintenance and repair, agricultural and energy production facilities, as well as environmental remediation. The collection, retention, reprocessing, and safe disposal of deicing fluids are important to ensure the natural environment is protected from potential water pollution. In many ways, airports have developed their own ecosystems and contain many functions that would allow them to exist and thrive as separate entities.

Of course, airports are not separate from the rest of the cities and regions they serve, and it is their connectivity to the outside world that provides their *raison d'être*. Indeed, their function as sites of long-distance connectivity to other cities around the world makes them and their surrounding areas attractive for urban development.

16.3 LAND USE NEAR AIRPORTS

The history of land use development around airports can be conceptualised in three temporal stages:

1. Simple extended outpost with airport-related low-order low-density activities, for example, parking, automobile service stations, rental cars, air mail facilities, air cargo, warehousing, light or aviation-related manufacturing, hotels/motels, restaurants/diners, amusements, scattered residential (Fig. 16.1).

From the first aerodromes and air fields in the early 1900s through the 1950s and 1960s, land use near airports was typically characterised by relatively simple low-density activities. The types of land uses were largely related to functions connected to the airport, including traffic to and from the airport, or to general space-extensive needs. These were usually lower order activities that provided frequently needed lower cost goods and services catering largely to airport traffic. These land use activities took advantage of proximity to the airport, improved ground transportation due to the need to access the airport, and relatively low land values because airports were most often located in the peripheries of cities. Airport areas were not significantly higher or lower in their overall land values from other outlying areas of the city. There had been a persistent myth that airports actually lowered land values overall, but empirical studies were unable to verify this alleged effect (Barrett, 1987; Karsner, 1997). Residential property values near airports declined largely due to noise impacts, but business land values rose (Barrett, 1987; Cidell and Adams, 2001).

Airport areas were peripheral in several ways. Besides being geographically peripheral, airports and their surrounding areas were viewed as functionally distant and separate from the city. In most cities, the airport was typically located away from the elite residential sector and commercial districts of the city, and usually in the direction of a

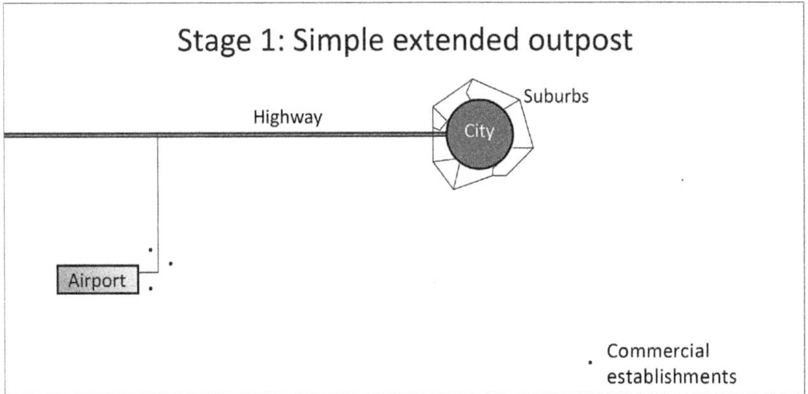

FIG. 16.1 The history of land use development around airports—Stage 1. *(Source: Designed by the author.)*

transportation/warehousing corridor (Goetz, 2015). Since most passenger traffic in the early years was business oriented, airports were viewed as remote Central Business District (CBD) commuter depots, tenuously linked together by single strands of highways and/or rail lines. Many urban planners and designers either considered airports and their environs as a specialised afterthought or did not consider them at all in their plans (Barrett, 1987; Freestone and Baker, 2011; Karsner, 1997). Traditional models of internal urban spatial structure, such as the concentric zone, sector, or multiple-nuclei models, did not explicitly mention airports as an important land use or transportation element.

2. Diversifying outer node with middle-order low-density activities, for example, planned office complexes, industrial parks, electronics and high-tech manufacturing, communications facilities, conference rooms, hotels, restaurants (Fig. 16.2).

From the 1960s to the 1980s, the character of land use around airports changed considerably. Together with generalised processes of suburbanisation and decentralisation, urban growth moved outward towards airports, and airport areas became sites of more numerous and diversified land uses. In addition to expanding the number of establishments catering to airport traffic, more specialised and higher-valued goods and services were produced and available near airports. Planned industrial parks and office complexes were increasingly developed near airports featuring companies that benefitted directly from proximity to airports, such as electronics and high-tech manufacturing and air freight forwarders. The airport areas became sites for conferences and meetings, featuring more higher-end hotels and restaurants. For example, by 1973, one-quarter of arriving passengers who flew into Chicago for business went no further than the hotels and office buildings located next to O'Hare International Airport (Karsner, 1997).

As urban areas grew outward and transportation access improved, airport areas became somewhat less peripheral and more connected with the city. Of course, the growth in importance of air transportation to local and regional economies contributed greatly to the increased role of airport areas in the urban environment. Functional connectivity increased and relative distance to the CBD and other urban centres was shortened due to more local transportation access. Urban planners and city officials began to incorporate airports to a greater extent in their land use, transportation, and economic development plans. Models of urban spatial structure from this time period, such as urban realms, suburban downtowns, or edge cities, explicitly included airports as one of several outlying centres, or nodes, within the urban environment, reflecting their increased importance.

3. Globalised metropolitan centre with high-order medium-density activities, for example, corporate headquarters, producer services, mixed-use activity centres, convention and hotel complexes, high-end restaurants, sports complexes (Fig. 16.3).

In the period from the 1980s to the early 2000s, development in airport areas took another step towards greater diversification, specialisation, and intensification. As political economies became more globalised, increasing international interaction elevated the status of airports and their surrounding areas as explicit sites of global activities. International business could be conducted easily at or near airports without having to travel to downtowns or central business districts. Other supporting services could also locate offices near the airport for easy access. More and higher-end hotels, restaurants, and other upscale facilities were increasingly found at or near airports. Specialised convention and hotel complexes, as well as sports and entertainment facilities, were developed around the largest airports. Increasing tourist demand, partly as a result of deregulation and liberalisation trends in the global airline industry, led to larger volumes of air passengers and more commercial opportunities at or near airports.

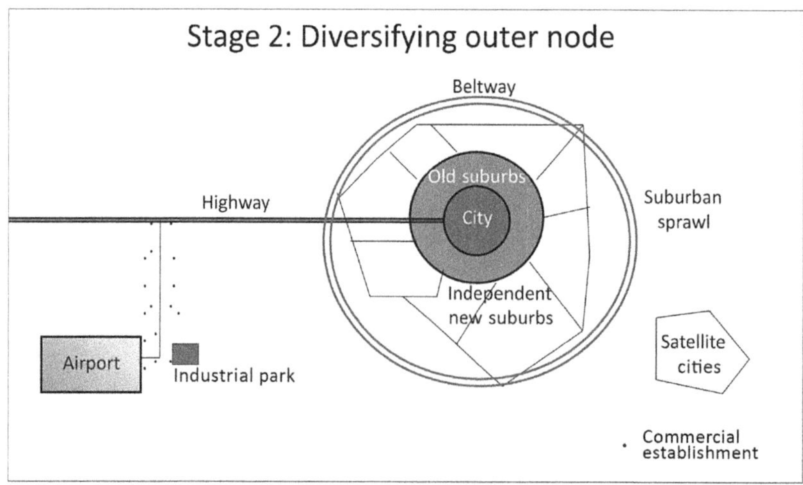

FIG. 16.2 The history of land use development around airports—Stage 2. *(Source: Designed by the author.)*

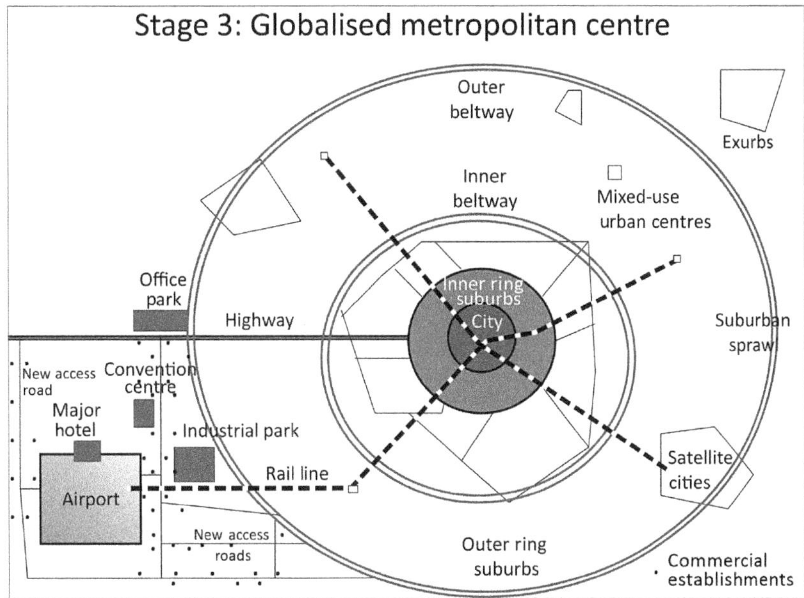

FIG. 16.3 The history of land use development around airports—Stage 3. *(Source: Designed by the author.)*

Whilst still peripheral in location within an urban area, the airport and its environs became a more important node of activity. These areas became larger centres of regional employment, and local transportation planners needed to address growing demand for ground transportation for both air passengers and employees who worked at or near the airport. Expanded road, highway, and rail projects became a more important preoccupation for cities to incorporate airports as major nodes on their critical transportation networks. Urban spatial models during this time referenced extended urban megaregions, postmodern forms, and global and world cities, in which the airport was increasingly recognised as an integral part of the new urban tapestry.

16.3.1 Regional Economic Impacts

In addition to the airport and the areas directly adjacent to airports, economic impacts affect a larger area throughout the region served by the airport. These economic effects are particularly evident for certain industries that value access to large global markets, including many advanced producer services,[1] especially international banking, finance, insurance, legal services, computer services, consulting, research and development, and other business services. Many consumer service industries are also heavily dependent upon air transport, none more so than tourism and the related entertainment, recreation, lodging, and restaurant industries. High-value and lighter-weight manufactured items from the medical, electronics, computer, and other high-technology industries, as well as high-value perishable commodities, including specialised food items and cut flowers, rely on the shipment of products by air (Goetz, 2015). Some of these activities have chosen locations directly adjacent to airports, but many others have located within the larger region based on other factors. Many businesses prefer to be located in central business districts or other urban centres to be closer to businesses and/or customers. Businesses will generally choose locations that are more convenient for executives and other employees to access from their residences. So long as good access to the airport is possible through local ground transportation, these activities can locate anywhere throughout a large region, but still benefit from relative proximity to the airport and the air service it provides.

16.4 LIMITS TO AIRPORT ATTRACTIVENESS

Whilst it is clear that airports have become greater attractions for economic development, there are limits to how much development can and should be destined for airports and their surrounding areas. These limits have much to do with hazards, safety, and environmental impacts from airport operations.

[1] Producer services are forms of service activity sold primarily to business and government clients. In contrast to retailing and consumer services that have their primary markets with households for final consumption, producer services are sold as inputs to the production process of various industries (Beyers, 2006).

16.4.1 Airports and Incompatible Land Uses

Since aircraft need space to take off and land, suitable sites for airports require large swaths of open space without obstructions. Airport compatible land uses are defined as uses that can coexist with a nearby airport without either constraining the safe and efficient operation of the airport or exposing people living and working nearby to unacceptable levels of noise or hazards (Ward et al., 2010). Land use at and around airports is subject to regulation in the following areas of concern:

1. Noise-related concerns. The goal is to limit noise-sensitive land uses to avoid issues such as annoyance and sleep disturbance to persons on the ground. These would include the following land uses:
   - Residences
   - Schools
   - Hospitals
2. Safety-related concerns. The goal is to limit uses that have potential impacts in the following two categories:
   - Those land uses hazardous to airspace and overflights
     - Tall structures (cell towers, wind turbines, vegetation, tall buildings)
     - Visual obstructions (smoke, glare, steam, dust, lights)
     - Wildlife and bird attractants (wetlands, crops, open water)
   - Those uses that affect accident severity
     - High concentrations of people (schools, churches, arenas)
     - Risk-sensitive uses (nursing homes, hospitals, flammable materials)

Aircraft taking off and landing cause significant noise impacts in flight paths around airports. Exposure to high levels of noise is one of the most serious local environmental impacts from aviation and can affect public health, including sleep disturbance, annoyance, stress, and related illnesses. Most communities try to follow suggested regulations to restrict land uses within the noise impact zones around airports so as to avoid the most harmful effects on people. These regulations typically emphasise limits on residential land use near airports, but also extend to other uses, such as schools and hospitals, in which annoyance and sleep disturbance can occur. Other responses include using building materials and techniques to limit noise intrusion (e.g. soundproofing windows).

In order to maintain safe operations at airports, nearby tall structures and visual obstructions are prohibited from aircraft approach and departure zones around airports. Likewise, land uses that might attract wildlife onto airport runways, or birds into flight paths, should be restricted in aircraft zones. Wildlife strikes killed more than 194 people and destroyed over 163 aircraft in the United States from 1988 to 2005 (US Department of Transportation Federal Aviation Administration, 2006). Other land uses, such as those that involve high concentrations of people or high risk-sensitive uses, do not have the potential to cause or contribute to the cause of aircraft accidents themselves, but they can greatly affect the consequences of accidents when they occur (Ward et al., 2010). These land uses should also be limited in approach and departure zones.

As a result of air transport's specific operational restrictions, land use at and around airports has been constrained, especially for residential uses. The location of airports within urban areas historically has been peripheral to the rest of the city, usually in sectors away from elite residential areas and high-density development. Whilst there has been increasing amounts of commercial, office, logistics, and light manufacturing development at or near airports as air transport has grown in importance, the nature of that development has been limited necessarily in density and intensity, especially as compared to central business districts and other urban centres.

16.4.2 Sustainability

Another potential limit to the attractiveness of airports is their role in promoting or impeding sustainable development. Based on the definition first proposed by the Brundtland Commission report (World Commission on Environment and Development, 1987), sustainable development can be defined as meeting current needs without compromising the ability of future generations to meet their needs, and encompasses economic, environmental, and social equity goals. A sustainable transport system is one that provides transport and mobility with renewable fuels whilst minimising emissions detrimental to the local and global environment, and preventing needless fatalities, injuries, and congestion (Black, 2010).

Whilst the transportation advantages of aviation are readily apparent, its sustainability externalities, including total reliance on an increasingly expensive nonrenewable resource (i.e. petroleum), together with relatively poor fuel economy (in comparison with other transport modes), serious noise issues, significant local air pollution and growing global greenhouse gas emissions diminish aviation's long-term sustainability profile (Palling et al., 2014; Upham et al., 2003; Goetz 2015). Adding to these concerns is the location of airports on the outskirts of cities, and their contribution to a more sprawling pattern of urban development which can have negative sustainability ramifications. Airports and nearby lower density development tend to induce more roadway traffic, which in many cases involves single-occupant vehicles contributing to increased traffic congestion and pollution (Schiller and Kenworthy, 2018). Fortunately, many of the largest airports in the world are connected by rail, bus, and transit systems, so that more sustainable ground transport options are available. Still, at most airports around the world, the largest share of ground access by passengers and employees is by automobile.

16.5 PLANNED AIRPORT CITIES AND THE AEROTROPOLIS CONCEPT: THE NEXT STAGE OF AIRPORT DEVELOPMENT?

Another step in the evolution of airports and their nearby land use started in the early 2000s with planned airport cities and the popularity of the aerotropolis concept. Planned airport cities usually refer to commercial and real estate development on the airport site itself whilst the aerotropolis is broader in geographic scope. Originally introduced by early visionaries including Le Corbusier in the 1920s, Nicholas DeSantis in the 1930s, and aeronautical engineer H. McKinley Conway in the 1970s, the aerotropolis concept has been popularised most recently by University of North Carolina Professor John Kasarda (Freestone and Baker, 2011; Perry, 2013). An aerotropolis is an airport-oriented commercial, office, and business development area that relies on proximity to a major airport and the air transport accessibility it provides (Aerotropolis Business Concepts LLC, 2017). Kasarda and Lindsay (2011, p. 174) further define an aerotropolis as:

"an airport-integrated region, extending as far as sixty miles from the inner clusters of hotels, offices, distribution, and logistics facilities. ... All kinds of activities are served by and enhanced by the airport. Whether it's supply chains, whether it's enterprise networks, whether it's biosciences and pharmaceuticals and time-sensitive organic materials, the airport itself is really the nucleus of a range of 'New Economy' functions, bolstering a city's competitiveness, job creation, and quality of life".

Instead of being considered simply as a peripheral infrastructure function in a city, Kasarda envisions the airport as the centre of a new urban form—separate from but still connected to traditional central business districts and other urban centres by highways and/or rail—emphasising high-speed, knowledge-intensive 'New Economy' activities that would be the economic growth engine of a large urbanised region. In the idealised model, the airport and its terminals, shopping arcades, business offices, conference centres, and hotels are the nucleus of the aerotropolis surrounded by logistics parks, free trade zones, wholesale merchandise marts, and e-commerce fulfilment facilities. Ground transportation corridors called 'aerolanes' and 'aerotrains' connect the airport with business parks, research/technology parks, industrial parks, warehouse districts, distribution centres, hotel and entertainment districts, office corridors, and information–communication technology (ICT) corridors, as well as residential areas located farther away (Aerotropolis Business Concepts LLC, 2017; Goetz, 2015). According to Kasarda, airports will shape business location and urban development in the 21st century as much as highways did in the 20th century, railroads in the 19th and seaports in the 18th (Kasarda and Lindsay 2011).

The aerotropolis is just one of several contemporary models of airport-driven urban development identified by Freestone and Baker (2011). The *airfront* has been defined as an airport-related commercial zone near the airport (Blanton, 2004). The *decoplex,* derived from 'development–ecology complex', is a new airport community in a regional setting catering to private aircraft owners (Conway, 1993). The *airport city* has been defined as planned mixed use development on the airport site itself (Guller and Guller, 2003). The *airport corridor* involves the coordinated provision of infrastructure and commercial development along the axis between the CBD and the airport (Schaafsma et al., 2008). Additionally the *aerea* is comprised of discrete spatial clusters of airport-related development throughout the metropolitan subregion (Schlaack, 2010). Each of these models is a variation on the general theme of airport-centred development.

Whilst the aerotropolis concept has become increasingly popular, it has also met with some criticism, particularly with regard to its sustainability. Basing future urban development on a mode of transport that scores poorly on a sustainability scale is not a sound strategy (Charles et al., 2007). Freestone and Baker (2011, p. 271) acknowledge that "the aerotropolis model more tacitly endorses an extensive pattern of land use development along lines most evident in American cities. ... At best, the result is an anodyne suburban landscape of commercial campuses, chain hotels, and generic commercial structures. At worst, the aerotropolis may well represent a jumbled map of what not to do in airport regions as the exemplification of what Hudnut (2003) terms the American 'exit ramp economy.'" Leinbach

(2004, p. 47) noted that airport-driven urban development adds to 'already existing externalities of noise, pollution, and increased traffic congestion' and thus residents living 'within the influence of these developments must shoulder the costs'.

Charles et al. (2007) comment on the vulnerability of airports and concentrated aerotropolis developments to possible terrorist attacks and military incursions. They also argue that the primacy of air transport inherent in the aerotropolis concept ignores the importance of other transport modes in economic development, especially freight movement by maritime transport. Whilst air cargo has been growing rapidly and carries predominantly low-weight high-value commodities, most of the world's freight is still carried by water transport, and that is likely to remain true for the foreseeable future. For this reason, developments near both airports and seaports have better prospects than at airports alone (Perry, 2013).

In another analysis, Cidell (2015) challenged a study by Appold and Kasarda (2013) that aimed to determine the extent to which airports were becoming the centres of economic activity in their metropolitan areas in comparison to traditional central business districts (CBDs). Appold and Kasarda compared the number of jobs within certain distances from the airports and the CBDs across 25 US cities. They found that employment within 2.5 miles of the airports was 50.6% as large as that within 2.5 miles of the city centres, thus suggesting that airports were becoming new focal points of development in US metropolitan areas. Cidell conducted a similar analysis using the airport as well as the region's largest shopping mall, the largest wastewater treatment plant, and the point directly opposite the CBD from the airport to compare employment location proximity. Cidell found that there were more jobs within the vicinity of the wastewater treatment plant than the airport for about half of the cities studied, and the random point in the reverse direction from the airport was roughly equivalent to the airport in terms of job generation. Whilst Cidell admits that this analysis is overly simplistic to analyse such a complex process, she warns that this type of analysis has been used in several aerotropolis studies and has considerable influence on airport policy and development, given the reach of the aerotropolis idea into local and national governments.

Indeed, the aerotropolis concept has become quite popular amongst city politicians, economic development officials, and real estate developers throughout the world. A growing number of cities have developed or are developing aerotropolis plans. Applications range from large-scale development of a greenfield site to development of large tracts of available land at an existing airport, to incremental development of business parks on airport property (Perry, 2013). Amongst the most famous are New Songdo City, near Incheon International Airport outside of Seoul, South Korea, and Dubai South (formerly Dubai World Central) adjacent to Al-Maktoum International Airport in Dubai, United Arab Emirates, which are both examples of large-scale greenfield site development. Zuidas, near Amsterdam Airport Schiphol in the Netherlands is an example of incremental development of land in an airport corridor. Other significant emerging aerotropolis development can also be found in Bangkok, Beijing, Dallas–Ft. Worth, Denver, Detroit, Hong Kong, Kuala Lumpur, Shanghai, and Singapore, amongst other cities (Kasarda and Lindsay, 2011).

16.5.1 New Songdo City and Seoul Incheon International Airport

New Songdo City, also known as Songdo International City including the Songdo International Business District (Songdo IBD), is a planned aerotropolis, located 65 km southwest of Seoul, South Korea, but only 12 km from Seoul Incheon International Airport. New Songdo City was built on land reclaimed from the Yellow Sea along the Incheon coastline and is connected to the airport by a highway bridge over the sea. Songdo construction began in 2005 on a 6 km^2 site designed to become an international business centre with 80,000 apartments, 5 million square metres of office space, and nearly 1 million square metres each of retail space and open public space. According to the Songdo IBD website, 36,000 residents live in the Songdo IBD with a total of 90,000 in greater Songdo City. Over 1000 retail and hospitality businesses are open and operating, and over 60,000 employees are working in over 1600 companies in Songdo City (Songdo IBD, 2017). Songdo is the largest and most well-known master-planned urban development amongst those that have evolved around three growth poles adjacent to the Incheon airport—Yeongjong, Cheongra, and Songdo. Kasarda (2004, p. 19) acknowledged the scale of this urban development as 'the most ambitious effort to develop an airport-centric urban form' (Kim, 2010).

Seoul Incheon International Airport opened in 2001 and is the major airport serving the Seoul capital region. It is located 48 km west of Seoul and is built on land reclaimed from the sea between two islands. It is the 19th largest passenger airport in the world with nearly 58 million total passengers in 2016 (ACI, 2017). Whilst most of the passengers either begin or end their flights at the airport, 13% were transferring passengers (Incheon International Airport Corporation, 2016). It is the principal hub for Korean Air, amongst the world's top 20 airlines based on passengers carried, and a member of the SkyTeam global airline alliance. Asiana Airlines and low-cost carriers Jeju Air and Jin Air also have principal hubs there. Incheon is a major freight airport, ranked 5th in the world with 2.7 million tons of cargo transported in 2016 (ACI, 2017). Korean Air is the world's 5th largest air cargo carrier based on ton-kms. Over 70 passenger airlines and over 35 cargo carriers serve Incheon, providing direct service to numerous destinations throughout Asia and the world.

Proximity to Incheon International Airport and the extensive air transport service it provides is a major feature in Songdo's promotion: '1/3 of the world's population is accessible within a 3 ½ hr flight away' (Kim, 2010; Songdo IBD 2017). The original plan was to create an international business district and free economic zone that would attract foreign direct investment as a 'Gateway to Northeast Asia', especially China (Kasarda and Lindsay 2011; Kim 2010). After receiving a $58 billion bank bailout by the International Monetary Fund in the wake of the Asian financial crisis of the late 1990s, the South Korean government needed foreign investment, and decided on a development strategy to make Seoul 'the financial and creative hub of northeast Asia' (Kasarda and Lindsay 2011, p. 354). The South Korean government enlisted the services of New York-based real estate developer Gale International, US architects Kohn Pederson Fox, and South Korean POSCO Engineering and Construction Co. to design, build, and market New Songdo City. The intention was to create an environment that would appeal to international businesses. 'New Songdo promises to be more American than any of its neighbours—an English-speaking island stocked with prep schools from Boston, malls from Beverly Hills, and a golf course designed by Jack Nicklaus' (Kasarda and Lindsay 2011, p. 355).

Songdo has also been promoted as a Ubiquitous City (U-City), in reference to its ubiquitous computing environment reflective of a Smart City, and more recently for its sustainability. In partnership with US-based CISCO Systems, much of the infrastructure has been embedded with smart technology that allows monitoring and information dissemination for transportation, safety and security, disaster management, facilities management, and educational services. The Leadership in Energy and Environmental Design (LEED) Green Building Rating System developed by the US Green Building Council has certified nearly 2 million square metres of space in Songdo, including over 100 LEED-certified buildings, representing 40% of all LEED-certified space in South Korea. Songdo has a pneumatic waste disposal system that uses a network of pipes to collect and process garbage from households, thus no need for garbage can collection from garbage trucks. Approximately 40% of Songdo's land area is designed as green public space (Arbes and Bethea, 2014; Songdo IBD, 2017).

Reports and assessments of Songdo have highlighted its proximity to Incheon Airport, its global accessibility, and its innovative technological and environmental features, but also some of the ways in which it has fallen short of its goals (Arbes and Bethea, 2014; Borowiec, 2016; Campbell, 2005; James, 2016; Kim, 2010; Mesmer, 2017; Shapiro, 2015; Williamson 2013). Whilst all of Songdo's planned infrastructure and buildings are still not yet completed, it is acknowledged that actual utilisation has been less than projected. It now has about 90,000 residents, less than half of what it was designed to hold. Developers say there are just 70,000 daily commuters, well short of the 300,000 they envisioned (Borowiec, 2016). In the wake of the 2007–08 Global Financial Crisis, international investment did not materialise as originally projected, and by far most of the residents in Songdo are South Koreans, especially young families attracted by the high quality of schools. Other residents have chosen Songdo because it is 'new and clean' and cheaper than parts of central Seoul (Mesmer 2017). For others, Songdo is perceived to be too far from Seoul—it takes well over an hour by bus or subway to reach most neighbourhoods there—'too far to commute, but too close to compete' (Borowiec, 2016; James, 2016; Mesmer, 2017). It has been criticised for being a ghost town, too silent, sterile, soul-less, and postapocalyptic with an 'oppressive, Chernobyl-like emptiness' (James, 2016; Mesmer, 2017). It differs markedly from the bustling and vibrant central areas of Seoul. Yet, for some, the peace and solitude is preferred. Similar to other new towns and 'instant cities', it will take more time for Songdo to evolve into what it will eventually become. However, it is clear that the original intention of a thriving airport-oriented international business city has not yet been achieved.

16.5.2 Dubai South (Dubai World Central) and Al-Maktoum International Airport

Dubai South, formerly known as Dubai World Central, is a 145 square km master-planned logistics, commercial and residential development planned in conjunction with Al-Maktoum International Airport in Dubai, United Arab Emirates. This aerotropolis project is located 37 km southwest of central Dubai, just south of the Jebel Ali Seaport. Al-Maktoum Airport (IATA code: DWC), which opened in 2010, is the second major airport in Dubai, in addition to Dubai International Airport (IATA code: DXB).

Dubai International Airport (DXB) has experienced meteoric growth in recent years as the principal hub for Emirates Airline. It is also the main hub for low-cost carrier flydubai. As of 2016, DXB was the third busiest passenger airport in the world serving nearly 84 million total passengers. In 2010 it was ranked 13th in the world with 47 million passengers, and as recently as 2005, it was much less active, ranking only 42nd with nearly 25 million passengers.

It also serves as a major air cargo facility, ranking as the 6th busiest cargo airport in the world in 2016 handling over 2.5 million tons of freight (ACI, 2017). The phenomenal growth of Dubai International can be attributed to an ambitious strategy by Emirates to become the leading carrier in the world by serving international traffic initially between Europe and Asia and then to the rest of the world through its geographically well-positioned hub airport. Emirates advertises Dubai's central location by noting 'over half of the world's population lives less than eight hours away', and is an ideal location for an airline hub connecting East and West (Derudder et al., 2013, p. A6), Emirates is the world's 4th largest passenger airline based on passenger-kms flown and the 2nd largest air cargo carrier based on ton-kms carried. In addition to Emirates, more than 140 airlines provide direct service to over 260 destinations across 6 continents from DBX (Dubai Airports, 2017a,b).

The extremely rapid growth of Dubai International, and the physical limitations of possible expansion due to its site location in central Dubai, led to the decision to build the more remotely located Al-Maktoum International Airport. Al-Maktoum has been built on a 140 km^2 site which includes five parallel runways capable of handling simultaneous operations of aircraft as large as Airbus A-380s, thus making it the world's largest airport in physical size. It is designed to accommodate over 160 million passengers and up to 12 million tons of cargo per year by 2030, and could have additional capacity for up to 220 million passengers per year if needed (Dubai Airports, 2017a,b). Opened in 2010 initially for cargo flights, Al-Maktoum has experienced limited use, mostly involving cargo traffic, although some passenger service has been operating since 2013. Whilst Dubai International will continue to function as the principal airport of Dubai, it is expected that an increasing amount of air traffic over time will be shifted to Al-Maktoum. The low-cost carrier flydubai started operating flights at Al-Maktoum in 2015, and was planning to shift the bulk of its operations there by the third quarter of 2017, whilst Emirates is expected to transition its hub operations to Al-Maktoum in 2025 (The National, 2017).

The site for Al-Maktoum Airport includes the Dubai South (formerly Dubai World Central) aerotropolis development. As part of its renaming and rebranding, Dubai South—'The City of You'—defines itself based on 'the happiness of the individual', and aspires to the following goals (Dubai South, 2017):

1. To become a city of happy, creative and empowered people
2. To become the preferred place to live, work and invest
3. To create an inclusive and cohesive society
4. To build a smart and sustainable city
5. To become a pivotal hub in the global economy

According to Dubai South (2017), the entire development is 'projected to sustain a population of a million. As an economic platform, it is designed to support every conceivable kind of business and industry and create 500,000 jobs'. The airport is at the centre of a proposed development that includes several specialised land use zones, including:

- Aviation District: a 6.7 km^2 area directly west of the air field dedicated to the aviation sector, featuring free zones for maintenance, repair, and operations (MROs), fixed-base operators (FBOs), light industries, education, and research and development. This district will also be the permanent home of the Dubai Airshow, the Middle East Business Aviation Show, and the VIP terminal.
- Logistics District: a 21 km^2 area directly northwest of the air field designed for multimodal logistics and supply chain company facilities. Connected to air cargo operations, the area services contract logistics firms, integrators, freight forwarders, and agents. Proximity to Jebel Ali Seaport facilitates intermodal freight connectivity.
- Business Park: a free zone in the Logistics District that features office space for firms of varying size, including a Business Centre providing round-the-clock services.
- Commercial District: a mixed-use development west of the Logistics District incorporating commercial, residential, and leisure activities.
- Exhibition District: a 4.4 km^2 area directly northeast of the air field dedicated to hosting meeting, incentive, conference and exhibition (MICE) activities. This will be the venue for World Expo 2020.
- Residential District: a 6.7 km^2 area directly east of the air field that will feature residential complexes, schools, clinics, hospitals, malls, as well as leisure and hospitality facilities.
- Golf District: a high-end residential development built around a world-class golf course, in conjunction with UAE-based Emaar Properties.
- Humanitarian District: a small area at the northern end of the Logistics District that will be used for logistics operations of international humanitarian aid agencies to coordinate responses to natural and other disasters. Its location between the air field and the Jebel Ali Seaport will facilitate shipments of medical and food supplies by sea and air.

The Government of Dubai aims to increase the number of tourists from 14 million a year in 2017 to 20 million by 2020, and the Dubai South complex (which will host World Expo 2020) is a major part of this strategy (LookUp.ae, 2017). Dubai Parks and Resorts, an integrated leisure and theme park on a 2.3 km^2 site located just west of Dubai South, opened in December 2016 and features theme parks including Motiongate Dubai, Bollywood Parks Dubai, Legoland Dubai, and Legoland Waterpark, as well as over 100 rides and attractions. The Six Flags Dubai amusement park is expected to open there in 2019. The Polynesian-themed Lapita Hotel opened in 2017, and a Lego themed hotel is also planned. The development of tourist attractions, as well as business functions, fits with Dubai's strategy to be more than just a connecting hub airport, but a destination as well. Proximity to the airport is intrinsic to this strategy since almost all of the projected tourist demand will come from business and leisure visitors arriving by air.

As of 2017, however, the level of airport activity at Al-Maktoum and the nearby development at Dubai South is still limited. Whilst air cargo traffic has reached an annual figure of just over 1 million tons in 2016, ranking Al-Maktoum as the 27th busiest cargo airport in the world, passenger traffic has lagged. In 2016 only 850,000 passengers used Al-Maktoum Airport, mostly as a result of low-cost carrier flydubai's service. At the same time, passenger traffic at Dubai International grew to over 83 million in 2016 (ACI, 2017). When it opened for passenger service in 2013, Al-Maktoum had an annual passenger capacity of only 7 million, but will be expanded to 26 million by 2018 (Dubai Airports, 2017b). It is expected that more flights will be shifted to Al-Maktoum as Dubai International approaches its 100 million per year passenger capacity (Legnani, 2016; Warrayat, 2017). Together with the growth of Jebel Ali Seaport (the 9th largest container port in the world as of 2015), the Jebel Ali Free Zone Authority (JAFZA), and air cargo growth at Al-Maktoum, there are warehousing and office facilities for over 5000 companies in the extended Logistics Corridor, including such major logistics firms Aramex, Hellman Calipar, Kuehne + Nagel, and Panalpina and shippers Nestlé and IKEA (Al-Kaabi 2015). However the lagging passenger traffic and the effects of the global financial crisis on real estate have thus far resulted in slower growth for other development at Dubai South.

It should be recognised that the airport-oriented development plans of Dubai are part of a larger state-led boosterist strategy employed by the ruling Al-Maktoum family. In contrast to the Emirate of Abu Dhabi, the Emirate of Dubai had limited access to oil resources, and consequently pursued a development model similar to city-states such as Singapore and Hong Kong. 'The Dubai model essentially envisioned the attraction of capital flows through a strategy of rapid and massive infrastructural developments, the implementation of a business-friendly regulatory framework, and intense place marketing targeted at international luxury tourism' (Derudder et al., 2013, p. A6). Dubai has indeed created massive projects in addition to its airport developments, including the construction of new artificial islands in the Persian/Arabian Gulf (e.g. Palm Islands, World Islands), the only 7-star luxury hotel in the world (Burj Al Arab), and the world's tallest skyscraper (Burj Khalifa). According to Derudder and Witlox (2014, p. 119), the Dubai model "implied introducing state-of-the-art infrastructures as 'phallic' symbols for international prominence, essential to realize a self-fulfilling prophecy that goes well beyond Kasarda's Aerotropolis discourse". Dubai's airport development and other infrastructure investment have triggered competitive responses throughout the Gulf region, including in Abu Dhabi, Qatar, Bahrain, and Kuwait. Derudder et al. (2013, p. A6) warn that "Dubai's 'successful' strategy has been mimicked by other (quasi) city-states in the region, whereby the rationale of being competitive amongst peers further normalises speculative infrastructure developments" thus inviting "the danger of a classical tragedy of the commons".

16.5.3 Amsterdam Airport Schiphol and Zuidas

Amsterdam Airport Schiphol in the Netherlands has long been one of the largest and most important airports in the world. Schiphol is the 12th busiest passenger airport in the world with nearly 64 million total passengers in 2016, of which 37.8% were transferring passengers (Schiphol Group, 2017). It is the principal hub for Dutch carrier KLM which is now part of the Air France–KLM group, the world's 6th largest passenger airline based on passenger-kms flown, as well as the SkyTeam global airline alliance. It is also a major air cargo facility, ranking 18th in the world with 1.7 million tons of freight handled in 2016 (ACI, 2017).

A key part of the Netherlands' economic development strategy historically has been to serve as a hub for global trade, relying on its major seaports at Amsterdam and Rotterdam, its rail and road terminals, and its principal airport at Schiphol (Schaafsma, 2015).

The Netherlands has consistently advocated for global free trade policies, including airline deregulation and liberalisation thus opening up more air service opportunities. The Netherlands and KLM have benefitted especially from the expansion of 6th freedom air service rights which allow an airline to carry passengers or cargo between two foreign countries via its own country. KLM has used 6th freedom rights effectively to serve connecting traffic through its Schiphol hub, making it one of the most important connecting hub airports in the world. It is a strategy that other major hub airports, such as in Singapore, Dubai, and Seoul have also utilised to great effect. Combined with major seaports, as well as road and rail terminals, airport trade and traffic has translated into considerable economic development impacts throughout the airport area and surrounding region.

The Dutch government's mainport policy that started in the 1980s emphasised airport development at Schiphol. 'The mainport was roughly defined as an airport with a global hub function and excellent network as well as optimal economic, social and living conditions in the surrounding metropolitan area' (Burghouwt and Dobruszkes 2014, p. 614). In 1991 a package deal signed by the Dutch Ministry of Transport, the Ministry of Housing, Spatial Planning and the Environment, the Ministry of Economic Affairs, the Province of North Holland, the Municipalities of Amsterdam and Haarlemmermeer and KLM Royal Dutch Airlines created a plan for the development of the airport that sought to strike a balance between maximising airport capacity whilst maintaining environmental quality and improving living conditions in the airport region (Burghouwt, 2007; Burghouwt and Dobruszkes, 2014). Recognising the potential of airport-related development, several Schiphol Airport development groups were started. Initial efforts took the form of Schiphol AirportCity which encouraged real estate development directly at the airport. Schiphol Real Estate (2017) was formed to develop land inside the airport boundary and is responsible for the Schiphol Central Business District which now contains more than 500 businesses and 65,000 employees working in offices, hotels, business centres, and catering facilities. Schiphol Area Development Company, a partnership involving airport operator Schiphol Group and nearby public jurisdictions, has sought to make the area around the airport an internationally competitive business district (Kasarda and Lindsay, 2011; Schiphol Area Development Company, 2017a). In 1994 the Amsterdam Airport Area association was formed as a partnership of public and private organisations involved in the development of business locations in the Amsterdam Metropolitan Area. With specific expertise in aerospace and logistics, its aim is to attract and facilitate international companies to locate in the Amsterdam area (Schiphol Area Development Company, 2017b).

The largest integrated development near Schiphol is Zuidas, a 27 km^2 international business district and multi-functional centre for living, working and recreation. Zuidas, meaning 'south axis' in Dutch, is located 10 km south of central Amsterdam along the A10 ring highway, and only 6 km from Schiphol Airport. Since central Amsterdam has building height and other restrictions, new large developments must locate in areas outside the centre, and Zuidas has become one of the city's main business districts due to its proximity to both the centre and the airport. Its location between central Amsterdam and Schiphol has created an opportunity for an 'airport corridor' pattern of development (Schaafsma, 2015; Schaafsma et al., 2008). It features numerous office buildings (including the World Trade Centre Amsterdam), restaurants, residential units, VU Amsterdam university and medical centre, and the RAI international conference and exhibition centre (City Film TV, 2012). Roughly 39,000 people find employment in approximately 700 large and small businesses, especially banks and financial institutions, legal services, and other business services (Zuidas Amsterdam Development Office, 2017). Multinational firms, including Google, Philips, TMF Group, AkzoNobel, ABM/AMRO, and ING have headquarters or major regional offices there.

Whilst it is clear that Zuidas has been successful in attracting business, residential, commercial, educational, and other activities, it is nevertheless subject to the same concerns raised for large-scale urban development projects in general. As part of a book exploring Zuidas, Swyngedouw (2005) reflected upon the experiences of other large-scale urban development projects (UDPs) in Europe that share many common features.[2] He notes that new UDPs have emerged in Amsterdam and other European cities as a result of new economic policies that favour free trade, deregulation, and privatisation, as well as new urban policies featuring entrepreneurialism, elite coalitions, growth machines, and public–private partnerships. As a result, urban regeneration is increasingly framed in a common language of competitiveness, flexibility, efficiency, state entrepreneurship, strategic partnerships, and collaborative advantage. Swyngedouw (2005) also makes the following observations about many of the new UDPs:

1. Despite the emphasis on private entrepreneurial development, new UDPs are usually state-led and largely state-financed.
2. One of the key objectives is to increase rents for urban land by closing existing 'rent gaps' through major public infrastructure development. Private investors and landholders stand to benefit greatly from the public investment.

[2] Amongst the projects analysed were London's South Bank, Rotterdam's Kop van Zuid, Berlin's Adlershof-City of Science, Brussels' Espace Leopold-European Union District, Lisbon's Expo 1998, Copenhagen's Orestaden, Vienna's Donau City, Dublin's Docklands-International Financial Services Centre, Athens' Olympic Village, Bilbao's Abandoibarra, Birmingham's Central Business District, Naples' Centro Direzionale, and Lille's Euralille (Swyngedouw, 2005).

3. The new UDPs are characterised by the formation of new planning and development institutions and organisations. In the process, formal government structures are subordinated to these new institutions and public participation is stilted. The new project is prioritised over other objectives and becomes an extraordinary and transcendent initiative.
4. There have rarely been significant 'grass-roots' contestations of large UDPs. A veil of secrecy, typical of public-private partnerships, tends to preempt criticism.
5. UDPs target places rather than people. There is very little, if any, concern with social equity objectives.
6. By targeting places, UDPs reinforce the city as a 'patchwork' where islands of elite activity are created amidst a sea of mixed neighbourhoods, contributing to greater polarisation. Global elites in UDPs, some in gated communities, live a separate existence within a 'splintered urban' environment (Graham and Marvin, 2001).

Since aerotropolis developments can be considered a subset of large urban development projects, many of these observations are applicable. In an article about the Ørestad new town development in Copenhagen, Olsson and Loerakker (2013) mentioned that "the critiques of Amsterdam Zuidas show similarities to those of Ørestad: being a very large-scale development, with a strong *business* orientation and a particular focus on *infrastructural* requirements – factors that involve large public investments and factors that raise the urge for high profits. As a consequence, negative pressure is put on the urban quality".

16.5.4 Analysis of Actors in the Case Studies

In each of the three aerotropolis case studies discussed before, the state played a leading, if not determinative, role in the development projects. In the case of New Songdo City, the South Korean government was intent on creating a new financial and creative hub near Seoul Incheon Airport that would be attractive to foreign investment. They brought in private real estate, architectural, and construction firms to design, build, and market New Songdo City, but the impetus for and control of the project remained with the national government, with little, if any, local government involvement. In Dubai, the ruling Al-Maktoum family is spearheading an ambitious international development strategy of massive infrastructure investment, emphasising airline and airport expansion. This is clearly operated by and for the national state, with private partners brought in as supplementary players, and no local government role. In Amsterdam, whilst the national government initiated the mainport strategy that included plans to develop Schiphol Airport and the area around it, a coalition of national ministries, local governments, the major private airline (KLM), and airport development groups collaborated to create and implement specific plans. There was more local government involvement in Amsterdam than in either Seoul or Dubai, but the national government and private sector played definitive roles. Criticisms of recent urban development projects raised by Swyngedouw (2005) are applicable to all three of the aerotropolis case studies.

In each of these cases, the aerotropolis concept was used either explicitly or implicitly by the actors to support and sell the project to potential investors. Whilst not going so far to claim that these developments were creating a new urban form with airports at the centre, they each relied on proximity to the airport and the international accessibility afforded by it to market their development potential. In this sense, these three development initiatives, whilst larger in scale and scope than previous airport-related developments, are still more evolutionary than revolutionary.

16.6 CONCLUSIONS

The airport has become more of an attraction over time due to its expanded role beyond a simple aviation facility to incorporate commercial and other service functions. Airport privatisation has accompanied increasing commercialisation to generate larger nonaeronautical revenues by catering to the retail and other service needs of travellers, employees, and visitors to the airport. The growth of global tourism has led to an expansion of airport functionality to encompass more goods and services specifically targeted to tourists. Not only have airports themselves become a greater attraction over time, but land areas surrounding airports have also emerged as sites of increased development. As the scale and importance of air transport has grown over time, its economic development impacts have also grown, which has led to greater land use development around airports and wider catalytic effects throughout urban regions that are served by the airport. Land use change around airports has proceeded through a series of stages, starting with limited low-density development evolving into more specialised and diversified land uses in later stages.

Most recently, much attention has been focused on the airport city and the aerotropolis concept, as perhaps the next stage of development for airports and their surrounding areas. Popularised by John Kasarda, the aerotropolis concept envisions the airport as the centre of a new urban form and the growth engine for the next wave of economic development relying on high-speed, knowledge-intensive 'New Economy' activities. A number of cities around the world have used the aerotropolis or related airport-centric concepts and are developing new centres at or near their airports. Amongst the most well known are New Songdo City near Seoul Incheon Airport in South Korea, Dubai South near Al-Maktoum Airport in the United Arab Emirates, and Zuidas near Amsterdam Airport Schiphol in the Netherlands.

Whilst these and other aerotropolis-related projects are quite ambitious in their goals, their actual development thus far has not yet met expectations. Aerotropolis projects have been criticised for their remote locations, lack of vibrant activity, unsustainability, vulnerability, overstated claims, and for concerns that are typical of other large public–private urban development projects regarding their social, economic, and political implications. In an age of urban entrepreneurialism and competition, many city and state leaders, economic development officials, and real estate agents have become enamoured with the aerotropolis concept in much the same way as they have latched onto other schemes such as: (1) building major sports facilities to attract mega sporting events (e.g. the Olympic Games), (2) using state policies and incentives to attract large corporate headquarters and/or production facilities, and (3) developing projects intended to attract members of the 'creative class'. The aerotropolis fixation can be viewed as yet another 'next big thing' that state, city, and economic development interests are desperate to discover to generate investment excitement. The aerotropolis concept has been hyped to a great extent, and actors in the urban growth machine have been very willing and eager accomplices.

That said, it is important to recognise that the attraction of airports and nearby urban development is more of an evolutionary, rather than revolutionary, process. The growth and importance of air transport over time has led to increasing economic activity at and near airports. Certain economic activities, especially logistics, light manufacturing, producer services, and other specialised businesses catering to travellers will find locations near airports to be most advantageous. Airports and the areas around them will continue to be important centres of activity within metropolitan regions. However, they will be one of many centres of activity, in addition to traditional central business districts, historic districts, suburban downtowns, cultural centres, and other areas of economic and social importance. If air transport and airports can successfully address their principal sustainability impediments, the outlook for future airport-related development will be much more robust.

References

Aerotropolis Business Concepts LLC, 2017. Available at http://www.aerotropolis.com/. (Accessed November 12, 2017).

Airports Council International [ACI], 2017. Annual Airport Traffic Statistics, 2016. Airports Council International, Geneva.

Al-Kaabi, K., 2015. The air transport system of United Arab Emirates during the global financial crisis and Arab Spring. In: Conventz, S., Thierstein, A. (Eds.), Airports, Cities, and Regions. Routledge, London and New York, pp. 47–67.

Appold, S., Kasarda, J., 2013. The airport city phenomenon: evidence from large US airports. Urban Stud. 50, 1239–1259.

Arbes, R., Bethea, C., 2014. Songdo, South Korea: city of the future? Atl. Mag.. September 27. Available at https://www.theatlantic.com/international/archive/2014/09/songdo-south-korea-the-city-of-the-future/380849/. (Accessed November 2, 2017).

Barrett, P., 1987. Cities and their airports: policy formation, 1926–1952. J. Urban Hist. 14, 112–137.

Beyers, W., 2006. Producer services. In: Warf, B. (Ed.), Encyclopedia of Human Geography. Sage Publications, Thousand Oaks, CA. Available at http://du.idm.oclc.org/login?url=https://search.credoreference.com/content/entry/sagehg/producer_services/0?institutionId=1676. (Accessed May 26, 2018).

Black, W.R., 2010. Sustainable Transportation. The Guilford Press, New York.

Blanton, W., 2004. On the airfront. Planning 70, 34–36.

Borowiec, S., 2016. Skyscrapers? Check. Parks? Check. People? Still needed. Los Angeles Times. May 31, 2016. Available at http://www.latimes.com/world/asia/la-fg-korea-songdo-snap-story.html. (Accessed November 3, 2016).

Burghouwt, G., 2007. Flexible strategic planning: the case of Amsterdam Airport Schiphol. In: Burghouwt, G. (Ed.), Airline Network Development in Europe and its Implications for Airport Planning. Ashgate, Aldershot, pp. 209–254.

Burghouwt, G., Dobruszkes, F., 2014. The (mis)fortunes of exceeding a small local air market: Comparing Amsterdam and Brussels. Tijdschr. Econ. Soc. Geogr. 105 (5), 604–621.

Campbell, S., 2005. Metropolis from scratch: South Korea's New Songdo City. The Next American City vol. 8, 9–11.

Charles, M.B., Barnes, P., Ryan, N., Clayton, J., 2007. Airport futures: towards a critique of the aerotropolis model. Futures 39, 1009–1028.

Cidell, J., 2015. The role of major infrastructure in subregional economic development: an empirical study of airports and cities. J. Econ. Geogr. 15, 1125–1144.

Cidell, J., Adams, J., 2001. The Groundside Effects of Air Transportation. Center for Transportation Studies, Minneapolis, MN.

City Film TV (2012). Amsterdam District Zuidas. Available at https://www.youtube.com/watch?v=r4owgtHmJ8I (Accessed November 11, 2017).

Conway, M.K., 1993. Airport Cities 21: The New Global Transport Centers of the 21st Century. Conway Data Inc, Atlanta.

de Neufville, R., Odoni, A.R., 2003. Airport Systems: Planning, Design, and Management. McGraw Hill, New York.

Derudder, B., Witlox, F., 2014. Global cities and air transport. In: Goetz, A.R., Budd, L. (Eds.), The Geographies of Air Transport. Ashgate, Aldershot, pp. 103–123.

Derudder, B., Bassens, D., Witlox, F., 2013. Political-geographic interpretations of massive air transport developments in Gulf cities. Polit. Geogr. 36, A4–A7.

Dubai Airports, 2017a. Available at http://www.dubaiairports.ae/corporate/about-us/dubai-international-(dxb. (Accessed November 7, 2017).

Dubai Airports, 2017b. http://www.dubaiairports.ae/corporate/about-us/dwc-dubai-world-central. (Accessed November 8, 2017).

Dubai South (2017). https://www.dubaisouth.ae/en/About-Us/MasterPlan. https://www.dubaisouth.ae/en/About-Us/Our-Story (Accessed November 6, 2017).

Freestone, R., Baker, D., 2011. Spatial planning models of airport-driven urban development. J. Plan. Lit. 26 (3), 263–279.

Frethy, P., 2004. The changing airport environment: past, present and future imperfect? In: Lumsdon, L., Page, S. (Eds.), Tourism and Transport: Issues and Agenda for the New Millenium. Routledge, London and New York, pp. 105–116.

Goetz, A.R., 2015. The expansion of large international hub airports. In: Hickman, R., Givoni, M., Bonilla, D., Banister, D. (Eds.), Handbook on Transport and Development. Edward Elgar, Cheltenham.

Graham, A., Ison, S., 2014. The role of airports in air transport. In: Goetz, A.R., Budd, L. (Eds.), The Geographies of Air Transport. Ashgate, Aldershot, pp. 81–101.

Graham, S., Marvin, S., 2001. Splintering Urbanism: Networked Infrastructures, Technological Mobilities and the Urban Condition. Routledge, London.

Guller, M., Guller, M., 2003. From Airport to Airport City. Editorial Gustavo Gill, Barcelona.

Hudnut, W.H., 2003. Half Way From Everywhere: A Portrait of America's First Tier Suburbs. Brookings Institution, Washington, DC.

Incheon International Airport Corporation (2016). Annual Report 2016. Available at https://www.kdevelopedia.org/Resources/territorial-development/incheon-international-airport-corporation-annual-report-2016--04201702200147213.do?fldIds=TP_TER%7CTP_TER_TR#.WqBdZiPwa70 (Accessed March 7, 2018).

James, Ian (2016). Songdo: no man's city. Korea Expose, October 14. Available at https://koreaexpose.com/songdo-no-mans-city/ (Accessed November 3, 2017).

Jankovec, O., 2016. The Ownership of Europe's Airports. Airports Council International, Europe. March 2016.

Karsner, D., 1997. Aviation and airports: the impact on the economic and geographic structure of American cities, 1940s-1980s. J. Urban Hist. 23, 406–436.

Kasarda, J.D., 2004. Asia's emerging airport cities. Urban Land Asia, 18–21. December.

Kasarda, J.D., Lindsay, G., 2011. Aerotropolis: The Way We'll Live Next. Farrar, Straus and Giroux, New York.

Kim, C., 2010. Place promotion and symbolic characterization of New Songdo City, South Korea. Cities 27, 13–19.

Legnani, M., 2016. Dubai World Central: poised to become the world's largest in a region where luxury is the norm. Airways Magazine. May 4. Available at https://airwaysmag.com/best-of-airways/dubai-world-central/. (Accessed November 4, 2017).

Leinbach, T.R., 2004. City interactions: the dynamics of passenger and freight flows. In: Hanson, S., Giuliano, G. (Eds.), The Geography of Urban Transportation, third ed. The Guilford Press, New York, pp. 30–58.

LookUp.ae (2017). A guide to investing in Dubai South. March 13. Available at https://lookup.ae/article/32/a-guide-to-investing-in-dubai-south (Accessed November 7, 2017).

Mesmer, Philippe (2017). Songdo, ghetto for the affluent. Le Monde, May 29. Available at http://www.lemonde.fr/smart-cities/article/2017/05/29/songdo-ghetto-for-the-affluent_5135650_4811534.html (Accessed November 3, 2017).

Olsson, Lea and Loerakker, Jan (2013). The story behind failure: Copenhagen's business district Orestad. Failed architecture: researching urban failure, September 12. Available at https://www.failedarchitecture.com/the-story-behind-the-failure-copenhagens-business-district-orestad/ (Accessed November 9, 2017).

Palling, C., Hooper, P., Thomas, C., 2014. The sustainability of air transport. In: Goetz, A.R., Budd, L. (Eds.), The Geographies of Air Transport. Ashgate, Farnham, pp. 125–140.

Perry, Linda (2013). The emergence of the airport city in the United States. Focus, LeighFisher (consulting), October. Available at http://www.leighfisher.com/sites/default/files/free_files/focus_-_the_emergence_of_the_airport_city_in_the_united_states_-_oct_2013.pdf (Accessed November 12, 2017).

Poole, Jr., Robert W. (2016). Annual Privatization Report 2016: air transportation. Reason Foundation, August.

Schaafsma, M., 2015. Amsterdam Mainport and metropolitan region. In: Conventz, S., Thierstein, A. (Eds.), Airports, Cities, and Regions. Routledge, London and New York, pp. 68–85.

Schaafsma, M., Amkreutz, J., Guller, M., 2008. Airport and city. In: Airport Corridors: Drivers of Economic Development. Schiphol Real Estate, Amsterdam.

Schiller, P., Kenworthy, J., 2018. An Introduction to Sustainable Transportation: Planning, Policy and Implementation, second ed. Routledge, London and New York.

Schiphol Area Development Company, 2017a. Available at https://www.sadc.nl/en/about-sadc/. (Accessed November 9, 2017).

Schiphol Area Development Company, 2017b. Available at https://www.sadc.nl/en/about-sadc/partner-projects/amsterdam-airport-area-aaa/. (Accessed November 9, 2017).

Schiphol Group (2017). Annual Report 2016. Available at http://www.annualreportschiphol.com/about-us (Accessed March 7, 2018).

Schiphol Real Estate, 2017. Available at https://www.schipholcbd.com/#over. (Accessed November 9, 2017).

Schlaack, J., 2010. Defining the area: evaluating urban output and forms of interaction between airport and region. In: Knippenberger, U., Wall, A. (Eds.), Airports in Cities and Regions: Research and Practise. KIT Scientific Publishing, Karlsruhe, pp. 113–126.

Shapiro, Ari (2015). A South Korean city designed for the future takes on a life of its own. National Public Radio. October 1. Available at http://www.npr.org/sections/parallels/2015/10/01/444749534/a-south-korean-city-designed-for-the-future-takes-on-a-life-of-its-own (Accessed November 3, 2017).

Songdo International Business District, 2017. Available at http://songdoibd.com/about/. (Accessed November 2, 2017).

Swyngedouw, E., 2005. A New Urbanity? The ambiguous politics of large-scale urban development projects in European cities. In: Salet, W., Majoor, S. (Eds.), Amsterdam Zuidas: European Space. 010 Publishers, Rotterdam.

The National (2017). Dubai's Al Maktoum International Airport expansion delayed until 2018, May 17. Available at https://www.thenational.ae/business/dubai-s-al-maktoum-international-airport-expansion-delayed-until-2018-1.31543 (Accessed November 6, 2017).

United States Department of Transportation Federal Aviation Administration (2006). Wildlife strikes to civil aircraft in the United States 1990–2005. Serial Report Number 12. Washington, DC. June 2006..

United States Government Accountability Office [GAO] (2014). Airport privatization: limited interest despite FAA's pilot program, GAO-15-42. Washington, DC, November.

Upham, P., Maughan, J., Raper, D., Thomas, C. (Eds.), 2003. Towards Sustainable Aviation. Earthscan, London.

Ward, S.A.D., Massey, R.A., Feldpauch, A.E., Puchacz, Z., Duerksen, C.J., Heller, E., Miller, N.P., Gardner, R.C., Gosling, G.D., Sarmiento, S., Lee, R.W., 2010. Enhancing airport land use compatibility, volume 1: land use fundamentals and implementation resources. In: Airport Cooperative Research Program Report 27, Transportation Research Board. National Academy of Sciences, Washington, DC.

Warrayat, Jinan (2017). Dubai Airport posts record passenger traffic in August. Bloomberg News, September 26. Available at https://www.bloomberg.com/news/articles/2017-09-26/dubai-airport-posts-record-passenger-traffic-in-august (Accessed November 8, 2017).

Williamson, L., 2013. Tomorrow's cities: just how smart is Songdo? BBC News. September 2, Available at http://www.bbc.com/news/technology-23757738. (Accessed November 3, 2017).

World Commission on Environment and Development, 1987. Our Common Future. Oxford University Press, Oxford.

Zuidas Amsterdam Development Office (2017). Available at https://www.amsterdam.nl/zuidas/english/working/(Accessed November 9, 2017).

CHAPTER

17

The Role of Niche Aviation Operations as Tourist Attractions

Isaac Levi HENDERSON, Wai Hong Kan TSUI

Massey University School of Aviation, Palmerston North, New Zealand

CHAPTER OUTLINE

17.1 INTRODUCTION

Hall (1999) suggests that there are four different roles of transport within tourism: (1) to link the source market with the destination; (2) to provide mobility within a destination area, region, or country; (3) to provide mobility and access within an actual tourism attraction; and (4) to facilitate travel along a recreational route that is in itself the tourist experience. Most publications that link aviation and tourism tend to outline the role of airlines and airports within the first two roles that Hall (1999) identifies (e.g. Costa et al., 2010; Davison and Ryley, 2010; Li, 2008); however, niche aviation operators do not entirely fit within this framework. Some niche aviation operations relate to the third role identified by Hall (1999); however, this chapter would contend that there is also a fifth role of air transport within tourism: to be the tourism attraction or experience itself. This chapter will first define tourist destinations, tourist products, and tourist experiences. It will also explore different types of niche aviation operations that relate to four key areas of tourism activities: (1) adventure tourism, (2) scenic tourism, (3) heritage tourism, and (4) space tourism.

17.1.1 Tourist Destinations Versus Tourist Products

It is important to understand the difference between a tourist destination and a tourist product. A tourist destination is a geographic location where a tourist product is consumed or experienced, whereas the tourism product

Air Transport—A Tourism Perspective. https://doi.org/10.1016/B978-0-12-812857-2.00017-8

is either an attraction or activity, an amenity, or accessibility to a destination or product (Collier, 2006). Attractions can be separated into one of four different categories: (1) natural attractions, (2) man-made attractions built for other purposes other than attracting tourists, (3) man-made attractions built to attract tourists, and (4) special events (Swarbrooke, 1995). Whilst niche aviation operations will often incorporate looking at attractions, they could be better classified as activities. Becken and Simmons (2002) separate tourist activities into the following categories: (1) air activities, such as scenic flights; (2) motorised water activity, such as diving or whale watching; (3) adventure recreation, such as kayaking or bungee jumping; and (4) nature recreation, such as cycling or golf. It should be noted, however, that some niche aviation operations may overlap across these activities. Accordingly, tourists will evaluate niche aviation operations in terms of their trip planning as this is what usually happens for tourist activities (Rao et al., 1992).

17.1.2 Tourist Experiences

Part of understanding the relationship between niche aviation operations and tourism is understanding what constitutes 'a memorable tourist experience'. Tung and Ritchie (2011, p. 1369) define a tourism experience as 'an individual's subjective evaluation and undergoing (i.e. affective, cognitive, and behavioural) of events related to his/her tourist activities which begins before (i.e. planning and preparation), during (i.e. at the destination), and after the trip (i.e. recollection)'. Using this definition, they conclude that the key role of tourism planning needs to be around the facilitation of tourists to develop their own memorable tourism experiences. To this end, it can be said that a memorable tourism experience cannot be created using a 'one-size-fits-all' approach. Kim et al. (2012) find 24 factors that create a memorable tourism experience and they separate these into seven key areas: (1) hedonism, (2) novelty, (3) local culture, (4) refreshment, (5) meaningfulness, (6) involvement, and (7) knowledge. Since the strength of each of these areas is subjectively assigned by each individual tourist, some experiences may be hedonistic to one tourist, and not hedonistic to another tourist. The key areas are also not mutually exclusive, in the sense that an experience can be both hedonistic and novel at the same time.

Other experiential aspects that contribute towards the perceived value of a tourist experience are (1) the authenticity of the interaction between the environment and the people-based experiences (Pearce and Moscardo, 1986); (2) social and emotional value (Colton, 1987); (3) the behaviour of other tourists (Graefe and Vaske, 1987); (4) intrinsic comparison with ideal, equitable, minimum, and expected standards (Vittersø et al., 2000); and (5) social and physical encounters, that is, interactions with the service provider, other consumers, and the servicescape (Prebensen and Foss, 2011).

The highly subjective and individualised nature of tourist experiences is the primary reason for the existence of certain niche aviation operations. Over the next few sections, different types of tourist experiences will be discussed, and examples of niche aviation operations will be provided to show how niche aviation operations contribute towards tourist experiences.

17.2 ADVENTURE TOURISM

Adventure activities are becoming increasingly popular in the tourism industry, with growth rates of roughly 15% per annum up until 2006 worldwide (Buckley, 2007). The appeal of adventure activities tends to lie in their emotional value to participants (Schlegelmilch and Ollenburg, 2013). For example, the desire to undertake adventure activities has been shown to be dependent on the desire to experience emotions such as rush, risk, fear, and thrill (Buckley, 2012; Schlegelmilch and Ollenburg, 2013). Rush, which is a function of flow and thrill, has been shown to be more important than risk, despite many adventure activities being risky in nature (Buckley, 2012). Flow can be broadly defined as an instance where mental focus coincides with physical activity so that one becomes intensely absorbed within that activity (Heo et al., 2010). Flow is closely related to skill, in that one must have enough skill to become intensely absorbed within an activity. Due to flow's subjective nature, it is not limited to adventure activities, but can also be experienced by musicians, professional athletes, and so on. Thrill, on the other hand, refers to a 'purely adrenalin-based physiological response' that is unrelated to the skill of the person performing the physical activity (Buckley, 2012, p. 963). Another study shows that intention to undertake adventure activities is related to satisfaction from previous adventure activity experiences, value for money of the adventure activity, and the emotional value to the person undertaking the adventure activity (Williams and Soutar, 2009). Interestingly, the novelty value of an adventure activity is not significantly related to intention to undertake an adventure activity.

17.2.1 Adventure Aviation

Adventure aviation encompasses a number of niche aviation operations that exist primarily to meet the needs of adventure tourists. The exact definition of what activities can be considered part of adventure aviation is not clear from the literature. In a study of the safety of adventure tourism in New Zealand, Bentley et al. (2001) include parasailing, hang gliding, skydiving, scenic flights, and helicopter flights within the category of aviation-related adventure tourism. The Civil Aviation Authority of New Zealand (CAANZ) provides some guidance from a legal point of view (New Zealand is the only country to treat adventure aviation operators under a different civil aviation rule part to other commercial air operators). According to CAANZ (2017a), "an adventure aviation operation involves carrying passengers for hire or reward, where the purpose of the operation is for the passenger's recreational experience of participating in the flight, or engaging in the aerial operation" (para. 1). Included as part of this are hot air balloon operations, parachute-drop aircraft operations, tandem parachute operations, glider operations, hang glider and paraglider operations, special category aircraft operations (e.g. aerobatics), and microlight aircraft operations (CAANZ, 2017a). In New Zealand, there are 29 certificated adventure aviation operators (CAANZ, 2017b), statistics from other countries cannot be obtained as they are not treated differently from other commercial air operators. These examples show that there are wide-ranging types of aviation operations that can be considered as 'adventure aviation'. It should also be noted that there is some overlap in that an adventure aviation operator can also provide scenic flights, heritage aviation experiences, and other novelty aviation experiences. Acknowledging that there is overlap between the areas of niche aviation operations, it is useful to look at some examples that relate to specific areas, whilst not ruling out that they may also relate to others.

17.2.2 Skydiving

A clear example of a niche aviation operation that caters to adventure tourists is skydiving. With regard to skydiving, there are different reasons why a tourist may engage in skydiving for the first time compared with tourists who regularly skydive. Celsi et al. (1993) identify that first-time skydivers are usually motivated by curiosity, thrill seeking, social compliance (i.e. are peer pressured into it by friends/family) and/or a desire for adventure. This contrasts with regular skydivers who may also be motivated by efficacy (i.e. wanting to develop their technical skill for intrinsic and extrinsic rewards), identity construction (i.e. providing a means of changing personal identity and become different from others), overcoming fear, and/or feeling a mixture of emotional and physical responses (Celsi et al., 1993; Lipscombe, 1999). Skydiving usually takes place at drop zones (DZs), which are typically small aerodromes with a runway, a few hangars, and an area for skydivers to land their parachutes (Laurendeau and Van Brunschot, 2006). The use of small aircraft as well as small and sometimes remote airfields distinguishes skydiving operations from other commercial aviation operations. Additionally, rather than passengers, skydivers can be thought of as participants, and only remain on the aircraft for takeoff as they return to the DZ by jumping out of the aircraft. Skydiving is a popular tourist activity across the world. For example, the United States Parachute Association (USPA) estimates that their members along with first time jumpers make around 3.2 million jumps per year across more than 220 of their affiliated DZs in the United States (USPA, 2017).

17.2.3 Adventure Destinations

Xie and Schneider (2004, p. 57) introduce the notion of adventure destinations as 'a bundle of tourism facilities and services composed of a number of multi-dimensional attributes'. New Zealand, for example, is often marketed as an adventure destination, with Queenstown being its adventure capital due to the large number of established and diversified adventure activities on offer (Cater, 2006; Cloke and Perkins, 1998; Schott, 2007). The Queenstown Lakes District Council (2017) says "The Queenstown Lakes District is a popular destination for visitors all from the world – whether you are an adventure seeker or just looking for somewhere to unwind, we've got something special for everyone". In addition, destination image and positioning both are affected by the presence of adventure activities in a destination (Baloglu and McCleary, 1999; Beerli and Martín, 2004; Pike and Ryan, 2004). Inevitably, for tourists to associate a destination with adventure, there needs to be a variety of adventure activities on offer. Adventure aviation operators, therefore, can be argued to contribute towards this variety and thus enhance a destination's image in terms of adventure (Page et al., 2006).

17.3 SCENIC TOURISM

Scenic tourism (also known as sightseeing) is one of the simpler types of tourism to understand and thus has not been studied in great detail in the literature (e.g. Denstadli and Jacobsen, 2011; Little, 2009; Nvíri, 2006). Nonetheless, it has been an important part of travel for at least the last few centuries (Adler, 1989; Little, 2009). Within the transport paradigm, Denstadli and Jacobsen (2011) investigate motivation for tourists to travel on two different scenic highways within Norway. The results of this study show that the three highest rated motives for tourists in this segment were beautiful views, interesting landscapes, and natural attractions. These were categorised into 'visual experiences' using a total factor analysis. This study shows that those who were categorised into being motivated primarily by visual experiences did not desire quick passage, but rather the opposite, slow travel. Dunn Ross and Iso-Aloha (1991) find that for bus sightseeing tours, the key determinants of satisfaction were knowledge (e.g. learning about location), escape (e.g. forgetting troubles and worries), tour pace (e.g. time to take pictures), social interaction (e.g. enjoy company of other tour members), social security (e.g. feeling safer in a group), and practical aspects (e.g. cleanliness of the vehicle). The requirement for scenic tourism or sightseeing to occur is that there is some form of 'scene' or 'sight' that provides some form of value for tourists in that they want 'to see it'. In this sense, there is no limitation on what this specific sight is. For example, scenery from movies has been recognised as a valuable source of movie-induced tourism (Riley et al., 1998; Riley and Van Doren, 1992).

17.3.1 Scenic Flights

In geographic locations that offer sufficient scenery, scenic flight operators are often present. For example, in New Zealand, 26.1% of first time tourists and 11.4% of repeat visitors undertook scenic flights, whereas 39.6% of first time visitors and 21.4% of repeat visitors undertook scenic boat cruises (Oppermann, 1997). Whilst these figures might be somewhat outdated, they still offer some insight to the importance of transport offerings that allow for effective sightseeing. Whilst some classify scenic flights as part of adventure aviation (e.g. Bentley et al., 2001), this chapter would argue that scenic flights are different in that the value of the experience is not derived from the activity as with adventure aviation, but rather through the value of the scenery or sights. This notion is somewhat supported by a study of Chinese tourists visiting the South Island of New Zealand who included activities such as kayaking or a scenic flight in photographs, not for the activity but for the value of the selected beautiful landscape (Sun et al., 2015). One of the important factors for being able to exploit the economic potential of scenery is accessibility, that is, actually being able to access the geographic location of the scenery (Crouch and Ritchie, 1999). To this end, aviation can provide the advantage of accessing scenery without needing infrastructure in the scenic location, provided that a runway or helipad is within reasonable proximity from the scenery.

CASE STUDY 17.1 EXAMPLES OF SCENIC FLIGHT OPERATORS

A good example of a scenic flight operation that takes advantage of movie-induced tourism is Heliworks Queenstown Helicopters, which offers Lord of the Rings tours in the South Island of New Zealand (see Heliworks Queenstown Helicopters, 2017). Alongside their more standard scenic flight packages, they also offer three specific Lord of the Rings packages: The 'Flight to the Ford' (45 min) package costing NZ$540 per person, 'The Great Forests' package (75 min) costing NZ$975 per person, and the 'Best of the Lord of the Rings Locations' package (3 h) costing NZ$2000 per person. All of these scenic flights are operated using helicopters, where their 'pilots have an intimate knowledge of the area and can transport you into Middle Earth'. Fictional place names from Lord of the Rings, such as Lothlorien, Khazad-dum, and Amon Hen feature alongside actual geographic locations for the tours.

In Switzerland, Scenic Air offers scenic flights around the Swiss Alps. As noted earlier, there is often overlap between the different categories of niche aviation operations. Whilst this operator primarily offers scenic flights in helicopters and small aircraft, they also offer experiences such as skydiving, landing on a glacier, and/or flying in a historic Swiss Air Force aircraft (see Skydivesswitzerland, 2017).

Papillon Grand Canyon Helicopters is the world's largest and oldest aerial sightseeing company, having been in continuous operation since 1965 (see Papillon, 2016). The company has a fleet of 48 aircraft (including helicopters and small fixed-wing aircraft), over 600 staff and carries an estimated 600,000 passengers annually. The tours focus on the natural beauty of the Grand Canyon and attractions in the surrounding area (such as Lake Mead and the Hoover Dam). The company operates out of five different airports and can also integrate aerial sightseeing tours with various land-based options.

Manhattan Helicopters is an operator that provides 'one-of-a-kind' helicopter tours of New York City (see Manhattan Helicopters, 2018). There are three standard packages offered by the company: (1) the 'Classic Manhattan Helicopter Tour' that lasts for between 12 and 15min, costing US$209 per person and featuring the must-see attractions (e.g. Statue of Liberty and Empire State Building); (2) the 'Deluxe Manhattan Helicopter Tour' that lasts for between 18 and 20min, costing US$289 per person and featuring Uptown Manhattan and The Bronx on top of the must-see attractions; and (3) the 'VIP Manhattan Helicopter Tour' that lasts for 30min, costing US$349 per person and featuring flight over Coney Island Beach and a panorama of the Palisades Mountains in addition to the must-see attractions. The company also offers several marriage proposal packages and charters.

17.4 HERITAGE TOURISM

Before going into more detail about heritage tourism, it is important to distinguish between two terms that are often used interchangeably in aviation: 'vintage' and 'heritage'. To the authors' best knowledge there is no definition in existing literature for these terms in relation to aviation. Given the lack of existing definitions, this chapter would suggest that 'vintage' refers to something of the past that is perceived as high quality, such as how the term is applied to wine; whereas 'heritage' is better applied to something that has been passed down from past generations, including both objects (aircraft) and customs (how they are used). In this sense, whilst the restoration of vintage aircraft may be an important factor in attracting tourists to visit museums or air shows, there is very little in the way of consistent operations.

On the contrary, commercial flights using either historic or modern aircraft to recreate historic aviation experiences are on offer around the world. However, historic aviation experiences have not been well addressed in the literature, meaning that a more generic discussion of heritage tourism is needed to understand this niche segment. Unfortunately, a lot of literature views heritage tourism attractions within the confines of physical attractions (e.g. Garrod and Fyall, 2000; Poria et al., 2003). However, heritage tourism has also been applied to the recreation or restaging of traditions in the modern day (e.g. Chhabra et al., 2003). There can be many different factors that can motivate a tourist towards a heritage attraction. For example, McCain and Ray (2003) use the term 'legacy tourists' to refer to those who engage in heritage tourism as a genealogical or ancestral endeavour. In the context of heritage aviation, some tourists have the desire to travel on a particular aircraft or to recreate a historic experience because they have a family connection to such activities (e.g. an ancestor that fought in World War I or worked for a historic airline). In other cases, movies that include historic images of areas, attractions, and activities have had positive effects on heritage tourism activities (e.g. Frost, 2006; Sargent, 1998).

Heritage aviation has not been widely studied in the literature (Deal et al., 2015; Historic England, 2016; Knott, 1997), perhaps because powered, controlled, and sustained flight was only achieved in the early 1900s, meaning that aviation is a relatively new phenomenon compared to other heritage tourist activities. However, now is a suitable time to be discussing the importance of heritage aviation. Aircraft and associated aviation operations played pivotal roles in all major conflicts of the 20th century as well as facilitating globalisation, international trade, and the modern tourism industry. As these events come to be further and further in the past, there is an imperative to preserve this rich heritage and this is what heritage aviation operations seek to do. A niche segment of tourists who place subjective value on aviation heritage, whatever the reason, sustain such operations.

17.4.1 Heritage Aviation Operations

With most heritage tourism activities, the issue of authenticity is a major concern (Chhabra et al., 2003; Halewood and Hannam, 2001). Whilst not empirically validated, the same concept is likely to apply to heritage aviation. In practice, there are two types of heritage aviation operations: (1) those that use a modern aircraft but recreate a historic experience; and (2) those that use a historic aircraft to recreate a historic experience. In this sense, the authenticity of the experience either comes from the authenticity of the aircraft, the authenticity of the onboard experience, or a combination of the two. To offer a better understanding of heritage aviation operations, two examples of heritage aviation operators are provided along with an explanation as to their historical significance.

CASE STUDY 17.2 EXAMPLES OF HERITAGE AVIATION OPERATIONS

The Zeppelin Experience

In 1900 Count Ferdinand Adolph Heinrich von Zeppelin launched his creation, the Luftschiff Zeppelin 1 (LZ 1) for the first time over Lake Constance, near Friedrichshafen in Germany. The flight lasted 18min and covered over 5km. This was the world's first controlled, powered, and sustained lighter-than-air flight, with the Wright Brothers being the first to achieve the same with heavier-than-air flight three years later. Zeppelin went through several other renditions of his technology and in order to demonstrate the soundness of his concept, he started the German Airship Transportation Company (German acronym: DELAG) in 1908 (Stephenson, 2010). This became the world's first airline, carrying over 34,000 passengers across 1500 flights without injury between the company's inauguration and the outbreak of World War I (Grossman, 2009). Passengers flew in luxury with food and drinks being served onboard as they looked out at the scenery of Germany. Following World War I, airships in the form of the Graf Zeppelin and the Hindenburg cruised between continents until the Hindenburg Disaster of 1937 effectively ended the airship era.

In 1993, in Friedrichshafen, Germany the Zeppelin company was reborn in the form of the ZLT Zeppelin Luftschifftechnik. The company began manufacturing airships under the Zeppelin name, producing the Zeppelin NT (where NT stands for new technology). In 2001 the company began scheduled passenger flights (see Zeppelin NT, 2017). Since then, the company has carried more than 130,000 passengers on its flights, carrying 20,100 passengers in 2016. The flights using the new airship seek to replicate the original 'Zeppelin experience' of quiet and gentle scenic flights, usually of short duration (30–120 min). The company bases itself out of one of the original Zeppelin hangars in Friedrichshafen, where the historic company was headquartered. Technologically speaking, the Zeppelin NT (Fig. 17.1) is far superior to the historic airships used in the time of DELAG. Despite using a modern airship, the company claims to operate in the spirit of Zeppelin's legacy. Adult fares range from €245 (30-min flight) through to €825 (120-min flight), with 2- to 12-year-olds getting 20% off adult fares. Flights are not on offer year-round, but can only be purchased for dates during the operation's 'flight season' (this does not mean that bookings cannot be made in the off season). For example, 'Flight Season 2018' will go from the 9th of March through until mid-November.

FLY DC3

FLY DC3 is a company in New Zealand that offers scenic and charter flights in a restored Douglas DC-3 (see FLY DC3, 2017). DC-3s were one of the most significant transport aircraft ever made, revolutionising air transport in the 1930s and 1940s. Whilst not repeated here for the sake of brevity, FLY DC3 can tell the entire story of their aircraft's service from its delivery to the United States Army Air Force in 1944 through to its extensive rebuild and restoration in New Zealand (Fig. 17.2). The company offers half hour scenic flights around Auckland, providing tourists with the opportunity to be a passenger in one of the world's most revolutionary aircraft. Fares range from NZ$80 (for children), through to NZ$120 (for adults) and the aircraft can also be chartered for longer flights. The operation is based out of Ardmore Airport in Auckland, which is primarily used for general aviation activities. Flights can be booked from 12 months to 2 days ahead by calling or using the operator's website.

FIG. 17.1 A Zeppelin NT shortly after take-off in Friedrichshafen, Germany. *(© Dietrich Krieger/CC-BY-SA-3.0.)*

FIG. 17.2 FLY DC3's Douglas DC-3 aircraft on a scenic flight. (*© Gavin Conroy. Photo supplied by FLY DC3.*)

17.5 SPACE TOURISM

Space tourism is another niche segment of the aviation industry that seeks to give tourists the ability to become astronauts and experience space travel for recreational, leisure, or business purposes. Since space tourism is extremely expensive, it is a case of a very small segment of consumers that are able and willing to purchase a space experience. There are several options for space tourists. For example, Crouch et al. (2009) investigate the choice behaviour between four types of space tourism: high altitude jet fighter flights, atmospheric zero-gravity flights, short-duration suborbital flights, and longer duration orbital trips into space. Reddy et al. (2012) find the following motivational factors behind space tourism (in order of importance): vision of earth from space, weightlessness, high speed experience, unusual experience, and scientific contribution. Currently, only high-altitude jet fighter flights and atmospheric zero-gravity flights are commercially available to tourists in the space tourism sector. Accordingly, this section provides an example of each, whilst the potential for suborbital and longer duration orbital trips into space are discussed later in this chapter.

CASE STUDY 17.3 EXAMPLES OF SPACE TOURISM

MiG-29 Edge of Space Flight

One current option for space tourists is to be taken up into the stratosphere in a supersonic fighter jet (see MiGFlug, 2017a). MiGFlug acts as a sales agent for this unique space tourism activity, which usually involves reaching an altitude of 20–22 km. At such an altitude, the curvature of the earth can be seen, the sky is dark, and it is possible to see into space. As part of this space travel experience, tourists are also given an opportunity to control the aircraft and there are a number of aerobatic manoeuvres that are performed by an experienced pilot. This operation is based out of Russia. The Mikoyan MiG-29 Fulcrum is a Russian military fighter jet that allows for rates of climb of 330 m/s and a top speed of Mach 2.25 (2390 km/h). MiGFlug sells three different services in this aircraft. For €12,500 a passenger can enjoy a 25-min flight featuring a number of aerobatic manoeuvres but without supersonic flight. For €14,500 a passenger can enjoy a 45-min flight that includes higher aerobatics and supersonic flight. The 'Edge of Space' flight includes aerobatics, supersonic flight, and the experience of being taken up into the stratosphere and is sold for €17,500.

The Weightless Experience

The Zero Gravity Corporation offers zero gravity experiences in the United States (see Zero Gravity Corporation, 2017). This unique tourism activity involves using a specially modified Boeing 727 where trained pilots perform aerobatic manoeuvres known as parabolas. The company promises to provide an opportunity for 'true weightlessness' without going to space. MiGFlug also acts as a sales agent for a similar experience on an Ilyushin IL-76 MDK aircraft in Russia (see MiGFlug, 2017b). In both instances, the aircraft are modified with padded cabins to prevent injuries during weightless flights.

The Zero Gravity Corporation sells its ZERO-G Experience®, which includes 15 parabolic manoeuvres that each provides roughly 20–30 s of weightlessness for US$4950 + 5% in tax. This package also includes ZERO-G merchandise, pre and post flight catering, photos, videos, and a certificate of weightless completion. The corporation also offers a nonflyer package for those who only want to participate in the pre and post flight activities, selling for US$195.

MiGFlug offers a package that includes more than just the weightless experience. The day before the flight, passengers undergo a medical checkup at the Yuri Gagarin Cosmonaut Training Centre. Passengers will also receive a guided tour of Star City, which includes viewing the world's largest centrifuge, the Hydrolab (where cosmonauts train to move in space suits) and a 1:1 scale replica of the Mir space station (operated by the Soviet Union and then Russia between 1986 and 2001). On the day of the flight, a bus takes passengers along with a crew of cosmonauts, pilots, and physicians across the Chkalovsky airfield to the IL-76 MDK, where the weightless experience takes place. MiGFlug sells this package for €4900 for a single person, or the whole aircraft can be booked for €49,000, allowing for a group of up to 12 people.

17.6 THE IMPORTANCE OF NOVELTY

Novelty-seeking behaviour is a well-documented human behaviour. Hirschman (1980) shows that there is a link between novelty seeking and purchasing innovative products. Berlyne (1970) also shows that novelty increases the pleasantness and interestingness of coloured shapes during an experiment using verbally expressed preference. Novelty seeking has also been used as a construct within tourism. Lee and Crompton (1992) define six dimensions of novelty for a tourist: (1) change from routine, (2) escape, (3) thrill, (4) adventure, (5) surprise, and (6) boredom alleviation. Novelty seeking has been shown to be a significant antecedent of mid-term and long-term revisit intentions with regard to tourist destinations (Jang and Feng, 2007). One difficulty with novelty seeking, however, is that different segments of people appear to seek novelty in different ways (Chang et al., 2006; Snepenger, 1987). This makes it difficult in practical terms to make a tourist experience novel in such a way that its novelty will appeal to most tourists. In this sense, novelty-seeking behaviour depends upon the subjective situations of tourists.

17.6.1 Novelty in Aviation Experiences

Due to the inherent subjectivity of the term 'novel', this term can be applied to the examples already covered in this chapter. The area of the novelty can vary markedly depending on the specific niche aviation operations. According to Kim et al. (2012), novelty consists of the four key scale items with regard to a memorable experience: (1) once-in-a-lifetime experience, (2) unique, (3) different from other experiences, and (4) get to experience something new. This helps narrow down the sorts of activities that tourists might describe as novel. For example, one might skydive because they see it as an once-in-a-lifetime experience, or perhaps want to fly in a hot air balloon because they see this as unique. No specific example is provided here because niche aviation operations provide novel experiences to tourists by their very nature. This chapter would argue that the aspects that make a niche aviation operator successful or not is whether enough tourists see the value in the type of novelty that is on offer. This lack of standardisation amongst niche aviation operators is one of the features that differentiates them from commercial airlines and the types of aviation operators that are more commonly addressed in relation to tourism.

17.7 INNOVATION IN NICHE AVIATION OPERATIONS

Thus far, this chapter has covered four different types of tourism and explained how niche aviation operations can help tourists form memorable experiences within each type. One issue is clear: there has been minimal empirical research that investigates the role of niche aviation operators or the idea that the novel air transport can be a tourist attraction in itself. As a consequence, there is potential for innovation in these areas in order to better meet the needs of tourists who seek unique and memorable experiences. The next few sections outline some potential sources of innovation for niche aviation operations, which in turn may be areas for future research with regard to the role of aviation within tourism.

17.7.1 Applying Existing Technologies in New Ways

One idea in this regard is to provide scenic airship services. Airships are a technology that was once very popular around the world. Airships are quiet, environmentally friendly, can be designed in almost any way, and have some safety advantages over more conventional aircraft (Pant, 2010). Whilst their slow flying speeds rule them out of performing the role of conventional airliners, slow flying speeds are not considered as a disadvantage for scenic flights and the novelty aspect of scenic airship services could be significant. Due to their long endurance, airship cruises for tourists are also a possibility and this would also hold some heritage value in that this was the purpose of historic airships such as the Hindenburg.

In recent times, Hybrid Air Vehicles (HAV) have been showing their Airlander 10 model, which is an example of a hybrid airship. Unlike conventional airships that use only buoyant lift to achieve flight, hybrid airships also produce direct lift with their pivoting engines and dynamic lift due to being in the shape of an aerofoil. This allows for higher flying speeds, whilst maintaining the quietness and efficiency of lighter-than-air aircraft. The Airlander 10 has primarily been proposed to be used for cargo operations, but there is no reason why a passenger-carrying version could not be developed. As discussed earlier, the Zeppelin NT is an existing airship model that could also be used for smaller scale operations. It will be interesting to see whether airships might be reintroduced to passenger operations (e.g. scenic flights and cruises) as tourism grapples with issues of environmental sustainability and innovation. Henderson et al. (2018) provides a case study of how innovations like scenic airship services can generate significant consumer interest. The technology is there, but further research is needed to see how to best apply it within the tourism industry.

17.7.2 Applying New Technologies to Niche Aviation Operations

The introduction of new technologies always presents opportunities. There are three transport technologies that have the potential to innovate niche aviation operations. Notably, these are Remotely Piloted Aircraft Systems (RPAS), which are often referred to as drones, spaceliners, which are aircraft that can be used on scheduled space flights (similar to the term of airliners) and supersonic airliners. RPAS have been applied to flight operations that were once performed by more conventional aircraft, such as aerial mapping, agricultural spraying, search and rescue, and so on. The next big step in this technology could potentially be the introduction of passenger-carrying RPAS, known more commonly as passenger drones. Nominally, the introduction of these in the form of Uber-like taxis has been suggested in Dubai. However, due to the novelty of being flown in a drone, it is possible that these services could also provide short-duration scenic flights.

In addition, spaceliners are likely to be applied to niche aviation operations (i.e. space travel) and will soon become a reality. Virgin Galactic (a subsidiary company of the Virgin Group) is about to bring tourists into space commercially. Space tourists may experience unique or once-in-a-lifetime suborbital spaceflight travel and explore the universe. There are roughly 700 Virgin Galactic future astronauts who have already paid deposits for their flights on SpaceShip Two—the suborbital spacecraft that is air launched from beneath a carrier airplane (see Virgin Galactic, 2017).

Supersonic experiences could potentially make a comeback as the notion of new supersonic airliners is being raised. In the past, Air France, British Airways, and Aeroflot have offered flights on supersonic airliners (Concorde and Tupolev Tu-144, respectively), with the last commercial airline flight on a supersonic aircraft taking place in 2003. Boom Technology is working on a new supersonic airliner, capable of reaching Mach 2.2, but remaining affordable enough for routine air travel (see Boomsupersonic, 2017a). They are currently building a prototype aircraft called the XB-1 that will be one-third the size of their anticipated passenger airliner and is hoped to fly in 2018. Both Japan Airlines and Virgin Group have invested in Boom. On 5 December 2017, Japan Airlines made an investment of US$10million for an option to purchase up to 20 Boom aircraft through a preorder arrangement. It is understood from their joint press release that Japan Airlines is also working with boom to refine the design of the aircraft and define the passenger experience (see Boomsupersonic, 2017b).

17.7.3 Relating Niche Aviation Operations to the Destination

The notion of adventure destinations was discussed earlier, with the example of Queenstown, New Zealand. However, unique activities that take place at a destination inevitably will affect the destination's brand. In order to brand a destination, the marketer for a destination needs to emphasise the features and activities of a destination that differentiate it from others (Qu et al., 2011). Niche aviation operations can form part of this differentiation. For example, hot air ballooning has been identified as an important tourist activity that affects tourist associations with Turkey

(Tasci et al., 2007) and Central Florida (Milman and Pizam, 1995). Even small and rural areas can be associated with niche aviation operations. For example, the ideal geographical and meteorological conditions in Linhares da Beira, Portugal make it ideal for paragliding (Costa and Chalip, 2005). There is also a relationship between a destination and whether certain types of niche aviation operations would be successful. The most obvious case in point is scenic tourism. For a scenic tourism offering to be successful, there must be scenery in or around a destination that provides a memorable visual experience that tourists are willing to pay for. These interrelationships between niche aviation operations and a destination's brand are less researched and will be an interesting area for future research.

17.8 CONCLUSIONS

This chapter has highlighted the important relationship between tourism and niche aviation operations. Four key areas of unique tourism activity served by niche aviation operations are discussed and examples related to each type of tourism activity are provided. They include adventure tourism, scenic tourism, heritage tourism, and space tourism. Adventure tourism and scenic tourism (or sightseeing) are becoming increasingly popular in the tourism industry worldwide, offering tourists with adventure activity experiences (e.g. skydiving) as well as the ability to view natural scenery (e.g. scenic flight services). In addition, niche aviation operators help to promote and offer exceptional heritage tourism experiences to tourists through the use of historic aircraft (e.g. FLY DC3) or the recreation of historical aviation experiences (e.g. Zeppelin NT). Space tourism is a new segment of future tourism activity that offers tourists the once-in-a-lifetime experience of becoming astronauts, experiencing space travel, and suborbital spaceflight (e.g. Virgin Galactic). Importantly, these four unique and novel tourism activities are perceived to offer memorable tourist experiences to tourists, and the innovation within niche aviation operations is indeed going to help create and bring remarkable tourist experiences into reality in the near future. Overall, it is clear that niche aviation operations play a vital role in growing and promoting the tourism industry by creating and bringing unique, memorable, once-in-a-lifetime tourist experiences for tourists who are able and willing to pay for such services.

References

Adler, J., 1989. Origins of sightseeing. Ann. Tour. Res. 16 (1), 7–29.

Baloglu, S., McCleary, K.W., 1999. A model of destination image formation. Ann. Tour. Res. 26 (4), 868–897.

Becken, S., Simmons, D.G., 2002. Understanding energy consumption patterns of tourist attractions and activities in New Zealand. Tour. Manag. 23 (4), 343–354.

Beerli, A., Martín, J.D., 2004. Factors influending destination image. Ann. Tour. Res. 31 (3), 657–681.

Bentley, T., Page, S., Meyer, D., Chalmers, D., Laird, I., 2001. How safe is adventure tourism in New Zealand? An exploratory analysis. Appl. Ergon. 32 (4), 327–338.

Berlyne, D.E., 1970. Novelty, complexity, and hedonic value. Percept. Psychophys. 8 (5), 279–286.

Boomsupersonic (2017a). Boom, the future is supersonic. Available at https://boomsupersonic.com (Accessed January 18, 2018).

Boomsupersonic (2017b) Japan Airlines, & Boom. Japan Airlines and Boom announce partnership for supersonic air travel. Available from https://boomsupersonic.com/jal-press-release/ (Accessed January 18, 2018).

Buckley, R., 2007. Adventure tourism products: price, duration, size, skill, remoteness. Tour. Manag. 28 (6), 1428–1433.

Buckley, R., 2012. Rush as a key motivation in skilled adventure tourism: resolving the risk recreation paradox. Tour. Manag. 33 (4), 961–970.

CAANZ (2017a) Adventure aviation (Part 115). Available at https://www.caa.govt.nz/sport-and-rec/part-115-info/ (Accessed September 28, 2017).

CAANZ (2017b) Organisation statistics. Available at https://www.caa.govt.nz/script/orgstats/ (Accessed September 28, 2017).

Cater, C.I., 2006. Playing with risk? Participant perceptions of risk and management implications in adventure tourism. Tour. Manag. 27 (2), 317–325.

Celsi, R.L., Rose, R.L., Leigh, T.W., 1993. An exploration of high-risk leisure consumption through skydiving. J. Consum. Res. 20 (1), 1–23.

Chang, J., Wall, G., Chu, S.-T.T., 2006. Novelty seeking at aboriginal attractions. Ann. Tour. Res. 33 (3), 729–747.

Chhabra, D., Healy, R., Sills, E., 2003. Staged authenticity and heritage tourism. Ann. Tour. Res. 30 (3), 702–719.

Cloke, P., Perkins, H.C., 1998. Cracking the canyon with the awesome foursome: representations of adventure tourism in New Zealand. Environ. Plan. D Soc. Space 16 (2), 185–218.

Collier, A., 2006. Principles of Tourism: A New Zealand Perspective. Pearson Education New Zealand, Auckland, New Zealand.

Colton, C.W., 1987. Leisure, recreation, tourism: a symbolic interactionism view. Ann. Tour. Res. 14 (3), 345–360.

Costa, C.A., Chalip, L., 2005. Adventure sport tourism in rural revitalisation: an ethnographic evaluation. Eur. Sport Manag. Q. 5 (3), 257–279.

Costa, T.F.G., Lohmann, G., Oliveira, A.V.M., 2010. A model to identify airport hubs and their importance to tourism in Brazil. Res. Transp. Econ. 26 (1), 3–11.

Crouch, G.I., Ritchie, J.R.B., 1999. Tourism, competitiveness, and societal prosperity. J. Bus. Res. 44 (3), 137–152.

Crouch, G.I., Devinney, T.M., Louviere, J.J., Islam, T., 2009. Modelling consumer choice behaviour in space tourism. Tour. Manag. 30 (3), 441–454.

Davison, L., Ryley, T., 2010. Tourism destination preferences of low-cost airline users in the East Midlands. J. Transp. Geogr. 18 (3), 458–465.

Deal, M., Daly, L.M., Mathias, C., 2015. Actor-network theory and the practice of aviation archaeology. J. Confl. Archaeol. 10 (1), 3–28.

Denstadli, J.M., Jacobsen, J.K.S., 2011. The long and winding roads: perceived quality of scenic tourism routes. Tour. Manag. 32 (4), 780–789.
Dunn Ross, E.L., Iso-Aloha, S.E., 1991. Sightseeing tourists' motivation and satisfaction. Ann. Tour. Res. 18 (2), 226–237.
FLY DC3 (2017). Home. Available at http://www.flydc3.co.nz/ (Accessed November 17, 2017).
Frost, W., 2006. Braveheart-ed Ned Kelly: historic films, heritage tourism and destination image. Tour. Manag. 27 (2), 247–254.
Garrod, B., Fyall, A., 2000. Managing heritage tourism. Ann. Tour. Res. 27 (3), 682–708.
Graefe, A.R., Vaske, J.J., 1987. A framework for managing quality in the tourist experience. Ann. Tour. Res. 14 (3), 390–404.
Grossman, D. (2009) DELAG: the world's first airline. Available at http://www.airships.net/delag-passenger-zeppelins (Accessed November 6, 2017).
Halewood, C., Hannam, K., 2001. Viking heritage tourism: authenticity and commodification. Ann. Tour. Res. 28 (3), 565–580.
Hall, D.R., 1999. Conceptualising tourism transport: inequality and externality issues. J. Transp. Geogr. 7 (3), 181–188.
Heliworks Queenstown Helicopters (2017). Fly with the pilots who filmed the lord of the rings trilogy. Available at http://www.heliworks.nz/lord-of-the-rings (Accessed September 29, 2017).
Henderson, I.L., Avis, M., Tsui, W.H.K., 2018. Testing discontinuous innovations in the tourism industry: the case of scenic airship services. Tour. Manag. 66, 167–179.
Heo, J., Lee, Y., McCormick, B.P., Pedersen, P.M., 2010. Daily experience of serious leisure, flow and subjective well-being of older adults. Leis. Stud. 29 (2), 207–225.
Hirschman, E.C., 1980. Innovativeness, novelty seeking, and consumer creativity. J. Consum. Res. 7 (3), 283–295.
Historic England (2016). Historic military aviation sites: conservation guidance. Available at https://content.historicengland.org.uk/images-books/publications/historic-military-aviation-sites/heag048-historic-military-aviation-sites.pdf/ (Accessed November 17, 2017).
Jang, S.S., Feng, R., 2007. Temporal destination revisit intention: the effects of novelty seeking and satisfaction. Tour. Manag. 28 (2), 580–590.
Kim, J.-H., Ritchie, J.R.B., McCormick, B., 2012. Development of a scale to measure memorable tourism experiences. J. Travel Res. 51 (1), 12–25.
Knott, R.C., 1997. A Heritage of Wings: An Illustrated History of Navy Aviation. Naval Institute Press, Annapolis, MD.
Laurendeau, J., Van Brunschot, E.G., 2006. Policing the edge: risk and social control in skydiving. Deviant Behav. 27 (2), 173–201.
Lee, T.-H., Crompton, J., 1992. Measuring novelty seeking in tourism. Ann. Tour. Res. 19 (4), 732–751.
Li, G., 2008. The nature of leisure travel demand. In: Graham, A., Papatheodorou, A., Forsyth, P. (Eds.), Aviation and Tourism: Implications for Leisure Travel. Ashgate, Aldershot, pp. 7–20.
Lipscombe, N., 1999. The relevance of the peak experience to continued skydiving participation: a qualitative approach to assessing motivations. Leis. Stud. 18 (4), 267–288.
Little, J.I., 2009. Scenic tourism on the northeastern borderland: Lake Memphremagog's steamboat excursions and resort hotels, 1850–1900. J. Hist. Geogr. 35 (4), 716–742.
Manhattan Helicopters (2018) Home. Available at https://manhattanhelicopters.com/ (Accessed January 18, 2018).
McCain, G., Ray, N.M., 2003. Legacy tourism: the search for personal meaning in heritage travel. Tour. Manag. 24 (6), 713–717.
MiGFlug (2017a) MiG-29 edge of space flight. Available at http://www.migflug.com/en/jet-fighter-flights/flying-with-a-jet/mig-29-edge-of-space.html (Accessed November 13, 2017).
MiGFlug (2017b). Weghtlessness/zero-G: float like cosmonauts. Available at http://www.migflug.com/en/jet-fighter-flights/flying-with-a-jet/zero-gravity-in-russia.html (Accessed January 18, 2018).
Milman, A., Pizam, A., 1995. The role of awareness and familiarity with a destination: the Central Florida case. J. Travel Res. 33 (3), 21–27.
Nvíri, P., 2006. Scenic Spots: Chinese Tourism, the State, and Cultural Authority. University of Washington Press, Seattle, WA.
Oppermann, M., 1997. First-time and repeat vistors to New Zealand. Tour. Manag. 18 (3), 177–181.
Page, S.J., Steele, W., Connell, J., 2006. Analysing the promotion of adventure tourism: a case study of Scotland. J. Sport Tour. 11 (1), 51–76.
Pant, R.S., 2010. Transportation of goods and passengers to remote areas using airships: two case studies in India. In: Williams, G., Bråthen, S. (Eds.), Air Transport Provision in Remoter Regions. Ashgate, Farnham.
Papillon (2016). The world's largest aerial sightseeing company: the only way to tour the grand canyon. Available from https://www.papillon.com/ (Accessed January 18, 2018).
Pearce, P.L., Moscardo, G.M., 1986. The concept of authenticity in tourist experiences. J. Sociol. 22 (1), 121–132.
Pike, S., Ryan, C., 2004. Destination positioning analysis through a comparison of cognitive, affective, and conative perceptions. J. Travel Res. 42 (4), 333–342.
Poria, Y., Butler, R., Airey, D., 2003. The core of heritage tourism. Ann. Tour. Res. 30 (1), 238–254.
Prebensen, N.K., Foss, L., 2011. Coping and co-creating in tourist experiences. Int. J. Tour. Res. 13 (1), 54–67.
Qu, H., Kim, L.H., Im, H.H., 2011. A model of destination branding: Integrating the concepts of the branding and destination image. Tour. Manag. 32 (3), 465–476.
Queenstown Lakes District Council, 2017. Tourism. Available from, http://www.qldc.govt.nz/leisure-and-culture/tourism/. (Accessed November 14, 2017).
Rao, S., Thomas, E.G., Javalgi, R.G., 1992. Activity preferences and trip-planning behavior of the US outbound pleasure travel market. J. Travel Res. 30 (3), 3–12.
Reddy, M.V., Nica, M., Wilkes, K., 2012. Space tourism: research recommendations for the future of the industry and perspectives of potential participants. Tour. Manag. 33 (5), 1093–1102.
Riley, R.W., Van Doren, C.S., 1992. Movies as tourism promotion: a 'pull' factor in a 'push' location. Tour. Manag. 13 (3), 267–274.
Riley, R.W., Baker, D., andVan Doren, C.S., 1998. Movie induced tourism. Ann. Tour. Res. 25 (4), 919–935.
Sargent, A., 1998. The Darcy effect: regional tourism and costume drama. Int. J. Herit. Stud. 4 (3–4), 177–186.
Schlegelmilch, F., Ollenburg, C., 2013. Marketing the adventure: utilising the aspects of risk/fear/thrill to target the youth traveller segment. Tour. Rev. 68 (3), 44–54.
Schott, C., 2007. Selling adventure tourism: a distribution channels perspective. Int. J. Tour. Res. 9, 257–274.
Skydivesswitzerland (2017) Scenic air. Home. Available at http://www.skydiveswitzerland.ch/en (Accessed November 17, 2017).
Snepenger, D.J., 1987. Segmenting the vacation market by novelty-seeking role. J. Travel Res. 26 (2), 8–14.
Stephenson, C., 2010. Zeppelins: German Airships 1900–40. Osprey Publishing, Oxford, UK.

Sun, M., Zhang, X., Ryan, C., 2015. Perceiving tourist destination landscapes through Chinese eyes: the case of South Island, New Zealand. Tour. Manag. 46, 582–595.

Swarbrooke, J., 1995. The Development and Management of Visitor Attractions. Butterworth Heinemann, Oxford, England.

Tasci, A.D.A., Gartner, W.C., Cavusgil, S.T., 2007. Measurement of destination brand bias using a quasi-experimental design. Tour. Manag. 28 (6), 1529–1540.

Tung, V.W.S., Ritchie, J.B., 2011. Exploring the essence of memorable tourism experiences. Ann. Tour. Res. 38 (4), 1367–1386.

USPA (2017). USPA at a glance. Available at http://www.uspa.org/About-USPA/about-us (Accessed September 29, 2017).

Virgin Galactic (2017). Home. Available at https://www.virgingalactic.com/ (Accessed November 17, 2017).

Vittersø, J., Vorkinn, M., Vistad, O.I., Vaagland, J., 2000. Tourist experiences and attractions. Ann. Tour. Res. 27 (2), 432–450.

Williams, P., Soutar, G.N., 2009. Value, satisfaction and behavioral intentions in an adventure tourism context. Ann. Tour. Res. 36 (3), 413–438.

Xie, P.F., Schneider, P.P., 2004. Challenges and opportunities for adventure tourism: the case of Patagonia, Chile. Tour. Recreat. Res. 29 (1), 57–65.

Zeppelin NT (2017). Homepage. Available at https://zeppelin-nt.de/en/homepage.html (Accessed November 17, 2017).

Zero Gravity Corporation (2017). Index. Available at https://www.gozerog.com/index.cfm (Accessed November 13, 2017).

CHAPTER

18

Conclusions: Factors, Beliefs and Perspectives

*Frédéric DOBRUSZKES**, *Anne GRAHAM*†

*Free University of Brussels (ULB), Brussels, Belgium †University of Westminster, London, United Kingdom

CHAPTER OUTLINE

You have now travelled through the successive stages of the tourist's journey, from the very roots of air travel (including not flying) to decisions taken before flying, through the whole journey itself, and finally arrival at the destination or tourist attraction. The return trip could have been added, although arguably this involves less major decisions to be made. No mention has been made at this stage as to what then happens back at home, namely, the return to everyday life and its routines. This may well result in some tedium and restlessness, and subsequently lead to fresh thoughts about the next trip and the start of a new story.[1]

18.1 AIR TRANSPORT/TOURISM CROSS-RELATIONSHIPS AS A MULTIFACTOR, MULTILEVEL PROCESS

Beyond the diversity of topics, scale, and places considered, the series of chapters has shed a new, integrated light on the cross-relationships between air transport and tourism. These relationships have appeared as a function of three key components or families of factors that form a triangle and also interact with each other. First of all, there are place attributes at both ends, namely, departure and arrival areas. More precisely, these attributes are made up of a wide range of characteristics that refer to natural/physical patterns, people, and to the economy. Natural/physical patterns mostly relate to the weather (and thus to the fact that places have to be suitable for tourism and satisfy the tourists' preferences) and landscapes (notably sea vs. mountains). Key characteristics of people include income, social–occupational group, age, health and well-being, life cycle position, household size, and lifestyle. Economic patterns relate back to the propensity to generate tourism flows, both directly (through shaping needs for travel) and indirectly (through affecting people's characteristics, especially income and social–occupational group). Economic patterns are also important at the destination in the sense that they define a place's ability to attract and accommodate tourists.

Second, air transport/tourism interactions are shaped by numerous policies and strategies pursued by a myriad of public authorities, acting right through from the local to global level. This includes regulatory regimes of air services, of course, but also monetary policies (which affect exchange rates and thus the relative attractiveness of

[1] Thank you to Marina Efthymiou for having highlighted this to us.

destinations regarding purchasing power at the origin) and the degree of free movement of people. At the national and subnational level, strategies include investment in—and promotion of—transport services and/or tourist facilities. In most cases, these policies are part of entrepreneurial strategies, to the point that countries and local places all compete with each other. This directly relates to Harvey (1989)'s statements about the large move from management to entrepreneurialism in somewhat more general terms.

Finally, there are also all the strategies pursued by private stakeholders, which include most of the air transport industry (e.g. private airlines, aircraft manufacturers, privatised airports, the myriad of suppliers and subcontractors) and the tourism industry (e.g. hotels, tourist attractions, leisure parks, resorts, tour operators, travel agents).[2] These actors shape and transform places, travel practices and, ultimately, societies.

18.2 SUPPORTING AND CHALLENGING COMMON BELIEFS

This book has supported and built on some of the conventional understandings of the air transport and tourism relationship with new and extensive evidence. For example, Chapter 5 is one of a number of chapters that has confirmed that this relationship is far from simple and is in a near constant state of flux owing to shifting market conditions, political interests, and changes in economic developments. This very much links with the notion of a multifactor, multilevel process as discussed before. More specifically, Chapters 7 and 12 have demonstrated than even the choice of airport and surface access mode involves complex decisions to be made, whilst Chapter 14 has highlighted the complicated relationships that can develop even just between airlines and airports. In addition, Chapter 9 has shown that technology is playing an increasingly multifaceted role within the air transport and tourism sectors.

Meanwhile a number of other common beliefs have been challenged and put into perspective by the contributors. From a demand viewpoint, Chapter 3 has questioned the idea, supported by many, that air traffic is dominated by business passengers. Within the context of passenger flows and global figures, leisure travel is much more important, and amongst leisure travel, VFR passengers are often more numerous than those on business (although the authors acknowledge that the situation could be different on specific routes or in terms of revenues). Also Chapter 4 has demonstrated, from a mature market perspective, that not everyone flies and, likewise, not everybody will fly in the future. This suggests that models used to forecast air traffic or tourism based on established past behaviour could be biased and should better take into account the market's degree of maturity as well as the specific nature of frequent and infrequent flyers. Still focusing on demand but from a different angle, Chapter 13 has argued that the airport journey, rather than being considered as a fairly uninfluential feature of the tourist trip, now potentially plays a much more significant role in shaping the overall tourist experience.

Some other findings have shed a different light on tourism flows. For example, Chapter 6 has shown that at least in the context of Spain, high-speed rail (HSR) services can have a negative, indirect impact on domestic tourism. This is because HSR induces competition, leading to a significant drop in domestic air services that cannot be compensated for by rail services. More generally it is sometimes claimed that it is easy to travel by air virtually everywhere nowadays. However, Chapter 8 has argued vehemently that even for well-established cities and tourist destinations, self-connections improve connectivity.

As regards industry developments, Chapter 10 comprehensively highlighted numerous beliefs regarding the evolution of airline industry structures. However, Chapter 11 has suggested that actually the so-called charter airlines (now rebranded as 'leisure airlines') have not mostly shifted towards long-haul markets to escape competition from the low-cost airlines. At least in Europe and based on two key cases studies, the move is significant but certainly less substantial than is usually supposed. Meanwhile Chapter 15 has acknowledged that partnerships between destination management organisations (DMOs) and the air sector may be fruitful for developing tourism, destination stakeholders should first cooperate on developing tourism products and services in the destination to closely meet the needs of the passengers that are targeted by the airlines.

Finally, the exact role of airlines and airports has also been questioned. Whilst the air journey is normally considered as a means to an end to get to a destination, Chapter 17 has discussed how the flight can act as the actual tourist attraction. Moreover as regards airports, Chapter 16 has argued that whilst many of these have claimed that they are becoming new centres of large urban regions by transforming themselves into an airport city or aerotropolis, the evidence points to most of them not having yet reached the ambitions expectations placed upon them.

[2] Of course, in certain countries, airlines/airports and sometimes tourism organisations, belong to the State and cannot be considered as 'private' sensu stricto.

18.3 TRENDS, PERSPECTIVES, AND UNCERTAINTIES

Whilst aiming to be as comprehensive and far-reaching as possible, of course it is not realistic to claim that this book brings an end to the complex and dynamic story of the air transport/tourism relationship. As a result this last section identifies key ongoing, and to some extent only emerging, changes that could likely affect the very nature of both air travel and tourism in the future.

First of all, the growth of the new middle class in emerging countries involves a large amount of new travellers (Cohen and Cohen, 2015a). For instance, today there are a substantial number of tourists from mainland China in places such as Japan and Thailand. Not only does this new situation drive a large increase in tourist flows, but it also involves new challenges in terms of (local and global) environmental impacts, and in responding to particular needs related to both cultural habits and less mature markets. It can be argued that research will have to move away from some kind of 'Eurocentrism in tourism' (Cohen and Cohen, 2015b) to take into account these specific characteristics.

On the airline side, the extent to which the low-cost model will be replicated with long-haul markets is still debated. Evidence suggests that drops in costs and fares might not be as spectacular as in the short- and medium-haul markets, and that long-haul demand cannot be so easily stimulated. This is notably because most social and economic interactions remain intracontinental rather than intercontinental. However, it cannot be denied that lower cost airlines are penetrating the long-haul market and will change the rules of the games to some extent. In this context, the recent advent of longer range narrow-body aircraft (B737 Max and A321LR) is an important technological change that will certainly deserve attention from scholars in the forthcoming years. For instance, Norwegian (one of the leading European low-cost airlines) has ordered no less than 103 B737 Max 8 and 30 A321LR. Even though the distribution amongst its subsidiaries and related markets has not been unveiled yet, this nevertheless gives information about the potential magnitude of changes.

Digitalisation and new technologies have been discussed in Chapters 9 and 13. In this rapidly moving area, predicting trends with any degree of certainty is becoming increasingly challenging, but it is likely that there will be even more far-reaching and comprehensive techniques in place to sell tickets/products to tourists, accompany them on their journey and track their movements and purchases. More and more powerful and connected personal devices, along with artificial intelligence, may well make trips easier and more integrated from a door-to-door and multimodal perspective. However, all these tools also raise fundamental moral concerns. For instance, how much privacy will eventually remain? How will learning more about individuals make it possible for private interests to manipulate tourists' behaviour just to sell them services and, ultimately, make profits? As a tourist, would rejecting these tools involve not being allowed to travel anymore?

Another issue is about the environmental impacts of flying. Despite significant progress in fuel consumption, specific (i.e. per seat-km) emissions of GHGs and of pollutants, and in noise emissions, these gains have largely been offset by traffic growth. Also, the magnitude of the impact of aviation on climate change is still being debated, since high-altitude processes and non-CO_2 impacts are not fully understood (Lee et al., 2009; Dahlmann et al., 2015). In addition, estimations of GHG emissions postulate that aircraft should follow the shortest route, which is not the case (Dobruszkes and Peeters, 2018). Here a somewhat unexplored, but fundamental, debate is whether to pursue mitigation strategies or adaptation strategies. The former broadly involves changing lifestyles and models of consumption, and ultimately accumulation regimes. This could only involve flying less which is against all observed trends and hence is a very dramatic suggestion. The latter accepts business-as-usual trends, thus keeping the serious climate changes and inevitable adverse impacts that various nations will have to deal with. This may include relocating people and businesses because of rising sea levels and new damaging weather patterns. Felli (2016) argues that calls for adaptation dominated at the early times of concerns of climate changes, and does so more and more today. In between, the 1997 Kyoto Protocol, and its objective for developed countries to reduce GHG emissions, was maybe only an interlude. In any case, the balance between mitigation and adaptation strategies may well have very divergent impacts on air transport and tourism.

Beyond the debate between mitigation of, and adaptation to, climate change, disruptions may actually come from the so-called peak oil. Peak oil refers to the time when the maximum extraction rate of conventional oil is reached, after which it then only falls. Drops in output in a context of increasing demand would logically mean much higher energy costs, all other things being equal. Beyond vibrant debates (see Chapman, 2014), this would arguably dramatically challenge industries that are significantly dependent on oil—especially aviation (Kerschner et al., 2013) but also tourism (Becken, 2015). In this context, there are three main pathways for aviation in the case of a confirmed reached peak. First, switching to alternative energies provided they are available at reasonable costs, and preferably with limited social and environmental impacts. Second, a major technological revolution that would liberate air transport from oil at an attractive cost, whilst at the same time maintaining its current efficiency in terms of speed, distance range and capacity. Third, a dramatic hike in air fares so that both flying and long-distance tourism would be seen as a privilege again as in the early days of travel. In essence, peak oil could well force a change even more challenging than the mitigation policies that were once called for by the Kyoto Protocol.

Surprisingly, the tourism industry does not generally seem alarmed by the prospect of peak oil (Becken, 2016). However, the ability of societies to innovate at the time they face major challenges should not be underestimated. Nevertheless, should they fail to innovate, tourists may perhaps be forced to (re)think about the concept of 'slow' tourism, and focus on more local or regional tourism within a context where the distance decay function is meaningful again (Becken, 2015). In this case, it may well be that the story of the relationship between air transport and tourism might have to be significantly rewritten at some stage in the future.

References

Becken, S., 2015. Tourism and Oil: Preparing for the Challenge. Channel View Publications, Bristol.

Becken, S., 2016. Peak oil: a hidden issue? Social representations of professional tourism perspectives. J. Sustain. Tour. 24 (1), 31–51.

Chapman, I., 2014. The end of peak oil? Why this topic is still relevant despite recent denials. Energy Policy 64, 93–101.

Cohen, E., Cohen, S., 2015a. A mobilities approach to tourism from emerging world regions. A mobilities approach to tourism from emerging world regions. Curr. Issue Tour. 18 (1), 11–43.

Cohen, E., Cohen, S., 2015b. Beyond Eurocentrism in tourism: a paradigm shift to mobilities. Beyond Eurocentrism in tourism: a paradigm shift to mobilities. Tour. Recreat. Res. 40 (2), 157–168.

Dahlmann, K., Grewe, V., Frömming, C., Burkhardt, U., 2015. Can we reliably assess climate mitigation options for air traffic scenarios despite large uncertainties in atmospheric processes? Transp. Res. D 46, 40–55.

Dobruszkes, F., Peeters, D., 2018. Planes not flying the shortest route: causes, magnitude and consequences. In: 2018 International Geographical Union Regional Conference, Québec.

Felli, R., 2016. La grande adaptation. In: Climat, Capitalisme et Catastrophe. Le Seuil, Paris.

Harvey, D., 1989. From managerialism to entrepreneurialism: the transformation in urban governance in late capitalism. Geogr. Ann. B Hum. Geogr. 71 (1), 3–17.

Kerschner, C., Press, C., Feng, J., Hubacek, K., 2013. Economic vulnerability to peak oil. Glob. Environ. Chang. 23 (6), 1424–1433.

Lee, D.S., Fahey, D.W., Forster, P.M., Newton, P.J., Wit, R.C., Lim, L.L., Owen, B., Sausen, R., 2009. Aviation and global climate change in the 21st century. Atmos. Environ. 43 (22–23), 3520–3537.

Index

Note: Page numbers followed by *f* indicate figures, *t* indicate tables, *b* indicate boxes, and *np* indicate footnotes.

CPI Antony Rowe
Chippenham, UK
2019-02-20 22:16